CLYMER®

SUZUKI

LT-Z400 • 2003-2008

The world's finest publisher of mechanical how-to manuals

CLYMER®

P.O. Box 12901, Overland Park, Kansas 66282-2901

FIRST EDITION
First Printing October, 2006

SECOND EDITION
First Printing July, 2009
Second Printing July, 2012

Printed in U.S.A.

ISBN-10: 1-59969-295-3

ISBN-13: 978-1-59969-295-1

Library of Congress: 2009930911

AUTHOR: Jon Engelman.

TECHNICAL PHOTOGRAPHY: Jon Engelman.

TECHNICAL ILLUSTRATIONS: Mitzi McCarthy.

WIRING DIAGRAMS: Bob Meyer and Steve Thomas.

EDITOR: Steve Thomas and James Grooms.

PRODUCTION: Susan Hartington.

TOOLS AND EQUIPMENT: K & L Supply Co. at www.klsupply.com.

COVER: Mark Clifford Photography at www.markclifford.com.

P.O. Box 12901, Overland Park, KS 66282-2901 • 800-262-1954 • 913-967-1719

More information available at *clymer.com*

CONTENTS

QUICK REFERENCE DATA

MODEL:______________________________ YEAR:______________

VIN NUMBER:______________________________

ENGINE SERIAL NUMBER:______________________________

CARBURETOR SERIAL NUMBER OR I.D. MARK:______________________________

TIRE SPECIFICATIONS*

Front tire	
Size	AT22 x 7-10
Manufacturer	Dunlop KT 331
Minimum tread depth	4 mm (0.16 in.)
Rear tire	
Size	AT20 x 10-9
Manufacturer	Dunlop KT 335
Minimum tread depth	4 mm (0.16 in.)
Inflation pressure (cold)*	
Standard	
Front	30 kPa (4.4 psi)
Rear	27.5 kPa (4.0 psi)

*Tire inflation pressure for original equipment tires. Aftermarket tires may require different inflation pressures; refer to aftermarket manufacturer's specifications.

RECOMMENDED LUBRICANTS, FLUIDS AND CAPACITIES

Brake fluid classification	DOT 4
Engine coolant	
capacity	1200 ml (1.3 qts.)
mixture	50:50 (antifreeze/distilled water)
type	Ethylene glycol containing anti-corrosion agents for aluminum engines
Engine oil	
Capacity	
Engine overhaul	2.2 L (2.3 qt.)
Oil and filter	2.1 L (2.2 qt.)
Oil change	2.0 L (2.1 qt.)
Classification	API SF/SG or SH/SJ with JASO MA
Viscosity	SAE 10W-40
Fuel	
Capacity	10 L (2.6 gal.)
Octane	Regular unleaded; 87 octane minimum (R + M/2) Regular unleaded; 91 octane minimum (RON)
Reserve	2.7 L (0.7 gal.)

MAINTENANCE AND TUNE-UP SPECIFICATIONS

Battery	
Capacity	12 V – 8 AH
Voltage	
Fully charged	13.0-13.2 V
Needs charging	Less than 12.3 V
Charge current	
Normal	0.9 A/5-10 h
Quick[1]	4.0 A/1.0 h
Brake light activation	Rear brake pedal depressed 7-10 mm (0.3-0.4 in.)
Brake pad minimum thickness	1 mm (0.04 in.) to wear indicator
Brake pedal height	0-10 mm (0-0.4 in.)
Choke lever free play	0.5-1.0 mm (0.02-0.04 in.)
Clutch lever free play	10-15 mm (0.4-0.6 in.)
Cooling system	
Maximum test pressure	120 kPa (17 psi)
Radiator cap relief pressure	108-137 kPa (15.6-19.9 psi)
Drive chain free play	30-40 mm (1.2-1.6 in.)
Drive chain service limit	No more than 319.4 mm (12.57 in.) between 21 chain pins
Engine compression	1000 kPa (142 psi) w/ decompressor activated
Idle speed	1400-1600 rpm
Ignition timing[2]	10° BTDC at 1500 rpm
Oil pressure	40-140 kPa (5.8-20.3 psi) at 3000 rpm
Pilot screw[3]	
2003-2004 models	2 1/4 turns out
2005-on models	1 1/2 turns out
Spark plug	
Gap	0.7-0.8 mm (0.028-0.031 in.)
Type	NGKCR7E or ND U22ESR-N
Throttle lever free play	
2003-2004 models	3-8 mm (0.12-0.31 in.)
2005-on models	3-5 mm (0.12-0.20 in.)
Toe-in	5 mm (0.20 in.)
Valve clearance	
Exhaust	0.20-0.30 mm (0.0078-0.0118 in.)
Intake	0.10-0.20 mm (0.0039-0.0078 in.)

1. Quick charging can shorten battery life. Use it only in an emergency.
2. Not adjustable
3. California models are preset.

MAINTENANCE AND TUNE-UP TORQUE SPECIFICATIONS

Item	N•m	in.-lb.	ft.-lb.
Brake bleed valve			
2003 models	7.5	66	–
2004-on models	6.0	53	–
Brake hose union bolt	23	–	17
Cylinder head cover bolts	14	124	–
Engine		–	
Crankcase oil drain bolt	21	–	15.5
Oil tank drain bolt	12	106	–
Exhaust pipe nut	23	–	17
Front hub nut	65	–	48
Handlebar clamp bolt			
2003 models	23	–	17
2004-on models	26	–	19
Main oil gallery plug	18	–	13

(continued)

MAINTENANCE AND TUNE-UP TORQUE SPECIFICATIONS (continued)

Item	N•m	in.-lb.	ft.-lb.
Muffler connecting bolt	23	–	17
Muffler mounting bolt	23	–	17
Rear brake caliper mounting bolts	26	–	19
Rear hub nut	100	–	74
Rear axle housing bolt			
Drive chain side (M12)	100	–	74
Brake side (M10)	73	–	54
Spark plug	11	97	–
Tie rod end nut	60	–	44
Tie rod locknut	29	–	21
Wheel lug nuts			
2003-2004	50	–	37
2005-on	60	–	44

CHAPTER ONE

GENERAL INFORMATION

This detailed and comprehensive manual covers the Suzuki LT-Z400 all terrain vehicle (ATV) from 2003-2008.

MANUAL ORGANIZATION

A shop manual is a tool and, as in all Clymer manuals, the text provides complete information on maintenance, tune-up, repair and overhaul. Hundreds of photographs and illustrations, created during the complete disassembly of the ATV, guide the reader through every job.

All procedures are in step-by-step format and designed for the reader who may be working on the vehicle for the first time. The chapters are thumb-tabbed for easy reference. Main headings are listed in the table of contents and the index.

Frequently used specifications and capacities from individual chapters are in the *Quick Reference Data* section at the front of the manual.

During some of the procedures there will be references to headings in other chapters or sections of the manual. When a specific heading is called out in a step it will be *italicized* as it appears in the manual. If a sub-heading is indicated as being "in this section" it is located within the same main heading. For example, the sub-heading *Handling Gasoline Safely* is located within the main heading *SAFETY.*

This chapter provides general information on shop safety, tools and their usage, service fundamentals and shop supplies. Refer to **Tables 1-6** at the end of the chapter for ATV dimensions and general shop information.

Chapter Two provides methods for quick and accurate diagnosis of problems. Troubleshooting procedures present typical symptoms and logical methods to pinpoint and repair the problem.

Chapter Three explains all routine maintenance.

Subsequent chapters describe specific systems including the engine, transmission, clutch, drive system, fuel system, suspension, brakes, exhaust and body. Each disassembly, repair and assembly procedure is discussed in step-by-step form.

Specification tables, when applicable, are located at the end of each chapter.

WARNINGS, CAUTIONS AND NOTES

The terms WARNING, CAUTION and NOTE have specific meanings in this manual.

A WARNING emphasizes areas where injury or even death could result from negligence. Mechanical damage may also occur. *Take* WARNINGS *seriously.*

A CAUTION emphasizes areas where equipment damage could result. Disregarding a CAUTION could cause permanent mechanical damage, though injury is unlikely.

A NOTE provides additional information to make a step or procedure easier or clearer. Disregarding a NOTE could cause inconvenience, but would not cause equipment damage or injury.

SAFETY

Refer to the following guidelines and practice common sense when servicing the ATV.

1. Do not operate the ATV in an enclosed area. The exhaust gasses cont ain carbon monoxide, an odorless, colorless and tasteless poisonous gas. Carbon monoxide levels build quickly in enclosed areas and can cause unconsciousness and death in a short time. Make sure to properly ventilate the work area or operate the ATV outside.
2. Never use gasoline or any extremely flammable liquid to clean parts. Refer to *Handling Gasoline Safely* and *Cleaning Parts* in this section.
3. Never smoke or use a torch in the vicinity of flammable liquids, such as gasoline or cleaning solvent.
4. If welding or brazing on the vehicle, remove the fuel tank to a safe distance at least 15 m (50 ft.) away.
5. Do not remove the radiator cap or cooling system hoses while the engine is hot. The cooling system is pressurized and the high temperature coolant may cause injury.
6. Dispose of and store coolant in a safe manner. Do not allow children or pets access to open containers of coolant. Animals are attracted to antifreeze.
7. Avoid contact with engine oil and other chemicals. Most are known carcinogens. Wash your hands thoroughly after coming in contact with engine oil. If possible, wear a pair of disposable gloves.
8. Use the correct type and size of tools to avoid damaging fasteners.
9. Keep tools clean and in good condition. Replace or repair worn or damaged equipment.
10. When loosening a tight fastener, be guided by what would happen if the tool slips.
11. When replacing fasteners, make sure the new fasteners are the same size and strength as the original ones.
12. Keep the work area clean and organized.
13. Wear eye protection *anytime* eye safety is in question. This includes procedures that involve drilling, grinding, hammering, compressed air and chemicals.
14. Wear the correct clothing for the job. Tie up or cover long hair so it does not get caught in moving equipment.
15. Do not carry sharp tools in clothing pockets.
16. Always have a fire extinguisher rated for gasoline (Class B) and electrical (Class C) fires available.
17. Do not use compressed air to clean clothes, the ATV or the work area. Debris may be blown into the eyes or skin. *Never* direct compressed air at anyone. Do not allow children to use or play with any compressed air equipment.
18. When using compressed air to dry rotating parts, hold the part so it does not rotate. Do not allow the force of the air to spin the part. The air jet is capable of rotating parts at extreme speed. The part may disintegrate or become damaged, causing serious injury.
19. Do not inhale the dust created by brake pad and clutch wear. These particles may contain asbestos. In addition, some types of insulating materials and gaskets may contain asbestos. Inhaling asbestos particles is hazardous to health.
20. Never work on the ATV while someone is working under it.
21. When placing the ATV on a stand, make sure it is secure before walking away.

Handling Gasoline Safely

Gasoline is a volatile flammable liquid and is one of the most dangerous items in the shop. Because gasoline is used so often, many people forget it is hazardous. Keep in mind when working on the machine, gasoline is always present in the fuel tank, fuel line and throttle body. To avoid an accident when working around the fuel system, carefully observe the following precautions:

1. Never use gasoline to clean parts. Refer to *Cleaning Parts* in this section.

2. When working on the fuel system, work outside or in a well-ventilated area.

3. Do not add fuel to the fuel tank or service the fuel system while the ATV is near open flames, sparks or where someone is smoking. Gasoline vapor is heavier than air; it collects in low areas and is more easily ignited than liquid gasoline.

4. Allow the engine to cool completely before working on any fuel system component.

5. Do not store gasoline in glass containers. If the glass breaks, an explosion or fire may occur.

6. Immediately wipe up spilled gasoline with rags. Store the rags in a metal container with a lid until they can be properly disposed of, or place them outside in a safe place for the fuel to evaporate.

7. Do not pour water onto a gasoline fire. Water spreads the fire and makes it more difficult to put out. Use a class B, BC or ABC fire extinguisher to extinguish the fire.

8. Always turn off the engine before refueling. Do not spill fuel onto the engine or exhaust system. Do not overfill the fuel tank. Leave an air space at the top of the tank to allow room for the fuel to expand due to temperature fluctuations.

Cleaning Parts

Cleaning parts is one of the more tedious and difficult service jobs performed in the home garage. Many types of chemical cleaners and solvents are available for shop use. Most are poisonous and extremely flammable. To prevent chemical exposure, vapor buildup, fire and serious injury, observe each product warning label and note the following:

1. Read and observe the entire product label before using any chemical. Always know what type of chemical is being used and whether it is poisonous and/or flammable.

2. Do not use more than one type of cleaning solvent at a time. If mixing chemicals is required, measure the proper amounts according to the manufacturer.

3. Work in a well-ventilated area.

4. Wear chemical-resistant gloves.

5. Wear safety glasses.

6. Wear a vapor respirator if the instructions call for it.

7. Wash hands and arms thoroughly after cleaning parts.

8. Keep chemical products away from children and pets.

9. Thoroughly clean all oil, grease and cleaner residue from any part that must be heated.

10. Use a nylon brush when cleaning parts. Metal brushes may cause a spark.

11. When using a parts washer, only use the solvent recommended by the manufacturer. Make sure the parts washer is equipped with a metal lid that will lower in case of fire.

Warning Labels

The manufacturer's labels contain important safety, operating, servicing, transporting and storing instructions. Refer to the owner's manual for the description and location of labels. Order replacement labels from the manufacturer if they are missing or damaged.

SERIAL NUMBERS

Serial numbers are stamped onto the frame and engine. Record these numbers in the *Quick Reference Data* section at the front of the manual. Have these numbers available when ordering parts.

The frame number (**Figure 1**) or vehicle identification number (VIN) is stamped on the left frame rail just ahead of the shift lever. The engine number (**Figure 2**) is stamped on the right side of the engine under the exhaust pipe, near the starter.

FASTENERS

Proper fastener selection and installation is important to ensure the ATV operates as designed and can be serviced efficiently. The choice of original equipment fasteners is not arrived at by chance. Make sure replacement fasteners meet all the same requirements as the originals.

Threaded Fasteners

WARNING
Do not install fasteners with a strength classification lower than what was originally installed by the manufacturer. Doing so may cause equipment failure and/or damage.

CAUTION
To ensure that the fastener threads are not mismatched or cross-threaded, start all fasteners by hand. If a fastener is hard to start or turn, determine the cause before tightening with a wrench.

Threaded fasteners secure most of the components on the vehicle. Most are tightened by turning them clockwise (right-hand threads). If the normal rotation of the component being tightened would loosen the fastener, it may have left-hand threads. If a left-hand threaded fastener is used, it is noted.

Two dimensions are required to match the thread size of the fastener: the number of threads in a given distance and the outside diameter of the threads.

The two systems currently used to specify threaded fastener dimensions are the U.S. Standard system and the metric system (**Figure 3**). Pay particular attention when working with unidentified fasteners; mismatching thread types can damage threads.

Determine the length (L, **Figure 4**), diameter (D) and distance between thread crests (pitch) (T) to classify metric screws and bolts. A typical bolt may be identified by the numbers, 8—1.25 × 130. This indicates the bolt has a diameter of 8 mm, the distance between thread crests is 1.25 mm and the length is 130 mm. Measure bolt length as shown in L, **Figure 4**.

The numbers on the top of the fastener (**Figure 4**) indicate the strength of metric screws and bolts. The higher the number, the stronger the fastener. Typically, unnumbered fasteners are the weakest.

Many screws, bolts and studs are combined with nuts to secure particular components. To indicate the size of a nut, manufacturers specify the internal diameter and the thread pitch.

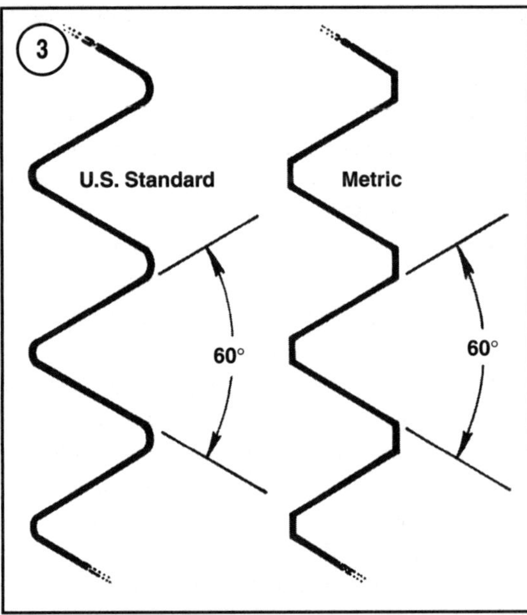

The measurement across two flats on a nut or bolt indicates the wrench size.

Torque Specifications

The materials used in the manufacturing of the ATV may be subjected to uneven stresses if the fasteners of the various subassemblies are not installed and tightened correctly. Fasteners that are improperly installed or work loose can cause damage. It is essential to use an accurate torque wrench as described in this chapter.

Torque specifications for specific applications are provided in Newton-meters (N•m), foot-pounds (ft.-lb.) and inch-pounds (in.-lb.).

If a specification is not provided, refer to **Table 6** for a recommended torque setting. To determine the

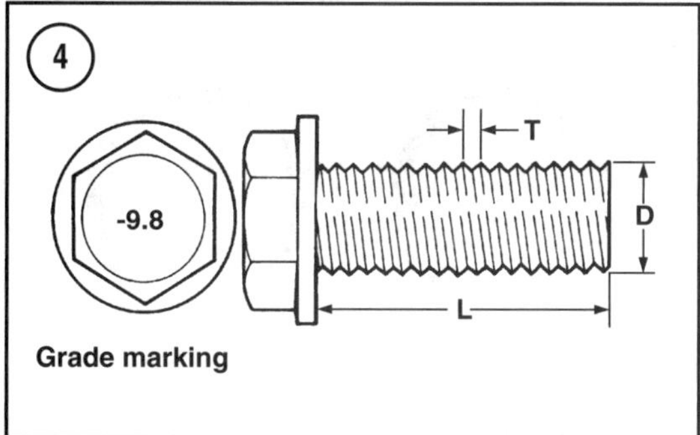

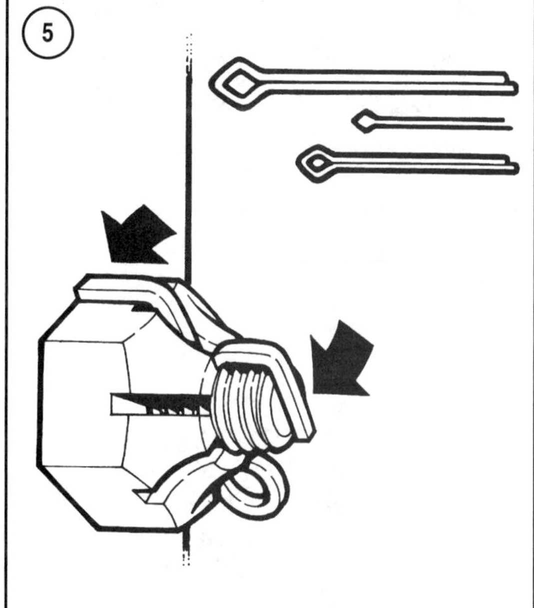

torque requirement, first determine the size of the fastener as described in *Threaded Fasteners* in this section.

Self-Locking Fasteners

Several types of bolts, screws and nuts incorporate a system that creates interference between the two fasteners. Interference is achieved in various ways. The most common types are the nylon insert nut and a dry adhesive coating on the threads of a bolt.

Self-locking fasteners offer greater holding strength than standard fasteners, which improves their resistance to vibration. Typically, a self-locking fastener cannot be reused. The materials used to form the lock become distorted after the initial installation and removal. Discard and replace self-locking fasteners after removing them. Do not replace self-locking fasteners with standard fasteners.

Washers

The two basic types of washers are flat washers and lockwashers. Flat washers are simple discs with a hole to fit a screw or bolt. Lockwashers are used to prevent a fastener from working loose. Washers can be used as spacers and seals, or can help distribute fastener load and prevent the fastener from damaging the component.

As with fasteners, when replacing washers make sure the replacement washers are of the same design and quality.

Cotter Pins

A cotter pin is a split metal pin inserted into a hole or slot to prevent a fastener from loosening. In certain applications, such as the rear axle nut on an ATV, the fastener must be secured in this way. For these applications, a cotter pin and castellated (slotted) nut are used.

To use a cotter pin, first make sure the diameter is correct for the hole in the fastener. After correctly tightening the fastener and aligning the holes, insert the cotter pin through the hole and bend the ends over the fastener (**Figure 5**). Unless instructed to do so, never loosen a tightened fastener to align the holes. If the holes do not align, tighten the fastener enough to achieve alignment.

Cotter pins are available in various diameters and lengths. Measure the length from the bottom of the head to the tip of the shortest pin.

Snap Rings and E-clips

Snap rings (**Figure 6**) are circular-shaped metal retaining clips. They are required to secure parts and gears in place on parts such as shafts, pins or rods. External type snap rings are used to retain items on shafts. Internal type snap rings secure parts within housing bores. In some applications, in addition to securing the component(s), snap rings of varying thicknesses also determine endplay. These are usually called selective snap rings.

The two basic types of snap rings are machined and stamped snap rings. Machined snap rings (**Figure 7**) can be installed in either direction, because both faces have sharp edges. Stamped snap rings (**Figure 8**) are manufactured with a sharp and a round edge. When installing a stamped snap ring in a thrust application, install the sharp edge facing away from the part producing the thrust.

E-clips are used when it is not practical to use a snap ring. Remove E-clips with a flat blade screwdriver by prying between the shaft and E-clip. To install an E-clip, center it over the shaft groove and push or tap it into place.

Observe the following when installing snap rings:

1. Remove and install snap rings with snap ring pliers. Refer to *Tools* in this chapter.
2. In some applications, it may be necessary to replace snap rings after removing them.
3. Compress or expand snap rings only enough to install them. If overly expanded, they lose their retaining ability.
4. After installing a snap ring, make sure it seats completely.
5. Wear eye protection when removing and installing snap rings.

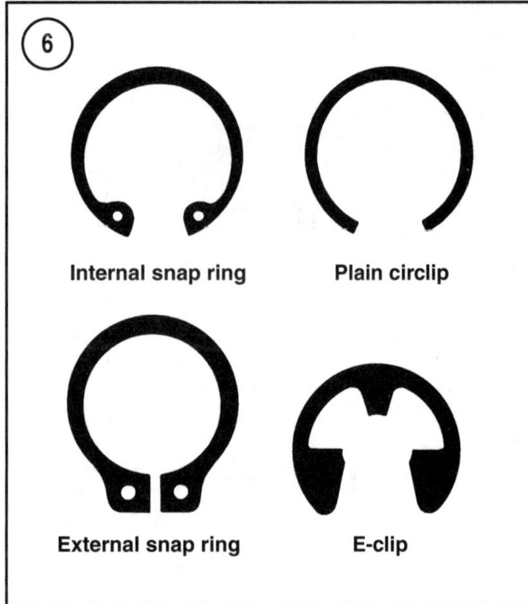

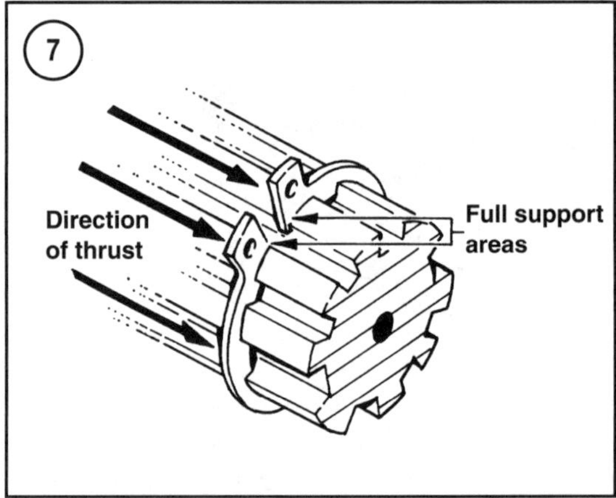

SHOP SUPPLIES

Lubricants and Fluids

The following section describes lubricants most often required. Make sure to follow the manufacturer's recommendations for lubricant types.

Engine oils

Engine oil for four-stroke engines use is classified by three standards: the American Petroleum Institute (API) service classification, the Society of Automotive Engineers (SAE) viscosity rating and the Japanese Automobile Standards Organization (JASO) T 903 Standard rating.

The API and the SAE information is on all oil container labels. JASO rating indicates the oil is specifically for ATV and ATV use. Two letters indicate the API service classification. The number or sequence of numbers and letter (10W-40 for example) is the oil's viscosity rating. The API service classification and the SAE viscosity index are not indications of oil quality.

The API service classification indicates that the oil meets specific lubrication standards. The S letter in the classification indicates the oil is for gasoline engines. The second letter indicates the standard the oil satisfies.

The JASO certification label identifies two separate oil classifications and a registration number to ensure the oil has passed all JASO certification standards for use in four-stroke engines. The classifications are: MA (high friction applications) and MB (low friction applications). Only oil that has passed JASO standards can carry the JASO certification label.

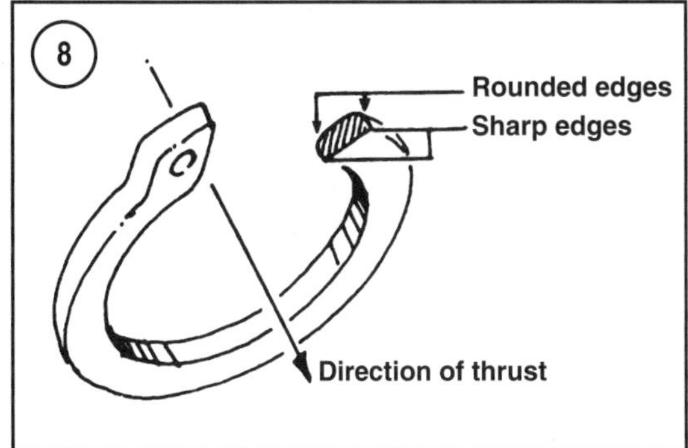

Always use an oil with a classification recommended by the manufacturer. Using an oil with a different classification can cause engine damage.

Viscosity is an indication of the oil's thickness. Thin oils have a lower number while thick oils have a higher number. Engine oils fall into the 5- to 50-weight range for single-grade oils.

Most manufacturers recommend multi-grade oil. These oils perform efficiently across a wide range of operating conditions. Multi-grade oils are identified by a W after the first number, which indicates the low-temperature viscosity.

Engine oils are most commonly mineral (petroleum) based, but synthetic and semi-synthetic types are used more frequently. When selecting engine oil, follow the manufacturer's recommendation for type, classification and viscosity.

Chain lubricant

An O-ring chain is standard equipment for the years covered by this manual. Since the links of an O-ring chain are permanently lubricated and sealed, O-ring chain lubricant is formulated to prevent exterior corrosion of the chain and to condition the O-rings. It is not tacky and resists the adhesion of dirt, which could damage the O-rings. Use a good quality chain lubricant that is compatible with the type of chain installed on the ATV. A heavy-viscosity engine oil is appropriate in some applications.

Air filter oil

Use either SAE 30 or SAE 10W-40 weight engine oil on the foam oil filter after it has been cleaned.

Greases

Grease is lubricating oil with thickening agents added to it. The National Lubricating Grease Institute (NLGI) grades grease. Grades range from No. 000 to No. 6, with No. 6 being the thickest. Typical multipurpose grease is NLGI No. 2. For specific applications, manufacturers may recommend water-resistant type grease or one with an additive such as molybdenum disulfide (MoS_2).

Brake fluid

WARNING
Never put a mineral-based (petroleum) oil into the brake system. Mineral oil causes rubber parts in the system to swell and break apart, causing complete brake failure.

Brake fluid is hydraulic fluid used to transmit hydraulic pressure (force) to the wheel brakes. Brake fluid is classified by the Department of Transportation (DOT). Designations for brake fluid include DOT 3, DOT 4 and DOT 5. This classification appears on the fluid container.

Each type of brake fluid has its own definite characteristics. Do not intermix different types of brake fluid as this may cause brake system failure. DOT 5 brake fluid is silicone based. DOT 5 is not compatible with other brake fluids or in systems for which it was not designed. Mixing DOT 5 fluid with other fluids may cause brake system failure. When adding brake fluid, *only* use the fluid recommended by the manufacturer. The ATVs covered in this manual use DOT 4 brake fluid.

Brake fluid will damage any plastic, painted or plated surface it contacts. Use extreme care when working with brake fluid and remove any spills immediately with soap and water.

Hydraulic brake systems require clean and moisture free brake fluid. Never reuse brake fluid. Keep containers and reservoirs properly sealed.

Coolant

Coolant is a mixture of water and antifreeze used to dissipate engine heat. Ethylene glycol is the most common form of antifreeze. Check the manufacturer's recommendations when selecting antifreeze. Most require one specifically designed for use in aluminum engines. These types of antifreeze have additives that inhibit corrosion. Only mix antifreeze with distilled water. Impurities in tap water may damage internal cooling system passages.

Cleaners, Degreasers and Solvents

Many chemicals are available to remove oil, grease and other debris from the ATV. Before using cleaning solvents, consider how they will be used and disposed of, particularly if they are not water-soluble. Local ordinances may require special procedures for the disposal of many types of cleaning chemicals. Refer to *Safety* in this chapter.

Use brake parts cleaner to clean brake system components. Brake parts cleaner leaves no residue. Use electrical contact cleaner to clean electrical connections and components without leaving any residue. Carburetor cleaner is a powerful solvent used to remove fuel deposits and varnish from fuel system components. Use this cleaner carefully, as it may damage finishes.

Generally, degreasers are strong cleaners used to remove heavy accumulations of grease from engine and frame components.

Most solvents are designed to be used with a parts washing cabinet for individual component cleaning. For safety, use only nonflammable or high flash point solvents.

Gasket Sealant

Sealant is used in combination with a gasket or seal. In other applications, such as between crankcase halves, only a sealant is used. Follow the manufacturer's recommendation when using a sealant. Use extreme care when choosing a sealant different from the type originally recommended. Choose sealant based on its resistance to heat, various fluids and its sealing capabilities.

A common sealant is room temperature vulcanization sealant, or RTV. This sealant cures at room temperature over a specific time period. This allows the repositioning of components without damaging gaskets.

Moisture in the air causes the RTV sealant to cure. Always install the tube cap as soon as possible after applying RTV sealant. RTV sealant has a limited shelf life and will not cure properly if the shelf life has expired. Keep partial tubes sealed and discard them if they have surpassed the expiration date.

Applying RTV sealant

Clean all old gasket residue from the mating surfaces. Remove all gasket material from blind threaded holes to avoid inaccurate bolt torque. Spray the mating surfaces with aerosol parts cleaner and then wipe with a lint-free cloth. The area must be clean for the sealant to adhere.

Apply RTV sealant in a continuous bead 2-3 mm (0.08-0.12 in.) thick. Circle all the fastener holes unless otherwise specified. Do not allow any sealant to enter these holes. Assemble and tighten the fasteners to the specified torque within the time frame recommended by the sealant manufacturer.

Gasket Remover

Aerosol gasket remover can help remove stubborn gaskets. This product can speed up the removal process and prevent damage to the mating surface that may be caused by using a scraping tool. Most of these types of products are caustic. Follow the gasket remover manufacturer's instructions for use.

Threadlocking Compound

CAUTION

Threadlocking compounds may damage plastic. Use caution when using these products in areas where there are plastic components.

A threadlocking compound is a fluid applied to the threads of fasteners. After tightening the fastener, the fluid dries and becomes a solid filler between the threads. This makes it difficult for the fastener to work loose from vibration or heat expansion and contraction. Some threadlocking compounds also provide a seal against fluid leaks.

Before applying a threadlocking compound, remove any old compound from both thread areas and clean them with aerosol parts cleaner. Use the compound sparingly. Excess fluid can run into adjoining parts.

Threadlocking compounds are available in a wide range of compounds for various strength, tem-

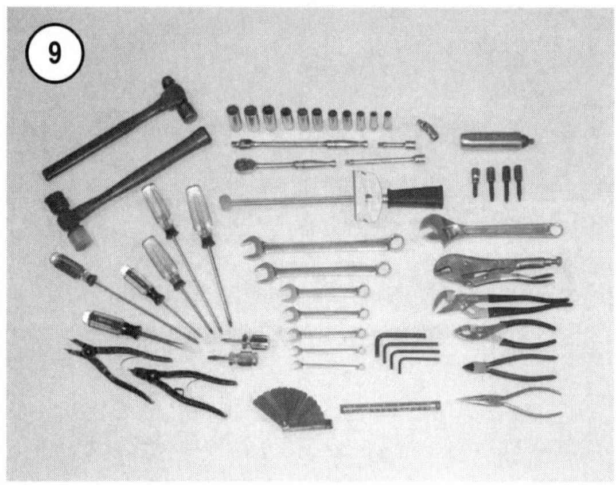

perature and repair applications. Follow the manufacturer's recommendations regarding compound selection.

TOOLS

Most of the procedures in this manual can be carried out with simple hand tools and test equipment familiar to the home mechanic. Always use the correct tools for the job at hand. Keep tools organized and clean. Store them in a tool chest with related tools organized together.

Quality tools are essential. The best are constructed of high-strength alloy steel. These tools are light, easy to use and resistant to wear. Their working surface is devoid of sharp edges and carefully polished. They have an easy-to-clean finish and are comfortable to use. Quality tools are a good investment.

Some of the procedures in this manual specify special tools. In many cases the tool is illustrated in use. Those with a large tool kit may be able to use a suitable substitute or fabricate a replacement. However, in some cases, the specialized equipment or expertise may make it impractical for the home mechanic to attempt the procedure. When necessary, such operations come with the recommendation to have a dealership or specialist perform the task. It may be less expensive to have a professional perform these jobs, especially when considering the cost of equipment.

When purchasing tools to perform the procedures in this manual, consider the tool's potential frequency of use. If a tool kit is just now being started, consider purchasing a basic tool set (**Figure 9**). These sets are available in many tool combinations and offer substantial savings when compared to individually purchased tools. As work experience grows and tasks become more complicated, specialized tools can be added.

Screwdrivers

Screwdrivers of various lengths and types are mandatory for the simplest tool kit. The two basic types are the slotted tip (flat blade) and the Phillips tip. These are available in sets that often include an assortment of tip sizes and shaft lengths.

As with all tools, use a screwdriver designed for the job. Make sure the size of the tip conforms to the size and shape of the fastener. Use them only for driving screws. Never use a screwdriver for prying or chiseling metal. Repair or replace worn or damaged screwdrivers. A worn tip may damage the fastener, making it difficult to remove.

Phillips-head screws are often damaged by incorrectly fitting screwdrivers. Quality Phillips screwdrivers are manufactured with their crosshead tip machined to Phillips Screw Company specifications. Poor quality or damaged Phillips screwdrivers can back out (camout) and round over the screw head. In addition, weak or soft screw materials can make removal difficult.

An effective screwdriver to use on Phillips screws is a ACR Phillips II screwdriver. Anti-camout ribs (ACR) on the driving faces or flutes of the screwdriver's tip (**Figure 10**) improve the driver-to-fastener grip. ACR Phillips II screwdrivers are designed to be used with ACR Phillips II screws, but they work well on all common Phillips screws. ACR Phillips II screwdrivers are available in different tip sizes and with interchangeable bits to fit screwdriver holders.

Another way to prevent camout and to increase the grip of a Phillips screwdriver is to apply valve grinding compound or Permatex Screw & Socket Gripper onto the screwdriver tip. After loosening/tightening the screw, clean the screw recess.

Wrenches

Open-end, box-end and combination wrenches (**Figure 11**) are available in a variety of types and sizes.

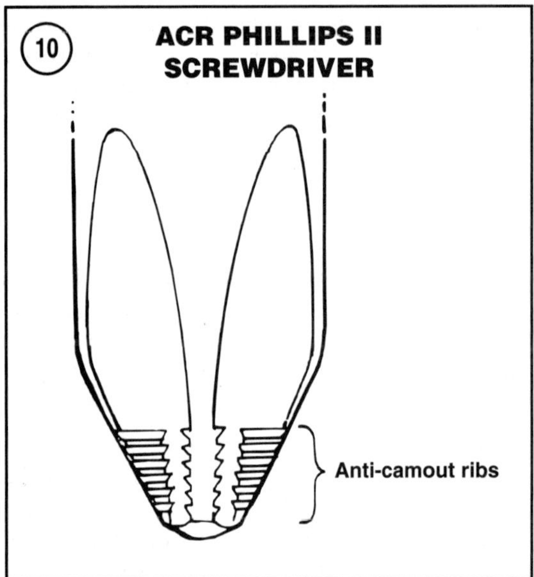

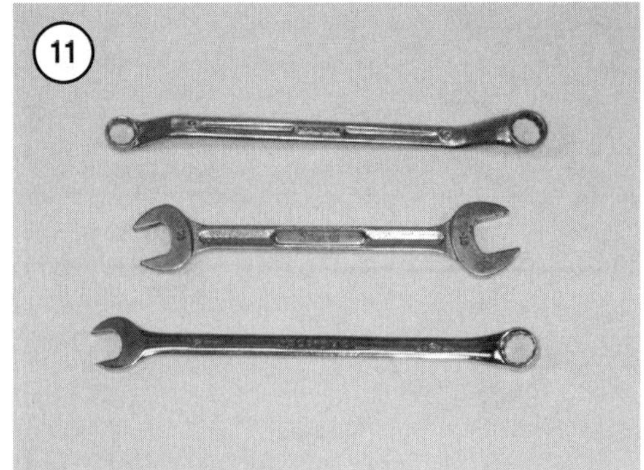

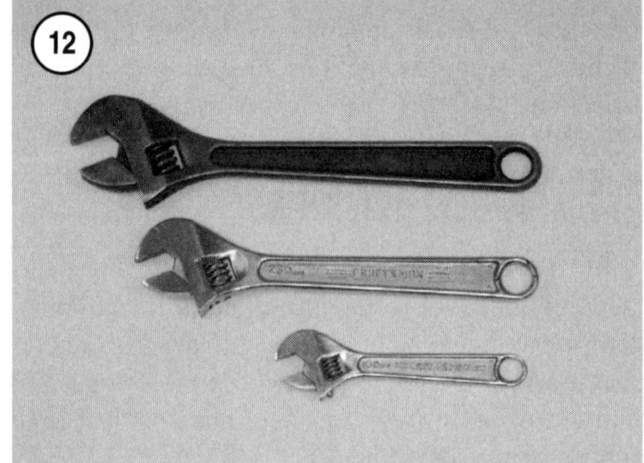

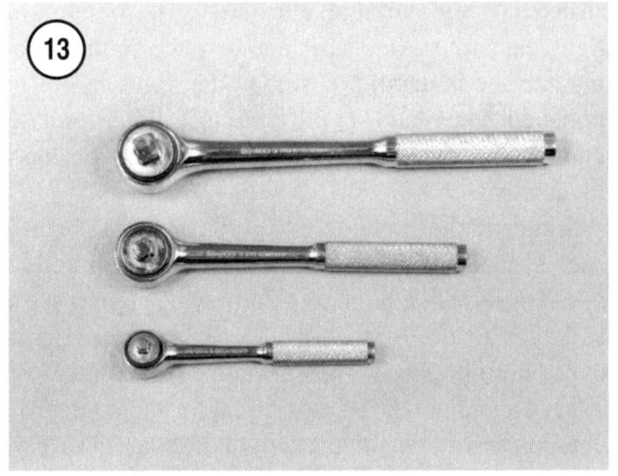

The number stamped on the wrench refers to the distance between the work areas. This size must match the size of the fastener head.

The box-end wrench is an excellent tool because it grips the fastener on all sides. This reduces the chance of the tool slipping. The box-end wrench is designed with either a 6- or 12-point opening. For stubborn or damaged fasteners, the 6-point provides superior holding because it contacts the fastener across a wider area at all six edges. For general use, the 12-point works well. It allows the wrench to be removed and reinstalled without moving the handle over such a wide arc.

An open-end wrench is fast and works best in areas with limited overhead access. It contacts the fastener at only two points and is subject to slipping if under heavy force, or if the tool or fastener is worn. A box-end wrench is preferred in most instances, especially when breaking loose and applying the final tightness to a fastener.

The combination wrench has a box-end on one end and an open-end on the other. This combination makes it a convenient tool.

Adjustable Wrenches

An adjustable wrench or Crescent wrench (**Figure 12**) can fit nearly any nut or bolt head that has clear access around its entire perimeter. An adjustable wrench is best used as a backup wrench to keep a large nut or bolt from turning while the other end is being loosened or tightened with a box-end or socket wrench.

Adjustable wrenches contact the fastener at only two points, which makes them more subject to slipping off the fastener. Because one jaw is adjustable and may become loose, this shortcoming is aggravated. Make certain the solid jaw is the one transmitting the force.

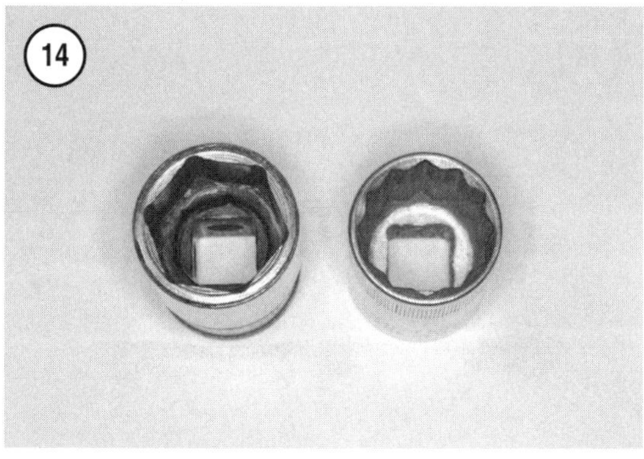

14

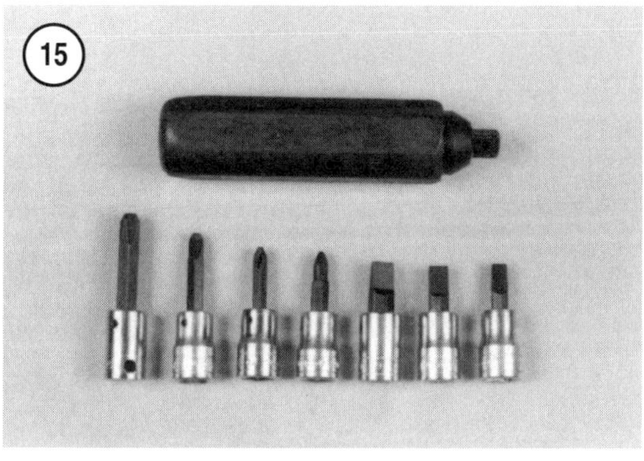

15

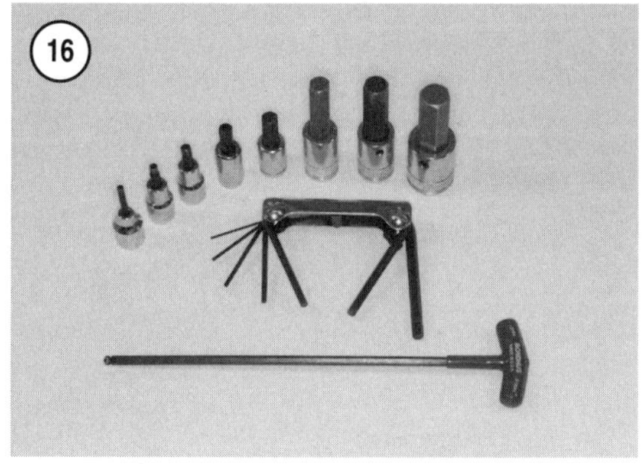

16

Socket Wrenches, Ratchets and Handles

WARNING
Do not use hand sockets with air or impact tools because they may shatter and cause injury. Always wear eye protection when using impact or air tools.

Sockets that attach to a ratchet handle (**Figure 13**) are available with 6-point or 12-point openings (**Figure 14**) and different drive sizes. The drive size indicates the size of the square hole that accepts the ratchet handle. The number stamped on the socket is the size of the work area and must match the fastener head.

As with wrenches, a 6-point socket provides superior-holding ability, while a 12-point socket needs to be moved only half as far to reposition it on the fastener.

Sockets are designated for either hand or impact use. Impact sockets are thicker than hand sockets. Use impact sockets when using an impact driver or air tools. Use hand sockets with hand-driven attachments.

Various handles are available for sockets. Use the speed handle for fast operation. Flexible ratchet heads in varying lengths allow the socket to be turned with varying force and at odd angles. Extension bars allow the socket setup to reach difficult areas. The ratchet is the most versatile. It allows the user to install or remove the nut without removing the socket.

Sockets combined with any number of drivers make them undoubtedly the fastest, safest and most convenient tool for fastener removal and installation.

Impact Drivers

WARNING
Do not use hand sockets with air or impact tools because they may shatter and cause injury. Always wear eye protection when using impact or air tools.

An impact driver provides extra force for removing fasteners by converting the impact of a hammer into a turning motion. This makes it possible to remove stubborn fasteners without damaging them. Impact drivers and interchangeable bits (**Figure 15**) are available from most tool suppliers. When using a socket with an impact driver, make sure the socket is designed for impact use. Refer to *Socket Wrenches, Ratchets and Handles* in this section.

Allen Wrenches

Use Allen or setscrew wrenches (**Figure 16**) on fasteners with hexagonal recesses in the fastener head. These wrenches are available in L-shaped bar,

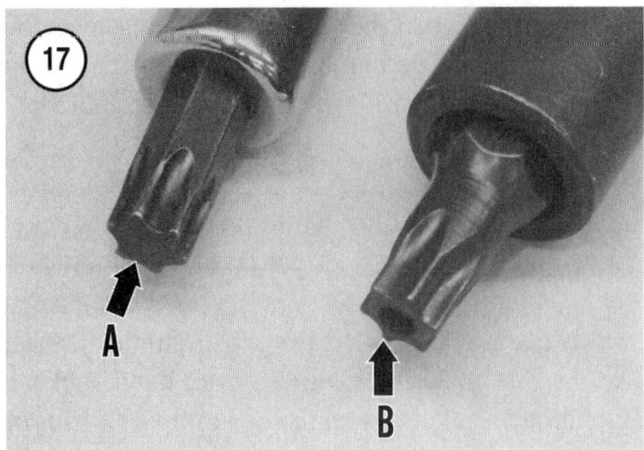

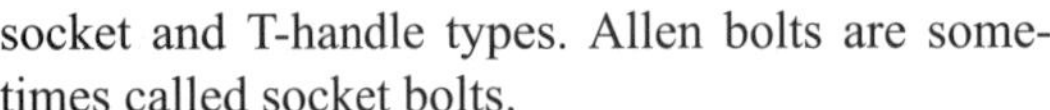

socket and T-handle types. Allen bolts are sometimes called socket bolts.

Torx Fasteners

A Torx fastener head is a 6-point star-shaped pattern (A, **Figure 17**). Torx fasteners are identified with a T and a number indicating their drive size. For example, T25. Torx drivers are available in L-shaped bars, sockets and T-handles. Tamper-resistant Torx fasteners are also used and have a round shaft in the center of the fastener head. Tamper-resistance Torx fasteners require a Torx bit with a hole in the center of the bit (B, **Figure 17**).

Torque Wrenches

Use a torque wrench (**Figure 18**) with a socket, torque adapter or similar extension to tighten a fastener to a measured torque. Torque wrenches come in several drive sizes (1/4, 3/8, 1/2 and 3/4) and have various methods of reading the torque value. The drive size indicates the size of the square drive that accepts the socket, adapter or extension. Common methods of reading the torque value are the deflecting beam, the dial indicator and the audible click .

When choosing a torque wrench, consider the torque range, drive size and accuracy. The torque specifications in this manual provide an indication of the range required.

A torque wrench is a precision tool that must be properly cared for to remain accurate. Store torque wrenches in cases or separate padded drawers within a toolbox. Follow the manufacturer's instructions for their care and calibration.

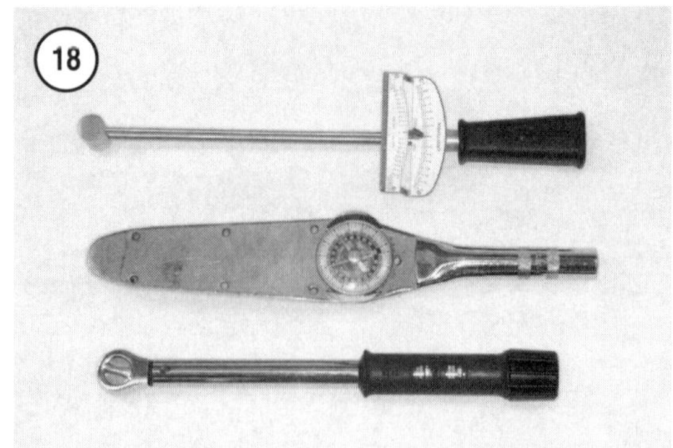

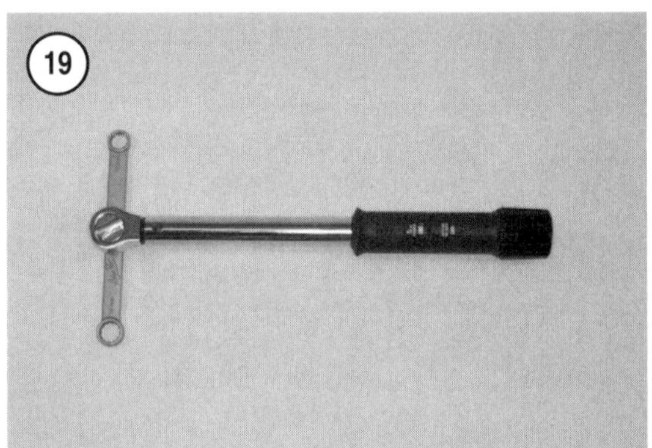

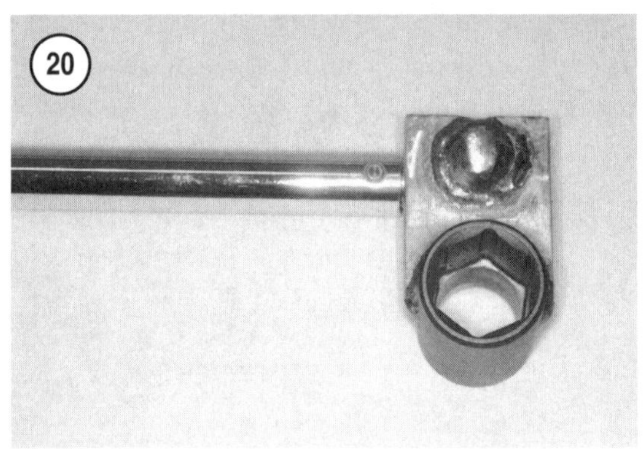

Torque Adapters

Torque adapters or extensions extend or reduce the reach of a torque wrench. The torque adapter shown in **Figure 19** is used to tighten a fastener that cannot be reached because of the size of the torque wrench head, drive, and socket. In some cases an adapter can be fabricated for specific applications (**Figure 20**). If a torque adapter changes the effective lever length (**Figure 21**), the torque reading on the wrench will not equal the actual torque applied

(21)

TORQUE WRENCH EFFECTIVE LENGTH

L A

L A

L + A = Effective length

L

L = Effective length

L

No calculation needed

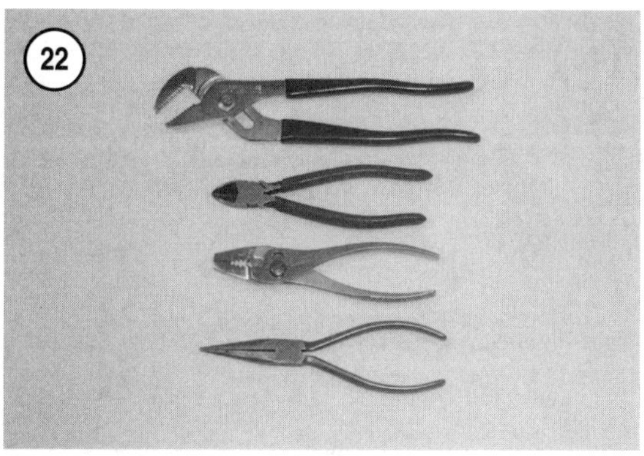

(22)

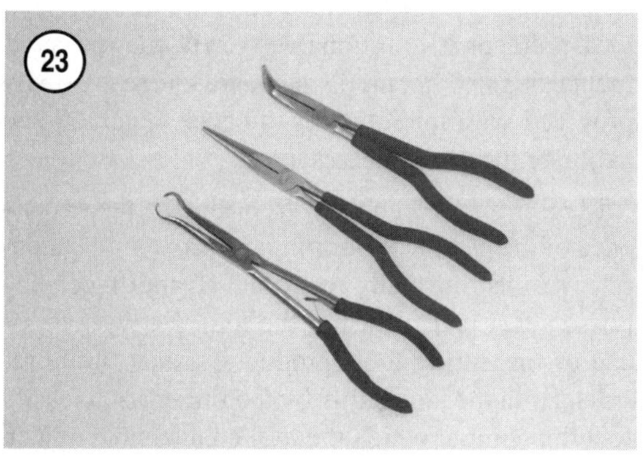

(23)

to the fastener. It is necessary to recalibrate the torque setting on the wrench to compensate for the change of lever length. When using a torque adapter at a right angle to the drive head, calibration is not required, because the effective length has not changed.

To recalculate a torque reading when using a torque adapter, use the following formula:

$$TW = \frac{TA \times L}{L + A}$$

TW is the torque setting or dial reading on the wrench.

TA is the torque specification and the actual amount of torque that is applied to the fastener.

A is the amount that the adapter increases (or in some cases reduces) the effective lever length as measured along the centerline of the torque wrench.

L is the lever length of the wrench as measured from the center of the drive to the center of the grip.

The effective length is the sum of L and A.

Example:

TA = 20 ft.-lb.

A = 3 in.

L = 14 in.

$$TW = \frac{20 \times 14}{14 + 3} = \frac{280}{17} = 16.5 \text{ ft.-lb.}$$

In this example, the torque wrench would be set to the recalculated torque value (TW = 16.5 ft.-lb.). When using a beam-type wrench, tighten the fastener until the pointer aligns with 16.5 ft.-lb. In this example, although the torque wrench is pre set to 16.5 ft.-lb., the actual torque is 20 ft.-lb.

Pliers

Pliers come in a wide range of types and sizes. Pliers are useful for holding, cutting, bending, and crimping. Do not use them to turn fasteners. **Figure 22** and **Figure 23** show several types of useful pliers. Each design has a specialized function. Slip-joint pliers are general-purpose pliers used for gripping and bending. Diagonal cutting pliers are needed to cut wire and can be used to remove cotter pins. Use needlenose pliers to hold or bend small objects. Locking pliers (**Figure 24**), sometimes called Vise-Grips, are used to hold objects very tightly. They have many uses ranging from holding two parts together, to gripping the end of a broken stud. Use caution when using locking pliers, as the sharp jaws will damage the objects they hold.

Snap Ring Pliers

WARNING
Snap rings can slip and fly off when removing and installing them. Also, the snap ring pliers' tips may break. Always wear eye protection when using snap ring pliers.

Snap ring pliers are specialized pliers with tips that fit into the ends of snap rings to remove and install them. Snap ring pliers (**Figure 25**) are available with a fixed action (either internal or external) or convertible (one tool works on both internal and external snap rings). They may have fixed tips or interchangeable ones of various sizes and angles. For general use, select a convertible type pliers with interchangeable tips.

Hammers

Various types of hammers (**Figure 26**) are available to fit a number of applications. Use a ball-peen hammer to strike another tool, such as a punch or chisel. Use soft-faced hammers when a metal object must be struck without damaging it. Never use a metal-faced hammer on engine and suspension components because damage occurs in most cases.

Always wear eye protection when using hammers. Make sure the hammer face is in good condition and the handle is not cracked. Select the correct hammer for the job and make sure to strike the object squarely. Do not use the handle or the side of the hammer to strike an object.

MEASURING TOOLS

The ability to accurately measure components is essential to perform many of the procedures described in this manual. Equipment is manufactured to close tolerances, and obtaining consistently accurate measurements is essential to determine which components require replacement or further service.

Each type of measuring instrument is designed to measure a dimension with a certain degree of accuracy and within a certain range. When selecting the measuring tool, make sure it is applicable to the task.

As with all tools, measuring tools provide the best results if cared for properly. Improper use can damage the tool and cause inaccurate results. If any measurement is questionable, verify the measurement using another tool. A standard gauge is usually provided with micrometers to check accuracy and calibrate the tool if necessary.

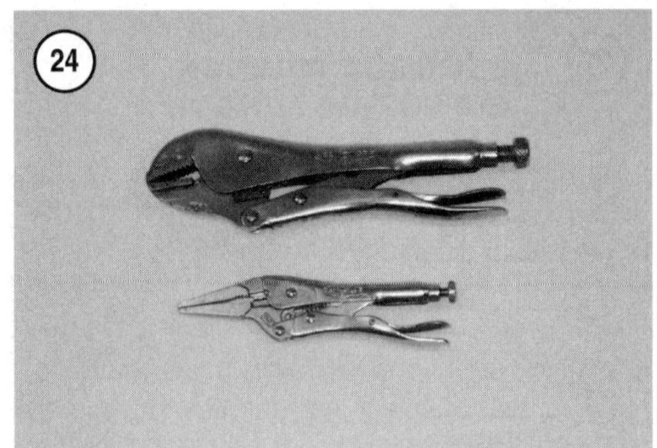
24

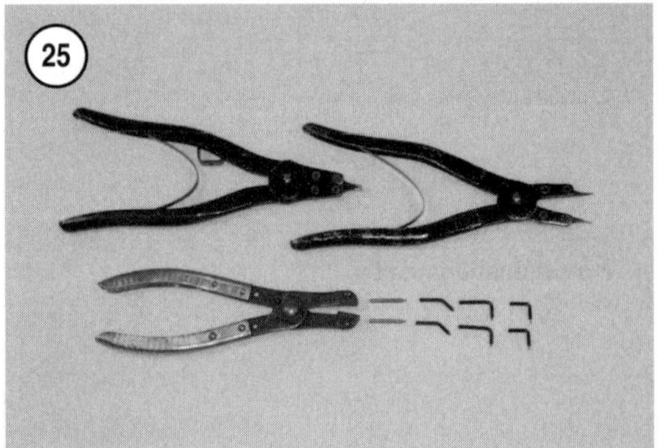
25

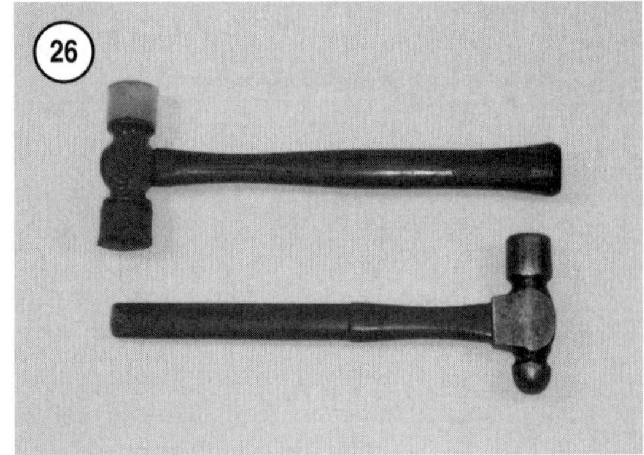
26

Measurements can vary according to the experience of the person performing the procedure. Accurate results are only possible if the mechanic possesses a feel for using the tool. Heavy-handed use of measuring tools produces less accurate results. Hold the tool gently by the fingertips to easily feel the point at which the tool contacts the object.

27

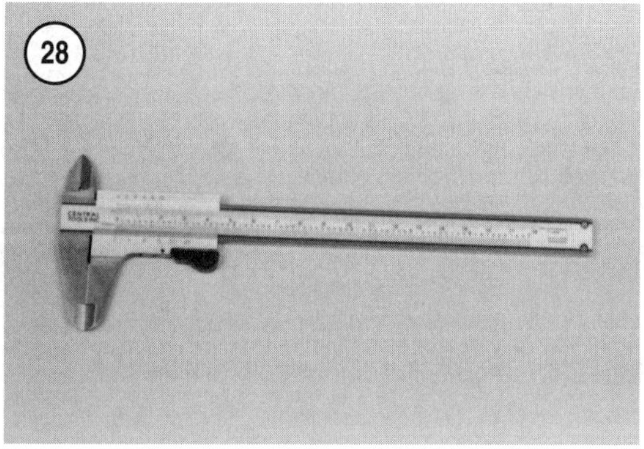

28

This feel for the equipment produces more accurate measurements and reduces the risk of damaging the tool or component. Refer to the following sections for specific measuring tools.

Feeler Gauge

Use feeler or thickness gauges (**Figure 27**) for measuring the distance between two surfaces. A feeler gauge set consists of an assortment of steel strips of graduated thickness. Each blade is marked with its thickness. Blades can be of various lengths and angles for different procedures. A common use for a feeler gauge is to measure valve clearance. Use wire (round) type gauges to measure spark plug gap.

Calipers

Calipers (**Figure 28**) are used to obtain inside, outside and depth measurements. Although not as precise as a micrometer, they allow reasonable precision, typically to within 0.05 mm (0.001 in.). Most calipers have a range up to 150 mm (6 in.).

Calipers are available in dial, vernier or digital versions. Dial calipers have a dial readout that provides convenient reading. Vernier calipers have marked scales that must be compared to determine the measurement. The digital caliper uses a liquid-crystal display (LCD) to show the measurement.

Properly maintain the measuring surfaces of the caliper. There must not be any dirt or burrs between the tool and the object being measured. Never force the caliper to close around an object. Close the caliper around the highest point so it can be removed with a slight drag. Some calipers require calibration. Always refer to the manufacturer's instructions when using a new or unfamiliar caliper.

To read a vernier caliper refer to **Figure 29**. The fixed scale is marked in 1-mm increments. Ten individual lines on the fixed scale equal 1 cm. The movable scale is marked in 0.05 mm (hundredth) increments. To obtain a reading, establish the first number by the location of the 0 line on the movable scale in relation to the first line to the left on the fixed scale. In this example, the number is 10 mm. To determine the next number, note which of the lines on the movable scale align with a mark on the fixed scale. A number of lines will seem close, but only one will align exactly. In this case, 0.50 mm is the reading to add to the first number. Adding 10 mm and 0.50 mm equals a measurement of 10.50 mm.

Micrometers

A micrometer (**Figure 30**) is an instrument designed for linear measurement using the decimal divisions of the inch or meter. While there are many types and styles of micrometers, most of the procedures in this manual call for an outside micrometer. Use the outside micrometer to measure the outside diameter of cylindrical forms and the thickness of materials.

A micrometer's size indicates the minimum and maximum size of a part that it can measure. The usual sizes are 0-25 mm (0-1 in.), 25-50 mm (1-2 in.), 50-75 mm (2-3 in.) and 75-100 mm (3-4 in.).

Micrometers that cover a wider range of measurements are available. These use a large frame with interchangeable anvils of various lengths. This type of micrometer offers a cost savings, but its overall size may make it less convenient.

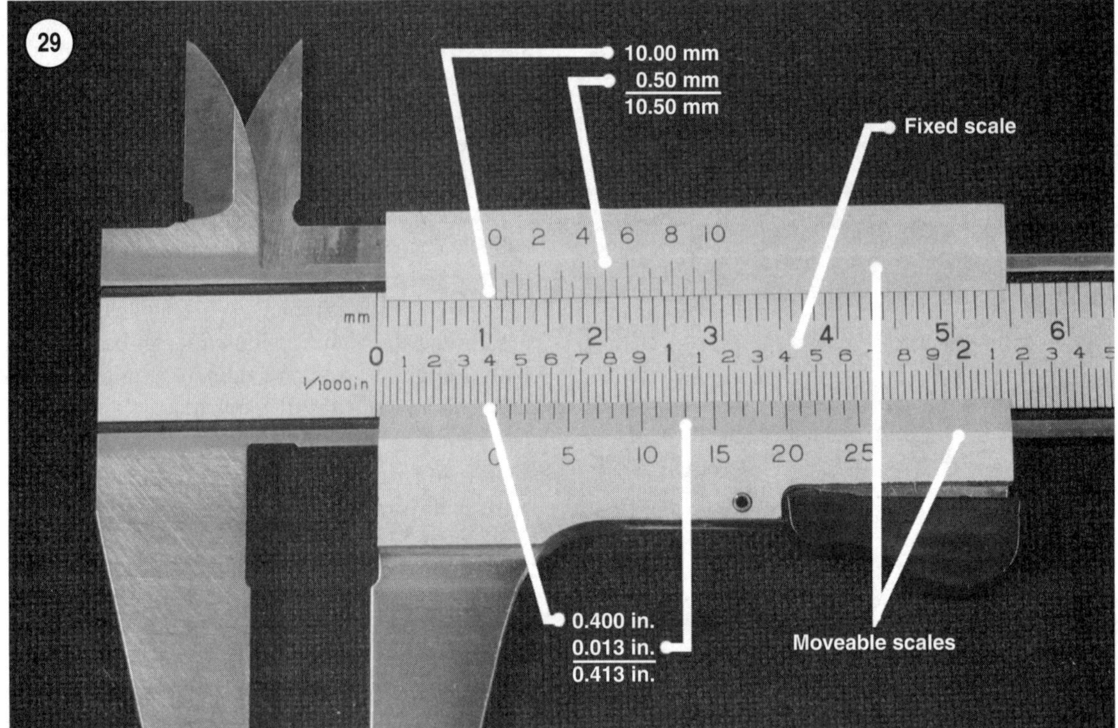

Adjustment

Before using a micrometer, check its adjustment as follows:

1. Clean the anvil and spindle faces.

2A. To check a 0-25 mm (0-1 in.) micrometer:

   a. Turn the thimble until the spindle contacts the anvil. If the micrometer has a ratchet stop, use it to ensure that the proper amount of pressure is applied.

   b. If the adjustment is correct, the 0 mark on the thimble will align exactly with the 0 mark on the sleeve line. If the marks do not align, the micrometer is out of adjustment.

   c. Follow the manufacturer's instructions to adjust the micrometer.

2B. To check a micrometer larger than 25 mm (1 in.), use the standard gauge supplied by the manufacturer. A standard gauge is a steel block, disc or rod that is machined to an exact size.

   a. Place the standard gauge between the spindle and anvil, and measure its outside diameter or length. If the micrometer has a ratchet stop, use it to ensure that the proper amount of pressure is applied.

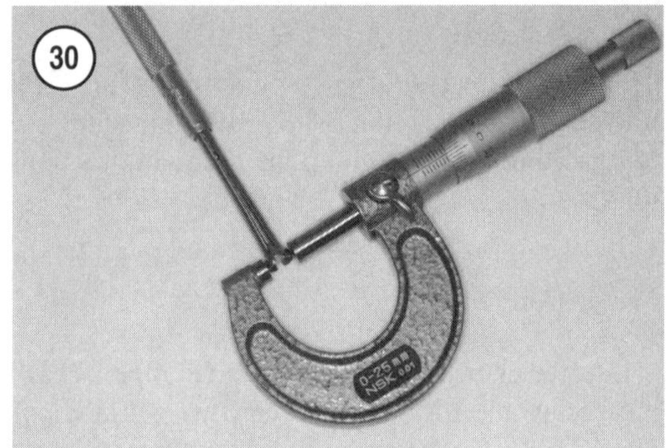

   b. If the adjustment is correct, the 0 mark on the thimble will align exactly with the 0 mark on the sleeve line. If the marks do not align, the micrometer is out of adjustment.

   c. Follow the manufacturer's instructions to adjust the micrometer.

Care

Micrometers are precision instruments. They must be used and maintained with great care. Note the following:

31

5.00 mm
0.50 mm
0.18 mm
5.68 mm

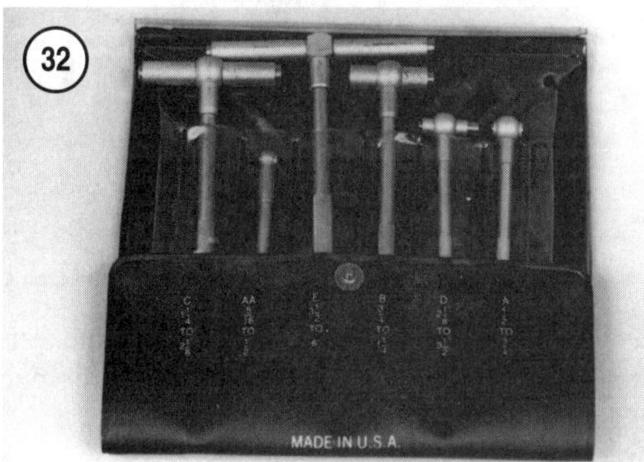

32

1. Store micrometers in protective cases or separate padded drawers in a toolbox.
2. When in storage, make sure the spindle and anvil faces do not contact each other or an other object. If they do, temperature changes and corrosion may damage the contact faces.
3. Do not clean a micrometer with compressed air. Dirt forced into the tool will cause wear.
4. Lubricate micrometers with WD-40 to prevent corrosion.

Reading

When reading a micrometer, numbers are taken from different scales and added together.

For accurate results, properly maintain the measuring surfaces of the micrometer. There cannot be any dirt or burrs between the tool and the measured object. Never force the micrometer to close around an object. Close the micrometer around the highest point so it can be removed with a slight drag.

The standard metric micrometer is accurate to one one-hundredth of a millimeter (0.01 mm). The sleeve line is graduated in millimeter and half millimeter increments. The marks on the upper half of the sleeve line equal 1.00 mm. Each fifth mark above the sleeve line is identified with a number. The number sequence depends on the size of the micrometer. A 0-25 mm micrometer, for example, will have sleeve marks numbered 0 through 25 in 5 mm increments. This numbering sequence continues with larger micrometers. On all metric micrometers, each mark on the lower half of the sleeve equals 0.50 mm.

The tapered end of the thimble has 50 lines marked around it. Each mark equals 0.01 mm. One complete turn of the thimble aligns its 0 mark with the first line on the lower half of the sleeve line or 0.50 mm.

When reading a metric micrometer, add the number of millimeters and half-millimeters on the sleeve line to the number of one one-hundredth millimeters on the thimble. Perform the following steps while referring to **Figure 31**.

1. Read the upper half of the sleeve line and count the number of lines visible. Each upper line equals 1 mm.
2. See if the half-millimeter line is visible on the lower sleeve line. If so, add 0.50 mm to the reading in Step 1.
3. Read the thimble mark that aligns with the sleeve line. Each thimble mark equals 0.01 mm.
4. If a thimble mark does not align exactly with the sleeve line, estimate the amount between the lines. For accurate readings in two-thousandths of a millimeter (0.002 mm), use a metric vernier micrometer.
5. Add the readings from Steps 1-3.

Telescoping and Small Hole Gauges

Use telescoping gauges (**Figure 32**) and small hole gauges (**Figure 33**) to measure bores. Neither gauge has a scale for direct readings. Use an outside micrometer to determine the reading.

To use a telescoping gauge, select the correct size gauge for the bore. Compress the movable post and carefully insert the gauge into the bore. Carefully move the gauge in the bore to make sure it is centered. Tighten the knurled end of the gauge to hold the movable post in position. Remove the gauge and measure the length of the posts. Telescoping gauges are typically used to measure cylinder bores.

To use a small hole gauge, select the correct size gauge for the bore. Carefully insert the gauge into the bore. Tighten the knurled end of the gauge to carefully expand the gauge fingers to the limit within the bore. Do not overtighten the gauge because there is no built-in release. Excessive tightening can damage the bore surface and damage the tool. Remove the gauge and measure the outside dimension (**Figure 34**). Small hole gauges are typically used to measure valve guides.

33

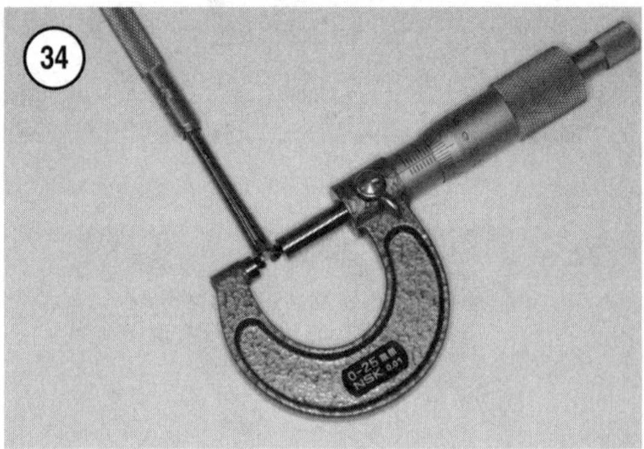

34

Dial Indicator

A dial indicator (**Figure 35**) is a gauge with a dial face and needle used to measure variations in dimensions and movements. Measuring brake rotor runout is a typical use for a dial indicator.

Dial indicators are available in various ranges and graduations and with three basic types of mounting bases: magnetic (**Figure 35**), clamp, or screw-in stud. When purchasing a dial indicator, select one with a continuous dial.

Cylinder Bore Gauge

A cylinder bore gauge is similar to a dial indicator. A bore gauge set consists of a dial indicator, handle, and different length adapters (anvils) to fit the gauge to various bore sizes. The bore gauge is used to measure bore size, taper and out-of-round. When using a bore gauge, follow the manufacturer's instructions.

Compression Gauge

A compression gauge (**Figure 36**) measures combustion chamber (cylinder) pressure, usually in psi or kg/cm^2. The gauge adapter is either inserted or screwed into the spark plug hole to obtain the reading.

Multimeter

A multimeter (**Figure 37**) is an essential tool for electrical system diagnosis. The voltage function indicates the voltage applied or available to various electrical components. The ohmmeter function tests circuits for continuity, or lack of continuity, and measures the resistance of a circuit.

Some manufacturers' specifications for electrical components are based on results using a specific test meter. Results may vary if using a meter not recommended by the manufacturer is used. Such requirements are noted when applicable.

Ohmmeter (analog) calibration

Each time an analog ohmmeter is used or if the scale is changed, the ohmmeter must be calibrated. Digital ohmmeters do not require calibration.

1. Make sure the meter battery is in good condition.
2. Make sure the meter probes are in good condition.
3. Touch the two probes together and observe the needle location on the ohms scale. The needle must align with the 0 mark to obtain accurate measurements.
4. If necessary, rotate the meter ohms adjust knob until the needle and 0 mark align.

35

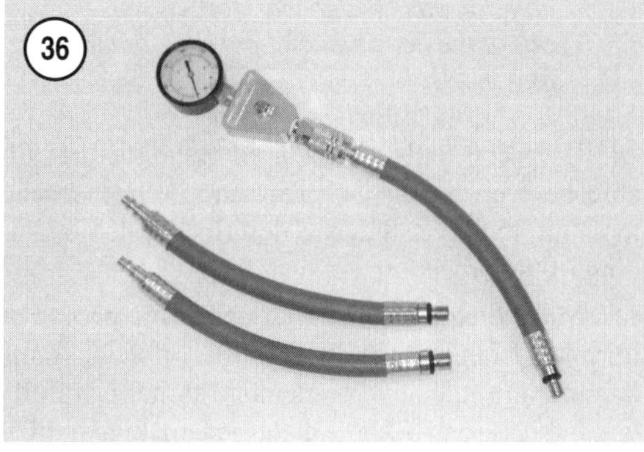
36

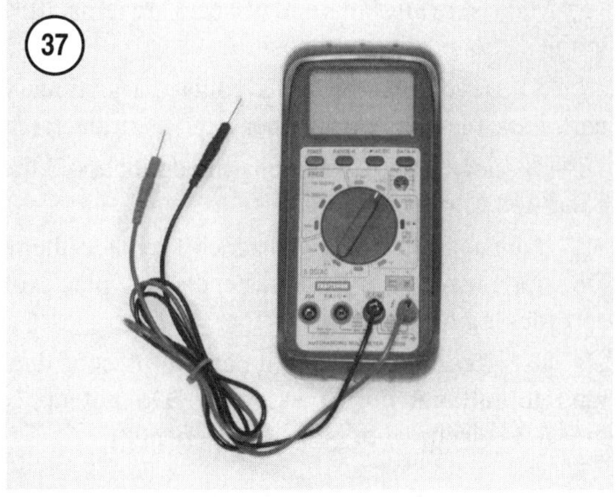
37

ELECTRICAL SYSTEM FUNDAMENTALS

A thorough study of the many types of electrical systems used in today's ATV is beyond the scope of this manual. However, a basic understanding of voltage, resistance and amperage is necessary to perform diagnostic tests.

Refer to Chapter Two for troubleshooting. Refer to Chapter Nine for specific test procedures.

Voltage

Voltage is the electrical potential or pressure in an electrical circuit and is expressed in volts. The more pressure (voltage) in a circuit, the more work can be performed.

Direct current (DC) voltage means the electricity flows in one direction. All circuits powered by a battery are DC circuits.

Alternating current (AC) means the electricity flows in one direction momentarily and then switches to the opposite direction. Alternator output is an example of AC voltage. This voltage must be changed or rectified to direct current to operate in a battery powered system.

Resistance

Resistance is the opposition to the flow of electricity within a circuit or component and is measured in ohms. Resistance causes a reduction in available current and voltage.

Resistance is measured in an inactive circuit with an ohmmeter. The ohmmeter sends a small amount of current into the circuit and measures how difficult it is to push the current through the circuit.

An ohmmeter, although useful, is not always a good indicator of a circuit's actual ability under operating conditions. This is because of the low voltage (6-9 volts) the meter uses to test the circuit. The voltage in an ignition coil secondary winding can be several thousand volts. Such high voltage can cause the coil to malfunction, even though it tests acceptable during a resistance test.

Resistance generally increases with temperature. Perform all testing with the component or circuit at room temperature. Resistance tests performed at high temperatures may indicate high resistance readings and cause unnecessary replacement of a component.

Amperage

Amperage is the unit of measurement for the amount of current within a circuit. Current is the actual flow of electricity. The higher the current, the more work can be performed up to a given point. If the current flow exceeds the circuit or component capacity, it will damage the system.

SERVICE METHODS

Most of the procedures in this manual are straightforward and can be performed by anyone reasonably competent with tools. However, consider personal capabilities carefully before attempting any operation involving major disassembly.

1. Front, in this manual, refers to the front of the vehicle. The front of any component is the end closest to the front of the ATV. The left and right sides refer to the position of the parts as viewed by the rider sitting on the seat facing forward.
2. Whenever servicing an engine or suspension component, secure the ATV in a safe manner.
3. Tag all similar parts for location and mark all mating parts for position. Record the number and thickness of any shims when removing them. Identify parts by placing them in sealed and labeled plastic sandwich bags.
4. Tag disconnected wires and connectors with masking tape and a marking pen. Do not rely on memory alone.
5. Protect finished surfaces from physical damage or corrosion. Keep gasoline and other chemicals off painted surfaces.
6. Use penetrating oil on frozen or tight bolts. Avoid using heat where possible. Heat can warp, melt or affect the temper of parts. Heat also damages the finish of paint and plastics.
7. When a part is a press fit or requires a special tool to remove, the information or type of tool is identified in the text. Otherwise, if a part is difficult to remove or install, determine the cause before proceeding.
8. To prevent objects or debris from falling into the engine, cover all openings.
9. Read each procedure thoroughly and compare the illustrations to the actual components before starting the procedure. Perform the procedure in sequence.
10. Recommendations are occasionally made to refer service to a dealership or specialist. In these cases, the work can be performed more economically by the specialist than by the home mechanic.
11. The term *replace* means to discard a defective part and replace it with a new part. *Overhaul* means to remove, disassemble, inspect, measure, repair and/or replace parts as required to recondition an assembly.
12. Some operations require using a hydraulic press. If a press is not available, have these operations performed by a shop equipped with the necessary equipment. Do not use makeshift equipment that may damage the vehicle.
13. Repairs are much faster and easier if the ATV is clean before starting work. Degrease the vehicle with a commercial degreaser; follow the directions on the container for the best results. Clean all parts with cleaning solvent when removing them.

CAUTION

Do not direct high-pressure water at steering bearings, fuel hoses, wheel bearings, suspension and electrical components. Water may force grease out of the bearings and possibly damage the seals.

14. If special tools are required, have them available before starting the procedure. When special tools are required, they are described at the beginning of the procedure.
15. Make diagrams of similar-appearing parts. For instance, crankcase bolts are often not the same lengths. Do not rely on memory alone. Carefully laid out parts can become disturbed, making it difficult to reassemble the components correctly.
16. Make sure all shims and washers are reinstalled in the same location and position.
17. Whenever rotating parts contact a stationary part, look for a shim or washer.
18. Use new gaskets if there is any doubt about the condition of old ones.
19. If using self-locking fasteners, replace them. Do not install standard fasteners in place of self-locking ones.
20. Use grease to hold small parts in place if they tend to fall out during assembly. Do not apply grease to electrical or brake components.

Heating Components

WARNING

Wear protective gloves to prevent burns and injury when heating parts.

CAUTION

Do not use a welding torch when heating parts. A welding torch applies excessive heat to a small area very quickly, which can damage parts.

38

Filed

Slotted

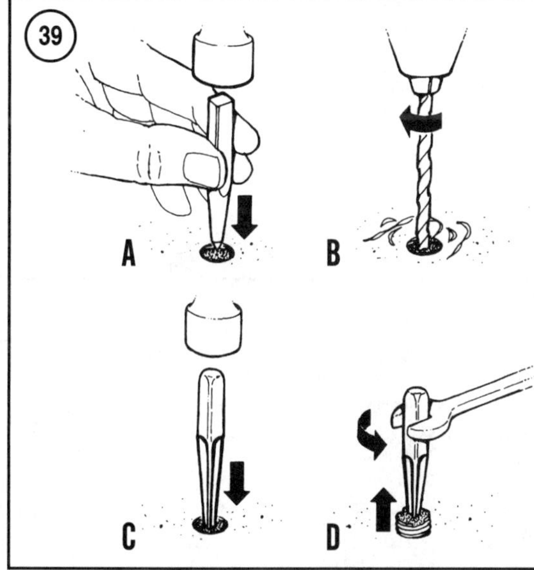

A heat gun or propane torch is required to disassemble, assemble, remove and install many parts and components in this manual. Read the safety and operating information supplied by the manufacturer of the heat gun or propane torch while also noting the following:

1. The work area should be clean and dry. Remove all combustible components and materials from the work area. Wipe up all grease, oil and other fluids from parts. Check for leaking or damaged fuel system components. Repair or remove these parts before beginning work.
2. Never use a flame near the battery, fuel tank, fuel lines or other flammable materials.
3. When using a heat gun, remember that the temperature can be in excess of 540° C (1000° F).
4. Have a fire extinguisher near the job.
5. Always wear protective goggles and gloves when heating parts.
6. Before heating a part installed on the ATV, check areas around the part and those hidden that could be damaged or possibly ignite. Do not heat surfaces than can be damaged by heat. Shield materials near the part or area to be heated. For example, cables and wiring harnesses.
7. Before heating a part, read the entire procedure to make sure the required tools are available. This allows quick work while the part is at its optimum temperature.
8. The amount of heat recommended to remove or install a part is typically listed in the procedure. However, before heating parts without a specific recommendation, consider the possible effects. To avoid damaging a part, monitor the temperature with heat sticks or an infrared thermometer, if possible. Another way, though not as accurate, is to place tiny drops of water on the part. When the water starts to sizzle, the part is hot enough. Keep the heat in motion to prevent overheating.

Removing Frozen Fasteners

If a fastener is difficult to remove, apply penetrating oil and let it penetrate for 10-15 minutes. Work the fastener in and out and reapply the penetrating oil if necessary.

For frozen screws, apply penetrating oil, then insert a screwdriver in the slot and rap the top of the screwdriver with a hammer. This loosens the rust so the screw can be removed in the normal way. If the screw head is damaged, grip the head with locking pliers and twist the screw out.

Refer to *Tools* in this chapter for Phillips screws.

If heat is required, refer to *Heating Components* in this section.

Removing Broken Fasteners

If the head breaks off a screw or bolt, several methods are available for removing the remaining portion. If a large portion of the remainder projects out, try gripping it with locking pliers. If the projecting portion is too small, file it to fit a wrench or cut a slot in it to fit a screwdriver (**Figure 38**).

If the head breaks off flush, use a screw extractor. To do this, centerpunch the exact center of the remaining portion of the screw or bolt (A, **Figure 39**), and then drill a small hole in the screw (B), and tap the extractor into the hole (C). Back the screw out with a wrench on the extractor (D, **Figure 39**).

Repairing Damaged Threads

Occasionally, threads are stripped through carelessness or impact damage. Often the threads can be repaired by running a tap (for internal threads on nuts) or die (for external threads on bolts) through the threads (**Figure 40**). To clean or repair spark plug threads, use a spark plug tap.

If an internal thread is damaged, it may be necessary to install a Helicoil or some other type of thread insert. Follow the manufacturer's instructions when installing their insert.

If it is necessary to drill and tap a hole, refer to **Table 5** for metric tap and drill sizes.

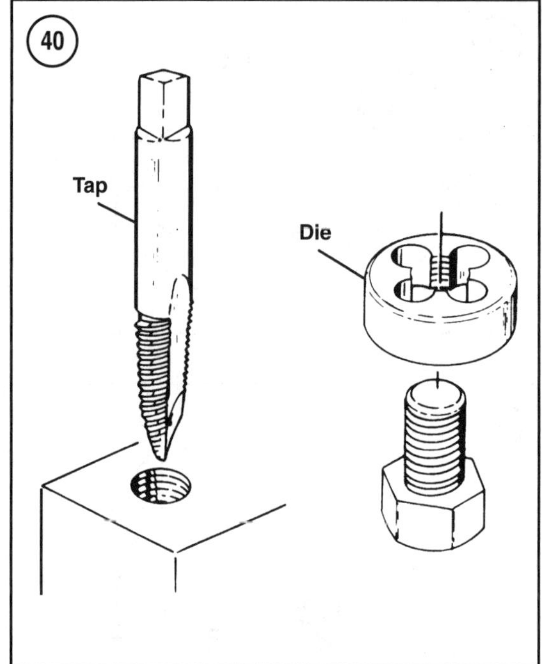

Stud Removal/Installation

A stud removal tool (**Figure 41**) is available from most tool suppliers. This tool makes the removal and installation of studs easier. If one is not available, thread two nuts onto the stud and tighten them against each other. Remove the stud by turning the lower nut.

1. Measure the height of the stud above the surface.
2. Thread the stud removal tool onto the stud and tighten it, or thread two nuts onto the stud.
3. Remove the stud by turning the stud remover or the lower nut.
4. Remove any threadlocking compound from the threaded hole. Clean the threads with an aerosol parts cleaner.
5. Install the stud removal tool onto the new stud or thread two nuts onto the stud.
6. Apply threadlocking compound to the threads of the stud.
7. Install the stud and tighten with the stud removal tool or the top nut.
8. Install the stud to the height noted in Step 1 or its torque specification.
9. Remove the stud removal tool or the two nuts.

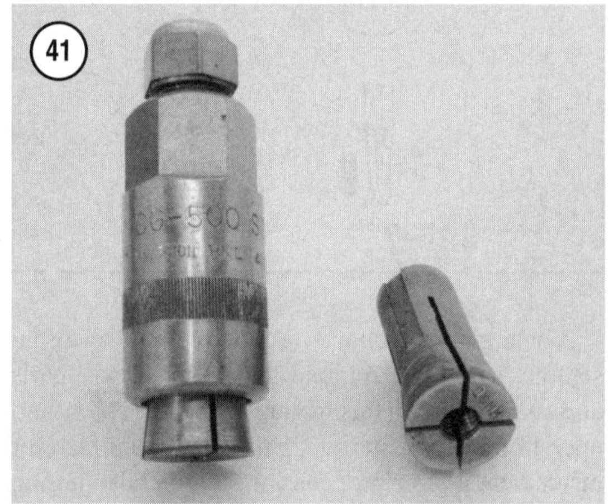

Removing Hoses

When removing stubborn hoses, do not exert excessive force on the hose or fitting. Remove the hose clamp and carefully insert a small screwdriver or pick tool between the fitting and hose. Apply a spray lubricant under the hose and carefully twist the hose off the fitting. Clean the fitting of any corrosion or rubber hose material with a wire brush. Clean the inside of the hose thoroughly. Do not use any lubricant when installing the hose (new or old). The lubricant may allow the hose to come off the fitting, even with the clamp secure.

Bearings

Bearings are precision parts, they must be maintained with proper lubrication and maintenance. If a

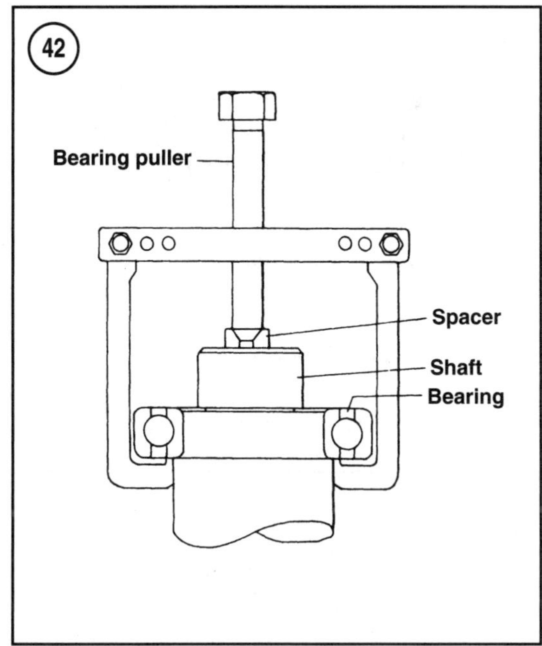

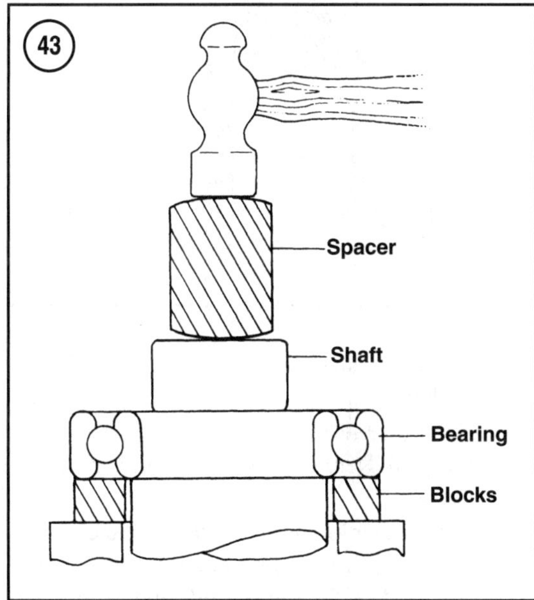

bearing is damaged, replace it immediately. When installing a new bearing, take care to prevent damaging it. Bearing replacement procedures are included in the individual chapters where applicable; however, use the following sections as a guideline. Unless otherwise specified, install bearings with the manufacturer's mark or number facing outward.

Refer to *Heating Components* in this section when heat is required.

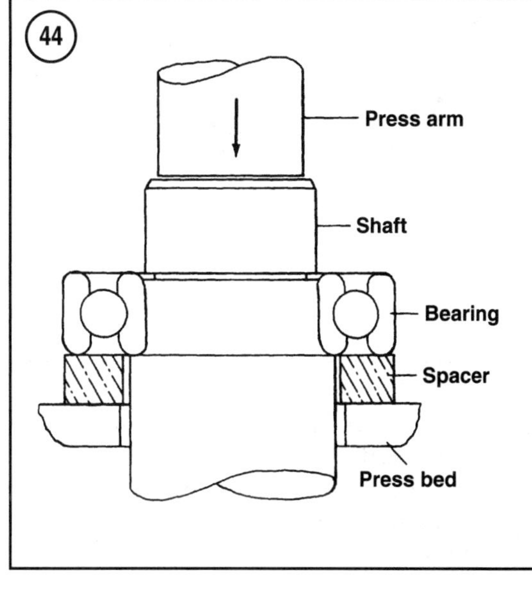

Removal

While bearings are normally removed only when damaged, there may be times when it is necessary to remove a bearing that is in good condition. However, improper bearing removal will damage the bearing and possibly the shaft or case. Note the following when removing bearings:

1. When using a puller to remove a bearing from a shaft, take care that the shaft is not damaged. Always place a piece of metal between the end of the shaft and the puller screw. In addition, place the puller arms next to the inner bearing race. See **Figure 42**.

2. When using a hammer to remove a bearing from a shaft, do not strike the hammer directly against the shaft. Instead, use a brass or aluminum rod between the hammer and shaft (**Figure 43**) and make sure to support both bearing races with wooden blocks as shown.

3. The ideal method of bearing removal is with a hydraulic press. Note the following when using a press:

   a. Always support the inner and outer bearing races with a suitable size wooden or aluminum spacer (**Figure 44**). If only the outer race is supported, pressure applied against the balls and/or the inner race will damage them.

   b. Always make sure the press arm (**Figure 44**) aligns with the center of the shaft. If the arm is

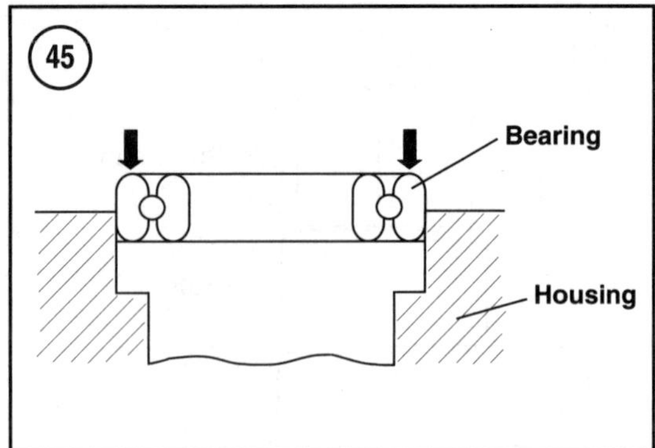

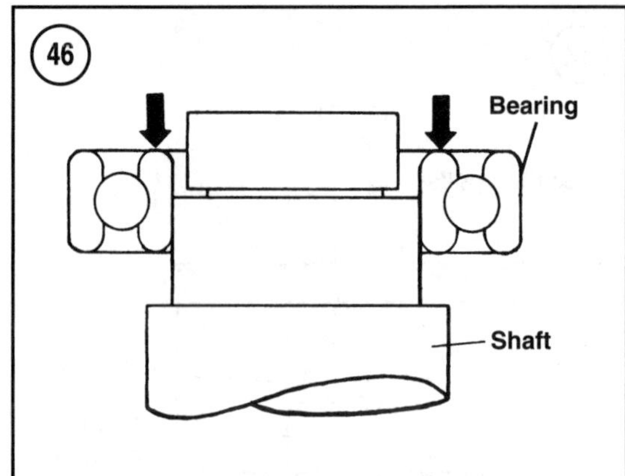

not centered, it may damage the bearing and/or shaft.

c. The moment the shaft is free of the bearing, it drops to the floor. Secure or hold the shaft to prevent it from falling.

Installation

1. When installing a bearing in a housing, apply pressure to the *outer* bearing race (**Figure 45**). When installing a bearing on a shaft, apply pressure to the *inner* bearing race (**Figure 46**).
2. When installing a bearing as described in Step 1, some type of driver is required. Never strike the bearing directly with a hammer or it will damage the bearing. When installing a bearing, use a piece of pipe or a driver with a diameter that matches the bearing inner race. **Figure 47** shows the correct way to use a driver and hammer to install a bearing.
3. Step 1 describes how to install a bearing in a case half or over a shaft. However, when installing a bearing over a shaft and into the housing at the same time, a tight fit is required for both outer and inner bearing races. In this situation, install a spacer underneath the driver tool so that pressure is applied evenly across both races. See **Figure 48**. If the outer race is not supported as shown, the balls will push against the outer bearing race and damage it.

Interference Fit

1. Follow this procedure when installing a bearing over a shaft. When a tight fit is required, the bearing inside diameter is smaller than the shaft. In this case, driving the bearing on the shaft using normal methods may cause bearing damage. Instead, heat the bearing before installation. Note the following:

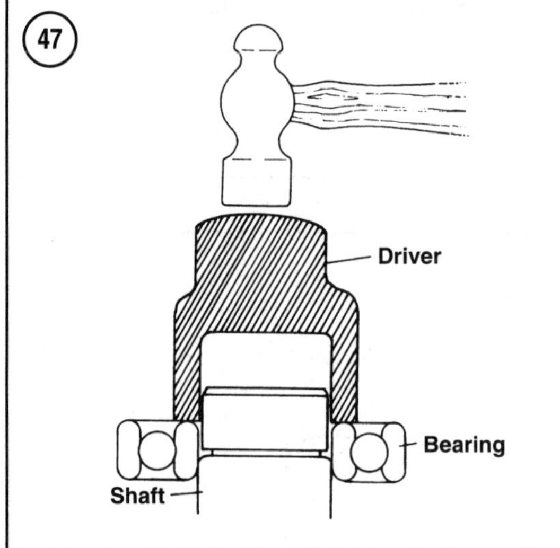

a. Secure the shaft so it is ready for bearing installation.
b. Clean all residues from the bearing surface of the shaft. Remove burrs with a file or sandpaper.
c. Fill a suitable pot or beaker with clean mineral oil. Place a thermometer rated above 120° C (248° F) in the oil. upport the thermometer so it does not rest on the bottom or side of the pot.
d. Remove the bearing from its wrapper and secure it with a piece of heavy wire bent to hold it in the pot. Hang the bearing in the pot so it does not touch the bottom or sides of the pot.
e. Turn the heat on and monitor the thermometer. When the oil temperature rises to approximately 120° C (248° F), remove the bearing from the pot and quickly install it. If neces-

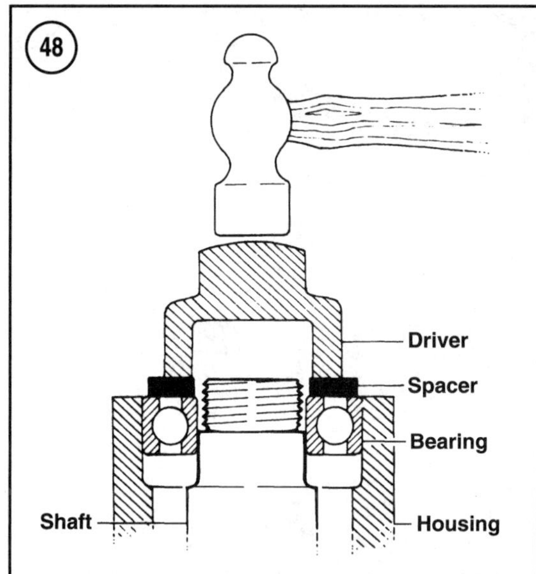

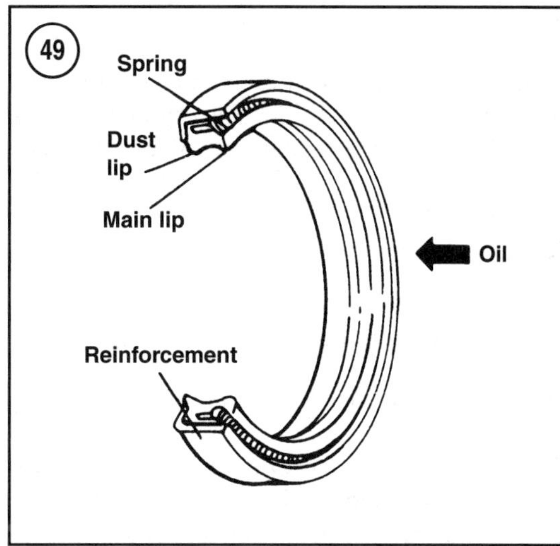

sary, place a socket on the inner bearing race and tap the bearing into place. As the bearing chills, it will tighten on the shaft, so installation must be done quickly. Make sure the bearing is installed completely.

2. Follow this step when installing a bearing in a housing. Bearings are generally installed in a housing with a slight interference fit. Driving the bearing into the housing using normal methods may damage the housing or cause bearing damage. Instead, heat the housing before the bearing is installed. Refer to *Heating Components* in this section and note the following:

a. Heat the housing to approximately 100° C (212° F) in an oven or on a hot plate. An easy way to check that it is the proper temperature is to place tiny drops of water on the housing; if they sizzle and evaporate immediately, the temperature is correct. Heat only one housing at a time.

b. Remove the housing from the oven or hot plate, and hold onto the housing with welding gloves.

c. Hold the housing with the bearing side down and tap the bearing out. Repeat for all bearings in the housing.

d. Before heating the bearing housing, place the new bearing in a freezer if possible. Chilling a bearing slightly reduces its outside diameter while the heated bearing housing assembly is slightly larger due to heat expansion. This makes bearing installation easier.

e. While the housing is still hot, install the new bearing(s) into the housing. Install the bearings by hand, if possible. If necessary, lightly tap the bearing(s) into the housing with a driver placed on the outer bearing race (**Figure 45**). Do not install new bearings by driving on the inner bearing race. Install the bearing(s) until it seats completely.

Seal Replacement

Seals (**Figure 49**) contain oil, water, grease or combustion gasses in a housing or shaft. Improperly removing a seal can damage the housing or shaft. Improperly installing the seal can damage the seal. Note the following:

1. Prying is generally the easiest and most effective method of removing a seal from the housing. However, always place a rag underneath the pry tool (**Figure 50**) to prevent damage to the housing. Note the seal's installed depth or if it is installed flush.

2. Pack waterproof grease in the seal lips before the seal is installed.

3. In most cases, install seals with the manufacturer's numbers or marks facing out.

4. Install seals with a socket or driver placed on the outside of the seal as shown in **Figure 51**. Drive the seal squarely into the housing until it is to the correct depth or flush as noted during removal. Never install a seal by hitting against the top of it with a hammer.

STORAGE

Several months of non-use can cause a general deterioration of the ATV. This is especially true in areas of extreme temperature variations. This deterioration can be minimized with careful preparation for storage. A properly stored ATV is much easier to return to service.

Storage Area Selection

When selecting a storage area, consider the following:

1. The storage area must be dry. A heated area is best, but not necessary. It should be insulated to minimize extreme temperature variations.
2. If the building has large window areas, mask them to keep sunlight off the ATV.
3. Avoid buildings in industrial areas where corrosive emissions may be present. Avoid areas close to saltwater.
4. Consider the area's risk of fire, theft or vandalism. Check with an insurer regarding coverage while in storage.

Preparing the Vehicle For Storage

The amount of preparation an ATV should undergo before storage depends on the expected length of non-use, storage area conditions and personal preference. Consider the following list the minimum requirement:

1. Wash the ATV thoroughly. Make sure all debris is removed.
2. Start the engine and allow it to reach operating temperature. Drain the engine oil regardless of the riding time since the last service. Fill the engine with the recommended type of oil.
3. Fill the fuel tank completely and add a fuel stabilizer. If the ATV will be in storage for an extended period, consider draining the fuel tank and running the engine until the fuel in the carburetor and lines is burned.
4. Remove the spark plug and pour a teaspoon (15-20 ml) of engine oil into the cylinder. Place a rag over the openings and slowly turn the engine over to distribute the oil. Reinstall the spark plug.
5. Remove the battery. Store the battery in a cool and dry location. Charge the battery once a month.
6. Cover the exhaust and intake openings.

7. Apply a protective substance to the plastic and rubber components. Make sure to follow the manufacturer's instructions for each type of product being used.
8. Rotate the tires periodically to prevent a flat spot from developing and damaging them.
9. Cover the ATV with old bed sheets or something similar. Do not cover it with any plastic material that will trap moisture.

Returning the Vehicle to Service

The amount of service required when returning the ATV to service after storage depends on the length of non-use and storage conditions. In addition to performing the reverse of the above procedure, make sure the brakes, clutch, throttle and engine stop switch work properly before operating the vehicle. Refer to Chapter Three and evaluate the service intervals to determine which areas require service.

Table 1 GENERAL VEHICLE DIMENSIONS

Overall length	1830 mm (72.0 in.)
Overall width	1165 mm (45.9 in.)
Overall height	1160 mm (45.7 in.)
Wheelbase	1245 mm (49.0 in.)
Ground clearance	265 mm (10.4 in.)
Seat height	810 mm (31.9 in.)
Track	
Front	935 mm (36.8 in.)
Rear	910 mm (35.8 in.)
Dry weight	169 kg (373 lbs.)
Maximum weight capacity	110 kg (243 lbs.)

Table 2 CONVERSION FORMULAS

Multiply:	By:	To get the equivalent of:
Length		
Inches	25.4	Millimeter
Inches	2.54	Centimeter
Miles	1.609	Kilometer
Feet	0.3048	Meter
Millimeter	0.03937	Inches
Centimeter	0.3937	Inches
Kilometer	0.6214	Mile
Meter	3.281	Feet
Fluid volume		
U.S. quarts	0.9463	Liters
U.S. gallons	3.785	Liters
U.S. ounces	29.573529	Milliliters
Imperial gallons	4.54609	Liters
Imperial quarts	1.1365	Liters
Liters	0.2641721	U.S. gallons
Liters	1.0566882	U.S. quarts
Liters	33.814023	U.S. ounces
Liters	0.22	Imperial gallons
Liters	0.8799	Imperial quarts
Milliliters	0.033814	U.S. ounces
Milliliters	1.0	Cubic centimeters
Milliliters	0.001	Liters
Torque		
Foot-pounds	1.3558	Newton-meters
Foot-pounds	0.138255	Meters-kilograms
Inch-pounds	0.11299	Newton-meters
Newton-meters	0.7375622	Foot-pounds
Newton-meters	8.8507	Inch-pounds
Meters-kilograms	7.2330139	Foot-pounds
Volume		
Cubic inches	16.387064	Cubic centimeters
Cubic centimeters	0.0610237	Cubic inches
Temperature		
Fahrenheit	(°F – 32) × 0.556	Centigrade
Centigrade	(°C × 1.8) + 32	Fahrenheit
Weight		
Ounces	28.3495	Grams
Pounds	0.4535924	Kilograms
Grams	0.035274	Ounces
Kilograms	2.2046224	Pounds

(continued)

Table 2 CONVERSION FORMULAS (continued)

Multiply:	By:	To get the equivalent of:
Pressure		
Pounds per square inch	0.070307	Kilograms per square centimeter
Kilograms per square centimeter	14.223343	Pounds per square inch
Kilopascals	0.1450	Pounds per square inch
Pounds per square inch	6.895	Kilopascals
Speed		
Miles per hour	1.609344	Kilometers per hour
Kilometers per hour	0.6213712	Miles per hour

Table 3 TECHNICAL ABBREVIATIONS

A	Ampere
AC	Alternating current
A•h	Ampere hour
C	Celsius
cc	Cubic centimeter
CDI	Capacitor discharge ignition
cm	Centimeter
cu. in.	Cubic inch and cubic inches
cyl.	Cylinder
DC	Direct current
F	Fahrenheit
fl. oz.	Fluid ounces
ft.	Foot
ft.-lb.	Foot pounds
gal.	Gallon and gallons
hp	Horsepower
Hz	Hertz
in.	Inch and inches
in.-lb.	Inch-pounds
in. Hg	Inches of mercury
kg	Kilogram
kg/cm^2	Kilogram per square centimeter
kgm	Kilogram meter
km	Kilometer
km/h	Kilometer per hour
kPa	Kilopascals
kW	Kilowatt
L	Liter and liters
L/m	Liters per minute
lb.	Pound and pounds
m	Meter
mL	Milliliter
mm	Millimeter
MPa	Megapascal
N	Newton
N•m	Newton meter
oz.	Ounce and ounces
p	Pascal
psi	Pounds per square inch
pt.	Pint and pints
qt.	Quart and quarts

(continued)

Table 3 TECHNICAL ABBREVIATIONS (continued)

rpm	Revolution per minute
TDC	Top dead center
V	Volt
VAC	Alternating current voltage
VDC	Direct current voltage
W	Watt

Table 4 METRIC, DECIMAL AND FRACTIONAL EQUIVALENTS

mm	in.	Nearest fraction	mm	in.	Nearest fraction
1	0.0394	1/32	26	1.0236	1 1/32
2	0.0787	3/32	27	1.0630	1 1/16
3	0.1181	1/8	28	1.1024	1 3/32
4	0.1575	5/32	29	1.1417	1 5/32
5	0.1969	3/16	30	1.1811	1 3/16
6	0.2362	1/4	31	1.2205	1 7/32
7	0.2756	9/32	32	1.2598	1 1/4
8	0.3150	5/16	33	1.2992	1 5/16
9	0.3543	11/32	34	1.3386	1 11/32
10	0.3937	13/32	35	1.3780	1 3/8
11	0.4331	7/16	36	1.4173	1 13/32
12	0.4724	15/32	37	1.4567	1 15/32
13	0.5118	1/2	38	1.4961	1 1/2
14	0.5512	9/16	39	1.5354	1 17/32
15	0.5906	19/32	40	1.5748	1 9/16
16	0.6299	5/8	41	1.6142	1 5/8
17	0.6693	21/32	42	1.6535	1 21/32
18	0.7087	23/32	43	1.6929	1 11/16
19	0.7480	3/4	44	1.7323	1 23/32
20	0.7874	25/32	45	1.7717	1 25/32
21	0.8268	13/16	46	1.8110	1 13/16
22	0.8661	7/8	47	1.8504	1 27/32
23	0.9055	29/32	48	1.8898	1 7/8
24	0.9449	15/16	49	1.9291	1 15/16
25	0.9843	31/32	50	1.9685	1 31/32

Table 5 METRIC TAP AND DRILL SIZES

Metric size	Drill equivalent	Decimal fraction	Nearest fraction
3 × 0.50	No. 39	0.0995	3/32
3 × 0.60	3/32	0.0937	3/32
4 × 0.70	No. 30	0.1285	1/8
4 × 0.75	1/8	0.125	1/8
5 × 0.80	No. 19	0.166	11/64

(continued)

Table 5 METRIC TAP AND DRILL SIZES (continued)

Metric size	Drill equivalent	Decimal fraction	Nearest fraction
5 × 0.90	No. 20	0.161	5/32
6 × 1.00	No. 9	0.196	13/64
7 × 1.00	16/64	0.234	15/64
8 × 1.00	J	0.277	9/32
8 × 1.25	17/64	0.265	17/64
9 × 1.00	5/16	0.3125	5/16
9 × 1.25	5/16	0.3125	5/16
10 × 1.25	11/32	0.3437	11/32
10 × 1.50	R	0.339	11/32
11 × 1.50	3/8	0.375	3/8
12 × 1.50	13/32	0.406	13/32
12 × 1.75	13/32	0.406	13/32

Table 6 TORQUE RECOMMENDATIONS*

Thread diameter	N•m	in.-lb.	ft.-lb.
5 mm			
Bolt and nut	5	44	–
Screw	4	35	–
6 mm			
Bolt and nut	10	88	–
Screw	9	80	–
6 mm flange bolt and nut	12	106	–
6 mm bolt with 8 mm head	9	80	–
8 mm			
Bolt and nut	22	–	16
Flange bolt and nut	27	–	20
10 mm			
Bolt and nut	35	–	26
Flange bolt and nut	40	–	30
12 mm			
Bolt and nut	55	–	40.5

*Torque recommendations for fasteners without a specification. Refer to the torque specification table at the end of each applicable chapter for specific applications.

CHAPTER TWO

TROUBLESHOOTING

The troubleshooting procedures described in this chapter provide typical symptoms and logical methods for isolating the cause(s). There may be several ways to solve a problem, but only a systematic approach will be successful in avoiding wasted time and possibly unnecessary parts replacement.

An engine needs the correct air/fuel mixture, compression and a spark at the correct time to run. If one of these is missing, the engine will not run. Gather as much information as possible to aid in diagnosis. Never assume anything and do not overlook the obvious. Make sure the stop switch is in the run position and there is fuel in the tank.

Learning to recognize symptoms makes troubleshooting easier. In most cases, expensive and complicated test equipment is not needed to determine whether repairs can be performed at home. On the other hand, be realistic and do not start procedures that are beyond your experience and equipment available. If the ATV requires the attention of a professional, describe symptoms and conditions accurately and fully. The more information a technician has available, the easier it is to diagnose the problem.

WATER DAMAGE

If the ATV is regularly operated in very wet conditions, the brakes, cables, wheel bearings, and engine oil may need to be serviced more often than specified. In addition, corrosion may increase the likelihood of electrical problems.

CAUTION

If the engine oil is contaminated with water it will foam and/or have a whitish appearance. Frequently this will be evident by a foam on the inside of the fill cap. Oil diluted with water will not lubricate properly.

Change the oil and if necessary, run the engine until it reaches operating temperature, and repeat the process until all contaminates are removed.

CAUTION

If the ATV has been completely submerged there is a chance that the cylinder can fill with water. Water does not compress, thus attempting to start the engine before pumping the water out can create hydraulic lock and result in engine damage.

If the ATV has been completely submerged and will no longer run, check the following:

1. Drain the fuel tank (Chapter Eight).
2. Clean the carburetor (Chapter Eight).
3. Drain and replace the engine oil (Chapter Three).

4. Remove the spark plug and crank the engine over to remove water from the cylinder.
5. Clean the air box (Chapter Three).
6. Clean or replace the air filter (Chapter Three).
7. Lubricate the cables (Chapter Three).
8. Clean the brakes and check brake fluid for contamination.
9. Clean and lubricate the chain (Chapter Three).

STARTING THE ENGINE

WARNING
Start the engine in a well-ventilated area with its muffler pointing away from all objects. Do not start a flooded engine in a garage or other closed area.

CAUTION
When trying to start the engine, do not operate the starter for more than five seconds at a time. This can cause the starter to overheat. Wait approximately 10 seconds before operating the starter button again.

Starting a Cold Engine

1. Shift the transmission into neutral and set the parking brake.
2. Move the choke lever on the left hand grip to the on position (**Figure 1**).
3. Turn the fuel valve on (**Figure 2**).
4. Turn the ignition switch on.
5. With the throttle slightly open, push the starter button.

6A. If the ambient air temperature is normal (10-35° C [50-95° F]), perform the following after the engine has started:

a. Move the choke lever to the halfway position.
b. Warm up the engine by working the throttle slightly.

6B. If the ambient air temperature is less than 10° C (50° F), perform the following after the engine has started:

a. Work the throttle slightly to keep the engine running.
b. When the engine begins to idle roughly, move the choke lever to the halfway position.

7. Idle the engine for approximately a minute or until the throttle responds cleanly, and then move the choke lever to off (**Figure 3**).

Starting a Warm or Hot Engine

1. Shift the transmission into neutral and set the parking brake.
2. Make sure the choke lever is off (**Figure 3**).
3. Turn the fuel valve on (**Figure 2**).
4. Turn the ignition switch on.
5. Open the throttle slightly and push the starter button.

Starting a Flooded Engine

If the engine is hard to start and there is a strong gasoline smell, the engine is probably flooded with fuel. This occurs when too much fuel is drawn into the engine and the spark plug fails to ignite the air/fuel mixture. If there are no obvious signs of fuel overflow from the carburetor, attempt to start the engine by fully opening the throttle (no choke) and operating the starter.

1. Make sure the choke lever is off. (**Figure 3**).
2. Turn the engine stop switch off (**Figure 4**).
3. Hold the throttle fully open.
4. Clear the engine by briefly pressing the starter button several times.
5. Wait ten seconds, turn the engine stop switch on, and perform the normal starting procedures.
6. If the engine is flooded badly, perform the following:
   a. Remove the spark plug and dry off its insulator, or replace the plug.
   b. Crank the engine over to remove excess fuel.
   c. Reinstall the plug and start the engine. Work the throttle until the engine runs cleanly.
7. If the engine refuses to start, check the carburetor overflow hose (A, **Figure 5**). If fuel is running out of the hose, the float valve is stuck open or leaking, Refer to Chapter Eight.

ENGINE DOES NOT START

If the engine does not start, perform the following steps in order. It is important to narrow the possibilities. After doing so, refer to the possible causes under *Electrical System*, *Fuel System* and *Engine Compression* in this section.

1. Make sure the choke lever is in the correct position. See *Starting the Engine* in this chapter.
2. Make sure there is fresh fuel in the tank. Check for a clogged fuel tank vent hose (**Figure 6**). Remove the tube from the filler cap, then wipe off one end and blow through it. Remove the filler cap and check for a plugged hose nozzle.
3. Disconnect the fuel line (B, **Figure 5**) from the carburetor and insert the end of the hose into a clear container. Turn the fuel valve (**Figure 2**) on. Fuel should flow freely from the fuel hose. If no fuel comes out, the fuel valve may be shut off, blocked by debris, or the fuel cap vent may be plugged. Remove and clean the fuel valve (Chapter Eight) and the fuel cap vent. Reconnect the fuel line to the carburetor fitting.
4. If there are signs that the cylinder is flooded, or there is a strong smell of gasoline, perform the procedures in *Starting a Flooded Engine* in this chapter.
5. Check the carburetor overflow hose (A, **Figure 5**) on the bottom of the float bowl. If fuel is running from the hose, the float valve is stuck open or leaking. Turn the fuel valve off and tap the carburetor a

few times. Then turn the fuel valve on. If fuel continues to run out of the hose, remove and repair the carburetor as described in Chapter Eight. Check the carburetor vent hoses to make sure they are clear. Check the end of the hoses for contamination.

6. If fuel is reaching the carburetor, the jets (pilot and main) could be plugged or the air filter could be severely restricted. However, before removing the carburetor, continue with Step 7 to check the ignition system.

7. Make sure the engine stop switch (**Figure 4**) is operating correctly. Make sure the stop switch wire is not broken or shorted. If necessary, test the engine stop switch as described in Chapter Nine.

8. Check to make sure the spark plug cap (**Figure 7**) is tight on the spark plug. Push it and slightly rotate it to clean the electrical connection between the spark plug and the cap. Remove the cap from the plug, hold the high-tension wire and screw the plug cap on tightly.

9. Perform a spark test as described in this section. If there is a strong spark, perform Step 10. If there is no spark or if the spark is very weak, troubleshoot the ignition system as described in this chapter.

10. Check cylinder compression as follows:
   a. Turn the engine stop switch (**Figure 4**) off.
   b. Remove the spark plug and ground the spark plug shell against the cylinder head.
   c. Hold your finger over the spark plug hole.
   d. Operate the starter. When the piston comes up on the compression stroke, pressure in the cylinder should force your finger from the spark plug hole. If there is no compression or it seems weak, perform the compression test described in Chapter Three.

Spark Test

A spark tester (**Figure 8**) is a useful tool for checking the ignition system. This tool is inserted in the spark plug cap and its base is grounded against the cylinder head. Because the tool's air gap is adjustable, it allows you to see and hear the spark while testing the intensity of the spark.

CAUTION
Before removing the spark plug, clean all debris from the plug base. Dirt that falls into the cylinder will cause engine wear.

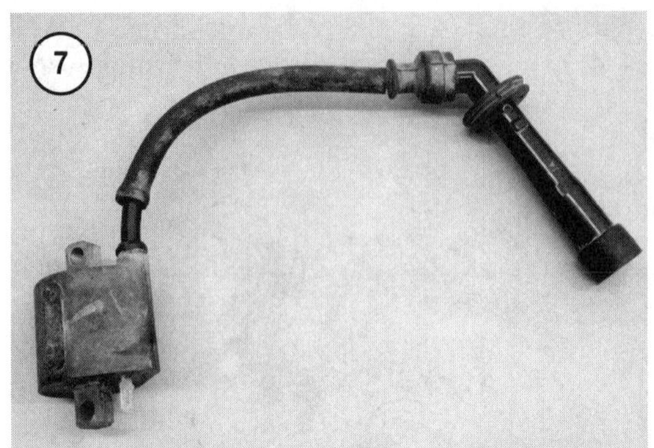
7

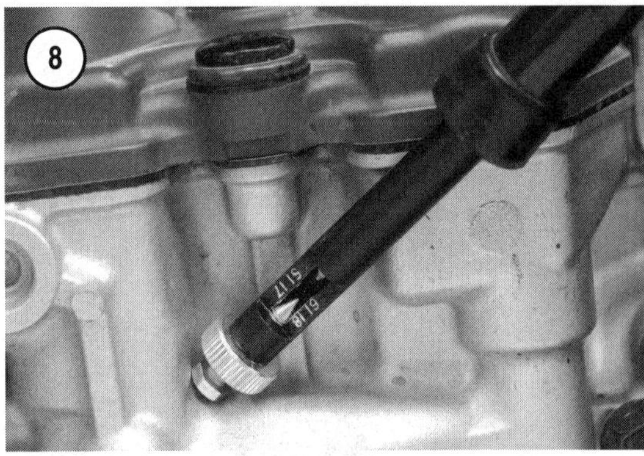
8

1. Disconnect the plug wire and remove the spark plug.

2. If using an adjustable spark tester, set its air gap to 6 mm (0.24 in.).

3. Insert the spark plug (or spark tester) into the plug cap and touch its base against the cylinder head (**Figure 9**) to ground it. Position the plug so the electrodes are visible.

WARNING
Mount the spark plug or spark tester away from the plug hole so the spark from the plug or tester cannot ignite the gasoline vapor in the cylinder.

WARNING
Do not hold or touch the spark plug (or spark tester), wire or connector when making a spark check. A serious electrical shock may result.

4. Turn the engine stop switch to run and the ignition switch on.

5. Turn the engine over with the starter button. A fat blue spark should be evident across the spark plug electrodes or across the spark tester terminals.

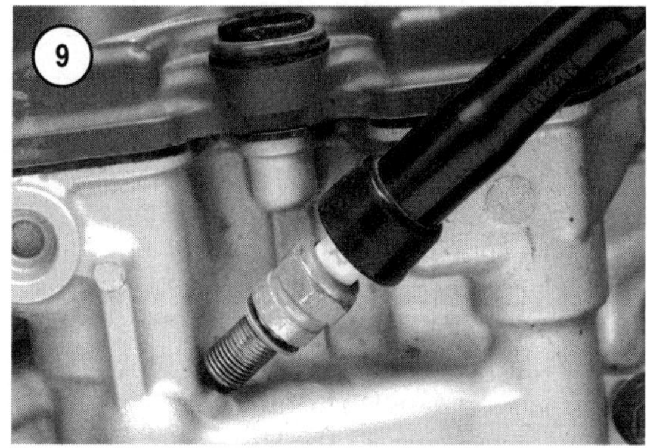

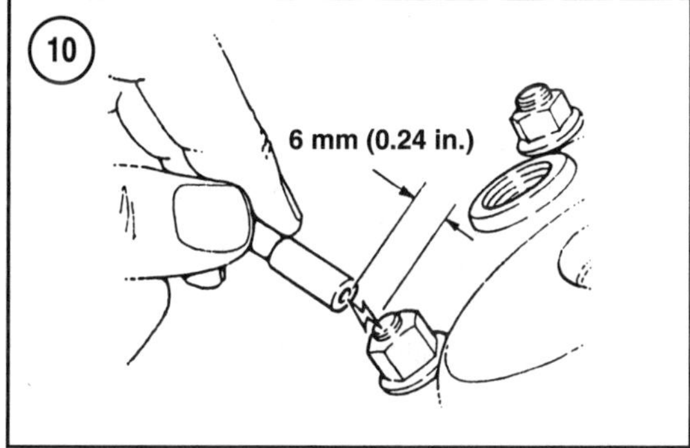

6. If the spark is good, check for one or more of the following possible malfunctions:
   a. Obstructed fuel line or fuel filter (if used).
   b. Low compression or engine damage.
   c. Flooded engine.

7. If the spark is weak (white or yellow in color) or if there is no spark, check for one or more of the following conditions:
   a. Fouled or wet spark plug. If there is a spark across a spark tester but not across the original spark plug, the plug is fouled. Repeat the spark test with a new spark plug.
   b. Loose or damaged spark plug cap connection. Hold the spark plug wire and turn the spark plug cap to tighten it. Then install the spark plug into the cap and repeat the spark test. If there is still no spark, bypass the plug cap as described in the next step.
   c. Check for a damaged spark plug cap. Hold the spark plug wire and unscrew the spark plug cap. Then hold the end of the spark plug wire 6 mm (0.24 in.) from the cylinder head as shown in **Figure 10**. Have an assistant turn the engine over and repeat the spark test. If there is a strong spark, the spark plug cap is faulty. Replace the plug cap and repeat the spark test.
   d. Loose or damaged spark plug wire connections (at coil and plug cap).
   e. Faulty ignition coil or faulty ignition coil ground wire connection.
   f. Faulty CDI unit or stator coil(s).
   g. Sheared flywheel key.
   h. Loose flywheel nut.
   i. Loose or dirty electrical connections.

8. If the engine backfires during starting attempts, the ignition timing, although not adjustable, may be incorrect. Check the following.
   a. Loose flywheel nut.
   b. Sheared flywheel key.
   c. Loose ignition pulse generator.
   d. Damaged ignition component (CDI unit).

2

Electrical System

1. Spark plug:
   a. Fouled spark plug.
   b. Incorrect spark plug gap.
   c. Incorrect spark plug heat range (too cold). See Chapter Three.
   d. Worn or damaged spark plug electrodes.
   e. Damaged spark plug.
   f. Damaged spark plug cap or spark plug wire.
2. Ignition coil:
   a. Loose or damaged ignition coil leads.
   b. Cracked ignition coil body—look for carbon tracks on the ignition coil.
   c. Loose or corroded ground wire.
3. Switches and wiring:
   a. Dirty or loose fitting terminals.
   b. Damaged wires or connectors.
   c. Damaged ignition switch.
   d. Damaged engine stop switch.
4. Electrical components:
   a. Damaged ignition pulse generator.
   b. Damaged CDI unit.
   c. Faulty exciter coil.

Fuel System

1. Air filter:
   a. Plugged air filter element.
   b. Plugged air filter housing.
   c. Leaking or damaged air filter housing-to-carburetor air boot.

2. Fuel valve:
   a. Plugged fuel hose.
   b. Plugged fuel valve filter.
3. Fuel tank:
   a. No fuel.
   b. Plugged fuel filter.
   c. Plugged fuel tank vent hose (**Figure 6**).
   d. Contaminated or old fuel.
4. Carburetor:
   a. Plugged or damaged choke system.
   b. Plugged main jet.
   c. Plugged pilot jet.
   d. Loose pilot jet or main jet.
   e. Plugged pilot jet air passage.
   f. Incorrect float level.
   g. Leaking or damaged float.
   h. Worn or damaged needle valve.

Engine Compression

Check engine compression as described in Chapter Three. If necessary, perform an engine leak down test as described in this chapter.

1. Cylinder and cylinder head:
   a. Loose spark plug.
   b. Missing spark plug gasket.
   c. Leaking cylinder head gasket.
   d. Leaking cylinder base gasket.
   e. Excessively worn or seized piston, piston rings and/or cylinder.
   f. Loose cylinder and/or cylinder head fasteners.
   g. Cylinder head incorrectly installed.
   h. Warped cylinder head.
   i. Valve(s) adjusted too tight.
   j. Bent valve.
   k. Worn valve and/or seat.
   l. Worn or damaged valve guide(s).
   m. Bent pushrod(s).
   n. Damaged cam follower.
2. Piston and piston rings:
   a. Worn piston rings.
   b. Damaged piston rings.
   c. Piston seizure or piston damage.
3. Crankcase and crankshaft:
   a. Seized connecting rod.
   b. Damaged crankcases.
   c. Damaged seals.

POOR IDLE SPEED PERFORMANCE

If the engine starts but off-idle performance is poor (engine hesitates or misfires), check for the following:

1. Clogged or damaged air filter element.
2. Carburetor:
   a. Plugged pilot jet.
   b. Loose pilot jet.
   c. Damaged choke system.
   d. Incorrect throttle cable adjustment.
   e. Incorrect pilot screw adjustment.
   f. Flooded carburetor (visually check carburetor overflow hose for fuel).
   g. Throttle valve does not slide smoothly in carburetor bore.
   h. Loose carburetor.
   i. Damaged intake manifold O-ring.
   j. Incorrect idle speed.
   k. Incorrect air/fuel mixture.
3. Fuel:
   a. Water and/or alcohol in fuel.
   b. Old fuel.
4. Engine:
   a. Valves are out of adjustment.
   b. Worn valve seats.
   c. Worn valve guides.
   d. Worn camshafts.
   e. Excessive spark plug gap.
   f. Defective ignition coil.
   g. Defective alternator.
   h. Defective CDI unit.
   i. Incorrect carburetor float level.
   j. Clogged carburetor idle jet.
   k. Low engine compression.
5. Electrical system:
   a. Damaged spark plug.
   b. Open or shorted spark plug wire.
   c. Damaged ignition coil.
   d. Faulty ignition or engine stop switch.
   e. Damaged ignition pulse generator.
   f. Damaged CDI unit.
   g. Damaged exciter coil.

POOR, MEDIUM AND HIGH SPEED PERFORMANCE

Check for the following:

1. Carburetor:
   a. Incorrect float level.

b. Incorrect jet needle clip position (if adjustable).
c. Plugged or loose main jet.
d. Plugged fuel line.
e. Plugged fuel valve.
f. Plugged fuel tank vent hose.
2. Plugged air filter element.
3. Engine:
a. Incorrect valve timing.
b. Weak valve springs.
4. Other considerations:
a. Overheating.
b. Clutch slippage.
c. Brake drag.
d. Engine oil level too high.

ELECTRICAL TESTING

WARNING
High voltage may be present during electrical testing. Do not hold wires or components while cranking the engine or when it is running.

This section describes electrical troubleshooting and the use of test equipment.

Never assume anything and do not overlook the obvious, such as a blown fuse or an electrical connector that has separated. Test the simplest and most obvious items first and try to make tests at easily accessible points on the ATV. Make sure to troubleshoot systematically. Refer to the color wiring diagram at the end of the manual for component and connector identification. Use the wiring diagram to determine how the circuit should work by tracing the current paths from the power source through the circuit components to ground. Also check any circuits that share the same fuse, ground or switch. If the other circuits work properly and the shared wiring is good, the cause must be in the wiring used only by the suspect circuit. If all related circuits are faulty at the same time, the probable cause is a poor ground connection or a blown fuse(s).

Preliminary Checks and Precautions

Before starting any electrical troubleshooting, perform the following:

1. Inspect the fuse for the suspected circuit, and replace it if blown. Refer to Chapter Nine.
2. Inspect the battery (Chapter Three). Make sure it is fully charged and the battery leads are clean and securely attached to the battery terminals.
3. Electrical connectors are often the cause of electrical system problems. Inspect the connectors as follows:
a. Disconnect each electrical connector in the suspect circuit and make sure there are no bent terminals in the electrical connector. A bent terminal will not connect to its mate, causing an open circuit.
b. Make sure the terminals are pushed all the way into the connector. If not, carefully push them in with a narrow blade screwdriver.
c. Check the wires where they attach to the terminals for damage.
d. Make sure each terminal is clean and free of corrosion. Clean them, if necessary, and pack the connectors with dielectric grease.
e. Push the connector halves together. Make sure the connectors are fully engaged and locked together.
f. Never pull the wires when disconnecting a connector. Pull only on the connector housing.
4. Never use a self-powered test light on circuits that contain solid-state devices. The solid-state devices may be damaged.
5. Never disconnect electrical connectors with the ignition on, or with the engine running or cranking.
6. When performing peak voltage tests make sure the connections are secure. Use caution when high voltage is present.

Intermittent Problems

Problems that do not occur all the time can be difficult to isolate during testing. For example, when a problem only occurs when the ATV is ridden over rough roads (vibration) or in wet conditions (water penetration). Note the following:

1. Vibration. This is a common problem with loose or damaged electrical connectors.

NOTE
An analog ohmmeter is useful when making this type of test. Slight needle movements are visibly apparent, which indicate a loose connection.

a. Perform a continuity test as described in the appropriate service procedure or under *Continuity Test* in this section.
b. Lightly pull or wiggle the connectors while repeating the test. Do the same when checking the wiring harness and individual components, especially where the wires enter a housing or connector.
c. A change in meter readings indicates a poor connection. Find and repair the problem or replace the part. Check for wires with cracked or broken insulation.

2. Heat. This is a common problem with connectors or joints that have loose or poor connections. As these connections heat up, the connection or joint expands and separates, causing an open circuit. Other heat related problems occur when a component starts to fail as it heats up.

a. Troubleshoot the problem to isolate the circuit.

CAUTION
A heat gun will quickly raise the temperature of the component being tested. Do not apply heat directly to the Motronic unit or use heat in excess of 60° C (140° F) on any electrical component.

b. To check a connector, perform a continuity test as described in the appropriate service procedure or under *Continuity Test* in this section. Then repeat the test while heating the connector with a heat gun. If the meter reading was normal (continuity) when the connector was cold, and then fluctuated or read infinity when heat was applied, the connection is bad.
c. To check a component, allow the engine to cool, and then start and run the engine. Note operational differences when the engine is cold and hot.
d. If the engine will not start, isolate and remove the suspect component. Test it at room temperature and again after heating it with a heat gun. A change in meter readings indicates a temperature problem.

3. Water. When the problem occurs when riding in wet conditions or in areas with high humidity, start and run the engine in a dry area. Then, with the engine running, spray water onto the suspected component/circuit. Water-related problems often stop after the component heats up and dries.

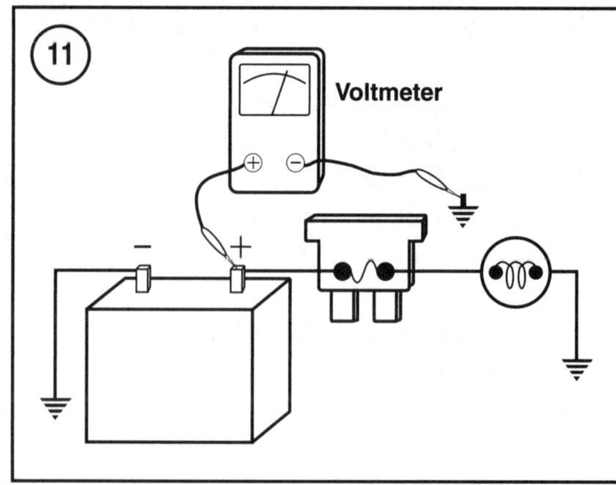

Test Light or Voltmeter

Use a test light to check for voltage in a circuit. Attach one lead to ground and the other lead to various points along the circuit. It does not make a difference which test lead is attached to ground. The bulb lights when voltage is present.

Use a voltmeter in the same manner as the test light to find out if voltage is present in any given circuit. The voltmeter, unlike the test light, also indicates how much voltage is present at each test point.

Voltage test

Unless otherwise specified, make all voltage tests with the electrical connectors still connected. Insert the test leads into the backside of the connector and make sure the test lead touches the electrical terminal within the connector housing. If the test lead only touches the wire insulation, it will cause a false reading. Always check both sides of the connector because one side may be loose or corroded, thus preventing electrical flow through the connector. This type of test can be performed with a test light or a voltmeter.

1. Attach the voltmeter negative test lead to a confirmed ground location. If possible, use the battery ground connection. Make sure the ground is not insulated.
2. Attach the voltmeter positive test lead to the point to be tested (**Figure 11**).

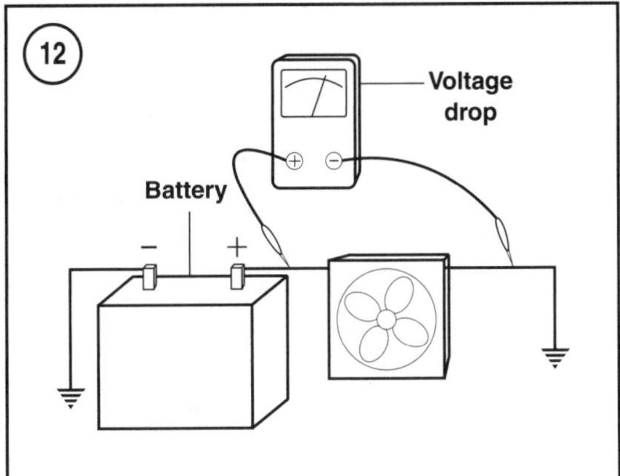

3. Turn the ignition switch on. If using a test light, the test light will come on if voltage is present. If using a voltmeter, note the voltage reading. The reading should be within 1 volt of battery voltage. If the voltage is less there is a problem in the circuit.

Voltage drop test

The wires, cables, connectors and switches in the electrical circuit are designed to carry current with low resistance. This ensures current can flow through the circuit with a minimum loss of voltage. Voltage drop indicates where there is resistance in a circuit. A higher-than-normal amount of resistance in a circuit decreases the flow of current and causes the voltage to drop between the source and destination in the circuit.

Because resistance causes voltage to drop, a voltmeter is used to measure voltage drop when current is running through the circuit. If the circuit has no resistance, there is no voltage drop so the voltmeter indicates 0 volts. The greater the resistance in a circuit, the greater the voltage drop reading.

To perform a voltage drop:

1. Connect the positive meter test lead to the electrical source (where electricity is coming from).
2. Connect the voltmeter negative test lead to the electrical load (where the electricity is going). Refer to **Figure 12**.
3. If necessary, activate the component(s) in the circuit.
4. Read the voltage drop (difference in voltage between the source and destination) on the voltmeter. Note the following:
   a. The voltmeter should indicate 0 volts. If there is a drop of 1 volt or more, there is a problem within the circuit. A voltage drop reading of 12 volts indicates an open in the circuit.
   b. A voltage drop of 1 or more volts indicates that a circuit has excessive resistance. For example, consider a starting problem where the battery is fully charged but the starter turns over slowly. Voltage drop would be the difference in the voltage at the battery (source) and the voltage at the starter (destination) as the engine is being started (current is flowing through the battery cables). A corroded battery cable would cause a high voltage drop (high resistance) and slow engine cranking.
   c. Common sources of voltage drop are loose or contaminated connectors and poor ground connections.

Testing for a short with a voltmeter

A test light may also be used.

1. Remove the blown fuse from the fuse panel.
2. Connect the voltmeter across the fuse terminals in the fuse panel. Turn the ignition switch on and check for battery voltage.
3. With the voltmeter attached to the fuse terminals, wiggle the wiring harness relating to the suspect circuit at approximately 15.2 cm (6 in.) intervals. Start next to the fuse panel and work systematically away from the panel. Note the voltmeter reading while progressing along the harness.
4. If the voltmeter reading changes (test light blinks), there is a short-to-ground at that point in the harness.

Peak voltage testing

Peak voltage tests check the voltage output of the ignition coil, ignition pulse generator and exciter coil and cranking speed. Refer to Chapter Nine.

Ammeter

Use an ammeter to measure the flow of current (amps) in a circuit (**Figure 13**). When connected in series in a circuit, the ammeter determines if current is flowing through the circuit and if that current flow is excessive because of a short in the circuit. Current flow is often referred to as current draw. Comparing actual current draw in the circuit or component to current draw specification (if specified by the manufacturer) provides useful diagnostic information.

Self-Powered Test Light

A self-powered test light can be constructed from a 12-volt light bulb, a pair of test leads and a 12-volt battery. When the test leads are touched together the light bulb should go on.

Use a self-powered test light as follows:

1. Touch the test leads together to make sure the light bulb goes on. If not, correct the problem.
2. Disconnect the ATV's battery or remove the fuse(s) that protects the circuit to be tested. Do not connect a self-powered test light to a circuit that has power applied to it.
3. Select two points within the circuit where there should be continuity.
4. Attach one lead of the test light to each point.
5. If there is continuity, the test light bulb will come on.
6. If there is no continuity, the test light bulb will not come on, indicating an open circuit.

Ohmmeter

CAUTION
To prevent damage to the ohmmeter, never connect it to a circuit that has power applied to it. Always disconnect the battery negative lead (Chapter Three) before using an ohmmeter.

Use an ohmmeter to measure the resistance (in ohms) to current flow in a circuit or component. Ohmmeters may be analog type (needle scale) or digital type (LCD or LED readout). Both types of ohmmeters have a switch that allows the user to select different ranges of resistance for accurate readings. The analog ohmmeter also has a set-adjust control which is used to zero or calibrate the meter (digital ohmmeters do not require calibration). Refer to the ohmmeter's instructions to determine the correct scale setting.

Use an ohmmeter by connecting its test leads to the circuit or component to be tested. If an analog meter is used, it must be calibrated by touching the test leads together and turning the set-adjust knob until the meter needle reads zero. When the leads are uncrossed, the needle should move to the other end of the scale, indicating infinite resistance. During a continuity test, a reading of infinite resistance indicates there is an open in the circuit or component. A reading of zero indicates continuity; that is, there is no measurable resistance in the circuit or component. A measured reading indicates the actual resistance to current flow that is present in that circuit. Even though resistance is present, the circuit has continuity.

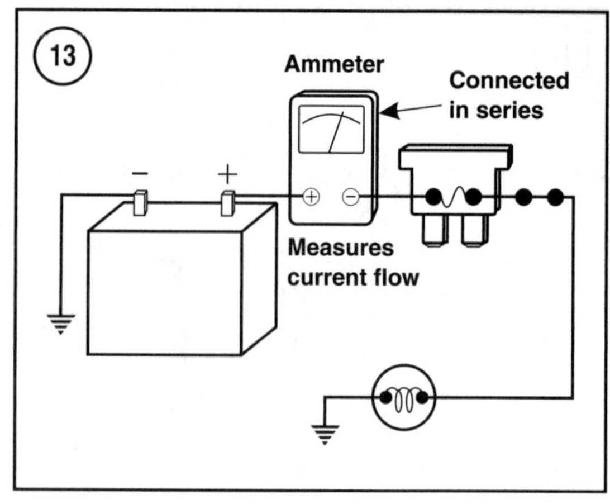

Continuity test

Perform a continuity test to determine the integrity of a circuit, wire or component. A circuit has continuity if it forms a complete circuit; that is, if there are no opens in either the electrical wires or components within the circuit. A circuit with an open, on the other hand, has no continuity. This type of test can be performed with a self-powered test light or an ohmmeter. An ohmmeter gives the best results.

1. Disconnect the negative battery cable (Chapter Three) or disconnect the test circuit/component from its power source.

2. Attach one test lead (test light or ohmmeter) to one end of the part of the circuit to be tested.

3. Attach the other test lead to the other end of the part or the circuit to be tested.

4. The self-powered test light comes on if there is continuity. An ohmmeter reads 0 or low resistance if there is continuity. A reading of infinite resistance indicates no continuity; the circuit is open.

5. If testing a component, note the resistance and compare this to the specification if available.

Testing for short with an ohmmeter

An analog ohmmeter or one with an audible continuity indicator works best for short testing. A self-powered test light may also be used.

1. Disconnect the negative battery cable (Chapter Three).
2. If necessary, remove the blown fuse from the fuse panel.
3. Connect one test lead of the ohmmeter to the load side (battery side) of the fuse terminal in the fuse panel.
4. Connect the other test lead to a confirmed ground location. Make sure the ground is not insulated. If possible, use the battery ground connection.
5. Wiggle the wiring harness relating to the suspect circuit at approximately 15.2 cm (6 in.) intervals. Watch the ohmmeter while progressing along the harness.
6. If the ohmmeter needle moves or the ohmmeter beeps, there is a short-to-ground at that point in the harness.

Jumper Wire

Use a jumper wire to bypass a potential problem and isolate it to a particular point in a circuit. If a faulty circuit works properly with a jumper wire installed, an open exists between the two jumped points in the circuit.

To troubleshoot with a jumper wire, first use the wire to determine if the problem is on the ground side or the load side of a device. Verify the ground by connecting the jumper wire between the lamp and a good ground. If the lamp comes on, the problem is the connection between the lamp and ground. If the lamp does not come on with the wire installed, the lamp's connection to ground is good, so the problem is between the lamp and the power source. To isolate the problem, connect the wire between the battery and the lamp. If it comes on, the problem is between these two points. Next, connect the wire between the battery and the fuse side of the switch. If the lamp comes on, the switch is good. By successively moving the wire from one point to another, the problem can be isolated to a particular place in the circuit. Note the following when using a jumper wire:

1. Make sure the wire gauge (thickness) is the same as that used in the circuit being tested. Smaller gauge wire rapidly overheats and could melt.
2. Make sure the jumper wire has insulated alligator clips. This prevents accidental grounding (sparks) or possible shock. Install an inline fuse/fuse holder in the jumper wire.
3. A jumper wire is a temporary test measure. Do not leave a jumper wire installed as a permanent solution. This creates a fire hazard.
4. Never use a jumper wire across any load (a component that is connected and turned on). This would cause a direct short and blow the fuse(s).

STARTING SYSTEM

CAUTION

Do not operate the starter continuously for more than 5 seconds. Allow the starter to cool for at least 10 seconds between starting attempts.

An electric starter (**Figure 14**) is used on all models. The starter is mounted horizontally at the left side of the engine.

The starting system requires a fully charged battery to provide the large current required to operate the starter. A charge coil on the stator plate and a voltage regulator, connected in circuit with the battery, keeps the battery charged while the engine is running.

The starting circuit consists of the battery, starter, neutral/reverse switch, neutral indicator, starter relay, ignition switch and engine stop switch.

The starter relay (**Figure 15**) carries the load current to the starter. Depressing the starter switch sends control current through the starter relay coil. The starter relay contacts close so load current flows from the battery through the starter relay to the starter.

When the ignition switch is turned on and the engine stop switch is in the run position, the starter can be operated only if the transmission is in neutral.

A fully charged battery, ohmmeter and jumper cables are required to perform the troubleshooting procedures in this section. Make sure the battery cables and electrical connections are in good condition.

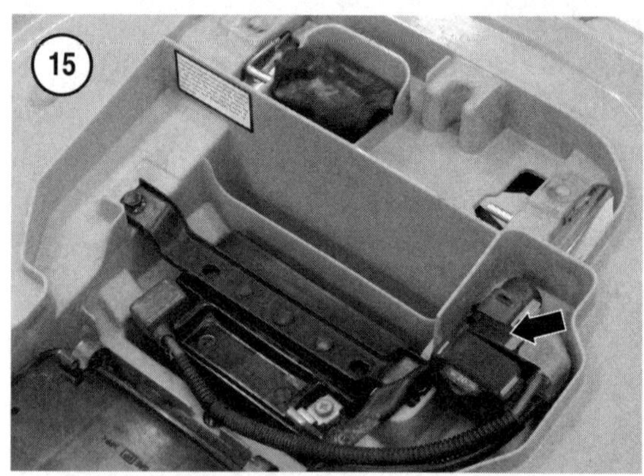

Starter Does Not Operate

1. Remove the seat, side covers, upper fuel tank cover, and front fender as described in Chapter Fourteen.
2. Check the 20-amp main fuse (**Figure 16**). Open the cap from the relay, pull out the fuse and visually inspect it. If the fuse is blown, replace it as described in Chapter Nine. If the main fuse is good, reinstall it and continue with Step 3.
3. Test the battery as described in Chapter Three. If the battery is damaged, replace it.
4. Check for loose, corroded or damaged battery cables. Check the cables at the battery, starter motor, starter relay and all cable-to-frame connections.
5. Turn the ignition switch on. Push the starter button and listen for a click at the starter relay switch (**Figure 15**).
   a. If the relay clicks, perform Step 6.
   b. If the relay did not click, go to Step 7.
6. Test the battery as follows:
   a. Park the vehicle on level ground and set the parking brake. Shift the transmission into neutral.
   b. Remove the fuel tank as described in Chapter Eight.
   c. Disconnect the cable (**Figure 17**) from the starter terminal.

WARNING

Because a spark will be produced in the following steps, perform this procedure away from all open flames. Make sure there is no spilt gasoline on the ATV or gasoline fumes in the work area.

   d. Momentarily connect a jumper cable (thick gauge wire) from the positive battery terminal to the starter motor terminal. The starter works properly if it turns when connected directly to the battery.
   e. If the starter did not turn, remove the starter and service it as described in Chapter Nine.
   f. If the starter turned, check for a loose or damaged starter cable. If the cable is good, the starter relay (**Figure 15**) is faulty. Replace the starter relay and retest.
7. Check that the neutral indicator light (**Figure 18**) comes on when the transmission is in neutral and the ignition switch is turned on. Note the following:
   a. If the neutral indicator light does not work properly, check for a blown bulb (Chapter Nine). If the bulb is good, perform Step 8.
   b. If the neutral indicator light works properly, go to Step 9.
8. Test the following items as described in Chapter Nine:
   a. Neutral/reverse switch.
   b. Ignition switch.
9. Check the voltage of the starter relay as described in Chapter Nine. Note the following:
   a. If the voltmeter shows battery voltage, continue with Step 10.

17

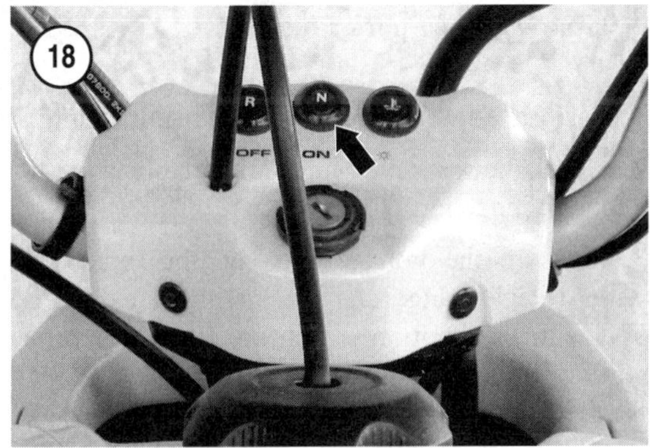

18

b. If there was no voltage reading, check the ignition switch and starter switch as described in Chapter Nine. If both switches are good, check the continuity of the yellow/black wire between the starter switch and the starter relay.

10. Perform the starter relay continuity test as described in Chapter Nine. Note the following:

a. If the starter relay passes both portions of the test, continue with Step 11.

b. If the starter relay fails either portion of the test, replace the starter relay.

11. If the starting system problem has not been located after performing these steps in order, recheck the wiring system for dirty or loose-fitting terminals or damaged wires. Clean and repair them as required.

12. Make sure all connectors disconnected during this procedure are corrosion free and reconnected properly.

Starter Turns Slowly

If the starter turns slowly and all engine components operate normally, perform the following:

1. Test the battery as described in Chapter Three.
2. Check for the following:
   a. Loose or corroded battery terminals.
   b. Loose or corroded battery ground cable.
   c. Loose starter cable.
3. Remove, disassemble and bench test the starter as described in Chapter Nine.
4. Check the starter for binding during operation. Disassemble the starter and check the armature shaft for bending or damage. Also, check the starter clutch as described in Chapter Five.

Starter Turns But the Engine Does Not

If the starter turns but the engine does not, perform the following:

1. Check for a damaged starter clutch (Chapter Five).
2. Check for damaged starter idle gears (Chapter Five).

CHARGING SYSTEM

The charging system consists of the battery, alternator and a voltage regulator/rectifier. A 20-amp main fuse protects the circuit.

Battery Discharging

1. Check all the connections. Make sure they are tight and corrosion free.
2. Refer to *Charging System* in Chapter Nine to perform the *Battery Voltage Test.*
   a. If the voltage is within specification, perform Step 3.
   b. If the voltage is outside the specified range, perform Step 5.
3. Refer to *Charging System* in Chapter Nine to perform the *Battery Current Draw Test.* Note the following:
   a. If the current draw exceeds 1.0 mA, isolate the cause.
   b. If the current draw is 1.0 mA or less, perform Step 4.
4. Disconnect the regulator/rectifier connector, and repeat the *Battery Current Draw Test.*

a. If the current draw exceeds 1.0 mA, check for a shorted wire harness or faulty ignition switch.
b. If the current draw is 1.0 mA or less, replace the regulator/rectifier.

5. Check the resistance of the stator coil as described in Chapter Nine.
a. If the resistance is within specification, replace the charging coil.
b. If the resistance is outside the specified range, check for dirty or loose fitting alternator connections.

Battery Overcharging

1. Check all the connections. Make sure they are tight and free of corrosion.
2. Refer to *Charging System* in Chapter Nine to perform the *Regulator/Rectifier Output Voltage Test*.
a. If the voltage is within specification, replace the battery.
b. If the voltage exceeds the specified range, perform Step 3.

3. Check the continuity of the regulator/rectifier connector as described in *Charging System* in Chapter Nine.
a. If the connector does not have continuity, check for a loose regulator/rectifier connector. If the connection is good, replace the regulator/rectifier.
b. If the connector has continuity, check for a poor connection or an open in the wire harness.

IGNITION SYSTEM

All models are equipped with a capacitor discharge ignition (CDI) system.

Test Notes

A multicircuit tester set (Suzuki part no. 09900-25008) or a commercially available digital multimeter (minimum impedance of 10M ohms/DVC) are required to troubleshoot the ignition system.

No Spark at the Spark Plug

1. Perform a spark test as described in this chapter.
2. Check the spark plug cap and spark plug wire for a loose connection.
3. Measure the voltage between the input lead wires (black/orange and black/white) at the CDI unit with the ignition switch on. If the voltage is correct continue with Step 4. If it is incorrect check for the following:
a. Faulty ignition switch.
b. Faulty engine stop switch.
c. Broken wire harness or poor connection.

4. Perform the ignition coil primary peak voltage test described in *Ignition System* in Chapter Nine. Record the results of the test. If the voltage is within specification, check the spark plug connection and replace the spark plug if necessary. If it is not, proceed with Step 5.
a. Replace the spark plug.
b. Check the ignition coil if it fails.

5. Measure the pickup coil and signal coil peak voltage and resistance. If they are within specification, proceed to Step 6. If they are out of specification, perform the following:
a. Replace the pickup coil and retest the system.
b. Signal coil and retest the system.

6. If all other tests have not revealed the fault, check the following:
a. Replace the CDI unit and retest the system.
b. Open circuit in wiring harness.
c. Improper ignition coupler connection.

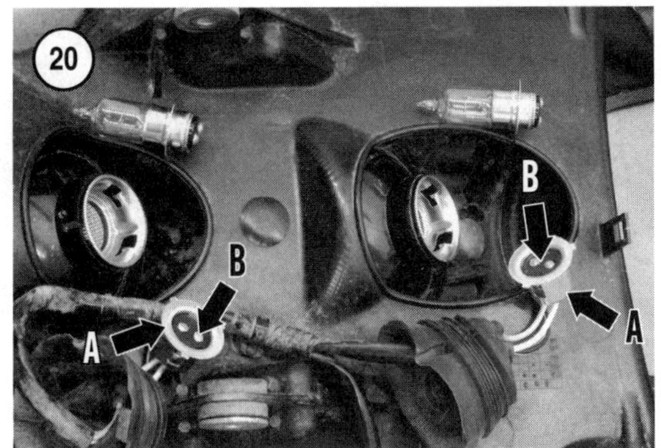

LIGHTING SYSTEM

Faulty Bulbs

If a headlight or taillight bulb(s) continually burn out, check for one or more of the following conditions:

1. Incorrect bulb type. Refer to Chapter Nine for bulb specifications.
2. Damaged battery.
3. Damaged rectifier/regulator.
4. Damaged ignition switch and/or light switch.

Headlight Operates Darker than Normal

Check for one or more of the following conditions:

1. Incorrect bulb type. Refer to Chapter Nine for bulb specifications.
2. Charging system problem.
3. Electric accessories added to the wiring harness. Disconnect each accessory one at a time, start the engine and check the headlight operation. If an accessory is the cause of the problem, contact the accessory manufacturer for more information.
4. Incorrect ground connection.
5. Poor main and/or light switch electrical contacts.

Lighting System Check

Headlight

If the headlights do not come on, perform the following test:

1. Remove the headlight bulb (Chapter Nine) and disconnect the headlight (**Figure 19**) from the main wiring harness.

   a. Connect an ohmmeter to the bulb socket (A, **Figure 20**). The reading should be zero ohms. Replace the bulb if the ohmmeter indicates an open circuit.

   b. Check the continuity of each wire in the headlight socket. Connect an ohmmeter to one of the terminals in the headlight socket (B, **Figure 20**) and to the same side of the headlight connector. Repeat this for the other wires. Each wire should have continuity. If any wire does have continuity, replace the headlight socket if it cannot be repaired.

2. Install the headlight bulb into its socket and reconnect the socket bullet connectors to their mates from the wiring harness. Do not install the socket into its headlight housing. The headlight bulb and socket must be connected to the wiring harness when making the following tests.

3. Switch a voltmeter to its DC20V scale. In Step 4 and Step 5, carefully test the bullet connectors while the are connected to the main wiring harness.

4. Connect the voltmeter positive lead to the headlight connector black/white lead and the voltmeter negative lead to the headlight connector white lead. Turn the ignition switch on and the dimmer switch to low. Note the voltmeter reading:

   a. If the voltmeter reads battery voltage, continue with Step 5.

   b. If the voltmeter does not read battery voltage, check the wiring harness from the ignition switch to the headlight socket for damage.

5. Turn the ignition switch off. Connect the voltmeter positive lead to the headlight connector black/white lead and the voltmeter negative lead to the headlight connector yellow lead. Turn the ignition switch on and the dimmer switch to high. Note the voltmeter reading:

   a. If the voltmeter reads battery voltage, continue with Step 6.

   b. If the voltmeter does not read battery voltage, check the wiring harness from the ignition switch to the headlight socket for damage.

6. Turn the ignition switch off and disconnect the voltmeter leads. If the voltmeter read battery voltage for both tests (Step 4 and Step 5), the headlight wiring is good.

Taillight

If the taillight does not turn on, perform the following test:

1. Remove the taillight bulb (**Figure 21**) as described in Chapter Nine, and disconnect the taillight bullet connectors from the wiring harness (**Figure 22**).
   a. Connect an ohmmeter to the bulb terminals. The reading should be zero ohms. Replace the bulb if the ohmmeter reads infinity.
   b. Check the continuity of the taillight wires. Connect an ohmmeter to one terminal in the taillight socket (**Figure 23**) and to the taillight side of its related bullet connector. Repeat for the other wire. Each reading should be zero ohms. If any reading indicates an open circuit, replace the taillight socket if it cannot be repaired.
2. Install the taillight bulb into its socket and reconnect the socket bullet connectors to the main wiring harness. Do not reinstall the socket into the taillight housing (mounting position). The taillight bulb and socket must be connected to the main wiring harness when making the following tests.
3. Switch a voltmeter to its DC20V scale. In Step 4, test the taillight socket bullet connectors with the taillight connectors connected to the main wiring harness.
4. Connect the voltmeter positive lead to the taillight connector black/white lead and the voltmeter negative lead to the taillight connector gray lead. Turn the ignition switch on and note the voltmeter reading:
   a. If the voltmeter reads battery voltage, continue with Step 5.
   b. If the voltmeter does not read battery voltage, check the wiring harness from the ignition switch to the taillight socket for damage.
5. Turn the ignition switch off and disconnect the voltmeter leads. If the voltmeter reads battery voltage in Step 4, the taillight wiring is good.

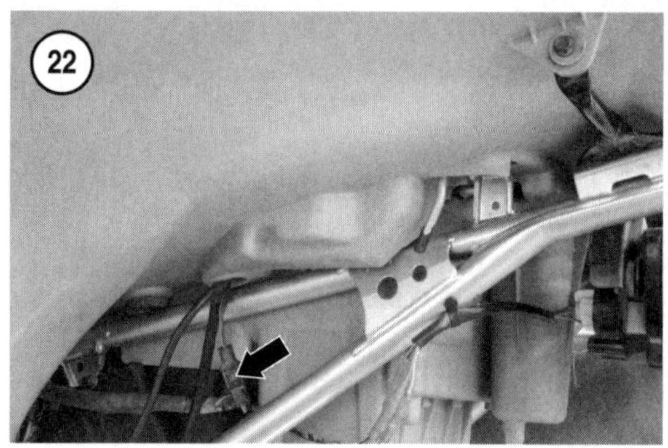

FUEL SYSTEM

When troubleshooting the fuel system, start at the fuel tank and work through the system, reserving the carburetor as the final point. Most fuel system problems result from an empty fuel tank, a plugged fuel valve or sour fuel. Fuel system troubleshooting is covered under *Starting the Engine, Engine Does Not Start, Poor Idle Speed Performance* and *Poor, Medium and High Speed Performance* in this chapter.

ENGINE OVERHEATING

Engine overheating can quickly cause damage. In water cooled engines most overheating problems are associated with the cooling system. The following section lists probable causes that can lead to engine overheating.

1. Cooling system:
   a. Low coolant level.
   b. Radiator core plugged.
   c. Defective temperature switch.
   d. Clogged engine coolant passage.
   e. Air trapped in the cooling circuit.
   f. Defective water pump.
   g. Incorrect engine coolant.
   h. Defective cooling fan thermoswitch.
   i. Blown cooling fan fuse (2004-on).
   j. Defective thermostat.
2. Engine:
   a. Incorrect spark plug heat range.

23

b. Low oil level.
c. Combustion chamber carbon deposits.
d. Brake drag.
e. Clutch slip.

ENGINE NOISES

1. A knocking or pinging during acceleration can be caused by using a lower octane fuel than recommended or a poor quality of fuel. Incorrect carburetor jetting or a spark plug that is too hot can also cause pinging. Refer to *Spark Plug* in Chapter Three. Check also for excessive carbon buildup in the combustion chamber or a faulty CDI unit.
2. A slapping or rattling noises at low speed or during acceleration can be caused by excessive piston-to-cylinder wall clearance. Check also for a bent connecting rod or worn piston pin and/or piston pin holes in the piston.
3. A knocking or rapping while decelerating is usually caused by excessive rod bearing clearance.
4. A persistent knocking and vibration or other noise is usually caused by worn main bearings. If the main bearings are good, consider the following:
   a. Loose engine mounts.
   b. Cracked frame.
   c. Leaking cylinder head gasket.
   d. Exhaust pipe leak at cylinder head.
   e. Stuck piston ring.
   f. Broken piston ring.
   g. Partial engine seizure.
   h. Excessive connecting rod small end bearing clearance.
   i. Excessive connecting rod big end side clearance.
   j. Excessive crankshaft runout.
   k. Worn or damaged primary drive gear.
5. If a rapid on-off squeal is heard, check for a compression leak around the cylinder head gasket or spark plug.

2

Preignition

Preignition is the premature burning of fuel and is caused by hot spots in the combustion chamber. The fuel ignites before spark ignition occurs. Glowing deposits in the combustion chamber, inadequate cooling or an overheated spark plug can all cause preignition. This is first noticed as a power loss but will eventually result in damage to the internal parts of the engine because of higher combustion chamber temperature.

Detonation

Commonly called spark knock or fuel knock, detonation is the violent explosion of fuel in the combustion chamber instead of the controlled burn that occurs during normal combustion. Excessive damage can result. Using low octane gasoline is a common cause of detonation.

Even when using a high-octane gasoline, detonation can still occur. Other causes are over-advanced ignition timing (not adjustable), lean fuel mixture at or near full throttle, inadequate engine cooling, or the excessive accumulation of carbon deposits in the combustion chamber and on the piston crown.

Power Loss

Several factors can cause a lack of power. Look for a clogged air filter or a fouled or damaged spark plug. A piston or cylinder that is galled, incorrect piston clearance or worn or sticking piston rings may be responsible. Look for loose bolts, defective gaskets or leaking machined mating surfaces on the cylinder head, cylinder or crankcase.

Piston Seizure

This may be caused by incorrect bore clearance, piston rings with an improper end gap, compression leak, incorrect air/fuel mixture, spark plug of the wrong heat range or incorrect ignition timing. Overheating from any cause may result in piston seizure.

Piston Slap

Piston slap is an audible slapping or rattling noise resulting from excessive piston-to-cylinder clearance. If allowed to continue, piston slap will eventually cause the piston skirt to crack and shatter.

To prevent piston slap, clean the air filter element on a regular schedule. If piston slap is heard, disassemble the engine top end and measure the cylinder bore and piston diameter. Replace parts that exceed service limits or show damage.

CYLINDER LEAKDOWN TEST

A cylinder leakdown test can determine if an engine problem is caused by leaking valves, a blown head gasket, or broken, worn or stuck piston rings. A cylinder leakdown test is performed by applying compressed air to the cylinder and then measuring the rate of leak. A cylinder leakdown tester (**Figure 24**) and an air compressor are required to perform this test. Follow the tester manufacturer's directions along with the following information when performing the test.

1. Run the engine until it reaches normal operating temperature, then turn the engine off.
2. Remove the air filter element as described in Chapter Three. Open and secure the throttle in the wide-open position.
3. Set the piston to TDC on its compression stroke. Refer to *Valve Clearance Inspection* in Chapter Three.
4. Remove the spark plug.
5. To prevent the engine from turning, shift the transmission into fifth gear and set the parking brake.
6. Install the cylinder leakdown tester into the spark plug hole.
7. Perform a cylinder leakdown test. Listen for air leaking while noting the following:
   a. Air leaking through the exhaust pipe indicates a leaking exhaust valve.
   b. Air leaking through the carburetor indicates a leaking intake valve.
   c. Air leaking through the crankcase breather tube indicates worn piston rings.
8. A cylinder with a reading of 10 percent or more requires further service.
9. Remove the tester and reinstall the spark plug.

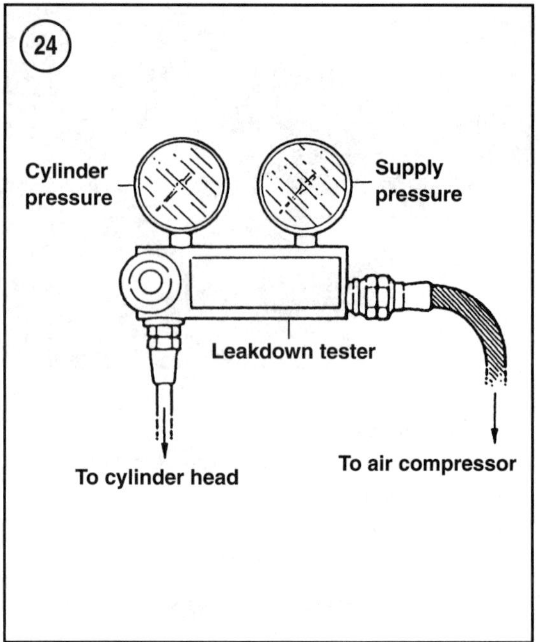

CLUTCH

The two main clutch problems are clutch slip (clutch does not fully engage) and clutch drag (clutch does not fully disengage). Both of these problems are usually caused by incorrect clutch adjustment, damaged cable, or damaged lever. Perform the following checks before removing the right crankcase cover to troubleshoot the clutch:

1. Check the clutch cable routing from the handlebar to the engine. Make sure the cable is free when the handlebars are turned lock to lock, and the cable ends are seated correctly.
2. With the engine off, pull and release the clutch lever. If the lever is hard to pull, or the action is rough, check for the following:
   a. Damaged/kinked cable.
   b. Incorrect cable routing.
   c. Cable not lubricated.
   d. Damaged lever at the handlebar.
   e. Damaged lifter arm at the engine.
3. If the parts in Step 1 and Step 2 are good, and the lever moves with excessive roughness or binding, check the clutch adjustment as described in Chapter Three.
4. If the clutch cannot be adjusted to specification, the clutch cable is stretched or damaged. If the clutch cable and its adjustment are good, the friction plates may be worn. Refer to Chapter Six.

Clutch Slip

If the clutch slips the engine will speed up without driving the vehicle forward. Because the clutch plates are spinning against each other, excessive heat is quickly built up in the assembly. This causes plate wear, warp and spring fatigue. One or more of the following can cause the clutch to slip:

1. Clutch wear or damage.
   a. Incorrect clutch cable adjustment.
   b. Weak or damaged clutch springs.
   c. Loose clutch springs.
   d. Worn friction plates.
   e. Warped steel plates.
   f. Worn/damaged clutch lifter arm.
2. Clutch/engine oil:
   a. Oil additives.
   b. Incorrect oil viscosity.
   c. Low oil level.

Clutch Drag

When the clutch drags, the plates are not completely separating from each other. This will cause the vehicle to creep or lurch forward when shifting the transmission into gear. Once underway, shifting is difficult. If this condition is not corrected, it can cause transmission gear and shift fork damage. All clutch service, except adjustment, requires partial engine disassembly to identify and cure the problem. Refer to Chapter Six.

One or more of the following can cause the clutch to drag.

1. Clutch wear or damage:
   a. Incorrect clutch adjustment.
   b. Weak or damaged clutch springs.
   c. Damaged clutch pushrod.
   d. Worn or distorted clutch pressure plate.
   e. Swollen friction plates.
   f. Warped pressure plate.
   g. Incorrect clutch spring tension.
   h. Incorrectly assembled clutch.
   i. Loose clutch nut.
   j. Galled primary drive gear bushing.
   k. Notched clutch hub splines.
   l. Notched clutch housing grooves.
2. Clutch/engine oil:
   a. Oil additives.
   b. Low oil level.
   c. Incorrect oil viscosity.

Rough Clutch Operation

1. Damaged clutch housing slots.
2. Damaged clutch center splines.
3. Incorrect engine idle speed.

Transmission is Hard to Shift

1. Clutch wear or damage:
   a. Incorrect clutch adjustment.
   b. Damaged clutch lifter mechanism.
2. Damaged shift drum shifter plate.

TRANSMISSION

Transmission symptoms can be difficult to distinguish from clutch symptoms. Make sure the clutch is not causing the trouble before working on the transmission.

Difficult Shifting

If the shift shaft does not move smoothly from one gear to the next, check the following:

1. Shift shaft:
   a. Incorrectly installed shift lever.
   b. Damaged gearshift linkage assembly where it engages the shift drum.
   c. Stopper arm binding on pivot.
2. Stopper arm:
   a. Seized or damaged stopper arm roller.
   b. Weak or damaged stopper arm spring.
   c. Loose stopper arm mounting bolts.
   d. Incorrectly assembled stopper arm assembly.
3. Shift drum and shift forks:
   a. Bent shift fork(s).
   b. Damaged shift fork guide pin(s).
   c. Seized shift fork (on shaft).
   d. Broken shift fork or shift fork shaft.
   e. Damaged shift drum groove(s).
   f. Damaged shift drum bearing surfaces.

Gears Pop Out of Mesh

If the transmission shifts into gear but then slips or pops out, check the following:

1. Worn gearshift pawls.
2. Shift drum:
   a. Incorrect thrust play.
   b. Worn or damaged shift drum groove(s).

3. Shift fork(s)
   a. Bent or damaged shift fork.
   b. Bent or damaged shift fork shaft.
4. Transmission:
   a. Worn or damaged gear dogs.
   b. Excessive gear thrust play.
   c. Worn or damaged transmission shaft circlips or thrust washers.

Transmission Fails to Shift into Reverse:

If the transmission fails to shift into or operate in reverse properly, check the following:

1. Incorrect reverse cable adjustment (Chapter Three).
2. Loose or damaged reverse selector shaft.
3. Damaged reverse selector shaft.

Oil Inspection

The transmission and clutch are lubricated with engine oil. Drain the oil (Chapter Three) into a clean container. Wipe a small amount of oil on one of your fingers, and then rub your finger and thumb together. Check for metallic particles. Also check the drain bolt for metal particles. While a small amount of particles in the oil is normal, an abnormal amount of debris means bearing or gear damage.

SUSPENSION

Poor suspension performance may cause loss of control. Check the following items when experiencing poor handling:

1. If the handlebars are hard to turn:
   a. Improper alignment.
   b. Poorly lubricated joints.
   c. Low air pressure in the front tires.
   d. Seized tie rod linkages.
2. If there is excessive handlebar shake or vibration:
   a. Improperly inflated tires.
   b. Loose hub nuts.
   c. Damaged or worn hub bearings.
   d. Worn or loose tie rod ends.
   e. Defective or incorrectly sized tires.
   f. Damaged or worn wishbone arms.
   g. Loose, missing or broken engine mount bolts and mounts.
   h. Cracked frame, especially at the steering head.
   i. Incorrect tire pressure.
   j. Damaged shock absorber damper rod.
   k. Leaking shock absorber damper housing.
   l. Sagged shock spring(s).
   m. Loose or damaged shock mount bolts.
3. If the rear suspension is too soft:
   a. Damaged shock absorber damper rod.
   b. Leaking shock absorber damper housing.
   c. Sagged shock spring.
   d. Loose or damaged shock mount bolts.
4. If the rear suspension is too hard:
   a. Rear tire pressure too high.
   b. Incorrect shock absorber adjustment.
   c. Damaged shock absorber damper rod.
   d. Leaking shock absorber damper housing.
   e. Sagged shock spring.
   f. Loose or damaged shock mount bolts.
   g. Improperly tightened swing arm pivot.
5. Frame:
   a. Damaged or broken frame.
   b. Cracked or broken engine mount brackets.
6. Wobbling wheel:
   a. Loose wheel nuts.
   b. Loose or incorrectly installed wheel hub.
   c. Excessive wheel bearing play.
   d. Loose wheel bearing.
   e. Bent wheel rim.
   f. Bent frame or other suspension component.
   g. Improperly tightened axle.
   h. Worn swing arm bearings.
7. If vehicle pulls to one side:
   a. Incorrect tire pressure.
   b. Incorrect tie rod adjustment.
   c. Bent or loose tie rod.
   d. Incorrect wheel alignment.
   e. Bent frame or other suspension component.
   f. Weak front shock absorber.

FRAME

Noises from the frame or suspension are usually caused by loose, worn or damaged parts. Check the following:

1. Front or rear shock absorber noise:
   a. Loose shock absorber mounting bolts.
   b. Cracked or broken shock spring.
   c. Damaged shock absorber.
2. Cracked or broken frame.

3. Broken swing arm or shock linkage.
4. Loose engine mounting bolts.
5. Damaged steering shaft bearings.
6. Loose mounting bracket.

BRAKES

Inspect the brakes frequently and repair any problem immediately. When replacing or refilling the brake fluid, use DOT 4 brake fluid from a sealed container. Refer to Chapter Thirteen for brake service.

If the front and/or rear disc brakes are not working properly, check for one or more of the following conditions:

1. Air in brake lines.
2. Brake reservoir fluid level low.
3. Loose brake hose banjo bolts allowing brake fluid leaks.
4. Loose or damaged brake hose or line.
5. Worn or damaged brake disc.
6. Worn or damaged brake pads.
7. Contaminated brake disc or brake pad surfaces.
8. Worn or damaged caliper(s).

CHAPTER THREE

LUBRICATION, MAINTENANCE AND TUNE-UP

MAINTENANCE SCHEDULE

Refer to **Table 1** for the maintenance schedule. These recommendations help ensure a long service. Perform service more often when operating the ATV in dusty or other harsh conditions.

Most of the services in **Table 1** are described in this chapter. However, some procedures that require more than minor disassembly or adjustment are covered in the appropriate chapters and are so indicated.

Tables 1-5 are at the end of the chapter.

PRE-RIDE INSPECTION

Perform the following checks before the first ride of the day. If a component requires service, refer to the appropriate section.

1. Inspect all fuel lines and fittings for leaks.
2. Make sure the fuel tank is full of fresh gasoline.
3. Make sure the engine oil level is correct.
4. Check the throttle for proper operation in all steering positions. Open the throttle all the way and release it. The throttle should close quickly with no binding or roughness.
5. Check that the brake lever and pedal operate properly with no binding.
6. Check the brake fluid level in the front and rear master cylinder reservoir. Add or DOT 4 brake fluid as necessary.
7. Check the parking brake operation and adjust it if necessary.
8. Inspect the front and rear suspension. Make sure they have a good solid feel with no looseness. Turn the handlebar from side to side to check steering play. Service the steering assembly if there is excessive play. Make sure the handlebar cables do not bind.
9. Check the tire pressure.
10. Check the exhaust system for looseness or damage.
11. Check the skid plates for damage.
12. Check the undercarriage for dirt, vegetation or other debris that might create a fire hazard or interfere with vehicle operation.
13. Check the tightness of all fasteners, especially engine, steering and suspension mounting hardware.
14. Make sure the headlight and taillight work properly.
15. Make sure each switch works properly.
16. Check the air filter drain tube for contamination.
17. Start the engine and stop it with the engine stop switch. If the engine stop switch does not work

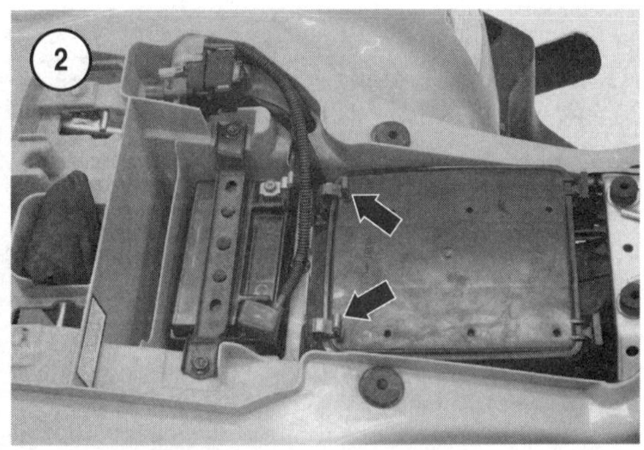

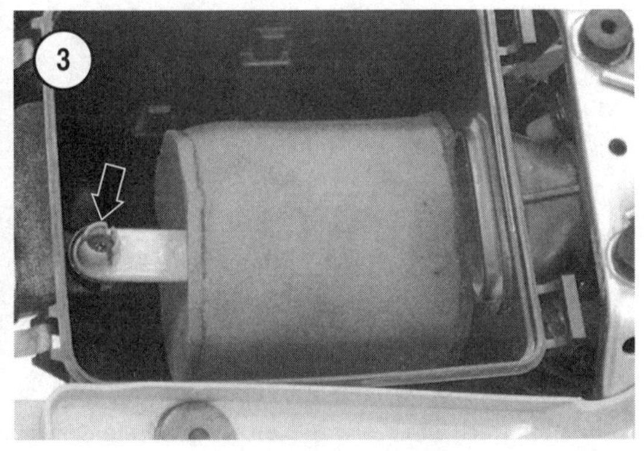

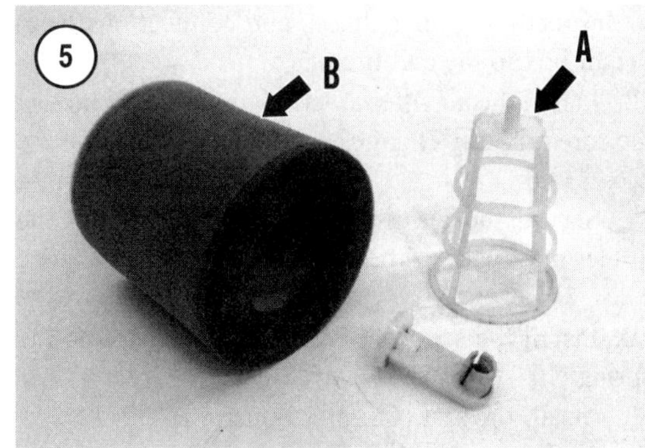

properly, test the switch as described in Chapter Nine.

AIR BOX DRAIN PLUG

Remove the air box drain plug to drain water out of the air box (**Figure 1**). If the air box fills with water, clean and oil the air filter.

AIR FILTER

A clogged air filter decreases the efficiency and life of the engine. Never run the engine without a properly installed air filter. Dust that enters the engine can cause severe engine wear and clog carburetor passages.

Removal/Installation

1. Remove the seat as described in Chapter Fourteen.
2. Release the spring clips (**Figure 2**) and remove the air box cover.
3. Remove the screw on the air filter holder (**Figure 3**).
4. Remove the air filter assembly (**Figure 4**) from the air box.
5. Disassemble, clean and oil the air filter (**Figure 5**) as described in this section.
6. Check the air box and carburetor boot for dirt or other contaminants.
7. Wipe the inside of the air box (**Figure 6**) with a clean rag. If it is not possible to clean the air box with it bolted to the frame, remove and clean the air box.
8. Cover the air box opening with a clean shop rag.

9. Inspect all fittings, hoses and connections from the air box to the carburetor.
10. Install the air filter assembly into the air box so the core properly engages the duct in the front of the box.
11. Secure the air filter with the holder and the holder into place with the mounting screw (**Figure 3**).
12. Install the air box cover and secure it with the spring clips (**Figure 2**).
13. Install the seat (Chapter Fourteen).

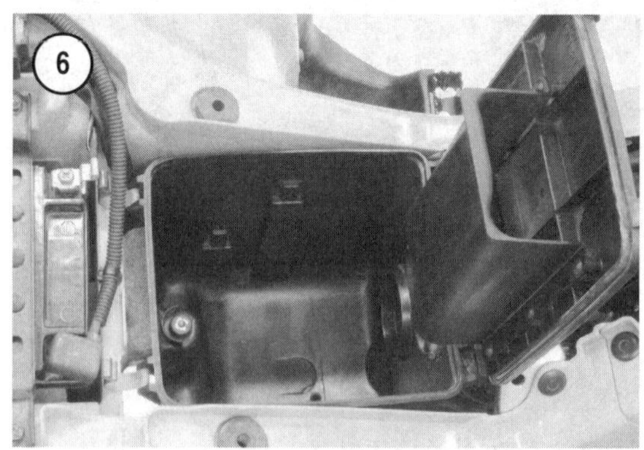

Cleaning

WARNING
Do not clean the filter element with gasoline.

Service the air filter element in a well-ventilated area away from all sparks and flames.

1. Lift the air filter from the air box and remove the frame (A, **Figure 5**) from inside the foam filter (B).
2. Clean the filter element with a non-flammable or high flash-point solvent to remove oil and dirt.
3. Inspect the filter element. Replace the element if it is torn or broken in any area.
4. Fill a clean pan with liquid detergent and warm water.
5. Submerge the filter element in the cleaning solution and gently work the cleaner into the filter pores. Soak and squeeze (gently) the filter element to clean it.

CAUTION
Do not wring or twist the filter element during cleaning. This could damage the filter pores or tear the filter loose at a seam. This would allow unfiltered air to enter the engine and cause rapid wear.

6. Rinse the filter element under warm water while soaking and gently squeezing it.
7. Repeat Step 5 and Step 6 until no dirt rinses from the filter element.
8. After cleaning the element, inspect it again carefully. If it is torn or broken in any area, replace it. Do not run the engine with a damaged filter element.
9. Set the filter element aside and allow to dry thoroughly. Make sure the filter element is completely dry before oiling it.

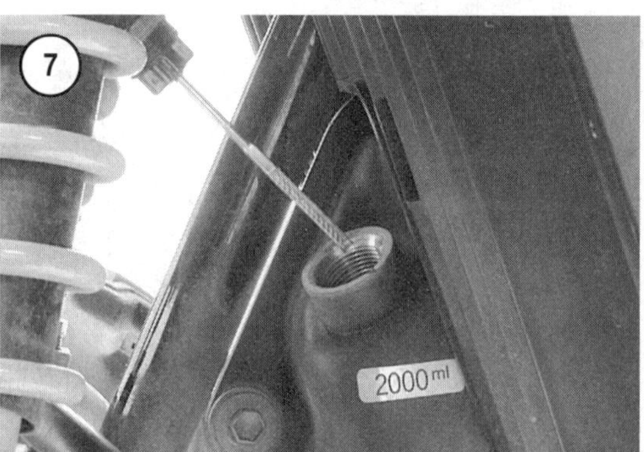

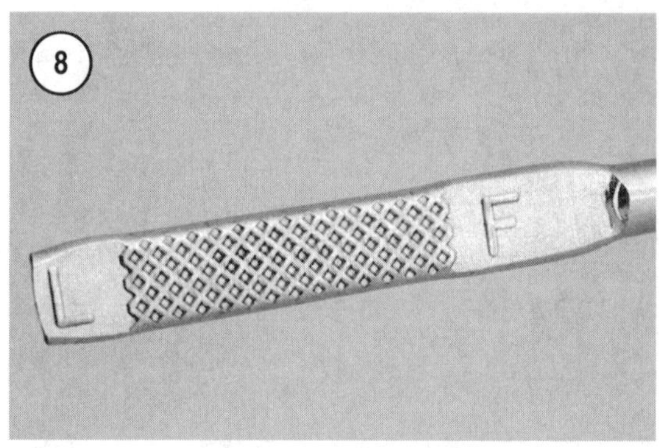

10. Wear a pair of disposable rubber gloves when performing this procedure. Oil the filter by performing the following:
    a. Place the filter element into a storage bag.
    b. Pour enough SAE 30 or SAE 10W-40 weight engine oil into the filter to soak it.
    c. Gently squeeze and release the filter to soak the oil into the filter's pores. Repeat this process until all of the filter's pores are saturated with oil.
    d. Remove the filter element from the bag and check the pores for uneven oiling. This is in-

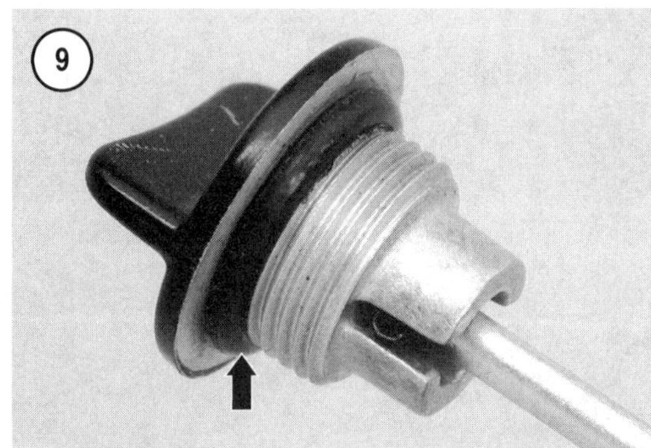

9

10

11

dicated by light or dark areas on the filter element. If necessary, soak the filter element and squeeze it again.

e. When the filter oiling is even, squeeze the filter element a final time.

f. Pour the leftover oil from the bag back into the bottle for reuse.

g. Dispose of the plastic bag.

11. Install the filter element (B, **Figure 5**) over the element frame (A).

12. Install the filter element assembly as described in this section.

ENGINE OIL

Level Check

Check the engine oil level with the dipstick/oil fill cap mounted in the external oil tank.

1. Park the vehicle on level ground and set the parking brake.
2. Start the engine and let it run approximately 2-3 minutes.
3. Shut off the engine, and let the oil drain into the crankcase and oil tank for a few minutes.
4. Unscrew and remove the dipstick/oil fill cap from the oil tank (**Figure 7**). Wipe it clean, and reinsert it onto the threads in the hole. Do *not* screw it in.
5. Remove the dipstick and read the oil level. The level is correct if it is between the two dipstick lines (**Figure 8**). If necessary, add the recommended type oil (**Table 3**) to correct the level.
6. Replace the dipstick O-ring (**Figure 9**) if damaged.
7. Install the dipstick/oil fill cap (**Figure 10**) and tighten it securely.

Oil and Filter Change

WARNING
Prolonged contact with used oil may cause skin cancer. Wash your hands with soap and water after handling or coming in contact with motor oil.

NOTE
Running the engine heats the oil, which enables the oil to flow more freely and carry contaminates out with it.

1. Park the vehicle on level ground and apply the parking brake.
2. Start the engine, and let it warm to normal operating temperature. Then shut the engine off.
3. Place a clean drain pan underneath the engine. Make sure the drain pan is large enough to catch the oil coming out of the crankcase and the oil tank.
4. Remove the drain plug from the crankcase (**Figure 11**) and the oil tank. Drain the oil.

3

5. Remove the dipstick/oil fill cap (**Figure 10**) to help speed up the flow of oil.
6. Allow the oil to drain completely.
7. Remove the bolts from the oil filter cover (A, **Figure 12**). Remove the cover.
8. Remove the filter and O-ring at the back of the housing (**Figure 13**).
9. Clean and inspect the filter housing and parts.
10. Install a new lubricated O-ring in the housing and on the filter cover. Install the filter and cover. Make sure the spring is in place on the cover.
11. Replace the drain plug gaskets if damaged or if the plug was leaking. Install the drain plugs. Tighten the oil tank drain plug to 12 N•m (106 in.-lb.). Tighten the crankcase drain plug to 21 N•m (15.5 ft.-lb.).
12. Fill the oil tank with the correct weight and quantity of oil (**Table 3**).
13. Screw in the dipstick/oil fill cap (**Figure 10**) securely.
14. Start the engine and run at idle speed.
15. Turn the engine off. Check the drain bolt and filter cover for leaks.
16. Check the oil level; adjust if necessary.

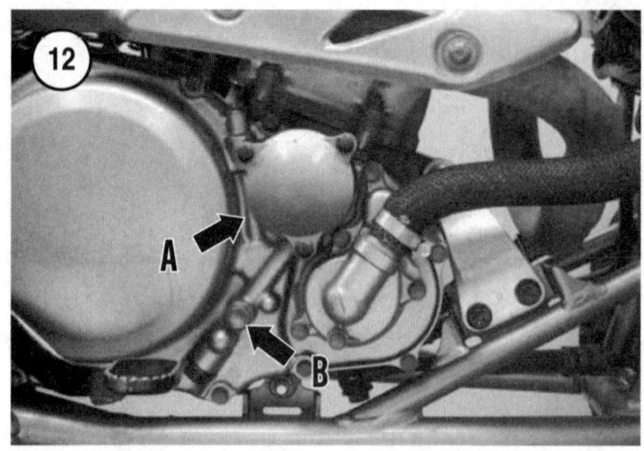

OIL PRESSURE CHECK

1. Warm the engine to operating temperature.
2. Attach a shop tachometer, following the manufacturer's instructions.
3. Remove the main oil gallery plug (B, **Figure 12**) and thread an oil pressure gauge into the fitting. An oil pressure gauge (Suzuki part No. 09915-74510) and adapter (part No. 09915-70610) are available.
4. Start the engine and raise the engine speed to 3000 rpm. Note the pressure reading on the gauge. Refer to **Table 4** for the oil pressure specifications.
5. Reinstall the main oil gallery plug and tighten it to 18 N•m (13 ft.-lb.).

SPARK PLUG

Cap

The spark plug cap should fit tightly to the spark plug and be in good condition. A cap that does not seal and insulate the spark plug terminal can lead to flashover (shorting down the side of the plug), particularly when the ATV is operated in wet conditions. To help prevent water from migrating into the spark plug well, wipe a small amount of dielectric grease around the edge of the rubber seal before seating it in the well.

Removal

Careful removal of the spark plug is important in preventing grit from entering the combustion chamber. It is also important to know how to remove a plug that is seized, or is resistant to removal. Forcing a seized plug can damage the threads in the cylinder head.

1. Remove the front bodywork (Chapter Fourteen) and fuel tank (Chapter Eight).
2. Clean the area around the spark plug cap, then grasp the cap and twist it loose from the spark plug. There may be slight suction and resistance while removing the cap.
3. Clean dirt from the plug well, preferably with compressed air.
4. Fit a spark plug socket onto the spark plug. If necessary, also use a jointed or flexible extension to reach to the bottom of the spark plug. The frame interferes with straight extensions. Remove the spark

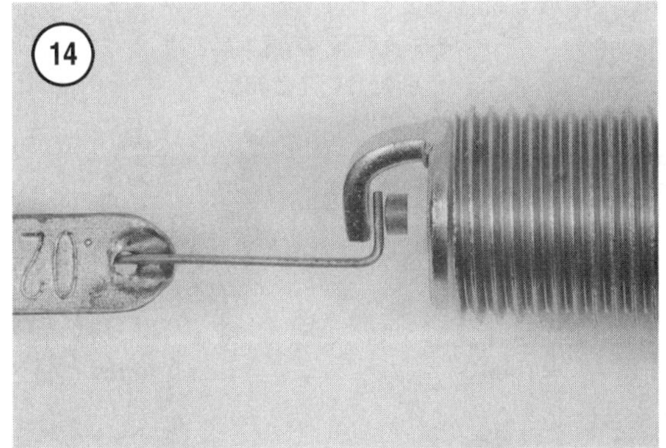
14

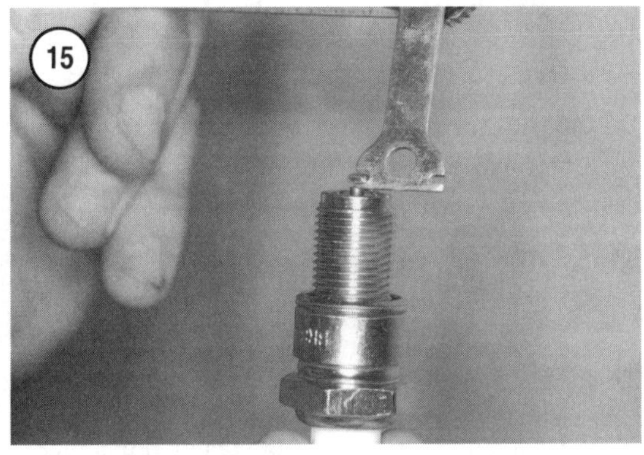
15

plug by turning the wrench counterclockwise. If the plug is seized or drags excessively during removal, stop and try the following techniques:

a. Apply a penetrating lubricant and allow it to stand for 15 minutes.

b. Apply moderate pressure in both directions with the wrench. Only attempt to break the seal so lubricant can penetrate under the spark plug and into the threads. If necessary, apply more penetrating lubricant around the spark plug threads. Slowly remove the plug, working it in and out of the cylinder head while adding lubricant.

c. If this does not work, and the ATV is still operable, install the spark plug cap and fuel tank, then start the engine. Allow it to completely warm up. The heat of the engine may be enough to expand the parts and allow the plug to be removed.

d. If available, clean and true the threads with a spark plug thread-chaser and extension.

5. Remove the spark plug. A magnetic tool is helpful in lifting the plug from the well.

6. Inspect the plug to determine if the engine is operating properly.

7. A spark plug in good condition can be reused after inspection. Clean the plug with electrical contact cleaner and a shop cloth. Do not use abrasives or wire brushes to clean the plug. Do not reinstall a spark plug that was seized in the cylinder head.

3

Gap and Installation

Carefully adjust the electrode gap on a new spark plug to ensure a reliable, consistent spark. Use a spark plug gapping tool and a wire feeler gauge.

1. Select a wire feeler gauge that is within the spark plug gap range specified in **Table 4**.

2. Insert the wire feeler gauge between the center and side electrode of the plug (**Figure 14**). If the gap is correct, a slight drag will be felt as the wire gauge is pulled through. If there is no drag or if the gauge does not pass through, bend the side electrode with a gaping tool (**Figure 15**) to set the proper gap.

3. Apply an antiseize compound to the plug threads before installing the spark plug. Do not use engine oil on the plug threads.

4. Screw the spark plug in by hand until it seats. Very little effort should be required. If force is necessary, the plug may be cross-threaded. Unscrew it and try again.

5. Use a spark plug wrench and tighten a new spark plug to the 11 N•m (97 in.-lb.). If a torque wrench is not available, tighten the plug an additional 1/2 turn after the gasket has made contact with the head. If installing a used spark plug, only tighten it an additional 1/8 to 1/4 turn. Do not overtighten the plug.

Reading

A careful examination of the spark plug can reveal information about engine and spark plug performance.

Normal condition

A plug that has a light tan- or gray-colored deposit and no abnormal gap wear or erosion indicates good engine, carburetion and ignition conditions.

This plug has the proper heat range. It may be serviced and returned to use.

Carbon fouled

Soft, dry, sooty deposits covering the entire firing end of the plug are evidence of incomplete combustion. Even though the firing end of the plug is dry, the plug's insulation decreases. The carbon forms an electrical path that bypasses the spark plug electrodes resulting in a misfire. Carbon fouling can be caused by one or more of the following:

1. Too rich fuel mixture.
2. Spark plug heat range too cold.
3. Clogged air filter.
4. Retarded ignition timing.
5. Ignition component failure.
6. Low engine compression.
7. Prolonged idling.

Oil fouled

The tip of an oil fouled plug has a black insulator tip, a damp oily film over the firing end and a carbon layer over the entire nose. The electrodes are not worn. Common causes for this condition are:

1. Incorrect carburetor jetting.
2. Low idle speed or prolonged idling.
3. Ignition component failure.
4. Spark plug heat range too cold.
5. Engine still being broken in.

Oil fouled spark plugs may be cleaned in an emergency, but it is better to replace them. It is important to correct the cause of fouling before the engine is returned to service.

Gap bridging

Plugs with this condition exhibit gaps shorted out by combustion deposits between the electrodes. If this condition exists, check for an improper oil type or excessive carbon in the combustion chamber. Make sure to identify and correct the cause of this condition.

Overheated

Badly worn electrodes and premature gap wear along with a gray or white blistered porcelain insulator surface are signs of overheating. This condition is commonly caused by a spark plug that is too hot. If you have not changed to a hotter spark plug but the plug is overheated, consider the following causes:

1. Lean fuel mixture.
2. Ignition timing too advanced.
3. Engine lubrication system malfunction.
4. Engine vacuum leak.
5. Improper spark plug installation (too tight).
6. No spark plug gasket.

Worn out

This occurs when corrosive gasses formed by combustion and high voltage sparks erode the electrodes. Spark plugs in this condition require more voltage to fire under hard acceleration. Install a new spark plug.

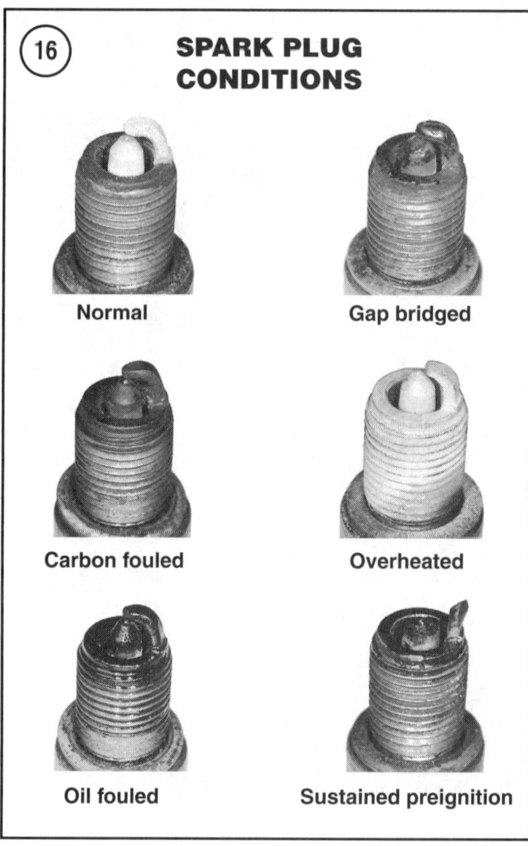

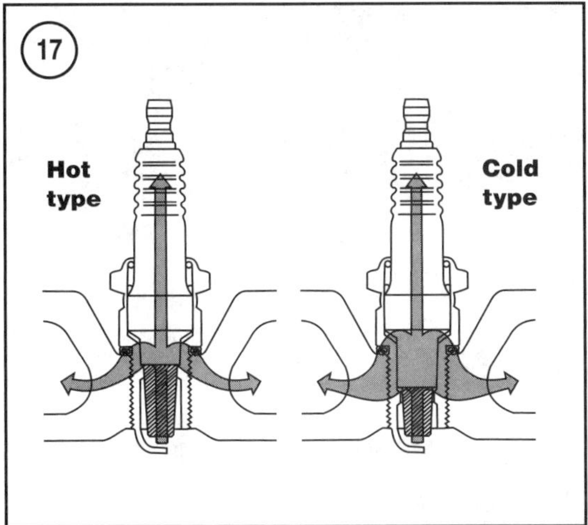

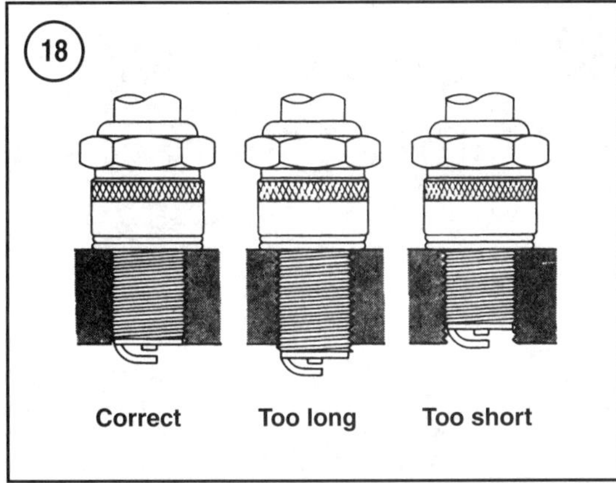

Sustained preignition

If the electrodes are melted, preignition is almost certainly the cause. Check for carburetor mounting or intake manifold leaks and over advanced ignition timing. A plug that is too hot can also cause this condition. Find and correct the cause of the preignition before returning the engine into service.

Heat Range

Spark plugs are available in several heat ranges to accommodate the load and performance demands put on the engine. The standard spark plug is usually a medium heat range plug that operates well over a wide range of engine speeds. As long as engine speeds vary, this plug will stay relatively clean and perform well.

If the engine is run in hot climates, at high speed or under heavy loads for prolonged periods, use a spark plug with a colder heat range. A colder plug quickly transfers heat away from its firing tip and to the cylinder head (**Figure 17**). By transferring the heat quickly, the plug remains cool enough to avoid overheating and preignition problems. If the engine is run slowly for prolonged periods, this type of plug may foul and cause poor performance.

If the engine is run in cold climates or at slow speed for prolonged periods, use a spark plug with a hotter heat range. A hotter plug slowly transfers heat away from its firing tip and to the cylinder head (**Figure 17**). By transferring heat slowly, the plug remains hot enough to avoid fouling. If the engine is run in hot climates or fast for prolonged period, this type of plug may overheat, cause preignition problems and possibly melt the electrode. Damage to the piston and cylinder assembly is possible.

If changing a spark plug to a different heat range, go one step hotter or colder from the recommended plug. When replacing the plug, make sure the reach (**Figure 18**) is correct. A longer than standard pug can interfere with the piston and cause engine damage. A shorter than standard type may foul due to the firing tip being shrouded within the spark plug hole. Do not try to correct poor carburetor or ignition problems by using a different spark plug.

Refer to **Table 4** for spark plug recommendations.

SPARK ARRESTOR CLEANING

CAUTION

Allow the muffler to cool to the touch before removing the spark arrestor. Clean the arrestor in an open area away from flammable material. Hot carbon particles trapped in the spark arrestor can start a fire.

1. Remove the three bolts (**Figure 19**) securing the spark arrestor in the muffler.
2. Remove the spark arrestor from the muffler.
3. Clean the spark arrestor with a stiff brush to remove carbon deposits.
4. Installation is the reverse of removal.

FUEL LINE INSPECTION

WARNING
Some fuel may spill when performing this procedure. Because gasoline is extremely flammable, perform the following procedure away from all open flames (including appliance pilot lights) and sparks. Do not smoke or allow someone who is smoking in the work area. Always work in a well-ventilated area. Wipe up any spills immediately. Refer to ***Safety*** *in Chapter One.*

1. Remove the side panel (Chapter Fourteen) and inspect the fuel line (A, **Figure 20**) for leaks, cracks, hardness, age deterioration or other damage.
2. Make sure each end of the hose is secured with a hose clamp (B, **Figure 20**).
3. Check the carburetor overflow and vent hose ends for contamination.
4. Replace any damaged or deteriorated fuel lines.

FUEL TANK VENT HOSE

Inspection

Check the fuel tank vent hose (**Figure 21**) for proper routing. Make sure the hose is not kinked, and that its end is free of contamination.

CARBURETOR

Idle Speed and Mixture Adjustment

Use the following procedure to adjust the idle speed and pilot mixture screw for the jets for the carburetor with *standard* jetting. Refer to Chapter Eight for carburetor rejetting.

1. Warm the engine to operating temperature.
2. Check the throttle cables for proper adjustment as described in this chapter.
3. Make sure the air filter is clean.
4. Attach a stop tachometer, following the manufacturer's instructions.
5. Locate the pilot mixture screw (**Figure 22**). The screw may be blocked by a plug. The plug may be plastic and easily removed with a screwdriver; however, some models may have a pressed in metal plug. Refer to Chapter Eight for metal plug removal.

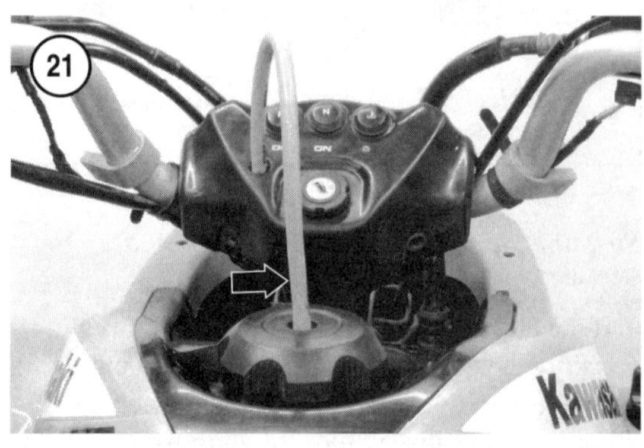

6. Lightly seat the pilot mixture screw, then turn the screw out the number of turns indicated in **Table 4**. This is a starting point for adjustment.
7. Start the engine and allow it to warm up.
8. Turn the idle adjustment knob (**Figure 23**) and set the engine idle speed to the specification in **Table 4**. Raise and lower the engine speed a few times to ensure that it returns to the set idle speed.
9. Note the position of the pilot mixture screw. From its initial setting, turn the pilot mixture screw in and out in small increments to find the points

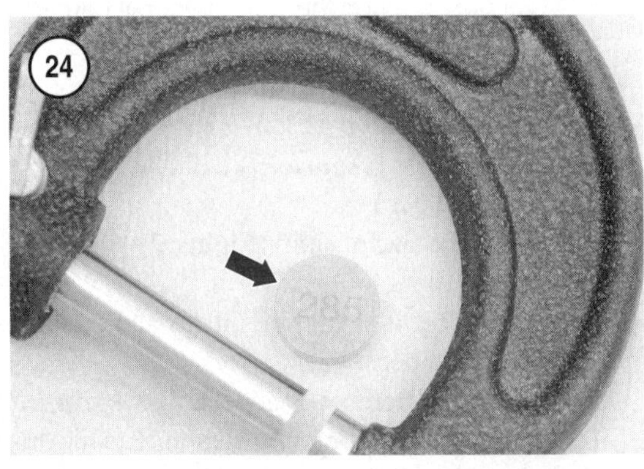

where the engine speed begins to decrease. Set the pilot mixture screw between the two points.

10. Reset the idle speed to bring it within its required setting.

11. Test ride the ATV and check throttle response. If throttle response is poor from an idle, adjust the pilot mixture screw out (richer) or in (leaner) by 1/8 turn increments until the engine accelerates smoothly.

Float Chamber Drain

Water can slowly build up in the float bowl. The float chamber can be drained without removing the carburetor. If the ATV will be put into storage, or not started for an extended period, drain the float chamber.

WARNING
Do not drain the float chamber while the engine is hot or running.

1. Support the vehicle so it is level.
2. Check that the fuel valve is off.
3. Place a suitable container under the end of the drain hose near the right foot peg.
4. Open the drain screw and allow the fuel to drain from the chamber. Do not remove the drain screw.
5. Close the drain screw; do not overtighten it.
6. Examine the fuel for water or other contaminants. If necessary, service the carburetor as described in Chapter Eight.

IGNITION TIMING

The ignition timing is controlled by the CDI unit. No adjustment is possible to the timing. The rotor is marked for top dead center.

VALVE CLEARANCE INSPECTION

The valves must be adjusted correctly so they will completely open and close during the combustion cycle. Valves that are out of adjustment can cause poor performance and engine damage. Valve clearance is adjusted by placing a calibrated shim (**Figure 24**) in the recess at the top of each valve assembly (**Figure 25**). The shim and valve assembly are covered with a cylindrical valve lifter (**Figure 26**), often called a *bucket*. Each valve lifter is aligned below one of the camshaft lobes (**Figure 27**), which opens and closes the valve. The camshaft lobe contacts only the valve lifter and not the shim or valve stem.

If the valve clearance is incorrect, remove the camshafts and valve lifters and install the correct shims to bring each valve within specification. When removing valve lifters and shims, always record the clearance and shim size for each valve location. Keep each shim and valve lifter set identified with their location in the cylinder head.

If the valve clearance is at or near the smallest acceptable clearance, typically, the clearance is increased, even though the valve is within the specification. Valves more often lose clearance than gain clearance between inspections, and therefore are adjusted toward the larger clearance specification.

Shims are available in increments of 0.05 mm (0.002 in.). Shim thickness ranges from 2.3 mm (a number 230 shim) to 3.5 mm (a number 350 shim). The number on the shim surface is the original thickness of the shim. Measure the shims with a caliper to verify their actual thickness.

Check the valve clearance when the engine is at ambient temperature.

1. Support the ATV so it is secure.
2. Remove the cylinder head cover and set the engine at TDC as described in Chapter Four.
3. For each valve:
   a. Refer to **Table 4** for the correct valve clearances.
   b. Use a flat feeler gauge to determine the clearance between the valve lifter and cam lobe (**Figure 28**). Clearance is correct when a slight resistance is felt when the gauge is inserted and withdrawn. Record the measurement and valve location.
4. If adjustment is required, refer to Chapter Four for camshaft and cam chain tensioner removal. Remove the camshaft from only the valve(s) that requires adjustment.
5. For each valve that requires adjustment, remove each valve lifter and shim set as follows:
   a. Use a magnetic tool and raise the lifter straight up (**Figure 26**).
   b. Lift out the valve shim resting on top of the valve stem.
   c. Inspect each set of parts as they are removed. Both parts should be smooth on all surfaces.

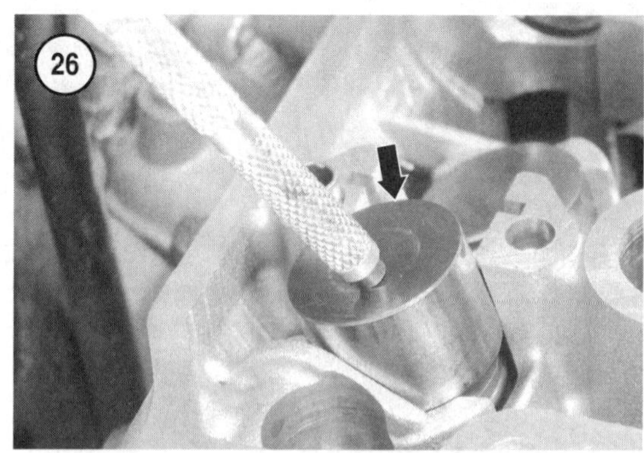

   Light polishing on the shim, where it contacts the valve stem, is normal.
   d. Clean and inspect the shim seat at the top of the valve assembly (**Figure 25**).
   e. Mark the parts (**Figure 29**) with their location in the cylinder head.
6. Determine the size of shim (**Figure 30**) to install on the valve lifter as follows:
   a. Refer to **Table 4** for the intake and exhaust valve clearances.
   b. Find the difference between the *specified* clearance and the *existing* clearance. This difference is the amount that must be added (loose valve) or subtracted (tight valve) from the value of the shim removed in Step 5.
   c. *For example*: If the existing clearance for an exhaust valve is 0.18 mm, and the specified clearance is 0.20-0.30 mm, the difference is 0.02-0.12 mm. In this example, the replacement shim should be this much *smaller* than the removed shim. If the removed shim is 2.85 mm thick (a number 285 shim), the replacement shim should be 2.75 mm thick (a number 275 shim). This would increase valve clearance to 0.28 mm (0.10 mm + 0.18 mm),

28

29

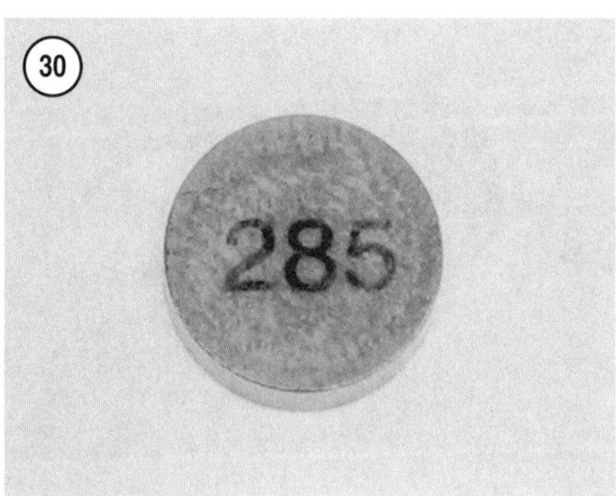

30

which is within the specification and near the maximum allowable clearance, which is preferable.

7. Lubricate the replacement shim with engine oil, then install the shim into the seat (**Figure 25**). Place the shim number facing up so it does not get worn away by the valve stem.

8. Lubricate the valve lifter (**Figure 26**) and install it over the shim and valve assembly.

9. Repeat the procedure for the remaining valves that are out of specification.

10. Install the camshaft(s) and cam chain tensioner as described in Chapter Four.

11. Check valve clearance as follows:

   a. Rotate the engine several times to seat the shims, valve lifters and camshafts. Place the engine at TDC.

   b. Measure the valve clearances. If clearance is not correct, remove the camshaft(s) and adjust the valves that are out of specification.

12. Install the cylinder head cover, timing plug and rotor nut plug as described in Chapter Four.

COMPRESSION CHECK

A cylinder compression check can help verify the condition of the piston, rings and cylinder head assembly without disassembling the engine. By keeping a record of the compression reading at each tune-up, readings can be compared to determine if normal wear is occurring. Refer to **Table 4** for the compression specification.

Since the compression release opens the right exhaust valve slightly during engine cranking, compression can vary. It is recommended that regular compression checks are performed and a record of the readings kept. If a current reading is extremely different from a previous reading, troubleshooting can begin to correct the problem.

1. Warm the engine to operating temperature.

2. Remove the spark plug. Insert the spark plug into the cap, then ground the plug to the cylinder. The spark plug must be grounded to prevent CDI unit damage.

CAUTION

Do not ground the spark plug on the cylinder head cover. The cover is coated and is a poor ground. Additionally, the magnesium alloy cover could be damaged.

3. Thread a compression gauge (**Figure 31**) into the spark plug hole. The gauge must fit airtight in the hole for an accurate reading.

4. Hold or secure the throttle fully open.

5. Operate the starter and turn the engine over until the highest gauge reading is achieved.

6. Record the reading. Compare the reading with previous readings, if available. Under normal oper-

ating conditions, compression will slowly lower from the original specification, due to wear of the piston rings and/or valve seats.

a. If the reading is higher than normal, this can be caused by the compression release. Commonly, carbon buildup in the combustion chamber is another cause of high compression. This can cause high combustion chamber temperatures and potential engine damage.
b. If the reading is lower than normal, this can be caused by worn piston rings, valves with no clearance, worn valves, damaged piston, leaking head gasket, or a combination of these parts. The compression release is less likely to be the problem in this case, since the release weights are probably not spinning fast enough to stop the release of compression. This would occur when the engine fired and camshaft speed increased.
c. To help pinpoint the source of compression loss, pour 15 cc (1/2 oz.) of four-stroke engine oil through the spark plug hole and into the cylinder. Turn the engine over to distribute the oil. Recheck compression. If compression increases, the piston rings are likely worn or damaged. If compression is the same, the piston, head gasket, valves or compression release are worn or damaged.

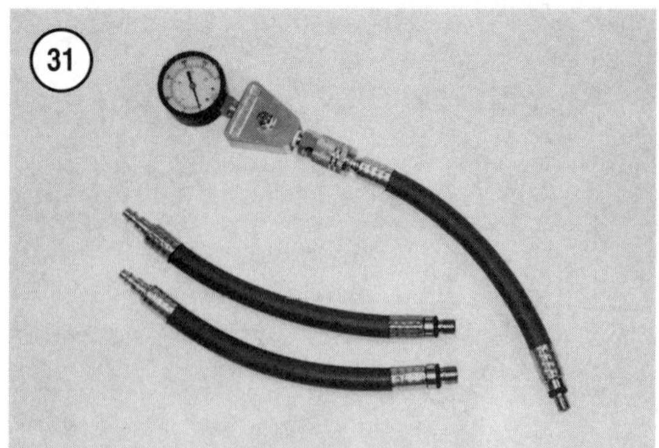

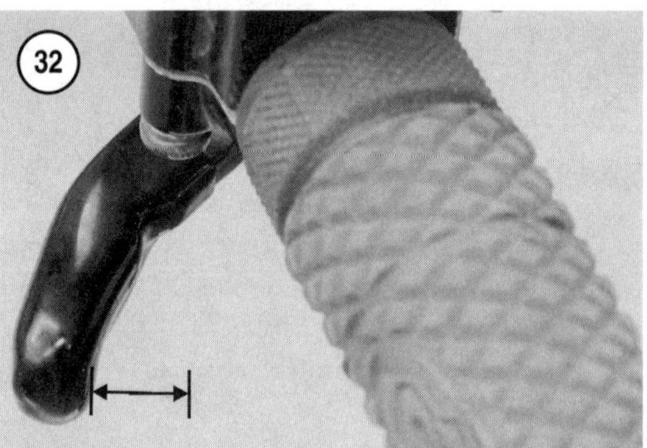

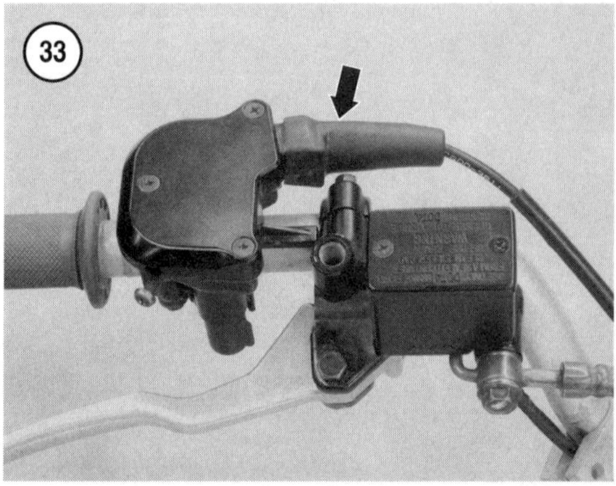

CONTROL CABLES

Control Cable Lubrication

Clean and lubricate the throttle, brake, choke and reverse cables at the intervals indicated in **Table 1**. In addition, check the cables for kinks, excessive wear, damage or fraying that could cause the cables to fail or stick. The most positive method of control cable lubrication involves the use of a cable lubricator and a can of cable lube or a general lubricant. Do not use chain lube as a cable lubricant. It is too thick and will not travel the length of the cable.

1. Disconnect the cable to be lubricated. Note the following:
   a. Refer to *Throttle Cable Replacement* in Chapter Eight.
   b. Refer to *Choke Cable Replacement* in Chapter Eight.
   c. Refer to *Clutch Cable Replacement* in Chapter Six.
   d. Refer to *Reverse Shift Cable Replacement* in Chapter Six.
   e. Refer to *Parking Brake/Clutch Lever* in Chapter Thirteen.
2. Attach a cable lubricator to the end of the cable following its manufacturer's instructions. Place a shop cloth at the end of the cable to catch the oil as it runs out.

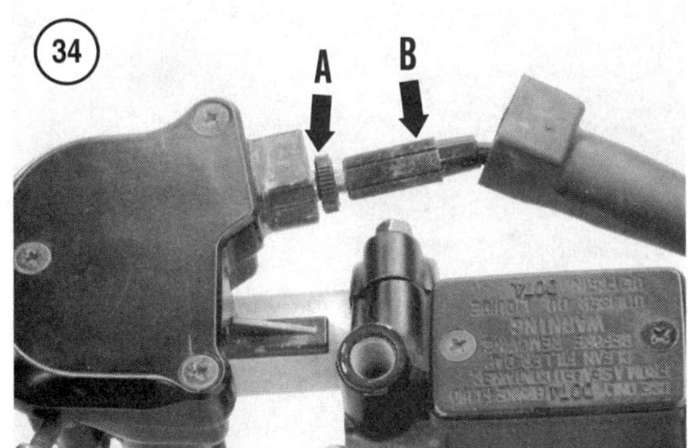

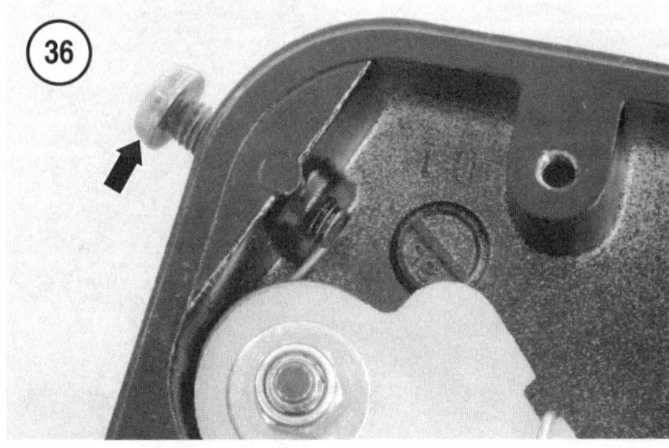

3. Inject cable lubricant into the cable until it begins to flow out of the other end of the cable.

4. Disconnect the lubricator.

5. Apply a light coat of multipurpose lithium grease to the cable ends before reconnecting them. Reconnect the cable, and adjust it as described in this chapter.

6. After lubricating the throttle cable, operate the throttle lever at the handlebar. It should open and close smoothly with no binding.

7. After lubricating the brake cable(s), check brake operation.

Throttle Cable Adjustment

1. Before adjusting the throttle cable, operate the throttle lever and make sure it opens and closes properly with the handlebar turned in different positions. If not, check the throttle cable for damage or improper routing. Check the throttle lever for damage. Replace or repair any damage before continuing with Step 2.

2. If necessary, lubricate the throttle cable as described in this section.

3. Operate the throttle lever and measure the amount of free play at the end of the lever (**Figure 32**) until the cable play is taken up and the carburetor lever starts to move. If the free play is outside the range specified in **Table 4**, continue with Step 4.

4. At the throttle housing on the handlebar, slide the rubber boot (**Figure 33**) off the adjuster and loosen the cable adjuster locknut (A, **Figure 34**). Turn the adjuster (B, **Figure 34**) in or out until the free play at the throttle lever is within specification. Hold the adjuster and tighten the locknut securely. Recheck the throttle lever free play while noting the following:

   a. If the free play measurement is correct, slide the rubber boot over the adjuster and go to Step 5.
   b. If the throttle cable free play cannot be adjusted properly, the cable has stretched. Additional slack can be removed from the cable at the carburetor with the barrel adjuster and locknut on the end of the cable (**Figure 35**).
   c. If the proper amount of free play cannot be achieved, replace it as described in Chapter Eight.

5. Apply the parking brake.

6. Start the engine and allow it to idle. Turn the handlebar from side to side. If the engine speed increases as the handlebar is turned, the throttle cable is routed incorrectly or there is not enough cable free play. Readjust the throttle cable, or if necessary, replace the throttle cable as described in Chapter Eight.

Speed Limiter Adjustment

The speed limiter screw (**Figure 36**) restricts the travel of the throttle lever and keeps the throttle from opening completely, limiting engine speed.

1. To adjust the limiter, loosen the locknut (**Figure 37**) and turn the limiter screw inward to restrict the throttle and outward to allow the throttle to open .
2. Check the throttle for proper operation.

Parking Brake Cable Adjustment

If necessary, lubricate the parking brake cable as described in this section.

1. Measure the cable length between the cable holder (A, **Figure 38**) and the center of the cable end (B). The length should be 47-51 mm (1.9-2.0 in.).
2. If necessary, adjust the cable as follows:
   a. At the handlebar, loosen the locknut (A, **Figure 39**) and turn the cable adjuster (B) until the proper length is achieved. Retighten the locknut.
   b. At the parking brake mechanism, loosen the locknut (C, **Figure 38**) and turn the bolt counterclockwise until no resistance is felt. Turn the adjuster bolt clockwise until resistance is felt, then turn it back 1/8 to 1/4 turn clockwise. Hold the adjuster bolt in this position and tighten the locknut. There should be no play in the cable at the handlebar lever after adjusting the cable. Once the adjuster bolt is secure, tighten the locknut securely.
3. Check the parking brake for proper operation.

Clutch Cable Adjustment

The clutch cable must be properly adjusted to ensure smooth shifting, full clutch engagement and minimal wear on the clutch plates. If necessary, lubricate the cable as described in this section. The ca-

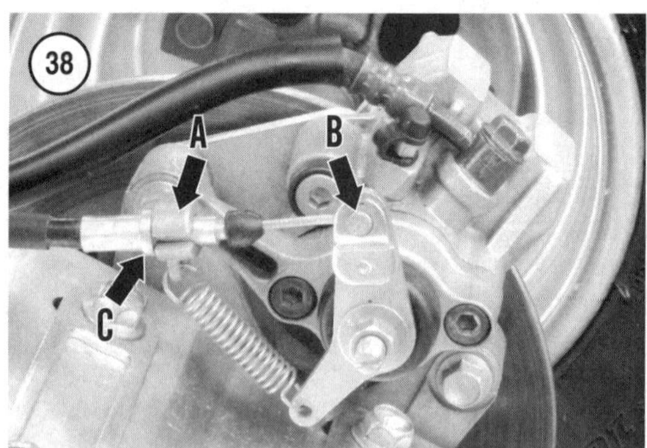

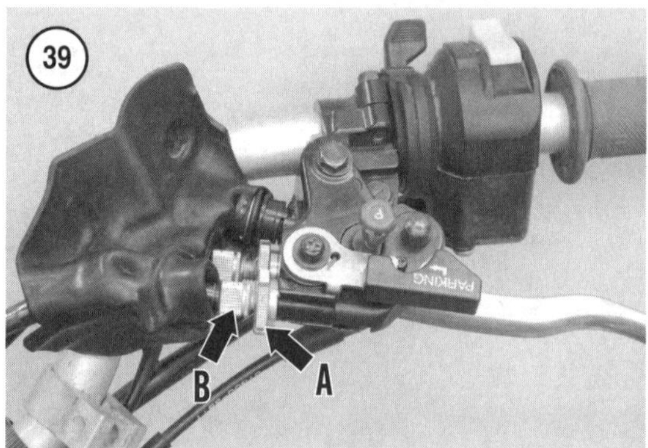

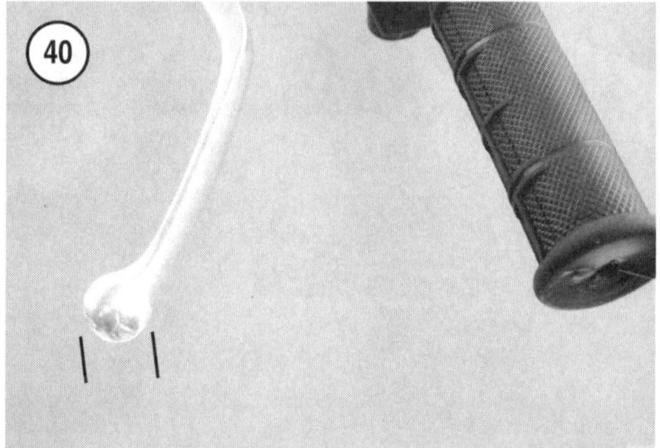

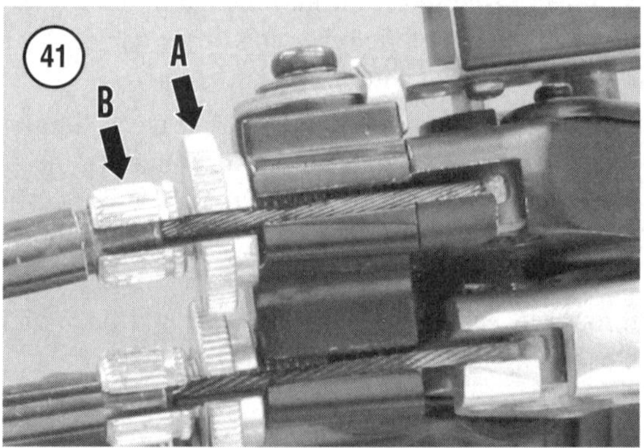

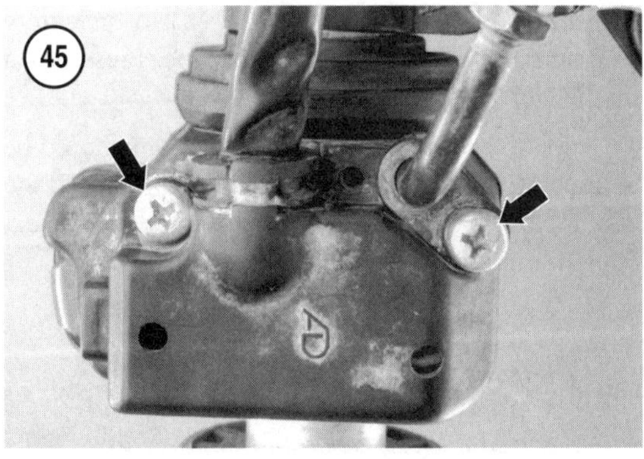

ble must not bind or drag. Adjust the clutch at the intervals specified in **Table 1**. Refer to Chapter Six for clutch cable replacement. If the clutch adjustment is difficult, the friction plates may be worn. Inspect the friction plates as described in Chapter Six.

1. Measure the amount of free play at the end of the lever (**Figure 40**). To adjust, pull the rubber cover back from the clutch cables.
2. Loosen the locknut (A, **Figure 41**) and turn the cable adjuster (B) to increase/decrease play in the cable and lever. Note the following:
    a. If correct play can be achieved, and the adjuster is close to the middle of its range of travel, tighten the locknut. Adjustment is complete.
    b. If correct play cannot be achieved with the adjuster, or if the adjuster is fully screwed in or out, set the adjuster to the middle of its travel. Proceed to Step 3 to make the adjustment on the release lever.
3. Pull back the cover (**Figure 42**) on the in-line cable adjustment located on the cable near the steering head.
    a. Loosen the locknut (A, **Figure 43**) and turn the barrel adjuster (B) until the cable free play is correct at the lever.
    b. Tighten the locknuts.
    c. If necessary, make fine adjustments at the handlebar (Step 2).
4. Start the engine and verify the transmission properly engages and disengages from the clutch.

Choke Cable Adjustment

1. Operate the choke lever (A, **Figure 44**). It should move smoothly from the fully closed the to fully opened position and back again.
2. If necessary, lubricate the choke lever as described in Chapter Eight.
3. Move the choke lever to its fully closed position.
4. Remove the two screws in the bottom of the left control housing (**Figure 45**).
5. Pull the top half of the control housing back to expose the end of the choke cable (**Figure 46**).
6. Loosen the locknut on the barrel adjuster just below the housing (B, **Figure 44**) until the cable has 1 mm (0.04 in.) of free play when the choke is fully closed. If the free play cannot be adjusted to within specification, replace the choke cable as described in Chapter Eight.

7. Reassemble the left hand control housing.

Reverse Shift Cable Adjustment

The reverse cable must be adjusted properly so it will fully disengage the lockout mechanism allowing the transmission to be shifted into reverse. The cable should have very little free play; however, if the cable is adjusted too tight it may prevent the shaft from fully returning to the seated lockout position. Check the reverse selector cable for loose or damaged cable ends and the reverse lever for damage. Repair or replace any damaged parts. If necessary, lubricate the reverse selector cable as described in this section. If there is more than 1 mm (0.04 in.) of play before the lever begins to engage the reverse selector mechanism, adjust as follows:

1. Remove the right side cover as described in Chapter Fourteen.
2. Locate the inline adjuster (**Figure 47**) in the reverse selector cable.
3. Loosen the locknut and turn the barrel adjuster to adjust the cable.
4. Before reassembling, test the adjustment by turning the lever and checking engagement.
5. Start the engine and make sure the transmission shifts into and out of reverse correctly.

46

47

48

COOLING SYSTEM

WARNING
Inspect the cooling system when the engine and coolant are cold. Injury could occur if the system is checked while it is hot. If the radiator cap must be removed while the coolant is still warm, cover the cap with a towel and open it slowly. Slowly remove the cap as the pressure is relieved.

CAUTION
Do not allow coolant to contact painted surfaces. If contact does occur, immediately wash the surface with water.

Coolant Level Inspection

Refer to **Table 3** for coolant capacity.

1. Support the ATV so it is level.
2. Remove the front bodywork (Chapter Fourteen).
3. Turn the radiator cap (**Figure 48**) to the safety stop and allow any pressure to escape. Press down on the cap and twist it free.
4. Inspect the coolant level. The coolant should be to the bottom of the filler neck on the radiator. If the coolant level is below the filler neck, add the correct coolant mixture to raise the level (**Figure 49**).

CAUTION
When the engine is at operating temperature, the coolant expands and coolant is diverted to the overflow

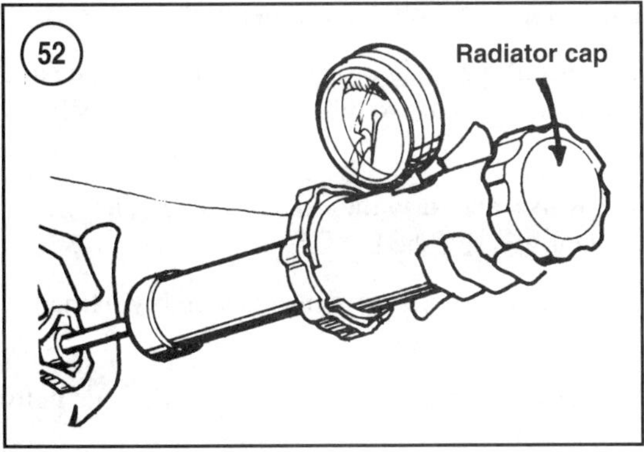

*tank (**Figure 50**). As the engine cools, most of the coolant is drawn back into the radiator. It is normal for a small amount of coolant to be in the overflow tank. Do not assume the coolant level in the radiator is correct because coolant is visible in the tank.*

3

5. If the coolant level is correct, install the radiator cap.
6. If the coolant level is low, make the following checks to determine the cause:
   a. Check the hoses for damage.
   b. Check the radiator for leaks.
   c. Install the radiator cap and start the engine. Inspect for leaks at all hoses and fittings when the engine is at operating temperature. Check for leaks near the bottom of the water pump. If coolant is visible, the water pump mechanical seal is leaking. If engine oil is visible, the water pump is leaking. Refer to Chapter Ten.

CAUTION

If the coolant level continues to drop, pressure test the cooling system. Engine damage can occur if the engine overheats.

Pressure Testing

The radiator cap and cooling system can be pressure tested, using a cooling system tester. Refer to **Table 4** for the cooling system pressure spcifications. Test the radiator cap and cooling system as follows:

1. Support the ATV so it is level.
2. Remove the radiator cap. Check the following on the cap (**Figure 51**).
   a. Rubber seals. Check for cracks, compression and pliability. Replace the cap if damage is evident.
   b. Relief valve. Check for damage. Replace the cap if damage is evident.
3. Wet the seal on the radiator cap, then attach the cap to the tester (**Figure 52**, typical). Apply the specified pressure to the cap. Observe the pressure gauge and note the following:
   a. If the gauge holds pressure up to the relief pressure range, the cap is good.
   b. If the gauge does not hold pressure, or the relief pressure is too high or low, replace the cap.

4. Make sure the radiator is filled to the bottom of the filler neck. Attach the tester to the radiator (**Figure 53**, typical), then pump the tester to the specification (**Table 4**).

CAUTION
Do not over pressurize the cooling system. Excessive pressure can damage components.

a. If the gauge holds the required pressure, the cooling system is in good condition. Install the radiator cap.
b. If the gauge does not hold the required pressure, check for leaks at the radiator and all fittings. If the pressure lowers and then stabilizes, check for swollen radiator hoses. Replace or repair the cooling system components so it maintains the specified pressure.

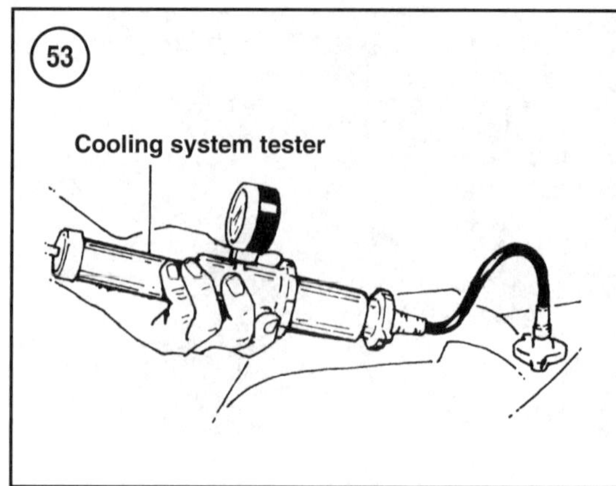

Coolant Replacement

1. Support the ATV so it is level.
2. Remove the front fender (Chapter Fourteen).
3. Place a drain pan under the right side of the engine, below the water pump. Remove the drain plug (**Figure 54**) from the water pump.
4. As coolant begins to drain from the engine, slowly loosen the radiator cap to increase flow from the engine. Be ready to reposition the drain pan.
5. Place a drain pan under the overflow tank. Disconnect the hose and drain the coolant from the tank.

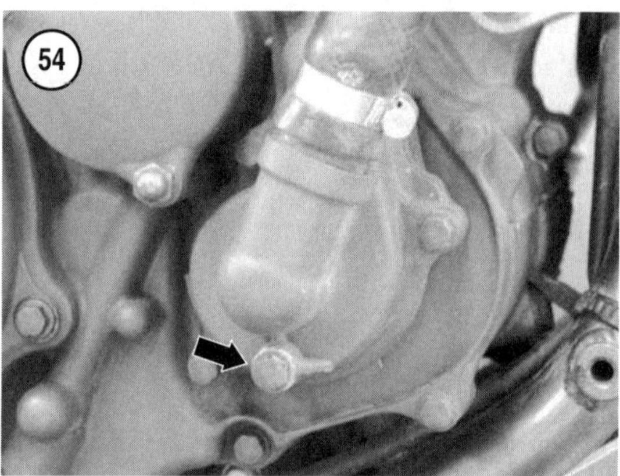

NOTE
Before flushing the radiator, look in the filler neck and inspect for buildup. If buildup is excessive, disconnect the lower radiator hose and flush thoroughly. Avoid passing the buildup from the radiators to the engine.

6. Flush the cooling system with clean water. Check that all water drains from the system.
7. Inspect the condition of:
   a. Radiator hoses. Check for leaks, cracks and loose clamps.
   b. Radiator core. Check for leaks, debris and tightness of mounting bolts.
   c. Radiator fan. Check for damaged wiring and tight connections.

8. Install a new seal washer on the water pump drain plug, then install and tighten the plug.

9. Connect the hose to the overflow tank.

10. Refill the radiator with the coolant specified in **Table 4**.

11. Start and warm the engine. As the coolant level no longer goes down, fill the radiator to the bottom of the filler neck (**Figure 55**). Shut off the engine and allow it to cool. Inspect for leaks at the hoses, radiators, drain bolt and bleeder bolts.

12. Install the radiator cap. Restart the engine and allow the system to pressurize and recheck for leaks.

13. Rinse and dry the frame and engine where coolant was splashed.

14. Install the front fender assembly (Chapter Fourteen).

15. Dispose of the coolant in an environmentally safe manner.

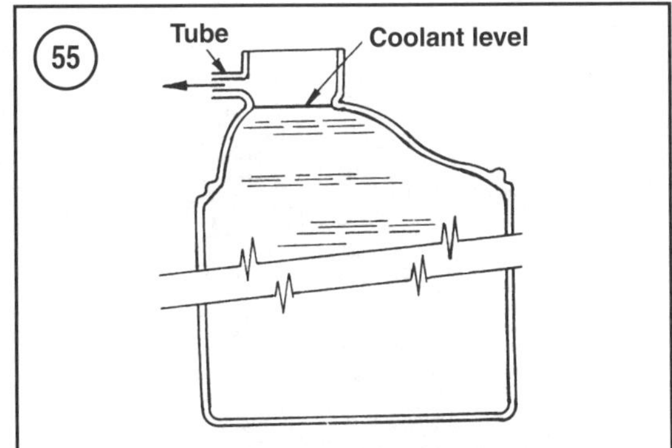

TIRES AND WHEELS

Tire Pressure

WARNING
Always inflate the tires—front and rear—to the correct pressure. If the vehicle is run with unequal air pressure, poor handling may result.

WARNING
Do not over inflate the tires. They can be permanently distorted and damaged.

Check and adjust tire pressure to maintain good traction, handling and to get the maximum life from the tire. Refer to **Table 2** for specifications. Check tire pressure when the tires are cold.

Tire Inspection

WARNING
Do not ride the vehicle with damaged or worn out tires. Replace damaged or severely worn out tires immediately.

Inspect the tires daily for wear, cuts, abrasions or punctures. If a nail or other object is in the tire, mark its location before removing it. Service the tire as described in Chapter Ten. To gauge tire wear, inspect the height of the tread knobs. If the average tread knob height is less than the minimum tread depth specification in **Table 2**, replace the tire as described in Chapter Eleven.

Wheel Inspection

Inspect the wheel for damage. Wheel damage can cause an air leak or knock a wheel out of alignment. Improper wheel alignment can cause vibration and cause an unsafe riding condition. Make sure the wheel nuts (**Figure 56**) are tightened securely on each wheel. Tighten the wheel nuts in a crisscross pattern to 50 N•m (37 ft.-lb.).

BATTERY

WARNING
Even maintenance-free batteries can leak due to damage. Always wear safety glasses. If electrolyte gets into your eyes, flush them thoroughly with clean water and get prompt medical attention.

CAUTION
The battery is maintenance-free and does not require additional water. Do not remove the sealing caps to add electrolyte or water; the battery may be damaged.

CAUTION
*Do not replace the maintenance-free battery with a standard battery. Always replace the battery with its correct type and designated capacity. Refer to the battery capacity specifications in **Table 4**.*

Even maintenance-free batteries can leak due to damage. If you spill or splash electrolyte on your clothing or skin, immediately neutralize the affected area with a solution of baking soda and water. Then flush the area with water.

Removal/Installation

1. Turn the ignition switch off.
2. Remove the seat as described in Chapter Fourteen.
3. Disconnect the negative battery cable (A, **Figure 57**) from the battery.
4. Disconnect the positive battery cable (B, **Figure 57**) from the battery.
5. Remove the two bolts securing the battery strap (C, **Figure 57**) and lift the battery from the compartment.
6. If necessary, service the battery as described in this section.
7. Lower the battery into the battery box so its terminals face the direction shown in **Figure 57**.
8. Secure the battery in place with the battery strap (C, **Figure 57**).
9. Coat the battery terminals with a thin layer of dielectric grease. This helps retard corrosion and decomposition of the terminals.
10. Attach the positive battery cable (B, **Figure 57**) to the battery.
11. Attach the negative battery cable (A, **Figure 57**) to the battery.
12. Install the seat.

Voltage Test

Connect a digital voltmeter to the battery negative and positive terminals (**Figure 58**) and measure the battery voltage. A fully charged battery reads between 13.0-13.2 volts. If the voltmeter reads 12.8 volts or less, the battery is undercharged. If necessary, charge the battery as described in this section.

Charging

Safety

During charging, explosive hydrogen gas forms in the battery. Some of this gas escapes from the vent. This condition can persist for several hours. Sparks or an open flame can ignite this gas and cause the battery to explode. When servicing the battery, note the following:

1. Remove the battery from the vehicle for charging.
2. Follow the manufacturer's instructions when using a battery charger.

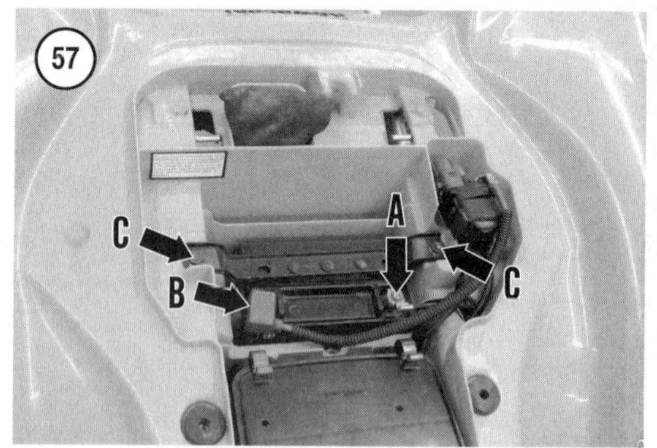

3. Do not smoke or have any open flame near the battery.
4. Do not disconnect live circuits at the battery.
5. Make sure the charger is off before connecting or disconnecting it to the battery.
6. Keep children and pets away from batteries and charging equipment.
7. Do not open a maintenance-free battery.

Procedure

1. Remove the battery as described in this section.
2. Connect the positive (+) charger lead to the positive battery terminal and the negative (–) charger lead to the negative battery terminal.

CAUTION
Do not exceed the recommended charging amperage rate or charging time on the label.

CAUTION
Do not charge the battery with a high rate charger. The high current will overheat the battery and damage the battery plates.

3. Set the charger to 12 volts. If the amperage is variable, select a low setting. Use the following suggested charging amperage and length of charging time:

CAUTION
Standard charging is the preferred charging method. Quick charging should only be used in emergencies.

   a. Standard charge: 1.2 amps at 5 to 10 hours.
   b. Quick charge: 5.0 amps at 1 hour.

4. Turn the charger on.

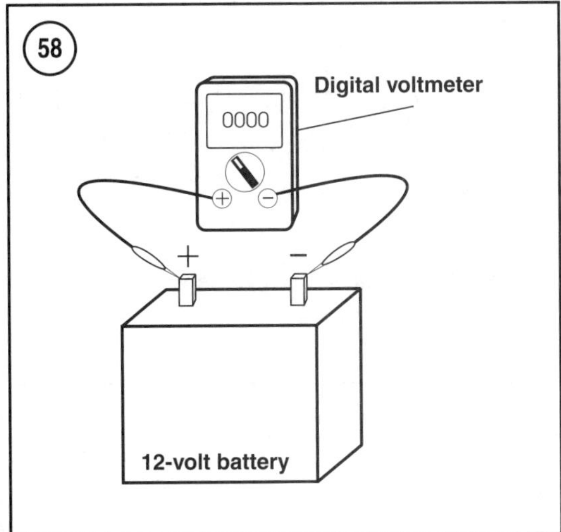

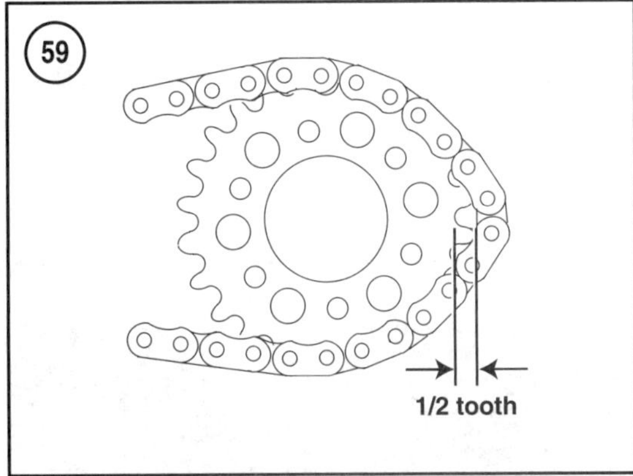

5. After charging the battery the specified amount of time, turn the charger off and disconnect the charger leads.
6. Connect a digital voltmeter to the battery terminals and measure battery voltage. A fully charged battery reads 13.0-13.2 volts.
7. If the battery voltage remains stable for one hour, the battery is charged.
8. Clean the battery cable connectors, battery terminals and case. Coat the terminals with a thin layer of dielectric grease. This helps prevent battery terminal corrosion.
9. Reinstall the battery.

Cable Service

1. If the battery cable terminals are badly corroded, disconnect them from the battery as described in *Removal/Installation* in this section.
2. Thoroughly clean the terminals with a wire brush and then with a water and baking soda solution. Wipe the area dry with a clean cloth.
3. Clean the battery posts in the same manner.
4. After cleaning, apply a thin layer of dielectric grease to the battery terminals and posts before reattaching the cables.
5. Reconnect the battery cables.
6. Apply another layer of dielectric grease to the terminal/post area.

New Battery Installation

NOTE
Recycle an old battery. Most motorcycle dealerships accept old batteries in trade when you purchase a new one.

Always replace the maintenance-free battery with a maintenance-free battery. The charging system is designed to operate with this type of battery. Before installing a new battery, make sure it is fully charged. Failure to do so shortens the useful life of the battery. Undercharging a new battery prevents a battery from ever obtaining a complete charge.

DRIVE CHAIN AND SPROCKETS

Drive Chain and Sprockets Inspection

Inspect the chain and rear sprocket for wear and replace if necessary. If there is wear, replace both sprockets and the chain. Mixing old and new parts will prematurely wear the new parts.
1. To determine if the chain should be measured for wear, perform this general check. At the rear sprocket, pull one chain link away from the sprocket. Generally, if more than 1/2 the height of the sprocket tooth is visible (**Figure 59**), the chain is worn. Accurately measusre the chain for wear.
2A. If the chain is not removed from the sprockets, remove the chain guard and loosen the axle nut. Turn the chain adjusters equally to take all free play out of the chain along its top run.
2B. If the chain is removed from the sprockets, lay the chain on a flat surface and pull the ends of the chain tight.
3. Measure the length of any 20-link (21 pin) span (**Figure 60**). Measure the pins from center-to-center.

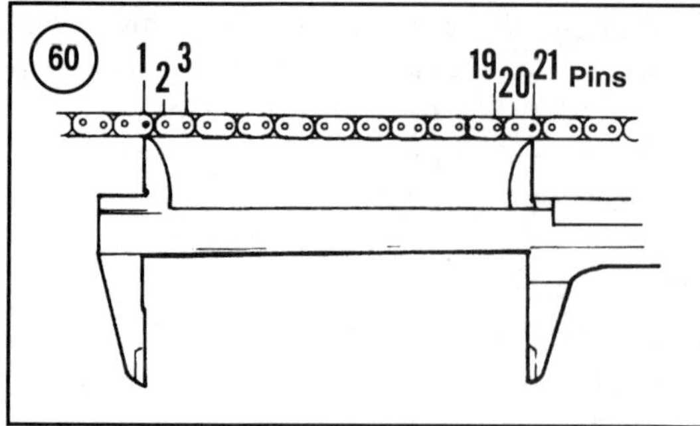

a. The service limit for the chain is 319 mm (12.6 in.). If the measured distance meets or exceeds the service limit, replace the chain.

b. If the chain is within the service limit, inspect the inside surfaces of the link plates. The plates should be shiny at both ends of the chain roller. If one side of the chain is worn, the chain has been running out of alignment. This also causes premature wear of the rollers and pins. Replace the chain if abnormal wear is detected.

4. Inspect the teeth on the front and rear sprockets. Compare the sprockets to **Figure 61**. A new sprocket will have symmetrical and uniform teeth. A used sprocket will wear on the back side of each tooth. Replace the sprocket if damage is evident or if a new chain is being installed. If either sprocket is worn out, replace both sprockets.

Drive Chain Adjustment

The drive chain must have adequate free play so it can adjust to the actions of the swing arm when the vehicle is in use. Too little free play can cause the chain to run tight and cause unnecessary wear to the driveline components. Too much free play can cause excessive looseness and possibly cause the chain to derail. The chain is ideally adjusted when the swing arm is stretching the chain to the maximum amount. This can be achieved by having a person sit on the vehicle while the free play is measured. Take the weight off the vehicle when loosening the adjuster nuts and axle carrier bolts.

1. Support the machine under the frame so the rear wheel is off the ground and the suspension is extended.

2. Rotate the rear wheel and determine when the chain is tightest along its lower length.

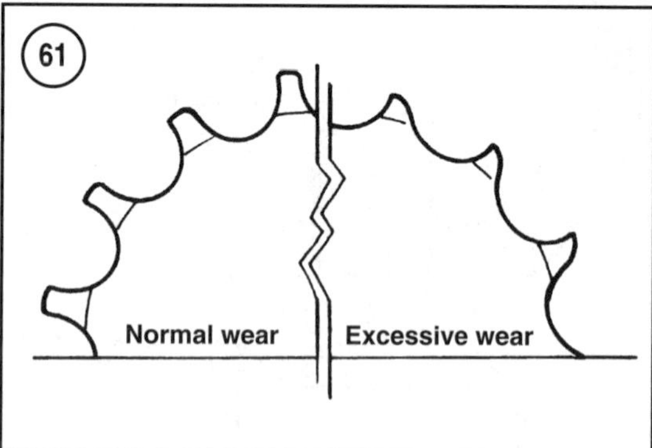

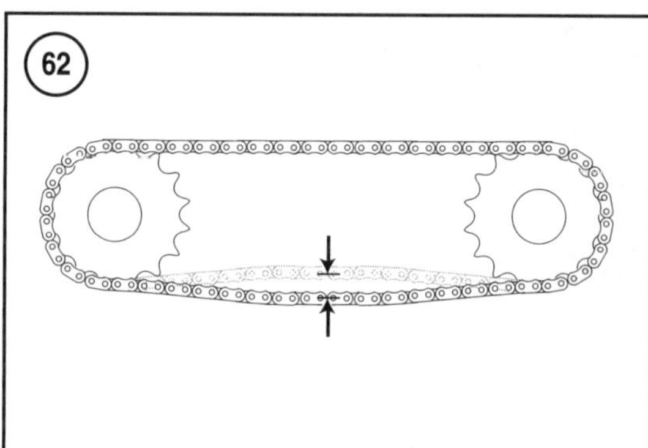

3. Measure the free play in the bottom length of the chain (**Figure 62**) as follows:

a. Place a tape measure so it is stable and vertical, below the chain midpoint.

b. Press the chain down and note where a chain link-pin aligns with the tape measure. Note the measurement.

c. Push the chain up and note where the same link pin aligns with the tape measure. Note the measurement.

64

65

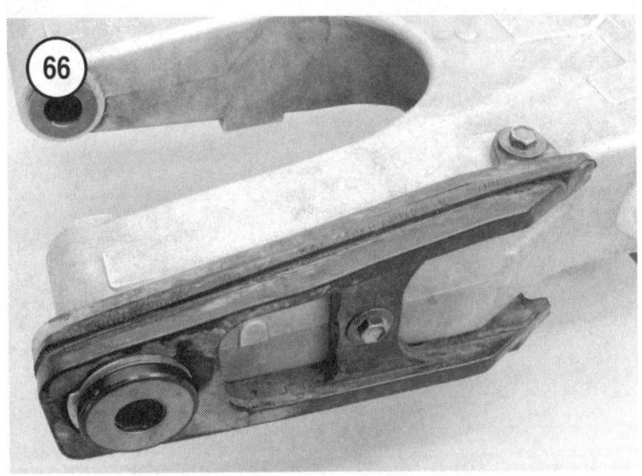
66

d. The difference between the two measurements is the chain free play. Required chain free play is 30-40 mm (1.2-1.6 in.).

4. If necessary, adjust the chain free play as follows:

a. Remove the two bolts securing the rear brake caliper (**Figure 63**) and move it out of the way.

b. Note the current setting on the stamped marks of the swing arm (**Figure 64**).

c. Loosen the bolts securing the rear axle housing in the swing arm.

d. To increase the tension on the chain, tighten the adjuster plate nuts (**Figure 65**).

e. Measure the chain free play. If the adjustment is too tight, loosen the adjusting plate nuts and push the axle forward until the adjusting plate is seated securely against the swing arm and readjust.

f. When the chain free play is correct, tighten the axle housing bolts. Tighten the drive chain side bolts to 100 N•m (74 ft.-lb.). Tighten the disc brake side bolts 73 N•m (54 ft.-lb.).

g. Reinstall the rear brake caliper and tighten the mounting bolts to 26 N•m (19 ft.-lb.).

5. Recheck the chain free play. Adjust if necessary.

NOTE

If the free play cannot be adjusted within the limits of the adjusters, the chain is excessively worn and should be replaced.

Drive Chain Slider, Guide and Guard Inspection

Inspect the chain slider, chain guide and chain guard (**Figure 66**) for wear or damage. The parts support or protect the drive chain.

1. Inspect the upper and lower surface of the chain slider for wear or damage. If the slider is worn through or missing, the chain will contact the swing arm, possibly causing damage. Check the mounting screws for tightness.

2. Inspect the sliding surface of the chain guide for wear or damage. A torn or broken guide can snag the chain, causing noise and possible damage. Check that the frame is straight and the bolts are tight.

BRAKE SYSTEM

Inspection

Regularly inspect the brake discs and pads to ensure they are in good condition. If damage is evident for any of the following inspections, refer to Chapter Thirteen.

3

To inspect the front brake pads and discs, the front wheels and calipers must be removed. Refer to Chapter Thirteen for the caliper removal procedure. The rear brake pads and disc can be visually inspected for wear without removing any parts. If disc scoring is evident, the caliper should be removed and the surface of the pads inspected.

1. Visually inspect the front discs for:
   a. Scoring–If scoring is evident, check for debris between the pads and disc.
   b. Drag–Turn each wheel and check for drag on the disc. *Light* drag on the disc is acceptable. If the drag substantially slows the wheel rotation, troubleshoot and repair the brake system.
   c. Runout–This is the lateral movement of the disc as it spins. It can be detected by spinning the wheel and listening for uneven drag on the disc. This pulsating drag usually indicates disc warp. If warp is suspected, measure the disc with a dial indicator. If the disc is not warped, look for loose or damaged wheel and/or axle components.
   d. Disc thickness–Measure the thickness of both discs and compare it to the specification in Chapter Thirteen.
2. Check the brake pads for even wear across the pad. If the brake pads are worn at an angle, the caliper is probably not sliding evenly on the caliper bracket. Buildup or corrosion on the parts can hold the caliper in one position, causing brake drag and excessive wear.
3. Check the brake pads for wear (**Figure 67**). The front pads should be replaced when they are within 1 mm (0.04 in.) of the backing plates. The rear pads are visible by looking into the caliper on both sides of the disc. If the pads are worn to the wear indicator grooves (**Figure 68**), the pads are less than 1 mm (0.04 in.) and require replacement.

Rear Brake Pedal Adjustment

Position the brake pedal 0-10 mm (0-0.4 in.) below the top of the footpeg. Adjust the pedal and linkage as follows:

1. Loosen the locknut at the master cylinder clevis (A, **Figure 69**), then turn the adjuster (B) to increase/decrease the height of the pedal.
2. Tighten the locknut.

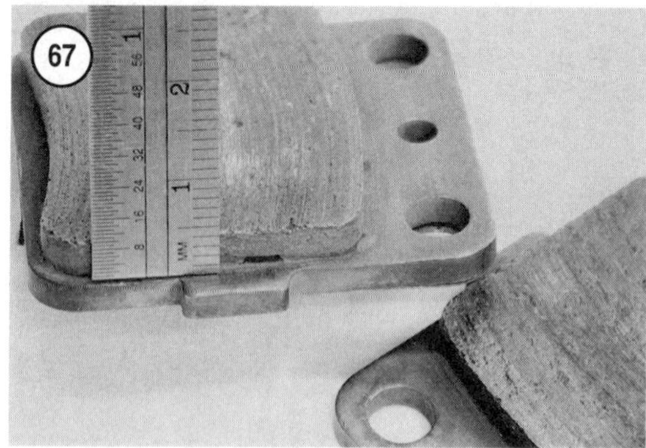

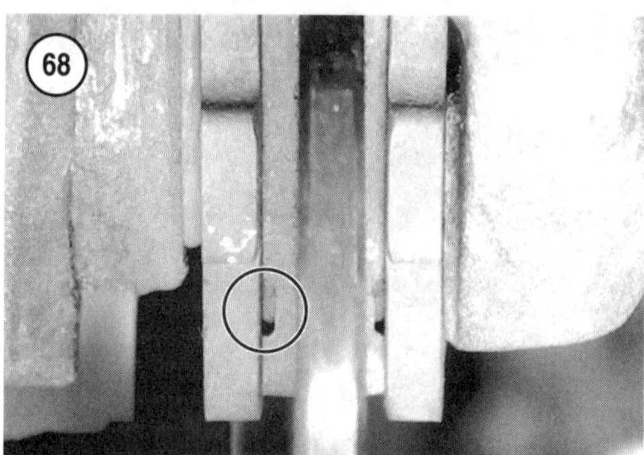

3. Readjust the brake light as described in this section if necessary.

Brake Fluid Level Check

CAUTION
Be careful when handling brake fluid. Do not spill it on painted, plastic or plated surfaces. Brake fluid damages these surfaces. Immediately wash the area with soap and water and thoroughly rinse it off.

NOTE
If the brake fluid is not clear to slightly yellow, the fluid is contaminated and should be replaced. Drain and bleed the brake system (Chapter Thirteen).

1. Park the machine on a level surface and position the handlebar so the brake fluid reservoirs are level.
2. Inspect the front reservoir as follows:
   a. The fluid level should be between the lower level mark and the top of the sight glass (**Figure 70**).
   b. If the fluid level is below the low mark, remove the cap and diaphragm (**Figure 71**), then add DOT 4 brake fluid. Replace the diaphragm and cap.
   c. Replace the cap and diaphragm.
   d. Check for master cylinder leaks and worn brake pads.
3. Inspect the rear reservoir (**Figure 72**) as follows:
   a. The fluid level should be between the upper and lower level marks embossed on the reservoir.
   b. If the fluid level is below the low mark remove the cap, diaphragm holder and diaphragm, then add DOT 4 brake fluid.
   c. Replace the diaphragm, diaphragm holder and cap, then bolt the guard into place.
   d. Check the master cylinder for leaks and worn brake pads.

Brake Hoses

Inspect the brake hoses for cracks, cuts, bulges, deterioration and leaks. Check the metal brake lines for cracks and leaks. Refer to Chapter Thirteen for service procedures.

Brake Fluid Change

WARNING
Use clearly marked DOT 4 brake fluid. Others may cause brake failure. Dispose of used fluid in an environmentally safe manner. Never reuse brake fluid. Contaminated brake fluid can cause brake failure.

Every time the master cylinder top cover is removed, a small amount of dirt and moisture can enter the brake fluid. The same thing happens if a leak occurs or if any part of the hydraulic system is loosened or disconnected. Dirt can clog the system and cause wear and brake failure. Water in the brake fluid causes corrosion inside the hydraulic system, impairing the hydraulic action and reducing the brake's stopping ability.

To maintain peak performance, change the brake fluid every two years or whenever rebuilding or replacing the master cylinder or a wheel cylinder. To change brake fluid, follow the brake bleeding procedure in Chapter Thirteen.

Rear Brake Light Switch Adjustment

The rear brake light should come on just after the rear brake pedal is slightly depressed. The switch (**Figure 73**) is located above the brake pedal and is attached to the pedal by a spring. Adjust the brake light switch position by turning the nut on the switch and moving it up and down in the mounting bracket. If the light does not come on after adjustment, check the bulb condition. If necessary, disconnect the switch wires and use an ohmmeter to check for continuity. The switch is in the on position when the switch plunger is extended.

1. To make the brake light come on earlier, hold the upper part of the switch and turn the plastic nut on the lower part of the switch clockwise.

2. To make the brake light come on later, hold the upper part of the switch and turn the plastic nut on the lower part of the switch counterclockwise.

3. Depress the brake lever several times to test the brake light, readjust if necessary.

SHOCK ABSORBERS

Spring Preload

The front and rear shocks are adjustable for spring preload, compression and rebound damping. Settings depend on the weight of the rider, riding conditions and riding habits. As each adjustment is made, make test rides until the desired ride is achieved. Always record the initial settings and the subsequent changes in order to create a record of settings for specific riding conditions.

Spring preload controls the amount a shock compression when the vehicle is at rest with the rider on it. With the rider aboard the shock should be compressed from 1/4 to 1/3 of the total travel. This allows the shock proper operation as it both compresses and extends. A lot of spring preload will increase the force needed to initially compress the spring, but will not change the rate at which the spring compresses. If the shock bottoms to the limit of its travel consistently, than the spring is likely too soft for the riding conditions and weight of the rider. Adding more spring preload will not improve the overall performance of the shock.

Shock Dampening

Compression and rebound damping adjustors control the rate at which the shock compresses and extends through its stroke. They allow the shock oil to flow through holes that are enlarged or reduced by the position of the adjustor. Because of their design, the rate at which the adjustment changes is not linear. In other words, when the adjuster is screwed all the way in, then backed out, there will be more noticeable changes than when the adjuster is backed all the way out and screwed in. When setting these adjusters it is easier to determine changes by starting all the way in or all the way out and working toward the middle. Incremental changes from the center position are difficult to sense.

Compression damping prevents the shock from sharply compressing to the bottom of the stroke. It can also aid in handling by resisting compression under acceleration, thus keeping the front wheels in better contact with the ground. Rebound damping effects how well the shock will keep the rear end on the ground over a series of bumps. If there is too little rebound dampening, the shock will tend to bounce up and allow the wheels to leave the ground. If there is too much dampening the wheels will tend to skip along the top of bumps. When testing shock settings, change only one adjustment at a time to more easily determine if the change was an improvement.

Front Shock Adjustments

Preload (2003-2004 models)

The front shock absorbers have five adjustment settings.

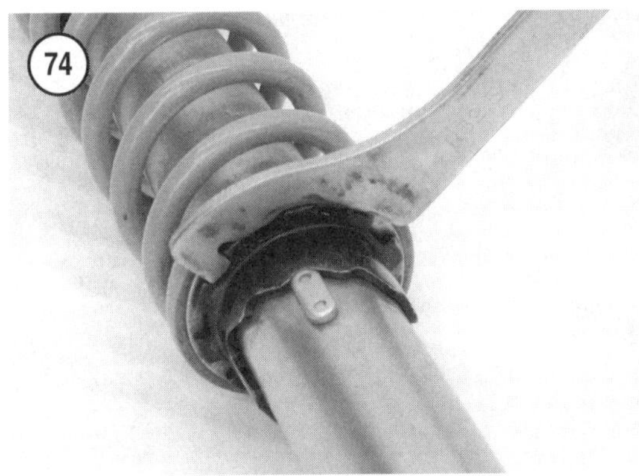
74

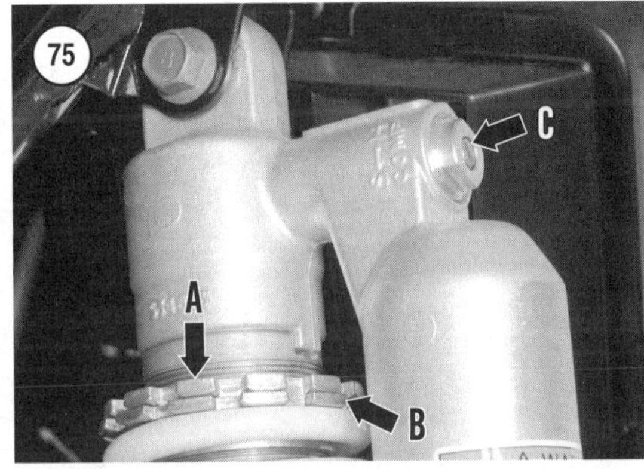

75

76

1. Place the ATV on level ground and set the parking brake.

2. Turn the spring preload adjuster by fitting a spanner wrench into the notch on the adjuster. If necessary, spray a penetrating lubricant between the adjuster and the shock body to make it easier to turn.

3. Rotate the base ring (**Figure 74**) in either direction to achieve the desired spring preload.

4. The base rings of both shocks must be set into the same adjuster notches, or the front suspension will not react evenly, creating unsafe riding conditions.

Preload (2005-on models)

1. Place the ATV on level ground and set the parking brake.

2. To adjust the spring preload, use a spanner wrench to loosen the upper lockring (A, **Figure 75**). If necessary, spray a penetrating lubricant between the adjuster and the shock body to make it easier to turn.

3. Add preload by adjusting the lower ring (B, **Figure 75**) clockwise and increasing tension on the shock spring. Remove preload by turning the lower ring counterclockwise and decreasing tension on the shock spring.

4. Before tightening the upper lockring, lower the vehicle to the ground and check the amount of sag on the shock. If necessary, readjust the lower ring.

5. When the adjustment is complete, tighten the upper ring.

6. Recheck the sag of the shock after tightening the lockring.

Compression damping

1. To adjust compression dampening, locate the adjuster (C, **Figure 75**) on the top of the shock at the shock reservoir.

2. Turn the adjuster clockwise to increase the damping effect, and turn it counterclockwise to decrease the damping effect.

Rebound damping

1. To adjust rebound dampening, locate the adjuster (**Figure 76**) on the bottom of the shock at the base.

2. Turn the adjuster clockwise to increase the damping effect, and turn it counterclockwise to decrease the damping effect.

Rear Shock Adjustments

Preload

1. Place a jack under the center of the vehicle and take all the weight off the rear wheels.
2. To adjust the spring preload, use a spanner wrench to loosen the upper lockring (A, **Figure 77**).
3. Add preload by adjusting the lower ring (B, **Figure 77**) clockwise and increasing tension on the shock spring. Remove preload by turning the lower ring counterclockwise and decreasing tension on the shock spring.
4. Before tightening the upper lockring, lower the vehicle to the ground and check the amount of sag on the shock. If necessary, readjust the lower ring.
5. When the adjustment is complete, tighten the upper ring.
6. Recheck the sag of the shock after tightening the lockring.

Compression damping

1. To adjust compression dampening, locate the adjuster (**Figure 78**) on the top of the shock at the shock reservoir.
2. Turn the adjuster clockwise to increase the damping effect, and turn it counterclockwise to decrease the damping effect.

Rebound damping

1. To adjust rebound dampening, locate the adjuster on the bottom of the shock at the base (**Figure 76**).
2. Turn the adjuster clockwise to increase the damping effect, and turn it counterclockwise to decrease the damping effect.

FRONT SUSPENSION

Inspection

Inspect the front suspension and steering at the interval indicated in **Table 1**. If any of the front suspension and steering fasteners are loose, refer to Chapter Eleven.

1. Park the vehicle on level ground and set the parking brake.

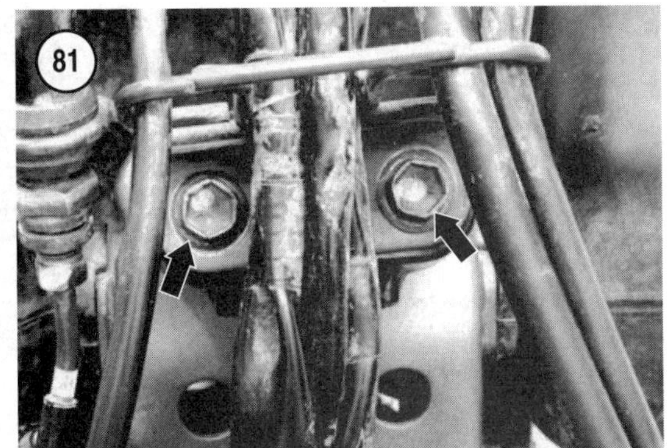

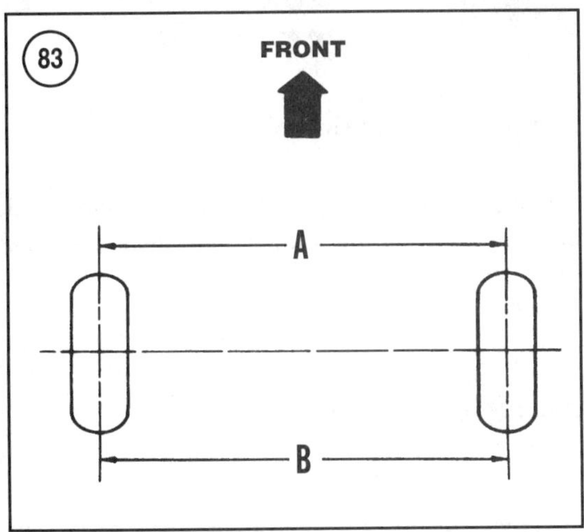

2. Visually inspect all components of the steering system. Repair or replace damaged components as described in Chapter Eleven.

3. Check the shock absorbers as described in this chapter.

4. Remove the handlebar cover (Chapter Fourteen). Check that the handlebar holder bolts are tight. Reinstall the handlebar cover.

5. Make sure the front hub nuts (**Figure 79**) are tight and that all cotter pins are in place.

6. Check that the cotter pins are in place on all steering components. If any cotter pin is missing, check the nut for looseness. Torque the nut and install a new cotter pin as described in Chapter Eleven.

7. Check the steering shaft play as follows:
   a. Support the vehicle with the front wheels off the ground.
   b. To check steering shaft radial play, move the handlebar from side to side (without attempting to move the wheels). If radial play is excessive, the upper bushing inside the steering shaft holder (**Figure 80**) is probably worn or the steering shaft holder bolts (**Figure 81**) are loose. Replace the upper bushing or tighten the holder bolts to the specification in **Table 5**.
   c. To check steering shaft thrust play, lift up and then push down on the handlebar. If there is excessive thrust play, check the lower steering shaft nut (**Figure 82**) for looseness. If necessary, tighten the nut to the specification in **Table 5**. If the nut is tightened properly, check the lower steering shaft bearing for excessive wear or damage.
   d. If necessary, service the steering shaft as described in Chapter Eleven.
   e. Lower the vehicle so all four tires are on the ground.

8. Check the steering knuckle and tie rod ends as follows:
   a. Turn the handlebar quickly from side to side. If there is appreciable looseness between the handlebar and tires, check the tie rod ends for excessive wear or damage.
   b. Service the steering knuckle and tie rods as described in Chapter Eleven.

9. Check the toe-in as described below.

Toe-In

Check the toe-in whenever inspecting the suspension, after servicing the front suspension or when replacing the tie rods.

Adjust toe-in by changing the length of the tie rods.

1. Inflate all four tires to the recommended pressure specified in **Table 2**.

2. Park the vehicle on level ground and set the parking brake.

3. Raise and support the front of the vehicle so both front tires just clear the ground.

4. Turn the handlebar so the wheels are facing straight ahead.

5. Using a tape measure, carefully measure the distance between the center of both front tires at axle height as shown in A, **Figure 83**. Mark the tires at these points. Record the measurement.

6. Rotate each tire exactly 180° so the center marks face rearward.

7. Measure the distance between the center of both front tires (B, **Figure 83**). Record the measurement.

8. Subtract the measurement taken in Step 5 (A, **Figure 83**) from the Step 7 measurement (B). Toe-in is correct if the difference equals the specification in **Table 4**.

WARNING

If the tie rods are not adjusted equally, the handlebar will not be centered while traveling straight ahead. This condition may cause loss of control. Turn both tie rods the same number of turns. This ensures that the tie rod length remains the same on each side. If the left and right side tie rod lengths are different, refer to ***Tie Rods*** *in Chapter Eleven. If toe-in cannot be properly adjusted, have it adjusted by a dealership.*

9. If the toe-in is incorrect, adjust it by performing the following:

   a. Loosen the locknut at each end of both tie rods (A, **Figure 84**).
   b. Use a wrench on the flat portion (B, **Figure 84**) of the tie rods, and slowly turn both tie rods the same amount until the toe-in measurement is correct.
   c. When the toe-in adjustment is correct, hold each tie rod in place and tighten the locknuts to 29 N•m (21 ft.-lb.).
   d. Recheck toe-in.

10. Lower the vehicle so both front wheels are on the ground.

11. Start the engine and make a slow test ride on level ground. Ride straight ahead while checking that the handlebar does not turn to the left or right side.

Steering Shaft Lubrication

Remove the steering shaft (Chapter Eleven) and lubricate the bushing with lithium grease. At the same time, check the lower bushing and seals for damage.

Front Upper and Lower Control Arm Lubrication

Remove the pivot bolts from the upper and lower arms. Lubricate the bolts and bushings with lithium grease. Refer to Chapter Eleven for service.

Shock Absorber Pivot Bolt Lubrication

Remove the front (Chapter Eleven) and rear (Chapter Twelve) shock absorbers and lubricate the mounting bolts with lithium grease.

SWING ARM BEARING INSPECTION

Periodically inspect the swing arm. If the following quick inspection indicates a problem with the swing arm bearings refer to *Swing Arm* in Chapter Twelve.

1. Support the ATV so the rear wheel is off the ground.
2. Have an assistant steady the ATV, then grasp the ends of the swing arm and leverage it from side to side. There should be no detectable play. If play is evident, refer to Chapter Twelve for servicing the swing arm.

REAR SUSPENSION INSPECTION

1. Support the vehicle so the rear wheels are off the ground.
2. Try to move the rear axle sideways while checking for excessive play at the swing arm bearings.
3. If there is any play, check the swing arm pivot bolts for looseness. If they are tightened properly, the swing arm bearings may require replacement. See Chapter Twelve.

SKID PLATE INSPECTION

Check the front (**Figure 85**), middle (**Figure 86**) and rear skid plates (**Figure 87**) for damage and loose fasteners. Repair or replace damaged skid plates. Replace missing or damaged mounting bolts. Tighten the mounting bolts securely.

Table 1 MAINTENANCE SCHEDULE

After the first month of operation:	Tighten the exhaust system fasteners Inspect the valve clearance Check the idle speed Check the throttle cable tension Drain and replace the engine oil Inspect the engine oil hoses Check the clutch adjustment Check the brakes for proper operation Inspect the steering system Tighten all chassis fasteners Lubricate the chain and cables

(continued)

Table 1 MAINTENANCE SCHEDULE (continued)

Every 3 months perform the following maintenance:	Clean the air filter Tighten the exhaust system fasteners Check the idle speed Check the throttle cable adjustment Inspect the fuel lines Inspect the engine oil hoses Check the brakes for proper operation Check the brake fluid and replace if necessary Inspect the wheels and tires for damage and wear Inspect the steering system Tighten all chassis fasteners Lubricate the chain and all cables
Every 6 months perform the following maintenance:	Clean the air filter Tighten the exhaust system fasteners Inspect the valve clearance Inspect the spark plug Clean the spark arrestor Check the idle speed Check the throttle cable adjustment Inspect the fuel lines Replace the engine oil and filter Inspect the engine oil hoses Check the clutch adjustment Inspect the coolant Inspect the radiator hose Check the brakes for proper operation Check the brake fluid and replace if necessary Inspect the brake hoses Inspect the wheels and tires for damage and wear Inspect the suspension Inspect the steering system Tighten all chassis fasteners Lubricate the chain and all cables
Every 18 months:	Replace the spark plug
Every 2 years:	Replace the coolant Replace the brake fluid
Every 4 years:	Replace the fuel hoses Replace the brake hoses

Table 2 TIRE SPECIFICATIONS

Front tire	
Size	AT22 × 7-10
Original equipment	Dunlop KT331
Minimum tread depth	4 mm (0.16 in.)
Rear tire	
Size	AT20 × 10-9
Original equipment	Dunlop KT335
Minimum tread depth	4 mm (0.16 in.)

(continued)

Table 2 TIRE SPECIFICATIONS (continued)

Inflation pressure (cold)*	
Standard	
Front	30 kPa (4.4 psi)
Rear	27.5 kPa (4.0 psi)

*Tire inflation pressure for original equipment tires. Aftermarket tires may require different inflation pressures.

Table 3 RECOMMENDED LUBRICANTS, FLUIDS AND CAPACITIES

Brake fluid classification	DOT 4
Engine coolant	
capacity	1200 ml (1.3 qts.)
mixture	50:50 (antifreeze/distilled water)
type	Ethylene glycol containing anti-corrosion agents for aluminum engines
Engine oil	
Capacity	
Engine overhaul	2.2 L (2.3 qt.)
Oil and filter	2.1 L (2.2 qt.)
Oil change	2.0 L (2.1 qt.)
Classification	API SF/SG or SH/SJ with JASO MA
Viscosity	SAE 10W-40
Fuel	
Capacity	10 L (2.6 gal.)
Octane	Regular unleaded; 87 octane minimum (R + M/2) Regular unleaded; 91 octane minimum (RON)
Reserve	2.7 L (0.7 gal.)

Table 4 MAINTENANCE AND TUNE-UP SPECIFICATIONS

Battery	
Capacity	12 V – 8 AH
Voltage	
Fully charged	13.0-13.2 V
Needs charging	Less than 12.3 V
Charge current	
Normal	0.9 A/5-10 h
Quick[1]	4.0 A/1.0 h
Brake light activation	Rear brake pedal depressed 7-10 mm (0.3-0.4 in.)
Brake pad minimum thickness	1 mm (0.04 in.) to wear indicator
Brake pedal height	0-10 mm (0-0.4 in.)
Choke lever free play	0.5-1.0 mm (0.02-0.04 in.)
Clutch lever free play	10-15 mm (0.4-0.6 in.)
Cooling system	
Maximum test pressure	120 kPa (17 psi)
Radiator cap relief pressure	108-137 kPa (15.6-19.9 psi)
Drive chain free play	30-40 mm (1.2-1.6 in.)
Drive chain service limit	No more than 319.4 mm (12.57 in.) between 21 chain pins
Engine compression	1000 kPa (142 psi) w/ decompressor activated
Idle speed	1400-1600 rpm
Ignition timing[2]	10° BTDC at 1500 rpm
Oil pressure	40-140 kPa (5.8-20.3 psi) at 3000 rpm
Pilot screw[3]	
2003-2004 models	2 1/4 turns out
2005-on models	1 1/2 turns out
Spark plug	
Gap	0.7-0.8 mm (0.028-0.031 in.)
Type	NGKCR7E or ND U22ESR-N

(continued)

Table 4 MAINTENANCE AND TUNE-UP SPECIFICATIONS (continued)

Throttle lever free play	
2003-2004 models	3-8 mm (0.12-0.31 in.)
2005-on models	3-5 mm (0.12-0.20 in.)
Toe-in	5 mm (0.20 in.)
Valve clearance	
Exhaust	0.20-0.30 mm (0.0078-0.0118 in.)
Intake	0.10-0.20 mm (0.0039-0.0078 in.)

1. Quick charging can shorten battery life. Use it only in an emergency.
2. Not adjustable
3. California models are preset.

Table 5 MAINTENANCE AND TUNE UP TORQUE SPECIFICATIONS

Item	N•m	in.-lb.	ft.-lb.
Brake bleed valve			
2003	7.5	66	–
2004-on	6.0	53	–
Brake hose union bolt	23	–	17
Cylinder head cover bolts	14	124	–
Engine		–	
Crankcase oil drain bolt	21	–	15.5
Oil tank drain bolt	12	106	–
Exhaust pipe nut	23	–	17
Front hub nut	65	–	48
Handlebar clamp bolt			
2003	23	–	17
2004-on	26	–	19
Main oil gallery plug	18	–	13
Muffler connecting bolt	23	–	17
Muffler mounting bolt	23	–	17
Rear brake caliper mounting bolts	26	–	19
Rear hub nut	100	–	74
Rear axle housing bolt			
Drive chain side (M12)	100	–	74
Brake side (M10)	73	–	54
Spark plug	11	97	–
Tie rod end nut	60	–	44
Tie rod locknut	29	–	21
Wheel lug nuts			
2003-2004	50	–	37
2005-on	60	–	44
Steering shaft holder bolts	23	–	17
Steering shaft nut	49	–	36

CHAPTER FOUR

ENGINE TOP END

The LT-Z400 engine features dual overhead cam shafts. The camshafts are mounted in the cylinder head and driven off the crankshaft by the timing chain.

All cylinder head components can be serviced with the engine in the frame.

This chapter describes service procedures for the following top end components:

1. Valve cover.
2. Camshafts.
3. Cam chain and guides.
4. Valves.
5. Exhaust system.
6. Cylinder head.
7. Pistons and piston rings.

Always clean the engine before starting repairs. If the engine will remain in the frame, clean the surrounding framework, cables and harnesses. Keep the work environment as clean as possible. Store parts and assemblies in well-marked plastic bags and containers. Keep reconditioned parts wrapped until they will be installed.

When inspecting components, compare measurements to the specifications in **Table 2**. Replace any component that is damaged, worn to the service limit or out of specification. During assembly, tighten fasteners to the provided torque specifications.

Tables 1-3 are located at the end of the chapter.

BREAK-IN PERIOD

On new and reconditioned engines, the performance and service life of the engine depends greatly on a careful and sensible break-in. Observe the following when breaking in an engine.

1. Check the oil frequently. Make sure the engine is filled with the correct amount and weight of engine oil.
2. Make sure the air filter is clean.
3. For the first 10 hours of operation, use no more than 1/2 throttle. Vary the speed as much as possible within this throttle range. Avoid running the machine at a steady speed. Avoid hard acceleration. The speed limiter screw can be adjusted to restrict throttle opening. Refer to *Control Cables* in Chapter Three.
4. For the next 10 hours of operation, use no more than 3/4 throttle. Vary the speed as much as possible within this throttle range. Intermittent use of full throttle is permissible, but do not maintain the engine at full throttle.

5. At the end of the break-in period, adjust the valves and change the engine oil and filter.

EXHAUST SYSTEM

Removal and Installation

The heat shields do not need to be removed to remove the exhaust pipe of muffler.

1. Support the ATV so it is stable and secure.
2. Remove the front fender, fuel tank cover and side covers as described in Chapter Fourteen.
3. Remove the fuel tank as described in Chapter Eight.
4. Remove the muffler as follows:
   a. Loosen the muffler clamp (**Figure 1**) connecting the muffler to the exhaust pipe.
   b. Remove the bolt (**Figure 2**) securing the muffler to the frame.
   c. Pull the muffler from the exhaust pipe and out of the frame. Do not hammer on the muffler if it is stuck to the exhaust pipe. Twist the muffler off the pipe. If necessary, apply penetrating oil around the connection.
5. Remove the exhaust pipe as follows:
   a. Remove the nuts (**Figure 3**) securing the exhaust pipe to the cylinder head. These fasteners are often corroded. To prevent thread damage, apply penetrating oil as needed during removal.
   b. Pull the exhaust pipe off the cylinder head.
   c. Remove the gasket (**Figure 4**) from the exhaust port .
6. Reverse these steps to install the system. Note the following:
   a. Clean the exhaust port and install a new exhaust pipe gasket (**Figure 5**), seating it in the port before installing the exhaust pipe.
   b. Apply antiseize compound to the threads of the muffler clamp bolt.
   c. Install and align the entire exhaust system with all fasteners finger-tight, then tighten the exhaust pipe squarely into the exhaust port. Tighten the nut and bolt to 23 N•m (17 ft.-lb.). Once the exhaust pipe is secured to the cylinder head tighten all other exhaust bolts to 23 N•m (17 ft.-lb.).

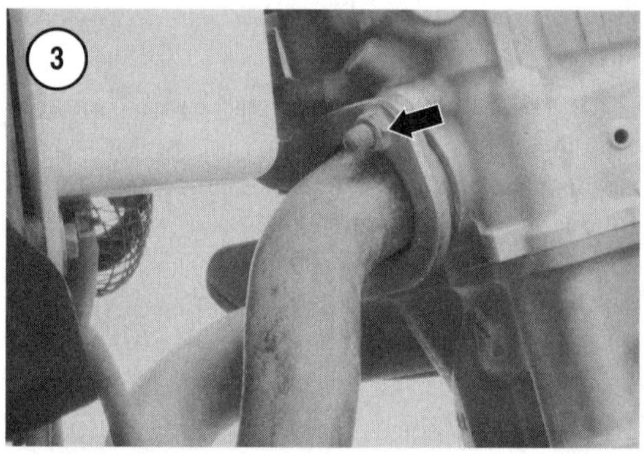

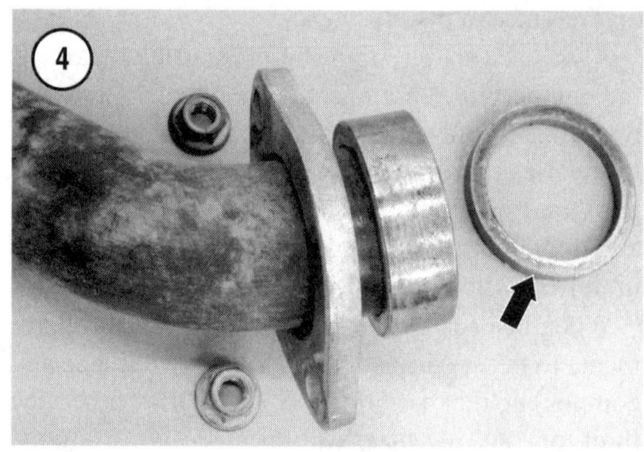

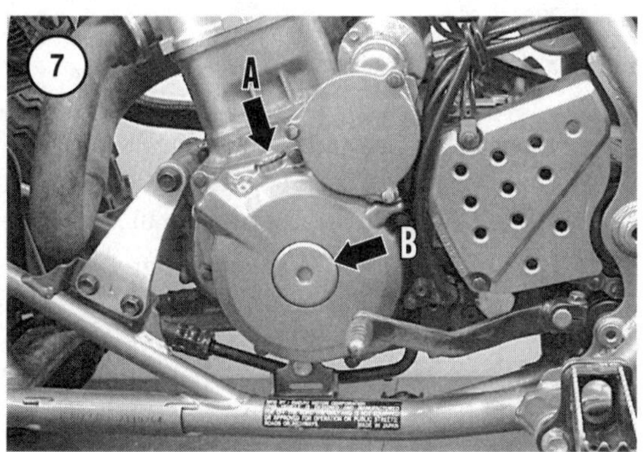

CYLINDER HEAD COVER

Removal and Installation

1. Support the vehicle so it is stable and secure.
2. Remove the fuel tank and breather hoses (Chapter Eight).
3. Remove the upper engine mounting bolt and bracket (**Figure 6**).
4. Temporarily tape the wires, cables and hoses to the frame, to provide maximum clearance.
5. Set the engine at top dead center (TDC) on the compression stroke as follows:

CAUTION

The cylinder head cover is bolted to the camshaft caps. Whenever the cover is removed or installed, set the engine at TDC (top dead center). This takes the camshaft pressure off the caps.

a. Remove the timing plug (A, **Figure 7**) and the rotor nut plug (B). When the rotor nut plug is removed, engine oil will slowly flow from the opening. If desired, drain the engine oil (Chapter Three).
b. Fit a socket onto the rotor nut and turn the crankshaft *counterclockwise* until the T mark on the rotor is aligned in the center of the timing hole (**Figure 8**). If compression is not felt when making the alignment, turn the crankshaft one more revolution.

6. Remove the spark plug from the cylinder (A, **Figure 9**).
7. Loosen the three cover bolts (B, **Figure 9**) in a crisscross pattern using several passes to relieve pressure on the gasket.

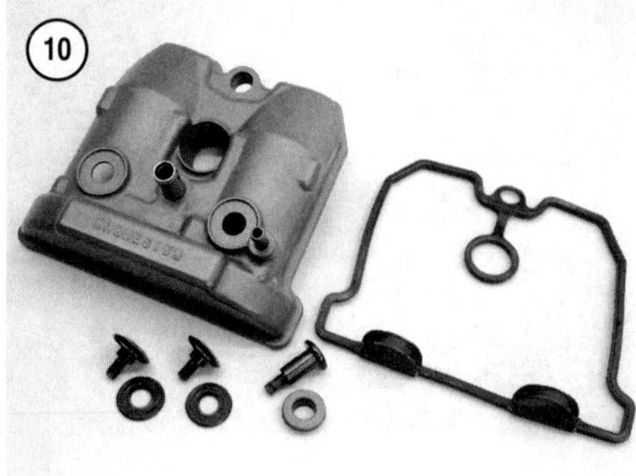
10

11

8. Raise the cylinder head cover slowly to prevent damaging the rubber gasket. The gasket is adhered to the right side of the cylinder head and may separate itself from the cover. The gasket can be cleaned and reused, if not damaged.

9. If necessary, refer to Chapter Three for performing the valve clearance check and adjustment. If valve adjustment is required, refer to this chapter for camshaft removal.

10. Inspect the cover, gasket, bolts and washers (**Figure 10**).

a. Clean all sealant and oil from the gasket.

b. Replace the washers if the rubber seals are damaged. The rubber seals prevent oil leaks past the bolt heads. Lubricate both sides of the washers before installing.

11. Reverse this procedure to install the cover. Note the following:

a. Verify the engine is at TDC by checking the camshaft lobes. If properly set, all camshaft lobes will point *away* from the spark plug hole (**Figure 11**). If necessary, rotate the crankshaft one full turn and realign the T mark (**Figure 8**).

b. Clean the gasket surface on the cylinder head. *Lightly* apply Suzuki Bond 1207B silicone sealant, or equivalent, to the entire length of the gasket surface on the right side of the cylinder head . This helps seal the plugs (**Figure 12**) that are a part of the gasket. Seat the gasket onto the cover (**Figure 13**), then seat the cover onto the cylinder head.

c. Install the washers onto the cover bolts so the rubber face will contact the cover. Install the bolts.

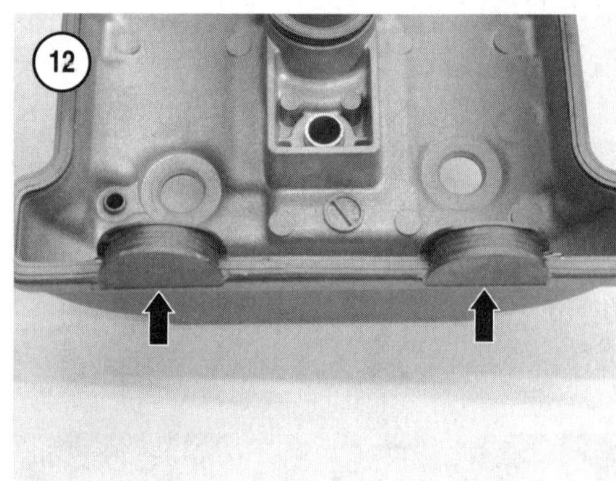
12

d. Tighten the bolts in several passes and in a crossing pattern. Tighten the bolts to 14 N•m (124 in.-lb.). Do not overtighten the bolts.

e. Check that the plugs are seated and not distorted.

f. Tighten the timing hole plug to 23 N•m (17 ft.-lb.).

g. Inspect the spark plug and replace, if necessary (Chapter Three).

h. Check the engine oil level (Chapter Three).

CAMSHAFTS AND CAM CHAIN TENSIONER

Removal

The camshafts and cam chain tensioner can be removed with the engine mounted in the frame. Before disassembly, measure and record the valve clearances. Refer to Chapter Three.

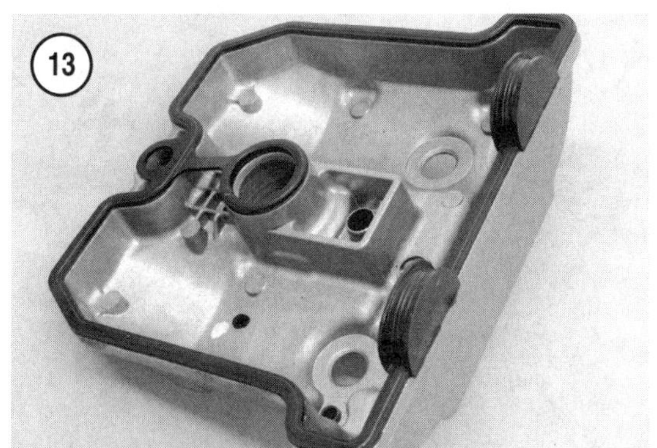

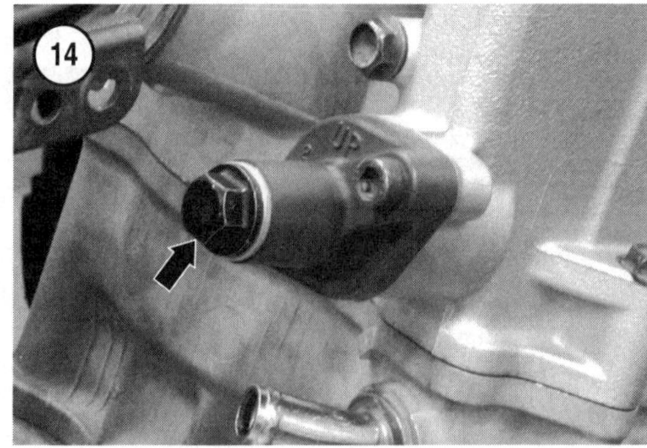

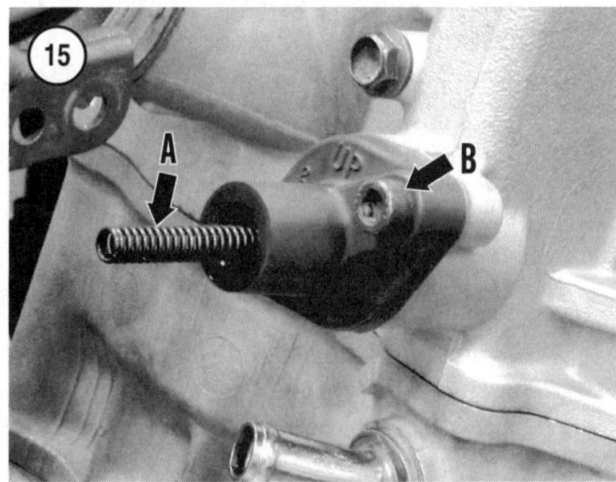

1. Remove the cylinder head cover as described in this chapter.

CAUTION
Anytime the tensioner mounting bolts are loosened, the tensioner must be removed and reset. Do not partially remove, then retighten the bolts. The one-way plunger will extend and lock. Retightening the bolts will cause the cam chain and tensioner to be too

tight, possibly causing engine damage if the engine is operated. Also, do not turn the crankshaft when the tensioner is removed from the engine. Camshaft timing could change with the chain loose.

2. Remove the cam chain tensioner from the cam chain tunnel as follows.
   a. Remove the center bolt (**Figure 14**) and remove the spring, under the center bolt (A, **Figure 15**).
   b. Remove the two mounting bolts (B, **Figure 15**), then remove the tensioner and gasket.
3. Remove the camshaft caps and cam chain guide as follows:
   a. Stuff clean shop cloths in the cam chain tunnel to prevent parts or debris from entering the engine. If parts do fall into the tunnel, they will not enter the crankcase. The tunnel leads to the right end of the crankshaft, in the right crankcase cover.
   b. Loosen the eight camshaft cap bolts (**Figure 16**). Loosen each set of bolts in several passes and in a crisscross pattern.

CAUTION
If the caps are tight, tap them with a small, soft mallet. Do not pry under the caps or damage the machined surfaces.

   c. Remove the chain guide and the bolt and cap sets. Raise the caps straight up and slowly. Account for the two dowels under each cap (**Figure 17**). The dowels may be loose and may fall from the cap. If the dowels are tight in either the cap or cylinder head, they may be left in place. Keep all sets of parts identified.

4. Attach a length of wire to the cam chain. This keeps tension on the chain when the camshafts are removed. The side bolt, on the right side of the cylinder head, prevents the chain from falling into the engine if the chain is mishandled.

CAUTION
If the crankshaft must be turned while the cam chain is loose, keep tension on the chain while turning the crankshaft. This will prevent possible chain binding at the crankshaft sprocket.

5. Raise the cam chain and remove the camshafts from the cylinder head. Secure the wire so it maintains tension on the cam chain.
6. Make sure the cylinder head openings are covered to prevent parts or debris from entering the engine.
7. Inspect the camshafts, caps and cam chain tensioner as described in this section.
   a. Reset the cam chain tensioner as described in the inspection procedure. The tensioner must be reset before installation.
   b. If necessary, refer to Chapter Five for cam chain removal and inspection.

Installation

1. Before installing the camshafts and cam chain tensioner, note the following:
   a. Adjust any valve clearances that are out of specification as described in Chapter Three. If the valves were reconditioned, install the original shims at this time and recheck the valve clearance. If necessary, readjust the clearances.
   b. Check that the cam chain tensioner is reset in the retracted position, as described in the inspection procedure.
   c. Lubricate parts with engine oil during assembly.
2. Inspect the cylinder head and ensure that all surfaces are clean. Remove any shop cloths from the cam chain tunnel.
3. Check that the engine is at TDC and is held in this position. If it is not at TDC, turn the crankshaft *counterclockwise* until the T mark on the rotor is aligned with the index mark in the timing hole (**Figure 8**). The engine must remain at TDC when installing and timing the camshafts.

4. Refer to **Figure 18** and **Figure 19** and install the camshafts as follows:
   a. Identify the number 1 and number 2 arrows on the exhaust camshaft sprocket. The exhaust camshaft is fitted with the compression release mechanism (**Figure 20**).
   b. Pull up on the tension side (front side) of the cam chain and install the exhaust camshaft. Place the chain on the sprocket. Check that the cam lobes point *away* from the spark plug.
   c. Check that the engine is still at TDC when the number 1 arrow is aligned with the top of the cylinder head. If necessary, reposition the camshaft.
   d. Beginning at the number 2 arrow on the exhaust camshaft sprocket, count and mark the fifteenth chain pin from the arrow. This pin must be aligned with the number 3 arrow on the intake camshaft sprocket.
   e. Identify the number 3 arrow on the intake camshaft sprocket.
   f. Keeping the chain taut, but seated on the exhaust cam sprocket, install the intake camshaft. Check that the cam lobes point *away* from the spark plug.
5. With the engine at TDC, inspect the installation.
   a. The cam chain should be taut at the front and across the cam sprockets. The excess chain slack at the rear, between the intake camshaft and crankshaft sprocket, will be taken up by the cam chain tensioner.
   b. The number 1 arrow on the exhaust camshaft sprocket should point forward and be parallel to the top edge of the cylinder head.
   c. The number 2 arrow on the exhaust camshaft sprocket should point straight up.

(18)

CAMSHAFT TIMING

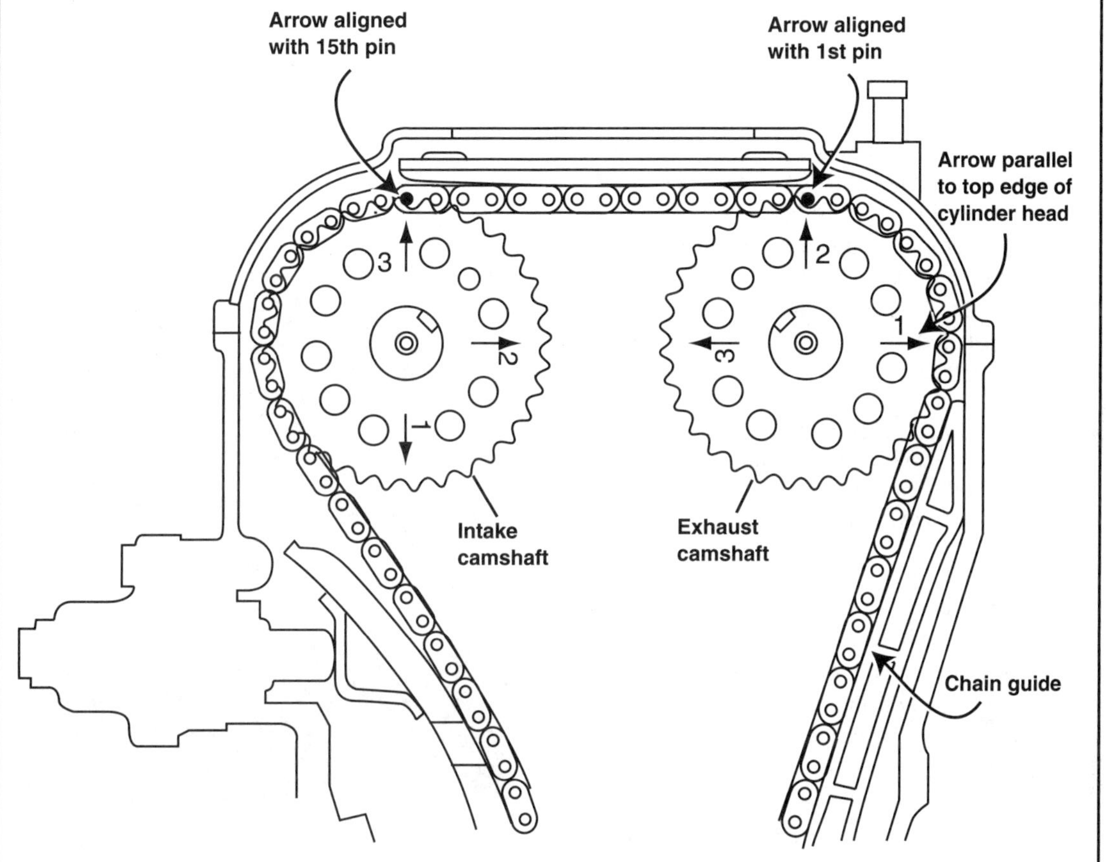

Arrow aligned with 15th pin

Arrow aligned with 1st pin

Arrow parallel to top edge of cylinder head

3 2 1

2 1 3

Intake camshaft

Exhaust camshaft

Chain guide

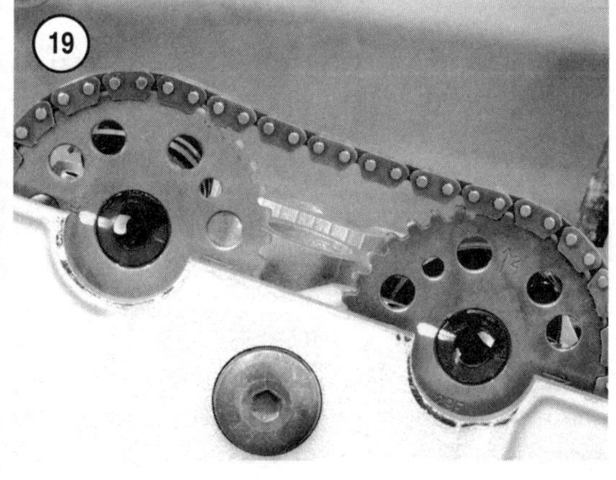

(19)

(20)

d. The number 3 arrow on the intake camshaft sprocket should point straight up and be engaged fifteen chain pins from the number 2 arrow on the exhaust camshaft sprocket.

6. Install the dowels, camshaft caps and cam chain guide as follows:

a. Cover the cam chain tunnel to prevent parts from entering the engine.

b. Install the two dowels (**Figure 21**) for each camshaft cap.

c. Identify and install the camshaft caps. The intake cap is marked IN (A, **Figure 22**) and the exhaust cap is marked EX (B).

d. Install the cam chain guide (**Figure 23**) on top of the camshaft caps, then install and finger-tighten the bolts. The two long bolts must be installed at the right end of the exhaust camshaft cap.

CAUTION
Failure to evenly tighten the camshaft cap bolts can damage the cylinder head, camshafts and caps.

e. For each camshaft, tighten the cap bolts in several passes and in a crisscross pattern. Tighten the bolts to 10 N•m (89 in.-lb.).

7. Install the cam chain tensioner as follows:

a. Inspect the housing and determine if there is an UP mark. Early tensioners are not marked.

b. Install a new gasket, the housing and the mounting bolts (**Figure 24**). Tighten the tensioner mounting bolts to 10 N•m (89 in.-lb.). Do not loosen the bolts without resetting the tensioner.

c. Install the seal washer and spring onto the center bolt then install and tighten the tensioner spring bolt to 30 N•m (22 ft.-lb.).

8. Remove any shop cloths from the cam chain tunnel, then slowly turn the crankshaft *counterclockwise* several times. Place the crankshaft at TDC as described in this chapter.

CAUTION
If abnormal resistance or noise is evident when turning the crankshaft, stop and recheck the camshaft alignments. Improper alignment can cause engine damage.

a. Check that the camshaft sprocket marks are aligned as described in Step 5.

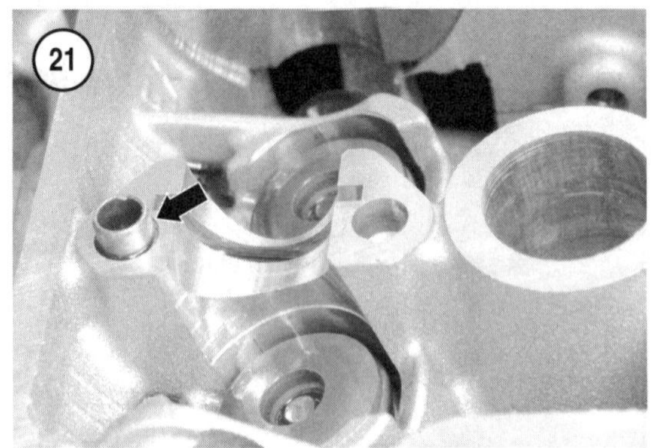

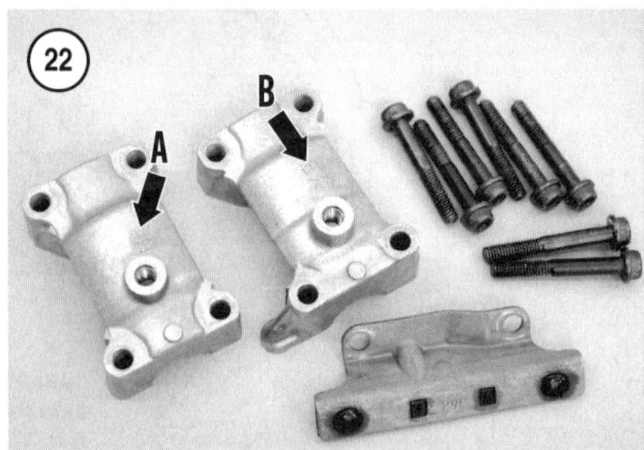

b. Check valve clearances (Chapter Three). If necessary, remove the camshafts and install the proper size valve lifter shim(s).

9. Install the cylinder head cover as described in this chapter.

Cam chain tensioner

The tensioner assembly is a spring-loaded, one-way tensioner. As the cam chain wears, the spring-loaded plunger extends and locks itself

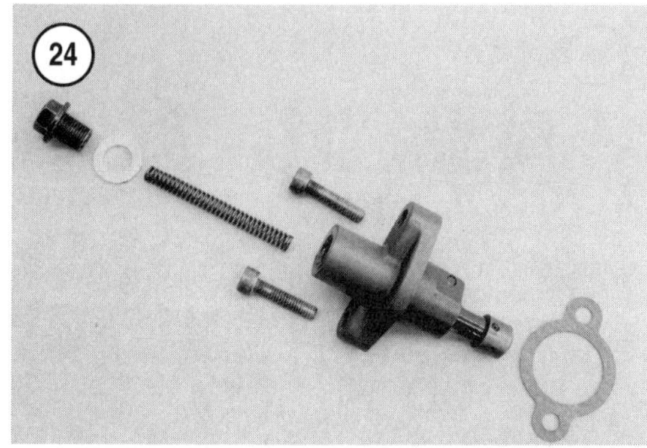
24

25

26

27

against the back of the rear chain guide. The guide then pivots forward and retightens the chain.

The tensioner is self-adjusting and no routine maintenance is required. However, any time the tensioner is loosened or removed the tensioner must be reset.

1. Perform the following when servicing the tensioner:
   a. Inspect the parts for cleanliness and damage.
   b. Apply engine oil to the plunger.
   c. Install a new gasket and seal washer during installation.
2. Reset the plunger as follows:
   a. Remove the center bolt and spring from the tensioner.
   b. Press and hold the ratchet release (**Figure 25**).
   c. Press and seat the plunger (**Figure 26**) into the tensioner housing. If the plunger does not fully retract or does not stay in the tensioner housing, replace the tensioner.
   d. Do not install the spring, washer and center bolt until the tensioner housing has been mounted.

Camshaft and compression release

The compression release is located at the right end of the exhaust camshaft. The release slightly opens the right exhaust valve during engine cranking. The reduction in compression makes starting easier. When the engine starts, the release is centrifugally disengaged.

In the following procedure, replace parts that are damaged or not within the specifications in **Table 2**.

1. Clean the camshafts in solvent and dry with compressed air. Use care when drying the compression release.
2. Inspect the camshafts for scoring or damage. If there is cam lobe damage, also inspect the mating valve lifter for damage.
3. For each camshaft, make the following checks. Record all measurements.
   a. Measure the cam lobe heights (**Figure 27**) with a micrometer.
   b. Measure the camshaft journal outside diameter (where the cap fits over the camshaft) (**Figure 28**).
   c. Support the camshaft in V-blocks and measure shaft runout.

4

d. Inspect the camshaft sprocket teeth (**Figure 29**) for wear or other damage. The profile of each tooth should be symmetrical. If a sprocket is worn, replace the camshafts and the cam chain as a set. When this type of damage occurs, also inspect the crankshaft sprocket, cam chain tensioner and chain guides for damage.

4. Inspect the automatic compression release (**Figure 20**).

a. Inspect the spring for damage.

b. Pivot the weights outward and check for smooth operation. When the weights are pivoted and released, the spring should fully retract the weights.

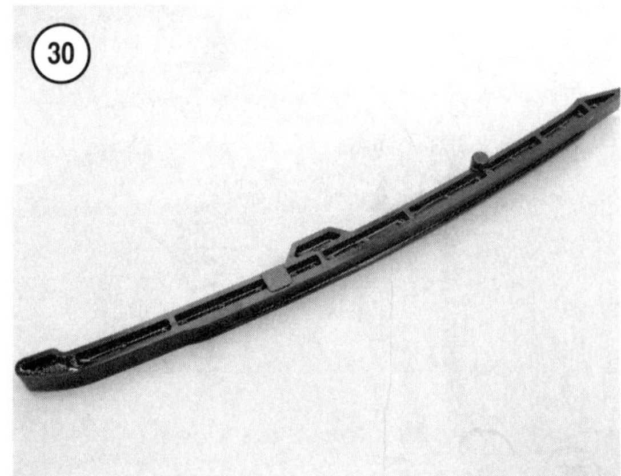

Camshaft cap

1. Clean the camshaft caps, bolts and chain guide (**Figure 30**) in solvent and dry with compressed air. Clean and handle the caps individually, preventing any damage to the bearing surfaces.

2. For each camshaft cap, perform the following:

a. Check all threads and bores for cleanliness.

b. Inspect the bearing surface in the cap (**Figure 31**) and the mating bearing surface in the journal holder (**Figure 32**). Check for scoring, galling or other damage. If either part is damaged, replace the caps and cylinder head as a set. The caps are machined with the cylinder head, so their dimensions and alignments are unique to that cylinder head.

c. Install the dowels and camshaft caps, then tighten the bolts in several passes and in a crisscross pattern. Tighten the bolts to 10 N•m (89 in.-lb.). Measure the inside diameter of the assembled camshaft journal holder in several directions (**Figure 33**). Record the measurements. Refer to **Table 2** for specifications.

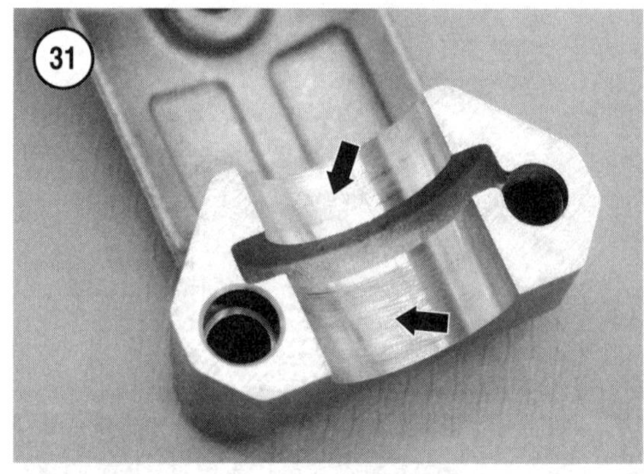

3. Determine the oil clearance between the camshaft and journal holder. Subtract the appropriate journal outside diameter from the appropriate journal holder inside diameter. Refer to **Table 2** for specifications.

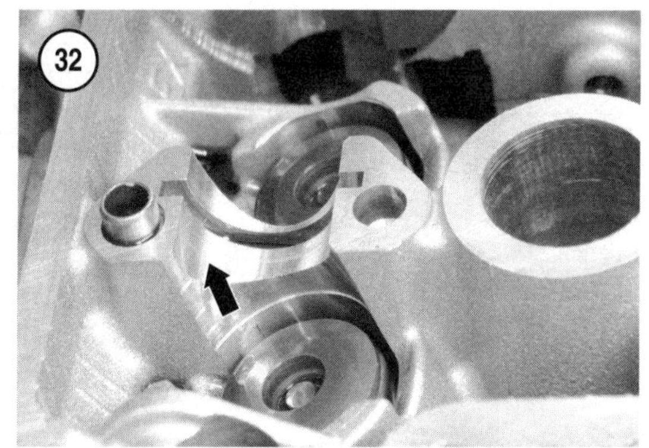

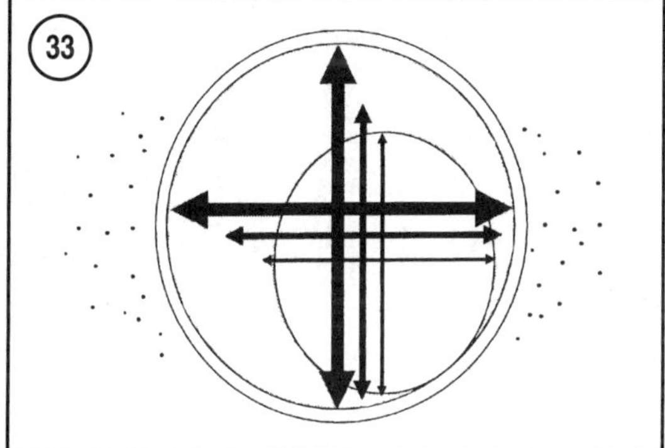

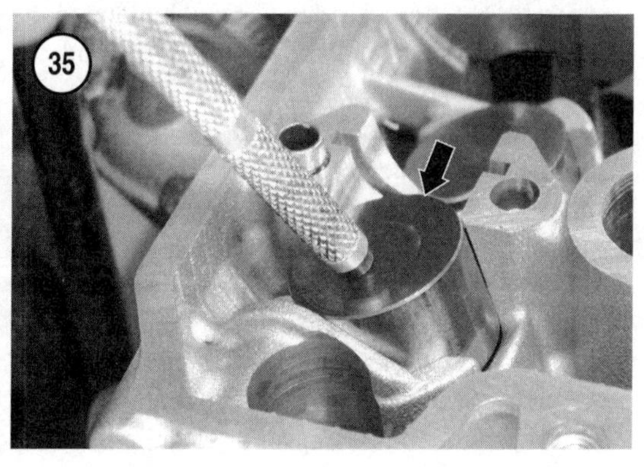

CYLINDER HEAD

Removal

The cylinder head can be removed with the engine mounted in the frame.

1. Remove the exhaust pipe as described in this chapter.
2. Remove the carburetor (Chapter Eight).
3. Drain the engine coolant (Chapter Three).
4. Disconnect the coolant hose (**Figure 34**) from the front of the cylinder.
5. Remove the cylinder head cover, camshafts and cam chain tensioner as described in this chapter.
6. Remove each valve lifter and shim set as follows:
   a. Use a magnetic tool and raise the lifter straight up (**Figure 35**).
   b. Lift out the valve shim resting on top of the valve stem.
   c. Inspect each set of parts while removing them. Both parts should be smooth on all surfaces. Light polishing on the shim, where it contacts the valve stem, is normal.
   d. Mark the parts with their location in the cylinder head (**Figure 36**). The shims vary in thickness and must be installed in their original position.
7. With the cam chain securely wired, remove the side bolt (A, **Figure 37**) from the cylinder. With the side bolt removed, the cam chain can fall into the right crankcase cover.
8. Loosen the two 6 mm cylinder head bolts (B, **Figure 37**) and the two cylinder mounting nuts, directly below the bolts.

9. Remove the four 10 mm cylinder head bolts (**Figure 38**). Loosen the bolts in several passes and in a criscross pattern. Account for the washer on each bolt.

10. Loosen the cylinder head by lightly tapping around its base with a soft mallet. Lift the head out of the engine while routing the cam chain out of the head. Secure the chain so it does not fall into the engine.

11. Stuff clean shop cloths into the cam chain tunnel, then remove the head gasket (A, **Figure 39**) and two dowels (B). If the cylinder will be removed, the front cam chain guide can be removed at this time.

12. At the workbench, remove the thermostat housing, thermostat and carburetor intake duct.

13. If necessary, remove and inspect the valve assembly as described in this chapter.

14. Wash the cylinder head components in solvent and dry with compressed air. Note the following:

   a. Remove all gasket residue from the cylinder head and cylinder. Do not scratch or gouge the surfaces.
   b. Remove all carbon deposits from the combustion chamber. Use solvent and a soft brush or a hardwood scraper. Do not use sharp-edged tools that could scratch the valves or combustion chamber. If the piston crown is cleaned, keep solvent and carbon deposits out of the gap between the piston and cylinder. If the valves are removed, do not damage the valve seats.
   c. If the cylinder head will be bead-blasted, wash the entire assembly in hot, soapy water after it has been reconditioned. This will remove blasting grit that is lodged in crevices and threads. Clean and chase all threads to ensure no grit remains.
   d. Check all oil and coolant passages for blockages.
   e. Check all parts for wear or damage.

15. Inspect the cylinder head as described in this section.

Inspection

1. Inspect the spark plug hole threads. If the threads are dirty or slightly damaged, use a spark plug thread tap to clean and straighten the threads. Keep the tap lubricated while cleaning the threads. If necessary, install a steel thread insert, such as a HeliCoil.

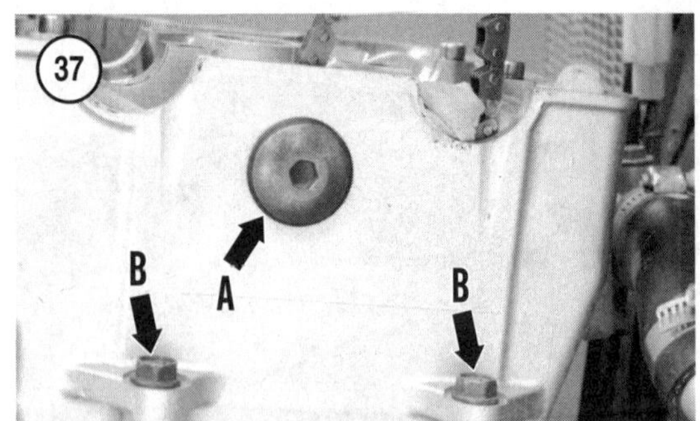

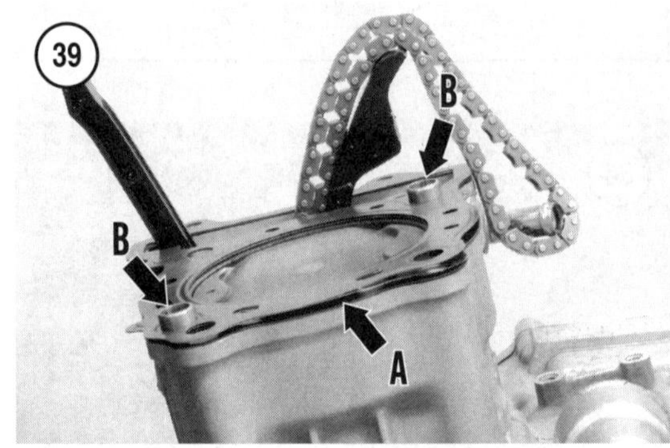

2. Inspect the inside of the cylinder head.
   a. Inspect for cracks, damage and buildup in the combustion chamber, water jackets and exhaust port.
   b. Inspect the threads for damage or looseness.
3. Inspect the outside of the cylinder head.
   a. Inspect for cracks or damage around the camshaft journal holders and spark plug hole. If cracks are found anywhere in the cylinder head, take the head to a dealership or machine shop to see if the head can be repaired. If not, replace the head and camshaft cap set.
   b. Inspect the oil passages for cleanliness.

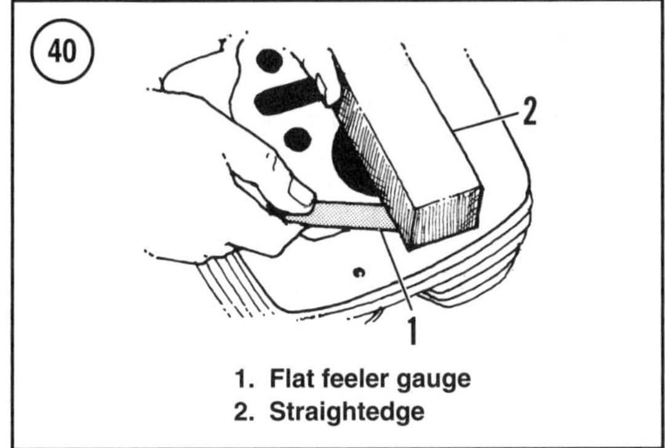

1. Flat feeler gauge
2. Straightedge

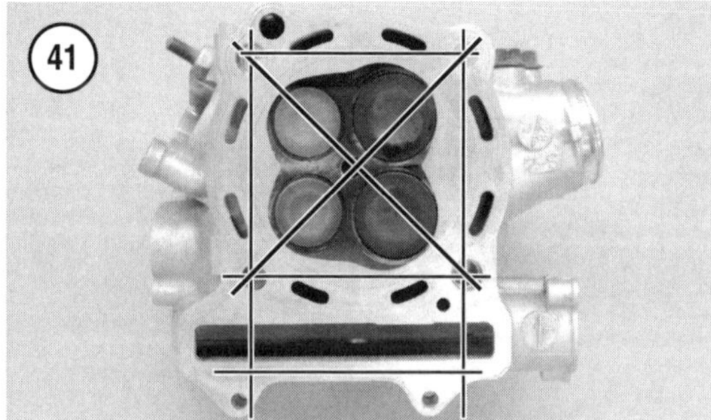

4. Inspect the cylinder head for warp as follows:

   a. Lay a machinest's straightedge across the cylinder head (**Figure 40**) and check the surface as shown in **Figure 41**.

   b. Try to insert a flat feeler gauge between the straightedge and the machined surface of the head. If clearance exists, record the maximum measurement.

   c. Compare the measurements to the service limit in **Table 2**. If the clearance is not within the service limit, take the cylinder head to a dealership or machine shop for further inspection and possible resurfacing.

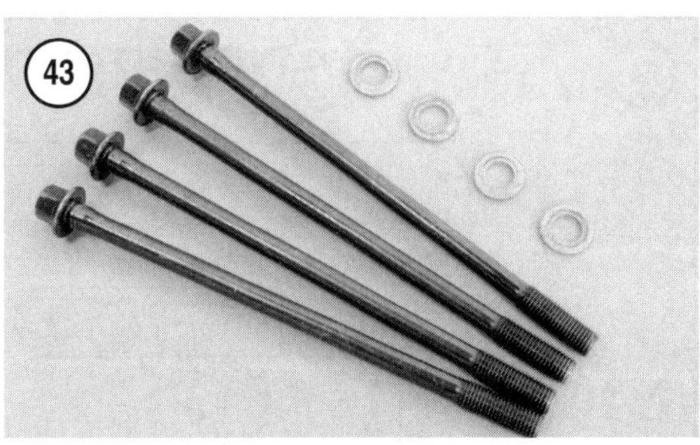

5. Inspect the cylinder head bolts, side bolt, washers and dowels (**Figure 42**) for damage. Check the fit of the cylinder head dowels and camshaft cap dowels prior to installing the cylinder head. Often, dowels fit in one location better than another. Match the dowels to their preferred bores to prevent binding during assembly.
6. Assemble and install the cylinder head as described in this section.

Installation

1. Note the following:
   a. Check that all gasket residue is removed from all mating surfaces. All cylinder head surfaces must be clean and dry.
   b. The valve lifters and shims can be installed after the cylinder head is installed.
2. Insert the dowels and a new cylinder head gasket onto the cylinder (**Figure 39**).
3. Lower the cylinder head onto the engine, routing the cam chain through the head.
   a. Keep adequate tension on the cam chain so it does bind at the crankshaft sprocket. Secure the cam chain when the cylinder head is seated. If desired, install and finger-tighten the side bolt, passing it between the chain. This prevents the chain from falling into the right crankcase cover if the chain is mishandled.
   b. Be careful not to dislodge the dowels as the cylinder head is positioned.
   c. Cover engine openings as needed.
4. Install and tighten the 10-mm cylinder head bolts as follows:
   a. Apply engine oil to the bolt heads, threads and washers (**Figure 43**).
   b. Install the washers with the rounded side facing up (against the bolt head).

4

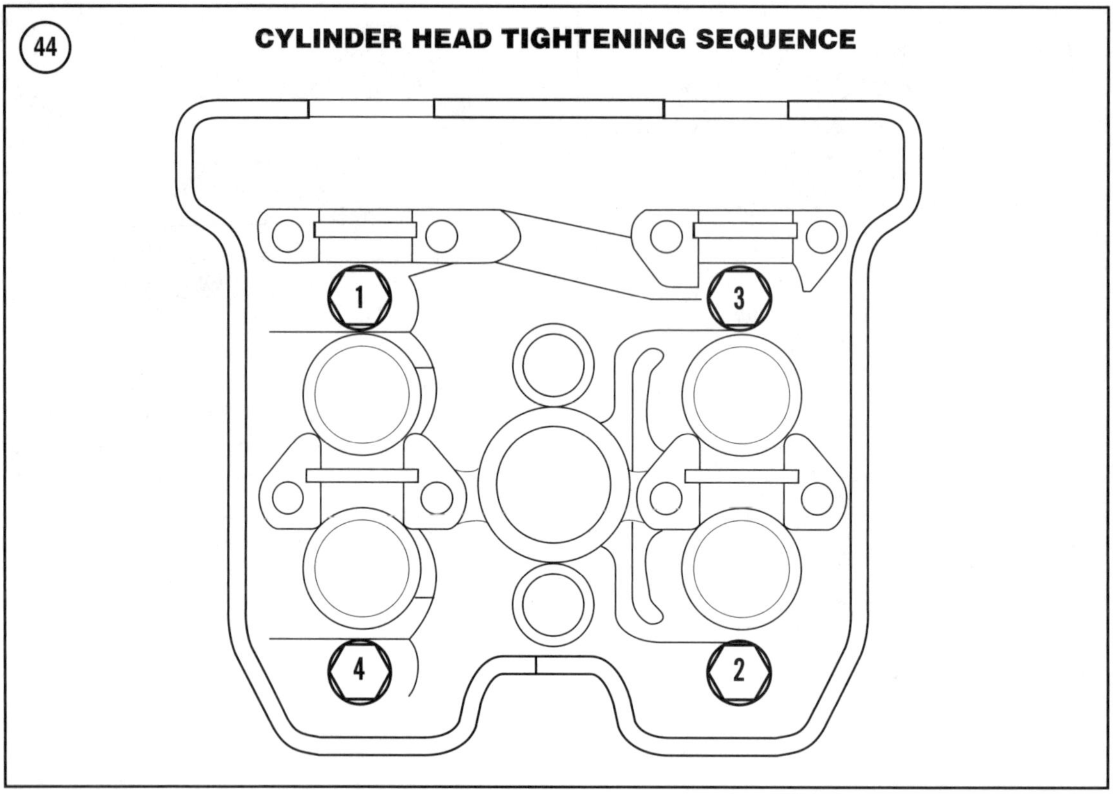

44 **CYLINDER HEAD TIGHTENING SEQUENCE**

1 3 4 2

c. Tighten the bolts in a diagonal sequence as shown in **Figure 44**.

d. Tighten the bolts in two passes. In the initial pass, tighten the bolts to 25 N•m (18 ft.-lb.). In the final pass, tighten the bolts to 46 N•m (34 ft.-lb.).

5. Tighten the two 6 mm cylinder head bolts (**Figure 38**) and the two cylinder mounting nuts, directly below the bolts. Tighten the bolts and nuts to 10 N•m (89 in.-lb.).

6. Tighten the side bolt to 14 N•m (124 in.-lb.).

7. Install the shim and valve lifter sets at their appropriate locations, lubricate the parts with engine oil, then seat the shim on top of the valve stem (**Figure 45**). If the shim size is visible (**Figure 46**), place the number facing up, so it does not get worn away by the valve. Note the following:

a. If the valve assembly was not reconditioned or disturbed when the cylinder head was removed, reinstall the original shim.

b. If the valve clearance was incorrect before the head was removed, refer to Chapter Three.

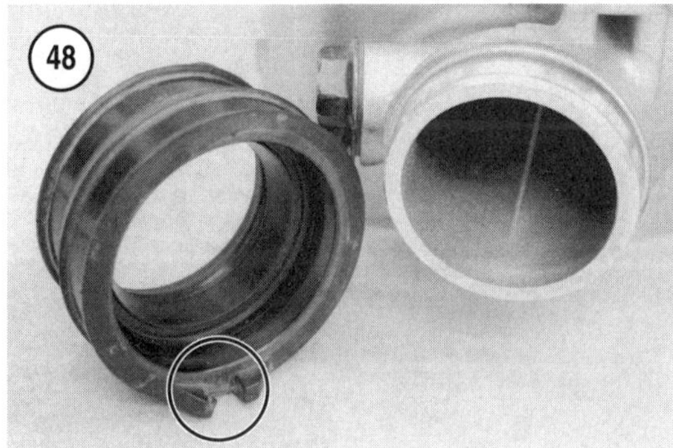

c. If the valves were reconditioned, install the original shim and check the valve clearance after the camshafts are installed.

d. Slide the valve lifter into place over the valve and shim assembly.

8. Install the camshafts, cam chain tensioner and cylinder head cover as described in this chapter.

9. Install the upper engine mounting bracket (**Figure 47**). Tighten the bracket-to-frame bolts to 40 N•m (30 ft.-lb.). Tighten the bracket-to-engine bolt to 66 N•m (49 ft.-lb.).

10. Install the following parts onto the cylinder head:

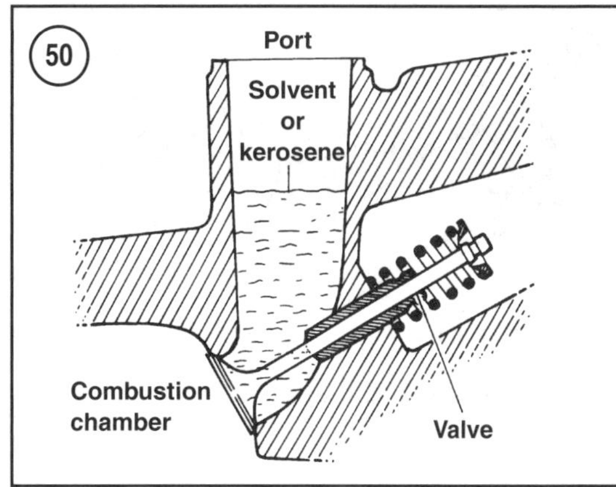

a. Carburetor intake duct. Make sure the cylinder head tab indexes with intake duct (**Figure 48**).

b. Thermostat housing. Tighten the bolts to 10 N•m (89 in.-lb.).

11. Install the engine coolant (Chapter Three).

12. Install the carburetor (Chapter Eight).

13. Install the exhaust pipe as described in this chapter.

VALVES

Solvent Test

A solvent test can reveal if valves are fully seating, and detect cracks in the cylinder head.

1. Remove the cylinder head as described in this chapter.

2. Check that the combustion chamber is dry and the valves are seated.

3. Support the cylinder head (**Figure 49**) so the port faces up.

4. Pour solvent or kerosene into the port (**Figure 50**).

5. Inspect the combustion chamber for leaks around the valve.

6. Repeat Steps 3-5 for the other valves.

7. If leaks are detected, this can be caused by:

a. A worn or damaged valve face.

b. A worn or damaged valve seat (in the cylinder head).

c. A bent valve stem.

d. A crack in the combustion chamber.

Valve Removal

1. Remove the cylinder head, valve lifters and shims as described in this chapter.

4

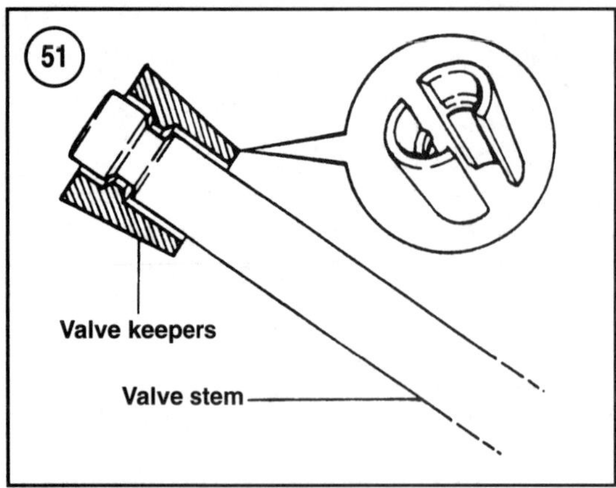

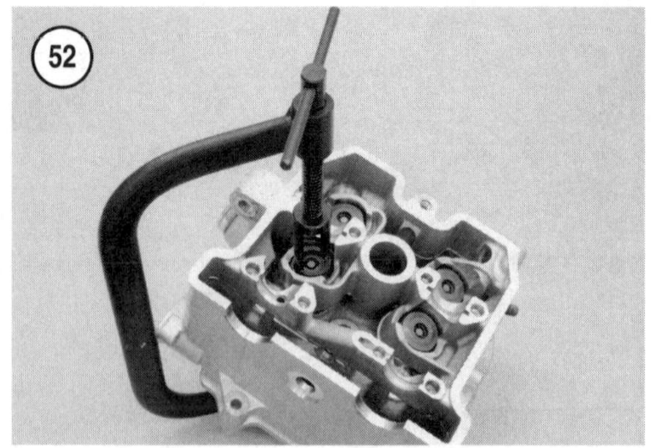

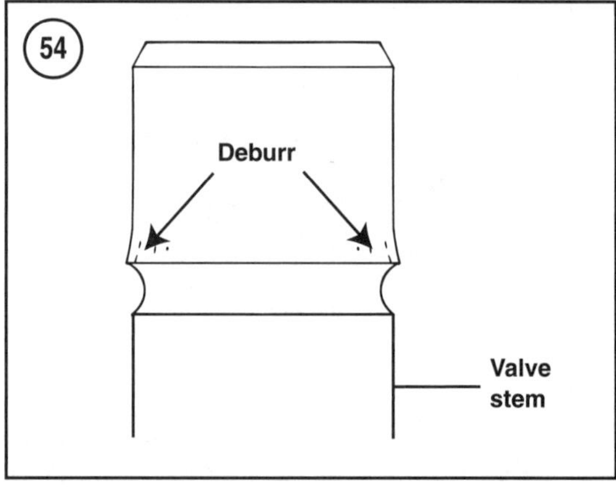

2. Perform the solvent test on the intake and exhaust valves as described in this section.
3. To disassemble the valve components, remove the valve keepers (**Figure 51**). Install a valve spring compressor (Suzuki part No. 09916-14510, or equivalent) and adapter (Suzuki part No. 09916-14910, or equivalent) over the valve assembly. Fit the stationary end of the tool squarely over the valve head. Fit the other end of the tool squarely on the spring retainer (**Figure 52**).
4. Tighten the compressor just enough to expose the valve keepers. Lift the keepers (**Figure 53**) from the valve stem. A tool with a magnetic tip works well.
5. Slowly relieve the pressure on the valve springs and remove the compressor from the head.
6. Remove the spring retainer, valve spring and spring seat.
7. Inspect the valve stem for sharp and flared metal (**Figure 54**) around the groove for the keepers. If necessary, deburr the valve stem before removing the valve from the head. Burrs on the valve stem can damage the valve guide.
8. Remove the valve from the cylinder head.
9. Remove the oil seal with needlenose pliers. Avoid gripping the inside of the valve guide.
10. While removing each valve assembly (**Figure 55**), store the parts with the shim and valve lifter for that location.
11. Repeat Steps 3-10 for the remaining valves.

Valve Component Inspection

During the cleaning and inspection of the valve assemblies, do not allow the sets of parts to get intermixed. Work with one set of parts at a time, repeating the procedure until all parts are inspected. After inspecting each set of parts, return them to their storage container.

In the following procedure, whenever the valves, valve guides and valve seats must be replaced or reconditioned, it is recommended that the work be done by a dealership. Replacing and servicing these parts requires special equipment. Refer to **Table 2** for specifications.

1. Clean the valve assembly in solvent.

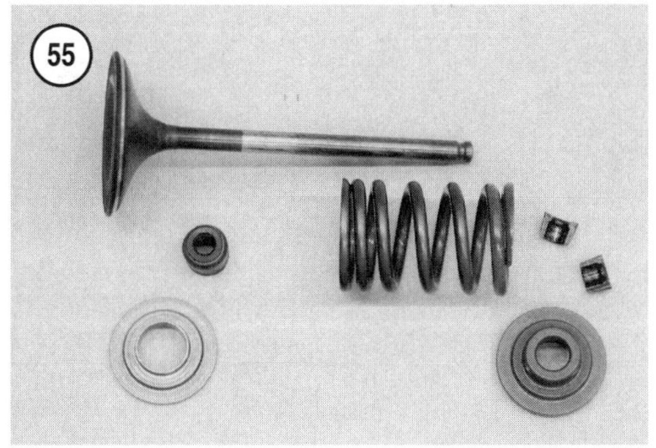
55

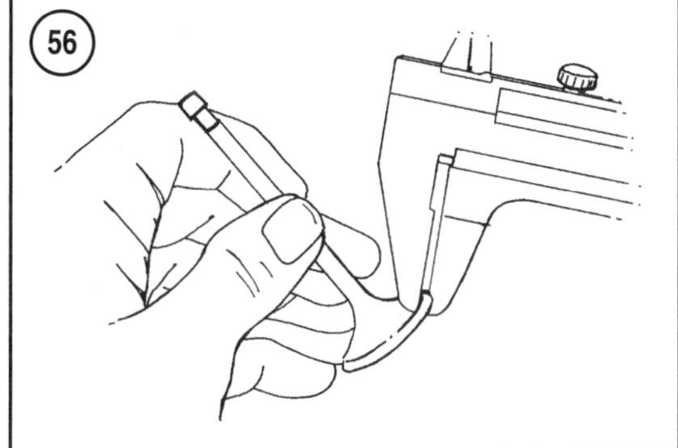
56

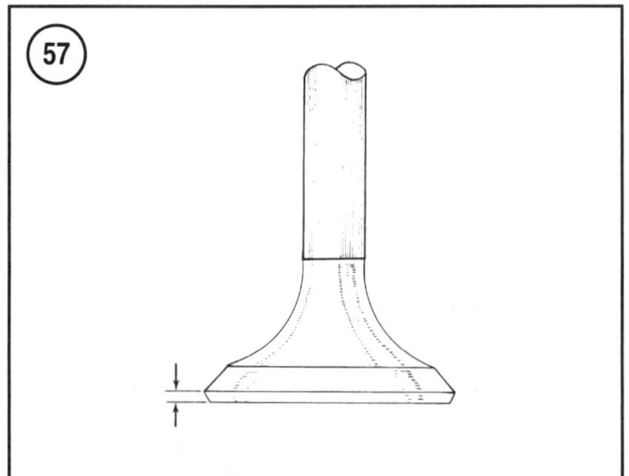
57

CAUTION
The valve seating surface is a critical surface and must not be damaged. Do not scrape on the seating surface or place the valve where it could roll off the work surface.

2. Inspect the valve head as follows:
   a. Inspect the top and perimeter of each valve. Check for burning or other damage on the top and seating surface. Replace the valve if damage is evident. If the valve head appears uniform, with only minor wear, the valve can be lapped and reused, if the other valve measurements are acceptable.
   b. Measure the valve seat width (**Figure 56**). Record the measurement.
   c. Measure the valve head thickness (**Figure 57**).
   d. Mount the valve in a V-block and measure the radial runout of the valve head (**Figure 58**). Record the measurement.

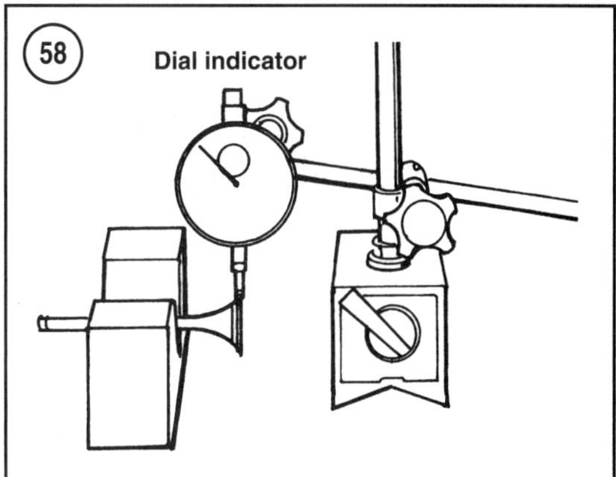

58

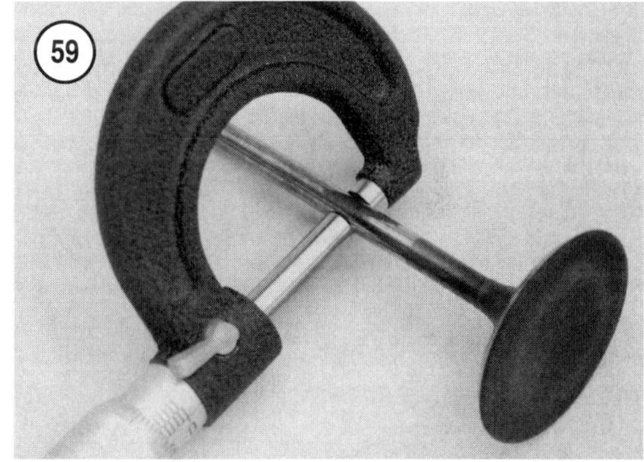
59

3. Inspect the valve stem as follows:
   a. Inspect the stem for wear and scoring. Also check the end of the valve stem for burrs (**Figure 54**).
   b. Measure the valve stem diameter in several locations that contact the valve guide (**Figure 59**). Record the measurements.
   c. Check the valve stem for runout. Place the valve in a V-block and measure runout with a dial indicator (**Figure 60**). Record the measurement.

4

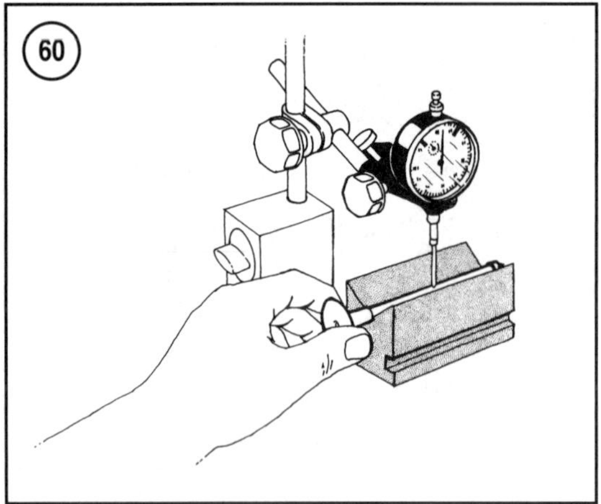

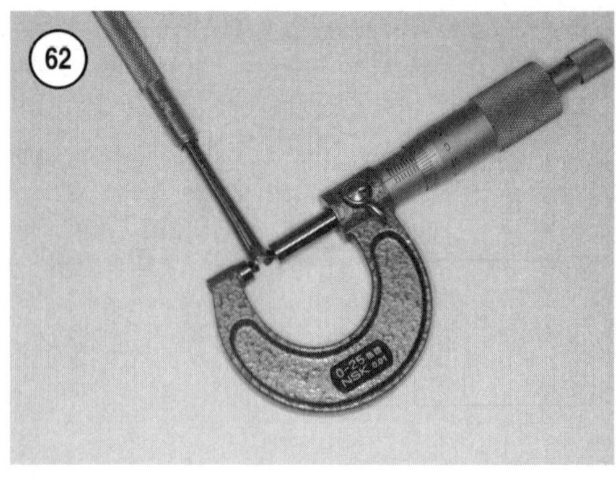

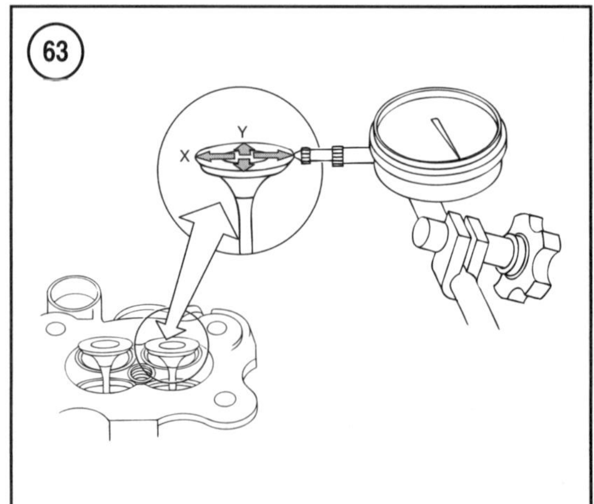

4A. Determine the valve guide to valve stem clearance as follows:

a. Clean the valve guides (**Figure 61**) so they are free of all carbon and varnish. Use solvent and a stiff, narrow brush.
b. Measure each valve guide hole at the top, center and bottom with a small hole guage and micrometer (**Figure 62**). Record the measurements. The difference between the outside diameter of the valve stem (Step 3b) and the inside diameter of the valve guide is the clearance.

4B. Measure the valve stem deflection as follows:

a. Clean the valve guide bores (**Figure 61**) so they are free of all carbon and varnish. Use solvent and a stiff, narrow brush.
b. Insert the appropriate valve into the guide, keeping the valve about 10 mm (0.040 in.) above the valve seat. Place the dial indicator in contact with the edge of the valve as shown in **Figure 63**.
c. Move the valve stem side to side in the valve guide. Record the measurement. Repeat the procedure, measuring in several directions. The largest measurement recorded is the valve stem deflection.

5. Check the inner and outer valve springs as follows:

65

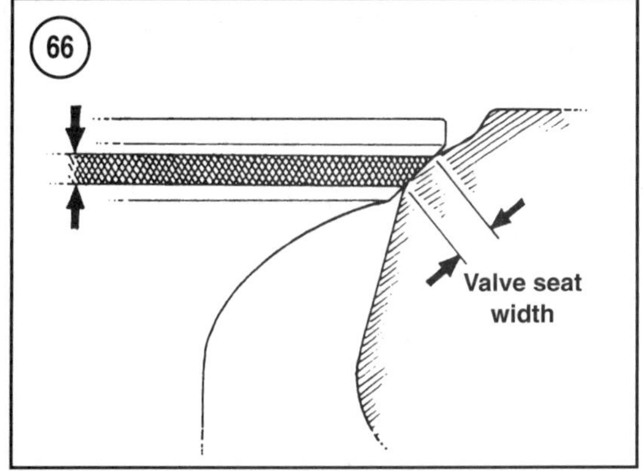

66

67

a. Visually check the springs for damage.

b. Measure the length of each valve spring (**Figure 64**).

6. Inspect the spring seat, spring retainer and keepers for wear or damage.

7. Inspect the seats on the valve and cylinder head (**Figure 65**) to determine if they must be reconditioned.

68

a. Clean and dry the valve seat and valve mating area with contact cleaner.

b. Coat the valve seat with machinist's marking fluid.

c. Install the appropriate valve into the guide, then *lightly* tap the valve against the seat so the fluid transfers to the valve contact area. Do not rotate the valve.

d. Remove the valve from the guide and measure the valve seat width (**Figure 66**) at several locations around the edge of the valve.

e. Clean all marking fluid from the valves and seats.

Valve Installation

Perform the following procedure for each set of valve components. All components should be clean and dry.

1. Coat the valve stem and interior of the oil seal with molybdenum disulfide grease.

2. Install a new oil seal onto the valve guide, checking that the retainer seats onto the seal and valve guide.

3. Install the spring seat.

4. Insert the appropriate valve into the cylinder head. Rotate the valve stem as it enters and passes through the seal. Check that the seal remains seated, then hold the valve in place.

5. Install the valve springs with the *small* coil pitch, facing down (**Figure 67**).

6. Install the spring retainer.

7. Install a valve spring compressor (**Figure 68**) over the valve assembly. Fit the tool squarely onto the spring retainer.

8. Tighten the compressor just far enough to install the valve keepers.

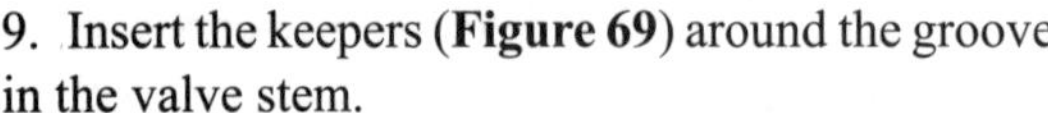

9. Insert the keepers (**Figure 69**) around the groove in the valve stem.
10. Slowly relieve the pressure on the spring retainer, then remove the compressor from the head.
11. Tap the end of the valve stem with a soft mallet to ensure that the keepers are seated in the valve stem groove (**Figure 70**).
12. After installing all valves, perform the solvent test as described in this section.
13. Install the cylinder head as described in this chapter.

Valve Lapping

Valve lapping can restore the seal between the valve seat and valve contact area, without machining if the components are within specifications. In addition, lap valves and valve seats that have been reconditioned.

1. Lightly coat the valve face with fine-grade lapping compound.
2. Lubricate the valve stem, then insert the valve into the head.
3. Wet the suction cup on the lapping tool and press it onto the head of the valve (**Figure 71**).
4. Spin the tool back and forth between your hands to lap the valve to the seat. Every 5 to 10 seconds, rotate the valve 180° and continue to lap the valve into the seat.
5. Frequently inspect the valve seat. Stop lapping the valve when the valve seat is smooth, even and polished. Keep each lapped valve identified so it can be installed in the correct seat during assembly.
6. Clean the valves and cylinder head in solvent and remove all lapping compound. Any abrasive remaining in the head will cause premature wear and damage to engine parts.

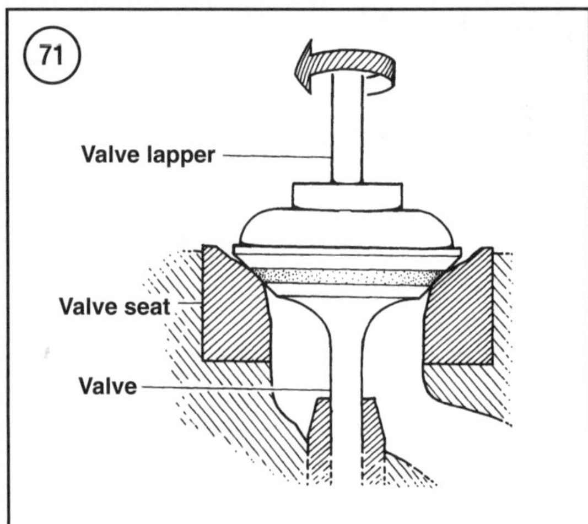

7. After installing the valves in the head, perform a solvent test as described in this chapter. If there are leaks, remove that valve and repeat the lapping process.

CYLINDER

Removal

The cylinder and piston can be removed with the engine mounted in the frame.

1. Remove the cylinder head as described in this chapter.
2. Remove the front cam chain guide.
3. Remove the oil return tank hose (**Figure 72**) at the back of the cylinder.
4. Remove the cylinder mounting nuts (**Figure 73**).

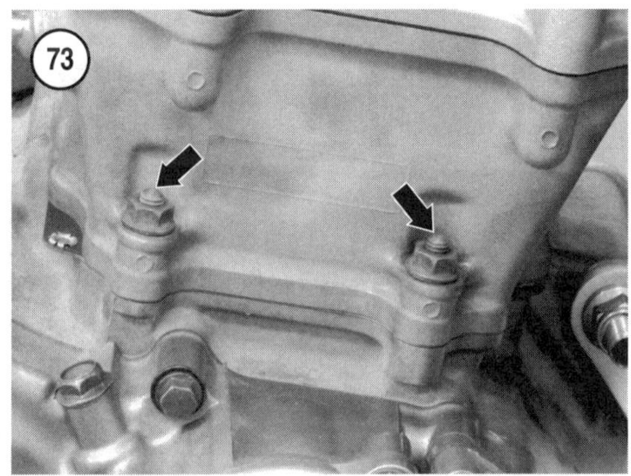

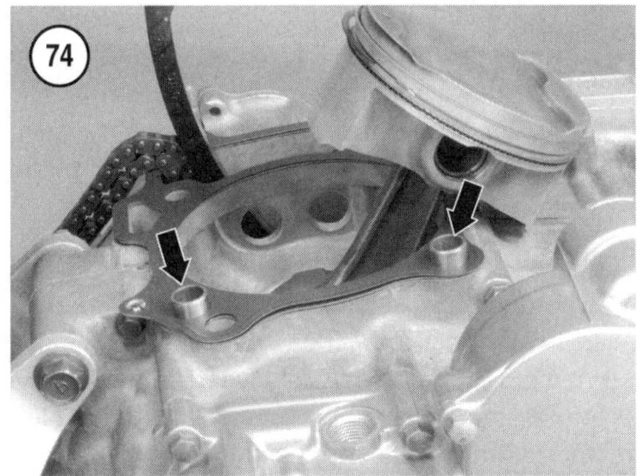

5. Loosen the cylinder by tapping around the base with a soft mallet. If necessary, apply penetrating oil to the joint.

6. *Slowly* lift the cylinder from the crankcase.

   a. Account for the two dowels under the cylinder (**Figure 74**). If loose, remove the dowels to prevent them from possibly falling into the engine.

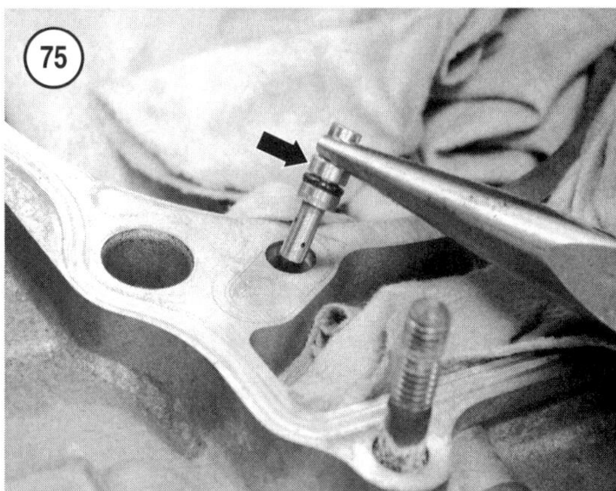

   b. Route and secure the cam chain out of the cylinder.

7. Remove the gasket.

8. Stuff clean shop cloths into the cam chain tunnel and around the piston. Support the piston and rod so they do not contact the crankcase.

9. Remove the oil jet at the right side of the engine (**Figure 75**).

10. Inspect the cylinder as described in this section.

Inspection

1. Remove all gasket residue from the top and bottom cylinder block surfaces.

2. Wash the cylinder in solvent and dry with compressed air.

NOTE

The cylinder is plated with nickel-silicon phosphorous carbide. If lightly damaged, the cylinder can be repaired and replated. If excessively damaged, the cylinder cannot be repaired. Check with a dealership for a recommendation on reconditioning or replacing the cylinder.

3. Inspect the overall condition of the cylinder for wear or damage.

   a. Inspect the cylinder bore for scoring or gouges.

   b. Inspect the water jackets for deposits.

   c. Inspect all threads for condition and cleanliness.

4. Measure and check the cylinder for wear. Measure the inside diameter of the cylinder with a bore gauge or inside micrometer as follows:

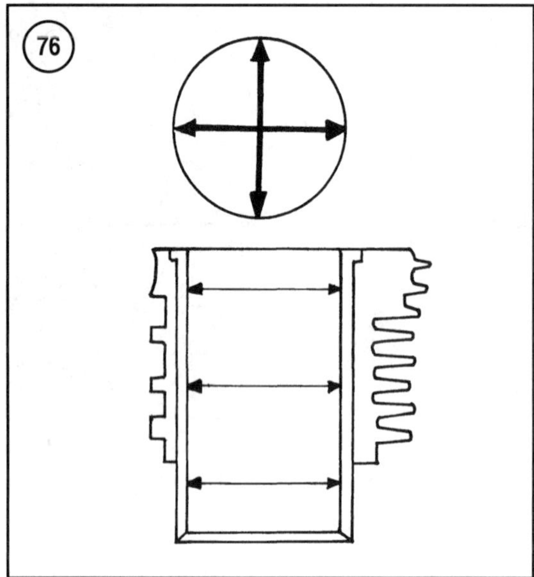

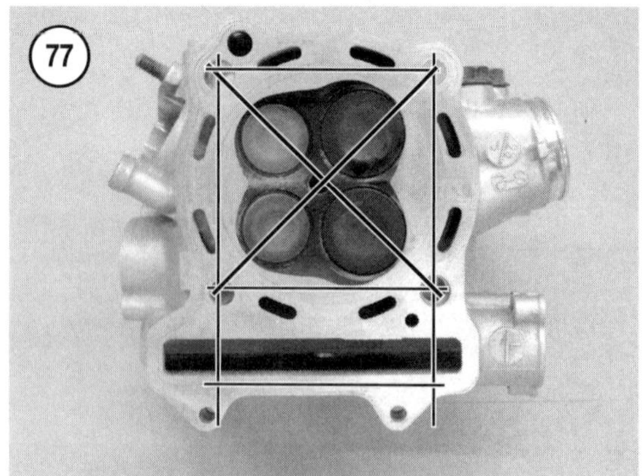

a. Measure the cylinder at 3 points along the bore axis (**Figure 76**). At each point, measure the cylinder front to back (measurement X) and side to side (measurement Y). Record the measurements for each location.

b. Compare the largest X or Y measurement recorded to the specifications in **Table 2**. If the cylinder bore is not within specification, replace the cylinder. The cylinder cannot be overbored.

5. Inspect the cylinder gasket surface for warp as follows:

a. Lay a machinist's straightedge across the cylinder at the positions shown in **Figure 77**.

b. Try to insert a flat feeler gauge between the straightedge and the machined surface of the cylinder. If clearance exists, record the maximum measurement.

c. Compare the measurements to the service limit in **Table 2**. If the clearance is not within the service limit, take the cylinder to a dealership or machine shop for further inspection and possible resurfacing.

6. If the cylinder is within all service limits, and the current piston and rings are reusable, clean the cylinder as described in Step 7. Do not remove the carbon ridge at the top of the cylinder (**Figure 78**). If new piston rings will be installed, hone the cylinder as follows:

a. Apply plenty of honing lubricant to the hone and cylinder surface.

b. Using a 240-grit Flex-Hone (**Figure 79**), move the hone quickly and smoothly in an up and down motion for 30 seconds. After the leading edge of the hone is in the cylinder, start the hone. The hone should continue to spin as it leaves the cylinder.

c. Hone the cylinder to a 45° crosshatch pattern.

7. Thoroughly wash and scrub the cylinder in hot, soapy water after inspection and service to remove all fine grit and material/residue left from machine operations. Solvents do not remove the fine grit left in the cylinder. Check cleanliness by rubbing a clean, white cloth over the bore. No residue should be evident. When the cylinder is thoroughly clean and dry, immediately coat the cylinder bore with oil to prevent corrosion. Wrap the cylinder until engine reassembly.

8. Inspect the front chain guide, dowels and cylinder mounting nuts (**Figure 80**) for wear or damage. Check the fit of the cylinder dowels prior to installing the cylinder. Often, dowels fit in one location better than another. Match the dowels to their pre-

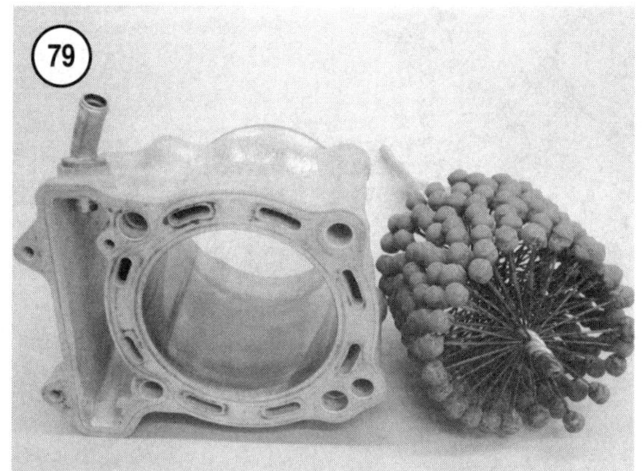

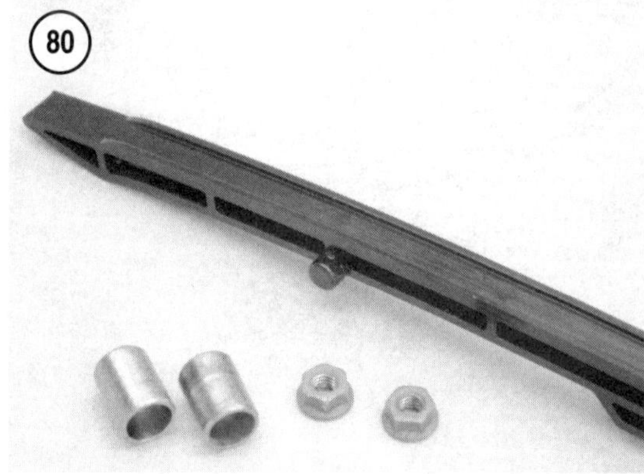

ferred bores to prevent jamming or binding during assembly.

9. Perform any service to the piston assembly before installing the cylinder.

Installation

1. Check that all gasket residue is removed from all mating surfaces.
2. Install a new, lubricated O-ring onto the oil jet (**Figure 75**), then seat the jet into the crankcase.
3. Install the dowels (**Figure 74**) and a new base gasket onto the crankcase.
4. Lubricate the following components with engine oil:
   a. Piston and rings.
   b. Piston pin and connecting rod.
   c. Cylinder bore.
5. Support the piston so the cylinder can be lowered into place.
6. Stagger the piston ring gaps on the piston as shown in **Figure 81**.

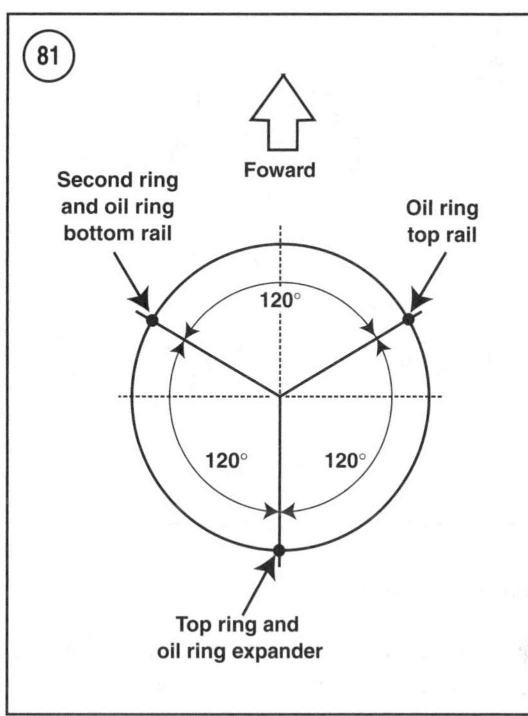

7. Lower the cylinder onto the crankcase.
   a. Route the cam chain and guide through the chain tunnel. Secure the cam chain so it cannot fall into the engine.
   b. As the piston enters the cylinder, compress each ring so it can enter the cylinder. A ring compressor can also be used. When the bottom ring is in the cylinder, remove any holding fixture and shop cloths from the crankcase.
8. Install and finger-tighten the cylinder mounting nuts (**Figure 73**). The nuts will be tightened after the cylinder head bolts are tightened.
9. Install the oil return tank hose (**Figure 72**) at the back of the cylinder.
10. Install the front cam chain guide. Check that the guide seats into its lower holder. If the guide is improperly installed, the cam chain may bind.
11. Install the cylinder head as described in this chapter.

PISTON AND PISTON RINGS

Refer to **Table 2** for specifications.

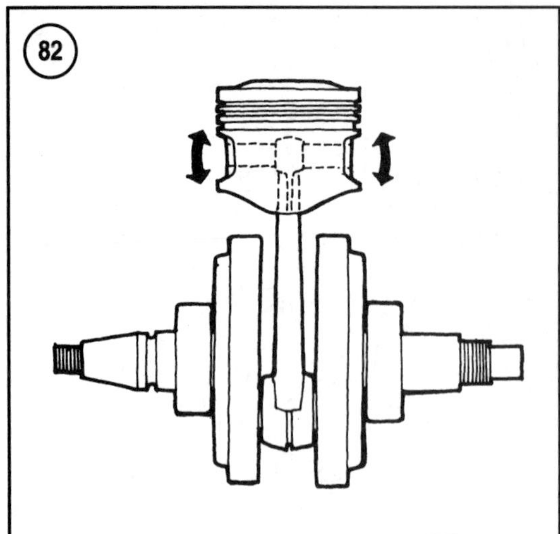
82

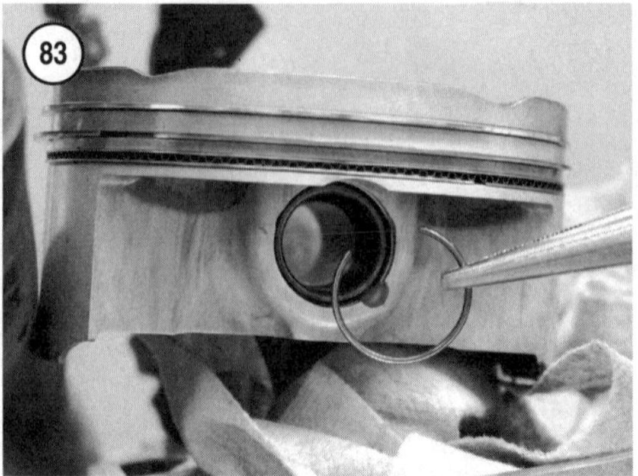
83

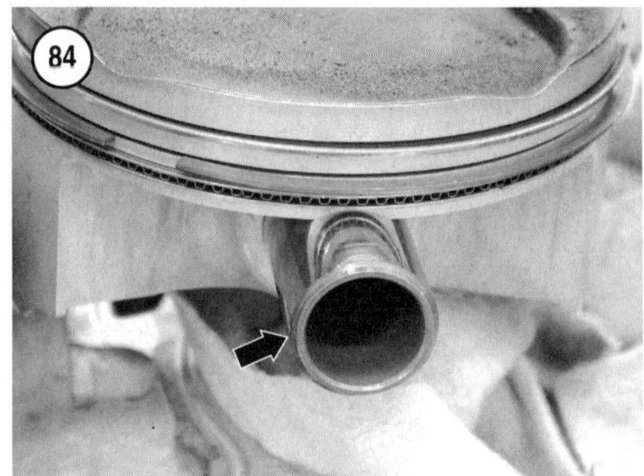
84

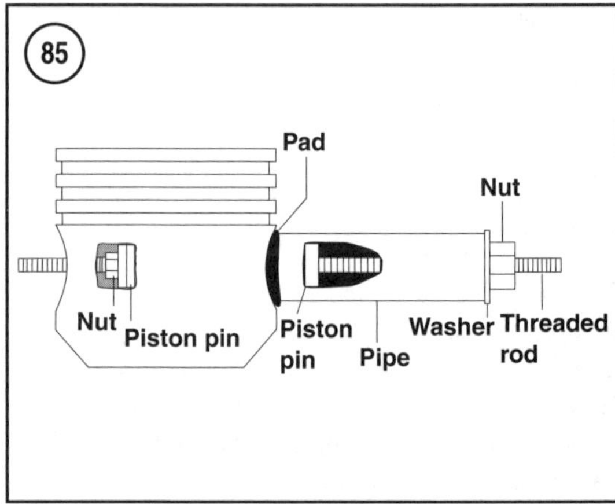

85

Piston Removal

1. Remove the cylinder as described in this chapter.
2. Before removing the piston, check the piston and piston pin for obvious play. Hold the rod and try to tilt the piston (**Figure 82**). If there is tilting (not sliding) motion, this indicates wear on either the piston pin, pin bore or connecting rod. Wear could be on any combination of the three parts.
3. Stuff clean shop cloths around the connecting rod and in the cam chain tunnel to prevent parts from entering the crankcase.
4. At the left side of the piston, rotate the ends of the circlip to the removal gaps, then remove the circlip from the piston pin bore (**Figure 83**). Discard the circlip. Install new circlips during assembly.
5. Press the piston pin (**Figure 84**) out of the piston by hand , then remove the piston. Do not drive the pin out with a hammer and drift. Remove the remaining circlip at the workbench. If the pin is tight, use a removal tool as shown in **Figure 85**. If this tool must be used, remove the remaining circlip before attempting pin removal.
6. Inspect the piston and piston pin as described in this section.

Piston Inspection

1. Remove the piston rings as described in this section.
2. Clean the piston.
   a. Clean the carbon from the piston crown. Use a soft scraper, brushes and solvent. Do not use tools that can gouge or scratch the surface. This type of damage can cause hot spots on the piston during engine operation.
   b. Clean the piston pin bore, ring grooves and piston skirt. Clean the ring grooves with a soft brush, or use a broken piston ring (**Figure 86**)

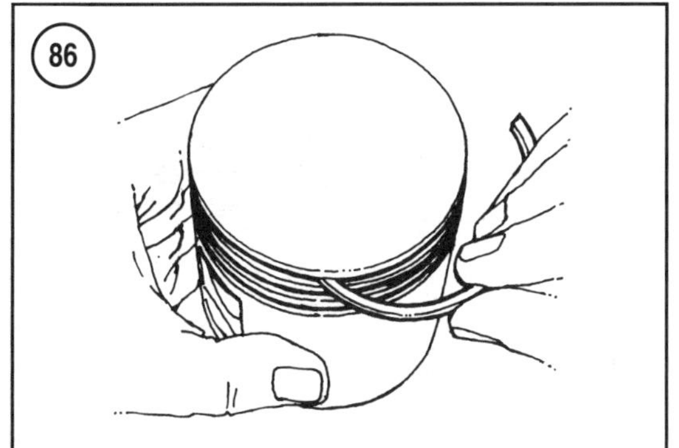
86

87

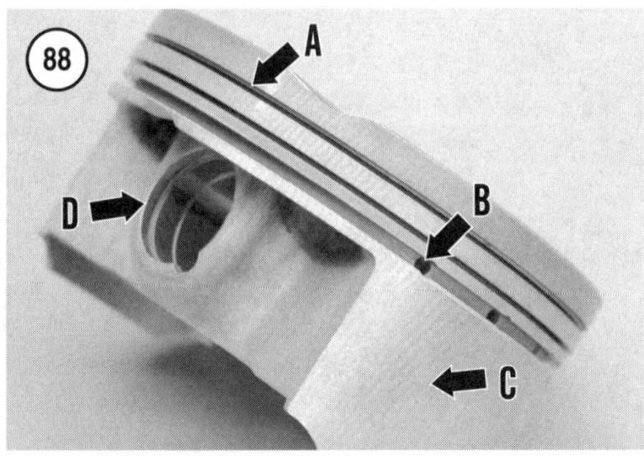

88

to remove carbon and oil residue. Mild galling or discoloration can be polished off the piston skirt with fine emery cloth and oil.

3. Inspect the piston. Replace the piston if there is damage.

   a. Inspect the piston crown (**Figure 87**) for wear or damage. If the piston is pitted, overheating is likely occurring.

   b. Inspect the ring grooves (A, **Figure 88**) for wear, nicks, cracks or other damage. The grooves should be square and uniform for the circumference of the piston. Inspect the top compression ring groove carefully. It is lubricated the least and is nearest to the combustion chamber. If the oil ring appears worn, or if the oil ring was difficult to remove, the piston has likely overheated and distorted.

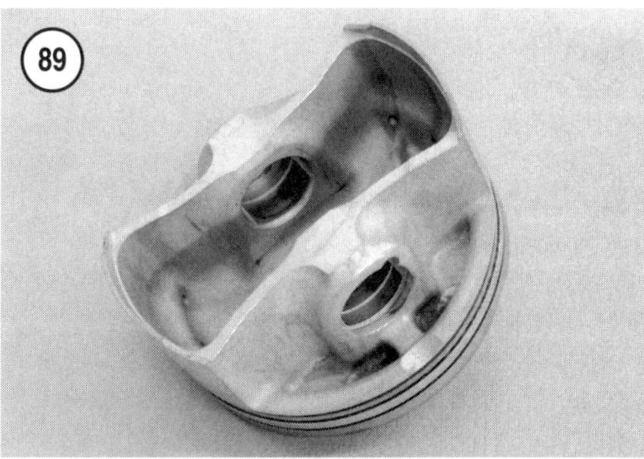
89

   c. Inspect the oil drain holes (B, **Figure 88**) for buildup. The holes must be clean to allow oil to return to the crankcase. Plugged holes can cause buildup in the oil control ring.

   d. Inspect the piston skirt (C, **Figure 88**). If the skirt has bits of metal embedded in the skirt or other signs of partial seizure, replace the piston.

   e. Check the pin bores and circlip grooves (D, **Figure 88**) for cleanliness and damage.

   f. Inspect the interior of the piston (**Figure 89**). Check the crown, skirt and bosses for cracks or other damage.

4. Measure the width of all ring grooves. Replace the piston if any measurement exceeds the specifications.

Piston to Cylinder Clearance Check

Measure the clearance between the piston and cylinder to determine if the parts can be reused. Clean and dry the piston and cylinder before measuring.

1. Measure the outside diameter of the piston (**Figure 90**). Make the measurement 15 mm (0.6 in.) from the bottom edge of the piston skirt and 90° to the direction of the piston pin. Record the measurement.

2. Determine clearance by subtracting the piston measurement from the largest cylinder measurement. If cylinder measurements are not yet known, refer to *Cylinder* in this chapter. If the clearance ex-

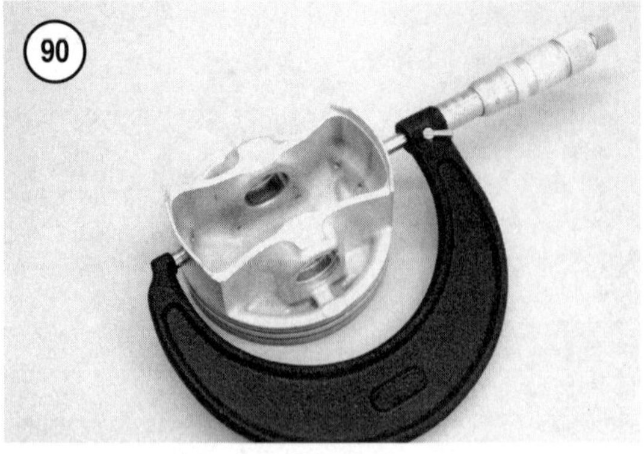

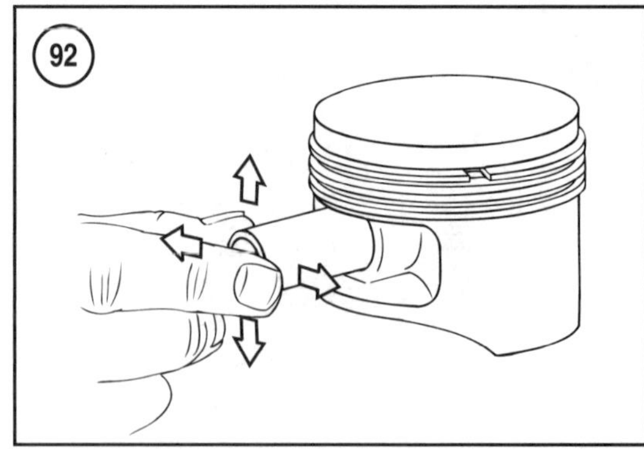

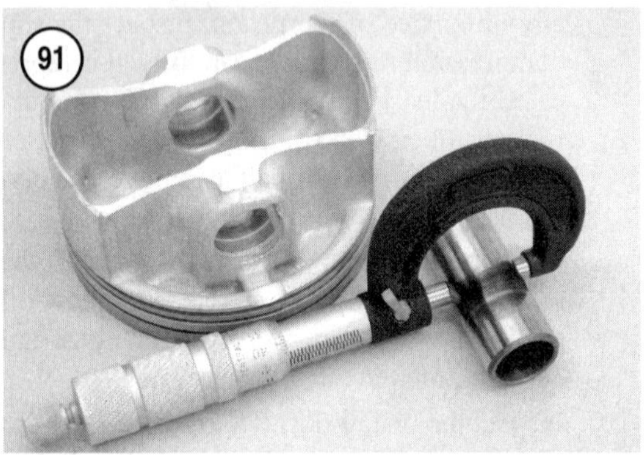

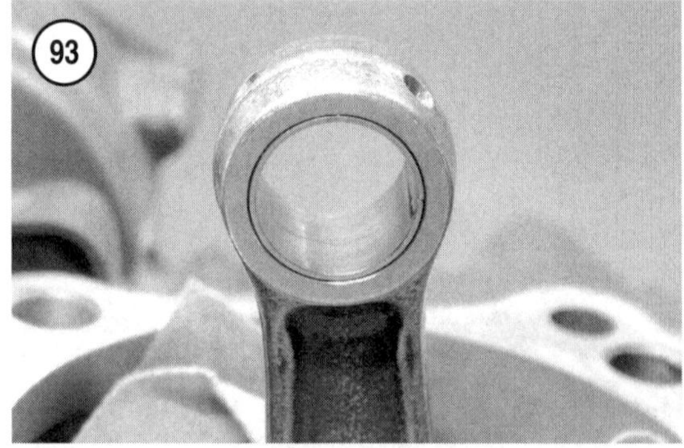

ceeds the specifications, determine which part(s) are worn.

Piston Pin Inspection

1. Clean the piston pin.
2. Inspect the pin for chrome flaking, wear or discoloration from overheating.
3. Measure the outside diameter of the piston pin (**Figure 91**). Measure the pin near both ends and in the middle. Record the measurements.
4. Inspect the pin bores in the piston.
   a. Check for scoring, uneven wear and discoloration from overheating. Lubricate the piston pin and slide it into the pin bores. Check for general fit and radial play (**Figure 92**). The pin should freely and smoothly slide and rotate.
   b. Measure the inside diameter of the piston bores. Record the measurements.
5. Inspect the bore in the small end of the connecting rod (**Figure 93**).
   a. Check for scoring, uneven wear and discoloration from overheating. Lubricate the piston pin with engine oil and slide it into the connecting rod (**Figure 94**). Check for general fit and radial play (**Figure 95**). The pin should freely and smoothly slide and rotate.
   b. Measure the inside diameter of the bore. Record the measurement.
6. If necessary, replace parts that are worn, damaged or out of specification.

Piston Ring Inspection and Removal

The piston is fitted with two compression rings and an oil control ring assembly. The oil ring assem-

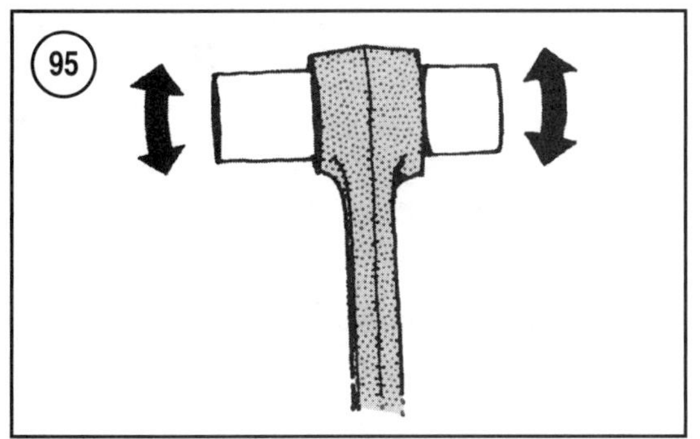

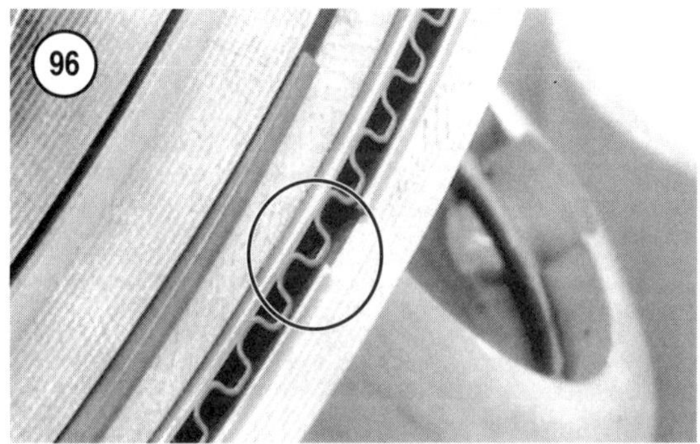

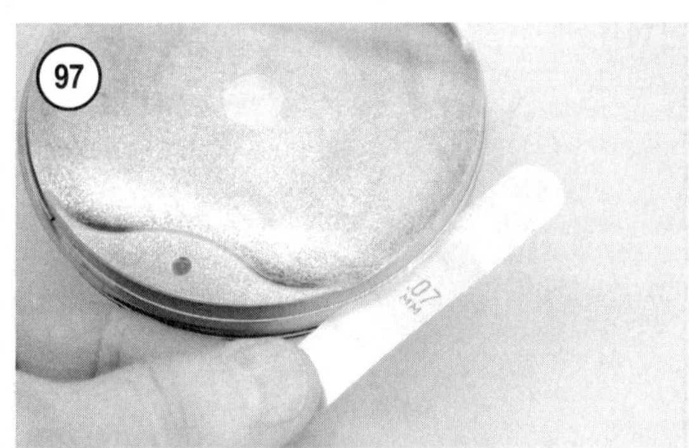

bly consists of two side rails and an expander ring (**Figure 96**).

1. Check the piston ring to ring groove clearance as follows:
   a. Clean the rings and grooves so accurate measurements can be made with a flat feeler gauge.
   b. Press the top ring into the piston groove.
   c. At the bottom side of the ring, insert a flat feeler gauge between the ring and groove (**Figure 97**). Record the measurement. Repeat this step at other points around the piston. If any measurement is out of specification, check the ring thickness, as described in Step 5. Also

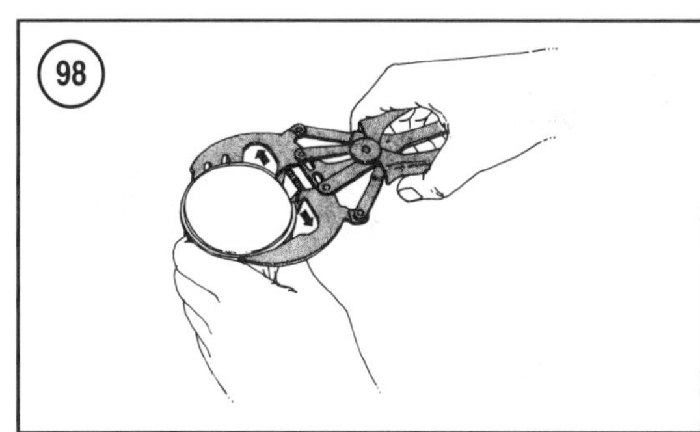

check the ring groove width as described in *Piston Inspection* in this section. Replace the worn or damaged part(s).
   d. Repeat substep b and susbstep c for the second compression ring. The oil control ring is not measured.
2. Remove the top and second rings with a ring expander (**Figure 98**) or by hand (**Figure 99**).
   a. Spread the rings only enough to clear the piston.
   b. As each ring is removed, mark the top surface if they will be reinstalled. The second ring is marked with an *R*; however, it will likely be worn away.
3. Remove the oil ring assembly by first removing the top rail, followed by the bottom rail. Remove (by hand) the expander ring last.
4. Clean and inspect the piston as described in *Piston Inspection* in this section.
5. Measure the thickness of the top and second rings (**Figure 100**). Note that the top ring is measured on its inner and outer thickness. Replace all the rings if any measurement is out of specification.
6. Inspect the end gap of the top and second rings as follows:
   a. Measure the free end gap of both rings (**Figure 101**).

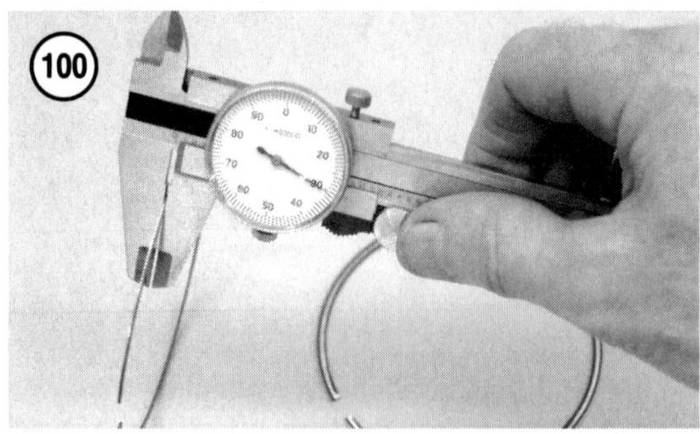

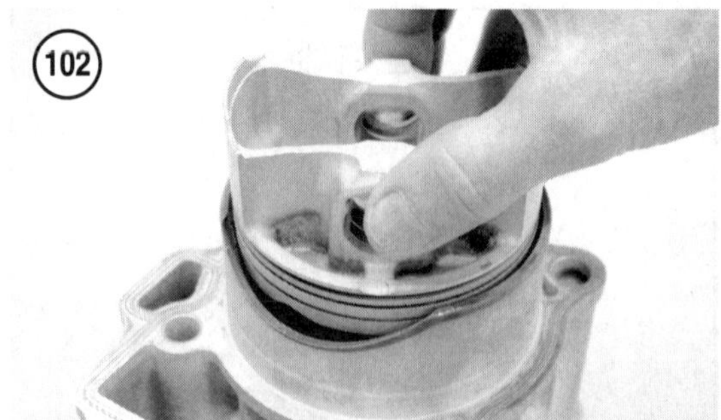

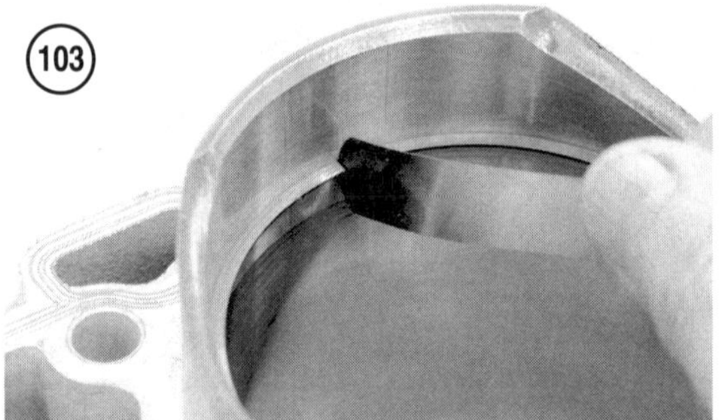

b. Measure the end gap of each ring as it is fitted in the cylinder. Insert a ring into the bottom of the cylinder. Then use the piston to square the ring to the cylinder wall (**Figure 102**). Measure the end gap with a feeler gauge (**Figure 103**). Replace the ring set if any measurement is out of specification. If new rings are to be installed, gap the new rings after the cylinder has been serviced. If the new ring gap is too narrow, carefully widen the gap using a fine-cut file as shown in **Figure 104**. Work slow and measure often.

7. Roll each ring around its piston groove and check for binding or snags. Repair minor damage with a fine-cut file.

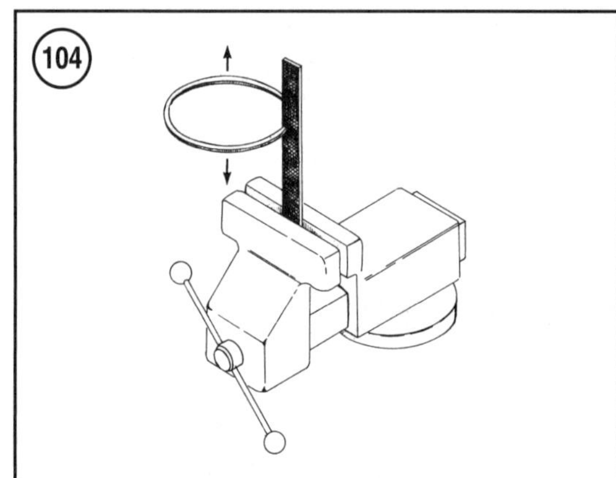

Piston Ring Installation

If new piston rings will be installed, hone the cylinder. Refer to *Cylinder* in this chapter.

1. Make sure the piston and rings are clean and dry. When installing, spread the rings only enough to clear the piston.
2. Install the rings as follows:
   a. Install the oil ring expander in the bottom groove, followed by the bottom rail and top rail. The ends of the expander must *not* overlap. The rails can be installed in either position and direction.
   b. Install the second ring. Make sure the *R* mark faces up (**Figure 105**).
   c. Install the top ring. If not marked, install the ring as shown in **Figure 106**. The lip on the outer edge must face up.
3. Check that all rings rotate freely in their grooves.

Piston Installation

1. Install the piston rings onto the piston as described in this section.

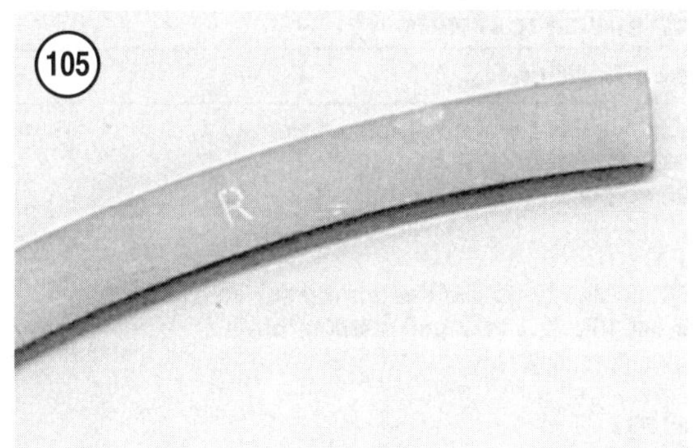

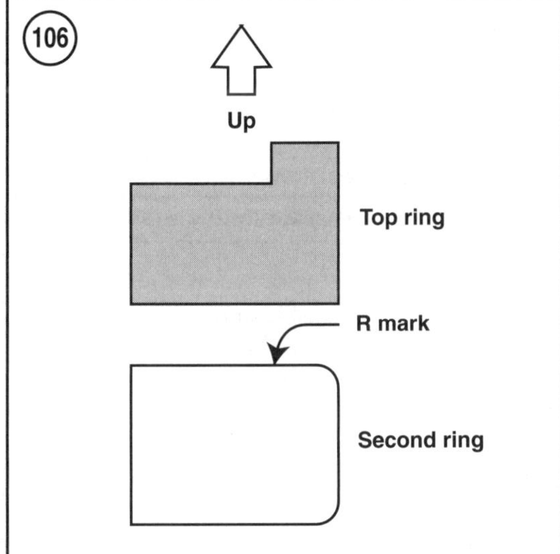

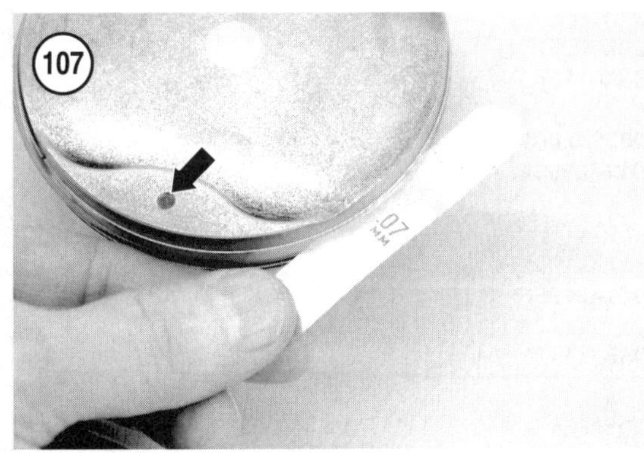

2. Check that all parts are clean and ready to be installed. Keep the engine openings covered and use new circlips when installing the piston.

CAUTION
Never install used circlips. Engine damage could occur. Circlips fatigue and distort when they are removed, even though they appear reusable.

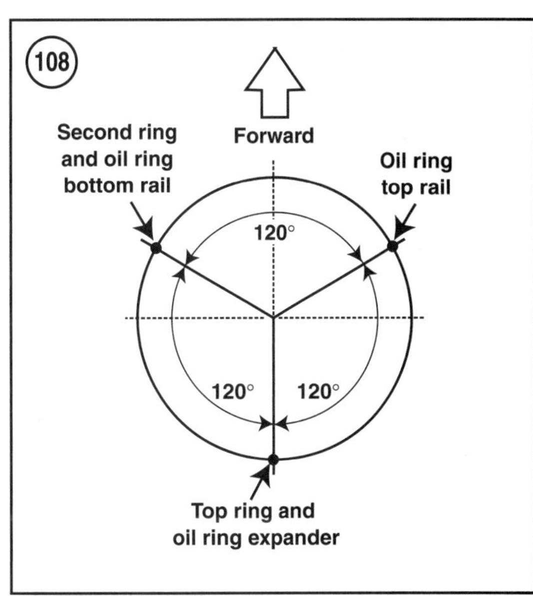

3. Install a new circlip into the right piston pin boss. Rotate the ends of the circlip away from the gap. By installing the circlip in the right boss, the remaining circlip can be installed at the left side of the engine, away from the cam chain tunnel.

4. Lubricate these components with engine oil:

   a. Piston pin.

   b. Piston pin bores.

   c. Connecting rod bore.

5. Start the piston pin into the open pin bore, then place the piston over the connecting rod. The indention on the piston crown (**Figure 107**) *must* point forward.

6. Align the piston with the rod, then slide the pin through the rod and into the other piston bore.

7. Install a new circlip into the left piston pin boss. Rotate the ends of the circlip away from the gap.

8. Stagger the piston ring gaps on the piston as shown in **Figure 108**.

9. Install the cylinder as described in this chapter.

10. Refer to Chapter Three for break-in procedures.

Table 1 GENERAL ENGINE SPECIFICATIONS

	Specification
Type	4-stroke, OHV, water cooled single
Bore × stroke	90.0 × 62.6 mm (3.543 x 2.464 in.)
Displacement	398 cc (24.3 cu. in.)
Compression	
Ratio	11.3:1
Pressure	1000 kPa (142 psi) w/ decompressor activated
Oil pressure	40-140 kPa (5.8-20.3 psi) at 3000 rpm
Valve timing	
Intake	
Open	19° BTDC
Closed	53° ABDC
Duration	252°
Exhaust	
Open	48° BBDC
Closed	11° ATDC
Duration	239°

Table 2 ENGINE TOP END SPECIFICATIONS

	Specification mm (in.)	Service limit mm (in.)
Camshaft		
Cam lobe height		
Intake	36.320-36.370 (1.429-1.431)	36.020 (1.418)
Exhaust	35.200-35.250 (1.385-1.387)	34.9 (1.374)
Cam journal oil clearance	0.019-0.053 (0.0007-0.0021)	0.150 (0.006)
Camshaft journal holder inside diameter	22.012-22.025 (0.8666-0.8671)	–
Camshaft journal outside diameter	21.972-21.993 (0.8650-0.8659)	–
Camshaft runout	–	0.10 (0.0039)
Cylinder head warp	–	0.05 (0.002)
Cylinder head cover warp	–	0.05 (0.002)
Valves and valve springs		
Valve tappet clearance (cold)		
Intake	0.10-0.20 (0.0039-0.0078)	–
Exhaust	0.20-0.30 (0.0078-0.0118)	–
Stem-to-guide clearance		
Intake	0.010-0.037 (0.00039-0.0015)	–
Exhaust	0.030-0.057 (0.0012-0.0022)	–
Valve stem deflection	–	0.35 (0.014)
Valve stem outside diameter		
Intake	4.975-4.990 (0.1957-0.1965)	–
Exhaust	4.955-4.970 (0.1951-0.1957)	–
Valve guide inside diameter (intake/exhaust)	5.000-5.012 (0.1968-0.1973)	–
Valve seat width (intake/exhaust)	0.9-1.1 (0.035-0.043)	–
Valve stem runout	–	0.05 (0.002)
Valve head thickness	–	0.5 (0.02)
Valve head radial runout	–	0.03 (0.001)
Valve spring free length	–	38.8 (1.53)
Valve seat surface angle	45°	
Valve seat cutting angle		
Intake	30°, 45°, 60°	
Exhaust	15°, 45°, 60°	

(continued)

Table 2 ENGINE TOP END SPECIFICATIONS (continued)

	Specification mm (in.)	Service limit mm (in.)
Cylinder		
Bore inside diameter	90.000-90.015 (3.5433-3.5439)	–
Distortion	–	0.05 (0.002)
Piston-to-cylinder clearance	0.030-0.040 (0.0012-0.0016)	0.120 (0.0047)
Piston		
Outside diameter	89.965-89.980 (3.5419-3.5425)	89.880 (3.5386)
Outside diameter measuring point	15 (0.6) from bottom of skirt	
Piston pin bore inside diameter	20.002-20.008 (0.7875-0.7877)	20.030 (0.7886)
Piston pin outside diameter	19.995-20.000 (0.7872-0.7874)	19.980 (0.7866)
Piston groove width		
Top	0.78-0.80 (0.0307-0.0315)	–
Top (with shoulder)	1.30-1.32 (0.0512-0.0520)	–
Second	0.81-0.83 (0.0319-0.0327)	–
Oil	2.01-2.03 (0.0791-0.799)	–
Ring-to-groove clearance		
Top	–	0.180 (0.007)
Second	–	0.150 (0.006)
Piston rings		
Ring free end gap (uncompressed)		
Top	Approx. 6.9 (0.27)	5.5 (0.22)
Second	Approx. 11.5 (0.45)	9.2 (0.36)
Ring end gap (compressed)		
Top	0.08-0.20 (0.003-0.008)	0.5 (0.020)
Second	0.08-0.20 (0.003-0.008)	0.5 (0.020)
Ring thickness		
Top	0.71-0.76 (0.0280-0.0299)	–
Top (with shoulder)	1.08-1.10 (0.0425-0.0433)	–
Second	0.77-0.79 (0.0303-0.0311)	–

Table 3 ENGINE TOP END TORQUE SPECIFICATIONS

Item	N•m	in.-lb.	ft.-lb.
Camshaft			
Cap bolts	10	89	–
Tensioner mounting bolts	10	89	–
Tensioner spring bolt	30	–	22
Cylinder head bolt			
M10			
Initial	25	–	18
Final	46	–	34
M6	10	89	–
Cylinder head cover bolt	14	124	–
Cylinder head side bolt	14	124	–
Engine mounting bracket bolts			
Bracket-to-frame	40	–	30
Bracket-to-engine	66	–	49
Engine oil drain bolt	25	–	18
Exhaust pipe nuts	23	–	17
Muffler clamp bolt	23	–	17
Muffler mounting bolt	23	–	17
Rocker arm holder acorn nut	30	–	22
Rocker arm holder bolt	30	–	22
Rocker arm shaft bolt	7	62	–
Thermostat housing bolts	10	89	–
Timing hole plug	23	–	17

CHAPTER FIVE

ENGINE LOWER END

This chapter describes procedures for the following:

1. Engine removal.
2. Crankcase bearings and seals.
3. Balancer and primary driven gears.
4. Transmission assembly.
5. Crankshaft and connecting rod.
6. Oil pump.
7. Oil strainer and oil screen.
8. Oil cooler.
9. Crankcase and crankshaft.

The text frequently mentions the front and rear sides of the engine. Remember, these terms refer to the engine as installed in the frame, not how it is on the workbench.

Refer to Chapter One for general procedures for engine overhaul.

When inspecting lower end components, compare measurements to the specifications in **Table 1**. Replace any component that is damaged, worn to the service limit or out of specification. During assembly, tighten fasteners to the torque specifications in **Table 2**. **Table 1** and **Table 2** are at the end of this chapter.

ENGINE

Engine Service in the Frame

NOTE
During engine removal, make note of mounting bolt directions and how cables and wire harnesses are routed.

If the engine requires crankcase disassembly, it is easier to remove all the sub-assemblies before removing the engine from the frame. By following this method, the frame holds the engine during disassembly. The following components can be removed while the engine is in the frame.

1. Left side:
   a. Front sprocket.
   b. Starter clutch and idle gear.
   c. Alternator rotor.
   d. Gear position switch.
   e. Reverse cable.
   f. Clutch release arm.
2. Right side:
   a. Exhaust pipe.
   b. Oil filter.
   c. Clutch.
   d. Primary drive gear assembly.
   e. Oil pump.
   f. Gearshift mechanism.
   g. Engine balancer driven gear.
3. Center:

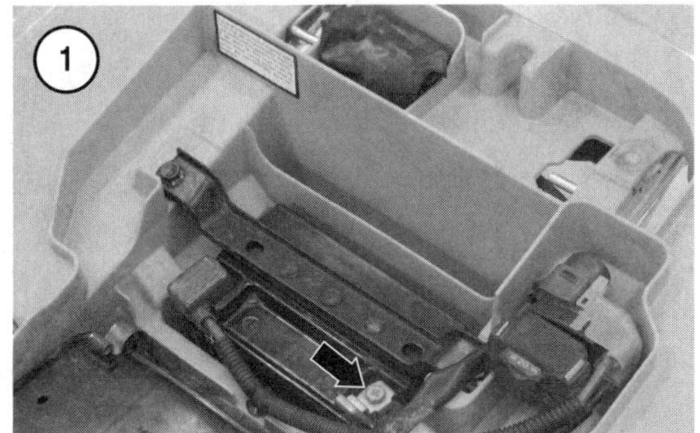

a. Carburetor.
b. Starter.
c. Cam chain tension adjuster.
d. Cylinder head/cover.
e. Camshaft/Automatic decompression assembly.
f. Cylinder head.
g. Cylinder.
h. Piston.
i. Cam chain.

Engine Removal

1. Park the vehicle on a level surface and set the parking brake.
2. Remove the seat, skid plate, bodywork, footguard assemblies and footpegs as described in Chapter Fourteen.
3. Remove the fuel tank as described in Chapter Eight.
4. Drain the engine oil as described in Chapter Three.
5. Remove the gearshift lever and spacers as described in Chapter Six.
6. Disconnect the negative battery cable (**Figure 1**).
7. Remove the spark plug wire.
8. Remove the crankcase breather hose and oil return tank with the hose attached as described in this chapter.
9. Drain the engine coolant as described in Chapter Three.
10. Disconnect the coolant hoses at the engine.
11. Remove the exhaust pipe as described in Chapter Four.
12. Remove the air box and carburetor as described in Chapter Eight.
13. Remove the starter cable and starter as described in Chapter Nine.
14. Remove the two bolts securing the engine sprocket cover. Remove the cable holder with the cover as described in Chapter Twelve. Remove the drive chain from the drive sprocket.
15. Remove the bracket securing the clutch cable and remove the cable from the clutch mechanism yoke as described in Chapter Three.
16. Disconnect the generator wire couplers and gear position switch wire couplers as described in Chapter Nine.
17. Remove the reverse selector cable and bracket as described in Chapter Three.
18. Remove the gear position switch as described in Chapter Nine.
19. Remove the oil outlet pipe (**Figure 2**) on the right side of the engine and the engine inlet pipe (A, **Figure 3**) on the bottom of the engine.
20. Remove the top end of the engine as described in Chapter Four.
21. Inspect the engine and verify that it is ready for removal.
22. Place a jack under the frame.
23. Remove the engine mounting bolts and brackets as follows:
    a. Loosen the right front engine mount but do *not* remove the bolts (**Figure 4**).

b. Remove the left front engine mount (**Figure 5**) and mark it so it can be installed in its correct position .
c. Remove the lower engine mounting bolt (A, **Figure 6**) and spacers (B, **Figure 3**).
d. Remove the swing arm bolt (B, **Figure 6**).

24. Remove the engine from the left side of the frame.
25. Push the swing arm pivot bolt back into the frame.
26. Clean and inspect the frame (**Figure 7**) for cracks and damage, particularly at the welded joints.
27. Refer to *Crankcase* in this chapter for further disassembly.

Engine Installation

1. Note the following before installing the engine:
   a. The swing arm pivots through the engine cases. There will need to be a jack in place under the frame of the vehicle for installation of the engine.
   b. If the chain is endless (no master link) and has been removed from the swing arm, check that it is routed over the swing arm pivot bolt before installing the new pivot bolt.
   c. Install new O-rings where they are used.
2. Mount the right engine mount but do not tighten the bolts (**Figure 8**) securing the mount.
3. Move the engine into the frame from the left side. Rotate the engine forward in the frame to allow the rear engine mounts to clear the swing arm pivot (**Figure 9**).
4. Insert the lower engine mounting bolt (A, **Figure 6**) and spacers (B, **Figure 3**).

NOTE
Do not leave out the spacers on the lower engine mounting bolt. The engine will not be secure in the frame without the spacers (B, ***Figure 3****).*

5. Place a jack under the frame to align the swing arm pivot with the crankcase (**Figure 10**).

CAUTION
The engine mounting nuts are self-locking. Once the nuts are removed, they must be replaced with new ones. Never reuse self-locking nuts.

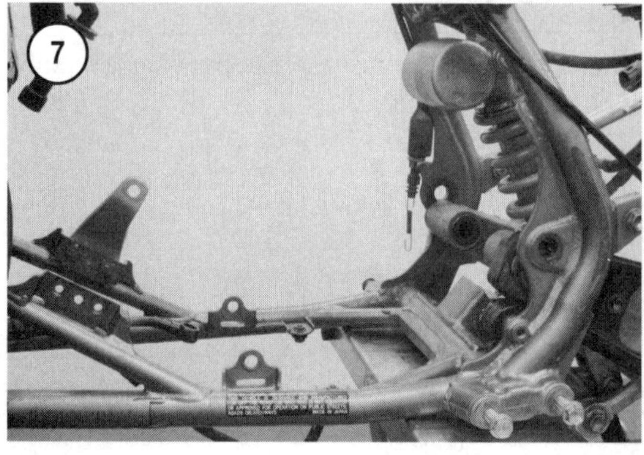

NOTE
The following step may require an assistant or an additional jack to align the swing arm, crankcase and frame.

6. Insert the swing arm bolt (B, **Figure 6**), but do not tighten it .

7. Install the left front engine mount (**Figure 5**) and finger- tighten the bolts.

8. Tighten the lower engine mounting bolt to 66 N•m (49 ft.-lb.).

9. Tighten the lower engine bracket bolts to 26 N•m (19 ft.-lb.).
10. Tighten the upper front engine mounting bolts to 66 N•m (49 ft.-lb.).
11. Tighten the swing arm bolt to 95 N•m (70 ft.-lb.).
12. Reassemble all sub-assemblies as described previously or in the appropriate chapter.

CRANKCASE

When the two halves of the crankcase are disassembled or split, the crankshaft, balancer and transmission assemblies can be removed for inspection and repair. All assemblies located in the crankcase covers must be removed to separate the crankcase.

Do not hammer or excessively pry on the crankcase. The crankcase will fracture or break. The case halves are aligned by dowels, and sealed with sealant.

Disassembly

While removing components, keep the parts organized and clean. Leave the left case half facing up until the balancer and transmission assembly have been removed.

1. Place the engine on wooden blocks and loosen the crankcase bolts on both sides of the engine (**Figure 11** and **Figure 12**). Loosen each bolt 1/4 turn, working in a crisscross pattern. Loosen the bolts until they can be removed by hand.
2. Remove the bolts as follows:
   a. Make a drawing of the crankcase shape on a piece of cardboard.
   b. Punch holes in the cardboard for each bolt location.
   c. Place each bolt and clamp in its respective hole in the cardboard (**Figure 13**).
3. Separate the crankcase halves as follows:
   a. With the right side of the engine facing up, install a crankcase separating tool (Suzuki part No. 09920-13120), or similar puller as shown in **Figure 14**. Thread the bolts into the crankcase, keeping the center bolt squarely positioned on the end of the crankshaft. Lubricate the tool threads and contact point on the crankshaft.
   b. Turn the center bolt and separate the case halves. If the case half does not raise evenly,

5

11

RIGHT SIDE CRANKCASE BOLTS

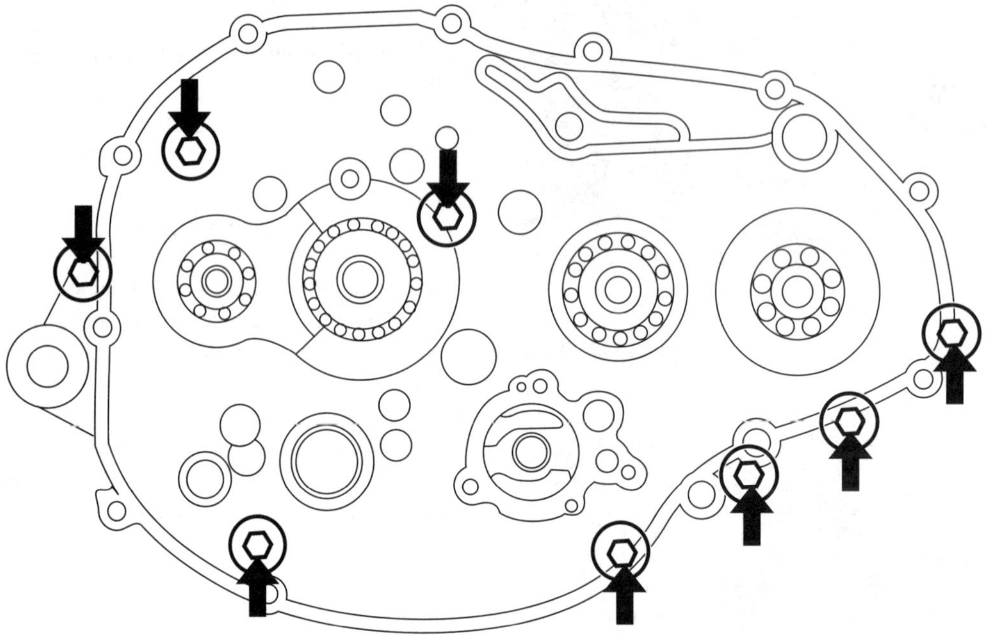

12

LEFT SIDE CRANKCASE BOLTS

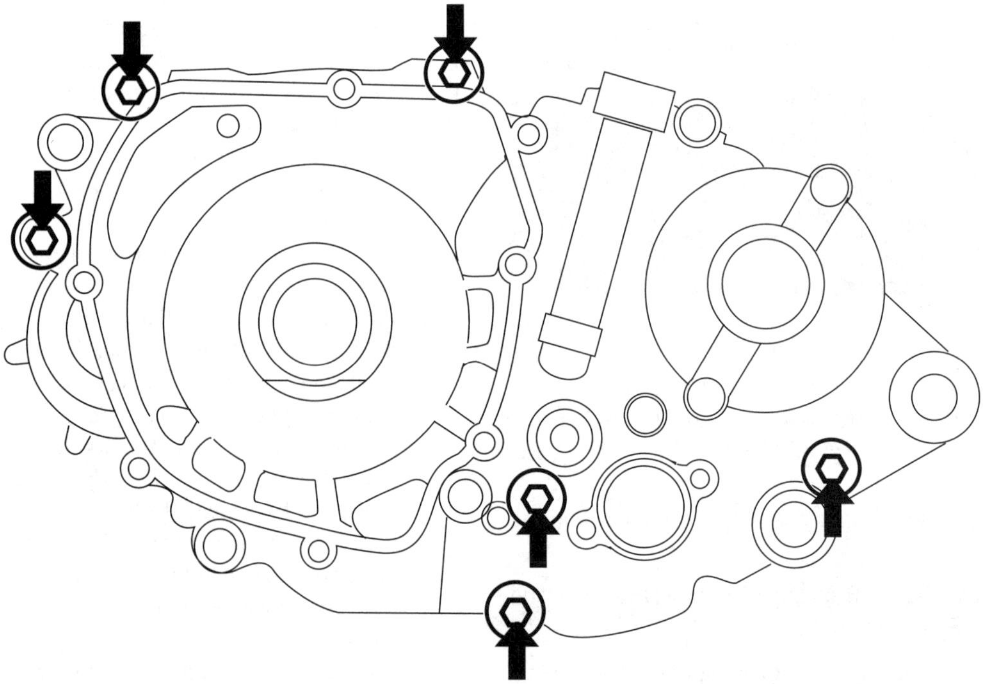

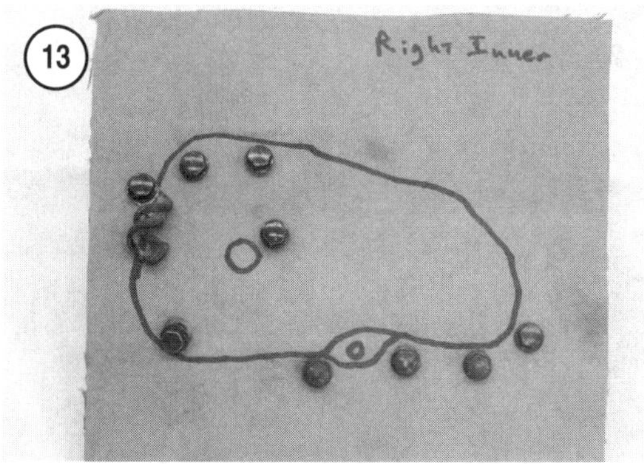

this can be caused by a seized dowel or a transmission shaft that is tight in its bearings. Do not force the crankcase apart. Lower and reseat the case halves. Apply penetrating lubricant around the shafts. Again, raise the case half a small amount, then insert a putty knife at the rear of the case half (**Figure 15**). Use the putty knife to help raise the case half equally. Do not pry with any tool that can damage the gasket surfaces. Using a mallet, tap the ends of the transmission shafts. Repeat the lowering and raising process until the case halves separate freely.

c. Account for the two dowels (**Figure 16**) between the case halves.

4. Remove the balancer (**Figure 17**). Inspect the balancer as described in this chapter.

5. Remove the transmission assembly as follows:

   a. Remove the two shift fork shafts (**Figure 18**).

   b. Spread the forks and remove the shift drum (A, **Figure 19**).

   c. Remove the No. 1 and No. 2 shift forks (B, **Figure 19**). Make note of the markings on each fork and its position in the crankcase.

d. Remove the No. 3 shift fork (**Figure 20**).
e. Remove the reverse shaft spring from the left case half (A, **Figure 21**).
f. Remove the first gear thrust washer (B, **Figure 21**) and first gear (C, **Figure 21**) and the first gear bushing.
g. Remove the thrust washer (**Figure 22**) from the reverse idle shaft.
h. Remove the spring washer (A, **Figure 23**) and reverse idle gear (B) from the reverse idle shaft.
i. Remove the reverse idle gear bushing and thrust washer (**Figure 24**).
j. Remove the reverse idle gear shaft (A, **Figure 25**), input shaft (B) and output shaft(C).
k. Disassemble and inspect the transmission components (Chapter Seven).

6. Remove the oil pipes from the right case half (**Figure 26** and **Figure 27**).

7. Remove the oil sump strainer (**Figure 28**) from the right case half .

8. If necessary, remove the crankshaft. Unless obviously damaged, the crankshaft does not have to be removed for most inspection procedures. To install the crankshaft, a crankshaft installer tool is required to pull the crankshaft into the case half. Remove the crankshaft as follows:

a. Attach a crankcase separating tool (Suzuki part No. 09920-13120), or similar puller as shown in **Figure 29**. Thread the bolts into the crankcase, keeping the center bolt squarely positioned on the end of the crankshaft. Lubricate the tool threads and contact point on the crankshaft.
b. If available, use a heat gun to heat the crankshaft bearing.

24

28

25

29

26

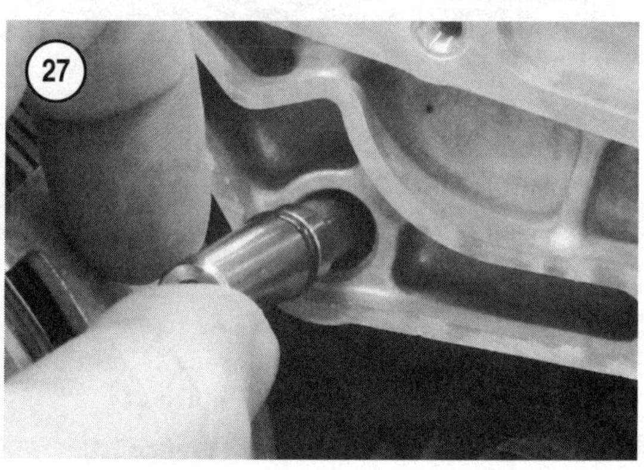
27

c. Working on a stable surface, turn the center bolt and pull the case half from the crankshaft.

d. Inspect the crankshaft as described in this chapter.

Assembly

1. During assembly, note the following:
   a. Make sure all mating surfaces are smooth, clean and dry. Minor irregularities can be repaired with an oil stone. After thorough removal of the old sealant, clean all mating surfaces with brake cleaner or electrical contact cleaner.
   b. Lubricate the crankshaft, bearings and transmission assembly with engine oil.
   c. Lubricate seal lips with grease.
   d. To install the crankshaft, a crankshaft installation set (crankshaft installer [Suzuki part No. 09910-32812] and attachment [Suzuki part no. 09940-52861]), or equivalent, is required.

30

31

e. To seal the crankcase halves, use Suzuki Bond 1207B. Do *not* use RVT sealant.

2. Install the crankshaft into the left case half as follows:

a. Lubricate the bearing bore, crankshaft and installer threads with engine oil.

b. Place the left crankcase on wooden blocks, with the open side of the case facing down.

c. If available, use a heat gun to heat the bearing bore.

d. Center the attachment over the crankcase bearing. Then thread the installer onto the crankshaft (**Figure 30**).

e. Hold the assembly stable and turn the T-handle to draw the crankshaft toward the bore. When the crankshaft is touching the bore, check all alignments.

f. Turn the T-handle (**Figure 31**) and fully seat the crankshaft into the bearing.

g. Remove the installer tools.

3. Seat the small oil pipe into the right case half (**Figure 32**). Install new, lubricated O-rings onto the pipe.

4. Install the oil sump strainer into the right case half (**Figure 28**). Apply threadlocking compound to the bolt threads, then securely tighten the bolts.

5. Place the left case half so the open side is facing up.

6. Install the transmission as follows:

a. Install the reverse idle gear shaft (A, **Figure 25**), input shaft (B) and output shaft (C).

b. Install the reverse idle gear bushing and thrust washer (**Figure 24**).

c. Install the spring washer (A, **Figure 23**) and reverse idle gear (B) on the reverse idle shaft.

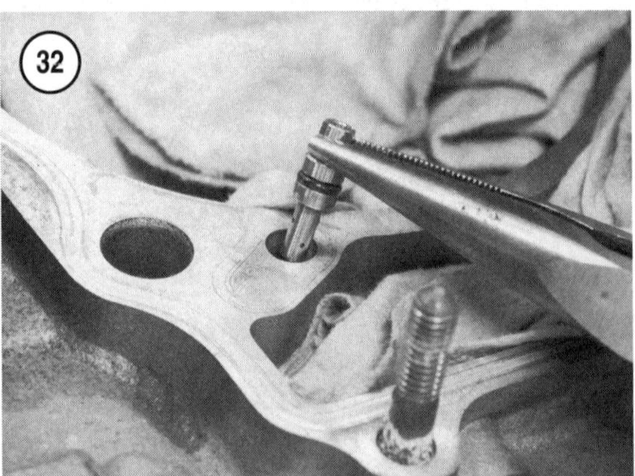
32

33

d. Install the thrust washer on the reverse idle shaft (**Figure 22**).

e. Install the first gear thrust washer (B, **Figure 21**) and first gear (C) and the first gear bushing.

f. Install the reverse shaft spring from the left half of the crankcase (A, **Figure 21**).

g. Install the No. 3 shift fork (**Figure 20**).

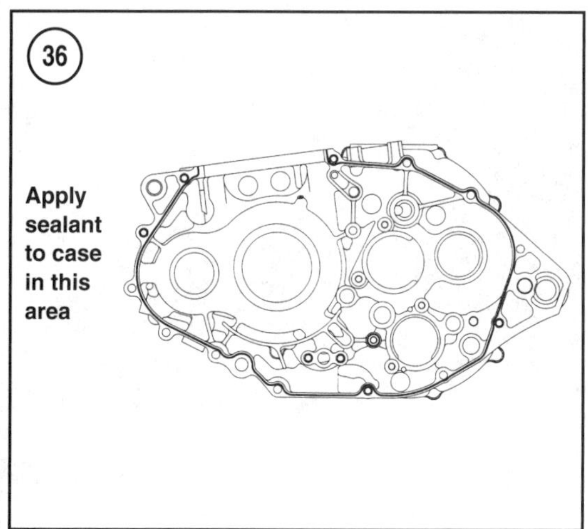

h. Install the No. 1 and No. 2 shift forks (B, **Figure 19**).

i. Engage the forks into their slots on the shift drum.

j. Install the two shift fork shafts (**Figure 33**).

7. Install the balancer (**Figure 34**).

8. Install the right case half onto the left case half as follows:

a. Check that all mating surfaces are clean and dry.

b. On the left case half, insert the two dowels (**Figure 35**).

c. On the right case half, apply the sealant to the mating surface as shown in **Figure 36**. Use only enough sealant to fill voids and provide a continuous seal on the entire joint.

d. Check that all shafts are aligned vertically, then fit the right case half squarely onto the left case half.

e. If necessary, *tap* the right case half with a mallet so it evenly seats. If the crankcase will not seat, a shaft is probably misaligned with its bore. Lift the right case half and slightly move it side to side until the shaft(s) are properly guided.

9. Install the large oil pipe (**Figure 37**) into the right case half. Install new, lubricated O-rings onto the pipe, then insert the pipe into the case. Use a small flashlight to verify that the long end of the pipe seats properly. Note that this pipe is secured by a crankcase bolt.

10. Remove each crankcase bolt from the template and insert the bolts and guides into the appropriate holes. Finger-tighten the bolts (**Figure 11** and **Figure 12**). Install any removed retainers to the exterior of the cases.

11. Tighten the bolts equally in several passes and in a crisscross pattern. Tighten the bolts to 11 N•m (97 in.-lb.).

12. Rotate the crankshaft and check for smooth operation. If binding is evident, lightly tap the ends of

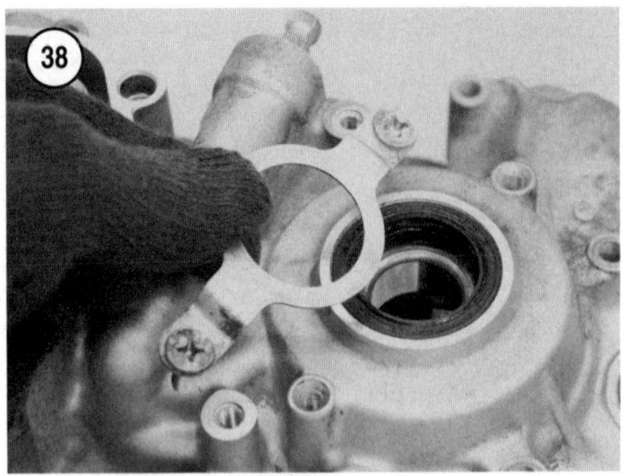

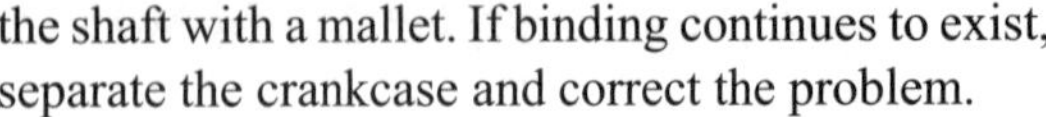

the shaft with a mallet. If binding continues to exist, separate the crankcase and correct the problem.

13. Rotate the transmission shafts and check for smooth operation. If binding or poor operation is evident, lightly tap the ends of the shafts with a mallet. If binding or poor operation continues to exist, separate the crankcase and correct the problem. Thread a bolt and locknut into the end of the shift drum and check for proper shifting through the gears. Rotate the shafts to aid in shifting. Since the shafts are not rotating very fast, it is normal for the gears to not engage as precisely as they do in actual operation. The transmission should be in neutral and both shafts should turn independently of one another.

14. Allow the sealant to set for a minimum of one hour. When the sealant is completely dry, trim the excess from the cylinder seating surface.

15. Install the crankcase into the frame or complete engine reassembly on the wokbench.

CRANKCASE SEALS

Output Shaft Seal Replacement

1. Remove the seal retainer (**Figure 38**).

CAUTION

*When prying, do not allow the end of the tool to touch the seal bore or snag the oil hole in the bore (**Figure 39**). Scratches in the bore will cause a leak and heavy-handed prying can break the casting.*

2. Pry out the seal (**Figure 40**). If necessary, place a block of wood on the crankcase for leverage and to

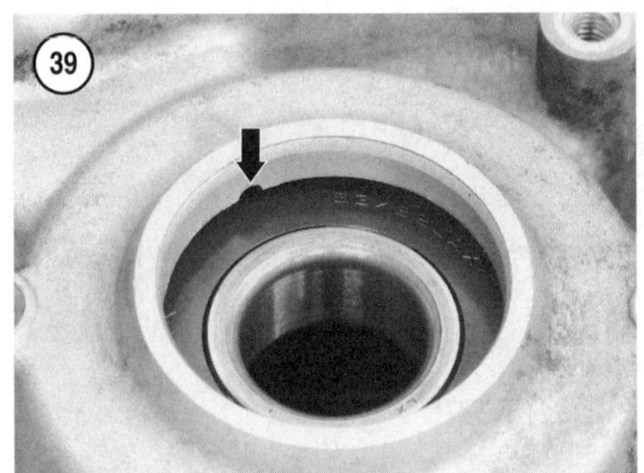

protect the crankcase from damage. Warming the seal with a heat gun will ease removal.

3. If a new bearing will be installed, replace the bearing before installing the new seal.

4. Clean the seal bore.

5. Apply grease to the lip and sides of the new seal.

6. Place the seal over the bore, with the closed side of the seal facing out. The seal must be square to the bore.

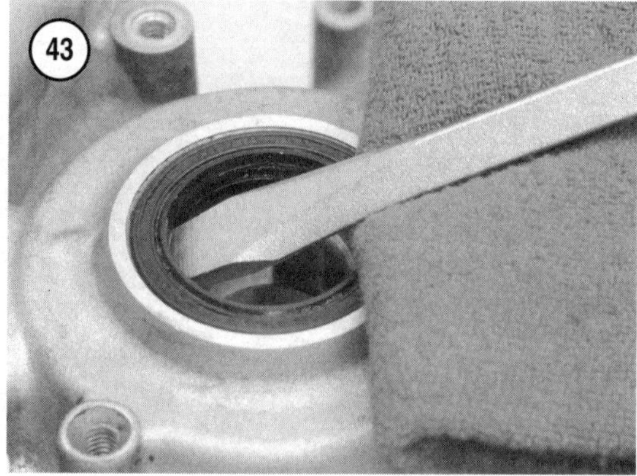

7. Drive the seal until it is flush with the outside edge of the bore.
   a. Use a driver that fits at the perimeter of the seal (**Figure 41**).
   b. Check that the oil hole in the bore is not blocked (**Figure 42**).
   c. Apply threadlocking compound to the retainer bolts, then install the retainer.

Shift Shaft Seal Replacement

CAUTION
This seal is typically replaced when the engine is assembled. If the shift shaft is installed, cover the shaft splines with plastic wrap, to prevent tearing of the seal lip when it is passed over the shaft.

CAUTION
When prying, do not allow the end of the tool to touch the seal bore.

Scratches in the bore will cause a leak.

1. Pry out the old seal (**Figure 43**). If necessary, place a block of wood on the crankcase for leverage and to protect the crankcase from damage.
2. If a new bearing will be installed, replace the bearing before installing the new seal.
3. Clean the oil seal bore.
4. Apply grease to the lip and sides of the new seal.
5. Place the seal in the bore, with the closed side of the seal facing out. The seal must be square to the bore.
6. Start the seal into the bore by hand, then use a socket or driver to squarely press the seal into the bore (**Figure 44**).

Reverse Shift Shaft Seal Replacement

CAUTION
This seal is typically replaced when the engine is assembled. If the shift shaft is installed, cover the shaft splines with plastic wrap, to prevent tearing the seal lip when it is passed over the shaft.

CAUTION
When prying, do not allow the end of the tool to touch the seal bore. Scratches in the bore will cause a leak.

1. Pry out the old seal (**Figure 45**). If necessary, place a block of wood on the case to improve leverage and protect the case from damage.
2. Clean the oil seal bore.
3. Apply grease to the lip and sides of the new seal.

5

4. Place the seal in the bore, with the closed side of the seal facing out. The seal must be square to the bore.
5. Start the seal into the bore by hand, then use a socket or driver to squarely press the seal into the bore.

CRANKCASE BEARINGS

Refer to Chapter One for general bearing removal and installation.

Crankcase Bearing Identification and Tools

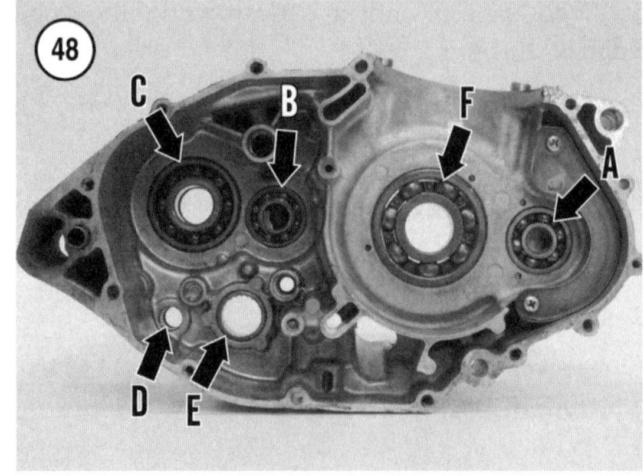

1. When replacing crankcase bearings, note the following:
   a. Where used, remove bearing retainers (A, **Figure 46**) before attempting bearing removal. When installing retainers, clean the screw threads and install the screws using threadlocking compound.
   b. Identify and record the size code (B, **Figure 46**) of each bearing before it is removed.
   c. Record the orientation of each bearing in its bore. Note if the size code faces toward the inside or outside of the crankcase. Typically, the markings should *face up* when installed. Also note the orientation of shielded bearings.
   d. Use a hydraulic press or a set of bearing drivers to remove and install bearings. All bearings in the crankcases are an interference-fit.
   e. Bearings that are only accessible from one side of the case are removed with a blind bearing puller.

2. To identify the *right* crankcase bearings (**Figure 47**). All of the bearings, except the shift drum bearing, can be removed using a bearing remover set (Suzuki part No. 09921-20240) and bearing installer set (Suzuki part No. 09913-70210). Use available drivers or sockets to remove and install the shift drum bearing.
   a. Balancer shaft bearing (A).

49

50

51

b. Crankshaft bearing (B).
c. Input shaft bearing (C).
d. Output shaft bearing (D).
e. Shift drum bearing (E).

3. Identify the *left* crankcase bearings (**Figure 48**).
   a. Balancer shaft bearing (A). Use bearing remover head (Suzuki part No. 09921-20210), sliding hammer (part No. 09930-30104) and bearing installer set (part No. 09913-70210).
   b. Input shaft bearing (B). Use bearing remover head (Suzuki part No. 09923-73210), sliding hammer (part No. 09930-30104) and bearing installer set (part No. 09913-70210).
   c. Output shaft bearing (C). Use bearing remover set (Suzuki part No. 09921-20240) and bearing installer set (part No. 09913-70210).
   d. Shift shaft bearing (D). Use available drivers or sockets.
   e. Shift drum bearing (E). Use available drivers or sockets.
   f. Crankshaft bearing (F). Use bearing remover set (Suzuki part No. 09921-20240) and bearing installer set (part No. 09913-70210).

Crankcase Bearing Replacement

1. Remove the seal from the bearing, if applicable.
2. Make note of which side of the bearing is facing up. Most bearings have numbers on one side. Note the direction of the numbers (**Figure 49**).
3. Heat the crankcase (**Figure 50**) as described in *Bearings* in Chapter One.
4. Support the crankcase on wooden blocks, allowing space for the bearing to fall from the bore (**Figure 51**).
5. Remove the damaged bearing from the bore, using a press, hand-driver set or bearing puller.
6. Clean and inspect the bore. Make sure all oil holes (where applicable) are clean.
7. Place the new bearing in a freezer and chill for at least one hour.
8. When the bearing is chilled, reheat the crankcase.
9. Support the crankcase on wooden blocks, then lubricate the mating surface of the bore and bearing. Place the bearing squarely over the bore and check that it is properly oriented. If the correct orientation of a bearing is not known, generally, bearings that are not sealed on either side should be installed with the manufacturer's marks (stamped on the side of the bearing) facing up (**Figure 49**). Bearings with one side shielded should have the sealed side facing the outside of the crankcase.

10A. With a press, install the bearing into place using a driver that fits on the outer bearing race (**Figure 52**).

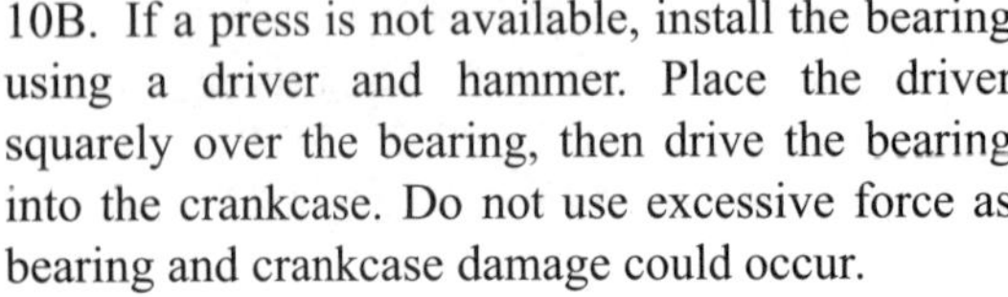

10B. If a press is not available, install the bearing using a driver and hammer. Place the driver squarely over the bearing, then drive the bearing into the crankcase. Do not use excessive force as bearing and crankcase damage could occur.

11. Install the seal (if applicable) as described in this chapter.

ENGINE BALANCER

Inspection

The balancer (**Figure 53**) is synchronized with the crankshaft and is driven by a gear on the right end of the crankshaft (**Figure 54**).

Inspect the balancer.

1. Install the balancer into its crankcase bearings and check for play between the parts.
2. Inspect the bearing surfaces (A, **Figure 55**), pin hole (B) and threads (C) for damage and cleanliness.
3. Inspect the fit of the drive gear, pin and nut on the balancer shaft.

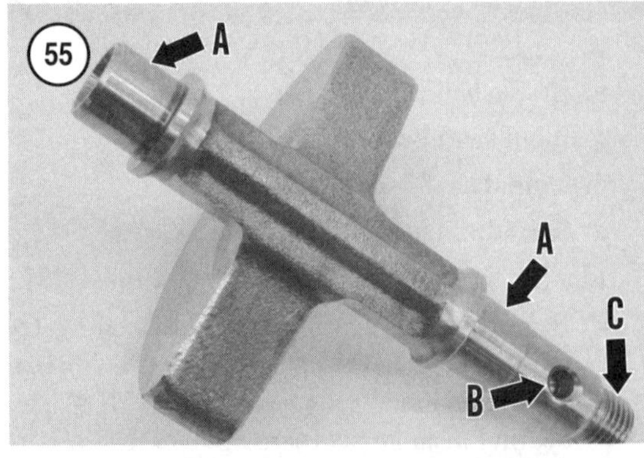

OIL PUMP

The oil pump (A, **Figure 56**) is behind the clutch housing and is driven by a gear on the clutch housing. The clutch assembly must be removed to service the oil pump.

Removal and Installation

1. Remove the right crankcase cover and clutch assembly as described in this chapter.
2. Remove the snap ring (B, **Figure 56**) and oil pump idle gear from the shaft. Do not remove the

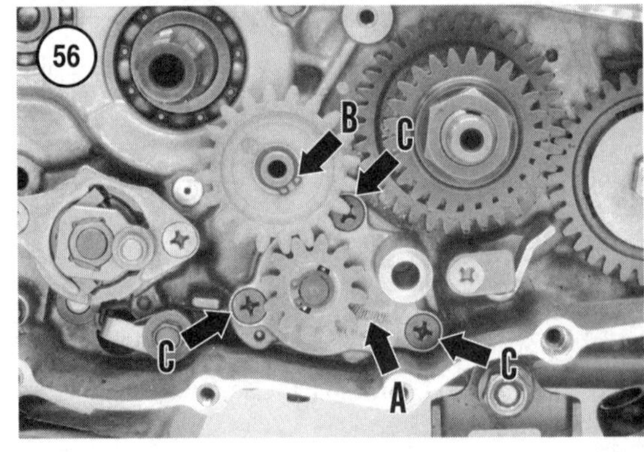

57

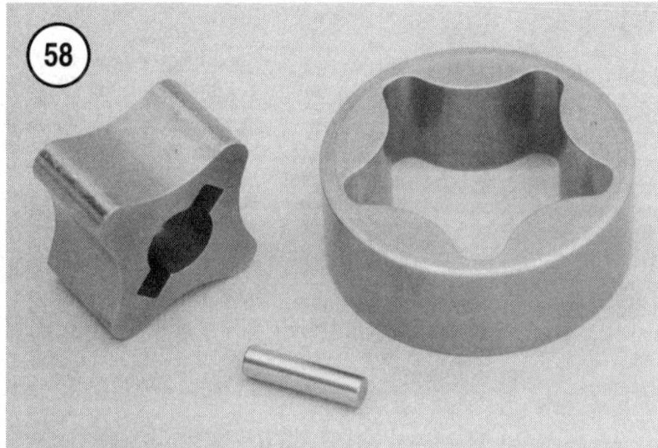
58

59

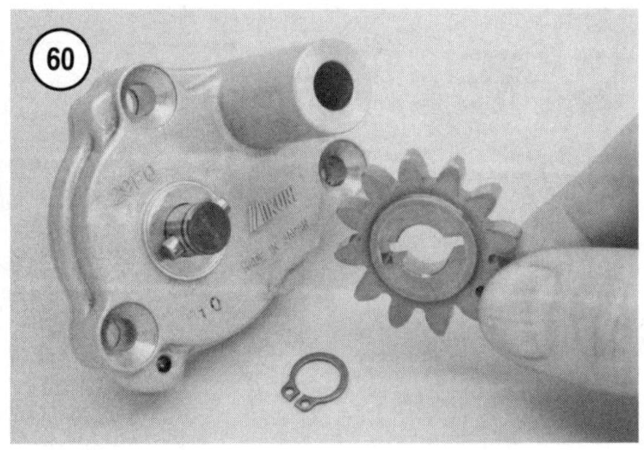
60

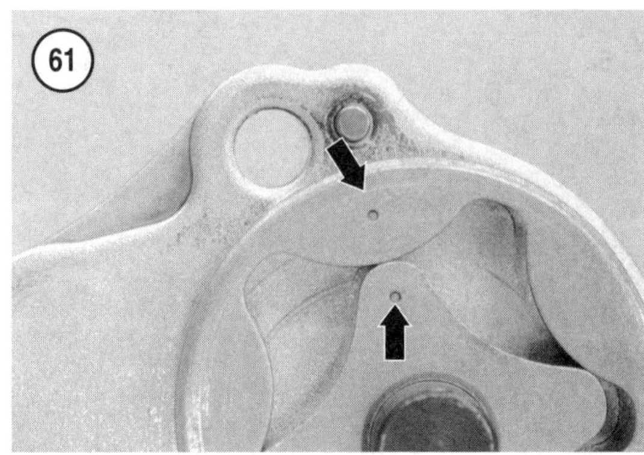
61

second snap ring on the idle gear shaft because it prevents the shaft from falling into the crankcase.

3. Remove the three mounting screws and the oil pump (C, **Figure 56**).
4. Remove the rotors (**Figure 57**). Account for the pin (**Figure 58**) on the pump shaft.
5. Remove the snap ring, gear, pin and washer from the oil pump (**Figure 59**).
6. Inspect the oil pump as described in this section.
7. Assemble and install the oil pump as follows:
   a. Lubricate the pump and rotors with engine oil.
   b. Install the washer and pin, then install the gear with the shouldered side facing in (**Figure 60**). Install a new snap ring, with the sharp edge facing out.
   c. Install the pin and rotors onto the pump shaft so the punch marks are visible.
   d. To ease installation of the pump, align the punch marks and pin as shown in **Figure 61**, then install the pump.
   e. Apply threadlocking compound to the mounting screws before tightening.
   f. Install the shouldered side of the idle gear facing in. Install a new snap ring with the sharp edge facing out.
8. Install the clutch and right crankcase cover as described in this chapter.

Inspection

1. Clean the parts in solvent. Flush the pump while rotating the shaft.
2. Visually inspect all parts for obvious wear or damage.
3. Inspect the pump. The shaft should turn freely and smoothly. If roughness is detected, and all de-

bris has been flushed from the pump, the complete pump must be replaced. The pump cover is sealed by a small screw installed with threadlocking compound. Individual parts for the pump are not available and disassembly is not recommended.

4. Inspect the washer, pin and gear (**Figure 59**).
   a. Inspect the parts for wear.
   b. Assemble the pin and gear onto the pump shaft. The parts should fit firmly on the shaft.
5. Inspect the rotor set (**Figure 58**).
   a. Inspect each rotor for wear or scoring.
   b. Assemble the inner rotor and pin onto the pump shaft. The parts should fit firmly on the shaft.
6. Clean and inspect the pump cavity in the engine (**Figure 62**). Inspect for wear and scoring in the rotor contact area.
7. Inspect the idle gear (**Figure 63**) for wear and damage. The gear should fit firmly on its shaft.
8. Install the oil pump as described in this section.

OIL STRAINER

Inspection

The strainer (**Figure 64**) is not designed to be disassembled. Flush the strainer with solvent and make sure the screen (**Figure 65**) is clean. Inspect the screen for damage. Clean the bolt threads.

OIL PRESSURE CHECK VALVE

The oil pressure check valve is located in the right crankcase cover (**Figure 66**). It is held in by a rubber bushing. It cannot be removed without damaging the rubber bushing. Refer to *Right Crankcase Cover* in Chapter Six.

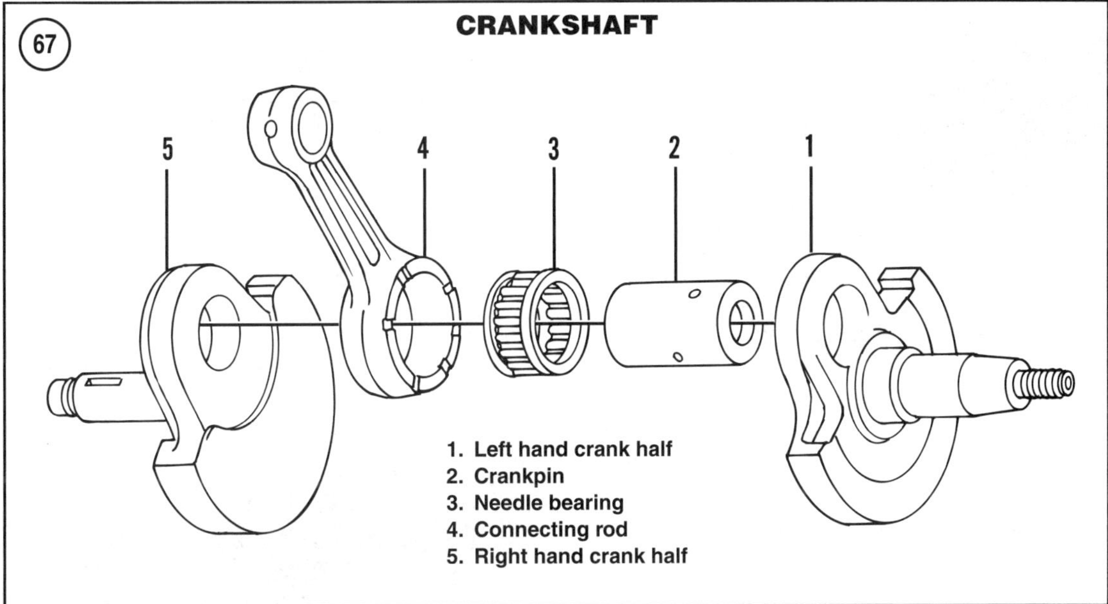

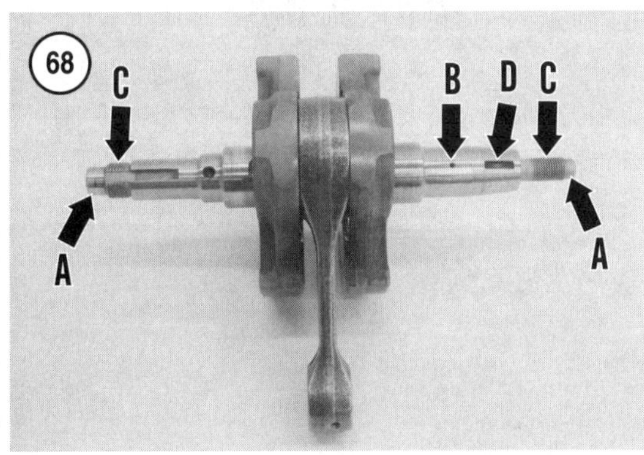

OIL TANK

Removal/Installation

1. Drain the engine oil (Chapter Three).
2. Remove the front fender (Chapter Fourteen).
3. Drain the coolant (Chapter Three).
4. Remove the radiator (Chapter Ten).
5. Remove the engine and oil tank skid plates.
6. Disconnect the oil hose from the crankcase.
7. Remove the two mounting bolts. Account for the collars in the mounting bushings.
8. Reverse these steps to install the oil tank: Note the following:
   a. Install new O-rings. Lubricate them with engine oil.
   b. When connecting the oil tank hose to the crankcase, place the base of the oil pipe against the stopper on the crankcase.
   c. Tighten the oil hose banjo bolt to 23 N•m (17 ft.-lb.).

CRANKSHAFT

Inspection

CAUTION
Carefully handle the crankshaft assembly during inspection. Do not place the crankshaft where it could accidentally roll off the workbench.

The crankshaft (**Figure 67**) is an assembly-type, with its two halves joined by a crankpin. The crankpin is pressed into the flywheels and aligned, both vertically and horizontally, with calibrated equipment.

If any part of the crankshaft assembly is worn or damaged, have a dealership evaluate all the parts to determine the practicality of repair. Each part is available separately.

Refer to **Table 1** for specifications.

1. Clean the crankshaft with *clean* solvent and dry with compressed air. Lubricate the rod bearing with engine oil.
2. Inspect both ends of the crankshaft (A, **Figure 68**) as follows:
   a. Inspect the oil passages (B, **Figure 68**) for cleanliness.

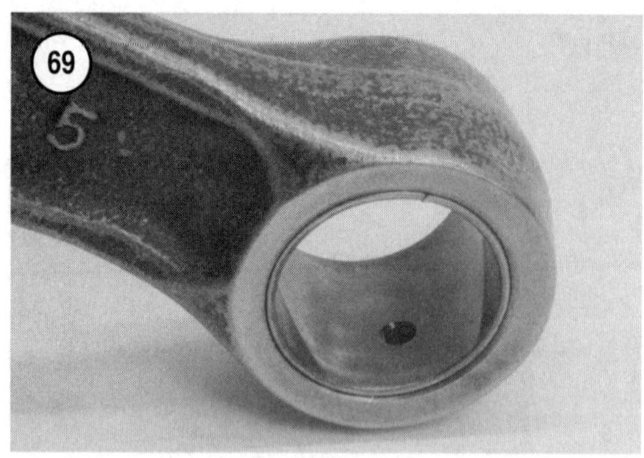

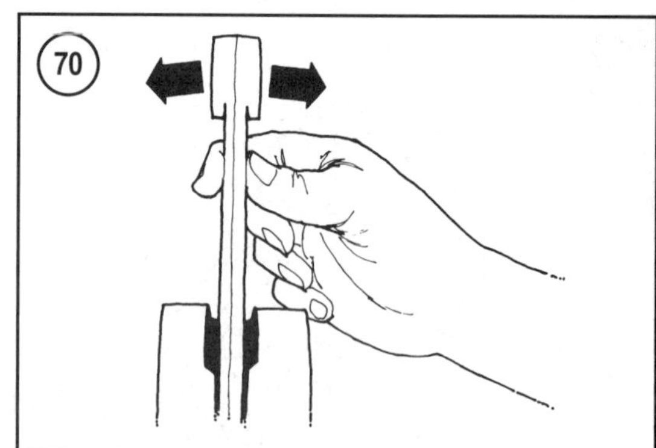

b. Inspect the shaft threads (C, **Figure 68**). Light damage can be corrected with a thread file .

c. Inspect the keyway (D, **Figure 68**). It should be square and the key should fit firmly.

d. Inspect the bearing surface for scoring, heat discoloration or other damage. Burnishing can be removed with 320-grit carborundum cloth and lubricant.

3. Inspect the connecting rod as follows:

a. Inspect the small end (**Figure 69**) for scoring, galling or heat damage as described in Chapter Four.

b. Inspect the rod for play (tilt) (**Figure 70**). Use a dial indicator, mounted on a stand, to make the check.

c. Inspect the big end and bearing for scoring, galling or heat damage.

d. Inspect the rod for radial clearance. Grasp the rod and feel for radial play in all directions. There should be no perceptible play. No specification is available.

e. Measure the connecting rod side clearance (**Figure 71**). Fully seat the feeler gauge against the crankpin to make the measurement.

4. Measure the crankshaft web-to-web width (**Figure 72**). If the width is not within specification, have a dealership evaluate and possibly true the crankshaft.

5. If removed from the crankcase, place the crankshaft in a flywheel alignment jig and measure crankshaft runout with a dial indicator. Measure at the bearing surface on each side of the crankshaft. If the runout exceeds the service limit, have a dealership evaluate and possibly true the crank shaft.

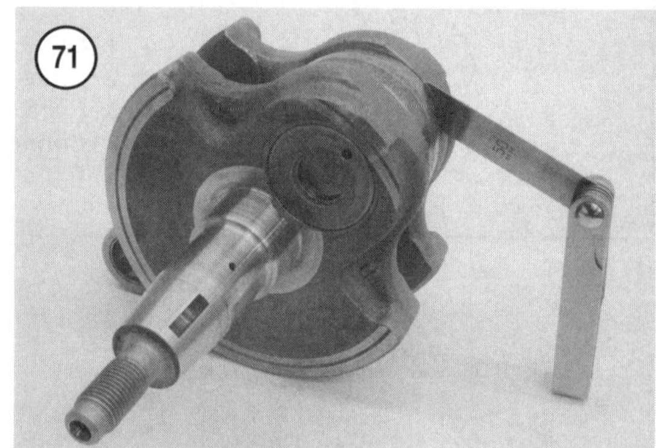

6. If the engine exhibited abnormal vibration, have the crankshaft alignment checked before assembling the engine.

CAM CHAIN AND REAR GUIDE

Removal, Inspection and Installation

There are two cam chain guides in the engine, one on the front of the cam chain and one on the rear. The rear guide pivots on a bolt and tensions the cam

73

74

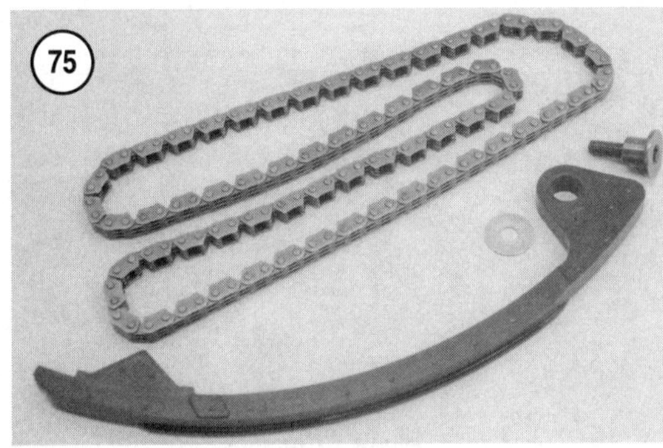
75

chain. The front cam chain guide (**Figure 73**) can be removed from the head once the cams are removed. If necessary, refer to Chapter Four for camshaft removal. The rear cam chain guide cannot be removed unless the right side cover and clutch are removed to access the pivot bolt. Refer to *Primary and Balancer Drive Gears* in this chapter for removal of the cam chain sprocket.

1. Remove the right crankcase cover and clutch assembly as described in this chapter.
2. Remove the bolt (**Figure 74**) securing the cam chain guide. Account for the washer between the guide and crankcase.

76

3. Route the guide down and out of the engine.
4. Remove the cam chain.
5. Inspect the parts (**Figure 75**).
   a. The face of the guide should be smooth. If it is torn or disintegrating, replace the guide.
   b. Inspect the chain for wear. If the chain or any sprockets are worn or damaged, replace all the parts. Using new and old parts could cause poor engine performance and possibly engine damage.
   c. Check the fit of the guide bolt in the guide bore. The bolt should fit firmly in the bore.
6. Reverse this procedure to install the cam chain and rear guide. Apply threadlocking compound to the guide bolt threads, then tighten the bolt to 10 N•m (89 in.).

BALANCER DRIVEN GEAR

The balancer shaft driven gear (A, **Figure 76**) is meshed with the balancer drive gear (B), located on the crankshaft. Whenever the balancer driven gear is removed, it must be synchronized with the balancer drive gear during assembly.

Removal and Installation

1. Remove the right crankcase cover and clutch assembly as described in Chapter Six.
2. Remove the balancer driven gear as follows:
   a. Turn the crankshaft so the synchronization marks on both gears are aligned (**Figure 77**).
   b. Hold the crankshaft. If this is difficult, insert a soft metal washer or penny between the gears. Then remove the driven gear nut and washer.
   c. Grip the gear and pull it straight out (**Figure 78**).

5

d. Remove the pin (**Figure 79**).

CAUTION

After removing the gear, the balancer weight will hang freely. With the weight in the down position, use caution if it is necessary to turn the crankshaft. The weight will bind against the crankshaft unless the weight is moved out of the way.

3. Inspect the parts (**Figure 80**).
   a. Clean the parts and shaft with solvent.
   b. Inspect the gear for worn or broken teeth.
   c. Check that the pins and springs are secure in the gear. If parts are broken, missing or excessively loose, replace the pins and springs (**Figure 81**). The gear halves can be driven apart and repaired.

CAUTION

If the gear is disassembled, align the inner and outer halves of the gear with their marks. Failure to align the parts will not allow the crankshaft and balancer to be synchronized correctly. Engine damage could occur.

   d. Check the fit of the pin in the gear and balancer shaft. The pin must not be worn and should fit in all parts with no excessive play.
   e. Inspect the shaft threads.
4. Install the parts as follows:
   a. Install the pin into the shaft.
   b. If not already positioned, turn the crankshaft so the synchronization marks on the drive gear and balancer driven gear can be aligned (**Figure 82**). Turn the shafts and seat the driven gear over the pin.
   c. Install the washer and nut. Hold the crankshaft nut and tighten the balancer nut to 50 N•m (37 ft.-lb.).
5. Install the clutch and right crankcase cover as described in this chapter.

PRIMARY AND BALANCER DRIVE GEARS

The primary drive gear, balancer drive gear and cam chain sprocket are located on the right end of the crankshaft. The primary drive gear (A, **Figure 83**) transmits power to the clutch housing while the balancer drive gear (B) powers the balancer shaft

77

78

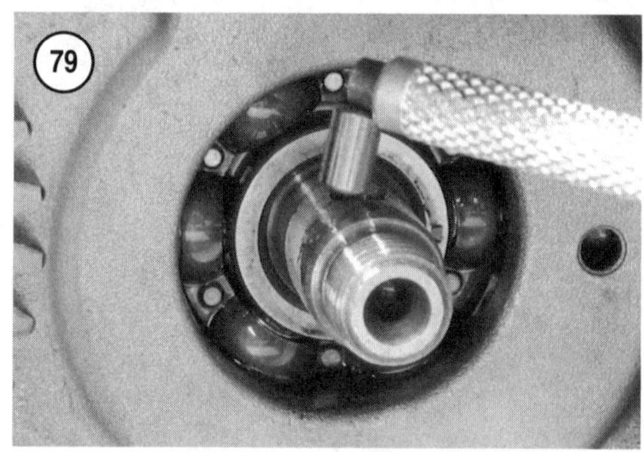
79

80

driven gear. Whenever the balancer drive gear is removed, it must be synchronized with the balancer driven gear during assembly.

The cam chain sprocket is located between the two gears on the crankshaft. The sprocket drives the cam chain, which rotates the camshafts.

Removal, Inspection and Installation

1. Remove the right crankcase cover and clutch assembly as described in Chapter Six.
2. Remove the cam chain and rear guide as described in this chapter.
3. Remove the primary drive-gear nut as follows:
   a. Remove the alternator cover as described in Chapter Nine. Hold the rotor with a 26 mm deep-well socket or offset wrench. The rotor must be held at the hub (**Figure 84**) and not by the nut on the end of the shaft. Holding this nut would overtighten it, as the primary drive gear nut uses left-hand threads.
   b. Using a 27 mm socket, remove the primary drive-gear nut by turning it *clockwise*.
   c. Remove the nut, washer, primary gear and Woodruff key (**Figure 85**).
   d. Remove the cam chain sprocket, balancer drive gear and pin (**Figure 86**).

CAUTION
After removing the gear, the balancer weight will hang freely. With the weight in the down position, use caution if it is necessary to turn the crankshaft. The weight will bind against the crankshaft unless the weight is first pivoted.

86

88

87

89

4. Clean the parts (**Figure 87**) and shaft with solvent.
5. Inspect the gears and sprocket for worn or broken teeth.
6. Inspect the Woodruff key and pin for damage. Both parts must not be worn and should fit firmly in the shaft.
7. Inspect the nut for damage and replace the lockwasher.
8. Inspect the shaft and shaft threads for damage.
9. Install the parts as follows:
   a. Install the pin into the shaft (**Figure 88**).
   b. Turn the shafts and seat the drive gear over the pin so the synchronization marks on the balancer gear and balancer drive gear are aligned (**Figure 82**). Install the balancer gear so the flat side faces out.
   c. Install the cam chain sprocket and Woodruff key (**Figure 89**). The square end of the key must be locked into the sprocket.
   d. Install the primary drive gear and a new lockwasher (**Figure 85**). Install the lockwasher with the cupped side facing in.
   e. Lubricate the shaft threads and primary drive-gear nut with engine oil.
   f. Thread the nut onto the shaft, turning the nut *counterclockwise.*
   g. Hold the rotor steady and tighten the primary drive-gear nut to 140 N•m (103 ft.-lb.).
10. Install the cam chain and rear guide as described in this chapter.
11. Install the clutch and right crankcase cover as described in this chapter.
12. Install the left side engine cover.

Table 1 ENGINE LOWER END SPECIFICATIONS

	Specification mm (in.)	Service limit mm (in.)
Balancer spring free length	–	10.3 (0.41)
Connecting rod		
Big end side clearance	0.30-0.65 (0.012-0.026)	1.0 (0.04)
Big end width	21.95-22.0 (0.864-0.866)	–
Deflection	–	3.0 (0.12)
Small end inside diameter	20.010-20.018 (0.7878-0.7881)	20.040 (0.7890)
Crankshaft		
Runout	–	0.08 (0.003)
Web-to-web width	62.0 (2.44)	–
Oil pump		
Body clearance	0.15-0.21 (0.006-0.008)	0.25 (0.010)
Side clearance	0.05-0.13 (0.002-0.005)	0.15 (0.006)
Tip clearance	0.15 (0.006)	0.20 (0.008)
Piston pin clearance	0.010-0.034 (0.0004-0.0013)	0.10 (0.004)

5

Table 2 ENGINE LOWER END TORQUE SPECIFICATIONS

Item	N•m	in.-lb.	ft.-lb.
Balancer driven gear nut	50	–	37
Cam chain guide (rear) pivot bolt*	10	89	–
Crankcase bolts	11	97	–
Engine mounting bolts and nuts			
Exhaust pipe nuts	23	–	17
Front engine mounting bolt	66	–	49
Lower engine bracket bolts	26	–	19
Lower engine mounting bolt	66	–	49
Muffler connecting bolt	23	–	17
Neutral switch bolt	6.5	56	–
Oil hose banjo bolt	23	–	17
Primary drive-gear nut	140	–	103
Swing arm pivot bolt	95	–	70

*Apply threadlock

CHAPTER SIX

CLUTCH AND EXTERNAL SHIFT MECHANISM

This chapter provides procedures for the following components:

1. Right crankcase cover.
2. Clutch.
3. Clutch release camshaft.
4. Shift lever.
5. Gearshift linkage.
6. Clutch cable replacement.
7. Clutch lever replacement.

Procedures for the reverse shift mechanism are in Chapter Five.

Refer to **Table 1** and **Table 2** for specifications.

RIGHT CRANKCASE COVER

Removal and Installation

1. Drain the engine oil and remove the oil filter (Chapter Three).
2. Drain the cooling system (Chapter Three).
3. Remove the water pump cover (Chapter Ten).
4. Remove the bolts from the perimeter of the crankcase cover (**Figure 1**).
5. Pull the cover straight out. If necessary, lightly tap the cover to loosen it from the crankcase.
6. Remove the gasket and account for the two dowels (**Figure 2**) that fit between the crankcase and cover .
7. If necessary, remove the remainder of the water pump assembly from the right side cover (Chapter Ten).
8. Inspect the cover as described in this section.
9. Reverse these steps to install the right crankcase cover. Note the following:
   a. Clean all oil from the cover gasket surfaces.
   b. Apply grease to the seal lips.

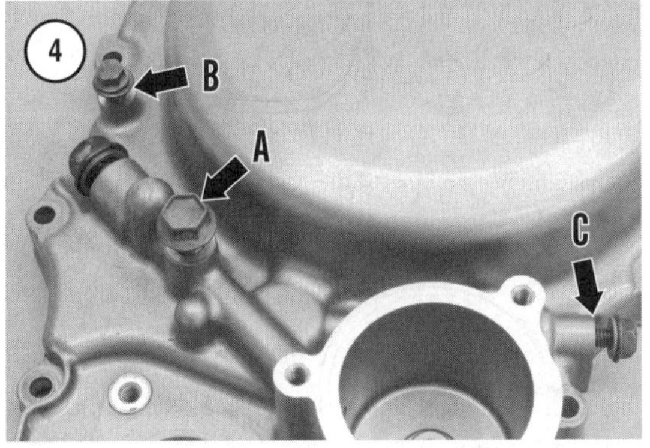

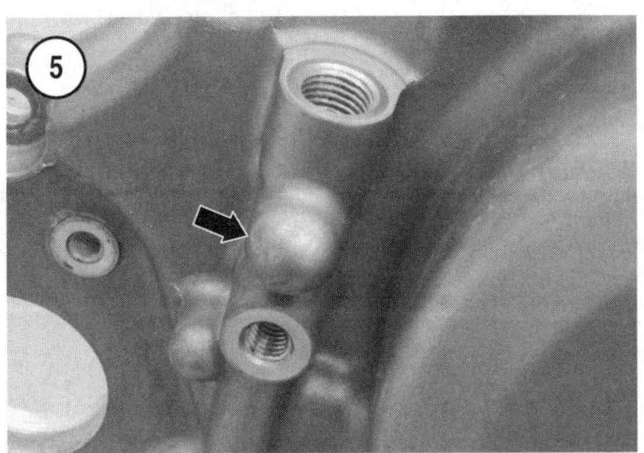

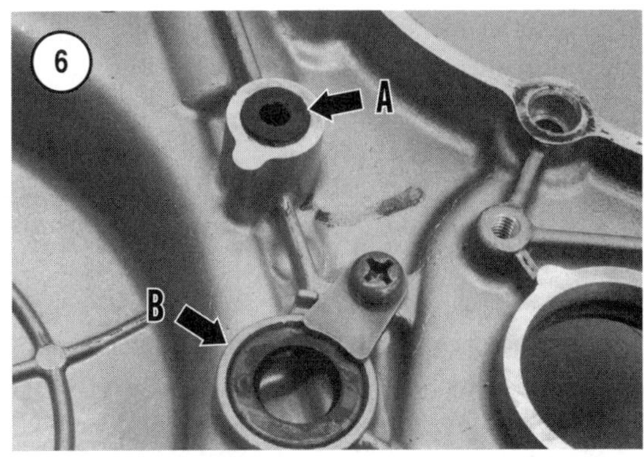

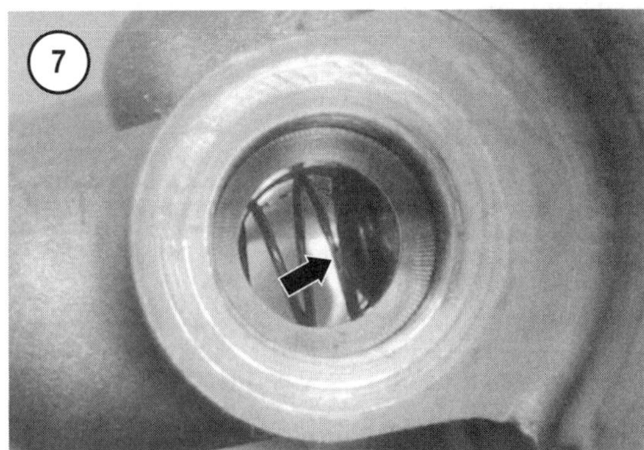

c. Install the dowels and a new cover gasket on the crankcase (**Figure 3**). To keep the gasket in place while installing the cover, apply small spots of sealant to the crankcase gasket surface. It is not necessary to apply sealant to the entire surface.

d. Tighten the right crankcase cover bolts to 10 N•m (88 in.-lb.).

Inspection

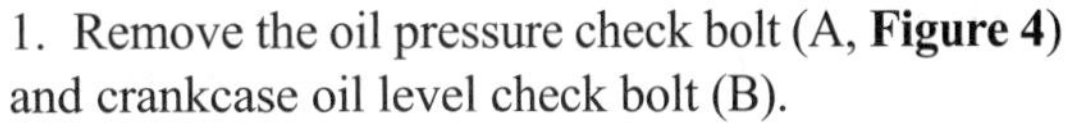

1. Remove the oil pressure check bolt (A, **Figure 4**) and crankcase oil level check bolt (B).

2. Remove the oil check bolt near the oil filter housing (C, **Figure 4**).

3. Inspect the oil pressure check valve in the cover (**Figure 5**) as follows:

a. Insert a small screwdriver into the rubber seat (A, **Figure 6**) and depress the ball (**Figure 7**) in the valve.

b. The ball should lift off the seat with some resistance and return when released. If the ball does not move, or does not operate smoothly, remove the seat, ball and spring for cleaning or parts replacement (**Figure 8**).

c. If the check valve operates smoothly and the oil passage is clean, the assembly can be left in place. If the check valve seat is removed, the rubber face must be out when the seat is installed in the cover.

4. Clean the cover in solvent and dry with compressed air. Check that all passages are clean.

5. Inspect both sides of the crankcase cover (**Figure 2** and **Figure 9**) for cracks and thread damage.

6. Inspect the crankshaft seal (B, **Figure 6**). If this seal leaks, oil pressure will be reduced. Replace the seal as follows:

a. Remove the seal retainer.
b. Pry the seal from its bore. Make sure not to damage the bore. Place a wooden block under the pry tool to create leverage. Avoid applying pressure to the cover.
c. Lubricate the new seal with grease.
d. Support the cover under the seal bore with a block of wood.
e. Place the seal over the bore.
f. Place a driver or socket over the seal. The driver should fit on the perimeter of the seal.
g. Drive the seal into place.
h. Install the seal retainer.

7. Install a new seal washer on the oil pressure check bolt (A, **Figure 4**) and crankcase oil level check bolt (B). Install the bolts into the cover.

8. Install a new seal washer on the oil check bolt (C, **Figure 4**). Install the bolt into the cover.

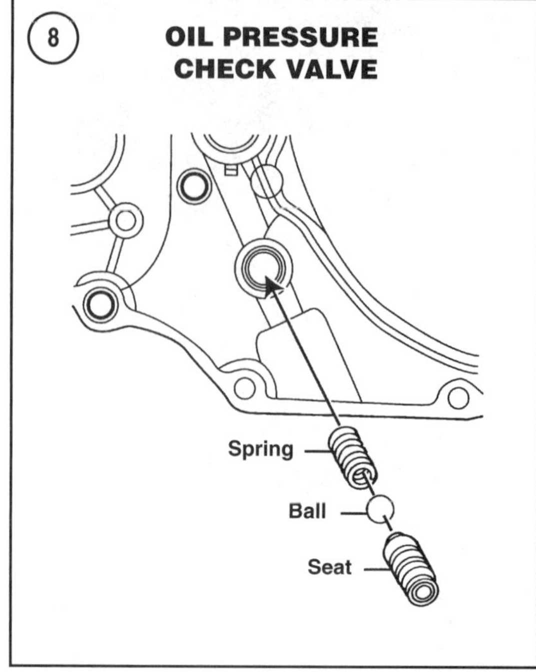

CLUTCH

The clutch assembly consists of an outer housing and a clutch hub. A set of clutch plates and friction plates are alternately locked to the two parts. The gear-driven clutch housing is mounted on the transmission input shaft and can rotate freely. The housing receives power from the primary drive gear mounted on the crankshaft. As the clutch is engaged, the housing and friction plates transfer the power to the clutch plates, locked to the clutch hub. The clutch hub is splined to the input shaft and powers the transmission. The plate assembly is engaged by springs and disengaged by a cable-actuated release lever and pushrod assembly.

Removal

Refer to **Figure 10** or **Figure 11**.

1. Drain the engine oil from the crankcase (Chapter Three). Although the engine is a dry sump engine, there will be some engine oil in the crankcase.

2. Drain the coolant (Chapter Ten).

3. Remove the right side crankcase cover as described in this chapter.

4. Check that there is play in the clutch lever and cable (Chapter Three).

5. Loosen the clutch spring bolts (**Figure 12**). Make several passes and work in a crisscross pattern to evenly relieve the pressure on the bolts. Remove the bolts and springs from the pressure plate.

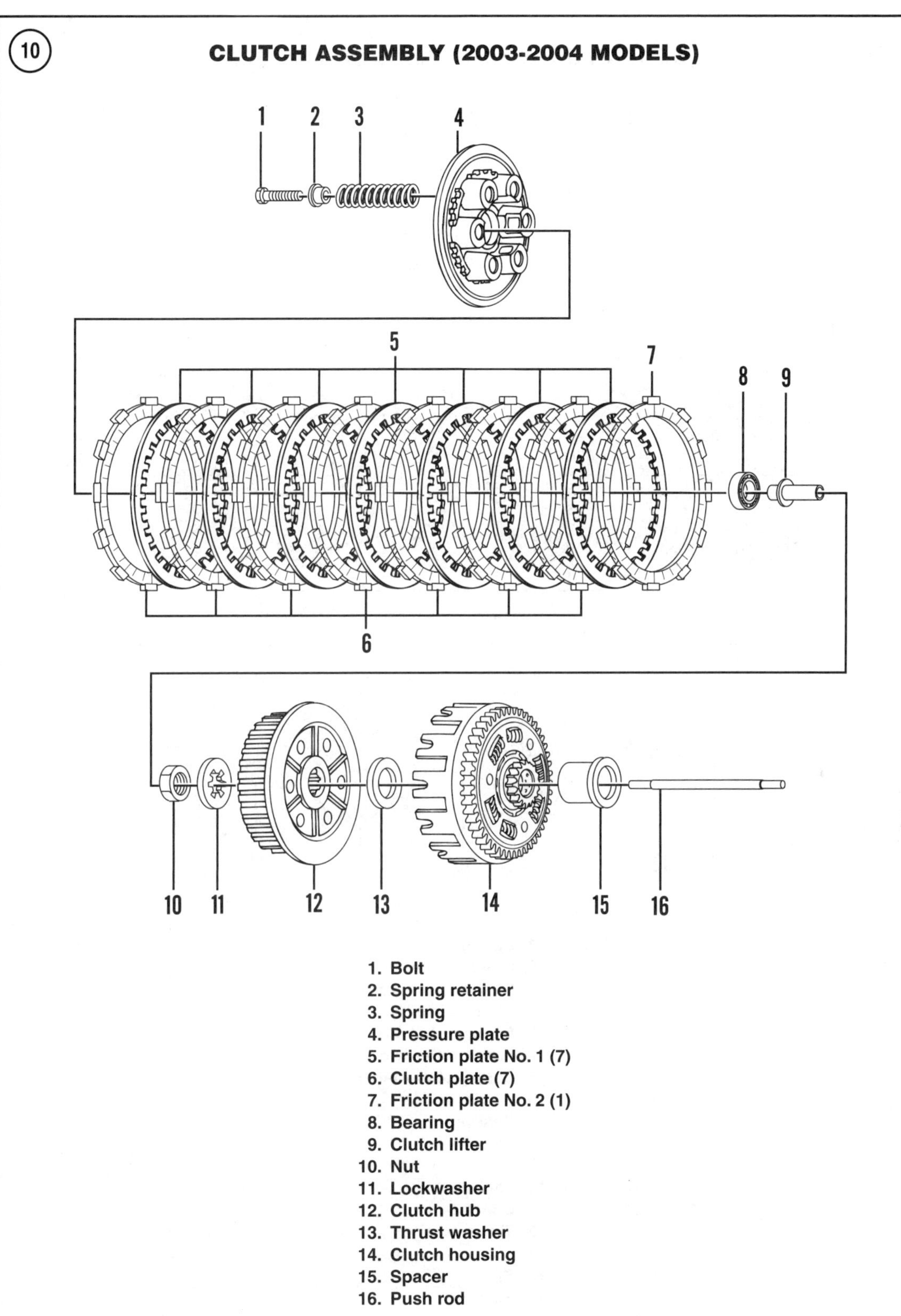

1. Bolt
2. Spring retainer
3. Spring
4. Pressure plate
5. Friction plate No. 1 (7)
6. Clutch plate (7)
7. Friction plate No. 2 (1)
8. Bearing
9. Clutch lifter
10. Nut
11. Lockwasher
12. Clutch hub
13. Thrust washer
14. Clutch housing
15. Spacer
16. Push rod

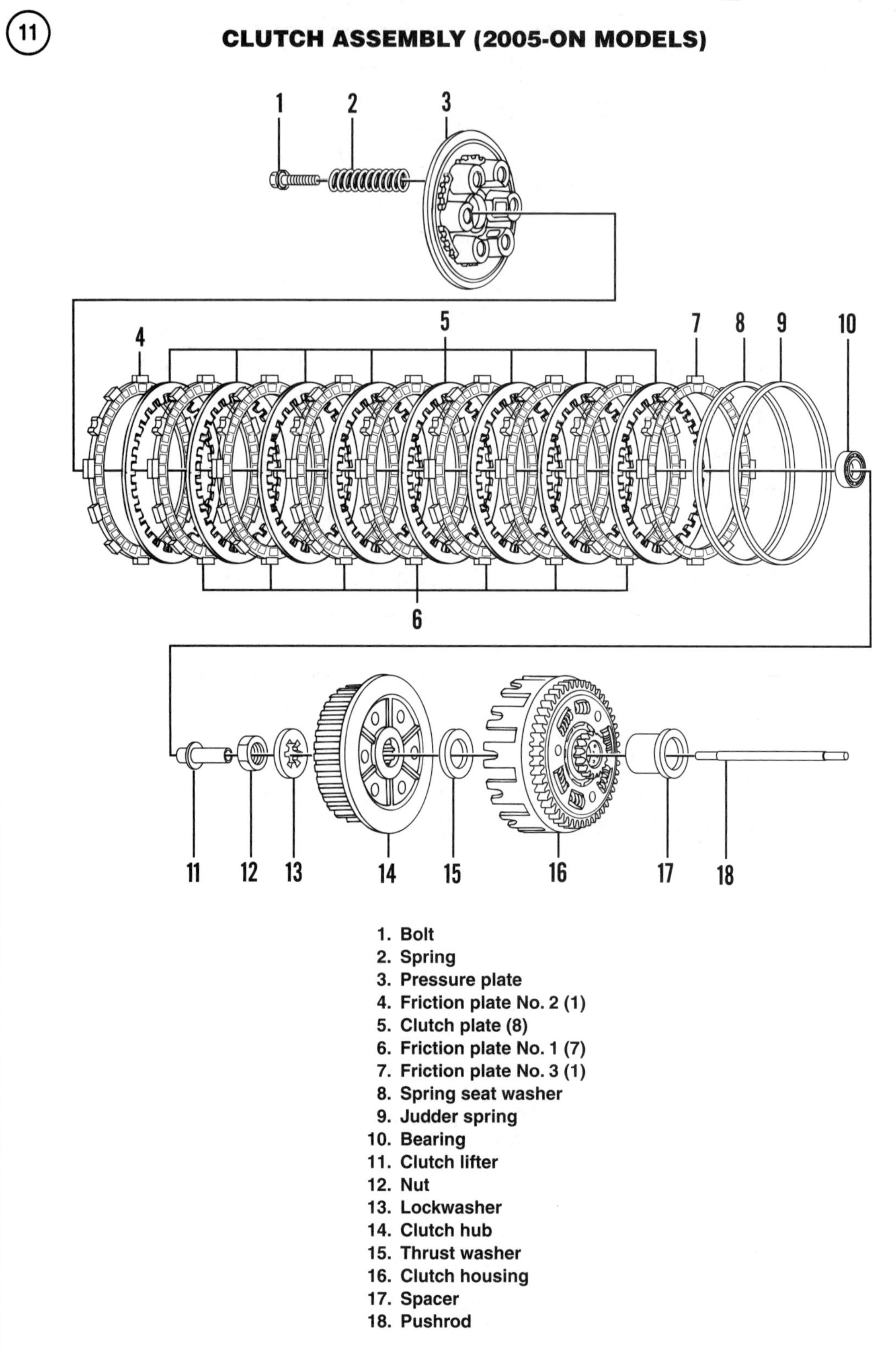

1. Bolt
2. Spring
3. Pressure plate
4. Friction plate No. 2 (1)
5. Clutch plate (8)
6. Friction plate No. 1 (7)
7. Friction plate No. 3 (1)
8. Spring seat washer
9. Judder spring
10. Bearing
11. Clutch lifter
12. Nut
13. Lockwasher
14. Clutch hub
15. Thrust washer
16. Clutch housing
17. Spacer
18. Pushrod

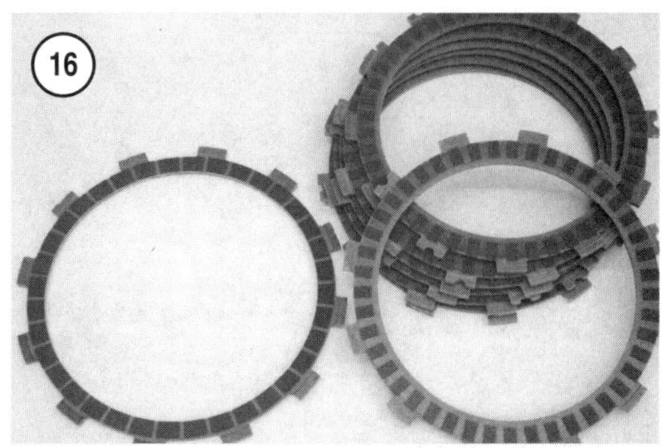

6. Remove the pressure plate (**Figure 13**), pushrod and push piece (**Figure 14**).
7. Remove the friction plates and clutch plates (**Figure 15**).

NOTE
*Not all the friction plates are the same and they may not be visually different (**Figure 16**). Refer to **Figure 10** and **Figure 11** for the order of the friction plates. If the friction plates are not being replaced, keep them in order front to back as they are removed.*

a. On 2003-04 models, there are eight friction plates and seven clutch plates (**Figure 10**).
b. On 2005-on models, there are nine friction plates, eight clutch plates and a Judder spring and spring seat washer (**Figure 11**).

8. Remove the clutch hub nut as follows:

a. Bend the lockwasher tab (**Figure 17**) away from the locknut.

CAUTION
Do not hold the gears with screwdrivers or other tools. This can cause gear

damage. Use a clutch holder (Suzuki part No. 09920-53740) or equivalent.

b. Attach a clutch holder tool to the clutch hub (**Figure 18**). The tool can be braced against the frame.

c. Remove the clutch hub nut and lockwasher.

9. Remove the clutch hub (**Figure 19**).
10. Remove the washer (**Figure 20**).
11. Remove the clutch housing (**Figure 21**).
12. Remove the spacer (A, **Figure 22**) from the input shaft (B) if it does not come off with the clutch housing (**Figure 23**).
13. Inspect the clutch assembly as described in this section.

Installation

During assembly, lubricate the parts and transmission shaft with engine oil. Refer to **Figure 10** and **Figure 11**.

1. Install the spacer (A, **Figure 22**) onto the input shaft (B).
2. Install the clutch housing (**Figure 21**).
3. Install the washer (**Figure 20**).
4. Install the clutch hub (**Figure 19**).
5. Install the clutch hub nut as follows:
   a. Install a new lockwasher **Figure 24**.
   b. Attach a clutch holder tool to the clutch hub (**Figure 18**).
   c. Tighten the clutch hub nut to 70 N•m (52 ft.-lb.).
   d. Bend the lockwasher tab against the locknut.
6. On 2005-on models, install the spring seat washer and Judder spring onto the clutch hub as follows:
   a. Install the Judder spring (A, **Figure 25**) first.

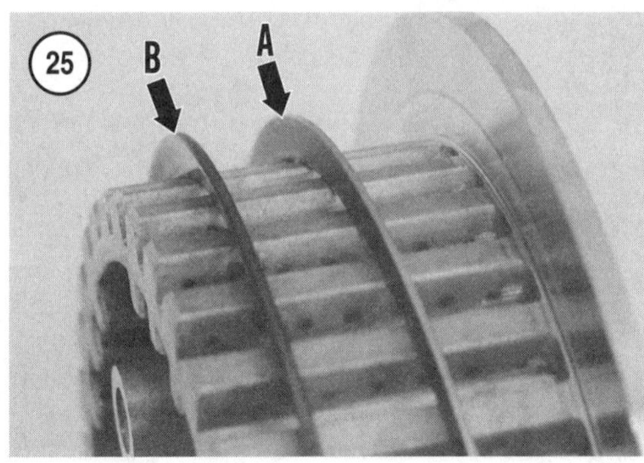

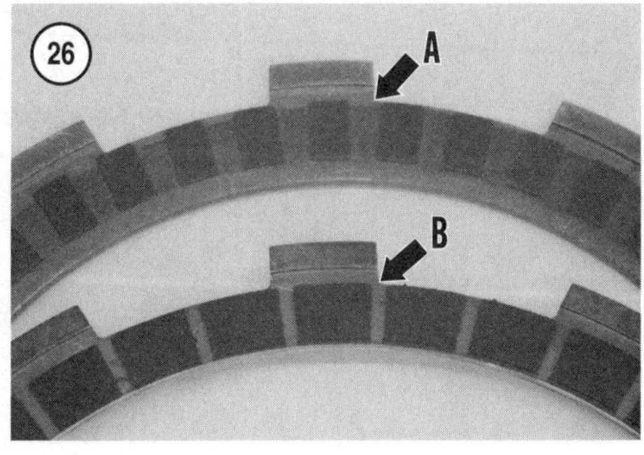

b. Install the spring seat washer (B, **Figure 25**) with the cupped side facing out.

6

7A. On 2003-2004 models, install the plates as follows:

a. Identify the No. 1 friction plates and the No. 2 friction plate. There are seven No. 1 friction plates (A, **Figure 26**) and one No. 2 friction plate. The No. 2 friction plate has a larger inside diameter (122.5 mm [4.822 in.]) and larger sections of friction material (B, **Figure 26**). Friction plate No. 2 must be the *first* plate installed.

b. To prevent possible seizure, particularly with new friction plates, it is important that the face of the friction plates be completely coated with oil. Soak the plates in engine oil.

c. Beginning with friction plate No. 2 (**Figure 27**), alternately install friction plates and clutch plates into the clutch housing and clutch hub.

7B. On 2005-on models, install the plates as follows:

a. Identify the No. 1, No. 2 and No. 3 friction plates. There is one No. 1 friction plate, seven No. 2 friction plates and one No. 3 friction plate. The No. 1 (A, **Figure 28**) and No. 2 (B) friction plates are visually identical so it is important to keep these plates in order upon disassembly or after purchase. The No. 3 friction plate has a larger inside diameter and larger sections of friction material (C, **Figure 28**). Friction plate No. 3 must be the *first* plate installed.

b. To prevent possible seizure, particularly with new friction plates, it is important that the

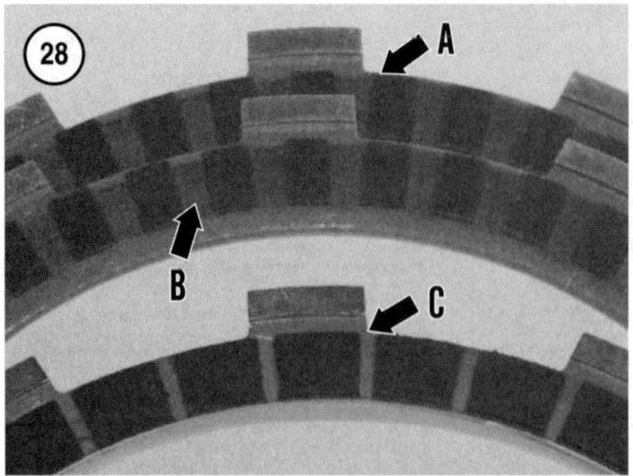

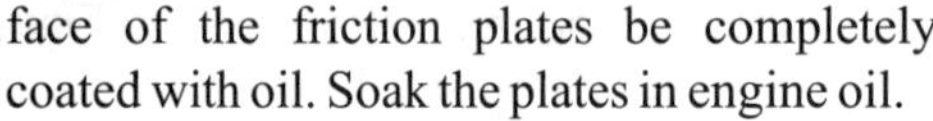

face of the friction plates be completely coated with oil. Soak the plates in engine oil.

c. Beginning with friction plate No. 3 (C, **Figure 28**), alternately install friction plates and clutch plates into the clutch housing and clutch hub.

8. Install the pushrod and push piece (**Figure 14**).
9. Install the pressure plate (**Figure 13**).
10. Lock the pressure plate to the clutch hub as follows:

a. Install the clutch springs, retainers and bolts (**Figure 29**).

b. Finger-tighten the bolts.

c. Tighten the bolts, working in a crisscross pattern. Make several passes so all bolts are tightened in equal steps. Tighten the bolts to 10 N•m (88 in.-lb.)

11. Install the right crankcase cover as described in this chapter.
12. Adjust the clutch cable (Chapter Three).

Inspection

Always replace clutch plates, friction plates or springs as a set if they do not meet specifications. If any part shows wear or damage, replace it, regardless of its specification. Refer to the specifications in **Table 1**.

1. Clean the parts in solvent and dry with compressed air. Also clean the transmission shaft.
2. Measure the thickness of each friction plate (**Figure 30**). Measure at several locations around the perimeter.
3. Measure the width of the claws on the friction plates (**Figure 31**).

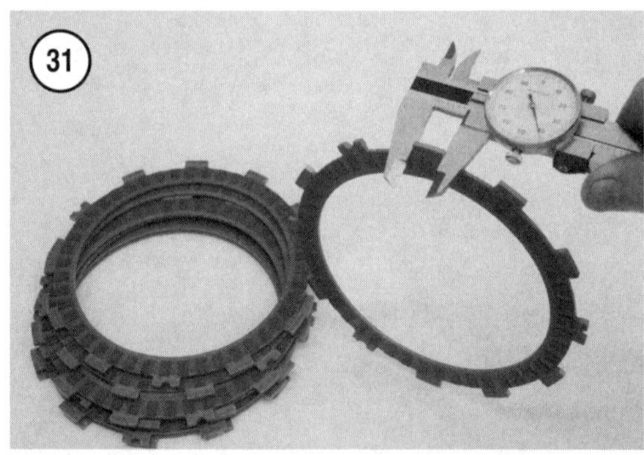

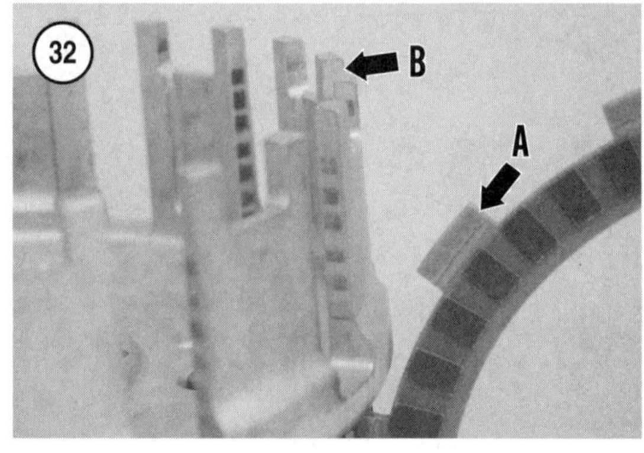

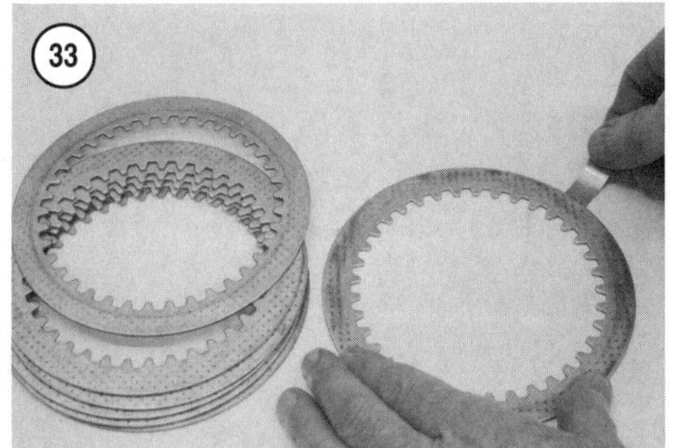

4. Inspect the claws on the friction plates (A, **Figure 32**) for damage. Check that each plate slides smoothly on the clutch housing.

5. Measure each clutch plate for warp. Lay each plate on a surface plate, or thick piece of glass, and measure any gap around the perimeter of the plate (**Figure 33**). Warped plates will cause erratic clutch operation.

6. Inspect the teeth on the clutch plates (**Figure 34**) for damage. Check that each plate slides smoothly on the clutch hub.

7. Inspect both sides of the clutch housing (**Figure 35** and **Figure 36**).
   a. Inspect the oil pockets in the housing bore for cleanliness and wear.
   b. Inspect the gear teeth for wear or damage.
   c. Inspect the damper springs and rivets on both sides of the housing for looseness or damage.
   d. Inspect the slots for nicks, wear and damage (B, **Figure 32**). The slots must be smooth and free of defects so the friction plates will smoothly engage and disengage. If chatter marks are evident, light damage can be smoothed using a fine-cut file or oilstone.

8. Inspect the condition of the spacer (**Figure 23**). Insert the spacer into the clutch housing and onto the transmission shaft (B, **Figure 22**). Check for excessive play, scoring and wear.

9. Inspect the clutch hub (**Figure 37**).
   a. Inspect the shaft splines. The hub should fit on the transmission shaft with no obvious play.
   b. Inspect the perimeter of the hub for wear and damage on the contact area.
   c. Inspect the bosses and threads for damage.
   d. Inspect the outer splines (B, **Figure 32**) for nicks, wear and damage. The splines must be

smooth and free of defects so the clutch plates will smoothly engage and disengage. If chatter marks are evident, light damage can be smoothed using a fine-cut file or oilstone.

10. Measure the free length of each clutch spring (**Figure 38**).

11. Inspect the pressure plate (**Figure 39**).

   a. Inspect the pressure plate for cracks, particularly around the bosses and bearing seat.
   b. Inspect the perimeter of the pressure plate for wear and damage on the contact area.
   c. Inspect the bearing for smooth operation.

12. Inspect the pushrod and push piece (**Figure 40**) for wear and damage.

13. Inspect the washer, nut, Judder spring and spring washer seat for wear and damage. The spring washer should be cupped on one side.

14. Inspect the oil hole, splines, threads and polished surfaces on the transmission shaft for damage (**Figure 41**).

15. At the left side of the engine, inspect the clutch release lever (**Figure 42**). The release lever shaft rotates against the end of the pushrod and disengages the clutch. Inspect the lever for tightness and seal leakage. If the seal is leaking, replace the seal as follows:

   a. Remove the starter (Chapter Nine).
   b. Make a reference mark on the shaft so the release lever can be installed in its original position (A, **Figure 43**).
   c. Remove the lever, screw and seal retainer plate.
   d. Pry out the seal (**Figure 44**).
   e. Apply grease to the new seal, then install the seal with the closed side facing out. Cover the shaft splines with plastic wrap to prevent tearing the seal when it is passed over the shaft.

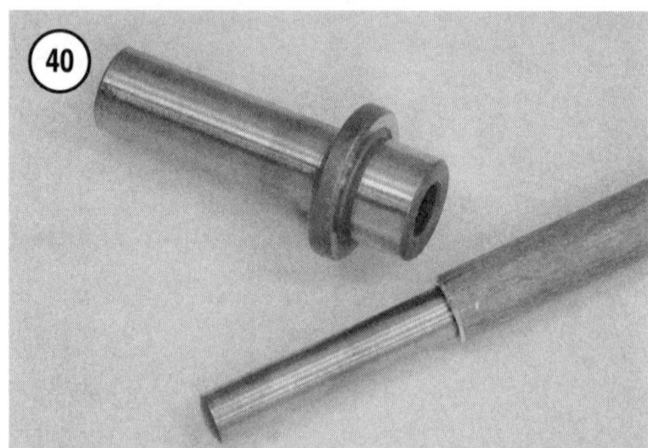

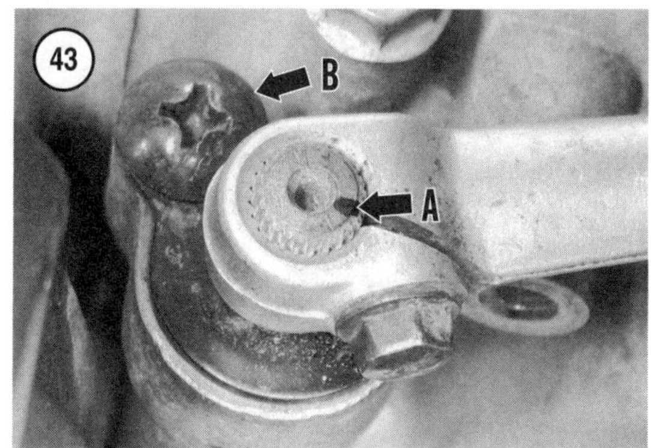

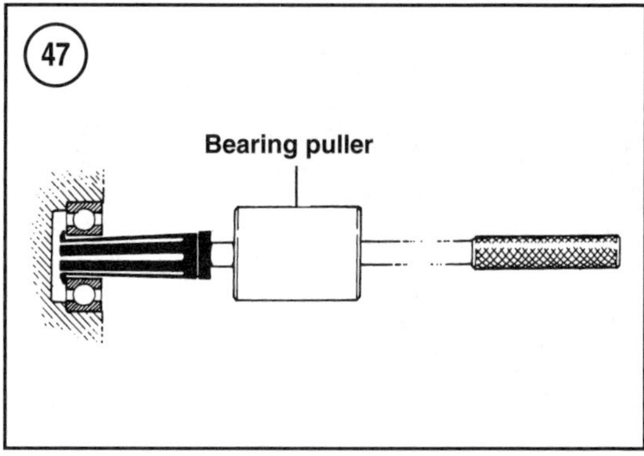

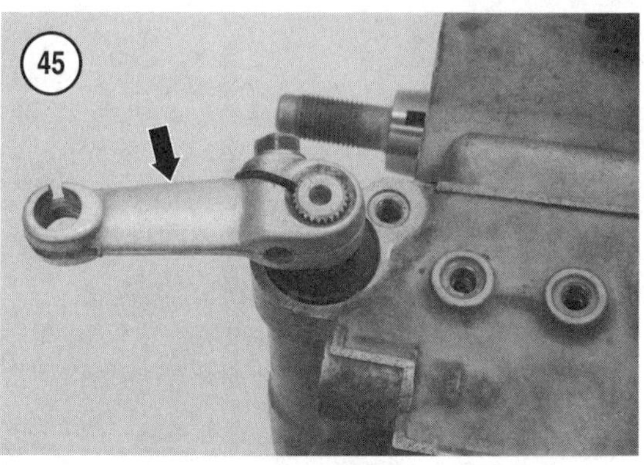

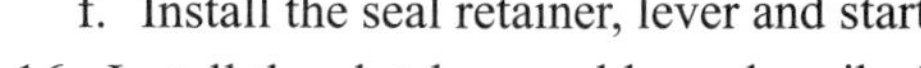

f. Install the seal retainer, lever and starter.

16. Install the clutch assembly as described in this section.

CLUTCH RELEASE CAMSHAFT

If the clutch release camshaft is damaged or has excessive play it will limit the release of the clutch. The clutch release camshaft can be removed if the pushrod for the clutch is removed.

Removal

1. Make a mark on the top of the shaft (A, **Figure 43**) to orient the camshaft lever during installation.
2. Remove the clutch pushrod as described in this chapter.
3. Loosen the clamp bolt and remove the lever from the end of the shaft.
4. Remove the screw (B, **Figure 43**) and the shaft seal retaining plate.
5. Reinstall the lever onto the shaft and lightly tighten the retaining bolt.
6. Turn the release lever (**Figure 45**) so it is at a right angle to the crankcase.
7. With a soft-faced mallet, gently tap the lever upward. The shaft, seal, washer and upper bearing will lift out of the crankcase together.
8. The lower bearing will remain in the crankcase (**Figure 46**). To remove it, use a long expandable bearing puller (**Figure 47**).
9. Examine the needle bearings for roughness or pitting.
10. Examine the shaft for wear. Make sure the area around the seal seat is free of burrs.

Installation

1. If the lower needle bearing was removed, use a deep well socket to install the new bearing into the engine crankcase.
2. Install the shaft into the hole, seating the lower end of the shaft into the crankcase.
3. Slide the needle bearing onto the shaft. Put a socket (**Figure 48**) over the end of the shaft and lightly drive the bearing into the crankcase.
4. Install the washer (**Figure 49**) onto the shaft.
5. Install the shaft seal carefully over the splines on the end of the shaft (**Figure 50**). Lightly seat the seal by using an appropriate sized socket and a soft faced hammer.
6. Install the seal retaining plate.
7. Install the shaft lever and align it with the mark on the top of the shaft (A, **Figure 43**).

SHIFT LEVER

Removal and Installation

The shift lever (**Figure 51**) is clamped to the transmission shift shaft. The shaft operates the gear-shift linkage inside the right crankcase cover.

1. To retain the current shift lever position, make an alignment mark on the shaft and lever so they can be installed in their original position.
2. Completely remove the lever bolt (**Figure 52**). The lever cannot be removed with the bolt in the lever.
3. Pull the lever from the splined shaft. If necessary, spread the lever open with a flat blade screw driver to ease removal.
4. Remove the two plastic shaft guards and the washer (**Figure 53**).

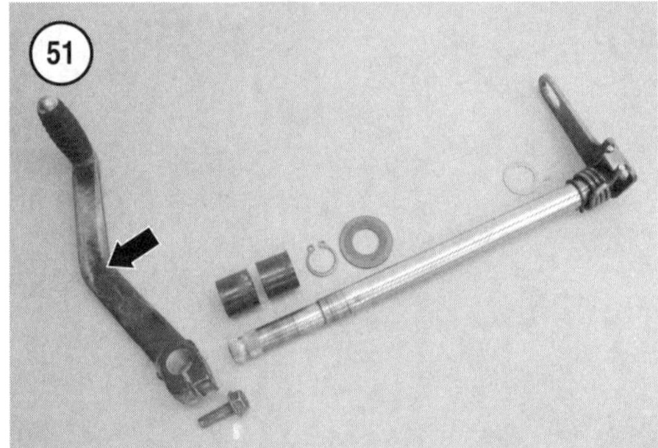

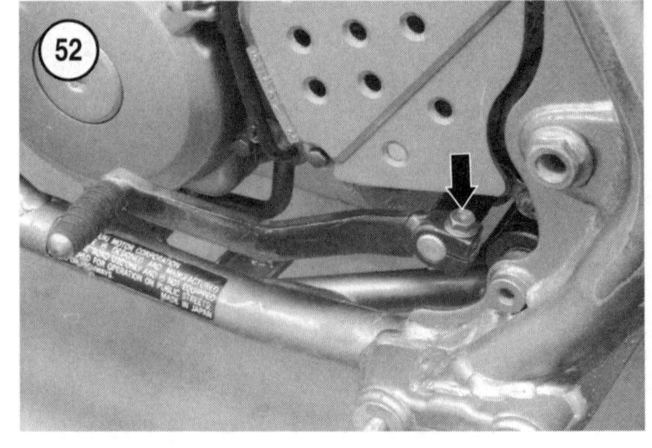

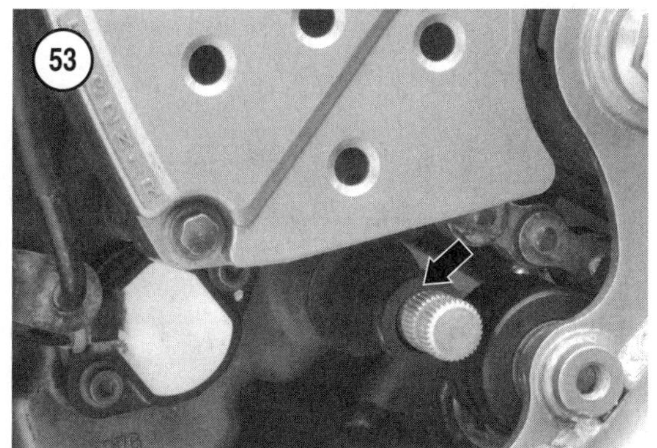

5. Clean the lever and shaft splines with solvent and a brush.

6. If seal replacement or shaft removal is necessary, remove the snap ring and washer (**Figure 54**). To replace the seal (**Figure 55**), refer to *Crankcase Seals* in Chapter Five. To remove the shift shaft, refer to *Shift Mechanism* in this chapter. During assembly, install a new snap ring with the sharp edge facing out.

7. Reverse these steps to install the shift lever.

SHIFT MECHANISM

The external shift mechanism includes all parts not within the crankcase. This includes the shift lever, shaft and components that connect to the shift drum (**Figure 56**). Other than the shift lever, all other components of the external shift mechanism are located in the right crankcase cover. The internal shift mechanism (shift drum and shift forks) are located in the crankcase. Refer to Chapter Five and Chapter Seven.

Refer to **Figure 57**.

6

Removal

1. Remove the right crankcase cover and clutch assembly as described in this chapter.

2. Remove the snap ring and oil pump idle gear from the shaft (**Figure 58**). Do not remove the second snap ring on the idle gear shaft, because it prevents the shaft from falling into the crankcase.

3. Put the transmission in neutral, then remove the shift lever from the shift shaft as described in this chapter.

4. Clean any dirt and grease from the shaft to prevent damage to the shaft seal as it is being removed.

5. Slowly pull the shift shaft and washer (**Figure 59**) from the engine. Account for the washer on the shaft.

6. Remove the gearshift cam stopper. Use a flat blade screwdriver to take the pressure off the spring (**Figure 60**).

7. Remove the bolts securing the shift selector plate and shift selector body assembly (**Figure 61**). The pawls of the selector are under spring pressure. To prevent the loss of these small parts, especially the springs, note the following:

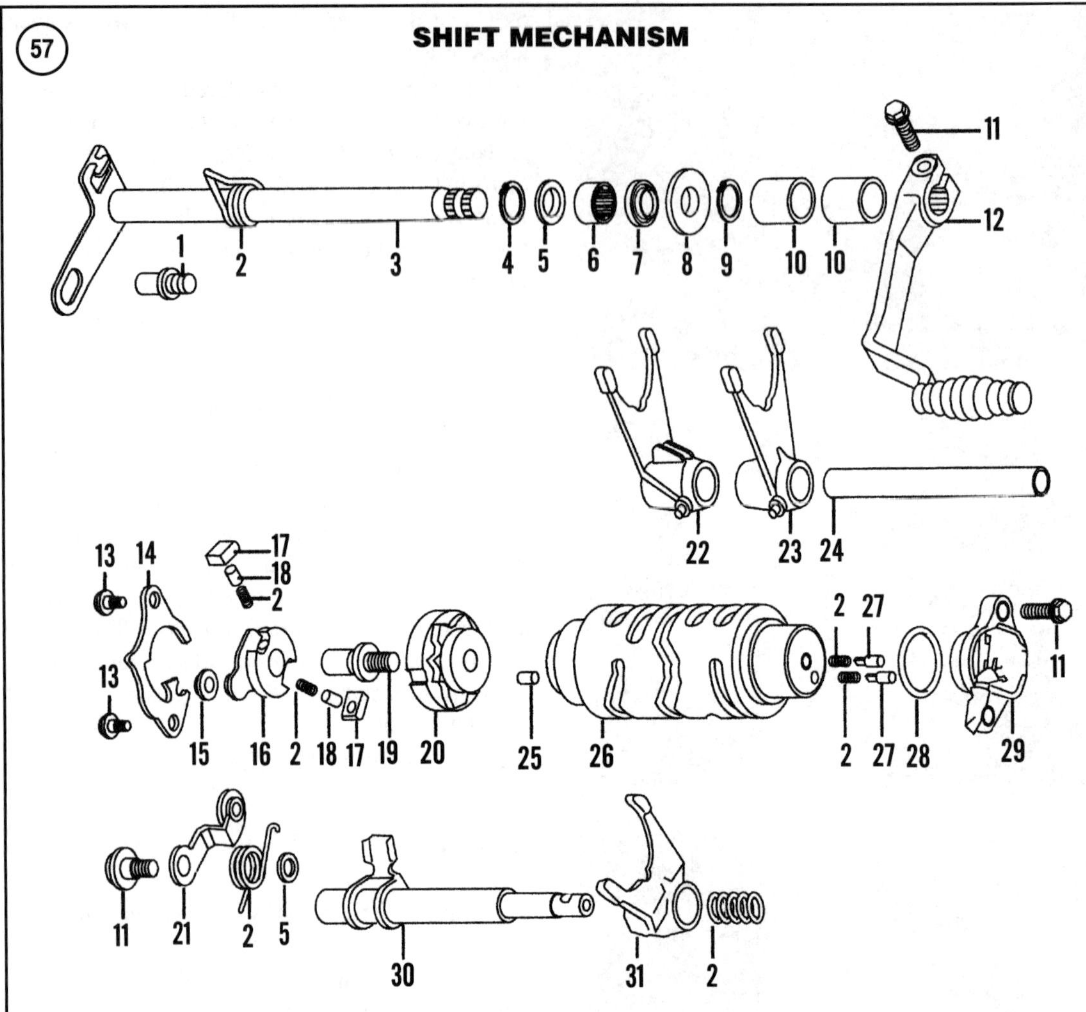

1. Spring stopper bolt
2. Spring
3. Gear shift shaft
4. Circlip
5. Washer
6. Bearing (crankcase)
7. Seal (crankcase)
8. Thrust washer
9. Circlip
10. Plastic collar
11. Bolt
12. Shift lever
13. Screw
14. Shift drum selector plate
15. Shift selector roller
16. Shift drum selector body
17. Pawl
18. Pawl pin
19. Center bolt
20. Shift drum cam
21. Cam stopper arm
22. No.1 Shift fork
23. No. 2 Shift fork
24. Shift fork shaft
25. Pin
26. Shift drum
27. Gear position switch contact
28. O-ring
29. Gear position switch
30. Reverse lock shaft
31. No. 3 Shift fork

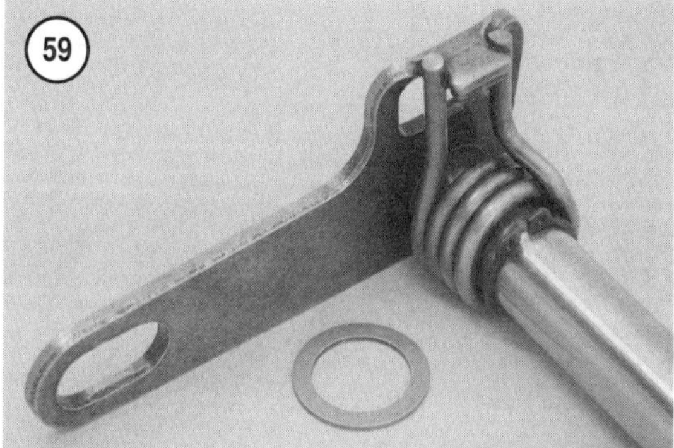

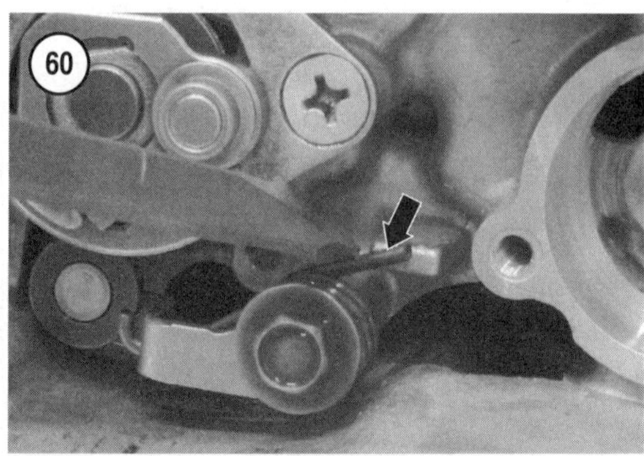

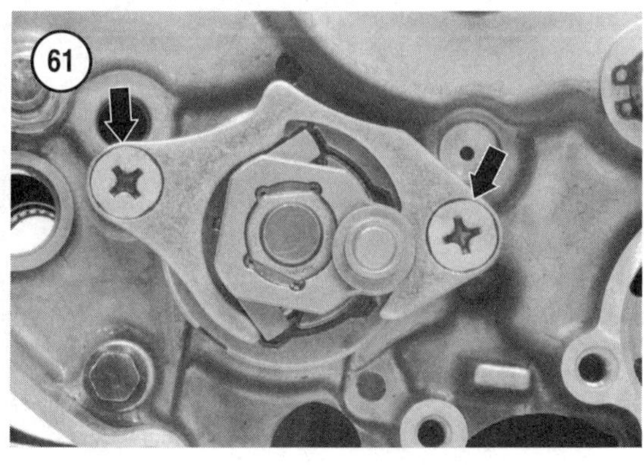

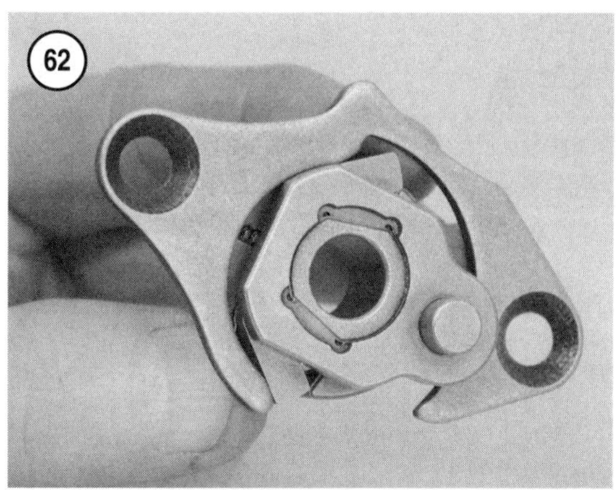

a. While removing the screws, hold the shift plate in place to prevent the selector assembly from falling.
b. When the screws are removed, slowly pull the plate and selector assembly from the shift drum stopper.
c. When the spring-loaded pawls are visible at the rear of the selector, grasp the pawls to prevent the pawl pins and springs from flying off the selector (**Figure 62**).

8. Remove the center bolt and shift drum cam (**Figure 63**).
9. Inspect the parts as described in this section.

Inspection

During inspection, replace parts that are worn or damaged.

1. Clean all parts in solvent.
2. Inspect the shift shaft assembly (**Figure 64**).
   a. Inspect the shaft for straightness.

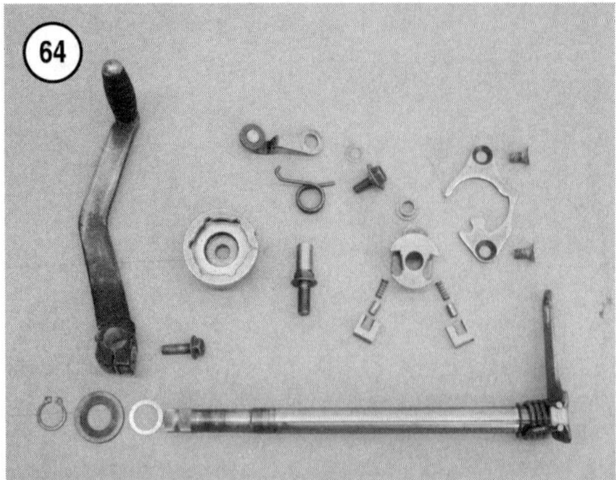

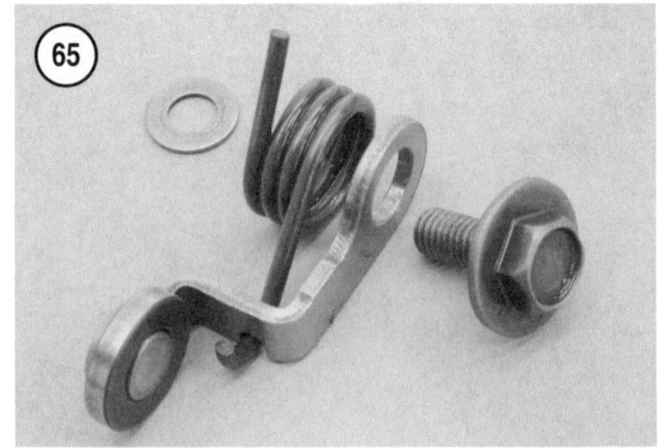

b. Inspect the roller engagement hole for wear. The hole should be symmetrical and not excessively worn.

c. Inspect the torsion spring for looseness, wear and fatigue cracks. If the spring is worn, inspect the condition of the spring post on the crankcase.

d. Inspect the washer and snap ring for wear and damage.

e. Inspect the shaft and lever splines for damage. The threads in the lever bolt must be in good condition. If necessary, use a tap and die to clean and straighten the threads.

3. Inspect the cam stopper assembly (**Figure 65**).

a. Inspect the roller on the stopper arm. It must be symmetrical and turn freely, but be firmly attached to the arm.

b. Inspect the fit of the shouldered bolt in the lever. The bolt must fit with minimal play. Excessive play can cause poor shifting.

c. Inspect the spring for wear or fatigue.

4. Inspect the shift drum cam and center bolt (**Figure 66**).

a. Inspect the detents inside the shift drum cam. The detents must be uniform and symmetrical. If wear is visible, the pawls may be jammed or damaged.

b. Inspect the center bolt. The shaft of the bolt must be smooth to allow the lever to pivot.

c. Inspect the shift detents and ramps on the outside of the shift drum cam (**Figure 67**). The detents and ramps must not be worn, or shifting will be imprecise.

d. Inspect the fit of the shift drum cam on the shift drum pin (**Figure 68**). The pin must be in good condition in order to properly engage

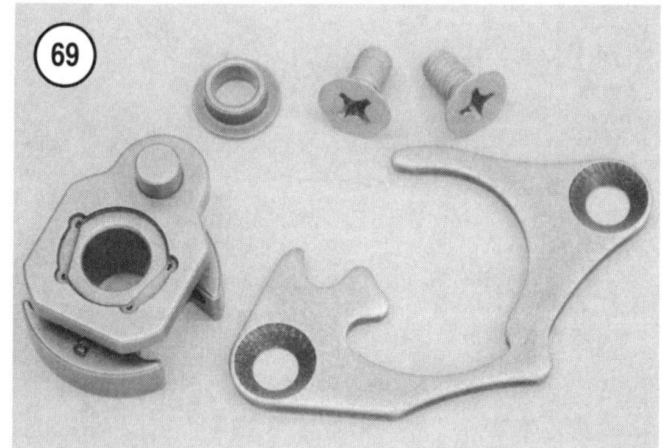

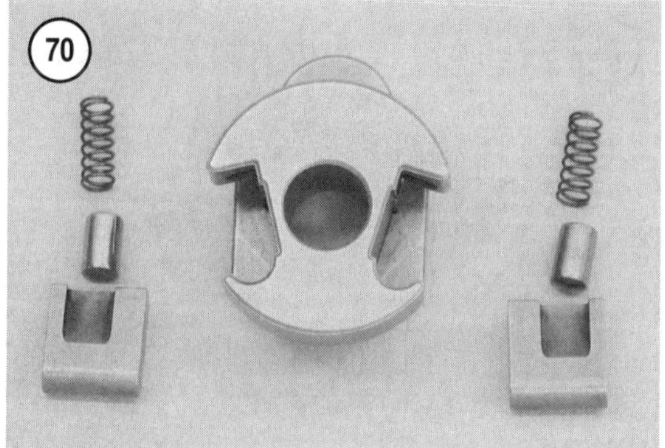

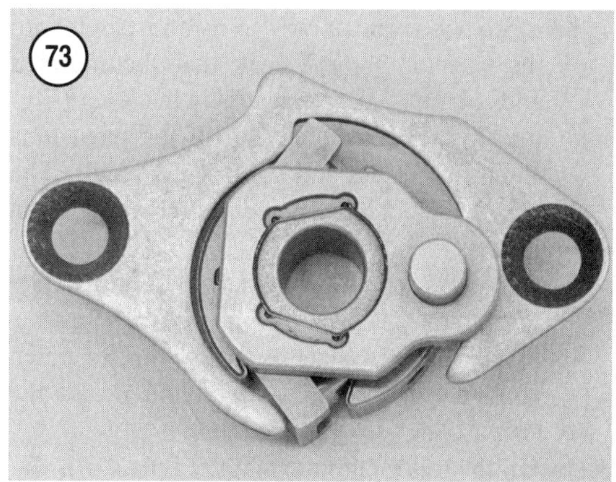

with the notch in the back of the shift drum cam.

5. Inspect the selector body, roller and shift drum plate (**Figure 69**).
   a. The roller should be symmetrical with no visible wear. The roller and selector body must fit together with minimal play.
   b. Inspect the shift drum plate for obvious wear.
6. Inspect the selector body and pawl assembly (**Figure 70**).
   a. Inspect the springs and pawl pins for wear and fatigue.
   b. Inspect the pawls for wear at their square end. The ends must be square in order to stay engaged in the shift drum stopper.
   c. Assemble the lever and pawl assembly (**Figure 71**), then insert it into the shift drum stopper. Check that the springs fully extend the pawls against the sides of the shift drum stopper.
7. Clean the threads in the shift drum and mounting bosses (**Figure 72**). Visually inspect the crankcase openings for debris.

Installation

1. Install the shift drum cam (**Figure 63**) and center bolt. Note the following:
   a. Engage the shift drum pin (**Figure 68**) with the notch in the shift drum stopper.
   b. Tighten the center bolt to 24 N•m (18 ft.-lb.).
2. Install the shift plate and shift drum selector assembly (**Figure 73**). Note the following:
   a. Apply threadlocking compound to the screw threads, then place the screws within reach of the installation point.

b. Insert the springs, pawl pins and pawls into the selector body. Check that the rounded ends of the pawls are seated in the lever (**Figure 74**). The rounded end of the pawl pins should point out and contact the pawls. The pawls must compress and retract smoothly in the lever.

c. Compress the pawls and install the shift selector into the shift drum cam (**Figure 75**).

d. Install the shift plate over the selector body. Hold the assembly in place and install the screws.

3. Install the roller onto the lever (**Figure 76**).
4. Install the stopper lever and spring (**Figure 65**).
   a. Install the washer behind the lever.
   b. Install the spring as shown in **Figure 60**.
   c. Check that the stopper lever pivots under spring pressure and the roller engages with the shift drum stopper.
5. Install the shift shaft assembly. Note the following:
   a. Install the washer on the shaft, against the snap ring (**Figure 77**).
   b. Lubricate the shaft and slide it through the crankcase. As the lever and spring approach the engine, engage the torsion spring with the post and the lever with the roller (**Figure 78**).
6. Install the shift lever as described in this chapter.
7. Check for proper shifting.
8. Install the oil pump idle gear. Install the shouldered side of the gear facing in (**Figure 79**). Install a new snap ring with the sharp edge facing out.
9. Install the clutch and right crankcase cover as described in this chapter.

CLUTCH CABLE REPLACEMENT

1. Remove the cable at the handlebar as follows:
   a. Pull back the dust cover from the clutch lever.
   b. Loosen the clutch cable locknut (A, **Figure 80**), then turn the adjuster (B) in until the cable can be removed from the lever and adjuster.
   c. If additional free play is needed, loosen the inline adjuster (**Figure 81**), then turn the adjuster in until the cable can be removed from the lever.
2. At the engine, remove the two bolts (A, **Figure 82**) securing the cable bracket and remove the cable from the release lever (B, **Figure 82**).

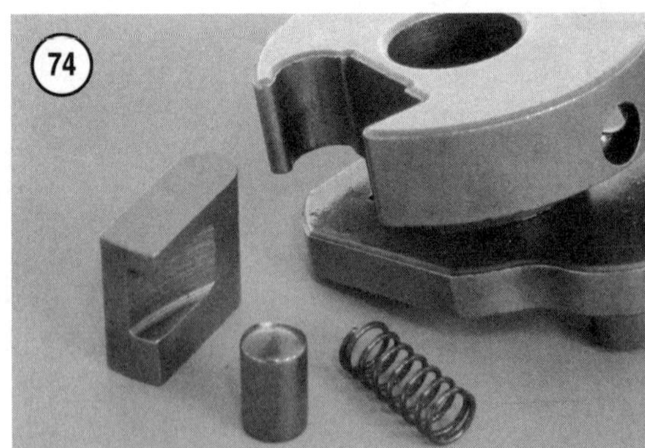
74

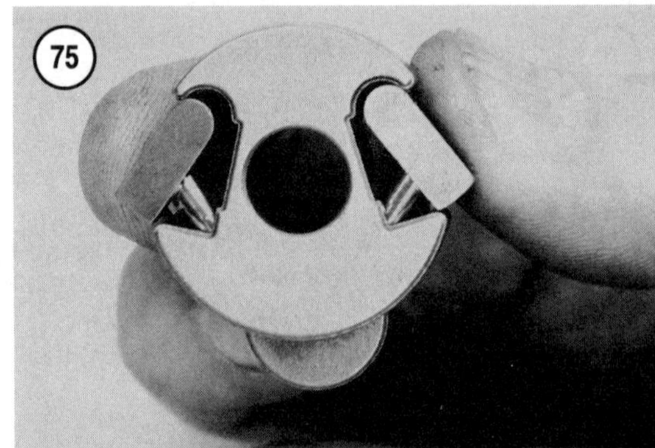
75

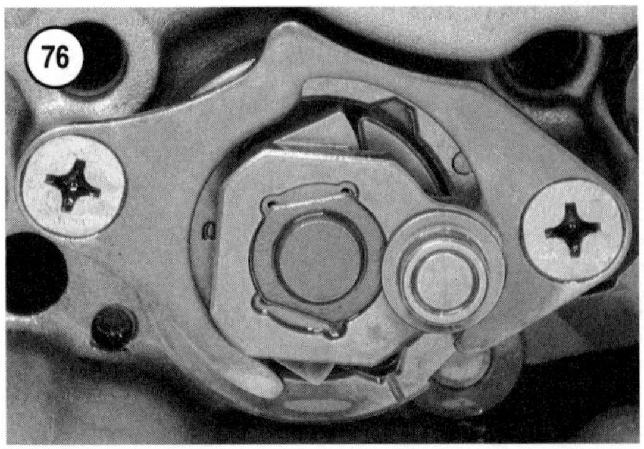
76

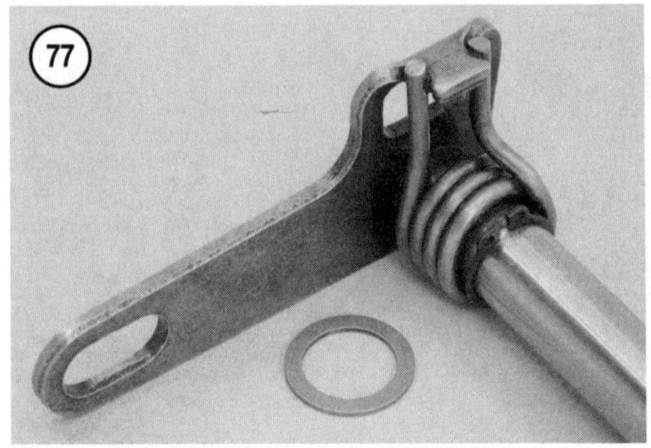
77

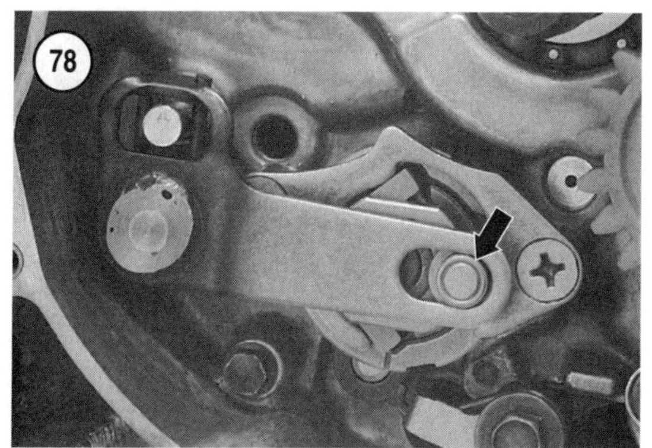

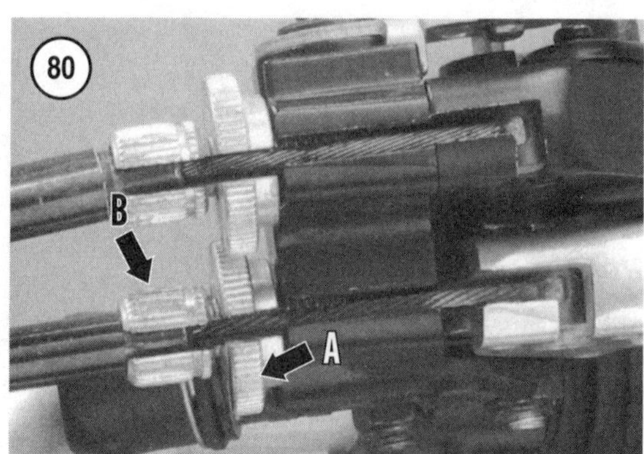

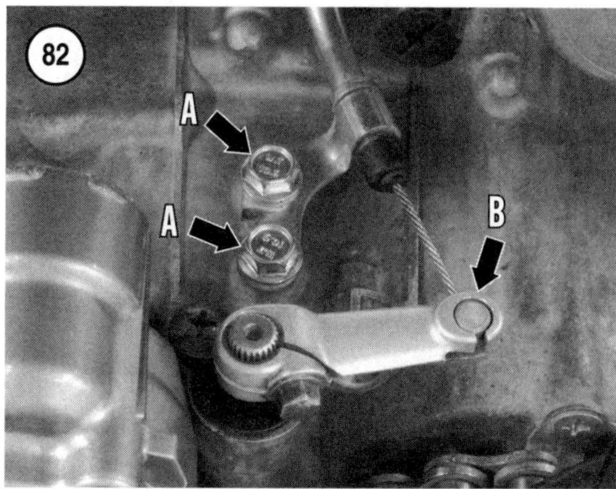

3. Remove the cable while noting the routing of the cable along the frame.
4. Clean the clutch lever, release lever and cable holder.
5. Lubricate the new cable with an aerosol cable lubricant as described in Chapter Three. Lubricate the cable ends with lithium grease.
6. Install and route the cable from the engine to the handlebar lever.
7. At the handlebar, attach the cable to the lever and thread the adjuster (B, **Figure 80**) to the middle of its travel.
8. Turn the cable adjuster (B, **Figure 80**) so there is approximately 12 mm (0.5 in.) of play at the end of the clutch lever. Tighten the locknut (A, **Figure 80**).
9. Refer to the clutch cable adjustment procedure in Chapter Three for final adjustment.

CLUTCH LEVER REPLACEMENT

Removal/Installation

1. Remove the clutch cable from the lever as described in this chapter and the parking brake cable as described in Chapter Thirteen.

NOTE
The clutch lever pivot bolt and parking brake pivot bolt are threaded into the clutch lever housing and then secured by a nut. The nut must be removed first in order to remove the pivot bolts.

2. To gain access to the clutch lever bolt (**Figure 83**), remove the parking brake mechanism from the lever as described in Chapter Thirteen.

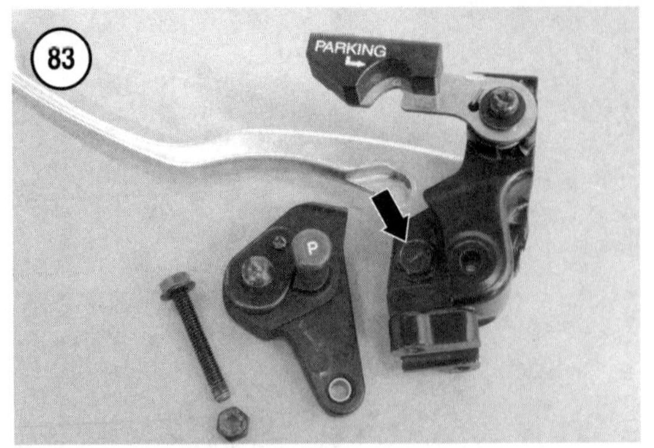
83
PARKING
P

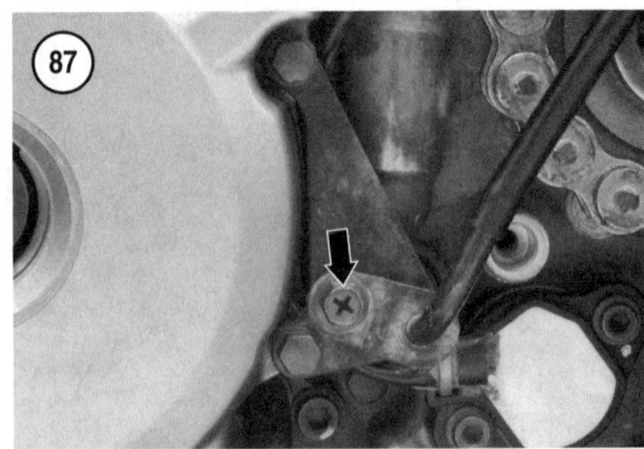
87

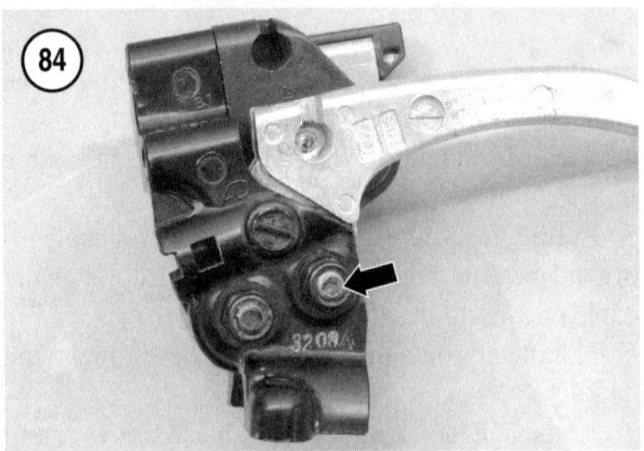
84

88

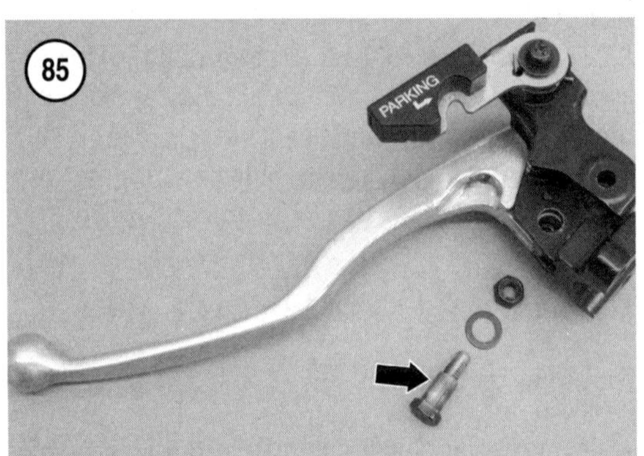
85
PARKING

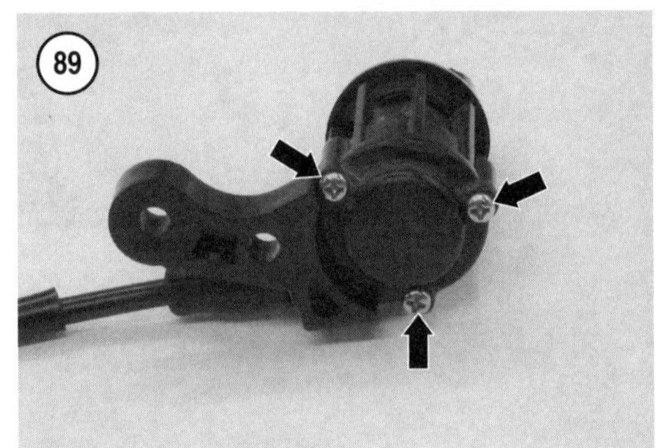
89

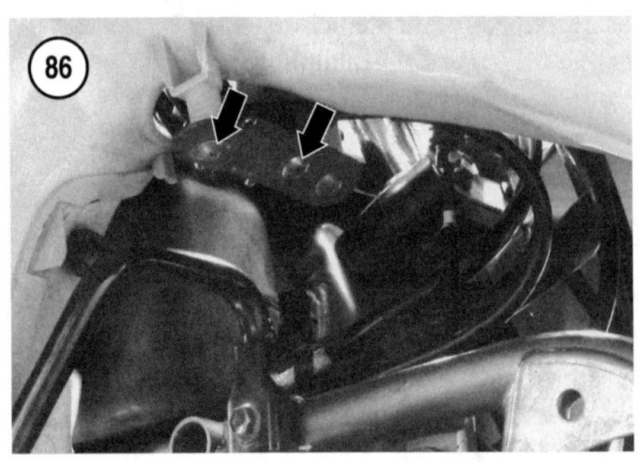
86

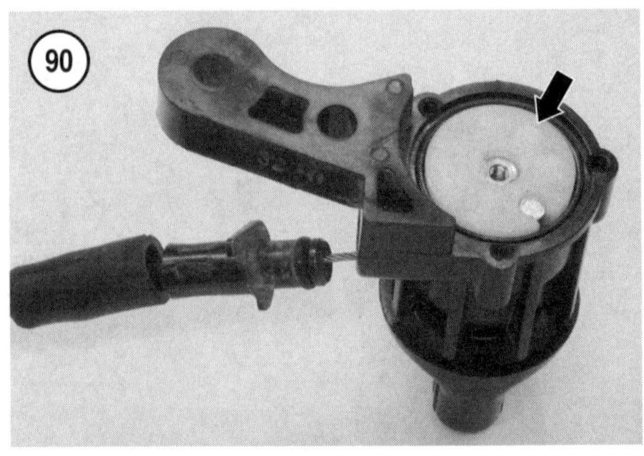
90

3. Remove the nut on the bottom of the clutch lever pivot bolt (**Figure 84**).
4. Remove the clutch lever pivot bolt (**Figure 85**).
5. Replace the clutch lever and examine the housing for cracks or damage.
6. Installation is the reverse of removal.

REVERSE SHIFT CABLE REPLACEMENT

Removal/Installation

1. Remove the upper fuel tank cover, side panels, and front fender as described in Chapter Fourteen. When removing the front fender, remove screws securing the reverse selection lever from the fender assembly (**Figure 86**)
2. Remove the fuel tank as described in Chapter Eight.
3. Remove the bolt securing the cable mount from the crankcase cover (**Figure 87**).
4. Remove the cable end from the reverse shift shaft (**Figure 88**).
5. Remove the screws securing the backing plate on the reverse selector lever (**Figure 89**).
6. Lift out the nylon cable holder and remove the cable from the selector body (**Figure 90**).
7. Installation is the reverse of removal.

Table 1 CLUTCH SPECIFICATIONS

	Specification mm (in.)	Service limit mm (in.)
Clutch cable free play	10-15 (0.4-0.6)	–
Clutch		
Spring free length	35.2 (1.39)	34.5 (1.36)
Friction disc thickness	2.9-3.0 (0.11-0.12)	2.6 (0.10)
Clutch plate warp	–	0.20 (0.008)
Clutch plates		
Drive plate thickness		
No. 1 and No. 2 and No. 3	2.92-3.08 (0.115-0.121)	2.62 (0.103)
Drive plate claw width		
No. 1 and No. 2	13.7-13.8 (0.539-0.543)	13.2 (0.520)
2003-2004 models		
Number of friction plates No. 1*	7	
Number of friction plates No. 2*	1	
Number of clutch plates	7	
2005-on models		
Number of friction plates No. 1*	1	
Number of friction plates No. 2*	7	
Number of friction plates No. 3	1	
Number of clutch plates	8	

*These clutch plates are composed of different compounds but are visually identical.

Table 2 CLUTCH TORQUE SPECIFICATIONS

Item	N•m	in.-lb.	ft.-lb.
Clutch hub nut	70	–	52
Clutch spring bolts	10	88	–
Crankcase cover bolts	10	88	–
Shift drum center bolt	24	–	18

CHAPTER SEVEN

TRANSMISSION AND INTERNAL SHIFT MECHANISM

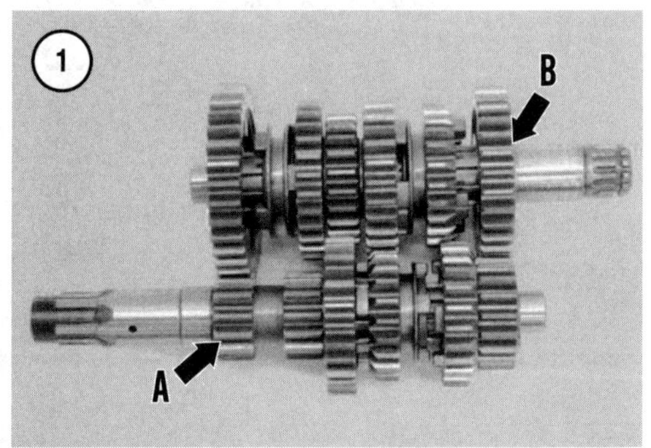

This chapter provides procedures for the transmission and internal shift mechanism. Specifications are in **Table 1** and **Table 2** at the end of this chapter.

Refer to Chapter Five to separate the crankcase.

TRANSMISSION OPERATION

The gears on the input shaft (A, **Figure 1**) are meshed with the gears on the output shaft (B). Each pair of meshed gears represents one gear ratio. For each pair of gears, one of the gears is splined to its shaft, while the other gear freewheels on its shaft.

Next to each freewheeling gear is a gear that is splined to the shaft. This locked gear can slide on the shaft and lock into the freewheeling gear, making that gear ratio active. Anytime the transmission is *in gear* one pair of meshed gears are locked to their shafts, and that gear ratio is selected. All other meshed gears have one freewheeling gear, making those ratios inoperative.

To engage and disengage the various gear ratios, the splined gears are moved by shift forks. The shift forks are guided by the shift drum, which is operated by the shift lever. As the transimission is up shifted and down shifted, the shift drum rotates and guides the forks to engage and disengage pairs of gears on the transmission shafts.

Reverse gear is locked out during normal forward operation and cannot be engaged. By activating the reverse gear selector, the lockout on the shift drum is moved and the vehicle can be shifted into reverse.

2

TRANSMISSION SERVICE

The crankcase must be separated to remove the transmission and internal shift mechanism (**Figure 2**).

Transmission work requires careful inspection of the parts, as well as keeping the parts oriented so they can be reinstalled in the correct direction on the shafts. The gears and snap rings *must* be installed in the same direction as they were before disassembly. If necessary, slide the parts onto a long dowel or screwdriver as the parts are removed, or, make an identification mark on each part to indicate position and orientation.

Always install new snap rings. The snap rings fatigue and distort when they are removed. Do not reuse them, even though they appear to be in good condition. To install a new snap ring without distorting or binding it, hold the closed side of the snap ring with a pair of pliers while the open side is spread with snap ring pliers (**Figure 3**). While holding the spread ring with both tools, slide it over the shaft and into position.

Usually, snap rings have one rounded edge, while the other side has a sharp edge (**Figure 4**). The inner sharp edge prevents the snap ring from lifting out of the shaft groove when lateral pressure is applied to the snap ring. Always look at the inner and outer edges of the snap ring. Some snap rings are manufactured with the inner and outer sharp edge on opposite sides. If a snap ring has no identifiable sharp edge, the snap ring can be installed in either direction. In all cases, new snap rings must be installed at assembly, and when applicable, must be installed in the same direction as the removed snap rings.

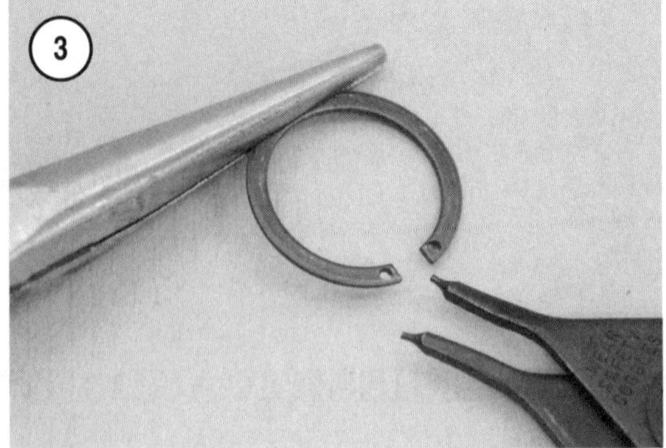

3

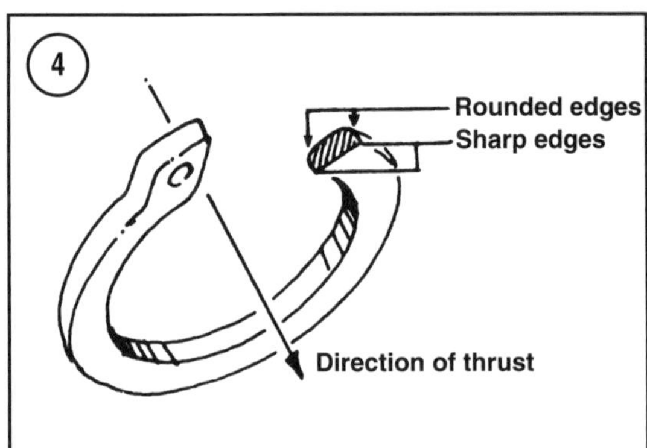

4

5

6

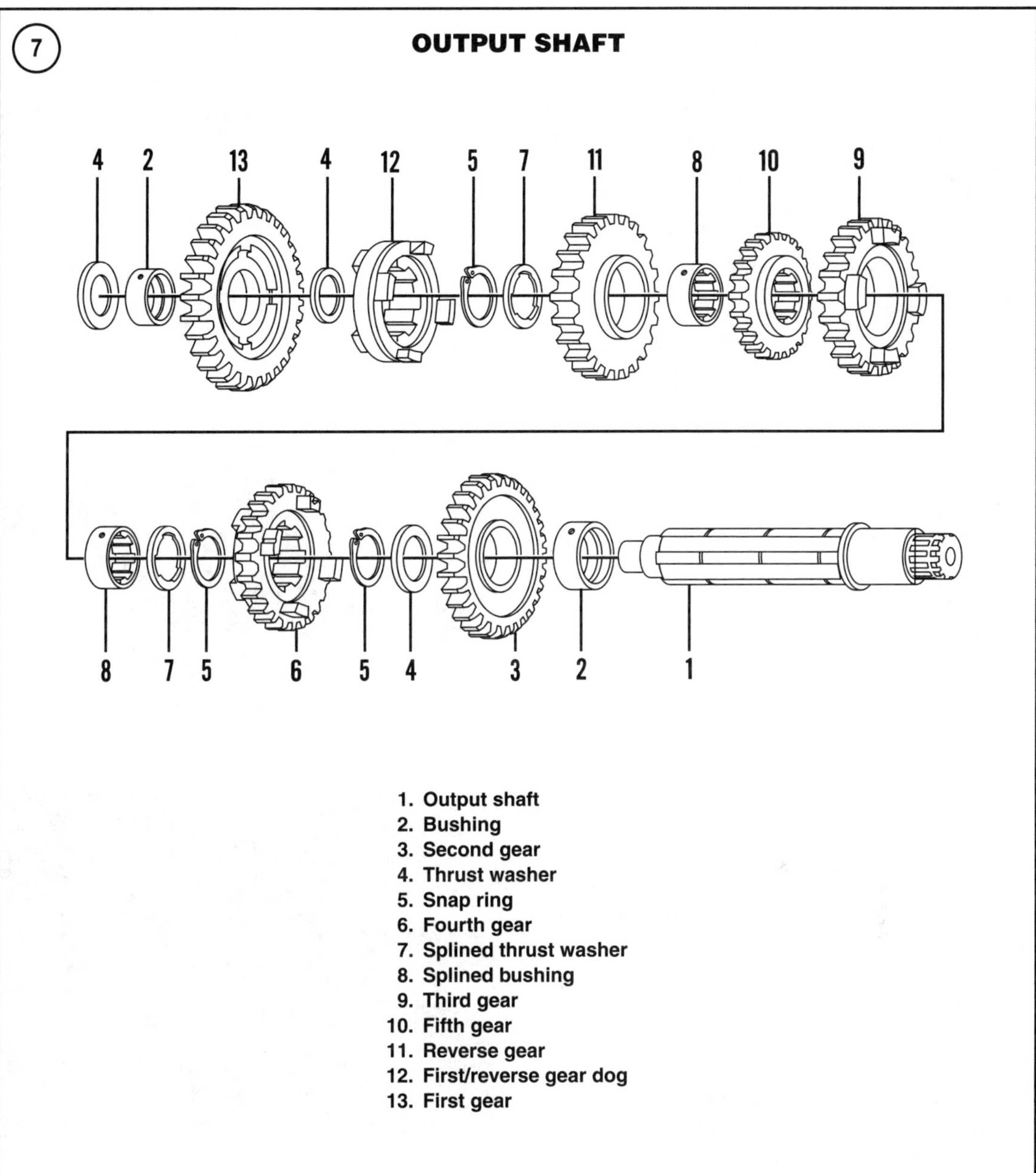

When installed on a splined shaft, make sure the snap ring is positioned over a groove in the shaft (**Figure 5**).

OUTPUT SHAFT

Disassembly

1. Disassemble the output shaft (**Figure 6** and **Figure 7**) in the following order:

a. Thrust washer.
b. First gear.
c. First gear bushing.
d. Thrust washer.
e. First and reverse gear dogs.
f. Snap rings.
g. Splined washer.
h. Reverse gear.
i. Reverse gear splined bushing.
j. Fifth gear.

k. Third gear.
l. Third gear splined bushing.
m. Splined washer.
n. Snap ring.
o. Fourth gear.
p. Snap ring.
q. Thrust washer.
r. Second gear.
s. Second gear bushing.

2. Inspect each part as described in this chapter. Store each part in order and in the correct orientation until assembly.

Assembly

Throughout the procedure, the orientation of the gears and snap rings is made in relation to the open end of the output shaft. Lubricate all parts with engine oil.

1. Clean and dry all parts before assembly. Lubricate all parts with engine oil.
2. Install the second gear bushing (**Figure 8**).
3. Install the second gear (**Figure 9**), with the gear dogs facing toward the open end of the shaft.
4. Install the thrust washer on the shaft (**Figure 10**).
5. Install the *new* snap ring on the shaft (**Figure 11**). The sharp edge must face *out* away from the gear. The snap ring must seat in the shaft groove. Position the snap ring gap over a groove in the shaft.
6. Install the thrust washer on the shaft (**Figure 12**).
7. Install the fourth gear onto the shaft (**Figure 13**) with the gear against second gear and the shift fork groove facing toward the open end of the shaft.
8. Install the *new* snap ring onto the shaft (**Figure 11**). The sharp edge must face *toward* the fourth

gear. The snap ring must seat in the shaft groove. Position the snap ring gap over a groove in the shaft.

9. Install the splined thrust washer on the shaft (**Figure 14**).

10. Install the splined third gear bushing onto the shaft (**Figure 15**) making sure the lubrication holes of the bushing align with the lubrication holes in the shaft.

11. Install the third gear onto the shaft (**Figure 16**) over the bushing.

12. Install the splined fifth gear onto the shaft (**Figure 17**).

13. Install the splined reverse gear bushing onto the shaft (**Figure 18**) making sure the lubrication holes of the bushing align with the lubrication holes in the shaft.

14. Install the reverse gear onto the shaft and over the bushing (**Figure 18**).

15. Install the splined thrust washer (**Figure 19**) onto the shaft.

16. Install the *new* snap ring (**Figure 20**) onto the shaft. The sharp edge must face *toward* the open end of the shaft. The snap ring must seat in the shaft

19

23

20

24

21

25

22

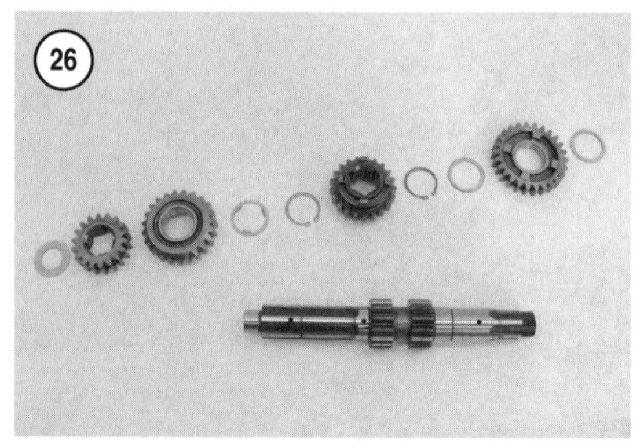
26

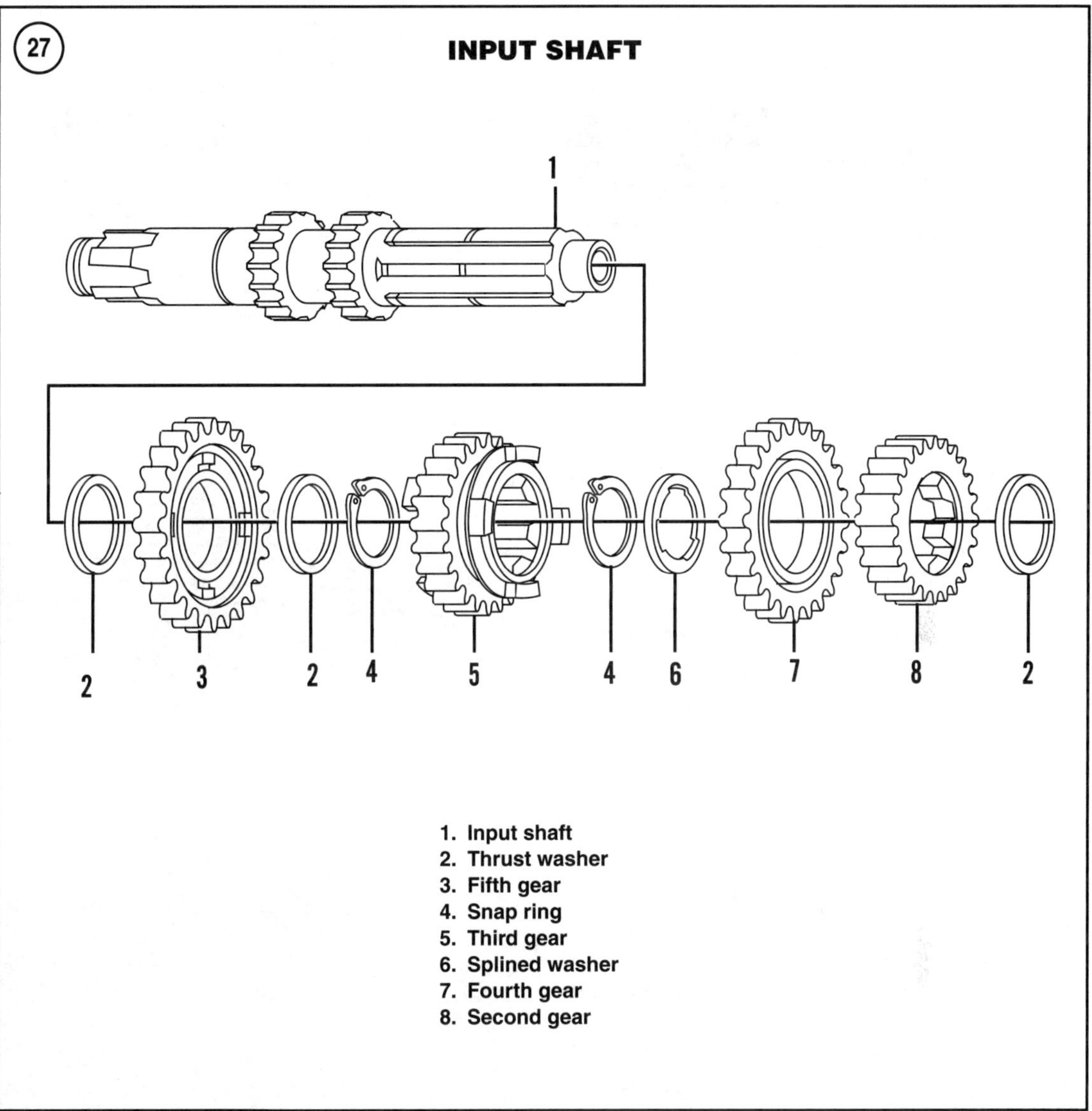

groove. Position the snap ring gap over a groove in the shaft.

17. Install the splined first/reverse gear dog (**Figure 21**) onto the shaft .

18. Install the thrust washer (**Figure 22**) onto the end of the shaft.

19. Install the first gear bushing (**Figure 23**) onto the shaft.

20. Install the first gear (**Figure 24**) over the bushing.

21. Install the thrust washer (**Figure 25**) onto the end of the shaft.

22. With the parts in their correct positions, wrap a rubber band around the end of the shaft. Check that all the parts are secure and that the gears spin, slide and engage freely on the shaft. Wrap and store the assembly until it is ready for installation.

INPUT SHAFT

Disassembly

1. Disassemble the input shaft (**Figure 26** and **Figure 27**) in the following order:
   a. Thrust washer.
   b. Second gear.
   c. Fourth gear.
   d. Splined washer.

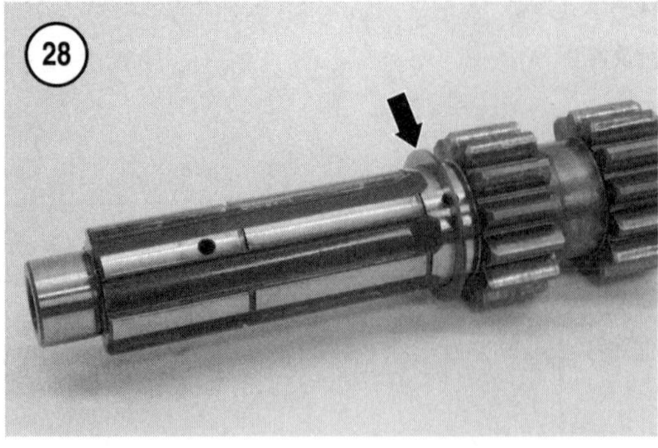

28

29

e. Snap ring.
f. Third gear.
g. Snap ring.
h. Thrust washer.
i. Fifth gear.
j. Thrust washer.

2. Inspect each part as described in this chapter. Store each part in order and in the correct orientation until assembly.

30

Assembly

Throughout the procedure, the orientation of many parts is made in relation to the splined end of the shaft.

1. Clean and dry all parts before assembly. Lubricate all parts with engine oil. Begin assembly at the smooth end of the shaft.
2. Install the thust washer (**Figure 28**) onto the shaft.
3. Install the fifth gear (**Figure 29**) onto the shaft with the dogs of the gear facing the open end of the shaft.
4. Install the thrust washer (**Figure 30**) onto the shaft.
5. Install the *new* snap ring (**Figure 31**) onto the shaft. The sharp edge must face *toward* the open end of the shaft away from the fifth gear. The snap ring must seat in the shaft groove. Position the snap ring gap over a groove in the shaft.
6. Install the third gear (**Figure 32**) onto the shaft. The side of the gear with the shift fork groove must face out toward the open end of the shaft.
7. Install the *new* snap ring (**Figure 33**) onto the shaft. The sharp edge must face *away* from the open end of the shaft towards the third gear. The snap ring must seat in the shaft groove. Position the snap ring gap over a groove in the shaft.

31

32

8. Install the splined thrust washer (**Figure 34**) onto the shaft.
9. Install the fourth gear (**Figure 35**) onto the shaft.
10. Install the splined second gear (**Figure 36**) onto the shaft.
11. Install the thrust washer (**Figure 37**) onto the end of the shaft.
12. With the parts in their correct positions, wrap a rubber band around the end of the shaft. Check that all the parts are secure and that the gears spin, slide and engage freely on the shaft. Wrap and store the assembly until it is ready for installation.

7

REVERSE IDLE GEAR AND SHAFT

Disassembly

1. Remove the parts from the reverse idle gear shaft (**Figure 38**) in the following order.
   a. Remove the thrust washer (A, **Figure 39**).
   b. Remove the spring washer (B, **Figure 39**).
   c. Remove the reverse idle gear.
   d. Remove the reverse idle gear bushing.
   e. Remove the thrust washer.
   f. If necessary remove the snap ring (**Figure 40**) from the shaft. If the snap ring is removed, replace it.
2. Inspect each part as described in this chapter. Store each part in order and in the correct orientation until assembly.

TRANSMISSION INSPECTION

Input and Output Shafts

1. Inspect the shafts for the following:
   a. Broken or damaged gear teeth (A, **Figure 41**) on the input shaft.

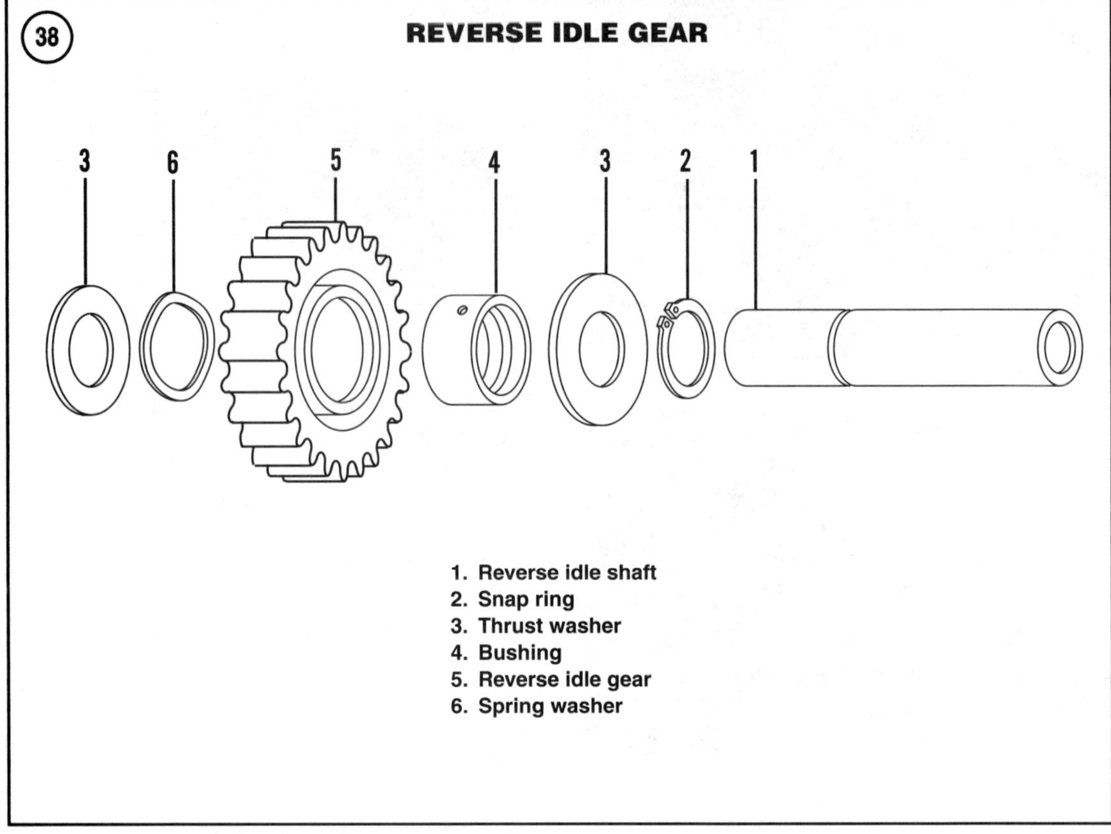

b. Worn or damaged splines (B, **Figure 41**).
c. Rounded or damaged snap ring grooves (C, **Figure 41**).
d. Clean oil holes (D, **Figure 41**).
e. Wear, galling or other damage on the bearing/bushing surfaces (E, **Figure 41**). A blue discoloration indicates excessive heat. The shafts should fit firmly in their crankcase bearings, with no evidence of play. It is common for some shafts to resist removal or installation into their bearings. If the shaft requires light seating with a soft mallet, this does not necessarily indicate a damaged bearing or shaft.
f. Damaged threads (F, **Figure 41**). Mildly damaged threads can be trued with a thread die.

2. Assemble the shafts as described in this chapter.

Gears, Bushings and Washers

1. Inspect the gears for the following:
   a. Broken or damaged teeth (A, **Figure 42**).
   b. Scored, galled or fractured bore (B, **Figure 42**). A blue discoloration indicates excessive heat. For gears that use a bushing on the shaft, check the fit of the bushing in the gear and on the shaft. Replace the bushing if it does not freely fit into the gear or onto the shaft.
   c. Worn or damaged splines (C, **Figure 42**).
   d. Worn, damaged or rounded gear dogs (D, **Figure 42**). Any wear on the dogs and mating recesses should be uniform. If the dogs are not worn evenly, the remaining dogs will be overstressed and possibly fail. Check the engagement of the dogs by placing the gears at their appropriate positions on the output shaft, then twisting the gears together. Check for positive engagement in both directions. If damage is evident, also check the condition of the shift forks, as described in this chapter.
   e. Worn or damaged shift fork groove. Measure the width of the groove (**Figure 43**). Refer to **Table 2** for the specification.
   f. Smooth gear operation on the shafts. Bored gears should fit firmly on the shaft, yet spin

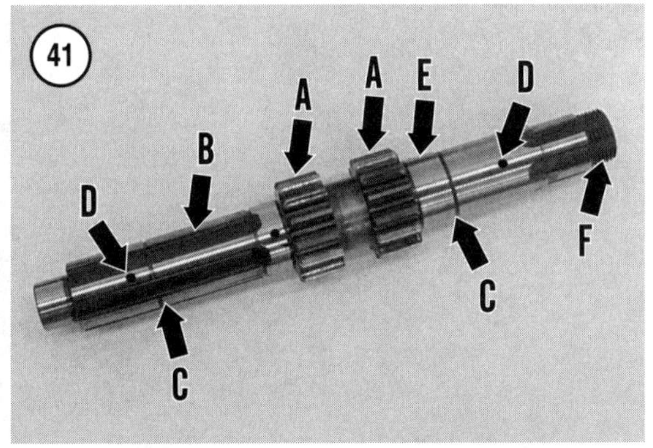

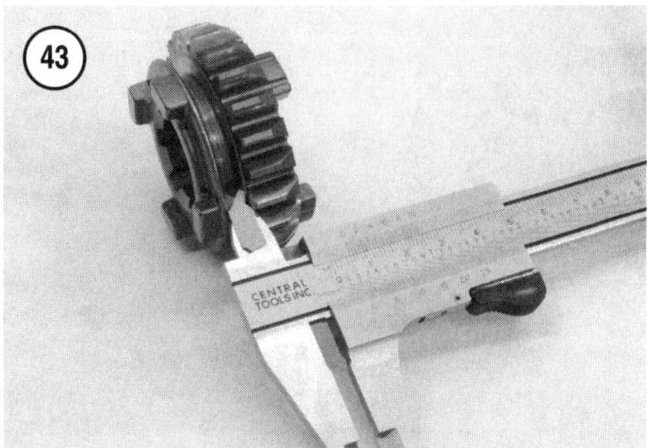

smoothly and freely. Splined gears should fit snugly at their position on the shaft, yet slide smoothly and freely from side to side. If a gear is worn or damaged, replace it and the gear it mates to on the other shaft.

2. Inspect the washers. The washers should be smooth and show no signs of wear or damage. The teeth on the spline washers should not be missing or damaged.

3. Install the parts onto their shafts as described in this chapter.

7

SHIFT DRUM AND FORKS

As the transmission is shifted, the shift drum and fork assembly engages and disengages pairs of gears on the transmission shafts. Gear shifting is done by the shift forks, which are guided by cam grooves on the shift drum.

It is important that the shift drum grooves, shift forks and mating gear grooves are in good condition. Excessive wear between the parts causes unreliable and poor engagement of the gears. This can lead to premature wear of the gear dogs and other parts.

Inspection

When inspecting the shift fork and drum assembly, replace parts that are worn, or marginally within specification.

1. Clean all parts in solvent and dry with compressed air.

2. Inspect the shift drum (**Figure 44**) for the following:

   a. Worn shift drum grooves and cam points. The grooves should be a uniform width. Worn

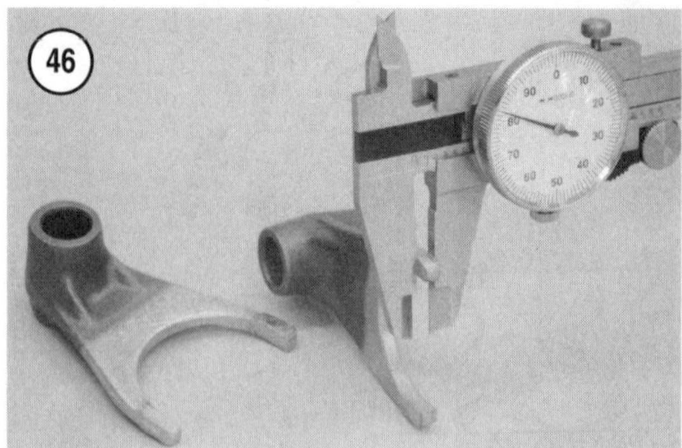

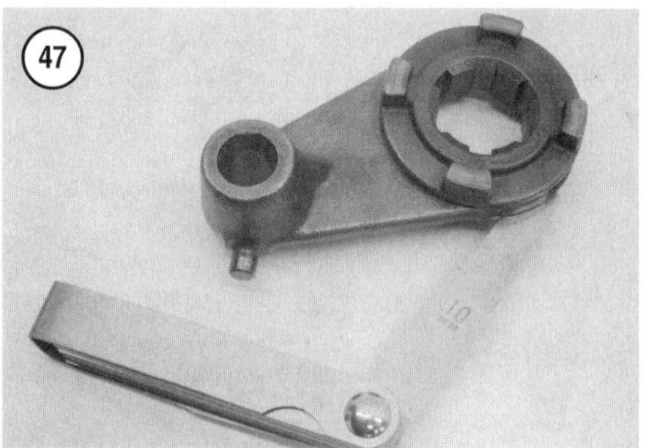

grooves can prevent complete gear engagement, which can cause rough shifting and allows the transmission to disengage.

b. Worn or damaged bearing surfaces. Besides wear, look for discoloration caused by overheating and lack of lubrication. Fit the shift drum into the crankcase bearings and check for play. If necessary, replace the shift drum bearings as described in Chapter Five.

c. Worn or loose end pin.

3. Inspect each shift fork for wear and damage. Inspect the:

a. Guide pin. The pin should be symmetrical and not flat on the side. Fit each fork guide pin into its groove (**Figure 45**) in the shift drum and check for lateral play. Although there is no specified clearance, the guide pin and groove should have a consistent, small amount of play along the length of the groove.

b. Shift fork thickness. Measure both claws at the end (**Figure 46**). Refer to **Table 2** for the specification.

c. Shift fork to gear groove clearance. Measure the side clearance between each fork and its mating gear groove (**Figure 47**). Refer to **Table 2** for specifications. Shift fork No. 1 mates with fifth gear and shift fork No. 2 mates with fourth gear on the drive shaft. Shift fork No. 3 mates with third gear on the output shaft.

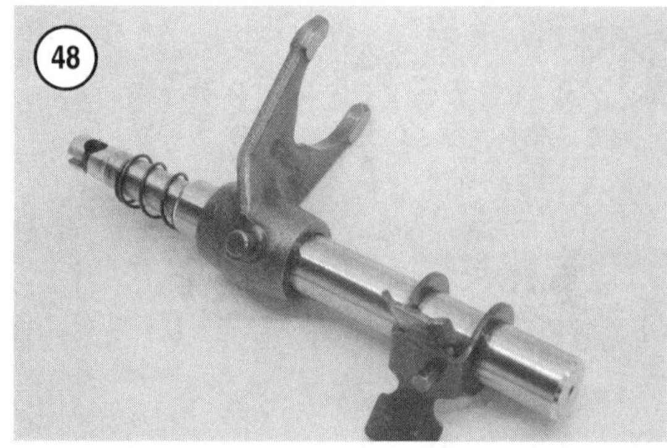

4. Inspect the shift fork shafts for wear and damage.

5. Install the shift forks onto their shafts (**Figure 48**). The forks should slide and pivot smoothly with no excessive play or tightness.

6. Install the shift drum, forks and transmission assembly as described in Chapter Five.

Table 1 TRANSMISSION SPECIFICATIONS

Item	Specifications
Primary reduction ratio	2.960 (74/25)
Final reduction ratio	2.857 (40/14)
Transmission	5-speed plus reverse, constant mesh
Shift pattern	R-N-1-2-3-4-5
Gear ratios	
First gear	2.538 (33/13)
Second gear	1.666 (30/18)
Third gear	1.238 (26/21)
Fourth gear	1.000 (23/23)
Fifth gear	0.846 (22/26)
Reverse	2.153 (28/13)

Table 2 SHIFT FORK SPECIFICATIONS

Item	New mm (in.)	Service limit mm (in.)
Shift fork finger thickness	4.8-4.9 (0.188-1.92)	–
Shift fork groove width	5.0-5.1 (0.196-0.20)	–
Shift fork to gear groove clearance	–	0.5 (0.19)

NOTES

CHAPTER EIGHT

FUEL SYSTEM

This chapter provides procedures for the carburetor, fuel valve, fuel tank, throttle position sensor and cable replacement. Also included is information on carburetor operation.

Refer to *Safety* in Chapter One before working on the fuel system. Refer to Chapter Three for air filter service, cable adjustment and cable lubrication.

Carburetor specifications are in **Tables 1-3** at the end of this chapter.

CARBURETOR

Operation

The Mikuni BSR is a vacuum-controlled, or constant velocity, carburetor. It uses both a throttle valve and diaphragm-operated slide to regulate fuel to the engine. The throttle valve (**Figure 1**) is located on the output side of the carburetor and is connected to the throttle cable. It is not connected to any fuel-regulating device. The slide and diaphragm assembly, located at the center of the carburetor, regulates fuel by a jet needle at the bottom of the slide (**Figure 2**). The diaphragm is sealed at the top of the carburetor by the vacuum chamber cover

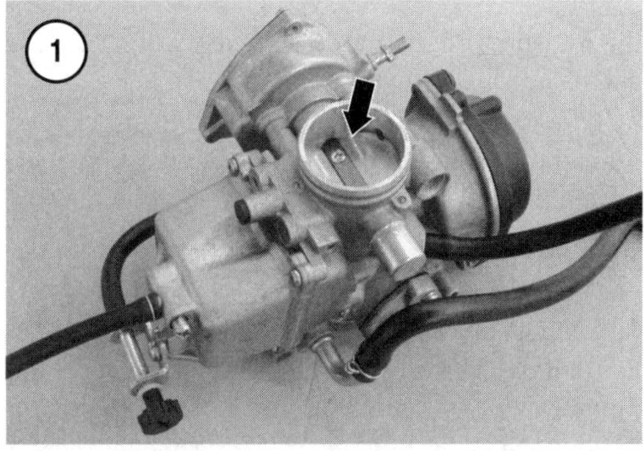

(**Figure 3**). The diaphragm divides and seals the large chamber into a lower and upper chamber (**Figure 4**).

During operation, when the throttle valve is opened, air demand and speed through the carburetor is increased. As air passes under the slide, air pressure drops in that area. This low air pressure is vented to the upper diaphragm chamber. The lower diaphragm chamber is vented to atmospheric pressure. This difference in pressure causes the slide and jet needle to rise, allowing fuel to pass into the carburetor throat. When the throttle valve is closed,

the pressure differential lowers, allowing the slide and jet needle to lower.

Refer to the *Carburetor Operation* in this chapter for carburetor circuit details.

Removal and Installation

1. Support the vehicle so it is stable and secure.
2. Remove the seat as described in Chapter Fourteen.
3. Remove the front fender as described in Chapter Fourteen.
4. Remove the fuel tank as described in this chapter.
5. Remove the bolt securing the oil return tank (**Figure 5**) and slide the hose clip down and remove the hose from the cylinder, then remove the tank vent hoses (**Figure 6**). Lift out the oil return tank.
6. Open the drain (**Figure 7**) on the bottom of the float chamber and drain any remaining fuel .
7. Remove the throttle cables as follows:
   a. Loosen the locknuts on the top of the cable near the throttle (**Figure 8**) and on the carburetor (**Figure 9**).

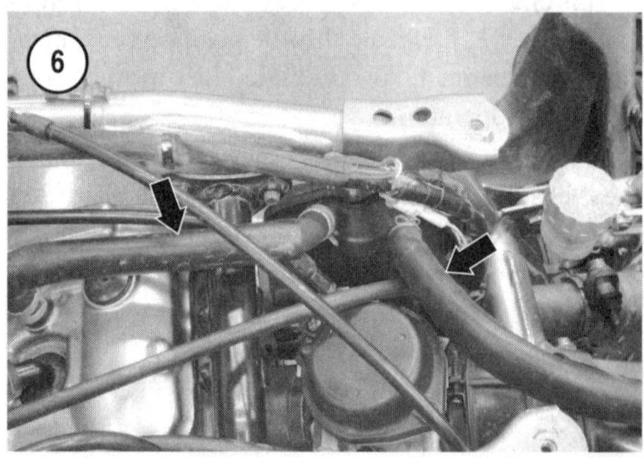

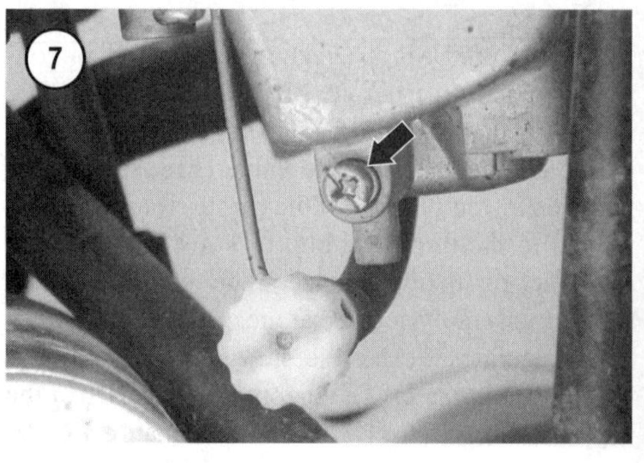

8

12

9

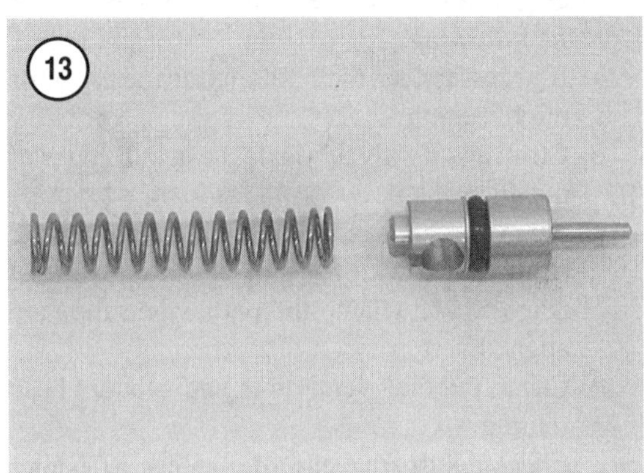
13

10

11

b. Remove the three screws on the throttle cam housing cover and remove the cover from the carburetor (**Figure 10**). Do not damage or loosen the O-ring on the cover.

c. Lift the throttle plate linkage up by operating the throttle thumb lever and inserting a small screwdriver to hold the throttle open, then work the slack in the cable around the cam until it frees the small brass keeper on the end of the throttle cable (**Figure 11**).

d. Remove the brass keeper and screw the barrel adjuster all the way out to remove the cable from the carburetor.

8. Remove the choke cable as follows:

a. Unscrew the large nut securing the choke cable (**Figure 12**) into the carburetor body.

b. Remove the choke mechanism (**Figure 13**) from the end of the choke cable. It is under spring tension and can easily fall off.

9. On 2005-on models, disconnect the throttle position sensor at the wire connector. Do not remove the sensor (**Figure 14**) from the carburetor.

10. Loosen the clamps from the air filter housing duct and intake duct (**Figure 15**).

11. Remove the carburetor from the ducts as follows:
   a. Pry up on the ducts to break them free from the carburetor. If necessary, lightly spray penetrating lubricant under the duct.
   b. Push the carburetor forward and back and pry the ducts off the carburetor. Pull the carburetor to the left side of the engine as the ducts are worked off. Keep the carburetor upright when it is removed or fuel may spill out.
12. Disassemble the carburetor as described in this section.
13. Reverse this procedure to install the carburetor. Note the following:
   a. If necessary, set the pilot mixture screw to its initial setting.
   b. Clean and lightly lubricate the inside edges of the ducts.
   c. Align and engage the boss on the carburetor (**Figure 16**) with the slot in the intake duct (**Figure 17**). Clamp the parts when they are aligned vertically.
   d. Check the fuel, vent, drain and vacuum hose routing.
   e. Check/adjust the throttle cables (Chapter Three).
   f. Check the throttle for proper operation.
   g. Open the fuel valve and check the carburetor for leaks.
   h. If necessary, adjust the idle speed and pilot mixture screw settings (Chapter Three).

Disassembly and Assembly

Refer to **Figure 18** or **Figure 19**.

1. Remove the vent and vacuum hoses (**Figure 20**).
2. On 2005-on models, determine if the throttle position sensor (**Figure 14**) should be removed, as follows:

CAUTION
If the sensor is left in the carburetor, do not submerge the carburetor body in solvent.

   a. If an ohmmeter is available, perform the resistance tests described in *Throttle Position Sensor* in this chapter. If the sensor is damaged or out of adjustment, further carburetor disassembly may not be necessary. If disassembly is necessary, remove the sensor.

14

15

16

17

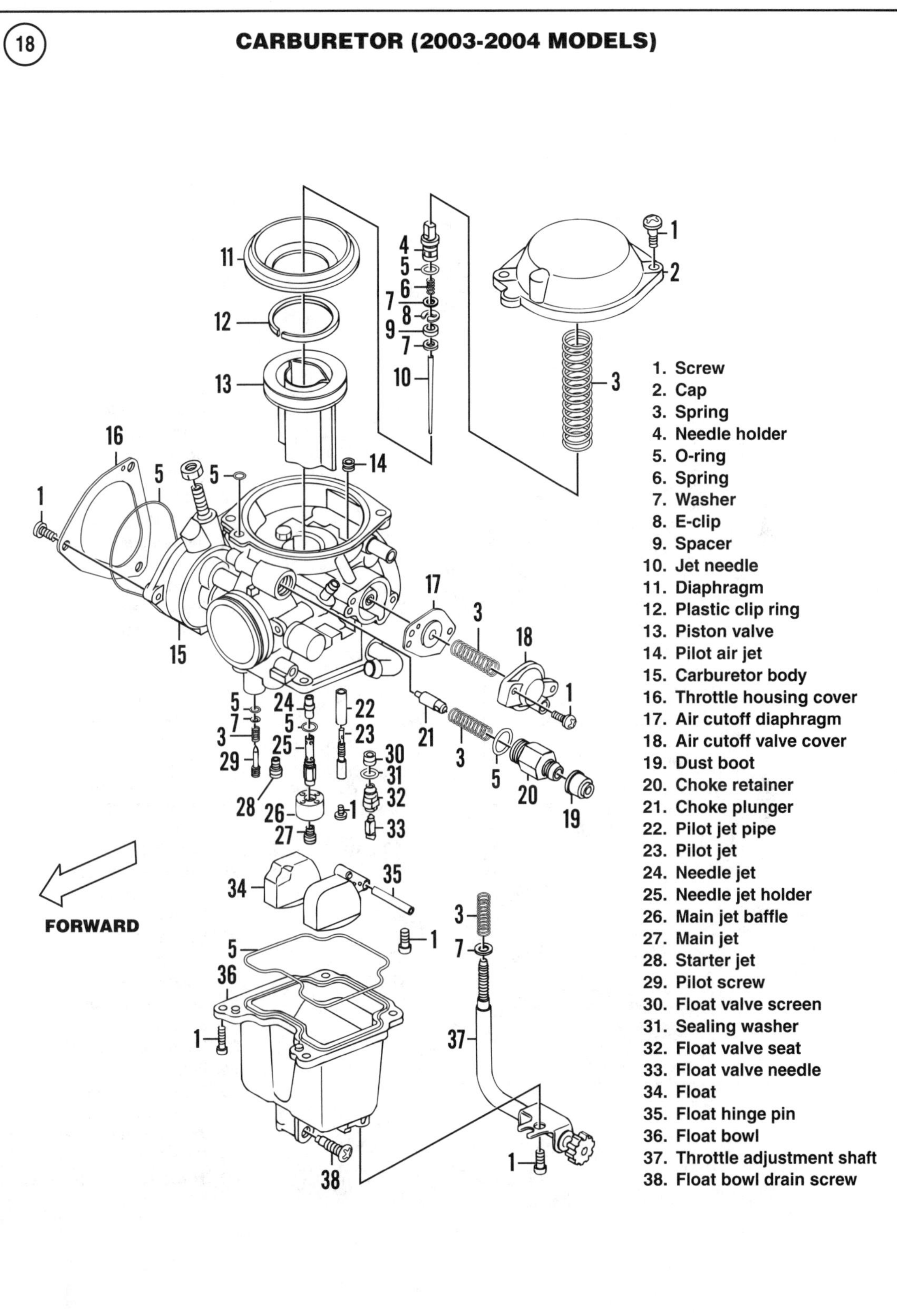
18
CARBURETOR (2003-2004 MODELS)
FORWARD
1. Screw
2. Cap
3. Spring
4. Needle holder
5. O-ring
6. Spring
7. Washer
8. E-clip
9. Spacer
10. Jet needle
11. Diaphragm
12. Plastic clip ring
13. Piston valve
14. Pilot air jet
15. Carburetor body
16. Throttle housing cover
17. Air cutoff diaphragm
18. Air cutoff valve cover
19. Dust boot
20. Choke retainer
21. Choke plunger
22. Pilot jet pipe
23. Pilot jet
24. Needle jet
25. Needle jet holder
26. Main jet baffle
27. Main jet
28. Starter jet
29. Pilot screw
30. Float valve screen
31. Sealing washer
32. Float valve seat
33. Float valve needle
34. Float
35. Float hinge pin
36. Float bowl
37. Throttle adjustment shaft
38. Float bowl drain screw

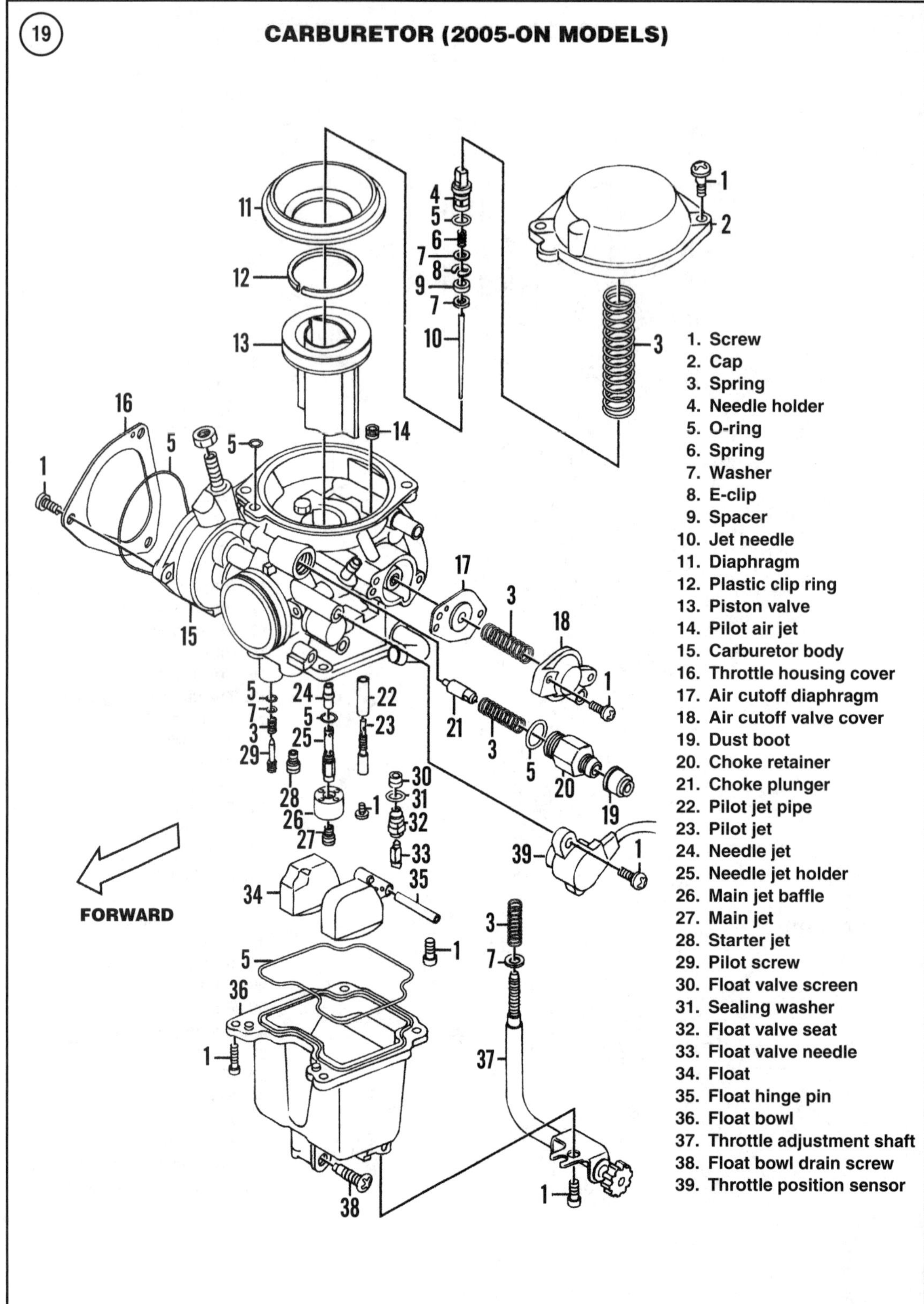
19
CARBURETOR (2005-ON MODELS)
FORWARD
1. Screw
2. Cap
3. Spring
4. Needle holder
5. O-ring
6. Spring
7. Washer
8. E-clip
9. Spacer
10. Jet needle
11. Diaphragm
12. Plastic clip ring
13. Piston valve
14. Pilot air jet
15. Carburetor body
16. Throttle housing cover
17. Air cutoff diaphragm
18. Air cutoff valve cover
19. Dust boot
20. Choke retainer
21. Choke plunger
22. Pilot jet pipe
23. Pilot jet
24. Needle jet
25. Needle jet holder
26. Main jet baffle
27. Main jet
28. Starter jet
29. Pilot screw
30. Float valve screen
31. Sealing washer
32. Float valve seat
33. Float valve needle
34. Float
35. Float hinge pin
36. Float bowl
37. Throttle adjustment shaft
38. Float bowl drain screw
39. Throttle position sensor

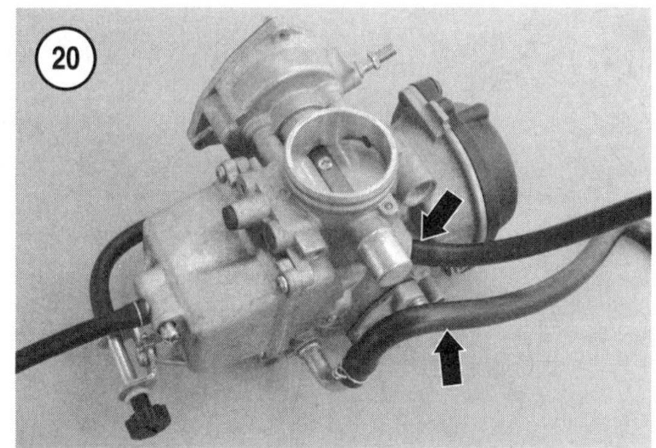

b. If an ohmmeter is not available, either do not remove the sensor or accurately mark the position of the sensor, then remove it from the carburetor.

c. Account for the rubber gasket on the back side of the sensor.

3. Remove the air cutoff valve assembly (**Figure 21**) as follows:

a. Remove the screws from the cover. The cover is under spring pressure. Keep pressure on the cover while removing the screws.

b. Remove the cover, spring and diaphragm.

4. Remove the diaphragm cover and the slide assembly as follows:

a. Remove the cover (**Figure 3**). The cover is under slight spring pressure. Hold the cover in place while removing the screws, then lift off the cover.

b. Remove the spring.

c. Remove the O-ring (**Figure 22**).

d. From the intake side, push up on the slide and lift it from the carburetor (**Figure 23**).

CAUTION

Do not lift or hold the slide by the diaphragm. Handle the jet needle carefully to prevent damage.

e. Remove the jet needle stopper from the slide (**Figure 24**), then remove the jet needle assembly (**Figure 25**).

5. Remove the throttle adjustment shaft (**Figure 26**) and float chamber (**Figure 27**). Remove the drain screw and O-ring from the chamber.

6. Remove and disassemble the float assembly as follows:

a. Remove the pin retaining screw (**Figure 28**).

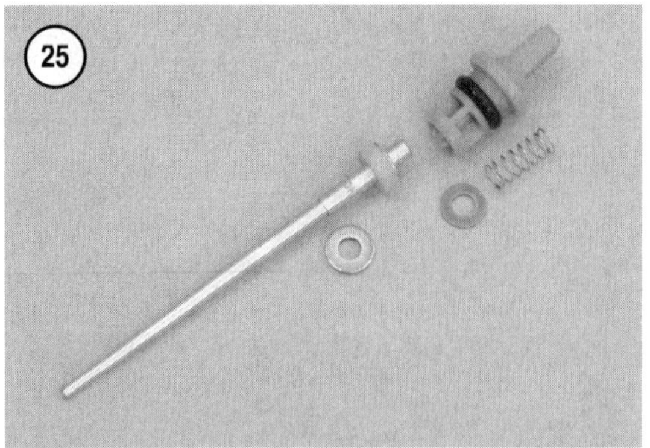

25

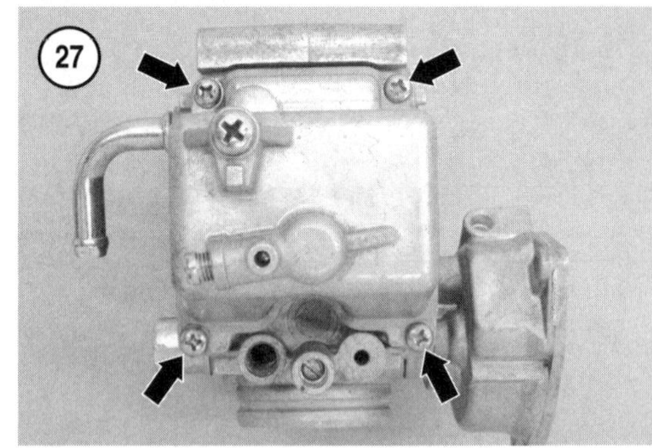

27

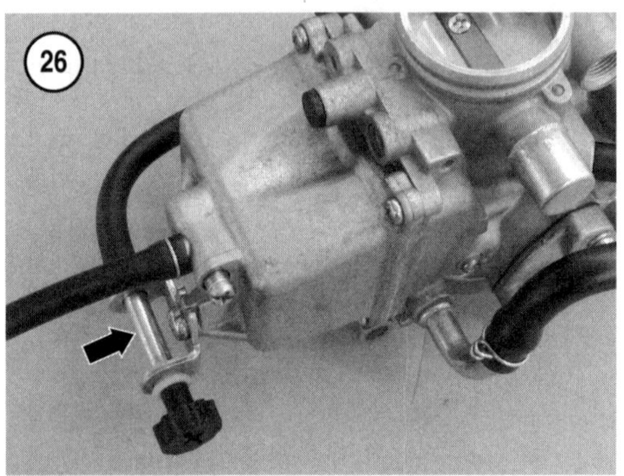

26

28

b. Carefully lift out the float, pin and float valve (**Figure 29**).

c. Slide the clip and float valve off the float tab.

7. Remove the float valve seat as follows:

a. Remove the retaining screw (**Figure 30**).

b. Twist and remove the float seat (**Figure 31**). Do not grip the seat inside the bore.

8. Remove the main jet assembly as follows:

a. Remove the baffle and main jet (A, **Figure 32**).

b. Remove the needle jet holder (**Figure 33**).

c. Remove the needle jet (**Figure 34**). Unseat the jet by hand. If necessary, use a wood or plastic dowel to help unseat the jet. Do not use tools that could scratch the inner surface of the jet.

9. Remove the pilot jet (B, **Figure 32**).

10. Remove the starter (choke) jet (C, **Figure 32**).

11. Remove the pilot mixture screw as follows:

a. Most models have a removable rubber plug installed over the screw. If the plug is metal and pressed in, remove it by drilling through it with a *small* drill bit. Do not use a bit larger

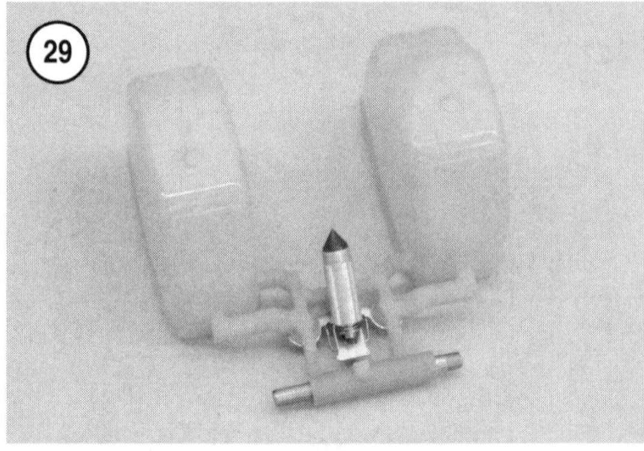

29

30

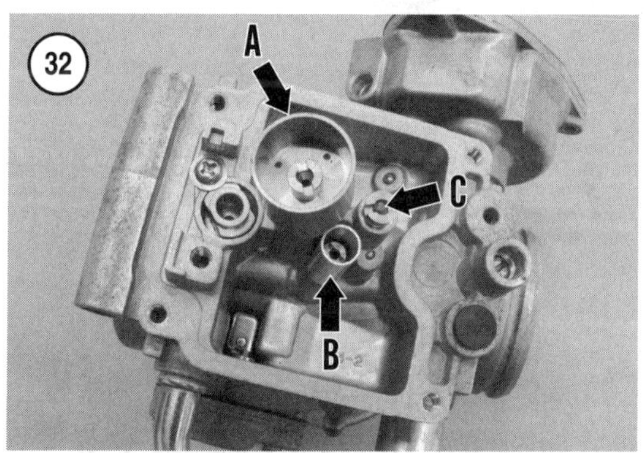

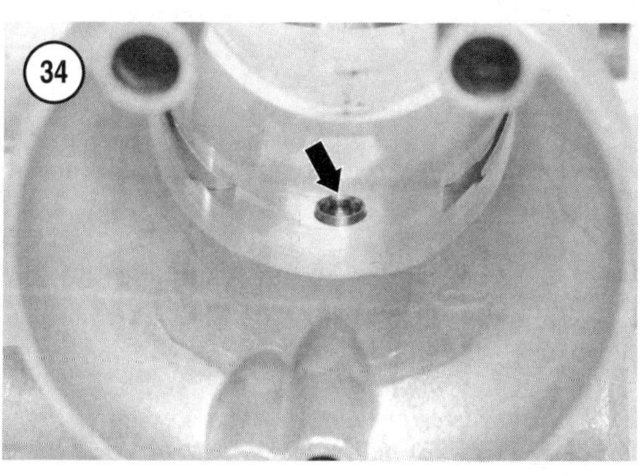

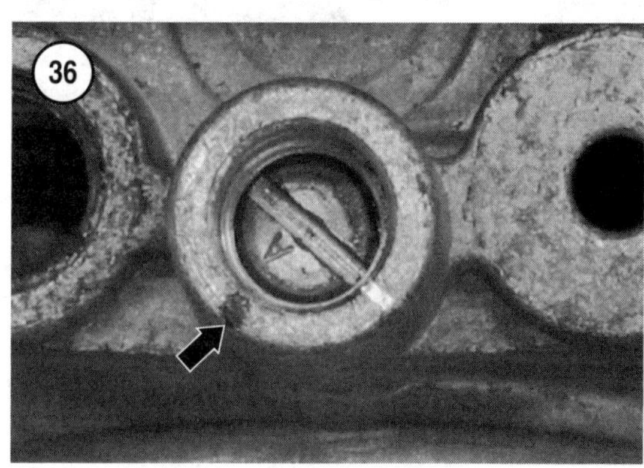

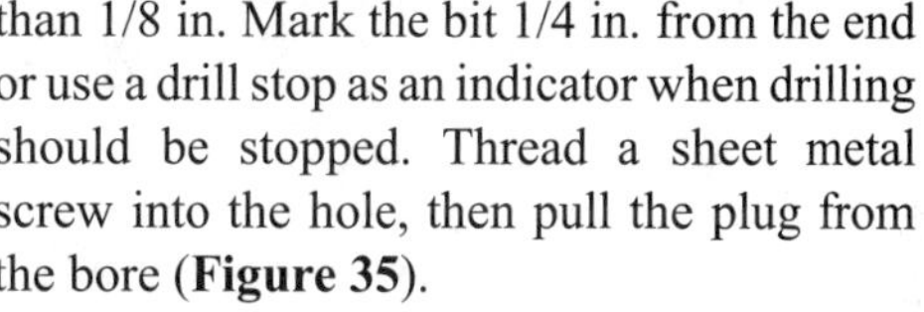

than 1/8 in. Mark the bit 1/4 in. from the end or use a drill stop as an indicator when drilling should be stopped. Thread a sheet metal screw into the hole, then pull the plug from the bore (**Figure 35**).

b. Make a mark on the edge of the bore, in line with the slot in the screw (**Figure 36**). This will be used as a reference point when installing the screw.

c. Turn the screw clockwise and count the number of turns it takes to *lightly* seat the screw.

d. Remove the pilot mixture screw, spring, washer and O-ring (**Figure 37**).

12. Remove the secondary pilot air jet (**Figure 38**).

13. Clean and inspect the parts as described in this section.

14. Reverse this procedure to assemble the carburetor. Note the following:

a. Install new, lubricated O-rings.

b. Do not confuse the starter jet and main jet. They are similar in appearance and fit in either location. The main jet has a *large* hole in its center.

c. When installing the pilot mixture screw, *lightly* seat the screw, then turn it out the number of turns recorded during disassembly. Refer to the reference mark on the carburetor for the original setting. If the number of turns is not known, refer to **Table 1** or **Table 2**.

d. Attach the float valve and clip to the float before installing the parts.

e. Check and adjust the float height as described in this chapter.

f. When installing the choke plunger, apply grease while assembling the parts.

g. On 2005–on models, engage the tangs in the throttle position sensor with the slots in the throttle shaft (**Figure 39**). Adjust the throttle position sensor as described in this chapter.

h. Install the slide assembly and diaphragm cover last. When installing the slide and diaphragm, the diaphragm must be seated at its edge (**Figure 40**) before installing the cover.

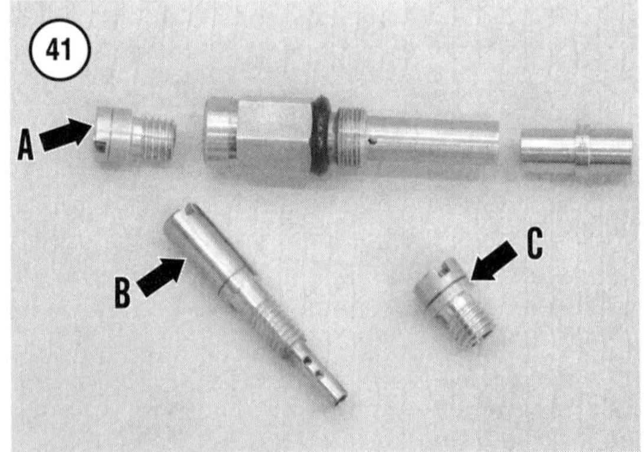

i. Install the carburetor as described in this section.

Cleaning and Inspection

CAUTION

Do not clean the jet orifices or seats with wire or drill bits. These items can

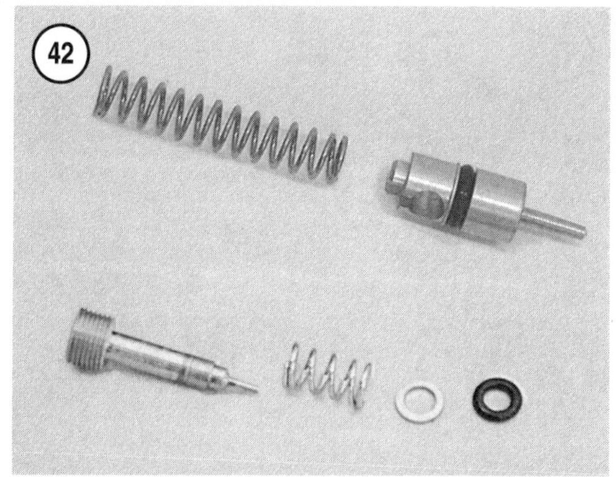

42

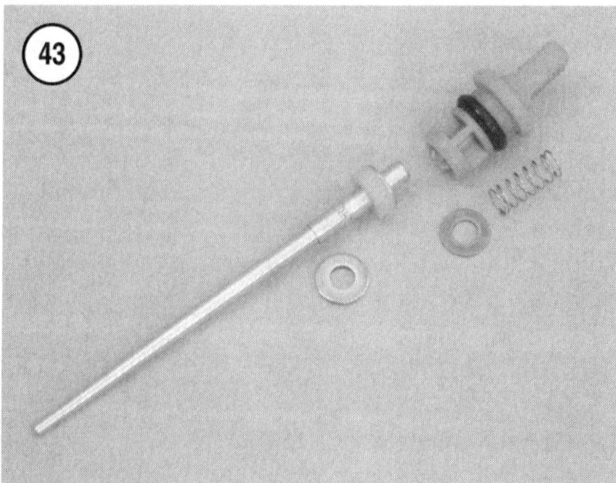

43

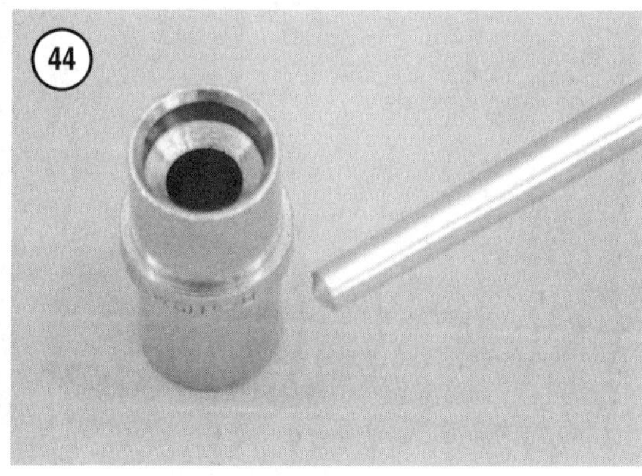

44

scratch the surfaces and alter flow rates, or cause leaking.

1. Clean all parts in carburetor cleaner. Use compressed air to clean all passages, orifices and vents in the carburetor body.

2. Inspect the main jet and needle jet assembly (A, **Figure 41**), pilot jet (B), starter (choke) jet (C) and secondary pilot air jet. Make sure all holes are clean and undamaged.

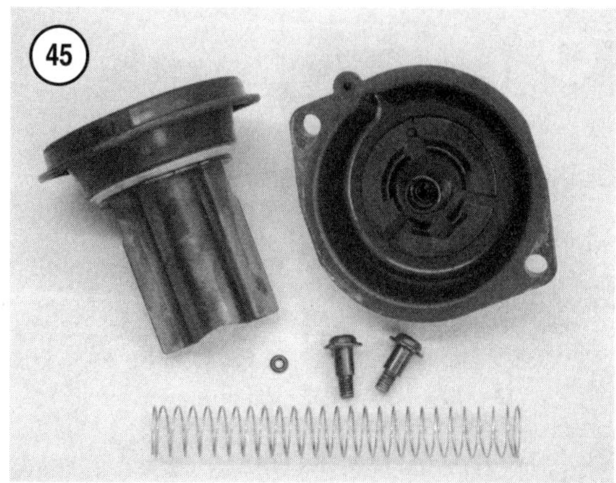

45

3. Inspect the pilot mixture screw assembly and choke plunger (**Figure 42**).
   a. Inspect the screw and plunger tips for dents or wear.
   b. The spring coils should be resilient and not crushed.
   c. The plunger should move freely in its bore in the carburetor.

4. Inspect the jet needle assembly (**Figure 43**). The jet needle must be smooth, straight and evenly tapered. If the needle or needle jet (**Figure 44**) is stepped, dented, worn or bent, replace the parts.

5. Inspect the diaphragm, slide, vacuum chamber cover and spring (**Figure 45**).
   a. Inspect the slide for wear and scratches. Fit the slide into the carburetor body and check for smooth vertical operation. The slide should have minimal front to back play.
   b. Inspect the diaphragm for dryness, tears and holes. A leaking diaphragm prevents the slide from reaching/maintaining its normal level.
   c. Inspect the vacuum chamber cover for cracks. A damaged or loose cover affects engine performance similar to a damaged diaphragm.

6. Inspect the float and float valve assembly (**Figure 46**).
   a. Inspect the rubber tip of the float valve (A, **Figure 47**). If it is stepped or dented, replace the float valve.
   b. Lightly press on the spring-loaded pin (B, **Figure 47**) in the float valve. The pin should easily move in and out of the valve. If it is varnished with fuel residue, replace the float valve.

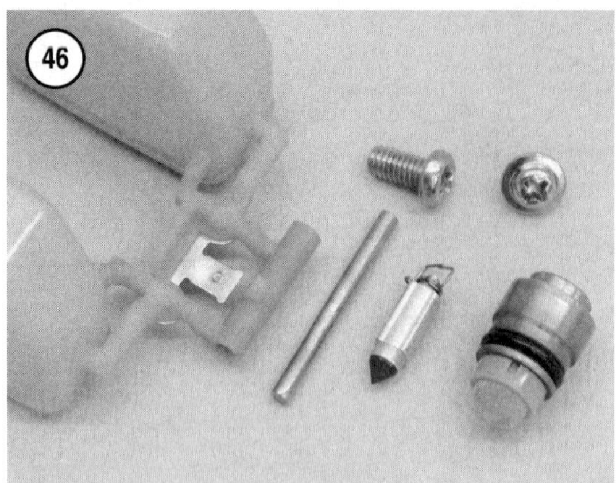

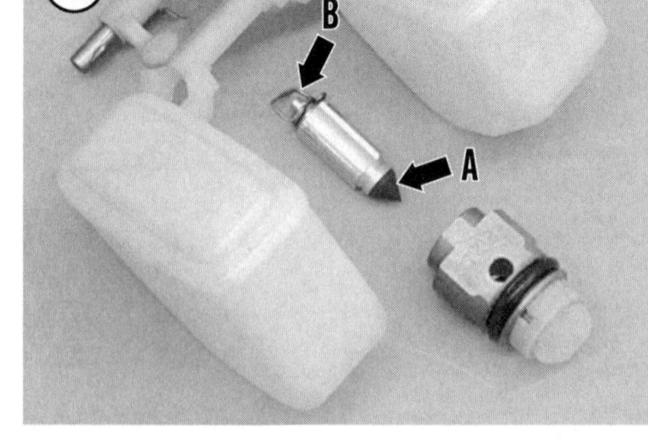

c. Inspect the float valve seat. The seat should be clean and scratch-free. If it is not, the float valve will not seat properly and the carburetor will overflow.

d. Inspect the screen on the float valve seat. The screen must be clean and not damaged.

e. Inspect the float and pin. Submerge the float in water and check for bubbles. Replace the float if water or fuel is detected inside the float. Check that the float pin is straight and smooth. It must be a slip-fit in the float.

7. Inspect the float chamber assembly (**Figure 48**).
   a. Check that all residue is removed from the interior of the bowl.
   b. Inspect screw threads for damage.
   c. Inspect the tip of the drain screw. If damaged, the drain screw will allow fuel to pass out the drain.
   d. Inspect the overflow tube for cleanliness.
8. Inspect the air cutoff valve assembly (**Figure 49**).
   a. The diaphragm must be free of damage in order to operate properly.
   b. The pin on the back of the diaphragm should not be worn.
   c. The air passages must be clean in order to operate properly.
9. Inspect the air cutoff valve chamber (**Figure 50**).
   a. Inspect the vent holes and ball valve for cleanliness.
   b. Check the ball valve for free movement. Apply light pressure to unseat the ball, then release pressure. The spring-loaded ball should seat itself.
10. On 2005-on models, inspect the throttle position sensor (**Figure 51**).

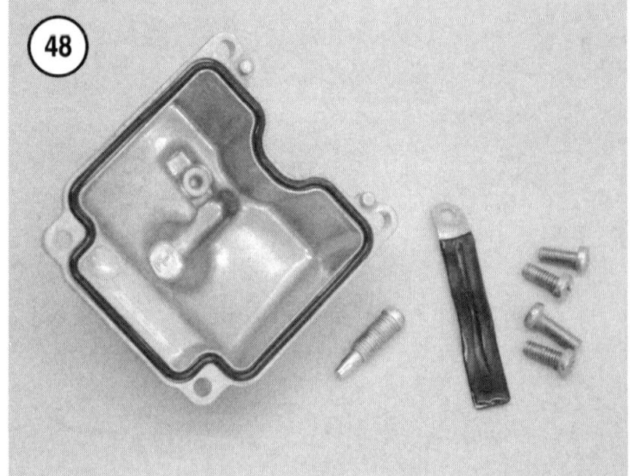

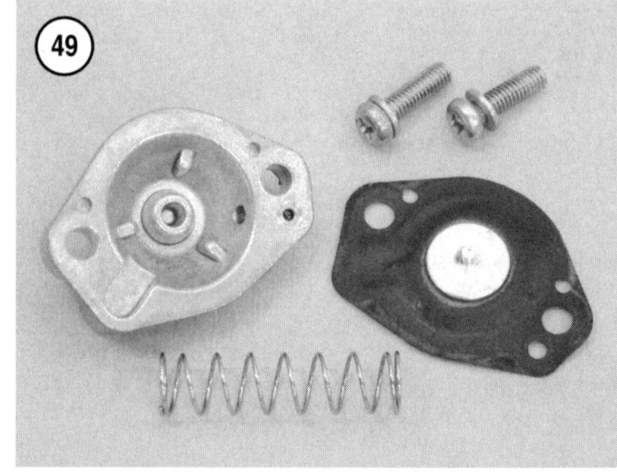

   a. Inspect the harness and connector terminals for damage.
   b. Turn the center of the sensor and inspect for free rotation. The sensor must rotate smoothly.
   c. Lightly lubricate the gasket with dielectric grease to prevent moisture entry.

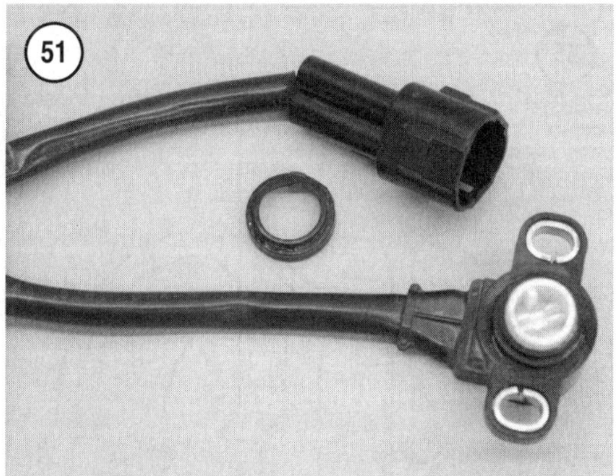

11. Inspect the throttle valve spring and cable holder (**Figure 52**). The spring must be clean between the coils and the cable holder must be tight on the shaft. The throttle valve must fully open and close.

12. Inspect the throttle adjustment shaft assembly and clamps (**Figure 53**).

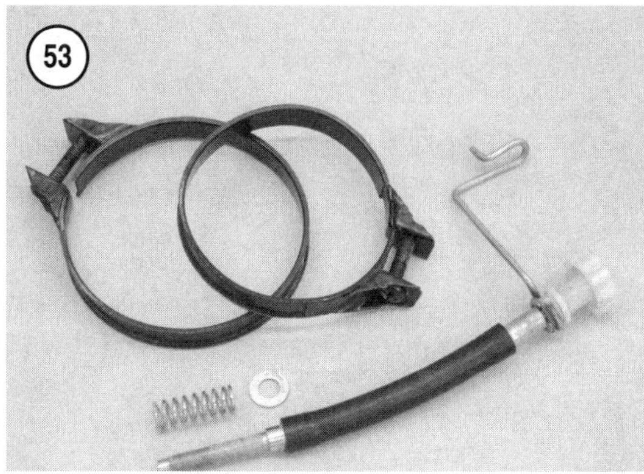

a. Inspect the throttle adjustment shaft screw for straightness and thread damage. The spring coils should be resilient and not crushed.
b. Replace clamps that are distorted or have stripped threads. The clamps must fit tightly on the ducts to prevent air leaks.

13. Inspect the vent and vacuum hoses for damage. The vacuum hose must fit tightly to the carburetor and fuel valve diaphragm. Air leaks will prevent the proper opening of the diaphragm to allow fuel to the carburetor.

Float Adjustment

The float and float valve maintain a constant fuel level in the float chamber. As fuel is used, the float lowers and allows more fuel past the valve. As the fuel level rises, the float closes the valve when the required fuel level is reached. If the float is out of adjustment, the fuel level will be too high or low. A low fuel level causes the engine to run as if the jetting is lean. A high fuel level causes the engine to run rich and may cause fuel overflow.

1. Remove the carburetor as described in this section.
2. Remove the float chamber.
3. Lightly touch the float to ensure the float valve is seated.
4. Lay the carburetor on its side so the float valve hangs freely. Tilt the carburetor until the tab on the float *lightly* touches the spring-loaded pin in the valve. The tab must not compress the pin.
5. Measure the distance from the carburetor gasket surface to the highest point on the float (**Figure 54**). Refer to **Table 1** or **Table 2** for the float height specifications.
6. If necessary, reset float height as follows:

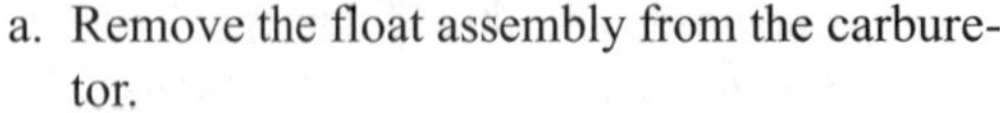

a. Remove the float assembly from the carburetor.
b. Remove the float valve and clip.
c. Bend the float tab in the appropriate direction to raise or lower the float. Use care when bending the tab to prevent breaking the plastic lugs or float.
d. Assemble the float and recheck the height. Adjust, if necessary.

7. Install the float chamber.

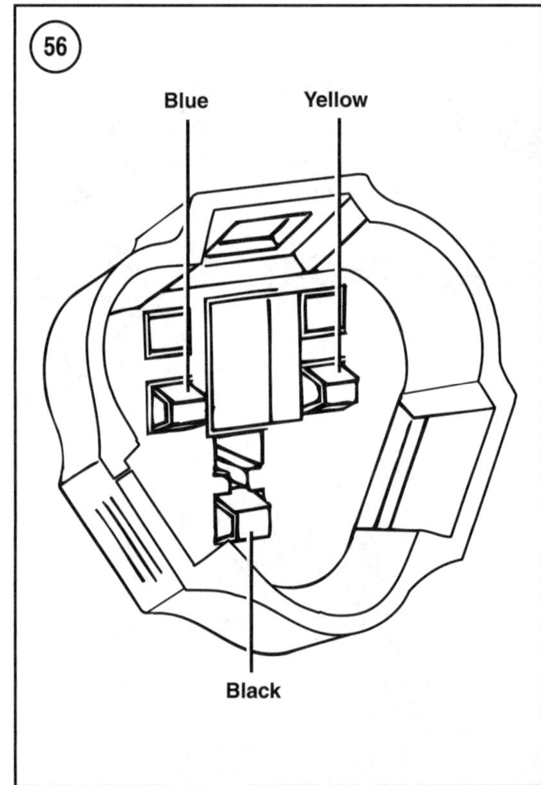

THROTTLE POSITION SENSOR (2005-ON MODELS)

Inspection and Adjustment

The throttle position sensor can be checked with the carburetor installed on the engine. Anytime the sensor is removed from the carburetor, use an ohmmeter to set the position of the sensor.

1. If the carburetor is installed on the engine, disconnect the wire connector leading to the sensor.
2. Turn the throttle stop screw out until it no longer touches the throttle valve (**Figure 55**, typical). The throttle must be fully closed.
3. Measure and record the fully closed resistance at the blue and black connector terminals shown in **Figure 56**. Refer to **Table 2** for the resistance specification.
   a. If the throttle resistance is within specification, proceed to the next step.
   b. If the throttle resistance is not within specification, check that the sensor is properly installed. The sensor must engage with the throttle shaft. Turn the sensor side to side and see if the specified resistance can be achieved. If it can, tighten the screws and proceed to the next step. If specified resistance cannot be achieved, replace the sensor.
4. Secure the throttle valve so it is in the fully open position.
5. Measure and record the fully open resistance at the yellow and black connector terminals shown in **Figure 56**. Refer to **Table 2** for the resistance specification.

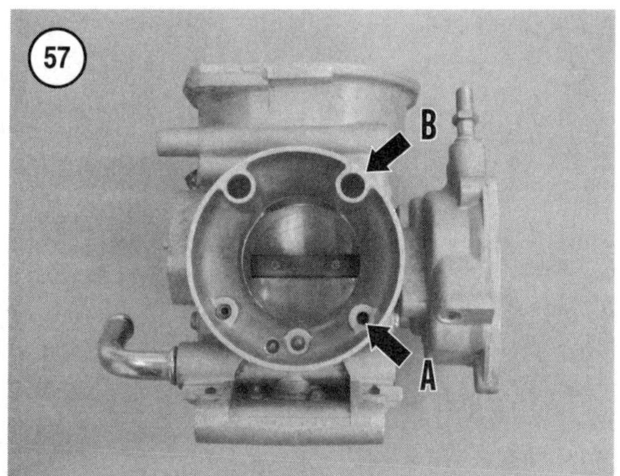

For example, if the fully closed resistance is 5000 ohms, the fully open resistance should be 3800 ohms ($0.76 \times 5000 = 3800$). If necessary, loosen the screws and adjust the sensor until the calculated specification is achieved. Tighten the screws and recheck the resistance measurement. If calculated resistance cannot be achieved, replace the sensor.

CARBURETOR OPERATION

Before disassembling the carburetor, understand the function of the pilot, needle and main jet systems.

Common factors that affect carburetor performance are altitude, temperature and engine load. If the engine is not performing up to expectations, check the following before adjusting or replacing carburetor components:

1. Make sure the throttle cables are not dragging and are correctly adjusted.
2. Make sure the choke fully opens and closes.

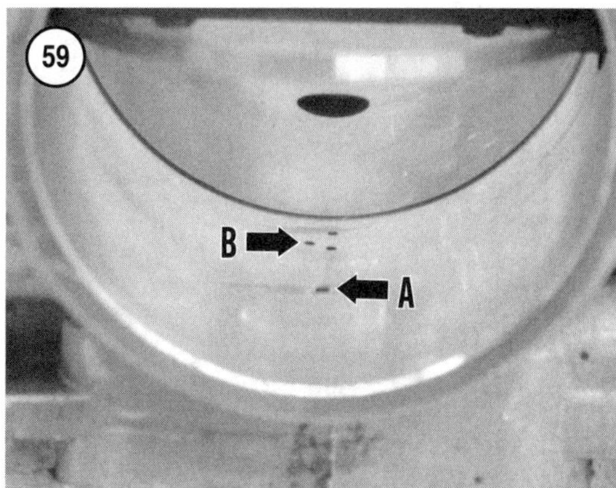

3. Make sure fuel is adequately flowing to the carburetor. Make sure that the vacuum hose leading to the fuel valve is tight.
4. Make sure the filter is clean.
5. Make sure the muffler is not restricting flow.
6. Make sure the brake pads are not dragging on the discs.

8

Pilot Jet System

The pilot jet system controls the air/fuel ratio from closed throttle to approximately 1/4 throttle. Air enters the pilot air jet (A, **Figure 57**), where it passes to the pilot jet (**Figure 58**). The pilot jet draws fuel from the float chamber and mixes it with the air from the pilot air jet. The atomized air/fuel mixture passes to the pilot mixture screw, where it is regulated into the throat of the carburetor. The mixture is discharged from the pilot hole (A, **Figure 59**). Turning the pilot mixture screw in will *lean* the air/fuel mixture entering the engine, while turning the screw out will *richen* the mixture.

As the throttle valve is opened, it uncovers the bypass pilot holes (B, **Figure 59**), which then become effective. These holes are connected to the passage between the pilot jet and pilot mixture screw. They are not affected by the mixture screw. As engine speed increases, fuel is drawn from these passages directly from the pilot jet.

Jet Needle System

The jet needle is connected to the slide (A, **Figure 60**) and controls the fuel mixture from approximately 1/8 to 3/4 throttle. Air enters the main air jet

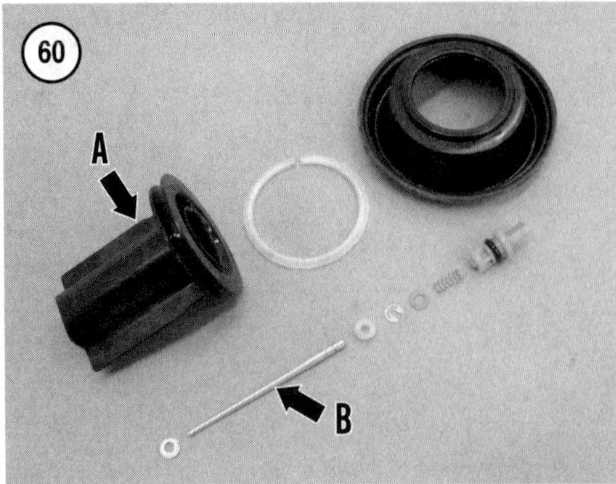

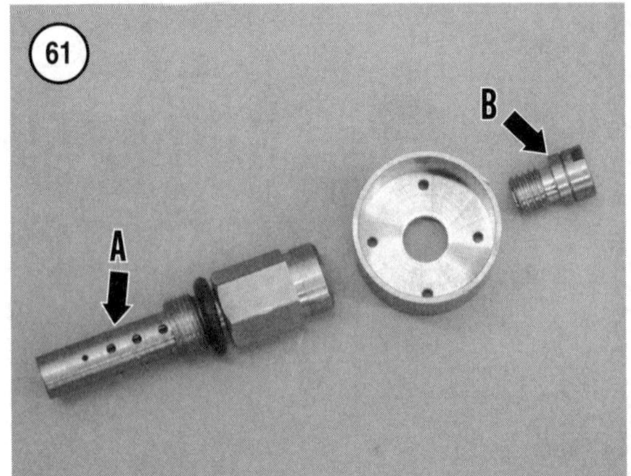

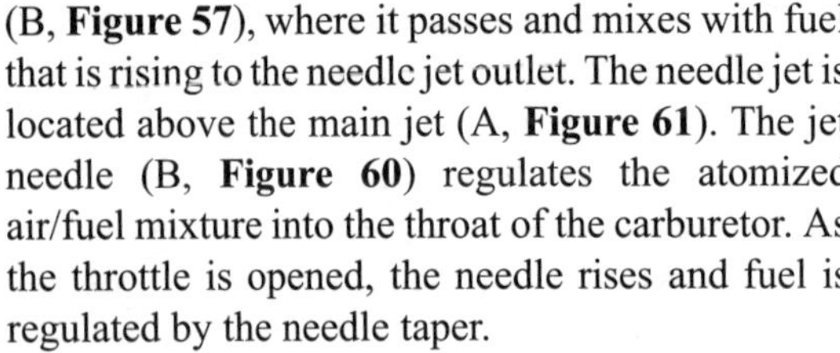

(B, **Figure 57**), where it passes and mixes with fuel that is rising to the needle jet outlet. The needle jet is located above the main jet (A, **Figure 61**). The jet needle (B, **Figure 60**) regulates the atomized air/fuel mixture into the throat of the carburetor. As the throttle is opened, the needle rises and fuel is regulated by the needle taper.

Main Jet System

The main jet (B, **Figure 61**) is screwed to the bottom of the needle jet and controls the mixture from approximately 3/4 to full throttle. When the jet needle is fully raised from the needle jet, the fuel is regulated into the throat of the carburetor by the size of the bore in the main jet. Main jets are usually numbered and are interchangeable with jets that will provide a leaner or richer air/fuel mixture.

Starter (Choke) System

The choke system is actually a starter by-pass system in which a plunger assembly and starter jet (**Figure 62**) pass fuel to an orifice in the plunger bore. A true choke system uses a plate in the carburetor to restrict air and richen the air/fuel mixture during cold start up. A starter by-pass system achieves this by introducing additional fuel.

When the choke knob is not being used, the plunger blocks the fuel orifice, as well as an air passage that intersects the bore.

When the choke knob is operated, the plunger is withdrawn from the fuel orifice and opens the air passage. As the engine is cranked, a rich air/fuel mixture is drawn through a passage and into the car-

buretor throat. The passage (**Figure 63**) is located on the outlet side of the carburetor, past the throttle valve. When the choke is closed, the plunger again blocks the air and fuel passages.

This type of system is most effective if the throttle remains closed during startup, in order to maintain high vacuum at the air and fuel passages.

Air Cutoff Valve System

The function of the air cutoff valve is to richen the pilot system air/fuel mixture during compression braking, such as descending steep grades, when the engine speed is high, but the throttle is closed. Without this valve, the engine will develop a lean air/fuel mixture in the pilot system, which will cause backfiring and possibly engine damage. The air cutoff valve consists of a diaphragm, spring and cover (**Figure 64**). The function of the assembly is to open and close an air passage that is a branch of the pilot air system.

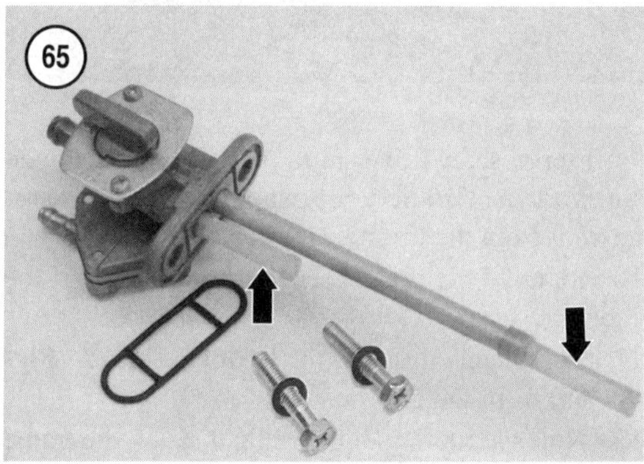

During acceleration and steady running speeds, the spring keeps the diaphragm in the down position, allowing air to pass to the pilot jet system. During deceleration, when the throttle valve is closed, engine vacuum vents through a passage leading to the air cutoff valve cover. The vacuum pulls the diaphragm out, causing it to block the air passage in the bore. This reduces the amount of air going to the pilot jet system, and a rich fuel mixture is discharged from the pilot hole (A, **Figure 59**).

When acceleration resumes, the vacuum holding the diaphragm out is reduced, and the spring pushes

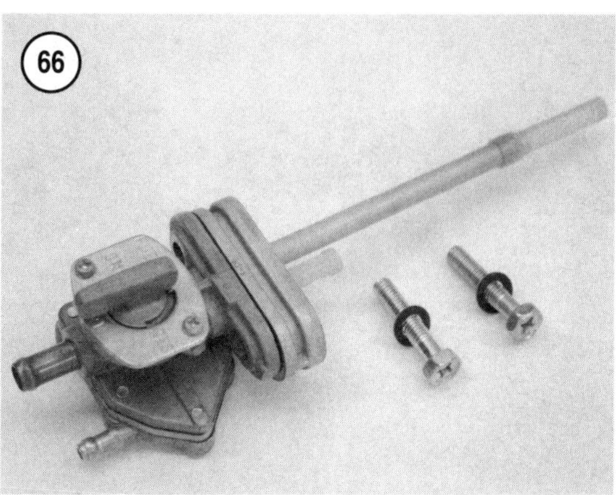

the diaphragm down, again creating a normal fuel mixture in the pilot jet system.

FUEL VALVE

Removal, Inspection and Installation

The vacuum-actuated fuel valve is always left in the on position. It only passes fuel when the engine is running. Fuel will flow freely from the valve when the lever is turned to the prime position. There are screen filters inside the valve (**Figure 65**, typical). To clean the filters, the fuel valve must be removed from the fuel tank. The fuel valve can be disassembled; however, the manufacturer does not provide replacement parts for the fuel valve. If it is not functioning, replace the whole unit.

1. Remove the fuel tank as described in this chapter.
2. Drain the fuel from the tank by setting the fuel valve to prime and putting the fuel line into an approved container.
3. Remove the two bolts securing the fuel valve to the tank, and then pull the valve and O-ring straight out of the tank (**Figure 66**, typical).
4. Clean the screens on the end of the fuel valve pickups with a soft plastic brush.
5. Installation is the reverse of removal.
6. Add small amounts of fuel to the tank at first to make sure there are no leaks.

THROTTLE CABLE REPLACEMENT

The throttle uses two cables. One cable pulls the throttle open during acceleration, while the other ensures the throttle closes during deceleration. In

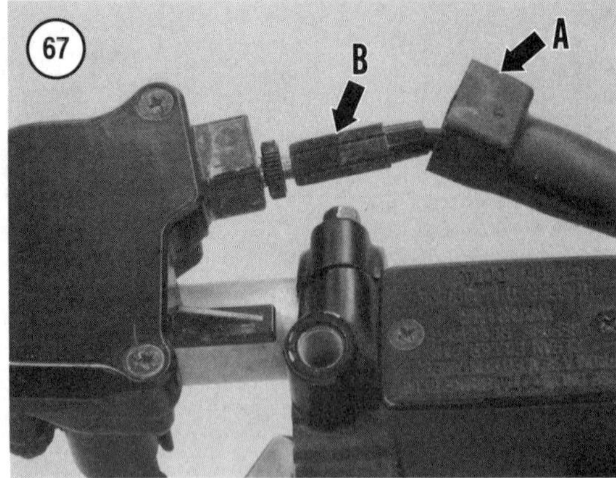

operation, the cables always move in opposite directions to one another.

1. Remove the front fender as described in Chapter Fourteen.

2. Remove the fuel tank as described in this chapter.

3. Pull back the throttle cable cover from the throttle housing (A, **Figure 67**).

4. Screw the cable adjuster as far in toward the throttle as it can go to create slack in the cable (B, **Figure 67**).

5. At the carburetor, screw the throttle cable adjuster all the way in to the carburetor body (A, **Figure 68**).

6. Remove the screws (B, **Figure 68**) securing the throttle housing cover and remove the cover.

7. Lift out the carburetor cable and note the routing to the carburetor.

8. Remove the screws in the throttle plate cover.

9. Insert a screwdriver in to hold the throttle open and work the throttle cable out of the groove and remove it from the throttle (**Figure 69**).

10. Remove the brass keeper from the end of the cable.

11. Completely unscrew the throttle cable (A, **Figure 68**) from the throttle.

12. Note the routing of the cable through the frame and handlebars before removing.

13. Clean the throttle assembly and handlebar.

14. Lubricate the cables with an aerosol cable lubricant. Lubricate the throttle mechanism and cable ends with lithium grease.

15. Install the new cables into their positions on the throttle lever.

16. Assemble the throttle housing around the cable.

17. Route the cable through the frame and to the carburetor.

18. Identify and install the cable onto the throttle valve and holder.

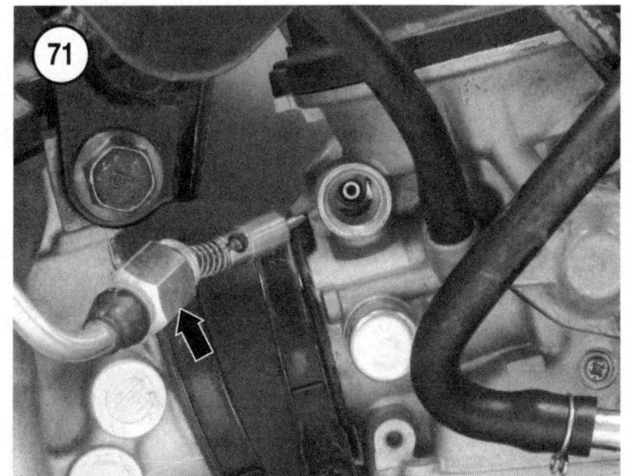

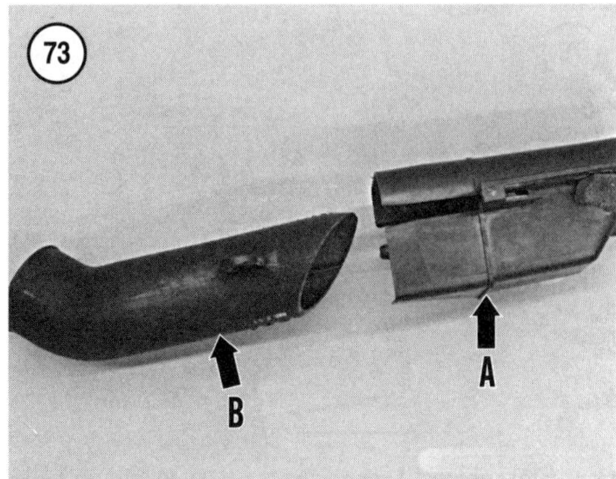

19. Adjust the cables as described in Chapter Three.
20. Install the fuel tank and front fender when adjustment and proper operation is verified.

CHOKE CABLE REPLACEMENT

Removal/Installation

1. Remove the front fender and fuel tank cover as described in Chapter Fourteen.
2. Remove the fuel tank as described in this chapter.
3. Remove the two screws on the bottom of the left hand control (**Figure 70**).
4. Pull the upper half of the left hand control from under the rubber seal of the choke lever.
5. Unscrew the nut securing the choke plunger in the carburetor (**Figure 71**).
6. Note the routing of the cables from the hand grip to the frame.
7. Remove the choke cable.
8. Installation is the reverse of removal. Note the follwing:
   a. When reassembling the left switch housing be certain to align the pin inside the housing (A, **Figure 72**) with the hole in the handlebar (B).
   b. Adjust the choke cable as described in Chapter Three.

FUEL TANK

Removal/Installation

1. Remove the front fender and fuel tank cover as described in Chapter Fourteen.
2. Remove the carburetor vent hose and slide the upper section (A, **Figure 73**) of the airbox intake from the lower section (B, **Figure 73**).
3. Turn the fuel valve on or to the reserve position (**Figure 74**). If the fuel valve is in the prime posi-

tion, fuel will spill when the hose is removed from the valve.

4. Remove the vacuum (A, **Figure 75**) and fuel line (B) from the fuel valve.

5. Remove the two bolts securing the fuel tank to the frame (**Figure 76**).

6. Pull the fuel tank toward the rear of the vehicle to disengage the front tabs from the frame (**Figure 77**).

7. Remove the fuel tank and inspect it for leaks or damage.

8. Installation is the reverse of removal.

Table 1 CARBURETOR SPECIFICATIONS (2003-2004 MODELS)

	U.S./Canada	California
Carburetor type	Mukuni BSR36	
Identification number	07G0	07G1
Throttle bore	36 mm	36 mm
Main jet	#130	#130
Pilot jet (slow jet)	#22.5	#22.5
Jet needle	5E26-1	5E26-1
Needle jet	P-OM	P-OM
Pilot screw setting	2 1/4 turns out	Pre-Set
Float level	12-14 mm (0.47-0.55 in.)	12-14 mm (0.47-0.55 in.)
Idle speed	1400-1600 rpm	1400-1600 rpm
Throttle lever free play	3-8 mm (0.12-0.31 in.)	3-8 mm (0.12-0.31 in.)
Starter enricher lever free play	0.5-1.0 mm (0.02-0.04 in.)	0.5-1.0 mm (0.02-0.04 in.)

Table 2 CARBURETOR SPECIFICATIONS (2005-ON MODELS)

	U.S./Canada	California
Carburetor type	Mukuni BSR37	Mukuni BSR37
Identification number	07G2	07G3
Throttle bore	37 mm	37 mm
Main jet	#130	#130
Pilot jet (slow jet)	#22.5	#22.5
Jet needle	5E26-1	5E26-1
Needle jet	P-OM	P-OM
Pilot screw setting	1 1/2 turns out	Pre-Set
Float level	12-14 mm (0.47-0.55 in.)	12-14 mm (0.47-0.55 in.)
Idle speed	1400-1600 rpm	1400-1600 rpm
Throttle lever free play	3-5 mm (0.12-0.20 in.)	3-5 mm (0.12-0.20 in.)
Starter enricher lever free play	0.5-1.0 mm (0.02-0.04 in.)	0.5-1.0 mm (0.02-0.04 in.)
Throttle position sensor		
Fully closed resistance	3500-6500 ohms	3500-6500 ohms
Fully open resistance	76 percent of closed reading	76 percent of closed reading

Table 3 FUEL AND EXHAUST SYSTEM TORQUE SPECIFICATIONS

Item	N•m	in.-lb.	ft.-lb.
Exhaust pipe nut	23		17
Muffler clamp bolt	23	–	17
Muffler mounting bolt	23		17

CHAPTER NINE

ELECTRICAL SYSTEM

This chapter covers procedures for the electrical system.

Refer to **Table 1** and **Table 2** at the end of the chapter for electrical system specifications.

Refer to *Electrical Testing* in Chapter Two for general troubleshooting information.

ELECTRICAL COMPONENT REPLACEMENT

Most motorcycle dealerships and parts suppliers do not accept the return of any electrical part. If the exact cause of any electrical system malfunction cannot be determined, have a dealership retest that specific system to verify your test results. If you purchase a new electrical component(s), install it, and then find that the system still does not work properly, you will probably be unable to return the unit for a refund. Consider any test results carefully before replacing a component that tests only slightly out of specification, especially resistance. A number of variables can affect test results dramatically. These include the testing meter's internal circuitry, ambient temperature and conditions under which the machine has been operated. All instructions and specifications have been checked for accuracy; however, successful test results depend to a great degree upon individual accuracy.

ALTERNATOR COVER

Removal and Installation

The alternator cover must be removed to access the lower idle gear for the starter motor, rotor and stator assembly. The stator assembly is mounted on the inside of the cover.

1. Drain the engine oil (Chapter Three).
2. Remove the shift lever (Chapter Six).
3. Disconnect the stator leads (**Figure 1**).
4. Remove the upper idle gear cover and gear as described in this chapter.
5. Remove the eight bolts securing the cover. One of the bolts is located in the upper idle gear cavity (**Figure 2**).
6. Pull the cover away from the engine. Magnetic resistance will be felt as the cover is unseated.
7. Remove the cover gasket and account for the two cover dowels (**Figure 3**).

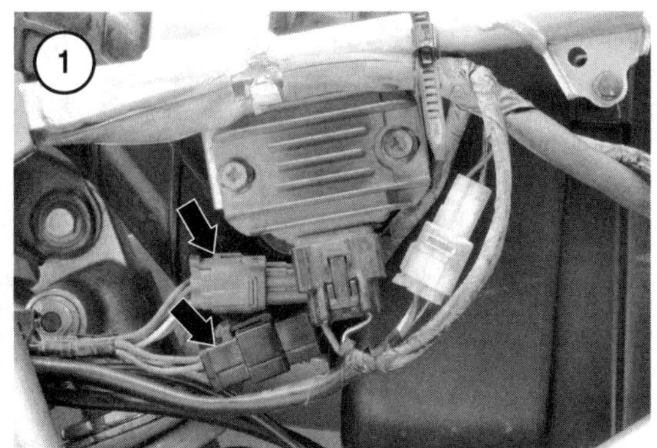

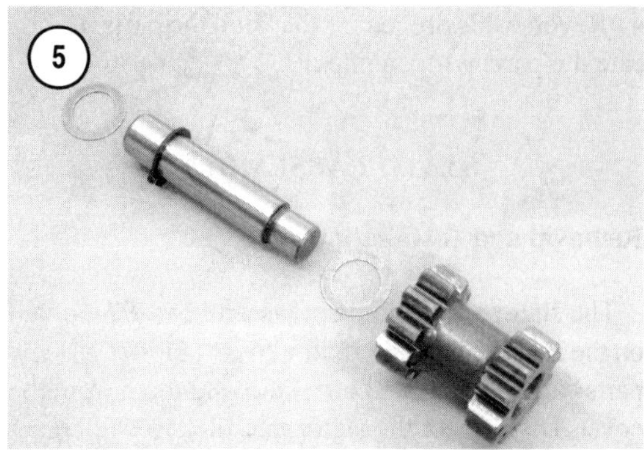

8. Remove and/or test the stator assembly as described in this chapter.
9. Reverse this procedure to install the stator and alternator cover. Note the following:
   a. Lubricate the gears and lower idle gear shaft with engine oil.
   b. Install a new cover gasket.
   c. If necessary, apply sealant to the stator lead grommet, then seat the grommet into the cover.
   d. Check that all wires are routed and secured.
   e. Clean electrical connections, then apply dielectric grease when assembling.
   f. Tighten the cover bolts to 10 N•m (89 in.-lb.). Make several passes and work in a crisscross pattern.

LOWER IDLE GEAR

The lower idle gear for the starter is accessed by removing the alternator cover.

Removal, Inspection and Installation

1. Remove the alternator cover as described in this chapter.
2. Remove the lower idle gear, shaft and washers (**Figure 4**).
3. Inspect the parts (**Figure 5**).
   a. Assemble the gear and shaft (**Figure 6**). The parts should operate smoothly with no play.
   b. Insert the shaft into the crankcase and cover bores. The shaft should fit firmly with no play.
   c. Inspect the gear teeth and bore. If the gear is worn, check the condition of the starter gear, upper idle gear and starter clutch gear.

9

4. Reverse this procedure to install the parts. Lubricate the parts with engine oil.

STATOR ASSEMBLY

Removal and Installation

The stator and pickup coil assembly are mounted on the inside of the alternator cover (**Figure 7**). The parts can be tested without removing them from the cover. Disconnect the stator and pickup coil/signal coil connectors, then test the parts at the connectors. Refer to *Charging System* to test the stator charging coil and *Ignition System* to test the signal coil and pickup coil.

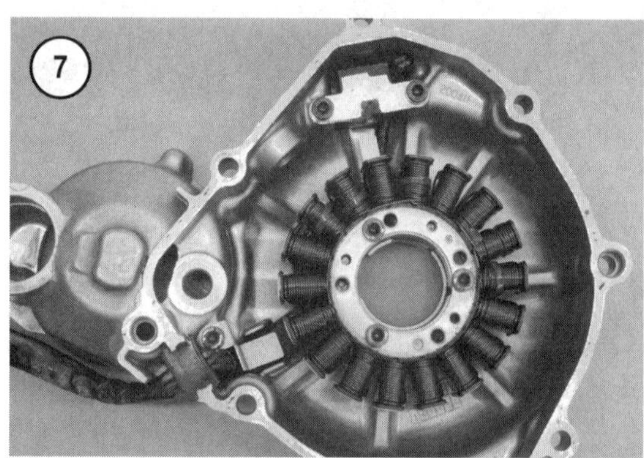

1. Remove the alternator cover as described in this chapter.
2. Remove the bolts securing the stator assembly (**Figure 8**).
3. Remove the wiring harness clamp from the cover.
4. Remove the wire grommet from the cover, then remove the parts.
5. Reverse this procedure to install the stator assembly. Apply threadlocking compound to the bolt threads when installing the parts in the cover. Tighten the stator bolts to 5 N•m (44 in.-lb.).

ROTOR AND STARTER CLUTCH

The starter clutch is mounted on the back of the rotor. The starter idle gears and rotor must be removed to access the clutch. In order to remove the rotor, it must be held with a 26 mm offset wrench to remove the nut. The rotor is then removed with a 38 mm rotor puller. If the right crankcase cover is removed, the primary drive gear nut can be held while the rotor nut is loosened.

NOTE

*If troubleshooting the starter clutch, check the clutch for freewheel and lockup without removing the rotor. Turn the clutch gear (**Figure 9**) clockwise (rearward). The clutch gear should turn freely and smoothly in that direction. Try to turn the gear counterclockwise (forward). The gear should not freewheel. If the gear turns in both directions or is always locked*

up, disassemble and inspect the clutch assembly.

Removal and Installation

1. Remove the alternator cover and lower idle gear as described in this chapter.
2. Remove the rotor nut as follows:
   a. Hold the rotor stationary with a 26 mm offset wrench. Seat the wrench on the hub (**Figure 10**).
   b. Remove the rotor nut and washer.
3. Loosen the rotor and starter clutch as follows:
   a. To aid in removal, spray penetrating lubricant into the rotor bore and Woodruff key area. Apply grease to the end and threads of the rotor puller.
   b. Install the rotor nut so it is flush with the end of the shaft. This will increase the area for the puller bolt to seat against (**Figure 11**).
   c. Thread the outer part of the puller onto the rotor threads.
   d. Thread the bolt into the puller and against the end of the crankshaft.
   e. Hold the puller with a wrench (**Figure 12**) and tighten the bolt to remove the rotor. Use wrenches that provide high leverage.
   f. When the rotor unseats, remove the puller and nut.
4. Remove the rotor (A, **Figure 13**), clutch gear (B) and Woodruff key (C) from the crankshaft.
5. Inspect and lubricate the parts as described in this section.
6. Reverse this procedure to install the rotor and starter clutch assembly. Note the following:
   a. Lubricate the clutch bearing and sprags with engine oil.
   b. Tighten the rotor nut to 120 N•m (89 ft.-lb.).

Inspection

1. Clean, lubricate and inspect the clutch assembly (**Figure 14**).
2. Inspect the clutch for proper operation as follows:
   a. Insert the clutch gear into the rotor. Turn the gear *counterclockwise* and twist it squarely into the rotor.
   b. With the clutch gear facing up, turn the gear *counterclockwise* (**Figure 15**). The gear

should turn freely and smoothly in that direction.

c. Try to turn the gear clockwise. The gear should not turn.

d. If the gear turns in both directions or is always locked up, disassemble and inspect the clutch assembly.

3. Remove the clutch gear from the rotor. Turn the gear counterclockwise and twist it squarely away from the rotor.

4. Inspect the clutch gear (**Figure 16**).

a. Inspect the gear teeth and sprag contact area for wear or damage.

b. Inspect the bearing for damage. Fit the gear onto the crankshaft and check for play or roughness.

5. Inspect the clutch sprags in the rotor. The sprags should be undamaged and operate smoothly.

CAUTION

The starter clutch sprags can potentially be damaged if the engine kicks back, particularly at engine startup. The reversal of the crankshaft direction puts a high load on the sprags. To minimize potential damage to the sprags, keep the starter button engaged until the engine is definitely started.

6. If the clutch sprags are damaged, remove the clutch from the rotor as follows:

a. Remove the bolts, then remove the clutch assembly from the rotor. Use a 26 mm offset wrench (**Figure 17**) to hold the rotor hub while loosening the bolts.

b. Install the new clutch assembly. The back of the clutch retainer has a notch on its outer edge (**Figure 18**). This side of the clutch retainer must face toward the rotor.

c. Apply threadlocking compound to the bolts, then tighten the bolts in several passes, working in a crisscross pattern. Tighten the bolts to 26 N•m (19 ft.-lb.).

d. Insert the clutch gear into the rotor and check for correct installation. The rotor should turn freely in the direction of the arrow stamped on the rotor (**Figure 19**).

e. Lubricate the clutch sprags with engine oil.

7. Clean and inspect the rotor (**Figure 20**).

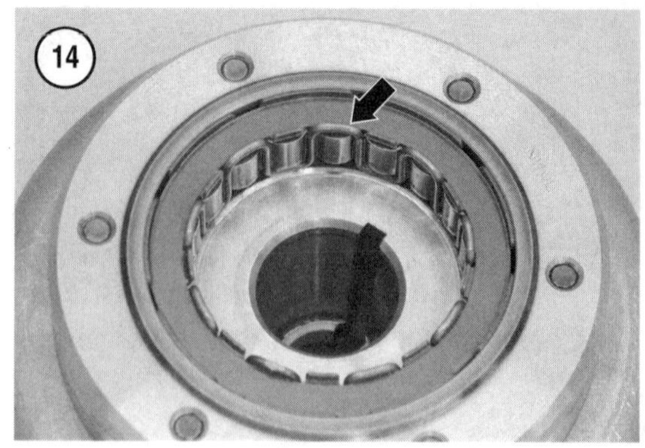

18

19

20

21

WARNING
Replace the rotor if it is damaged. The rotor can break apart at high crankshaft speeds, causing injury and engine damage.

a. Inspect the rotor for cracks and damage.
b. Inspect the bore, keyway and threads for damage.
c. Inspect the magnetic strip on the outside of the rotor. It must not be loose or missing.
d. Check that all clutch bolts are tight.

8. Inspect the crankshaft (A, **Figure 21**).
   a. Inspect the crankshaft for scoring or other damage.
   b. Inspect the shaft threads (B, **Figure 21**) and rotor nut for damage.
   c. Inspect the oil hole (C, **Figure 21**) for cleanliness.
   d. Inspect the keyway (D, **Figure 21**) and Woodruff key.
9. Install the parts as described in this section.

9

STARTER

Removal and Installation

Refer to **Figure 22**.

1. Disconnect the negative cable from the battery (**Figure 23**).
2. Remove the muffler (Chapter Four).
3. Disconnect the oil return tank hose and remove the oil return tank (**Figure 24**).
4. Disconnect the positive cable from the starter (**Figure 25**).
5. Remove the mounting bolts (**Figure 26**), then pull and twist the starter out of the alternator cover. The starter is sealed to the cover by an O-ring, which will cause resistance during removal. If necessary, use a block of wood and a mallet to tap the starter free.
6. Disassemble, inspect and test the starter as described in this section.
7. Reverse this procedure to install the starter. Note the following:
   a. Lubricate the O-ring on the end cover before inserting it into the alternator cover. If necessary, the starter can be seated in the cover using a block of wood and a mallet. Place the wood squarely against the back of the starter and tap it into place.

(22)

STARTER

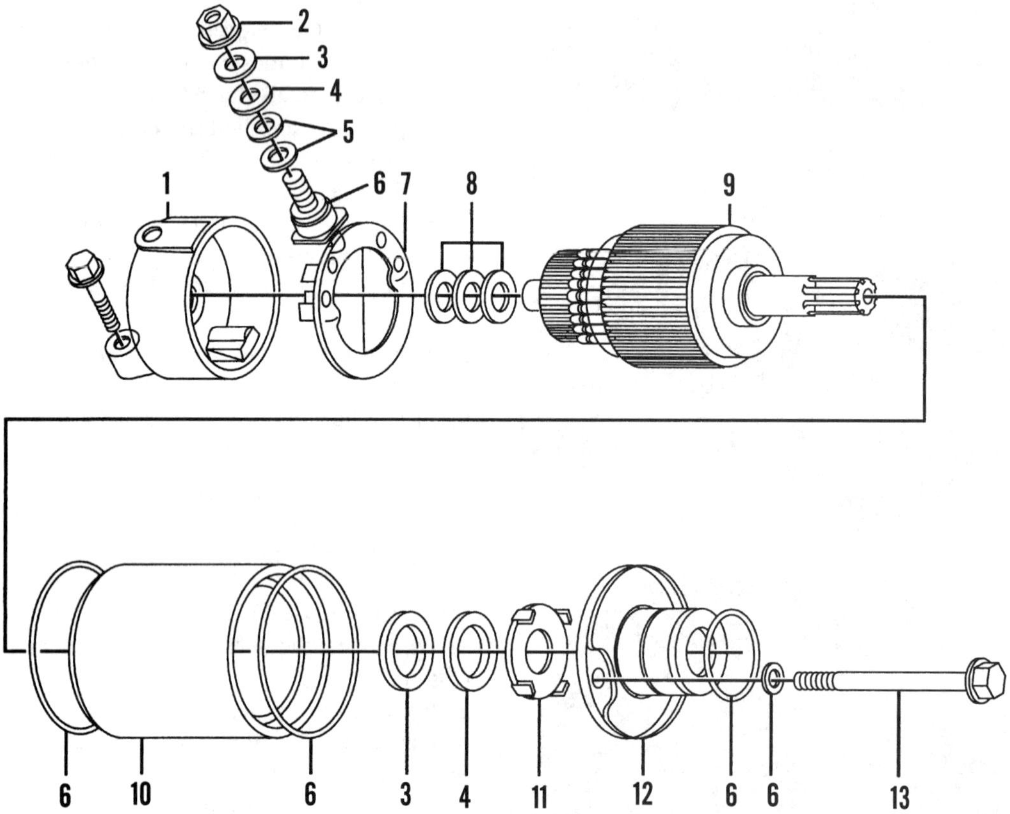

1. Cover
2. Nut
3. Metal washers
4. Large fiber washer
5. Small fiber washer
6. O-ring
7. Brushplate
8. Shims
9. Armature
10. Housing
11. Spacer
12. Cover
13. Housing bolt

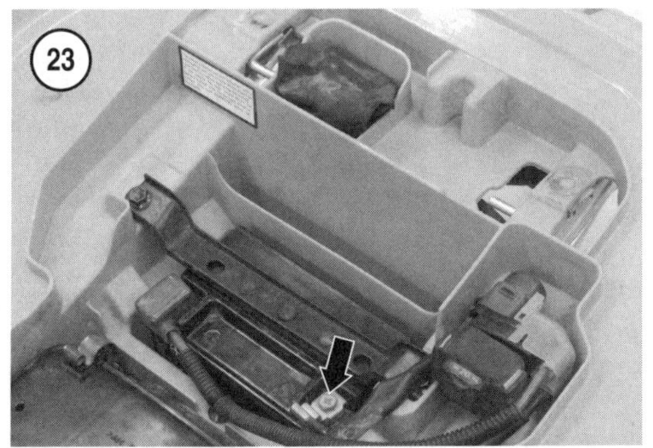

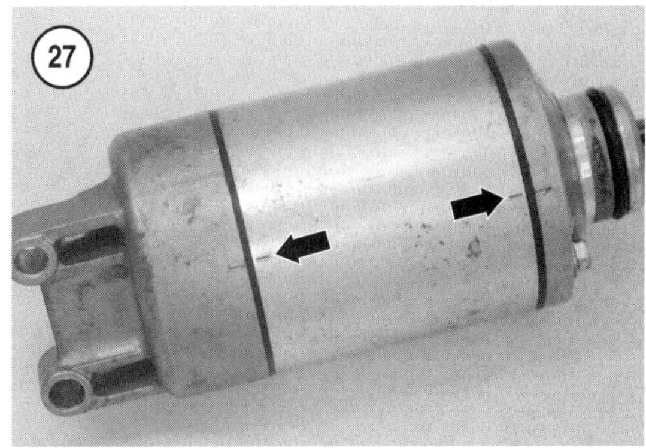

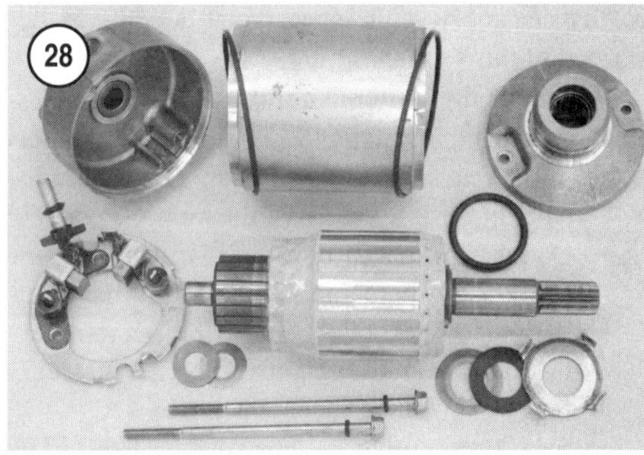

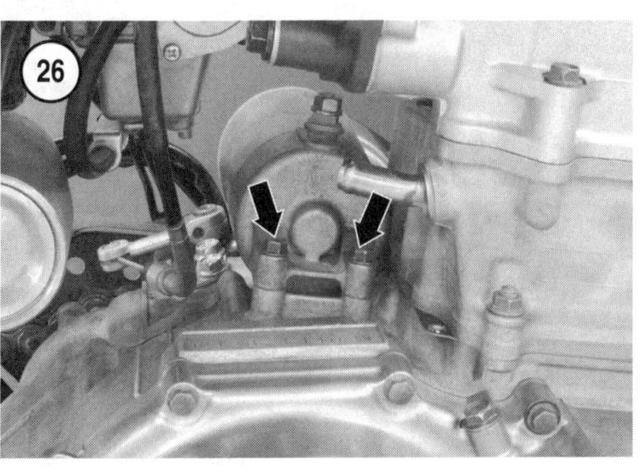

b. Check that the fiber washers on the cable post are in good condition. The washers must insulate the cable from the starter housing.

c. Clean all cable connections, then apply dielectric grease to the fittings and connectors before tightening.

d. Adjust the clutch (Chapter Three).

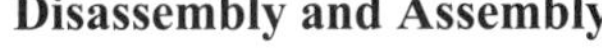

Disassembly and Assembly

Refer to **Figure 22**.

1. Note the alignment marks on the starter housing and end covers (**Figure 27**). Mark the rear end of the housing so it can be installed in its original position. The rear end of the housing is notched to accept the brush plate.

NOTE

If disassembling the starter to check brush condition, remove only the rear end cover.

2. Remove the two housing bolts and disassemble the starter (**Figure 28**).

3. Inspect and test the starter components as described in this section.
4. Assemble the starter as follows:
   a. Align and install the positive brushes and terminal into the rear end cover. The square insulator must be seated in the hole. Seat a new O-ring (**Figure 29**) around the terminal. Install the washers and lower nut on the terminal. The terminal must be completely insulated from the end cover to prevent shorting.
   b. Install the armature into the housing. The commutator should be located at the notched end of the housing (**Figure 30**). Lightly lubricate the ends of the armature shaft with waterproof grease.
   c. Install the shim(s) at the rear end of the armature shaft.
   d. Spread the brushes and seat the rear end cover onto the armature and housing.
   e. Install the washers on the armature and the spacer in the front end cover (**Figure 31**).
   f. Install the front end cover.
   g. Align the bolt holes and check the alignment marks (**Figure 27**).
   h. Apply threadlocking compound to the bolt threads, then install the bolts.
   i. Perform an operational test as described in this section.
   j. Install the starter as described in this section.

Inspection and Testing

1. Clean the parts, as required. Use a solvent specifically for electric components to remove buildup and contamination, particularly between the commutator bars.

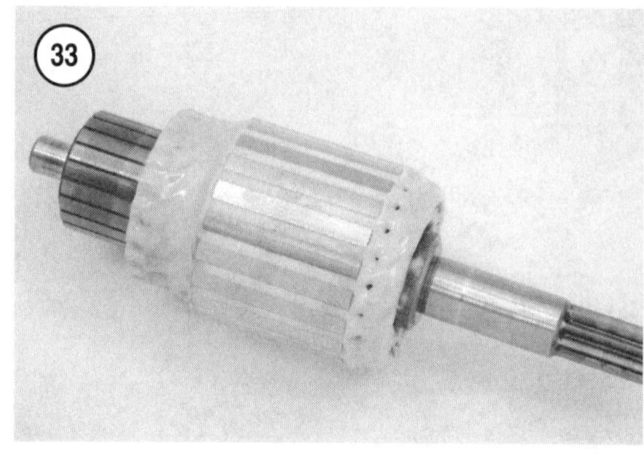

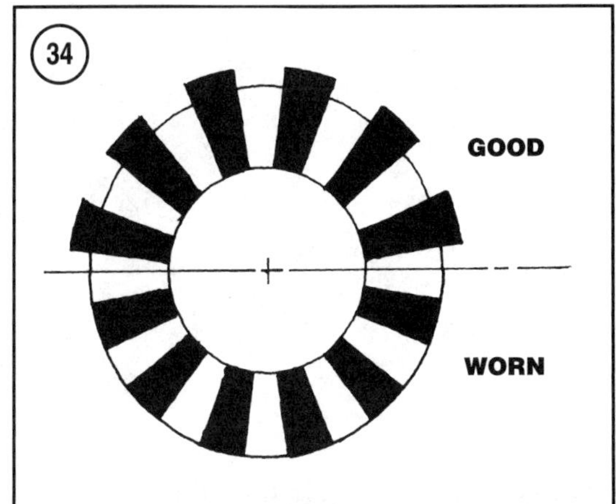

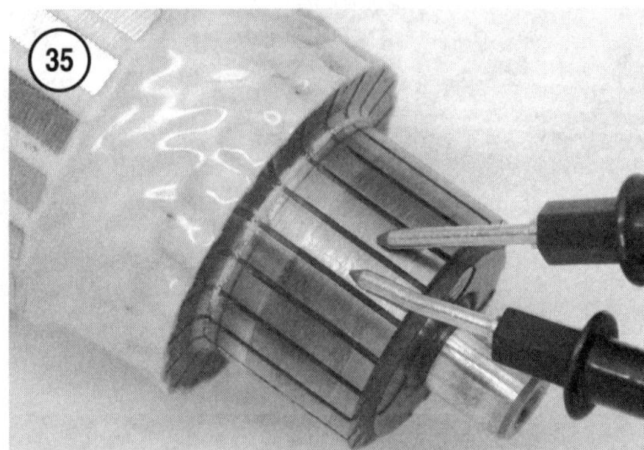

2. Inspect the condition of the housing and end covers (**Figure 32**).

   a. The armature should fit in the covers with little or no play.

   b. Inspect the condition of the bushing, bearing and seal. Lubricate the parts with waterproof grease. Remove excess grease that could migrate to the armature, commutator or brush assembly.

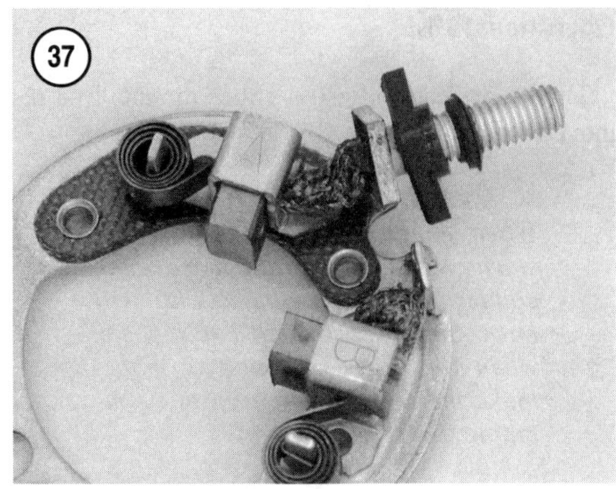

3. Inspect and test the commutator and armature (**Figure 33**).

   a. Inspect the bar height. The commutator bars should be taller than the insulation between the bars (**Figure 34**).

   b. Inspect the bars for discoloration. If a pair of bars is discolored, it indicates grounded armature coils.

   c. Inspect the bars for scoring. Mild scoring can be repaired with fine emery cloth.

   d. Check for continuity across all adjacent pairs of commutator bars (**Figure 35**). There should be continuity across all pairs of bars.

   e. Check for continuity between each commutator bar and the armature shaft (**Figure 36**). There should be no continuity.

   f. Inspect the armature shaft and drive splines for scoring, wear and other damage. If the splines are worn, check the condition of the idle gears, located in the upper idle gear cover and alternator cover.

4. Inspect the brush plate assembly (**Figure 37**).

   a. Inspect the condition of the brush springs. If rusted or broken, replace the brush plate.

   b. Inspect the length of each brush. Replace the brushes if they are chipped, rough, or when they are no longer secure in the brush housing.

5. Inspect the spacer, shims, washers and insulator for damage.

6. Install new, lubricated O-rings on the housing, front end cover and bolts (**Figure 38**).

7. Assemble the starter as described in this section.

9

Operational Test

The starter can be tested either mounted or removed from the engine.

WARNING
When connecting a battery to the starter, use jumper cables to make the connections. Light gauge wire will burn. Since sparks will likely occur when the test connection is made, make the check away from all flammable sources.

1. Shift the transmission into neutral if the starter is mounted in the engine.
2. Disconnect the positive cable from the starter (**Figure 39**).
3. Connect the negative cable from a 12-volt battery to the starter and cover.
4. Quickly touch and remove the positive battery cable to the positive terminal on the starter.
   a. If the starter turns, it is in good condition. Check the starter relay and cables for damage.
   b. If the starter does not turn, and the starter is not mounted in the engine, the starter is faulty.
   c. If the starter does not turn, and it is mounted in the engine, remove the starter and repeat the test. If the starter works after removing it, check for possible jamming of the starter idle gears or starter clutch.

STARTING SYSTEM SWITCHES

The starting system switches include the starter relay, ignition switch, engine stop switch, starter button, and clutch switch. Refer to the wiring diagram at the back of the manual to identify wire colors and connectors.

Switches and relays that require a specific test procedure, or special equipment, are described in this section. The remaining switches can be tested for continuity by referring to the wiring diagram.

Starter Relay Tests

The starter relay (**Figure 40**) is located under the right side cover. The starter relay connects the battery to the starter. The relay is activated when the

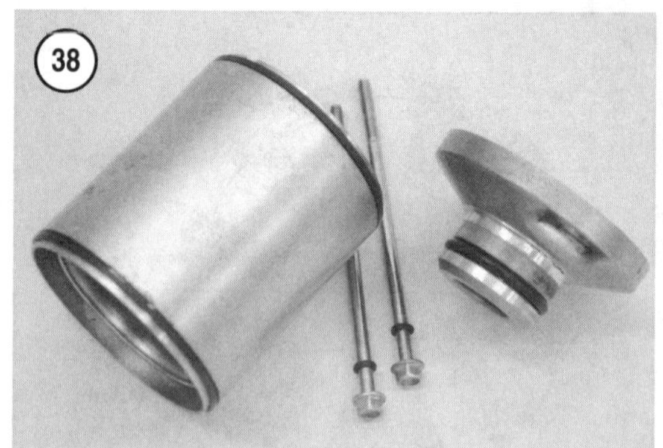

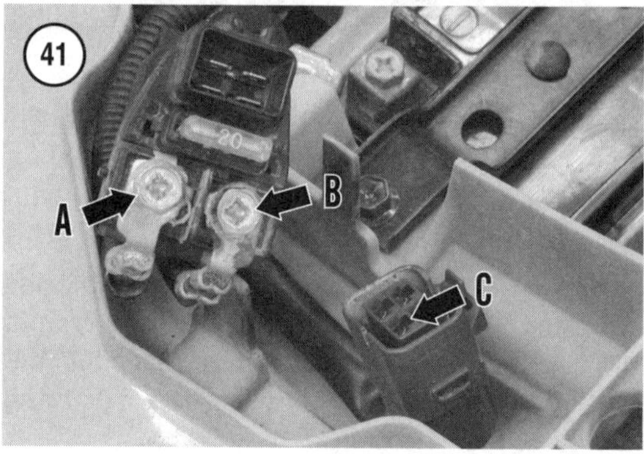

42

43

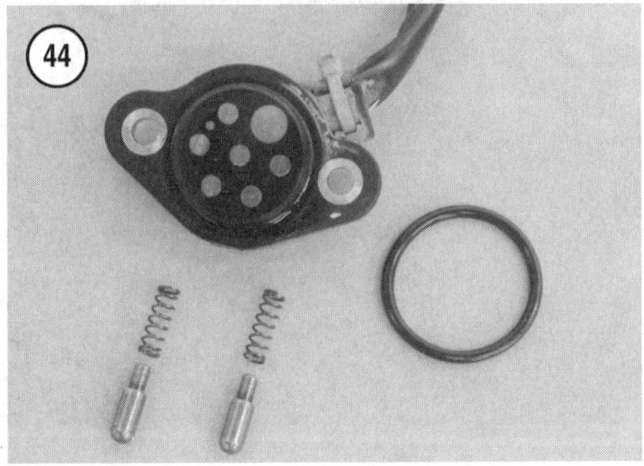

44

starter button is pressed. All other switches in the starting system must also be in the closed position.

1. At the battery, disconnect the negative cable.
2. At the relay, disconnect the positive (A, **Figure 41**) and negative (B) leads and connector (C).
3. Remove the starter relay.
4. Perform the relay coil resistance test as follows:
   a. Connect an ohmmeter to the wire connector terminals *closest* to the fuse (**Figure 42**).
   b. Refer to **Table 1** for specifications. Replace the relay if it is not within specifications.
5. Perform the relay operational test as follows:
   a. Connect an ohmmeter to the wire connector terminals *closest* to the fuse (**Figure 42**).
   b. Use a jumper wire to connect a fully charged, 12-volt battery to the relay wire connector. Connect the positive lead to the terminal for the red wire (A, **Figure 41**).
   c. Observe the meter, then touch the negative battery lead to the terminal for the black/orange wire (B, **Figure 41**). The relay should *click* when voltage is applied. Do not apply voltage to the relay for more than five seconds at a time. The relay coil can overheat.
   d. If the meter indicates continuity, the relay is in good condition. Check the starter, cables and other starting system switches for damage.
   e. If the meter does not indicate continuity, the relay is faulty.

Gear Position Switch Test

The gear position switch (**Figure 43**) is located on the lower left side of the engine near the shift lever. Test the switch in each position. If the switch fails one of the tests, replace it.

1. Identify the connector half that leads to the gear position switch.
2. Shift the transmission into neutral. Connect an ohmmeter to the blue wire and the black wire.
   a. The meter should indicate continuity when the transmission is in neutral.
   b. Shift the transmission into gear. The meter should not indicate continuity.
   c. If the meter has the same reading when the transmission is in neutral or in gear, remove the switch (**Figure 44**) and inspect the contacts on the end of the shift drum (**Figure 45**). The contacts are spring-loaded and must be free to fully extend against the switch. If the contacts are in good condition, replace the switch.
3. Shift the transmission into reverse. Connect an ohmmeter to the red wire and the black wire.
   a. The meter should indicate continuity when the transmission is in reverse.
   b. Shift the transmission into gear. The meter should not indicate continuity.

c. If the meter has the same reading when the transmission is in reverse or in neutral, remove the switch (**Figure 44**) and inspect the contacts on the end of the shift drum (**Figure 45**). The contacts are spring-loaded and must be free to fully extend against the switch. If the contacts are in good condition, replace the switch.

4. Shift the transmission into first gear. Connect an ohmmeter to the white wire and the black wire.

a. The meter should indicate continuity when the transmission is in reverse.

b. Shift the transmission into first gear. The meter should not indicate continuity.

c. If the meter has the same reading when the transmission is in reverse or in first gear, remove the switch (**Figure 44**) and inspect the contacts on the end of the shift drum (**Figure 45**). The contacts are spring-loaded and must be free to fully extend against the switch. If the contacts are in good condition, replace the switch.

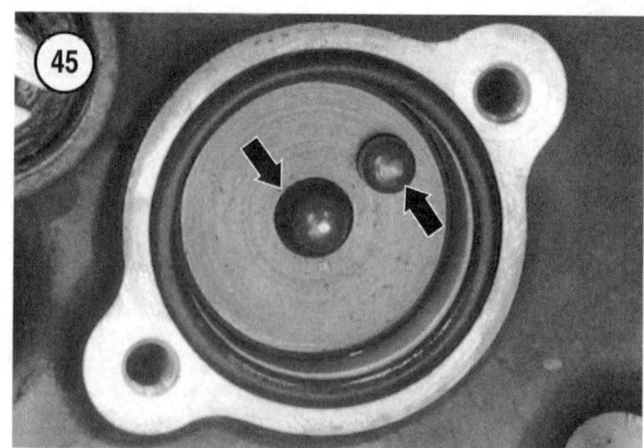

45

46

47

IGNITION SYSTEM

Before checking components in the ignition system, verify the condition of the battery, fuse, ignition switch and engine stop switch. Test the switches for continuity while referring to the wiring diagram.

Operation

A permanent magnet alternator on the left end of the crankshaft supplies power to the ignition and charging systems. The capacitor discharge ignition system (CDI) receives power from the signal coil. When the rotor is in the correct position, the pickup coil signals the CDI unit to release the stored voltage into the ignition coil's primary windings. This voltage is then increased in the secondary windings and fires the spark plug.

CDI Unit

No specifications are available for testing the CDI unit. If the voltage measured in the *Ignition Coil Primary Peak-Voltage Test* is out of specification, replace the CDI unit. The CDI unit (**Figure 46**) is located under the rear fender on the left hand side of the frame.

Ignition Coil Primary Peak-Voltage Test

The ignition coil (A, **Figure 47**) is located under the fuel tank. The test requires a multicircuit tester (Suzuki part No. 09900-25008) and peak voltage adapter, or an equivalent tester and adapter, and a new spark plug.

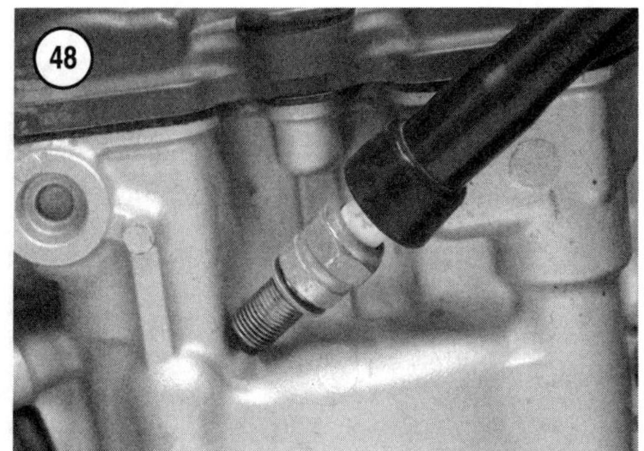

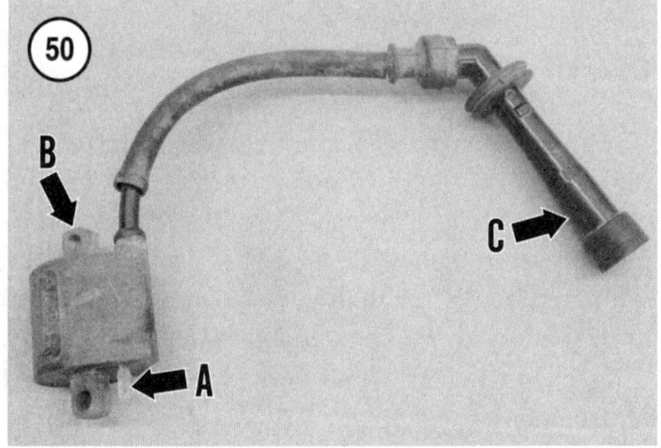

1. Connect a new spark plug to the spark plug cap and securely ground the plug against the cylinder head (**Figure 48**).

CAUTION
Do not ground the spark plug on the cylinder head cover. The magnesium alloy cover could be damaged by the spark plug voltage.

2. Connect the positive meter lead to the coil terminal for the black/white wire (B, **Figure 47**). The wire and lead must both be in contact with the terminal when performing the test.
3. Connect the negative meter lead to the black wire (C, **Figure 47**).
4. Set the tester to the voltage setting.
5. Shift the transmission into neutral and crank the engine. Allow the engine to crank for a few seconds, then note the voltage reading. Repeat this step several times and determine the highest voltage measured.
6. Refer to **Table 1** for specifications. If the voltage is below the specification, the CDI unit output is too low. Replace the CDI unit.

Ignition Coil Resistance Tests

The ignition coil (A, **Figure 47**) is located under the fuel tank. Use an ohmmeter and check the resistance in the primary and secondary coils.

1. Remove the spark plug cap from the spark plug (**Figure 49**).
2. Disconnect the black wire at the coil.
3. Measure primary coil resistance as follows:
   a. Connect one meter lead to the black wire terminal (A, **Figure 50**) on the coil and the other meter lead to the coil base (B), or ground.
   b. Measure the resistance. Refer to **Table 2** for specifications.
4. Measure secondary coil resistance as follows:
   a. Connect one meter lead to the black wire terminal on the coil and the other meter lead to the spark plug cap (C, **Figure 50**).
   b. Measure the resistance. Refer to **Table 1** for specifications.

9

Pickup Coil and Signal Coil Peak-Voltage Test

The pickup coil and signal coil connector (**Figure 51**) is plugged into the CDI unit, located on the left side of the frame. The Suzuki multicircuit tester (part No. 09900-25008) and peak voltage adapter, or an equivalent tester and adapter, are required for this test. Remove the plug from the CDI unit to perform the tests.

1. Perform the pickup coil voltage test as follows:
   a. Connect the negative meter lead to the blue wire and the positive meter lead to the green wire.
   b. Set the tester to the voltage setting.

c. Shift the transmission into neutral and crank the engine. Allow the engine to crank for a few seconds, then note the voltage reading. Repeat this step several times and determine the highest voltage measured.
d. Refer to **Table 1** for specifications.

2. Perform the signal coil voltage test as follows:
   a. Connect the negative meter lead to the yellow wire and the positive meter lead to the white wire.
   b. Set the tester to the voltage setting.
   c. Shift the transmission into neutral and crank the engine. Allow the engine to crank for a few seconds, then note the voltage reading. Repeat this step several times and determine the highest voltage measured.
   d. Refer to **Table 1** for specifications.

3. If the either voltage is out of specification, check the resistance of both coils for additional verification that the parts are damaged. If the parts are damaged, replace the complete stator assembly.

Pickup Coil and Signal Coil Resistance Test

The pickup coil and signal coil connector (**Figure 51**) is plugged into the CDI unit, located under the seat. Remove the plug from the CDI unit, then use an ohmmeter to perform the tests.

1. Measure pickup coil resistance as follows:
   a. Connect one meter lead to the blue wire terminal and the other meter lead to the green wire terminal.
   b. Measure the resistance. Refer to **Table 1** for specifications.
2. Measure signal coil resistance as follows:
   a. Connect one meter lead to the yellow wire terminal and the other meter lead to the white wire terminal.
   b. Measure the resistance. Refer to **Table 1** for specifications.

Ignition Timing

The ignition timing is controlled by the CDI unit. No adjustment is possible to the ignition timing. The rotor is marked for top dead center only. Advance timing is controlled by the CDI unit.

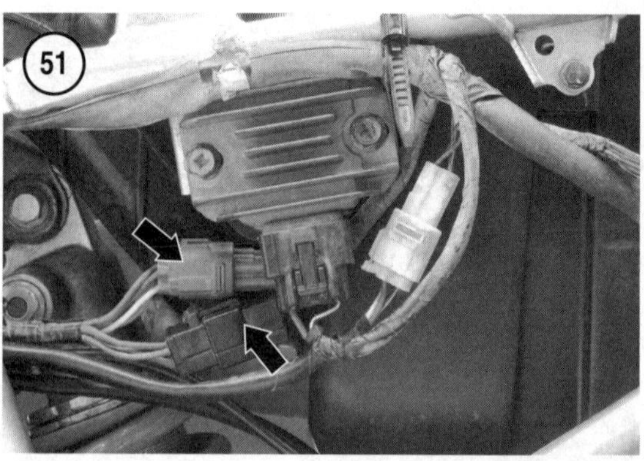

CHARGING SYSTEM

Operation

A permanent magnet alternator on the left end of the crankshaft supplies power to the ignition and charging systems. The charge coil generates charging system voltage while the engine is running. The voltage is converted to direct current and regulated to the battery by the regulator/rectifier.

Refer to Chapter Three for battery charging and replacement.

Fuse Holder

The fuse holder is located on top of the starter relay (**Figure 52**). Use an ohmmeter to check the fuse for continuity. A visual check may not reveal a fine break in the element.

Battery Voltage Test (Unloaded)

For a maintenance-free battery (original equipment), use a voltmenter to check the unloaded volt-

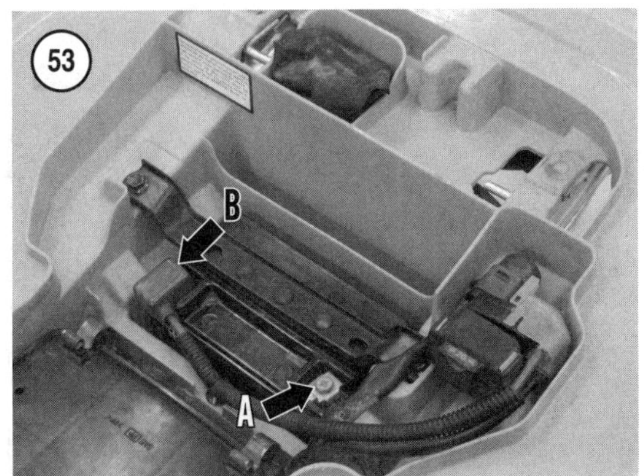

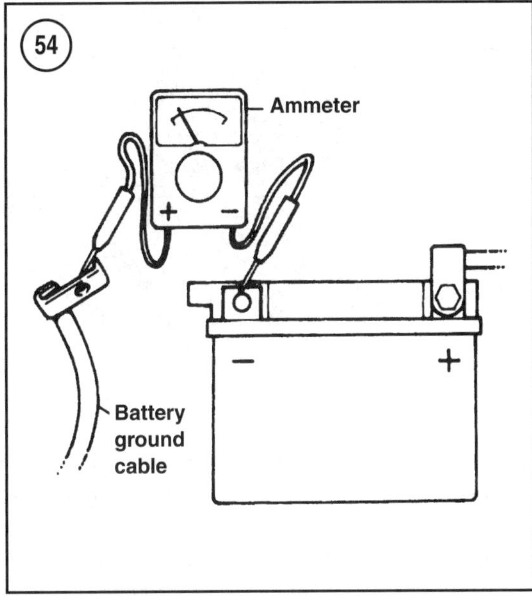

age. An unloaded test will indicate the basic state of charge.

1. Disconnect the battery cables and allow the battery to remain undisturbed for at least 4 hours.
2. Connect a voltmeter to the negative (A, **Figure 53**) and positive (B) terminals.
3. Measure the voltage. A fully charged battery will show 13.0-13.2 volts. If the voltage is 12.8 volts or less, the battery is undercharged.
4. If battery charging or replacement is required, refer to the procedures in Chapter Three.

Battery Voltage Test (Loaded)

For a maintenance-free battery (original equipment), use a voltmenter to check the loaded voltage. A load test requires the battery to discharge current. A load test will indicate whether the battery is adequate to operate the machine.

1. Connect a voltmeter to the negative (A, **Figure 53**) and positive (B) terminals.
2. Turn the headlight to the high beam.
3. Measure the voltage.
   a. A battery in good condition will have a minimum of 12.3 volts.
   b. If battery charging or replacement is required, refer to the procedures in Chapter Three.

Battery Current Draw Test

If the battery is in good condition, but it discharges at a rapid rate when the machine is not used, check the electrical system for a current draw or drain. A short in a wire or component in the electrical system can cause the battery to discharge to ground. Accumulations of dirt and moisture can also create a path to ground. It is normal for accessories to draw current when the machine is turned off.

To isolate a current draw, connect an ammeter to the battery (**Figure 54**). Observe the meter while disconnecting the wire connectors leading to components and circuits. When the meter stops indicating, inspect and test the component/circuit that affects the meter.

1. Remove the bodywork so all connectors and components can be accessed.
2. Turn the ignition switch off.
3. Disconnect the negative battery cable.
4. Check that the battery is fully charged.

CAUTION
Before connecting the ammeter in the next step, set the range selector to its highest setting. If there is an excessive amount of current flow, the meter could be damaged.

5. Connect the ammeter to the negative battery cable and terminal as shown in **Figure 54**.
   a. The meter should indicate a current draw of no more than 1.0 mA.
   b. If there is excessive current draw, continue the test.
6. Check the connectors.
   a. Refer to the wiring diagram at the back of the manual for circuits and part identifications.

b. Separate the individual connectors of the appropriate parts one at a time until the current draw is within specification. When this occurs, the problem circuit has been isolated.

Regulator/Rectifier Output Voltage Test

The regulator/rectifier is located on the left side of the frame (A, **Figure 55**). The regulator/rectifier converts the alternating current produced by the alternator into direct current to charge the battery and power the electrical system. The unit also regulates the charging voltage to the battery.

The following test checks regulator/rectifier output voltage for charging the battery. The battery must be in good condition and charged before performing the test.

1. Start the engine and allow it to reach operating temperature, then turn off the engine.
2. Check the regulator/rectifier output voltage as follows:
   a. Set a voltmeter to DC volts.
   b. Connect the voltmeter to the battery negative (A, **Figure 53**) and positive (B) terminals.
   c. Start the engine and momentarily raise the engine speed to 5000 rpm.
   d. The meter should indicate 14.0-15.5 volts (unloaded) when the engine speed is raised.
   e. If the output voltage is significantly higher than 15 volts, the regulator/rectifier may not be adequately grounded, or is faulty. If the output voltage does not rise with engine speed, the regulator/rectifier or stator coils are faulty. Before replacing parts, check the condition of the stator charging coils, wiring harness and battery.

Regulator/Rectifier Circuit Voltage Test

The regulator/rectifier connectors are located behind the front left side cover. Locate and separate the connector containing three brown wires (B, **Figure 55**) and the connector containing a red and black/white wire (C). The Suzuki multicircuit tester (part No. 09900-25008), or an equivalent tester, is required for this test.

1. Identify the connector halves that lead to the regulator/rectifier (A, **Figure 55**).

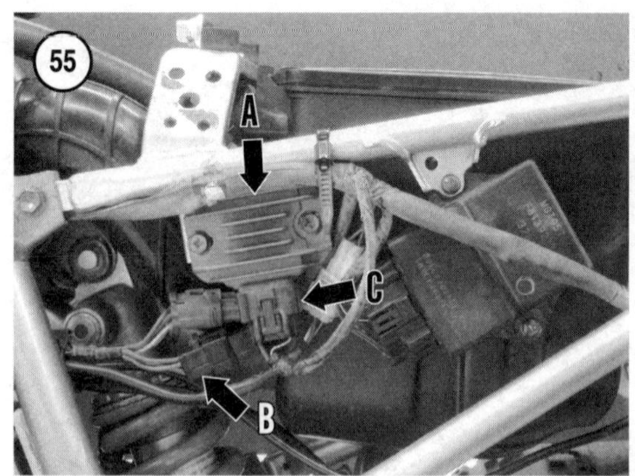

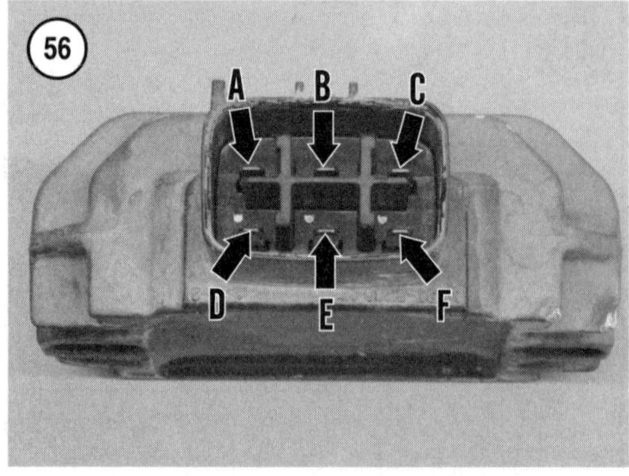

2. Connect the positive meter lead to the green wire terminal and the negative meter lead to the black/white wire.
3. Set the tester to the diode setting.
4. Measure the voltage between pairs of wire terminals labeled in **Figure 56**.
5. If the voltage is out of specification (**Figure 57**) for any measurement, the regulator/rectifier is damaged.

Stator Charging Coil Resistance Test

The stator coils are located in the alternator cover and are connected to the voltage regulator. Check the stator coils at the connector containing three brown wires (B, **Figure 55**), located on the left side of the frame. Use an ohmmeter to perform the test.

1. Identify the connector half that leads to the alternator cover.
2. Measure the resistance as follows:
   a. Insert the meter leads into the terminals of the brown wires. Check all three combinations of

57

REGULATOR/RECTIFIER CIRCUIT TESTS

	+ Tester Probe						
		A	B	C	D	E	F
– Tester Probe	A		*	0.5 – 1.2	0.4 – 0.7	0.4 – 0.7	0.4 – 0.7
	B	*		*	*	*	*
	C	*	*		*	*	*
	D	*	*	0.4 – 0.7		*	*
	E	*	*	0.4 – 0.7	*		*
	F	*	*	0.4 – 0.7	*	*	

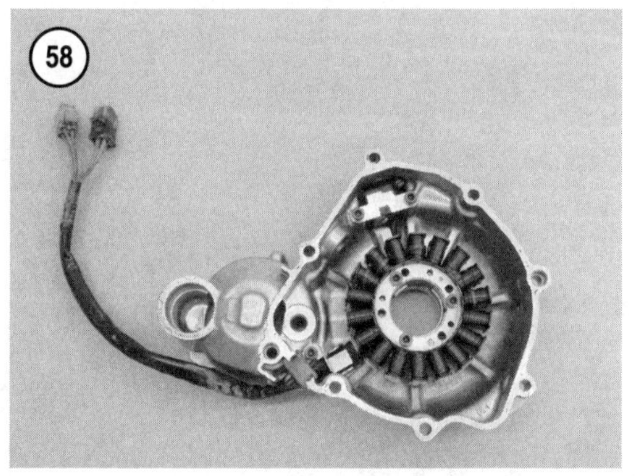

58

the brown wires. The resistance between all pairs of brown wires should be within the specifications in **Table 1**.

b. If the charging coils are not within specifications, check the wiring harness for damage and shorting.

c. If necessary, remove the alternator cover and recheck the wiring harness and coils (**Figure 58**). Individually check the full length of the harness wires for continuity. There should be near zero resistance in all wires. Flex the harness as the check is being made to detect erratic continuity.

d. If the harness is not shorted, check the coils at the brown wire connections on the stator. If the coils fail the check, replace the stator assembly.

3. Measure the resistance between the coils and ground. Ground one of the meter leads to the engine (or the alternator cover, if removed). Touch the other lead to each brown wire. There should be no continuity. Any other reading indicates a short. Remove the stator from the alternator cover and determine if repair is possible. If not, replace the stator assembly.

Alternator No-Load Voltage Test

The alternator is located in the alternator cover and consists of the stator coils and magnetic rotor. The stator coils are connected to the voltage regulator. Check the alternator voltage at the connector containing three brown wires, located along the left side of the frame (B, **Figure 55**). This test requires The Suzuki multicircuit tester (part No. 09900-25008), or an equivalent tester.

1. Start the engine and allow it to reach operating temperature, then turn off the engine.

2. Identify the connector half that leads to the alternator.

3. Measure the AC voltage as follows:

   a. Set the tester to the voltage setting.

   b. Insert the meter leads into a pair of the brown wires.

c. Start the engine and momentarily raise the engine speed to 5000 rpm.

d. The meter should indicate 65 volts or greater when the engine speed is raised.

e. Check all three combinations of the brown wires. The voltage between all pairs of brown wires should be 65 volts or greater.

f. If the output voltage is significantly lower than 65 volts, check the condition of the alternator wiring harness and connectors. Also check the stator charging coil resistance and the condition of the rotor.

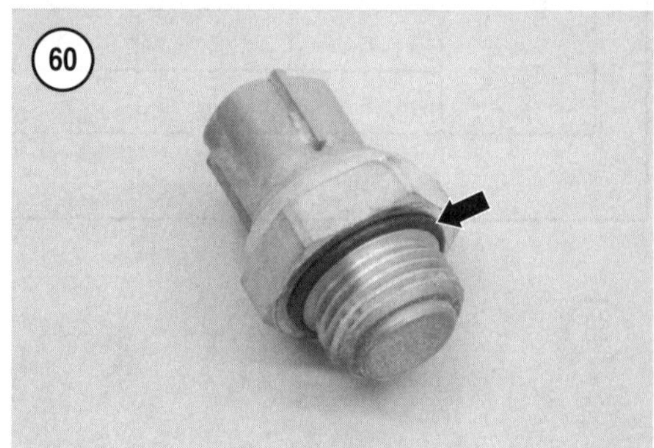

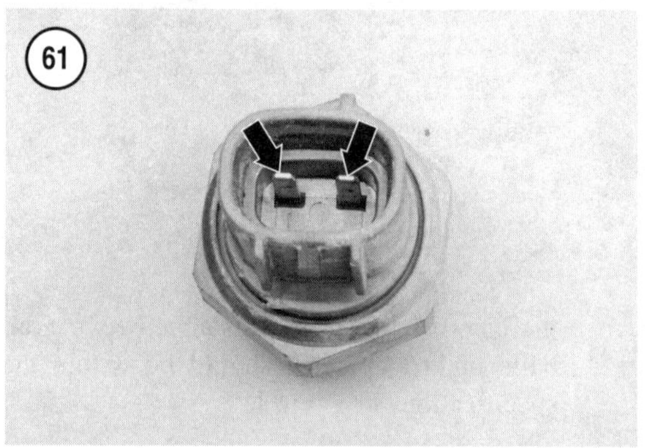

RADIATOR FAN SYSTEM

When coolant temperature cannot be maintained by air passing through the radiator, an electric fan (A, **Figure 59**) turns on to increase airflow through the radiator fins. The fan is turned on and off by a sending unit (B, **Figure 59**). The sending unit is thermally sensitive and controls power to the fan. When the engine coolant is cold, the sending unit has an open circuit and the fan is inoperative. As coolant temperature rises and begins to exceed normal operating temperature, resistance in the sending unit lowers and the circuit closes. The fan turns on and runs until the coolant temperature falls, causing resistance in the sending unit and opening the circuit.

When testing or troubleshooting the fan system, it is important that all connections are clean and tight. During assembly, apply dielectric grease to connections to prevent corrosion and the entry of moisture. 2004-on models have an inline 10 amp fuse to protect the fan. Always check the fuse first before performing any diagnostic tests.

Fan Test

1. Separate the fan connector.

2. Identify the half of the connector that leads to the fan (C, **Figure 59**).

3. Connect a 12-volt battery to the fan leads. Connect the positive lead to the red wire and the negative lead to the black/red wire.

a. If the fan does not turn on, replace the fan.

b. If the fan turns on, test the fan sending unit.

Fan Sending Unit Test

The following test requires that the sending unit (B, **Figure 59**) be placed in heated water to simulate actual operating conditions.

1. Remove the sending unit from the radiator (Chapter Ten).

2. Clean and inspect the sending unit for damage. Remove the O-ring (**Figure 60**).

3. Test the sending unit at ambient temperature as follows:

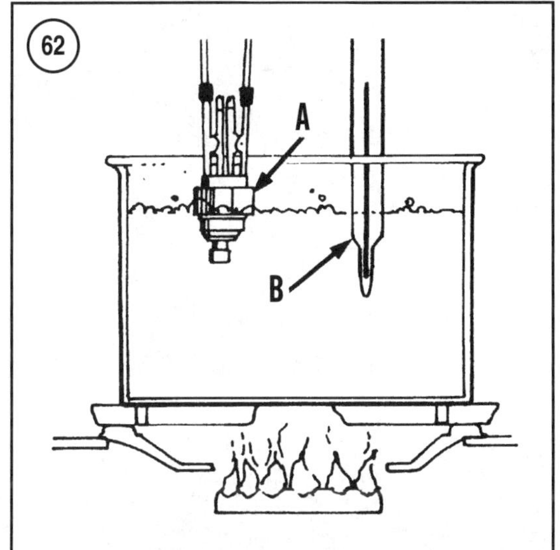

a. Connect an ohmmeter to the sending unit terminals (**Figure 61**). Note the meter reading.
b. If the reading indicates continuity, the sending unit is faulty. Low resistance in the part will cause the fan to come on too soon and/or not turn off.

4. Test the sending unit at operating temperature as follows:
   a. Connect an ohmmeter to the sending unit terminals.
   b. Suspend the part (A, **Figure 62**) and an accurate thermometer (B) in a container of water. The temperature sensor and threads must be submerged. Do not allow the parts to touch the bottom or side of the container.
   c. Slowly heat the water and observe the thermometer and ohmmeter readings. Do not excessively overheat the switch.
   d. As the sending unit is heated, there should be continuity at approximately 88° C (190° F).
   e. As the sending unit is cooled, there should be no continuity at approximately 82° C (180° F).
   f. Replace the sending unit if it does not operate within the specifications.
5. Install the sending unit (Chapter Ten).

COOLANT TEMPERATURE WARNING CIRCUIT

A coolant temperature warning circuit uses a warning light (**Figure 63**) to indicate that the coolant temperature is higher than it should be. It is turned on and off by the sending unit, located in the radiator (D, **Figure 59**). At normal operating temperatures, the sending unit has high resistance and the warning light remains off. If the coolant temperature rises above normal operating temperatures, the resistance of the sending unit lowers and the warning light indicates engine overheating. The light remains on until the coolant temperature falls, causing resistance in the sending unit and ungrounding the circuit. Refer to **Table 1** for specifications.

9

Warning Light Check

The warning light (**Figure 63**) should turn on only when the coolant temperature sending unit grounds the circuit. This should only occur when the coolant temperature sending unit detects high coolant temperature.

If the light is on at all times, or turns on soon after start up, test the sending unit. If the sending unit is in good condition, check for a short in the wire between the light and sending unit. If overheating is suspected and the light does not come on, make the following checks:

1. Remove the front fender (Chapter Fourteen) and the fuel tank (Chapter Eight) to access the wire connector leading from the sending unit.
2. Separate the black/green wire connector leading from the sending unit.
3. Identify the connector half (E, **Figure 59**) that leads to the warning light.
4. Turn on the ignition and ground the black/blue wire. Observe the warning light.

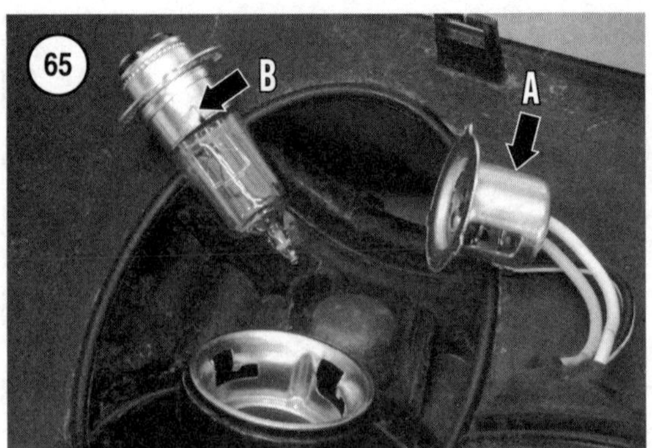

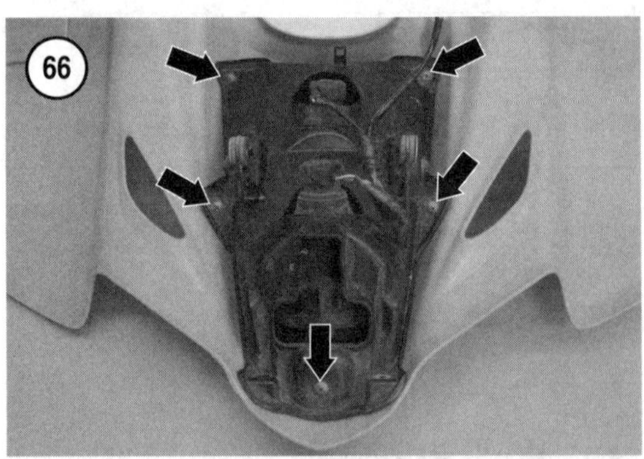

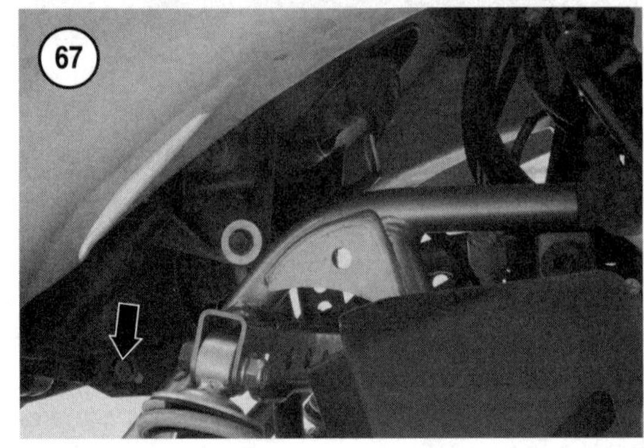

a. If the light does not turn on, inspect the meter cluster for damaged or broken wiring. Replace the water temperature bulb.

b. If the light turns on, check the wire connections for cleanliness, and if necessary, replace the sending unit.

Sending Unit Test

If the warning light is on all the time, or comes on soon after engine startup, perform the following:

1. Remove the front fender and the fuel tank to access the wire connector leading from the sending unit.

2. Separate the connectors leading from the sending unit (E, **Figure 59**).

3. Identify the connector halves that lead to the sending unit.

4. Connect an ohmmeter to the sending unit terminals.

5. If the reading indicates continuity, the sending unit is faulty. Replace the sending unit.

6. Start the engine and observe the meter as the engine coolant is brought to operating temperature.

7. If the meter indicates continuity at any time during the warmup, the sending unit is faulty. Replace the sending unit (Chapter Ten).

8. If the warning light does not turn on, and the light has been determined to be in good condition, replace the sending unit. Since the sending unit closes (creates continuity) at 120° C (248° F) to turn on the warning light, it is not practical or safe to heat the switch to this temperature.

HEADLIGHT

Bulb Replacement

CAUTION

Do not touch the bulb glass with bare hands. Handle the bulb with a clean cloth. Contaminants on the bulb surface prevent heat dissipation, which can cause shortened bulb life. If necessary, clean the bulb with isopropyl alcohol.

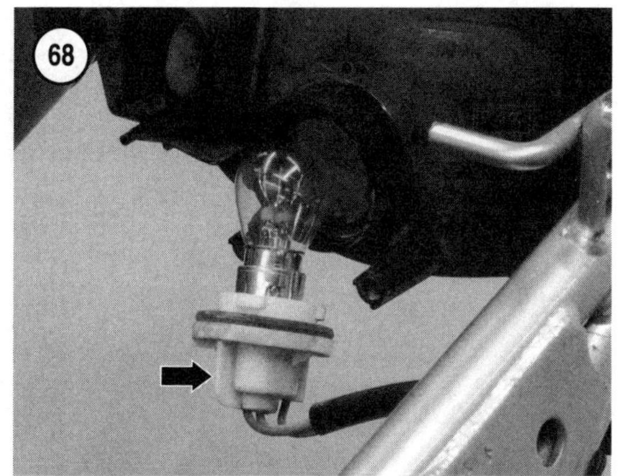

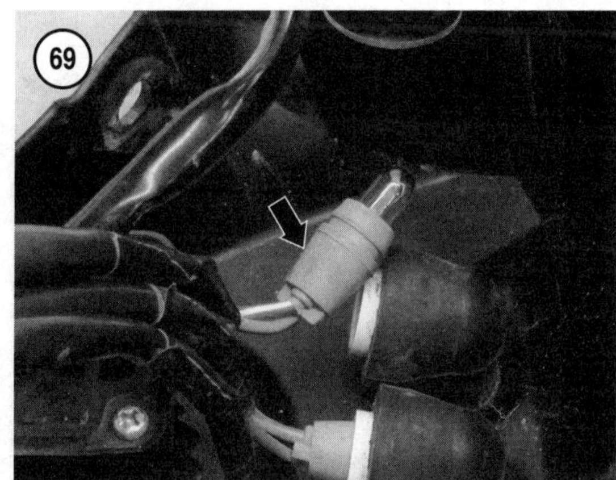

1. Remove the rubber boot from the back side of the socket (**Figure 64**).
2. To remove the bulb socket (A, **Figure 65**), push it in and turn it counterclockwise to remove it.
3. Remove the bulb (B, **Figure 65**) from the socket.
4. Seat the new bulb in the socket and reinstall the rubber boot.

Headlight Housing

If the headlight housing is damaged it can be removed from the front fender assembly as follows:

1. Remove the front fender assembly as described in Chapter Fourteen.
2. Remove the screws securing the headlight housing to the front fender (**Figure 66**).

Headlight Adjustment

To adjust the headlight loosen the screw on the bottom of the headlight housing under the front fender (**Figure 67**). The headlight can be adjusted by moving the headlight lens within the housing.

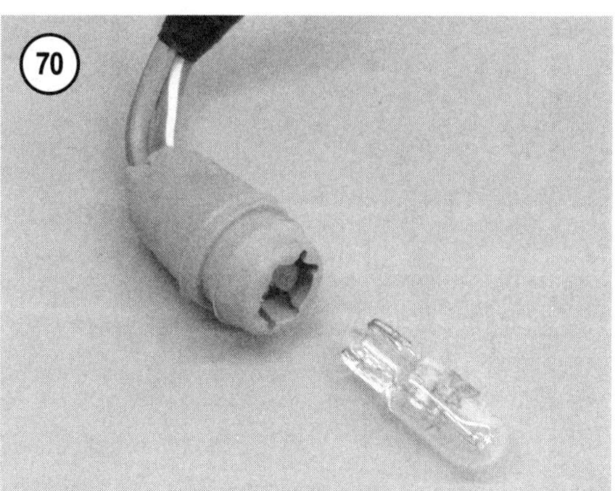

TAILLIGHT

Bulb Replacement

CAUTION
Do not touch the bulb glass with bare hands. Handle the bulb with a clean cloth. Contaminants on the bulb surface prevent heat dissipation, which can cause shortened bulb life. If necessary, clean the bulb with isopropyl alcohol.

1. Turn the socket (**Figure 68**) counterclockwise to remove it from the taillight housing.
2. To remove the bulb, push the bulb in and turn it counterclockwise.
3. Seat the new bulb in the socket by turning it clockwise.
4. Check that the rubber seal is in place, then install the socket into the taillight housing.

METER LIGHTS

1. Remove the two screws securing the meter housing to the handlbars and pull it straight up off the bars.
2. Pull the meter light socket from the meter body (**Figure 69**).
3. Remove the bulb from the socket (**Figure 70**).
4. Installation is the reverse of removal.

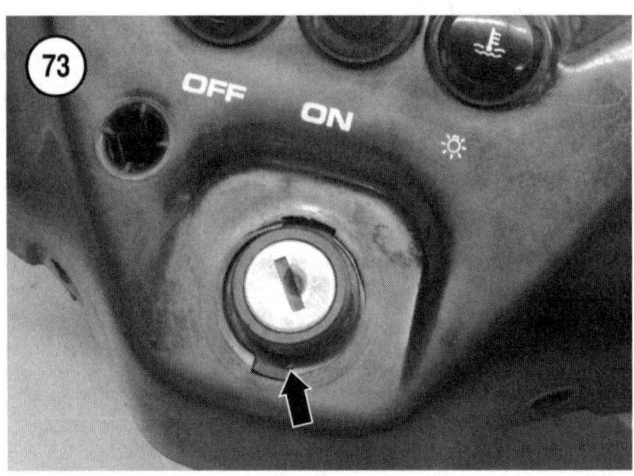

SWITCHES

Test switches by performing a continuity test with an ohmmeter (see Chapter Two) or a test light. Disconnect each switch connector and check the continuity while operating the switch in each of its positions. Refer to the wiring diagram for wiring colors.

Disconnect the negative battery lead from the battery if the switch connectors are not disconnected from the circuit.

Ignition Switch Replacement

1. Disconnect the ignition switch from the wiring harness.

2. Remove the two screws securing the meter housing to the handlebar.

3. Unscrew the plastic ring securing the switch to the meter body (**Figure 71**).

4. Remove the ignition switch (**Figure 72**).

5. Installation is the reverse of removal. Align the notch on the switch body with the slot in the meter body (**Figure 73**).

Left Switch Lever Replacement

1. Disconnect the switch from the wiring harness.
2. Remove the two screws on the bottom of the switch lever (**Figure 74**).
3. Separate the halves of the switch lever shell and remove the choke cable from the choke lever (**Figure 75**).
4. Installation is the reverse of removal. When reassembling the switch lever shell, align the pin in the shell with the hole in the handlebar (**Figure 76**).

Table 1 ELECTRICAL SYSTEM SPECIFICATIONS

Alternator	
Regulated voltage	14.0-15.5 V at 5000 rpm
Wattage	150 W at 5000 rpm
Battery	
Capacity	12 V – 8Ah
Current draw	1.0 mA maximum
Type	YTX9-BS
Coolant temperature sending unit	
On temperature	120° C (248° F)
Off temperature	113° C (235° F)
Fuses	
Main fuse	20 A
Cooling fan fuse (2004-on)	10 A
Ignition coil	
Primary peak voltage	130 V minimum
Resistance	
Primary	0.1-1.0 ohms
Secondary	12,000-20,000 ohms
Light bulbs	
Headlight (high/low beam)	12 V-30 W × 2
Taillight	12 V-21/5 W
Reverse/neutral/coolant indicator	12 V-3 W
Pickup coil	
Peak voltage	2.0 V minimum
Resistance	350-670 ohms
Radiator fan sending unit	
On fan temperature	88° C (190° F)
Off fan temperature	82° C (180° F)
Starter relay resistance	3-6 ohms
Stator coil	
Resistance	0.1-1.5 ohms
No load voltage	65 V at 5000 rpm
Signal coil	
Peak voltage	0.1 V minimum
Resistance	0.09-0.5 ohm

9

Table 2 ELECTRICAL SYSTEM TORQUE SPECIFICATIONS

Item	N•m	in.-lb.	ft.-lb.
Alternator cover bolts	10	89	–
Coolant temperature sending unit	13	115	–
Gear indicator	5	44	–
Neutral and reverse switches	13	115	–
Radiator fan sending unit	20	–	15
Starter bolt	5	44	–
Starter clutch bolts	26	–	19
Stator bolts	5	44	–
Stator rotor nut	120	–	89

CHAPTER TEN

COOLING SYSTEM

10

This chapter provides service procedures for the fan, fan sending unit, radiator, coolant temperature sending unit, thermostat and water pump.

Refer to Chapter Nine for electrical test procedures. Refer to **Table 1** and **Table 2** for specifications.

SAFETY PRECAUTIONS

Do not remove the radiator cap (**Figure 1**) immediately after or during engine operation. When the engine has been operated, the coolant is hot and under pressure. Removing the cap while the engine is hot can cause the coolant to spray violently from the radiator opening, possibly causing injury.

Wait for the engine to cool, then place a shop cloth over the cap. *Slowly* turn the cap to the safety stop to relieve any pressure. To remove the cap from the radiator, press down on the cap and twist it free.

FAN AND FAN SWITCH

A thermostatically controlled fan (A, **Figure 2**) is located between the engine and the radiator. The fan is turned on and off by the fan sending unit, located on the right side of the radiator (B, **Figure 2**). During engine operation, coolant from the engine circulates through the radiator. The coolant then returns to the engine to repeat the cycle. If the coolant entering the radiator is too hot (**Table 1**), the switch turns on the fan. The fan draws air through the radiator to aid in lowering coolant temperature.

Fan
Removal/Installation

1. Remove the front fender as described in Chapter Fourteen.
2. Remove the fuel tank as described in Chapter Eight.
3. Trace the wires leading from the fan, then disconnect the wires at the connectors (C, **Figure 2**).
4. Remove the single bolt on the left of the fan (**Figure 3**) and the two bolts on the right (**Figure 4**).
5. If necessary, refer to Chapter Nine to test the fan.
6. Installation is the reverse of removal.

Radiator Fan Sending Unit Removal/Installation

It is possible to remove the sending unit without removing the bodywork.

1. Drain the coolant from the radiator (Chapter Three).
2. Disconnect the sending unit (A, **Figure 5**) from the wiring harness by pressing down on the tab at the top of the connector. If the connector is difficult to remove, use a small screwdriver to gently pry it off the switch.
3. Unscrew the sending unit from the radiator.
4. Clean the sending unit (**Figure 6**) and the threads in the radiator.
5. Test the sending unit as described in Chapter Nine.
6. Installation is the reverse of removal. Note the following:
   a. Install a new, lubricated O-ring on the sending unit.
   b. Tighten the sending unit to 20 N•m (15 ft.-lb.).

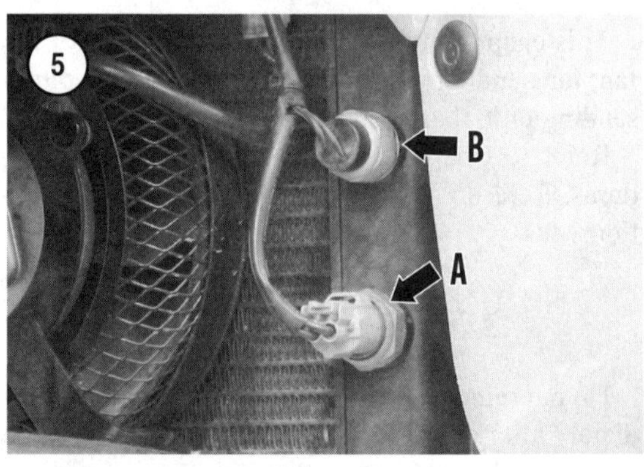

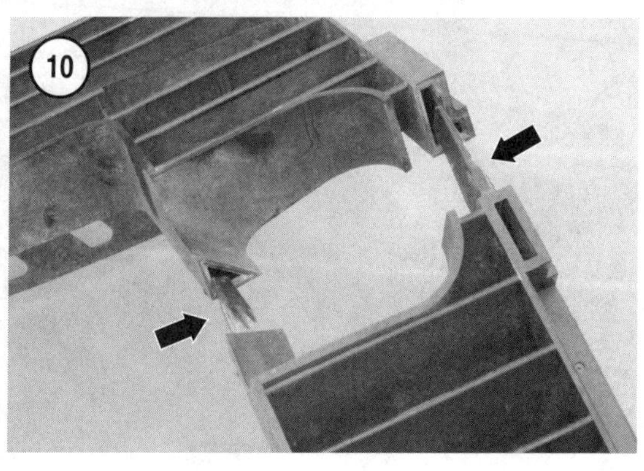

RADIATOR

Coolant is circulated from the bottom of the radiator, through the water pump, and up through the engine into the top end. A coolant temperature sending unit is located on the right side of the radiator. When coolant temperature is excessively high, the sending unit turns on the warning light at the handlebar.

Radiator Removal and Installation

1. Remove the front fender as described in Chapter Fourteen.
2. Remove the fuel tank as described in Chapter Eight.
3. Drain the cooling system as described Chapter Three.
4. Disconnect the wires leading from the fan (C, **Figure 2**), the fan sending unit (A, **Figure 5**) and the warning light sending unit (B, **Figure 5**).
5. Remove the upper (**Figure 7**) and lower radiator hoses (**Figure 8**). If the hoses are seized to the fittings, cut and split the hoses so they can be peeled from the fittings. Avoid scoring the fittings.
6. Remove the radiator shroud surrounding the radiator as follows:
   a. Unclip both sides of the radiator shroud from the frame (**Figure 9**).
   b. Separate the shroud in the middle (**Figure 10**) and pull each half out of the frame.
7. Remove the upper radiator bolt (**Figure 11**) from the right side.
8. Remove the upper (A, **Figure 12**) and lower radiator bolts (B) from the left side.
9. Inspect the radiator as described in this chapter.

10. Installation of the radiator is the reverse of removal. Note the following:
   a. Replace hoses that are hard, cracked or show signs of deterioration, both internally and externally. Hold each hose and flex it in several directions to check for damage. For a hose that is difficult to install on a fitting, dip the hose end in hot water until the rubber has softened, then install the hose.
   b. Install hose clamps in their original positions.
   c. Check that both sending units are installed. Tighten the radiator fan sending unit to 20 N•m (15 ft.-lb.). Tighten the coolant temperature sending unit to 13 N•m (115 in.-lb.).
   d. Fill and bleed the cooling system (Chapter Three).
   e. Start the engine and allow it to warm up. Check for leaks.

Inspection

1. Clean the exterior of the radiator with a low-pressure water spray. Allow the radiator to dry.
2. Check for damaged cooling fins. Straighten bent fins with a screwdriver (**Figure 13**). Replace a radiator with more than 20 percent damage in the cooling area.
3. Check the seams and other soldered connections for corrosion (green residue). If corrosion is evident, there could be a leak in that spot. Perform a cooling system pressure check as described in Chapter Three. If the equipment is not available, take the radiators to a radiator repair shop to have them flushed and pressure checked.
4. Fill each radiator with water and check the flow rate out of the radiator. If the flow rate is slow, or if corrosion or other buildup is seen, flush and pressure check the radiator.

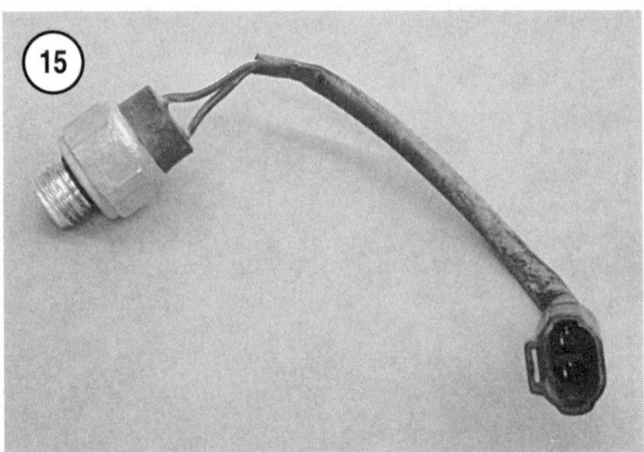

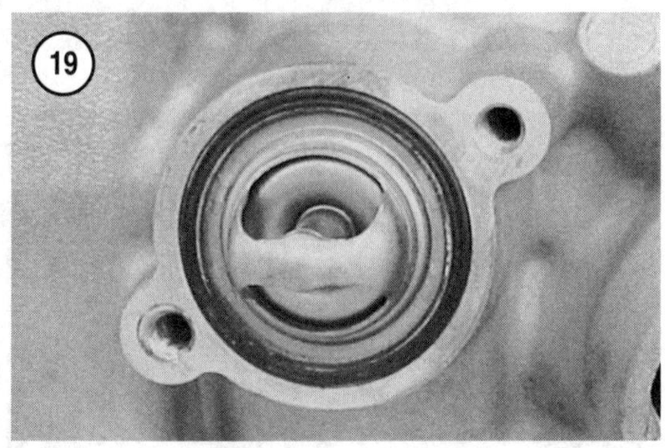

Coolant Temperature Sending Unit Removal and Installation

1. Remove the front fender (Chapter Fourteen).
2. Trace the wires leading from the sending unit (A, **Figure 14**), then disconnect the wires at the connector (B).
3. Partially drain the cooling system (Chapter Three). The coolant level in the radiators only needs to be below the switch.
4. Remove the sending unit from the radiator.
5. Clean the sending unit (**Figure 15**) and the threads in the radiator.

6. Test the sending unit as described in Chapter Nine.
7. Reverse this procedure to install the sending unit.
   a. Install a new, lubricated O-ring on the sending unit (**Figure 16**).
   b. Tighten the sending unit to 13 N·m (115 in.-lb.).

THERMOSTAT

The engine thermostat is located in a housing on the front of the cylinder head. The thermostat is a temperature-sensitive valve that opens and closes, depending on the coolant temperature in the cylinder head.

Removal, Inspection and Installation

1. Remove the fuel tank (Chapter Eight).
2. Remove the front fender (Chapter Fourteen).
3. Drain the cooling system (Chapter Three).
4. Remove the upper radiator hose (**Figure 17**). If the hose is seized to the fitting, cut and split the hose so it can be peeled away. Avoid scoring the fittings. Replace the hose if necessary.
5. Remove the bolts securing the thermostat housing to the cylinder head (**Figure 18**).
6. Remove the thermostat (**Figure 19**).
7. Inspect the inside of the water jacket for buildup that could cause restrictions or other cooling system damage. If necessary, open the drain bolt at the water pump and flush the water jackets. If heavy buildup is evident at the water pump drain, remove the water pump and clean all parts. Heavy buildup can cause water pump damage and plug the radiator.
8. Inspect and clean the thermostat and housing (**Figure 20**).

a. Visually inspect the valve in the thermostat. The valve should be closed when the thermostat is cold. If the valve is cold and open, replace the thermostat.
b. Wash the thermostat in cool water. If necessary, use a soft brush to scrub accumulation off the thermostat. If accumulation of rubber particles is evident, inspect the radiator hoses for internal deterioration.
c. Inspect the condition of the housing and the rubber seal on the thermostat.
d. Clean the bolts and threaded bores.
e. To test the thermostat, suspend it and an accurate thermometer in a container of water (**Figure 21**). Do not allow the parts to touch the bottom or side of the container. Slowly heat the water and observe the thermostat valve. The thermostat should begin to open at approximately 75° C (167° F). Continue to raise the temperature to approximately 90° C (194° F). At this temperature, the thermostat valve should have lifted at least 6 mm (0.24 in.). Replace the thermostat if it does not meet the conditions of the test.

9. Lubricate the rubber seal, then seat the thermostat in the cylinder head.
10. Install the housing and tighten the bolts to 10 N•m (89 in.-lb.).
11. Install the upper radiator hose.
12. Fill the cooling system (Chapter Three).
13. Install the fuel tank (Chapter Eight).
14. Start the engine and allow it to warm up. Check for leaks.

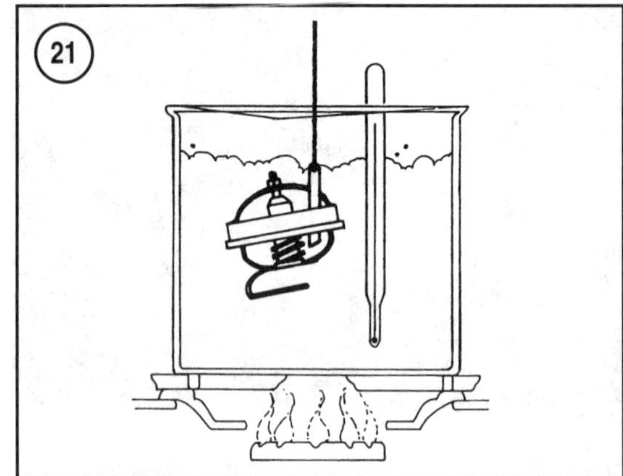

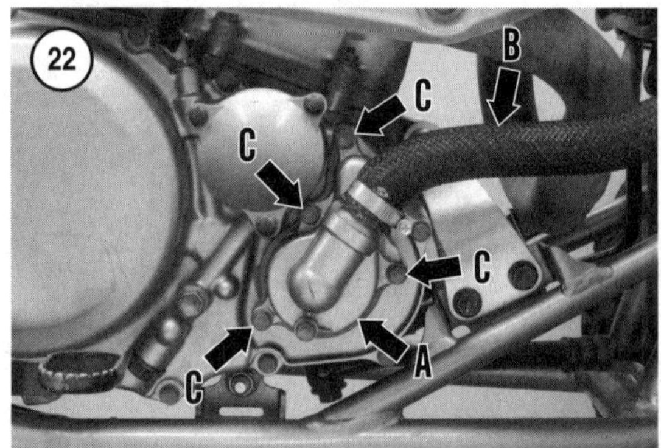

WATER PUMP

The water pump (A, **Figure 22**) is located in the right crankcase cover. To inspect the condition of the impeller (**Figure 23**), the water pump cover can be removed without removing the right crankcase cover. The cooling system must be drained before removing the water pump cover.

Although not visible, a drain hole is located on the back side of the pump plate. Any leaks from this hole will be visible at the bottom of the pump plate, where it joins the right crankcase cover. If there is coolant visible, the pump mechanical seal is leaking. If there is oil visible, the oil seal is leaking. Removal of the right crankcase cover is necessary to replace the seals.

Removal, Inspection and Installation

Refer to **Figure 24**.

1. Drain the cooling system (Chapter Three).
2. Remove the right engine cover (Chapter Five).
3. Drain the engine oil and remove the oil filter (Chapter Three).
4. Remove the hose (B, **Figure 22**) from the water pump cover and loosen the bolts securing the cover to the pump plate (C).

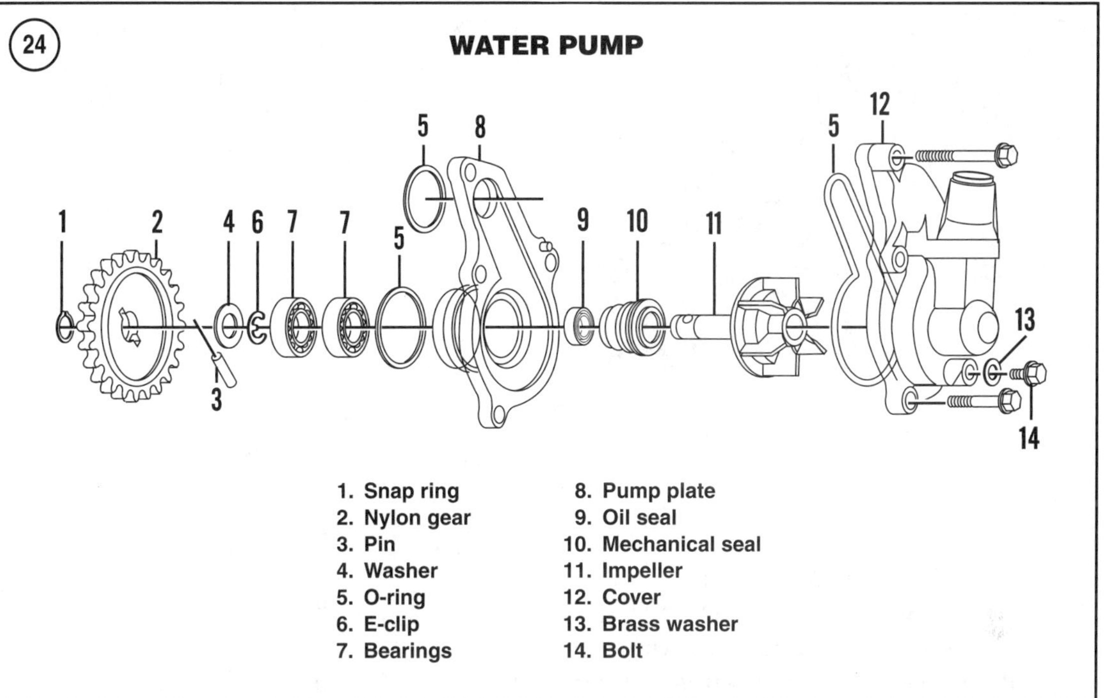

5. Remove the right crankcase cover (Chapter Six). It is not necessary to remove the clutch assembly.

6. Remove and disassemble the water pump as follows:

   a. Remove the water pump cover.

   b. Remove the snap ring (**Figure 25**), driven gear, pin and washer (**Figure 26**).

   c. Twist and press the pump plate from the right crankcase cover (**Figure 27**). An O-ring seals the two parts together.

   d. Remove the E-clip (**Figure 28**) and remove the impeller shaft from the bearings.

   e. Remove the O-rings from the parts.

7. Inspect the parts (**Figure 29**) for wear and damage. Note the following:
   a. Replace all O-rings.
   b. Replace the seal washer on the drain bolt.
   c. Replace the snap ring and E-clip.
8. Inspect the bearings in the water pump:
   a. Turn each bearing by hand and check for smooth, quiet operation. Insert the impeller shaft into the bearings and feel for play and roughness.
   b. Try to push each bearing in and out to check for axial play. Try to push each bearing up and down to check for radial play. Any play (**Figure 30**) should be difficult to feel. If play is easily felt, the bearing is worn out. Always replace bearings as a set. If necessary, replace the bearings as described in this section.
9. Inspect the impeller and mechanical seal (**Figure 31**) for obvious wear or damage. The face of the mechanical seal on the impeller and in the pump plate must be smooth and free of scoring or damage. When installed, the impeller seal should fit firmly against the seal in the pump plate. Since the seal in the pump plate is spring-loaded, it maintains pressure against the impeller and compensates for wear. If necessary, replace the mechanical seal and oil seal as described in this section.
10. Reverse Step 6 to assemble and install the water pump onto the right crankcase cover. Note the following:
   a. Apply waterproof grease to the impeller shaft.
   b. Install a *new* snap ring and E-clip with their sharp edge facing out.
   c. Lubricate the water pump bearings with engine oil.

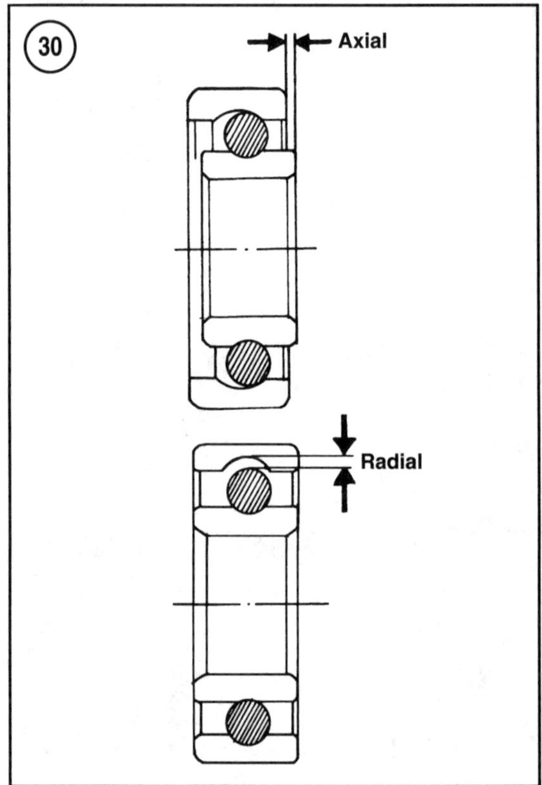

   d. Tighten the water pump cover bolts to 10 N•m (89 in.-lb.).
11. Reverse Steps 1-5 to install the right crankcase cover. Refer to the referenced chapters for installation procedures and for fluid requirements and capacities.

Mechanical and Oil Seal Replacement

The water pump has a two-piece mechanical seal (A, **Figure 32**) and an oil seal (B). The mechanical

31

32

33

34

seal prevents coolant in the pump chamber from passing into the right crankcase cover, which contains oil. Likewise, the oil seal prevents oil in the right crankcase cover from passing into the pump chamber, which contains coolant. A drain hole is located between the seals to allow leaking water or oil to drain to the outside of the engine. If there is a leak at the bottom of the pump plate, replace the seals. The mechanical seal must be removed from the pump plate in order to remove the oil seal.

1. Replace the mechanical seal in the impeller as follows:
   a. Lift the impeller seal from the impeller (**Figure 33**). Clean the seal bore.
   b. Lightly lubricate the rubber edge of the new seal with waterproof grease.
   c. Seat the new seal into the impeller by hand.
2. In the pump plate, remove the remaining half of the mechanical seal and the oil seal as follows:
   a. Support the pump plate on wooden blocks, with the mechanical seal facing down. Keep the blocks as close as possible to the seal, without touching the seal.
   b. If desired, use a heat gun to warm the area around the seal. The heat will soften the sealant at the outer edge of the seal, making it easier to remove.
   c. Place a narrow drift under the oil seal and onto the back of the mechanical seal (**Figure 34**). Work around the seal and drive it from the bore. Avoid any contact with the surface of the bore. Do not attempt to pry the seal from the front side of the pump plate.
   d. Drive out the oil seal.
   e. Clean the pump plate bore, drain hole and bearings. If bearing replacement is required, replace the bearings before installing a new oil seal and mechanical seal. Refer to *Bearing Replacement* in this section.
3. Install the oil seal as follows:
   a. Pack molydisulfide grease into the lip of the oil seal.
   b. Place the seal squarely over the bore, with the closed side of the seal facing up.
   c. Drive the seal into the bore using a driver that fits on the perimeter of the seal. Check that the seal is fully seated (**Figure 35**).
4. Install the mechanical seal as follows:
   a. To ease installation, *lightly* apply Suzuki Bond 1207B sealant to the outer edge of the

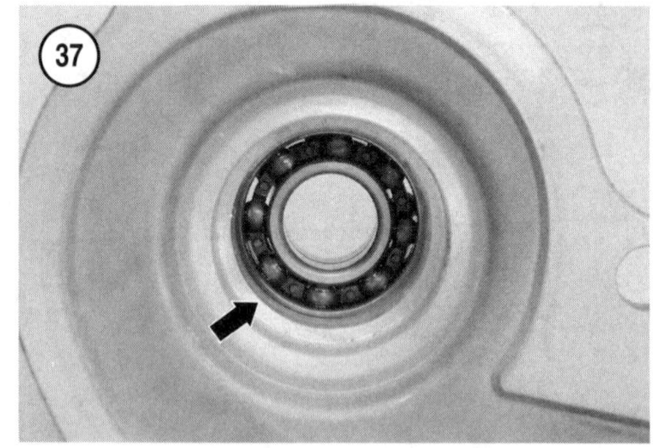

   seal. Use only enough to lubricate the parts as they are driven together. Excess sealant can plug the drain hole.
   b. Place the seal squarely over the bore (**Figure 36**).
   c. Drive the seal into the bore. Use a driver that fits on the flange at the perimeter of the seal.
   d. Wipe any sealant from the pump plate.

Bearing Replacement

1. Remove the mechanical seal and oil seal from the pump plate as described in this section.
2. Remove the bearings in the pump plate as follows:
   a. Support the pump plate on wooden blocks, with the bearings facing down. Keep the blocks as close as possible to the bearing housing.
   b. If desired, use a heat gun to warm the housing around the bearings. The heat will ease removal of the bearings.
   c. Place a driver that fits on the back side of the bearings (**Figure 37**), then remove the bearings using a hydraulic press, or hammer.
   d. Clean and lubricate the bearing bore.
3. Install the bearings as follows:
   a. Support the pump plate on a wooden block.
   b. If desired, use a heat gun to warm the housing around the bearings. The heat will ease installation of the bearings.
   c. Place a bearing squarely over the bore, with the manufacturer's marks facing up.
   d. Drive the bearing into the bore using a driver that fits on the perimeter of the bearing. Check that the bearing is fully seated, then install the remaining bearing (**Figure 38**).
4. Install the oil seal and mechanical seal as described in this section.

Table 1 COOLING SYSTEM SPECIFICATIONS

Cooling system	
Maximum test pressure	120 kPa (17 psi)
Coolant temperature sending unit	
On temperature	120° C (248° F)
Off temperature	113° C (235° F)
Engine coolant	
Capacity	1200 ml (1.3 gal.)
Mixture	50:50 (antifreeze /distilled water)
Type	Ethylene glycol containing anti-corrosion agents for aluminum engines
Radiator cap relief pressure	108-137 kPa (15.6-19.9 psi)
Radiator fan sending unit	
On fan temperature	88° C (190° F)
Off fan temperature	82° C (180° F)
Thermostat valve	
Lift	Over 6 mm at 90° C (over 0.24 in. at 194° F)
Opening temperature	75° C (167° F)

Table 2 COOLING SYSTEM TORQUE SPECIFICATIONS

Item	N•m	in.-lb.	ft.-lb.
Coolant temperature sending unit	13	115	–
Radiator fan sending unit	20	–	15
Thermostat housing bolts	10	89	–
Water pump cover bolts	10	89	–

CHAPTER ELEVEN

FRONT SUSPENSION AND STEERING

This chapter provides service procedures for the front wheel, hub, suspension and steering components. Refer to the **Tables 1-3** at the end of this chapter for specifications.

FRONT WHEEL

Removal/Installation

1. Park the ATV on level ground and set the parking brake.
2. Loosen the lug nuts (**Figure 1**).
3. Raise and support the machine. The front wheels must be off the ground.
4. Remove the lug nuts and washers from the studs, then remove the wheel from the hub. If removing more than one wheel, mark each wheel so it can be installed on its original location.
5. Clean the lug nuts, washers and studs. If there are broken or damaged studs, replace them.

WARNING

*If more than one wheel has been removed from the machine, check that the tire direction arrow (**Figure 2**) is pointing forward when the wheel is mounted.*

6. Install the wheel onto the studs, with the valve stem facing out.
7. Install the washers and finger-tighten the lug nuts.
8. Lower the machine to the ground.
9. Tighten the lug nuts in stages and in a crisscross pattern. On the final pass tighten them as specified in **Table 3**.

FRONT HUB

Removal/Installation

1. Remove the front wheel and outer brake disc guard (**Figure 3**).
2. Remove the cotter pin from the hub nut (**Figure 4**).
3. Remove the hub nut and washer (**Figure 5**).
4. Remove the brake caliper mounting bolts (**Figure 6**).

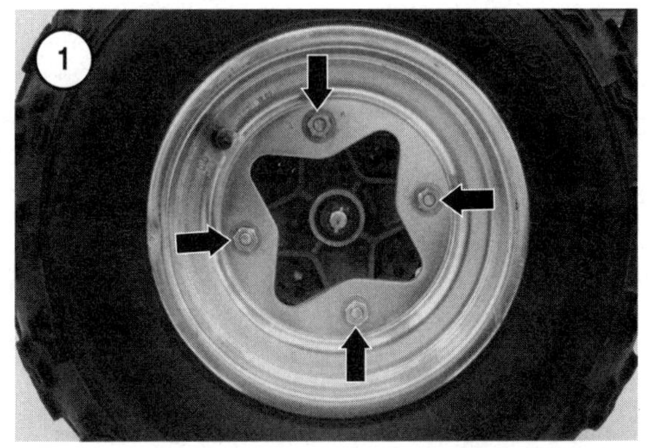

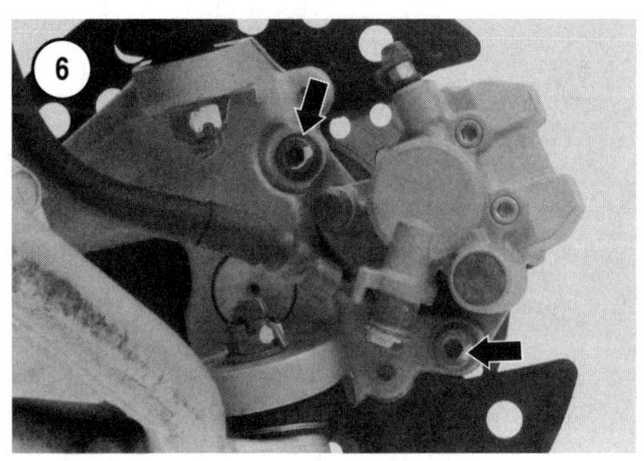

5. Remove the caliper from the disc.
   a. Suspend the caliper with a length of wire. Do not let the caliper hang by the brake hose.
   b. Insert a small wooden block between the brake pads. This prevents the caliper piston from extending out of the caliper if the brake lever is operated.

6. Remove the hub. If the hub is corroded to the axle, place a drift against the back of the hub and tap it free. Do not strike the outer edge of the brake disc.

7. Inspect and repair the front hub assembly as described in this section.

8. If additional suspension or steering components will be serviced, remove the inner brake disc guard (**Figure** 7).

9. If necessary remove the brake disc from the hub (**Figure 8**) as described in Chapter Thirteen .

10. Installation is the reverse of removal, note the following:
    a. Inspect the steering knuckle (**Figure 9**) condition before installing the hub. Check for cracks and damage on bearing surfaces and threads.

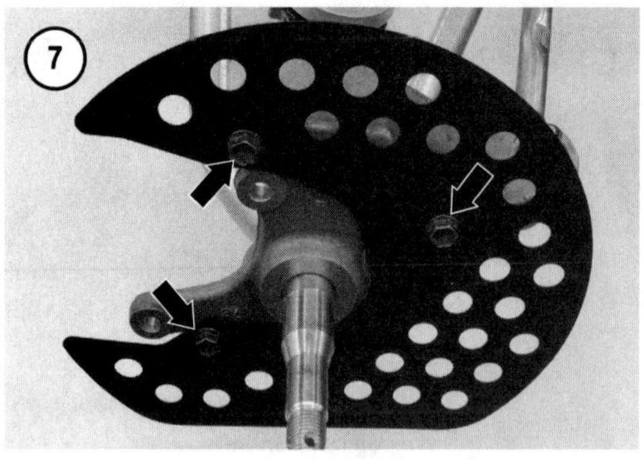

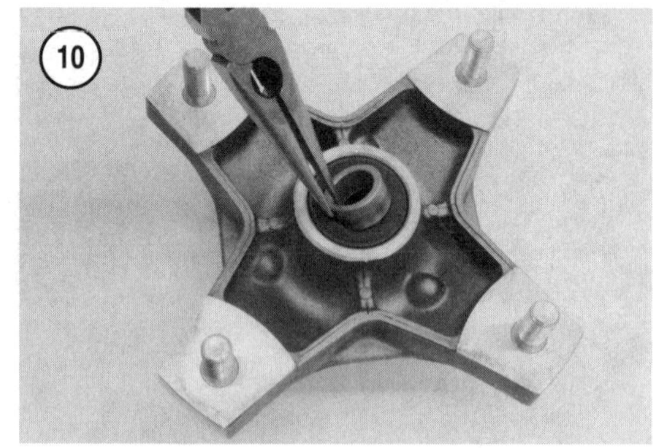

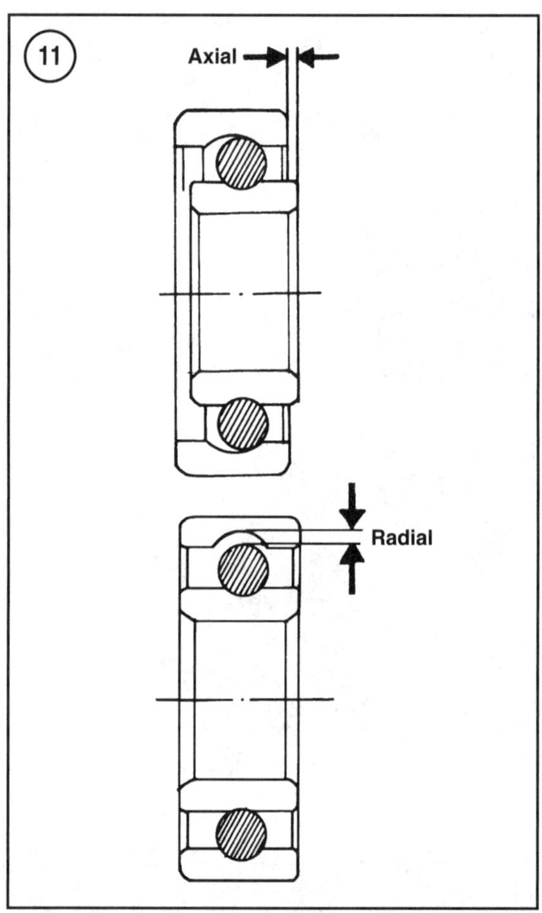

b. If the inner disc brake guard was removed, apply a threadlock agent to the bolts and tighten them securely.
c. Tighten the hub nut to 65 N•m (47 ft.-lb.).
d. Install a *new* cotter pin.
e. Install and tighten the brake caliper bolts to 26 N•m (19 ft.-lb.).
f. Operate the brake lever several times to seat the pads.
g. Check that the hub spins freely and the brake operates properly.

Inspection

1. Remove the collars from both sides of the hub (**Figure 10**).
2. Inspect the seals for damage.
3. Turn each bearing race by hand. The bearings should operate smoothly and quietly. If there is binding or roughness, replace both bearings.

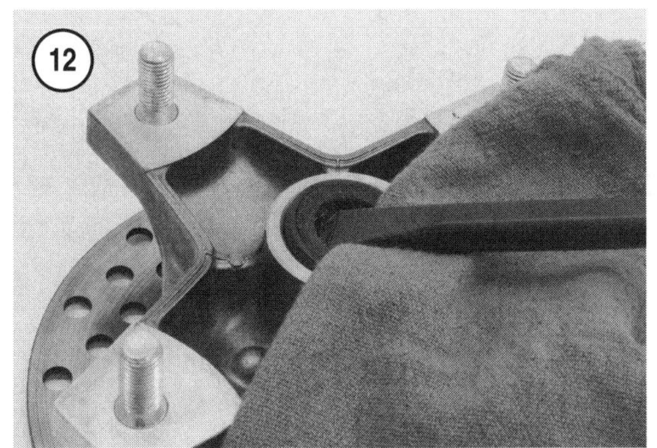

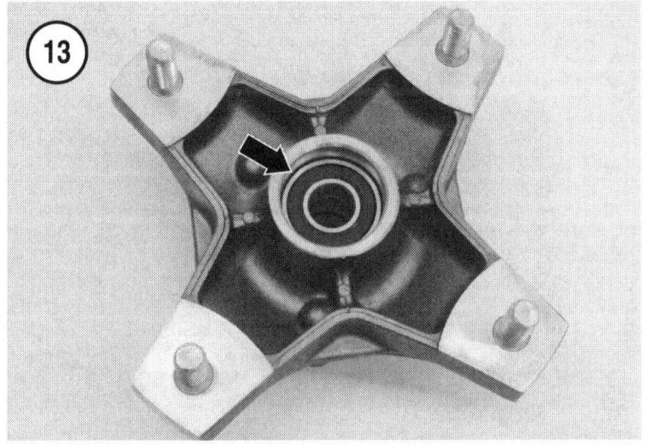

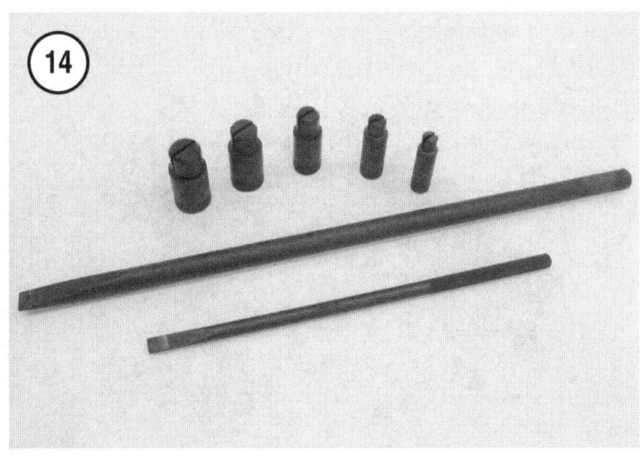

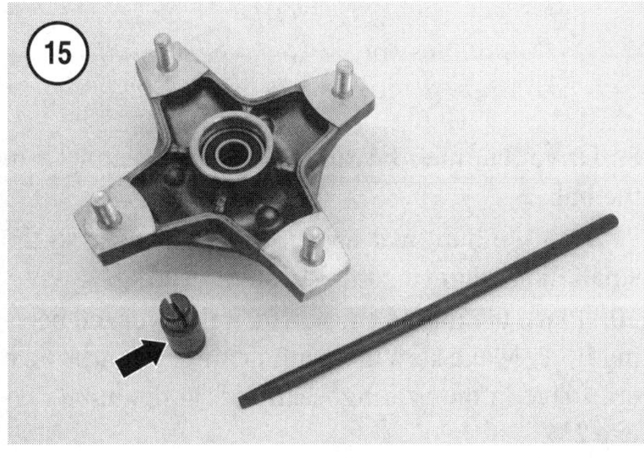

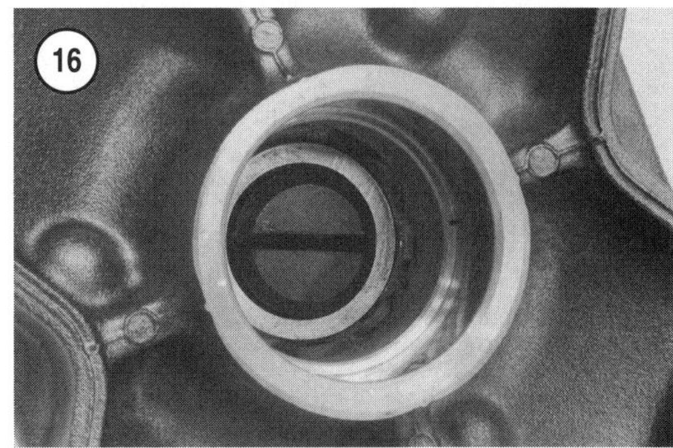

4. Check each bearing for axial and radial play (**Figure 11**). If there is obvious play, replace the bearing. Replace both bearings if either bearing is worn or damaged.
5. If the bearings are damaged, check the spindle.
6. Check the tightness of the bearings in the hub. Replace the bearings if they are loose.
7. Install the spacers if the bearings and seals are in good condition. Leave the spacers out if the bearings and/or the seals will be replaced.

Bearing and Seal Replacement

Two methods for removing bearings from the wheel hub are provided in the following procedure. The first method (Step 2A) uses special tools, while the second method (Step 2B) uses common shop tools.

1. Pry out the seals from both sides of the hub (**Figure 12**). Protect the hub and disc as shown.
2A. Remove the outside bearing (**Figure 13**) using special tools as follows:

NOTE
*The tools shown in the procedure are part of a wheel bearing remover set (**Figure 14**). A similar set can be ordered from a dealership (Suzuki part Nos. 09921-20240 and 09913-70210).*

a. Select the appropriate size remover head (**Figure 15**). The small split end of the remover must fit inside the bearing race (**Figure 16**).
b. Insert the small end of the remover head into the outer bearing.
c. Insert the tapered end of the driver through the back side of the hub (**Figure 17**). Fit the

tapered end into the slot of the remover head (**Figure 18**).

d. Position the hub so the remover head is against a solid surface, such as a concrete floor.

e. Strike the end of the driver so it wedges firmly in the remover head. The remover head should now be jammed tight against the inner bearing race.

f. Reposition the assembly so the remover head is free to move, and the driver can be struck again.

g. Strike the driver, forcing the bearing and remover head from the hub.

h. Remove the driver from the remover head.

i. Remove the spacer from the hub noting the direction that it is installed.

2B. To remove the outer bearing from the hub without special tools.

a. Insert a long drift into the hub from the brake side (**Figure 19**).

b. Carefully wedge the spacer to one side so the edge of the bearing race is exposed (**Figure 20**, typical).

c. Tap the bearing out of the hub, working around the race. Work slowly to avoid damaging the smooth surface of the spacer.

d. Remove the spacer (**Figure 21**) from the hub.

3. Drive the inner bearing on the brake side with a bearing driver or a large socket.

4. Clean and dry the hub and spacer.

5. Before installing the new bearings and seals, note the following:

a. Inspect the new bearings and determine which side faces out. This is usually the side with the manufacturer's numbers. If a shield is on one side of the bearing, the shield should face out.

b. Apply grease (NLGI #2) to bearings that are not lubricated by the manufacturer. Work the grease into the cavities between the balls and races.

c. Always support the bottom side of the hub, near the bore, when installing bearings.

6. Place the outer bearing squarely over the bearing bore.

7. Place a suitably sized driver or socket over the bearing. The driver should seat against the outside diameter of the bearing (**Figure 22**).

CAUTION

Do not press or strike the bearing directly. Bearing damage will occur.

8. Drive the inner bearing into place, seating it in the hub.

9. Turn the hub over and install the spacer so the small diameter is next to the outer bearing.

10. Place the inner bearing squarely over the bearing bore. Make sure the manufacturer's marks face up. Drive in the bearing, seating it in the hub (**Figure 23**).

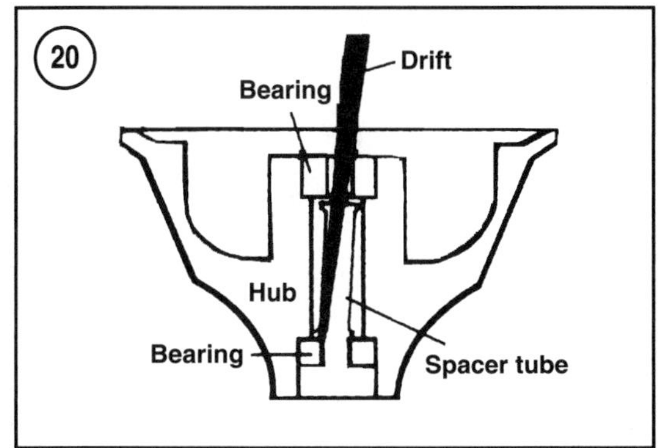

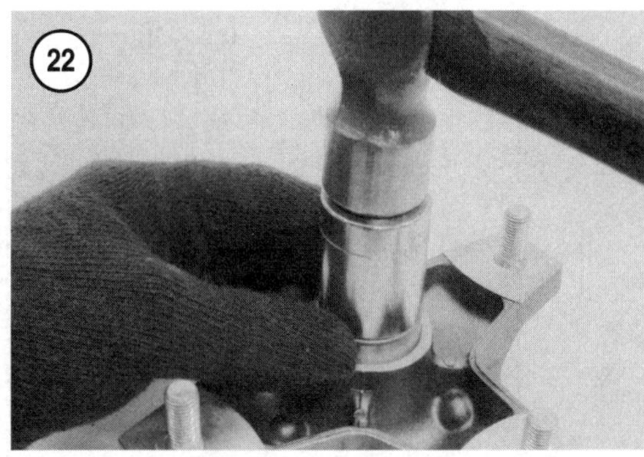

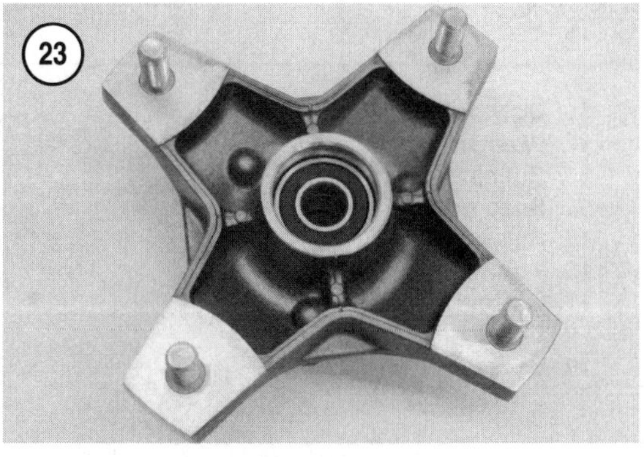

11. Install the seals as follows:
   a. Pack grease into the inner lips of the new seals.
   b. Lubricate the seal bores.
   c. Place a seal squarely over the bore.
   d. Press the seal into place.
12. Install the collars on both sides of the hub (**Figure 10**).

TIE RODS

Removal/Installation

Refer to **Figure 24**.

1. Before removing the tie rods, make the following check for play and wear.
   a. Park the ATV on level ground with the wheels pointing straight ahead.
   b. Lightly turn the handlebar toward the left, then right while observing the tie rod ends. If the tie rod ends move vertically (removing play) as pressure is applied, they are worn or damaged.
   c. Repeat the check with the wheels fully locked to the left then the right. If vertical play is observed in this position, this also indicates worn tie rod ends.
2. Remove the front wheel as described in this chapter. Access to the tie rod ends will be easier.
3. Remove the cotter pin from the nut on the tie rod end at the steering knuckle (**Figure 25**). Hold the ball joint of the tie rod by putting an open end wrench on the flats of the joint (**Figure 26**) and remove the nut from the tie rod end (**Figure 27**). Use a small drift and tap the center of the tie rod to free it from the steering knuckle. If the tie rod end is seized in the bore do the following:
   a. If a ball joint remover (**Figure 28**) is available, it can be used to separate the parts. If the tie rod end will be reused, there is a risk of tearing the rubber boot when using this tool.
   b. If a ball joint remover is not available, use a heat gun or propane torch to heat the area around the joint. Place a drift on the center of the tire rod and drive it out of the steering knuckle. If the tire rod end will be reused, avoid damaging the threads.
4. Repeat Step 3 to remove the tie rod from the steering shaft (**Figure 29**). If the tie rod end is seized in the bore, and must be driven out, it may be neces-

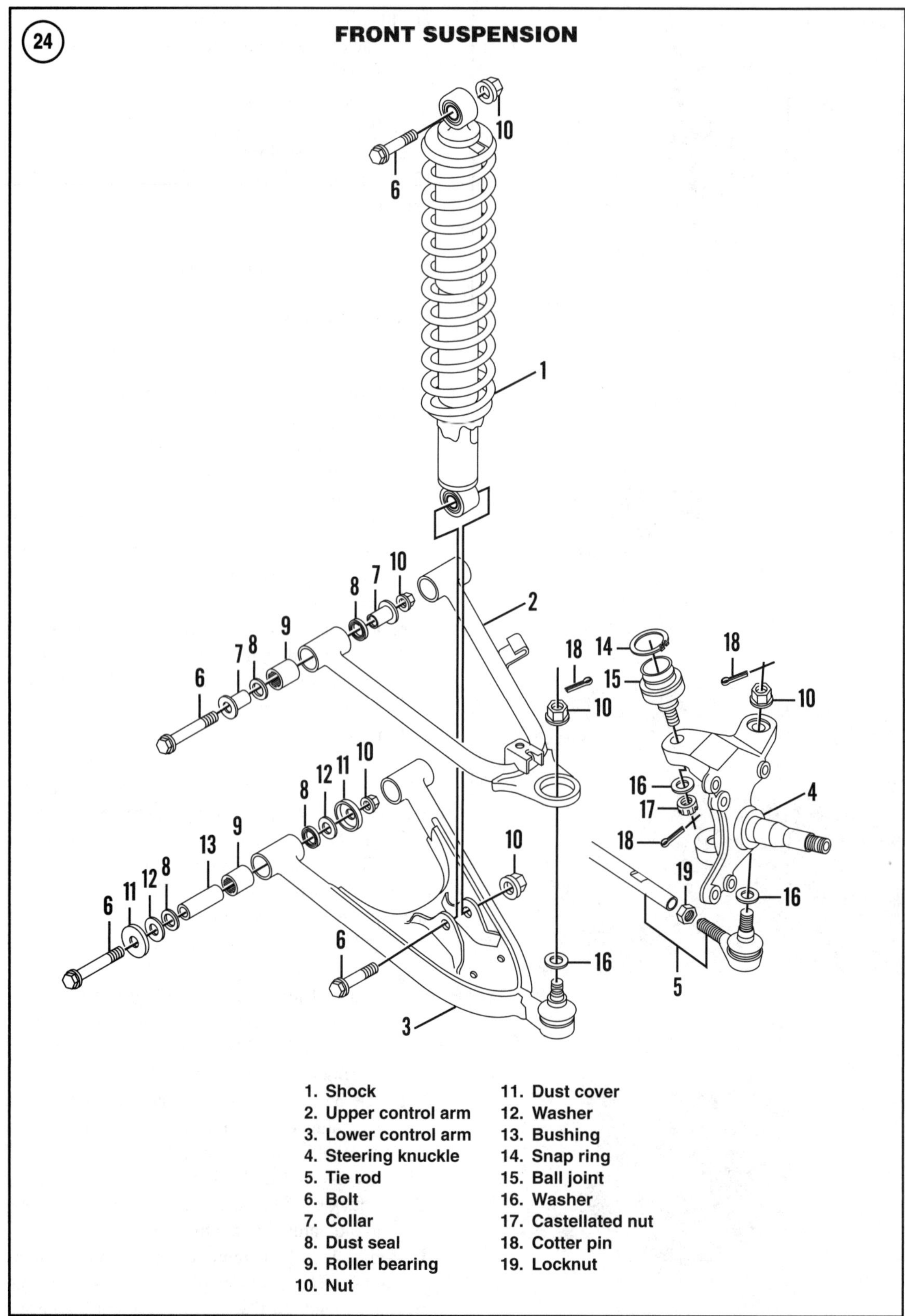
24
FRONT SUSPENSION
1. Shock
2. Upper control arm
3. Lower control arm
4. Steering knuckle
5. Tie rod
6. Bolt
7. Collar
8. Dust seal
9. Roller bearing
10. Nut
11. Dust cover
12. Washer
13. Bushing
14. Snap ring
15. Ball joint
16. Washer
17. Castellated nut
18. Cotter pin
19. Locknut

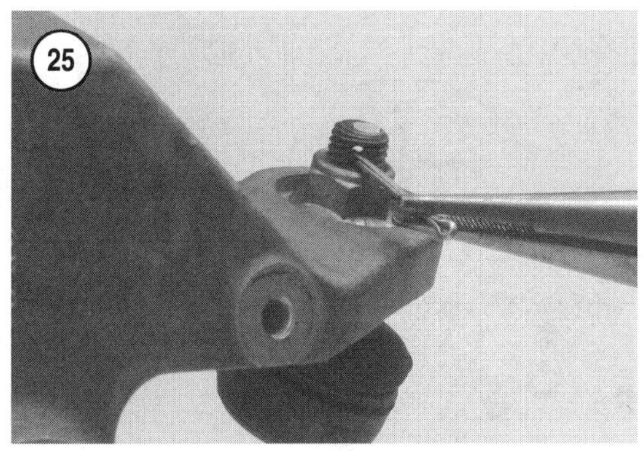
25

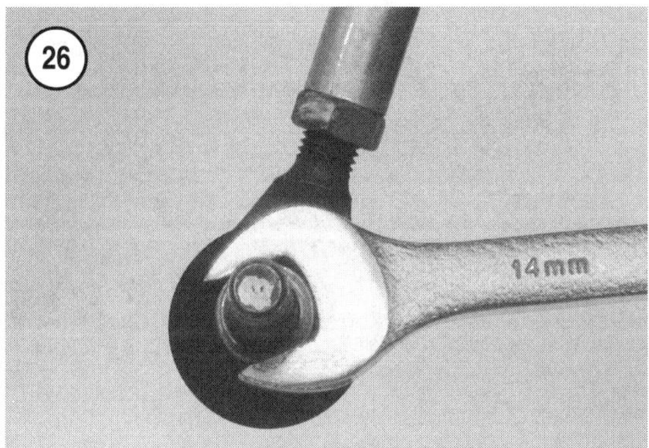

26

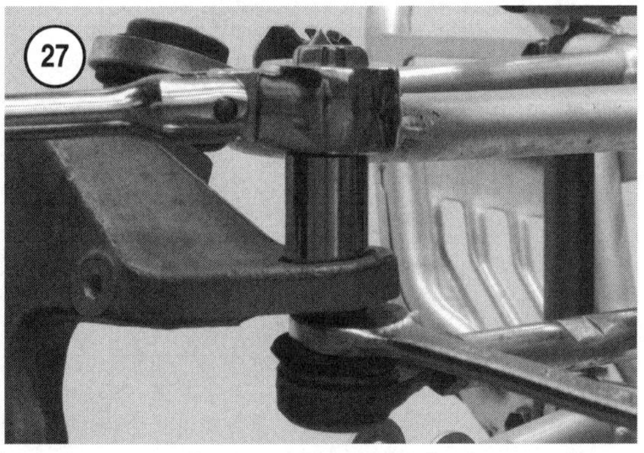
27

28

29

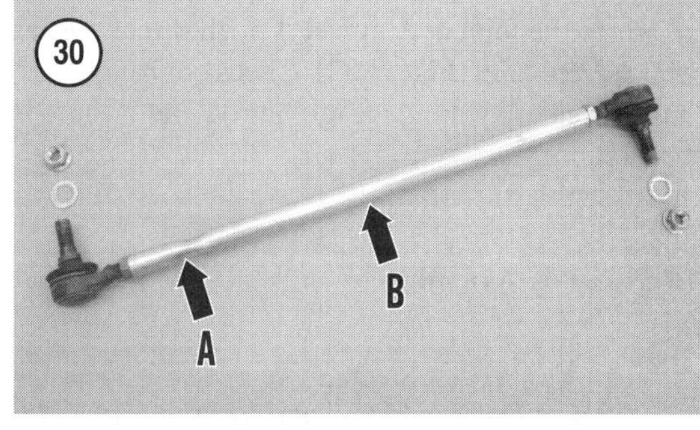

30

sary to remove the brush guard and upper control arm to gain the necessary clearance.

5. Reverse these steps to install the tie rods. Note the following:
   a. Install the tie rod ends so the wrench flats (A, **Figure 30**) are nearest the wheel.
   b. Tighten the nuts as specified in **Table 3**.
   c. Install new cotter pins.

Inspection

CAUTION
When cleaning the tie rods, do not immerse the joints in any chemical that could contaminate the internal lubricating grease and/or damage the protective rubber boots.

1. Inspect the tie rod shaft (B, **Figure 30**). Replace it if damaged.

2. Inspect the rubber boot (**Figure 31**). The ball joints are permanently packed with grease. If a rubber boot is damaged, dirt and moisture can enter the ball joint. If a boot is damaged in any way, disassemble the tie rod and replace the tie rod end(s) as described in the following procedure.

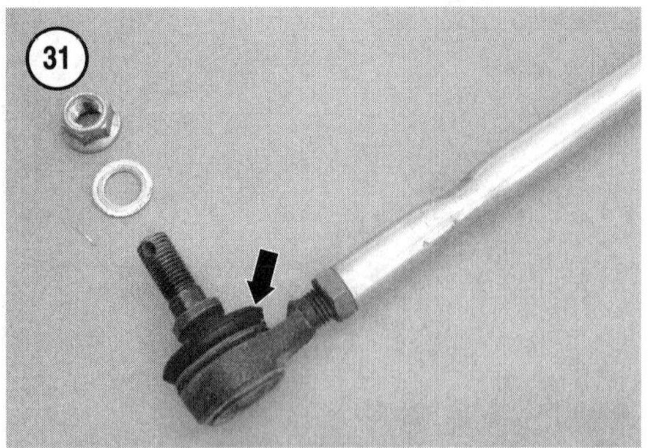

3. Grasp the joint and swivel it in all directions, as well as vertically (**Figure 32**). Check for roughness, dryness and play. Replace the tie rod end if there is wear.

Disassembly/Assembly

> *NOTE*
> *The outer tie rod end and locknut is a left hand thread. The inner tie rod end and locknut is a right hand thread. Note which direction each set of parts must be turned when loosening and tightening the parts.*

1. Hold the tie rod with a wrench placed on the rod flats (A, **Figure 33**).
2. Loosen the locknut (B, **Figure 33**) and remove the tie rod end.
3. Clean the tie rod threads.
4. Thread the correct tie rod end onto the tie rod.
5. Repeat the procedure for the remaining tie rod end.
6. Adjust the tie rod ends as follows:
   a. Equally adjust the tie rod ends so the number of exposed threads (C, **Figure 33**) is the same. Both tie rod assemblies must be identically adjusted.
   b. When the adjustment is achieved, finger-tighten the locknuts to hold the positions. Tighten the locknuts after the tie rods have been installed and the toe-in adjusted.
   c. Check the toe-in as described in Chapter Three.

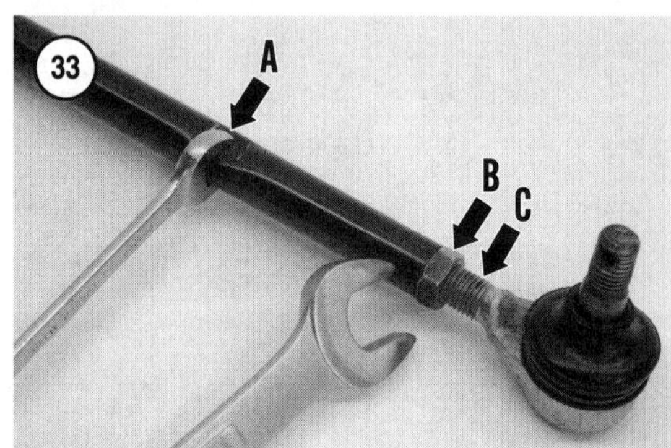

STEERING KNUCKLE

Removal/Installation

Refer to **Figure 24**.

1. Remove the front wheel as described in this chapter.
2. Remove the brake hose guide mounting bolt (**Figure 34**).
3. Remove the brake caliper bolts (**Figure 35**), and remove the brake caliper from the steering knuckle. Suspend the caliper with a length of wire. Do not let the caliper hang by the brake hose.

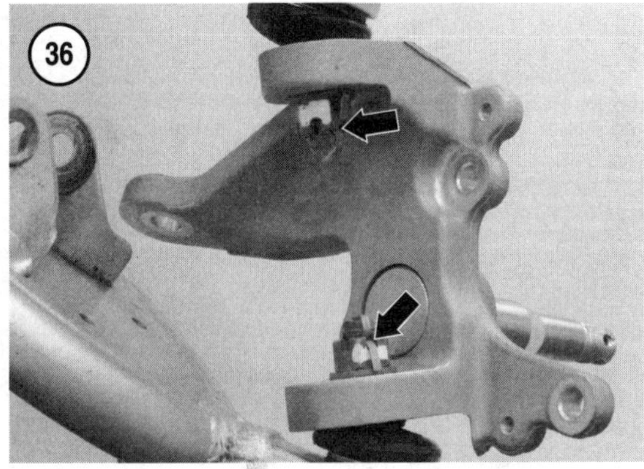

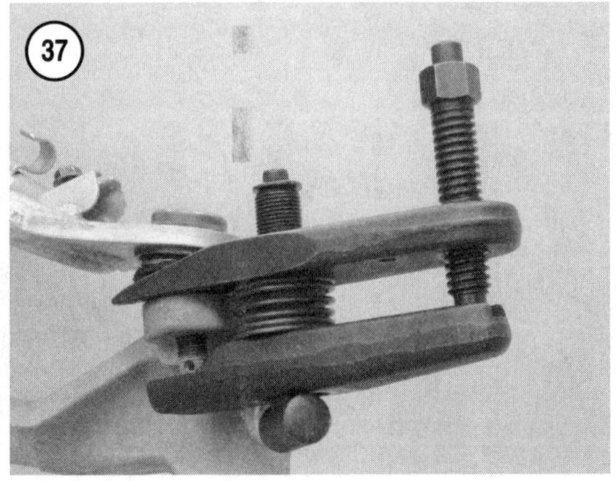

4. Remove the front hub as described in this chapter.

5. Disconnect the tie rod from the steering knuckle as described in this chapter.

6. Remove the cotter pins and nuts (**Figure 36**) from the upper and lower control arm ball joints.

7. Use a ball joint remover (Motion Pro part No. 08-0120) to disconnect the upper and lower control arm ball joints from the steering knuckle as follows:

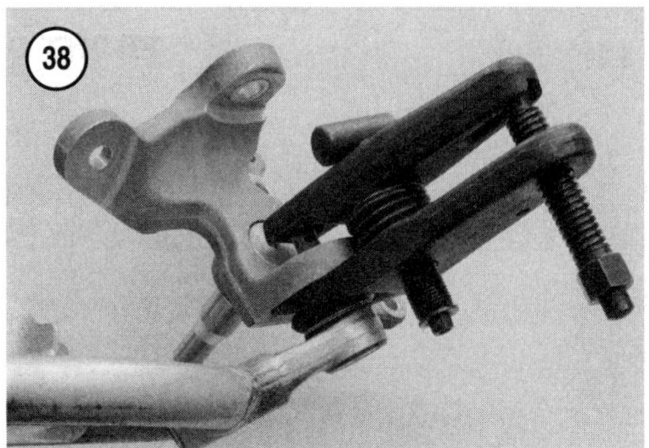

CAUTION
Do not strike the ball joint or its stud when removing it; otherwise, the ball joint will be damaged.

a. Turn each ball joint nut so it is flush with the end of the stud.
b. Thread the pressure screw into the tool body.
c. Mount the ball-joint separator between the ball joints and run the pressure screw up against the upper-arm nut as shown in **Figure 37**.
d. Hold the tool body and turn the pressure bolt until the upper arm ball joint breaks loose from the steering knuckle. If the ball joint does not break loose, stop at this point. Do not try to force it with the ball-joint separator. Instead, place a 2 × 4 against the control arm, and strike the 2 × 4 with a mallet. The ball joint should pop out of the steering knuckle.
e. Invert the tool and repeat this process for the lower control arm.
f. Remove the tool from the steering knuckle.

8. Remove each nut from its ball joint stud.

9. Remove the upper-arm ball joint from the steering knuckle, and remove the steering knuckle from the lower arm ball joint (**Figure 38**).

10. Inspect the steering knuckle as described in this section.

11. Install the steering knuckle by reversing these removal steps. Note to the following:

a. Position the steering knuckle on the lower-arm ball joint and then install the upper-arm ball joint into the knuckle.
b. Install the ball joint nuts and tighten them as specified in **Table 3**.
c. Install new cotter pins and bend the ends over completely.

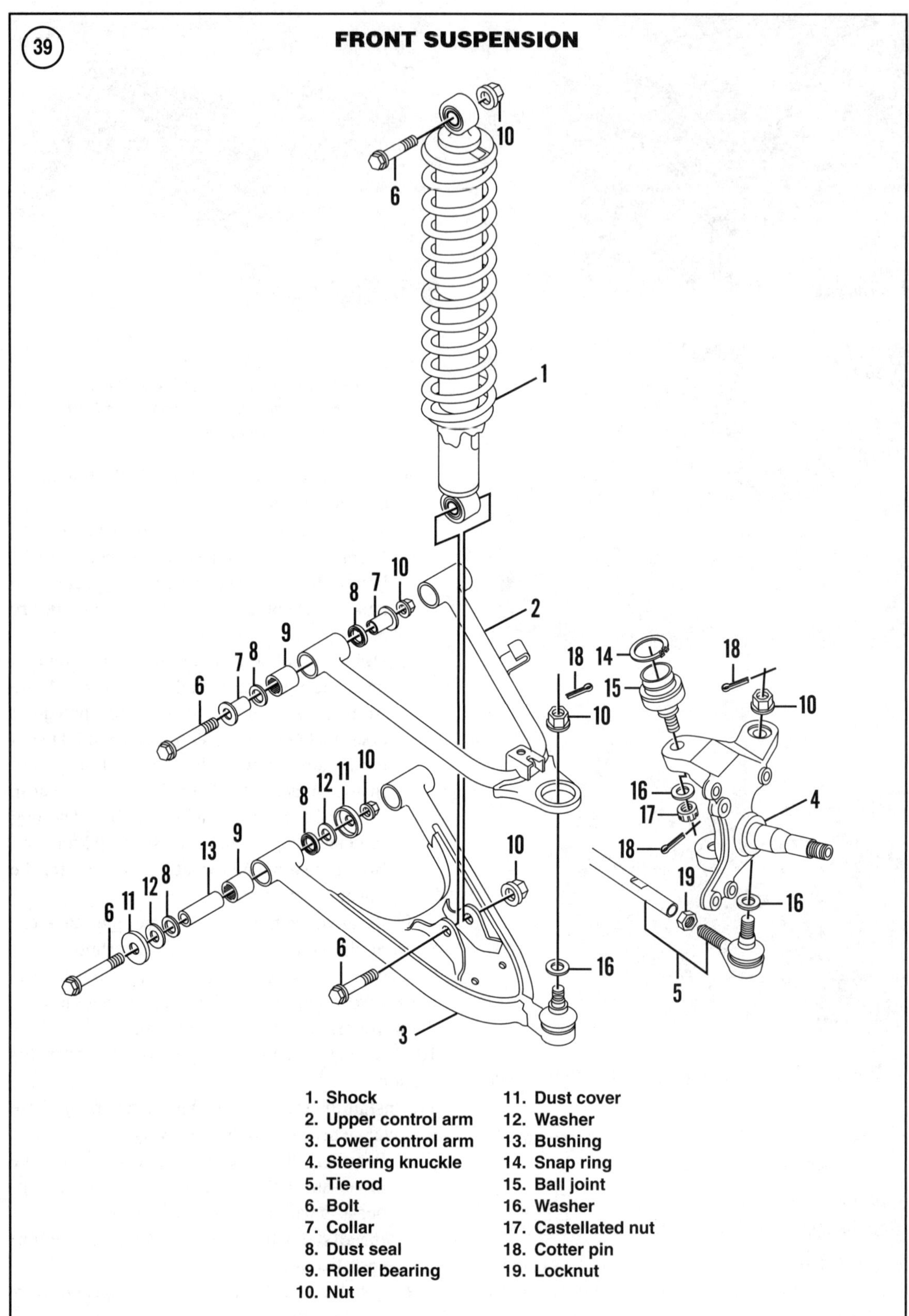
39
FRONT SUSPENSION
1. Shock
2. Upper control arm
3. Lower control arm
4. Steering knuckle
5. Tie rod
6. Bolt
7. Collar
8. Dust seal
9. Roller bearing
10. Nut
11. Dust cover
12. Washer
13. Bushing
14. Snap ring
15. Ball joint
16. Washer
17. Castellated nut
18. Cotter pin
19. Locknut

d. Install the tie rod as described in this chapter.
e. Install the brake-hose-guide bolt.
f. Install and tighten the brake caliper to 26 N•m (19 ft.-lb.).
g. Check front brake operation before riding the vehicle.

Inspection

1. Clean the steering knuckle in solvent and dry it with compressed air.
2. Inspect the steering knuckle for bending, thread damage, cracks or other damage.
3. Inspect the spindle bearing surfaces for wear or damage. A hard collision may cause the spindle to bend or fracture. If the spindle is damaged, replace the steering knuckle.
4. Check the cotter-pin hole at the end of the spindle. Make sure there are no fractures or cracks leading out toward the end of the steering knuckle. Replace the steering knuckle if damaged.

CONTROL ARMS

Removal/Installation

Refer to **Figure 39**.

1. Remove the front hub as described in this chapter.
2. Remove the lower mounting bolt from the shock absorber. If increased work space is desired, remove the entire shock absorber as described in this chapter.
3. Remove the brake hose guide and disconnect the control arm ball joints as described in this chapter.
4. Before removing the control arms, grasp each arm and leverage it side to side. If play is noticeable, check the bushings for wear.
5. Remove the bolts from the upper control arm (**Figure 40** and **Figure 41**), then remove the control arm. Note that the bolt heads point to the front of the control arm. If both upper control arms are removed, identify the arms so they can be installed in their original positions. 11
6. Remove the bolts from the lower control arm (**Figure 42**), then remove the control arm assembly. Note that the bolt heads point to the front of the vehicle. If both lower control arms are removed, identify the arms so they can be installed in their correct positions.
7. Inspect the control arms as described in this section.
8. Reverse these steps to install the control arms. Note the following:
   a. If both pairs of control arms have been removed, verify that they are being installed on the correct side of the machine.
   b. Install the control arm bolt heads so they face forward.
   c. Apply a threadlock agent to the control arm pivot bolts and tighten them to 65 N•m (47 ft.-lb.).

d. Tighten the ball joint nuts to 45 N•m (33 ft.-lb.) and secure them with new cotter pins.
e. Apply a threadlock agent to the shock absorber bolts and tighten them to 60 N•m. (44 ft.-lb.).

Inspection

CAUTION
The ball joints are packed with grease and sealed. Do not immerse the ball joints in solvent or any other liquid that could penetrate the boots. Wipe the ball joints clean with a shop cloth prior to inspection.

1. Remove the collars and dust seals from the upper control arm (**Figure 43**).
2. Remove the dust cover, washer and spacer from the lower control arm (**Figure 44**).
3. Clean the control arm parts. Keep all bolts identified in order to install them in their original positions.
4. Inspect all welded joints on the control arm. Check for fractures, bending or other damage. If there is damage, replace the control arm.
5. Inspect the ball joint boots for tears and the entry of moisture or dirt into the joint.
6. Grasp each ball joint and swivel it in all directions, including vertically (**Figure 45**). Check for roughness, dryness and play.

Bearing Replacement

1. Inspect the pivot bolts, spacers, seals and dust caps for wear or damage.
2. Check the fit of all bolts in their respective mating parts. Bolts should pass straight through the parts with no binding or difficulty.
3. Check the fit of all pivot spacers in their bearings. The spacers should turn freely and smoothly with no play. Replace if worn.
4. Inspect the bearings for wear and damage.
5. Remove the bearings using one of the following:
   a. An expanding bearing puller (Suzuki part No. 09923-73210) and slide hammer (Suzuki part No. 09923-30104).
   b. A draw bolt and a variety of sockets (**Figure 46**).
   c. A hydraulic press.
6. Install the bearings with one of the following:

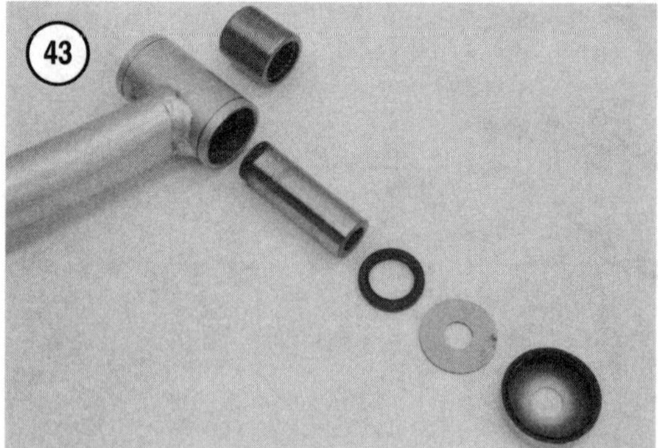
43

44

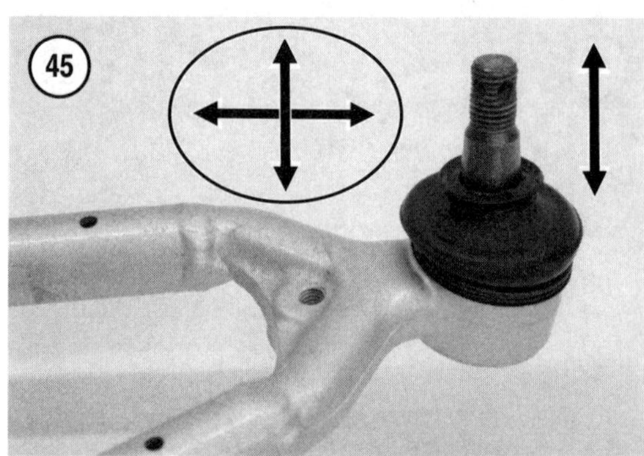
45

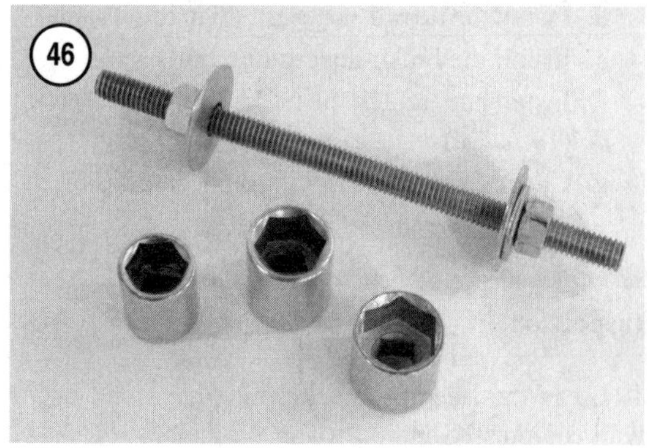
46

47

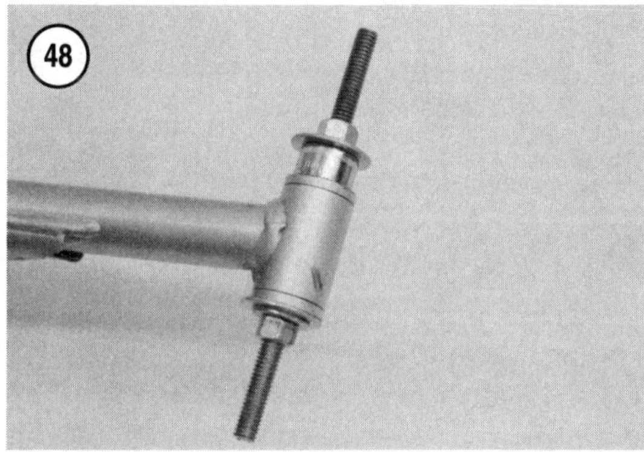

48

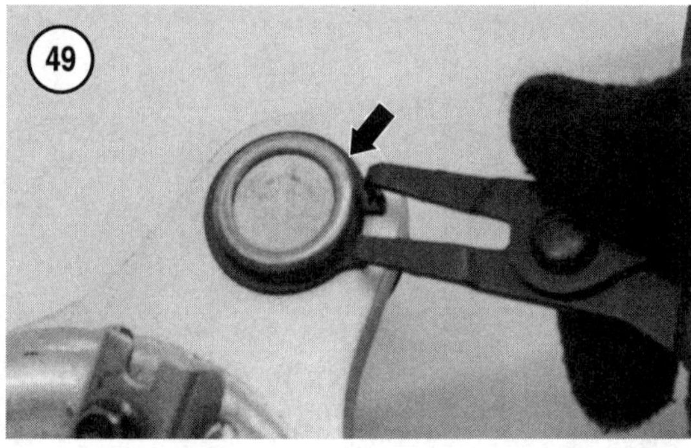

49

a. A bearing installer set (Suzuki part No. 09924-84510).

b. Using a hydraulic press.

c. A draw bolt and a variety of sockets (**Figure 46**).

7. Replace the bearings using a draw bolt as follows:

 a. To press the bearing out of the linkage, use a larger socket on one end of the draw bolt to receive the bearing.

 b. Use tape on the socket to mark the bearing depth (**Figure 47**).

 c. Turn the nuts of the draw bolt to press the bearing into the linkage to the tape mark (**Figure 48**).

8. Lubricate the bearings with waterproof grease.

9. Install new dust seals before reassembling.

BALL JOINT REPLACEMENT

Refer to **Figure 39**.

NOTE

Suzuki does not provide a replacement ball joint for the lower control arm. If this ball joint is no longer serviceable, replace the arm.

1. Remove the upper ball joint from the control arm with a hydraulic press or with a bearing installer set (Suzuki part No. 09924-84510 or equivelant).

2. Remove the snap ring (**Figure 49**) from the upper ball joint.

3. To remove the ball joint using a press, perform the following:

 a. Position the upper arm and the ball joint in a press.

 b. Slowly lower the press ram, and press the ball joint from the arm.

 c. Remove the tools and control arm from the press.

 d. Clean the ball joint receptacle in the upper arm with solvent. Dry it thoroughly.

 e. Correctly position a new ball joint into the arm.

 f. Position the upper arm in the press.

CAUTION

If there is strong resistance when lowering the press ram, stop immediately. Realign the ball joint and try again. The ball joint should press into place with a minimum amount of resistance.

 g. Slowly lower the press ram and press the ball joint straight into the upper arm until the joint bottoms. The snap ring groove must be completely visible so it can accept the snap ring.

4. To service the ball joint using a bearing driver, perform the following:

 a. Position the driver over the ball joint and drive it out of the control arm with several sharp blows.

b. Clean the ball joint receptacle in the upper arm with solvent. Dry it thoroughly.

c. Position the new ball joint squarely over the control arm and drive it into the arm with a bearing installer (Suzuki part No. 09924-84510).

5. Install the snap ring (**Figure 49**) so the flat side faces up away from the control arm. The snap ring must be completely seated in the groove.

SHOCK ABSORBERS

Removal/Installation

Refer to **Figure 39**.

1. Support the ATV with the front wheels off the ground.
2. Remove the upper (**Figure 50**) and lower (**Figure 51**) shock absorber mounting bolt.
3. Remove the shock absorber.
4. Inspect the shock absorber as described in this section.
5. Install the shock absorber by reversing the preceding removal steps while noting the following:
    a. Install the shock bolts into the front side of each mount.
    b. Install new self-locking nuts.
    c. Apply the threadlock to the upper and lower shock absorber nuts and tighten them to 60 N•m (51 ft.-lb.).

Inspection

NOTE
Replacement parts for the shock absorber are not available. If any part is damaged or worn, replace the shock absorber.

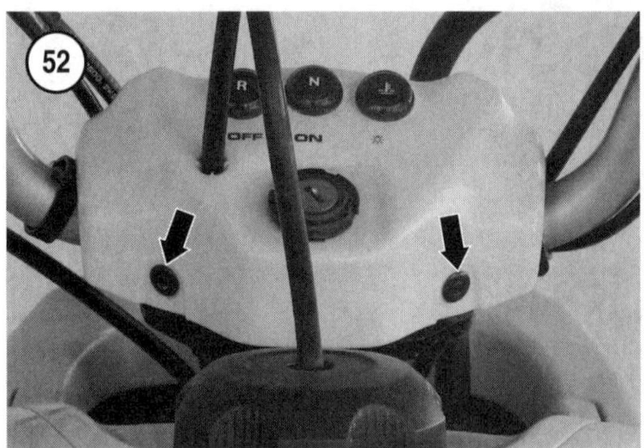

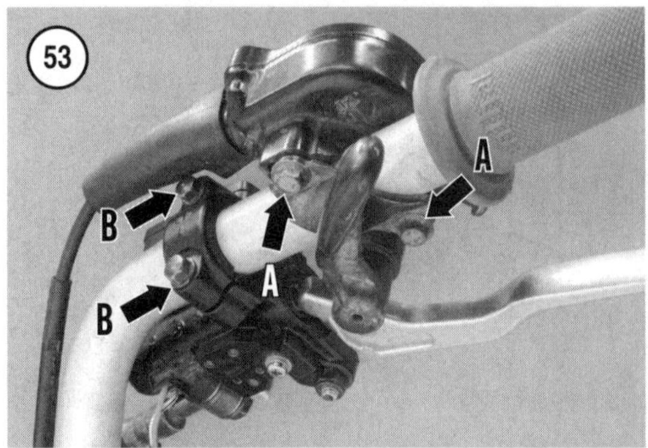

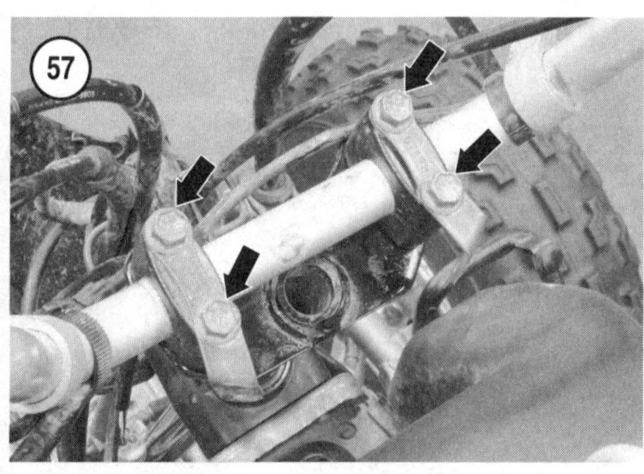

1. Clean and dry the shock absorber.
2. Inspect the shock for leaks or other damage.
3. Inspect the upper and lower rubber bushings for deterioration, excessive wear or other damage.
4. Inspect the shock spring for cracks or other damage.

HANDLEBAR

Removal

CAUTION
Cover the seat, fuel tank and front fender with a heavy cloth or plastic tarp to protect them from brake fluid spills. Clean up any spilled brake fluid immediately. Wash the area with soapy water and rinse thoroughly.

1. Remove the two plastic clips securing the handlebar cover (**Figure 52**).
2. Remove the bands securing the wiring harness to the handlebar.
3. Remove the two throttle housing clamp bolts (A, **Figure 53**) and the clamp. Remove the throttle housing and lay it over the front fender. Make sure the throttle cable is not kinked.
4. Remove the clamp bolts (B, **Figure 53**) from the front master cylinder. Remove the front master cylinder, and lay it over the front fender. Keep the reservoir in an upright position to minimize brake fluid loss and to keep air from entering the brake system. The hydraulic brake line does not have to be removed from the master cylinder.
5. Remove the clamp screws (**Figure 54**) from the clutch parking brake lever mount. Remove the lever and lay it over the front fender. Make sure the cables are not kinked.
6. Remove the switch housing screws (**Figure 55**). Separate the switch halves, and remove the choke cable (**Figure 56**). Set the assembly aside.
7. Remove the upper handlebar holder mounting bolts (**Figure 57**) from each handlebar holder. Remove the upper holders, and then remove the handlebar.

Installation

1. Position the handlebar on the lower handlebar holders and hold it in place (**Figure 58**).

61

STEERING SHAFT ASSEMBLY

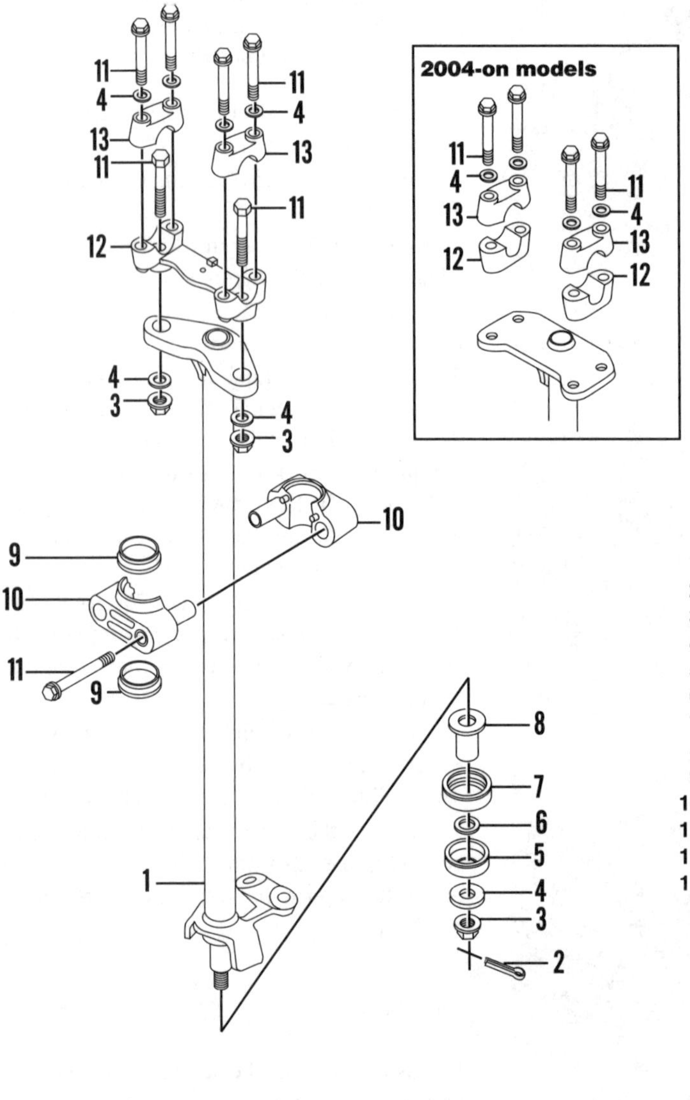

2004-on models

1. Steering shaft
2. Cotter pin
3. Nut
4. Washer
5. Lower dust seal
6. O-ring
7. Upper dust seal
8. Bushing
9. Upper dust seal
10. Steering shaft holder bushing
11. Bolt
12. Lower handlebar clamp
13. Upper handlebar clamp

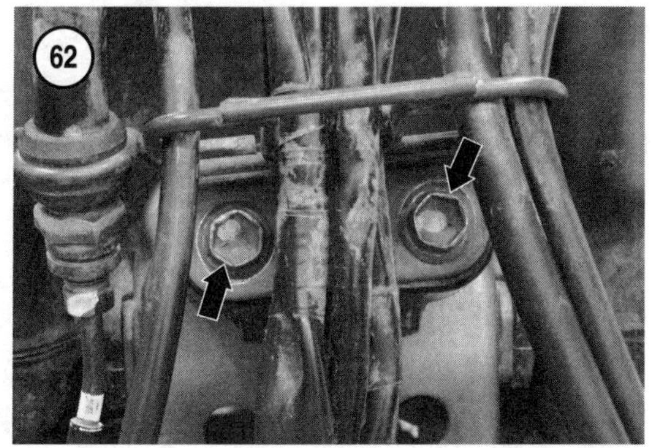
62

63

2. Align the punch mark on the handlebar with the top surface of the lower holders.

3. Install the handlebar holder bolts (**Figure 57**). Tighten the forward bolts first and then the rear bolts. Tighten each bolt as specified in **Table 3**.

4. Install the left switch housing by performing the following:

   a. Fit the pin on the rear switch housing half into the hole in the handlebar (**Figure 59**), and then install the switch housing.

   b. Tighten the housing screws (**Figure 55**).

5. Install the rear brake lever housing by performing the following:

   a. Fit the clutch/parking brake lever mount and its clamp into place on the handlebar. Position the clamp so its punch mark faces up.

   b. Align the edge of the housing with the punch mark on the handlebar.

   c. Install the clamp screws. Tighten the upper screw first and then the lower screw.

6. Install the master cylinder by performing the following:

   a. Fit the master cylinder and its clamp into place on the handlebar. Position the clamp so its UP mark (**Figure 60**) faces up.

   b. Align the edge of the master cylinder housing with the punch mark on the handlebar.

   c. Install the master cylinder clamp bolts. Tighten the bolts to 10 N•m (89 in.-lb.). Tighten the upper bolt first and then the lower bolt.

7. Install the throttle housing by aligning the line on the throttle housing with the edge of the master cylinder. Install the clamp and tighten the throttle housing clamp bolts (A, **Figure 53**) to 5 N•m (44 in.-lb.).

8. Secure the wiring harness to the handlebar with the wire bands.

9. Check all cable adjustments as described in Chapter Three.

10. Check that the front brake, clutch and parking brake work properly.

11. Check that each handlebar switch works properly.

12. Install the handlebar cover and secure it with the plastic clips (**Figure 52**).

STEERING SHAFT

11

Removal

Refer to **Figure 61**.

1. Remove the upper cover, side panels and front fender as described in Chapter Fourteen.

2. Remove the handlebar as described in this chapter. Pull the handlebar assembly back to not damage the brake hose, cables or wiring harness. Support the handlebar so the master cylinder remains upright. This minimizes brake fluid loss and keeps air from entering the brake system.

3. Remove the upper steering shaft bolts (**Figure 62**).

4. Disconnect the tie rods from the steering arm (**Figure 63**) by performing the following.

   a. Remove the cotter pin from each inner tie rod end.

   b. Hold the flats of each tie rod joint with a wrench, and remove the tie rod nut.

   c. Disconnect the tie rods from the steering arm.

5. Remove the cotter pin and nut (**Figure 64**) from the bottom of the steering shaft.

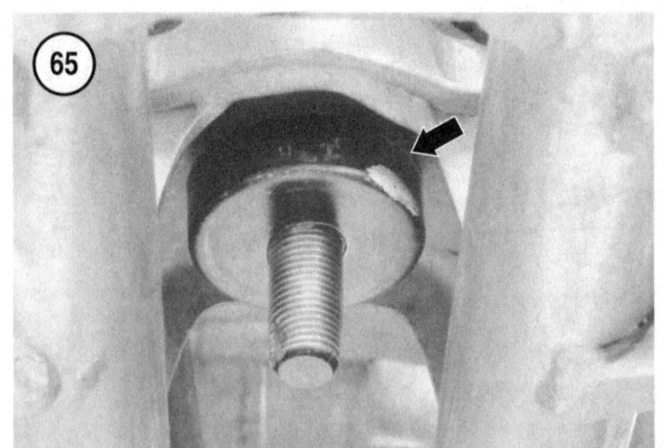

6. Remove the dust cap (**Figure 65**) from the end of the steering shaft.
7. Remove the O-ring (**Figure 66**) from the end of the steering shaft.
8. Remove the outer steering shaft holder bushing (**Figure 67**), the bolt collars (A, **Figure 68**) and the inner steering shaft holder bushing (B).
9. Remove the steering shaft from the frame.

Installation

1. Pack the lips of the steering shaft bushing and seals with lithium grease, and install the upper bushing (**Figure 69**).
2. Pack the steering shaft dust seal (**Figure 70**) with lithium grease.
3. Install the steering shaft into the frame.
4. Install the O-ring (**Figure 66**) onto the end of the steering shaft.
5. Install the dust cap onto the end of the steering shaft (**Figure 65**).
6. Install the upper bushing bolt spacers (**Figure 71**) into the bushing and install the bolts (**Figure 62**). Tighten the steering shaft holder bolts to 23 N•m (17 ft.-lb.).
7. Apply lithium grease to the flange and threads of the steering shaft nut. Install the steering shaft nut (**Figure 64**), and tighten it to 49 N•m (36 ft.-lb.). Secure the nut with a *new* cotter pin and bend the ends over completely.
8. Install the tie rods by performing the following:
   a. Fit each inner tie rod end into its mounting boss on the steering arm.
   b. Install the tie rod nut onto each tie rod. Tighten the nuts to 29 N•m. (21 ft.-lb.).
   c. Install a new cotter pin through the hole in the stud and bend the ends over completely.

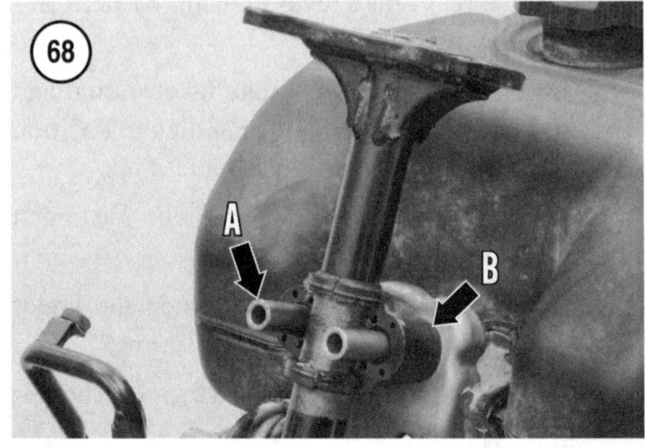

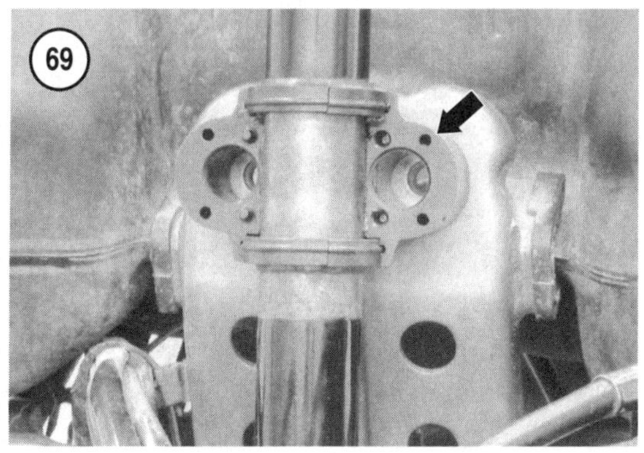
69

70

71

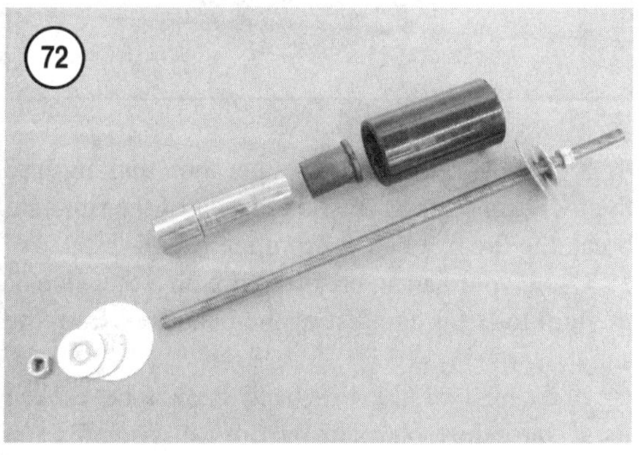
72

9. Set the handlebar assembly into place on the steering shaft. Check the routing of the brake hose, cables and wiring harness.

10. Install the handlebar holder as described in this chapter.

11. Install the front fender (Chapter Fourteen).

12. Check that the handlebar turns properly and that the throttle returns to its closed position after releasing it.

13. Adjust the toe-in as described in Chapter Three.

Inspection

Replace parts that are excessively worn or damaged as described in this section.

1. Clean and dry all parts.

2. Check the steering shaft for bending or thread damage.

3. Check the cotter pin hole at the end of the steering shaft. Make sure no fractures or cracks lead out toward the end of the steering shaft. If any are present, replace the steering shaft.

4. Check the steering arm for cracks, spline or other damage.

5. Inspect the steering bearing by turning its inner race with your finger. Replace the bearing if it turns roughly or has excessive play.

6. Inspect the dust seals for execessive wear or other damage.

7. Replace the dust seals and bushing as described in this section.

Dust Seal and Bushing Replacement

CAUTION
The steering shaft bushing is plastic and pressed into the frame. Do not remove the bearing unless it requires replacement.

1. Remove the steering shaft as described in this section.

2. Press the bushing out from the bottom using the bearing installer set and rotor remover, (Suzuki part Nos. 09924-84510 and 09930-30721) or a draw bolt, washers, socket and a 34 mm socket (**Figure 72**).

73

74

3. Use a smaller socket (**Figure 73**) on the bottom of the tool and draw the bushing upward into the larger socket (**Figure 74**).

4. Inspect the bushing for wear or damage and replace if necessary (8, **Figure 61**).

5. Installation is the reverse of removal.

TIRES AND WHEELS

Tire Changing

The design of an ATV tire can create a seal that makes tire bead and wheel separation difficult. A bead breaker tool, tire irons and rim protectors are required to remove and install the tire. If the tire is difficult to remove or install, do not take a chance on damaging the tire or wheel. Take the tire and wheel to a dealership with the proper equipment (**Figure 75**).

75

1. Remove the valve stem cap and core, and deflate the tire. Do not reinstall the core at this time.

WARNING

Only use water to lubricate the tire during removal and installation. Soap or other types of tire lubricants can leave a residue that can lead to tire slip, rapid pressure loss, and a possible accident.

2. Lubricate the tire bead and rim flanges with water. Press the tire sidewall/bead down so the water can run into and around the bead area. Also apply water to the area where the bead breaker arm will contact the tire sidewall.

3. Position the wheel into the bead breaker tool (**Figure 76**).

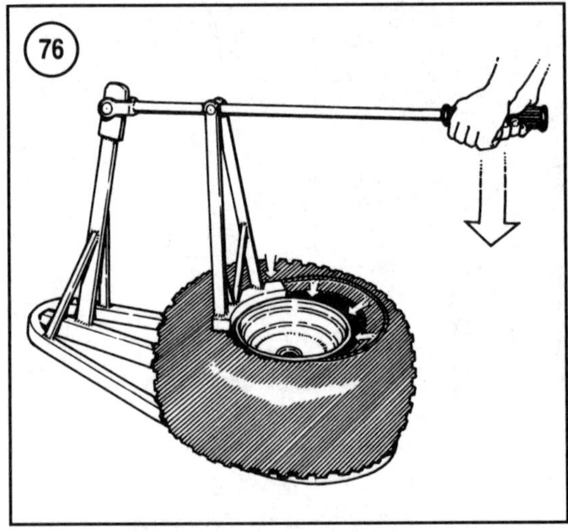
76

4. Slowly work the bead breaker tool, making sure the tool arm seats against the inside of the rim, and break the tire bead away from the rim.

5. Using your hands, press the tire on either side of the tool to break the rest of the bead free from the rim.

6. If the rest of the tire bead cannot be broken loose, raise the tool, rotate the tire/rim assembly and

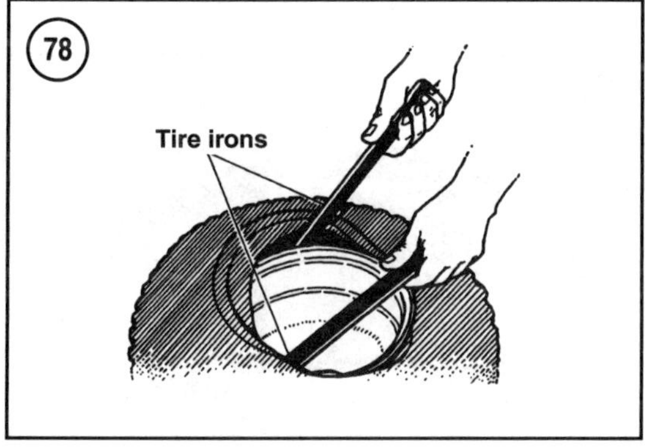

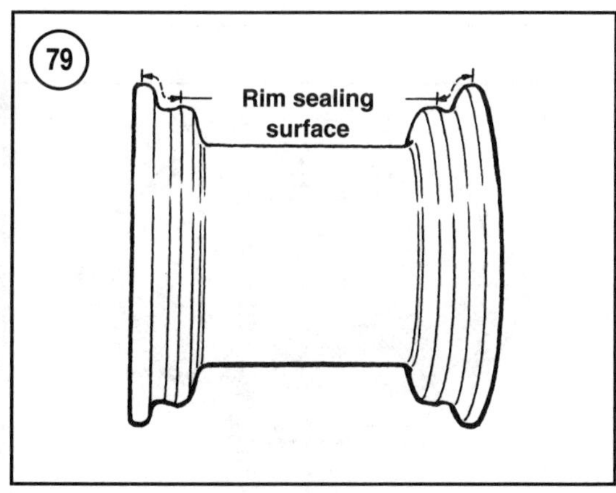

repeat Step 4 and Step 5 until the entire bead is broken loose from the rim (**Figure** 77).

7. Turn the wheel over and repeat the preceding steps to break the bead on the opposite side of the rim.

CAUTION
When using tire irons, work carefully so the tire or rim sealing surfaces will not be damaged. Any damage to these areas may cause an air leak and require replacement of the tire or rim.

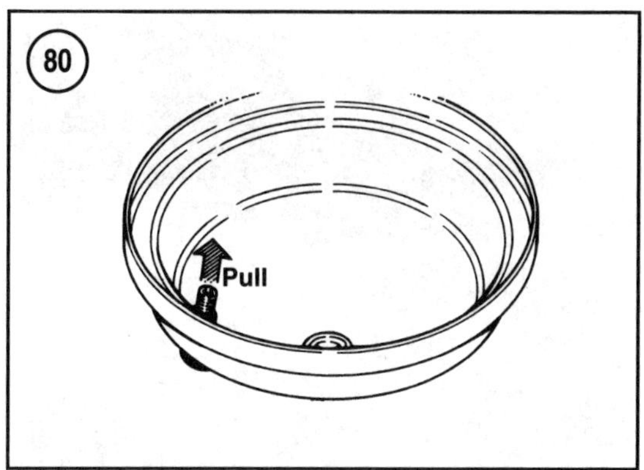

8. Lubricate the tire beads and rim flanges as described in Step 2. Pry the bead over the rim with two tire irons (**Figure 78**). Take small bites with the tire irons. Place rim protectors between the tire irons and the rim.

9. When the upper tire bead is free, lift the second bead up into the center rim well. Remove the second bead from the rim as described in Step 8.

10. Clean and dry the rim.

11. Inspect the sealing surface on both sides of the rim (**Figure 79**). If the rim is bent, it may leak air.

12. To replace the valve stem, perform the following:

  a. Support the rim and pull the valve stem out of the rim. Discard the valve stem.
  b. Lubricate the new valve stem with water.
  c. Pull a new valve stem into the rim, from the inside out, until it snaps into place (**Figure 80**).

13. Inspect the tire for cuts, tears, abrasions or any other defects.

WARNING
Only use clean water as a lubricant during tire mounting. Soap or other tire lubricants can leave a residue, which could cause the tire to slip on the rim and lose air pressure during operation.

14. Clean the tire and rim of any lubricant used during removal.

WARNING
The tread pattern is directional on most tires. Position the tire onto the

81

83

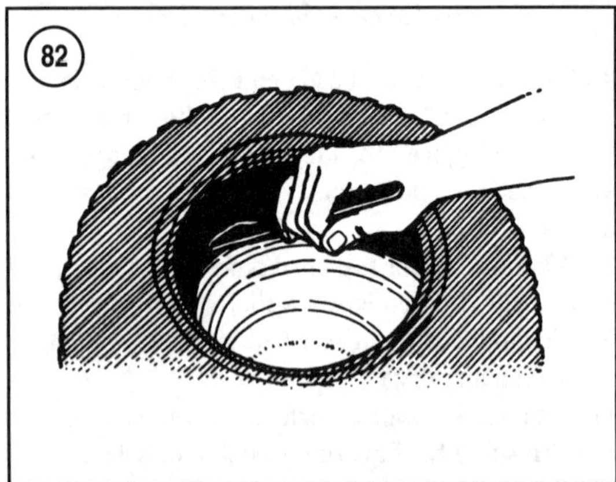
82

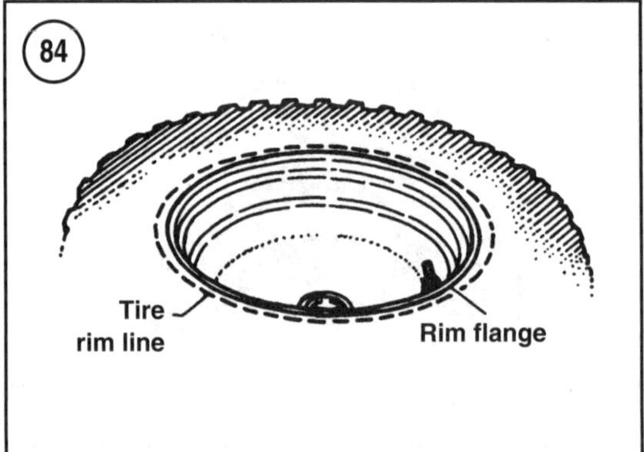

84

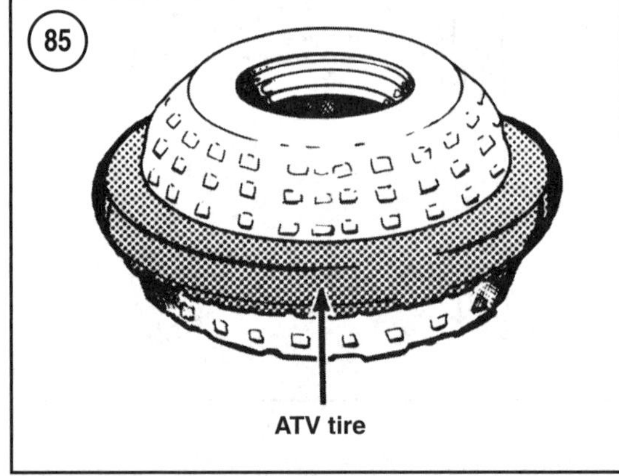

85

*rim so the arrow on the sidewall (**Figure 81**) points in the direction of the wheel's forward rotation.*

NOTE
If the tire is difficult to install, place the tire outside in the sun (or an enclosed car). The higher temperatures soften the tire and help ease installation.

15. Install the tire onto the rim from the side with the narrower rim shoulder. If this cannot be determined, start with the side opposite the valve stem. Push the first bead over the rim flange. Force the bead into the center of the rim to help installation (**Figure 82**).
16. Install the rest of the bead with tire irons.
17. Repeat the preceding steps to install the second bead onto the rim (**Figure 83**).
18. Install the valve stem core, if necessary.
19. Apply water to the tire bead and inflate the tire to seat the tire onto the rim. Check that the rim lines on both sides of the tire are parallel with the rim flanges as shown in **Figure 84**. If the rim flanges are not parallel, deflate the tire and break the bead. Lubricate the tire with water again and reinflate the tire.

NOTE
If the tire beads will not seat because of an air leak, a tight strap around

*perimeter of the tread will aid in the driving the beads into place. If correctly sized, a discarded ATV tire (**Figure 85**) will also work.*

20. When the tire is properly seated, do the following:
    a. Remove the valve core to deflate the tire.
    b. Wait one hour to allow adjustment of the tire on the rim.
    c. Install the valve core and inflate the tire to the operating specified pressure. See **Table 2**.
    d. Apply water to the beads and valve stem and check for air leaks.

Tire Repair

Use the manufacturer's instructions for the tire repair kit being used. If there are no instructions, use the following procedure.

1. Remove the tire as described in this section.
2. Prior to removing the object that punctured the tire, mark the puncture location. Then remove the object.
3. Working on the inside of the tire, roughen an area around the hole that is larger than the patch. Use the cap from the tire repair kit or a pocket knife. Do not scrape too vigorously or additional damage may occur.
4. Clean the area with a non-flammable solvent. Do not use an oil base solvent. It will leave a residue rendering the patch useless.
5. Apply a small amount of special cement to the puncture and spread it evenly.
6. Allow the cement to dry until tacky. Usually 30 seconds is sufficient.

CAUTION
Do not touch the newly exposed rubber or the patch will not stick firmly.

7. Remove the backing from the patch.
8. Center the patch over the hole. Hold the patch firmly in place for about 30 seconds to allow the cement to dry. If a roller is available, use it to press the patch into place.
9. Dust the area with talcum powder.

Table 1 FRONT SUSPENSION AND STEERING SPECIFICATIONS

Front suspension	
Type	Double wishbone
Caster	8.5°
Camber	-0.9°
Steering angle	41°
Trail	36 mm (1.42 in.)
Toe-in	5.0 mm (0.20 in.)
Tie-rod length	325.7-327.7 mm (12.82-12.90 in.)
Turning radius	3.1 m (10.2 ft.)
Wheel travel	215 mm (8.5 in.)

Table 2 TIRE SPECIFICATIONS

Front tire	
Size	AT22 × 7-10
Original equipment	Dunlop KT331
Minimum tread depth	4 mm (0.16 in.)
Rear tire	
Size	AT20 × 10-9
Original equipment	Dunlop KT335
Minimum tread depth	4 mm (0.16 in.)
Inflation pressure (cold)*	
Standard	
Front	30 kPa (4.4 psi)
Rear	27.5 kPa (4.0 psi)

*Tire inflation pressure for original equipment tires. Aftermarket tires may require different inflation pressures.

11

Table 3 FRONT SUSPENSION AND STEERING TORQUE SPECIFICATIONS

	N•m	in.-lb.	ft.-lb.
Ball joint nuts			
2003 models	43	–	32
2004 models	45	–	33
2005-on models	29	–	21
Brake caliper bolts	26	–	19
Control arm pivot nut*	65	–	47
Front hub nut	65	–	47
Front shock absorber nuts*	60	–	44
Handlebar clamp bolts			
2003 models	23	–	17
2004-on models	26	–	19
Master cylinder clamp bolts	10	89	–
Steering shaft holder bolts	23	–	17
Steering shaft nut	49	–	36
Throttle housing clamp bolts	5	44	–
Tie-rod end nut			
2003 models	60	–	44
2004-on models	45	–	33
Tie-rod lock nut	29	–	21
Wheel lug nuts			
2003-2004 models	50	–	37
2005-on models	60	–	44

*Apply threadlock.

CHAPTER TWELVE

REAR SUSPENSION

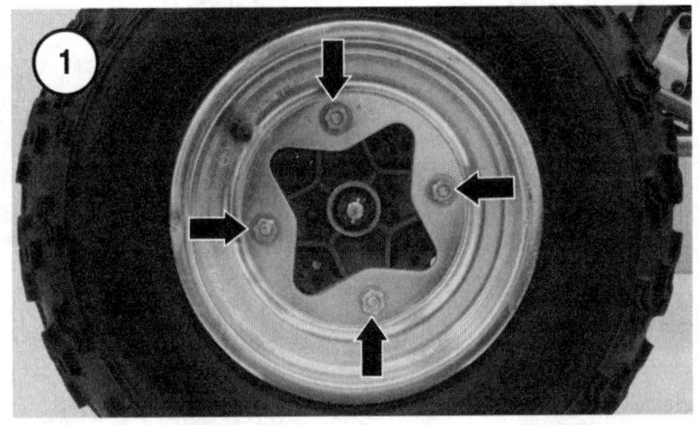

This chapter provides service procedures for the rear wheel, rear wheel hub, rear axle, rear axle hub, sprockets, drive chain, shock absorber, shock linkage and swing arm.

For tire and wheel procedures, refer to Chapter Eleven.

Refer to **Tables 1-3** at the end of the chapter for specifications.

REAR WHEEL

Removal/Installation

1. Park the ATV on level ground and block the front wheels.
2. Loosen the lug nuts (**Figure 1**).
3. Raise and support the ATV.
4. Remove the lug nuts and washers from the studs, then remove the wheel from the hub. If more than one wheel will be removed, mark each wheel so it can be installed on its original location.
5. Clean the lug nuts, washers and studs. If there are broken or damaged studs, replace them.

WARNING

*If more than one wheel has been removed from the machine, check that the tire direction arrow, on the tire sidewall (**Figure 2**), is pointing forward when the wheel is mounted. The arrow must point forward to prevent the possibility of tire ply failure during operation.*

6. Install the wheel onto the studs, with the valve stem facing out.
7. Install the washers and finger-tighten the lug nuts.
8. Lower the machine to the ground.
9. Equally tighten the wheel nuts in stages and in a crisscross pattern. On the final pass tighten as specified in **Table 3**.

12

REAR WHEEL HUBS

Removal/Installation

NOTE

The axle nut is very tight and removal can be difficult. Depending on the available tools, it maybe necessary to loosen and tighten the axle nut while the rear wheel is in place and the vehicle is on the ground. This makes it

easier to hold the vehicle steady during removal.

1. Remove the rear wheel as described in this chapter.
2. Set the parking brake to hold the rear axle when removing the axle nut. If the axle still spins, have an assistant apply the rear brake or hold the opposite wheel during removal.
3. Remove the cotter pin, nut and washer from the axle (**Figure 3**).
4. Pull the wheel hub from the axle splines. If removing the opposite hub, mark the hubs so they can be reinstalled in their original positions on the axle.
5. If the hub is seized to the splines, apply penetrating oil and lightly tap the back of the hub near the center. If a light tapping does not loosen the hub, use a puller to remove the hub from the axle.
6. Inspect the hub for cracks, damaged splines and broken studs (**Figure 4**).
7. Reverse this procedure to install the hub. Note the following.
   a. The hub washer (**Figure 5**) is very slightly concave. Install it on the axle with the domed side facing out.
   b. Apply grease to the hub splines.
   c. Tighten the hub nuts to 100 N•m (74 ft.-lb.).
   d. Install a *new* cotter pin.

REAR AXLE

Removal

The axle nuts are 47 mm (1.85 in.) and can be removed with rear axle nut holders (Suzuki part Nos. 09930-73180 and 57001-SO55). It is also possible to make a tool from any 1 3/4 in. wrench by grinding 2 mm (1/8 in.) off both sides (**Figure 6**).

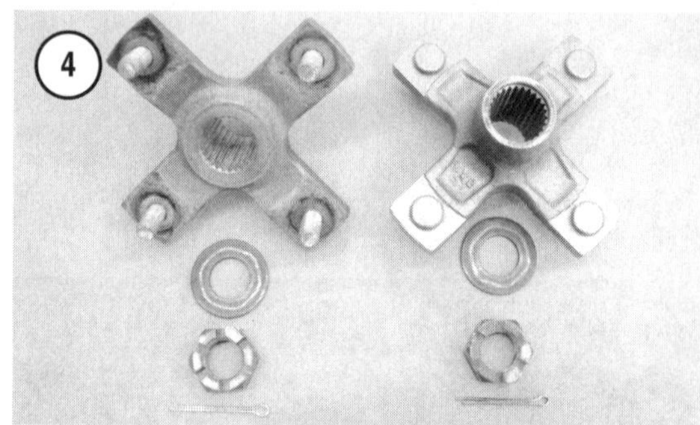

1. Park the ATV on level ground and set the parking brake.
2. While the ATV is on the ground loosen the rear axle nuts. They are difficult to remove and it is much easier to hold the vehicle steady. If they cannot be loosened without moving the ATV consider using tie down straps.
3. Remove the cotter pins from the hub nuts, then loosen the hub nuts and then the lug nuts on both wheels.
4. Place a jack under the center of the vehicle and raise the rear tires off the ground.
5. Remove the rear wheels and hubs as described in this section.
6. Remove the rear brake caliper as described in Chapter Thirteen.

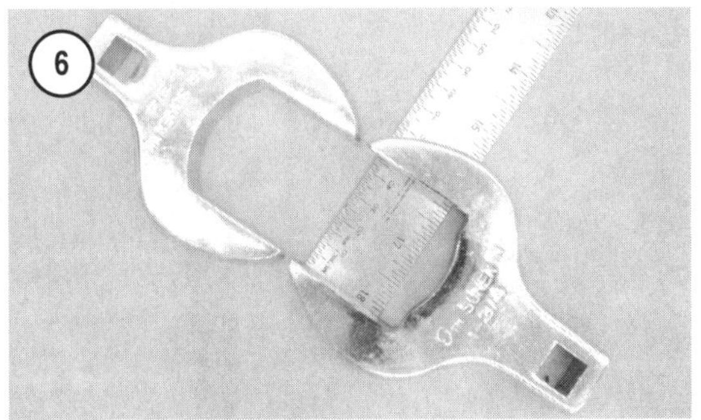

7. Loosen the chain adjustment bolts on the rear axle housing and take the tension off the chain (**Figure 7**).

8. While the chain is still on the sprocket, remove the bolts securing the rear sprocket to the carrier (**Figure 8**) and then lift the chain off the rear sprocket and remove it from the rear axle.

9. Loosen the axle nuts the rest of the way and slide them off the end of the axle.

10. Remove the rear sprocket carrier from the axle (**Figure 9**).

11. Pull the axle out of the right side of the axle housing.

12. Inspect the axle as described in this chapter.

13. Inspect the seals and bearing as described in this chapter.

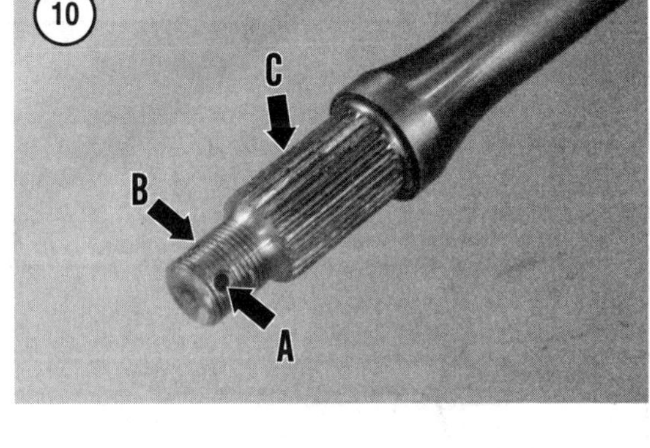

Inspection

1. Clean the axle and fasteners. All splines must be clean for inspection.
2. At each end of the axle inspect the following:
   a. Check for cracks or fractures around the cotter pin holes (A, **Figure 10**). Replace the axle if damage is evident.
   b. Check for uniform and symmetrical axle nut threads (B, **Figure 10**). Screw the axle nut onto the threads and check for roughness and play. If damage is evident, try restoring the threads with a thread die or small triangular file.
   c. Check for worn, distorted and broken wheel hub splines (C, **Figure 10**). Inspect the splines (**Figure 11**) in each wheel hub for damage. Fit each hub onto its respective end of the axle and feel for play. If play or wear evident, replace the parts.
3. Inspect the axle where it contacts the bearing in the axle hub (**Figure 12**). Check for scoring, galling and other damage. If damage is evident, inspect the bearings in the axle hub as described in this chapter.
4. Check the axle for straightness using a dial indicator and V-blocks as shown in **Figure 13**. Replace

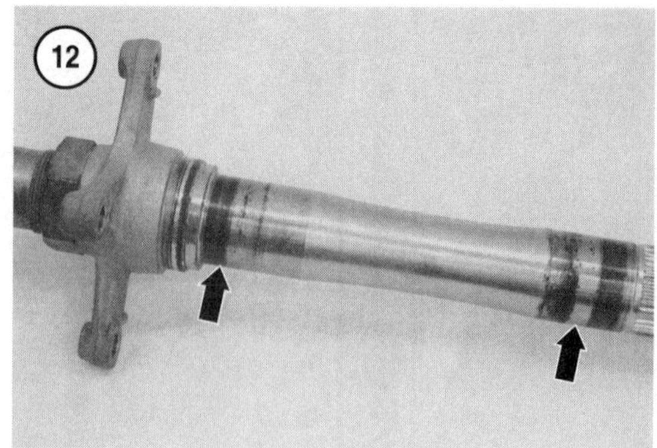

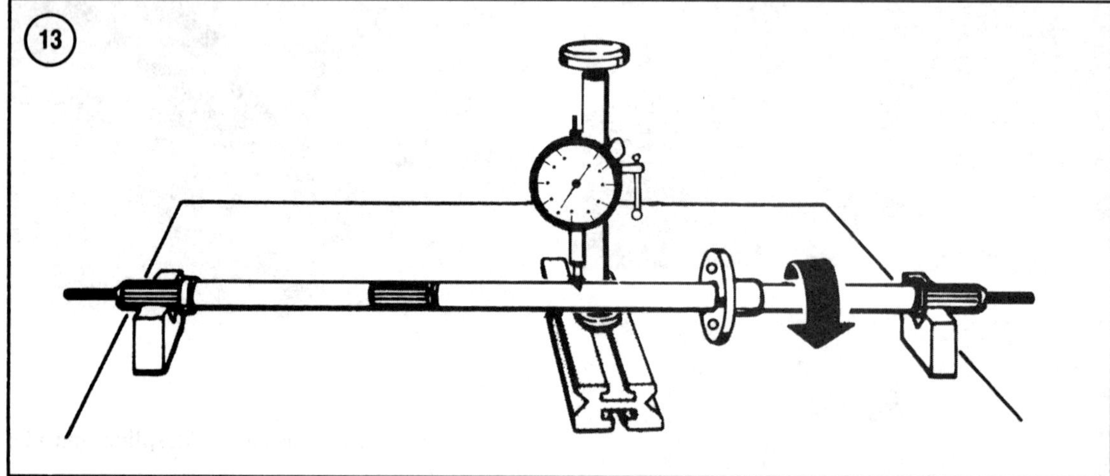

the axle if runout exceeds the service limit in **Table 1**.

Installation

1. Apply waterproof grease to the splines of the sprocket hub and axle bearing surfaces (**Figure 14**).
2. Insert the axle into the axle hub from the right side of swing arm and seat the lip of the disc brake hub into the axle housing seal.
3. If the chain was not broken when the axle was removed, loop the chain around the axle upon reassembly (**Figure 15**).
4. Install the sprocket carrier onto the left side of the axle (**Figure 9**).
5. Install the sprocket and loop the chain back around it, then insert the sprocket bolts into the sprocket carrier and tighten them finger-tight.
6. Temporarily tighten the axle housing in the swing arm to secure the axle.

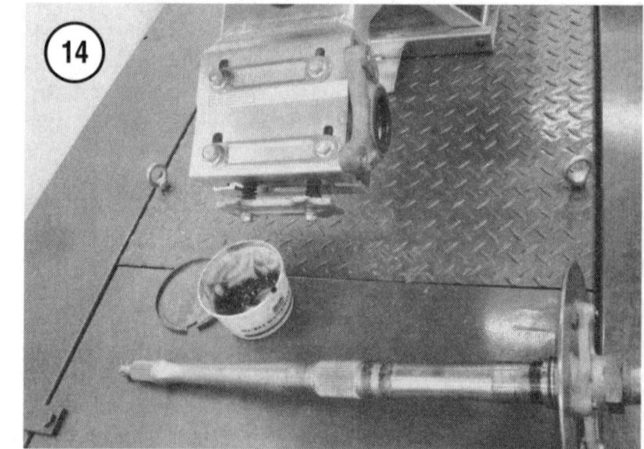

7. Apply a silicone sealant to the axle shaft at the base of the sprocket carrier.
8. Install the concave washers onto the axle (**Figure 16**) so the cupped sides are facing one another (**Figure 17**).
9. To tighten the axle shaft nuts to the necessary specification, perform the following:

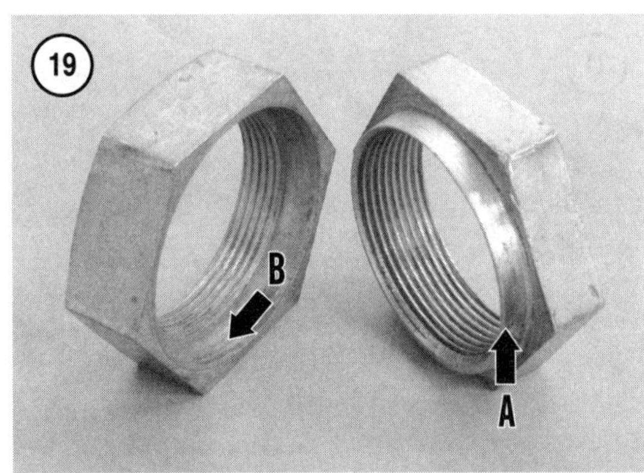

NOTE
When tightening the axle nuts in the following steps, the torque wrench reading may need to be calculated to reflect the actual torque being applied. Refer to Chapter One.

a. Apply a threadlocking compound to the axle threads.

b. Install and finger-tighten the inner locknut (**Figure 18**) with the shoulder side of the nut facing out (A, **Figure 19**).

c. Install and finger-tighten the outer locknut (**Figure 20**) with the recessed channel facing the inner nut (B, **Figure 19**).

d. Use tie down straps to secure both the disc brake hub (**Figure 21**) and the sprocket hub (**Figure 22**) to the footpegs or their mounting bolts.

e. Tighten the axle nuts as specified in **Table 3**.

f. Remove the straps securing the rear axle.

10. Check that the axle turns freely and runs true.

11. Install the rear disc brake caliper.

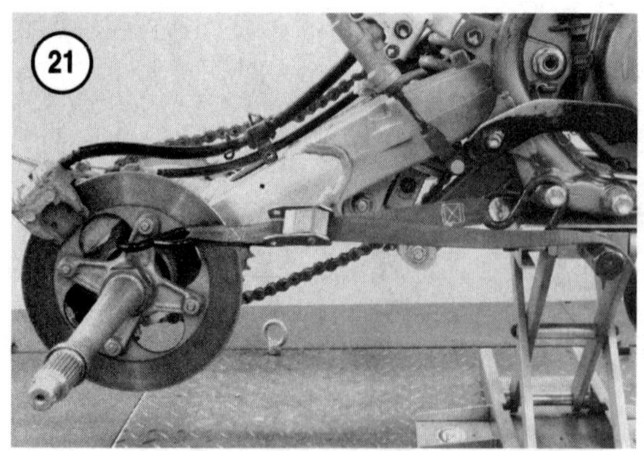
21

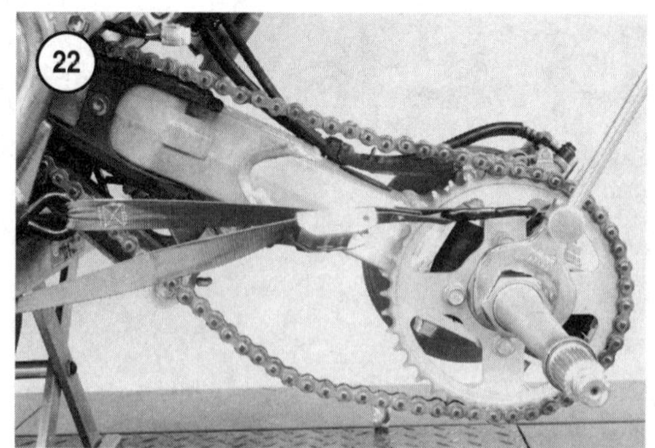
22

23

REAR AXLE HOUSING

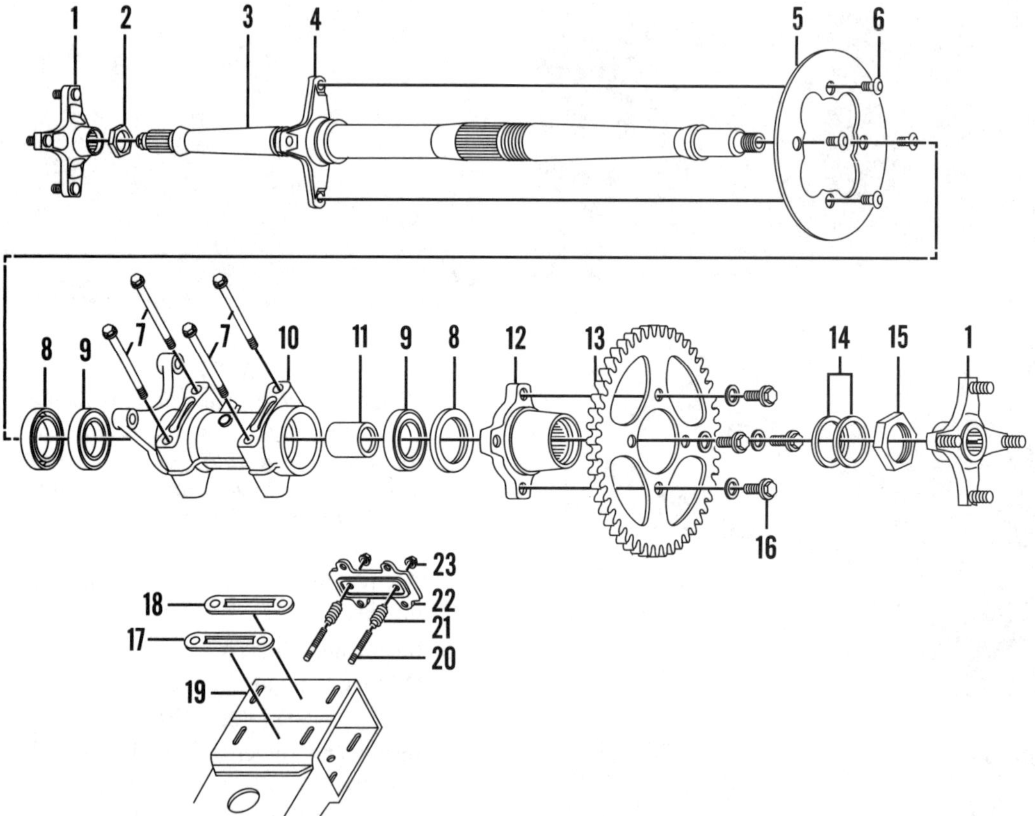

1. Rear wheel hub
2. Right axle nut
3. Rear axle
4. Disc brake carrier
5. Disc brake
6. Disc bolt
7. Bolts
8. Dust seal
9. Bearing
10. Rear axle housing
11. Spacer
12. Sprocket flange
13. Rear sprocket
14. Concave washers
15. Left axle nut and locknut
16. Sprocket mounting bolt
17. Front alignment plates (short)
18. Rear alignment plates (long)
19. Swing arm
20. Threaded stud
21. Dust cover
22. Adjuster plate
23. Nut

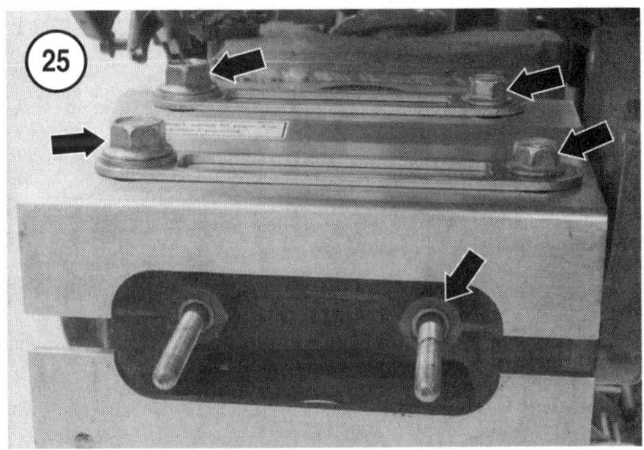

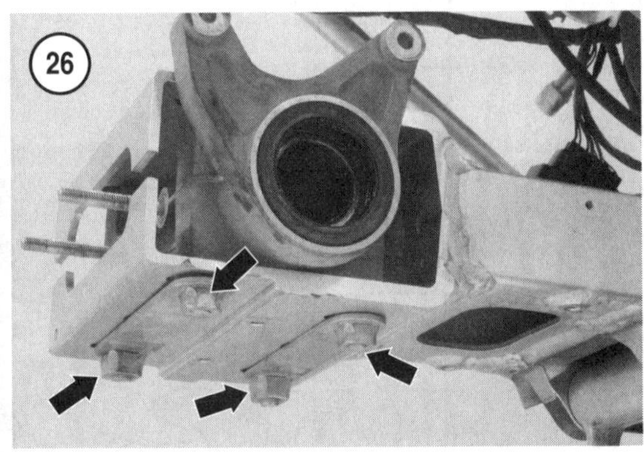

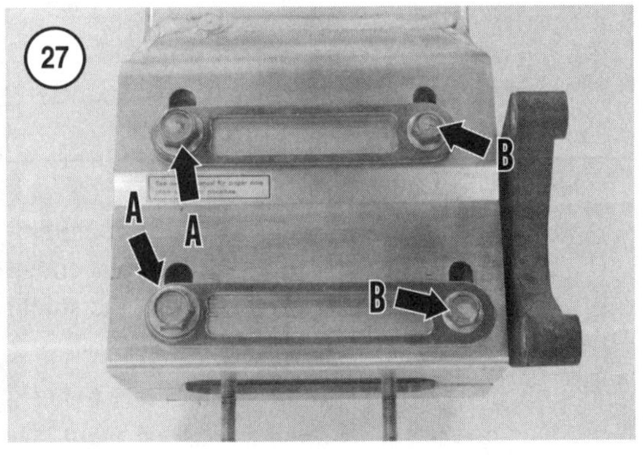

12. Install the rear hubs and wheels as described in this chapter.
13. Loosen the rear axle housing nuts and adjust the chain as described in Chapter Three.

REAR AXLE HOUSING

The rear axle housing (**Figure 23**) passes through the swing arm and contains the seals and axle bearings that support the rear axle. The hubs for the sprocket and brake disc are located to the left and right side of the axle housing respectively.

Removal/Installation

1. Park the ATV on level ground and set the parking brake.
2. Place a jack under the center of the ATV and raise the rear tires off the ground.
3. Remove the rear wheels and hubs as described in this chapter.
4. Remove the rear axle as described in this chapter.
5. Remove the chain adjuster plate and rubber boots from the bolts in the rear of the housing (**Figure 24**).
6. Remove the rear axle housing bolts (**Figure 25**) and the nuts from the underside of the swing arm (**Figure 26**).
7. Remove the rear axle housing from the swing arm.
8. Installation is the reverse of removal. Note the following:
   a. Grease the chain adjuster bolts before installing the rubber boots to protect the bolts from corrosion.
   b. Tighten the drive chain side axle housing bolts (A, **Figure 27**) to 100 N•m (74 ft.-lb.). Tighten the disc brake side bolts (B, **Figure 27**) to 73 N•m (54 ft.-lb.).
   c. Coat the contact surfaces of the bearing housing with a thin film of waterproof grease before installing it into the swing arm to aid in chain adjustment.

Inspection

1. Wipe the axle housing (**Figure 28**) clean. Do not immerse the hub in solvent unless the bearings and seals will be replaced.

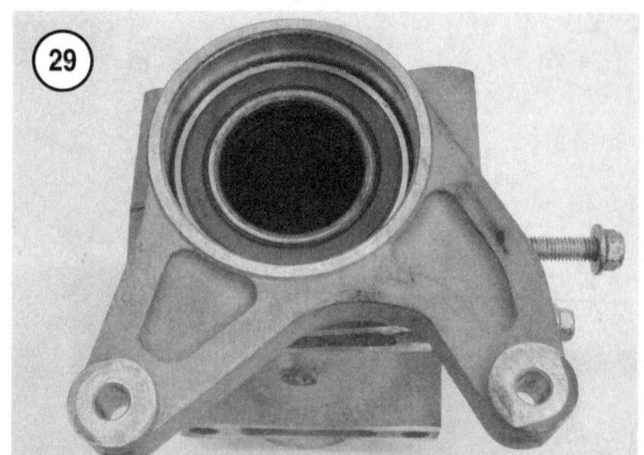

2. Inspect the dust seals for tears, distortion or damage. If rust, dirt or moisture is evident behind the seal, the seals are leaking. Replace the seals as described in this section.

3. Inspect the bearings as follows:

   a. Turn each bearing inner race (**Figure 29**). Feel for roughness, noise or binding. The bearings should turn smoothly and quietly.

   b. Check for axial and radial (**Figure 30**) play. Replace the bearings as a pair if worn or damaged. Remove and install the bearings as described in this section.

4. After the bearings and seals have been inspected/replaced, coat the surface of the bearing housing with a film of waterproof grease.

5. Inspect the bolts and nuts for corrosion and damage.

Bearing and Seal Replacement

1. Remove the seals from the housing using a seal puller or a long screwdriver (**Figure 31**).

2. Securely mount the axle housing in a soft jawed vice (**Figure 32**).

3. Place a drift on the edge of the inner bearing race (**Figure 33**) and tap it with a hammer. Work around the perimeter of the race, moving it in small increments until it is removed. Apply penetrating lubricant as necessary.

4. Remove the spacer from the axle housing.

5. Remove the remaining bearing, driving it out with a bearing driver or a socket that fits on the outer edge of the bearing race.

6. Clean and dry the axle hub and spacer.

7. Before installing the new bearings and seals, note the following:

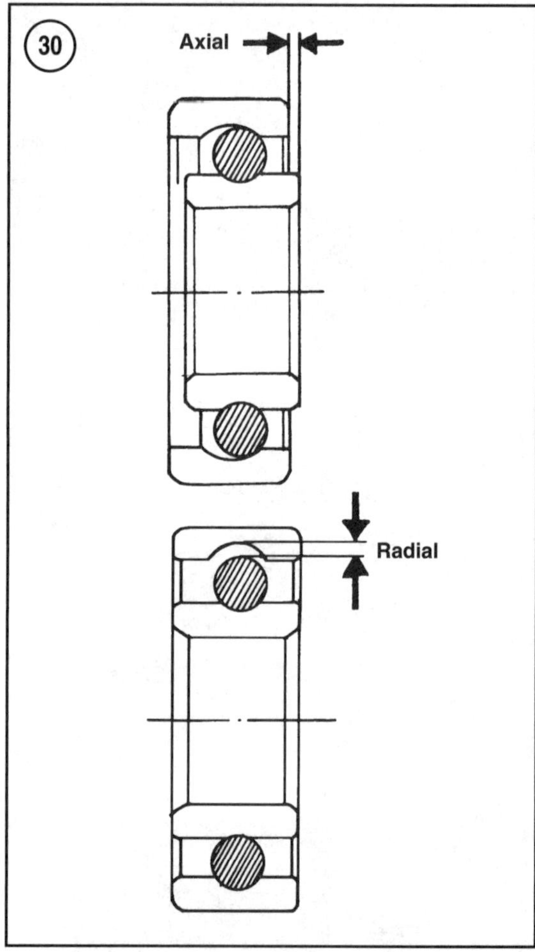

   a. Install the new bearings with the manufacturer's marks facing out. If the replacement bearings are shielded on one side, the shield faces out.

   b. If necessary, apply waterproof grease to bearings that are not lubricated by the manufac-

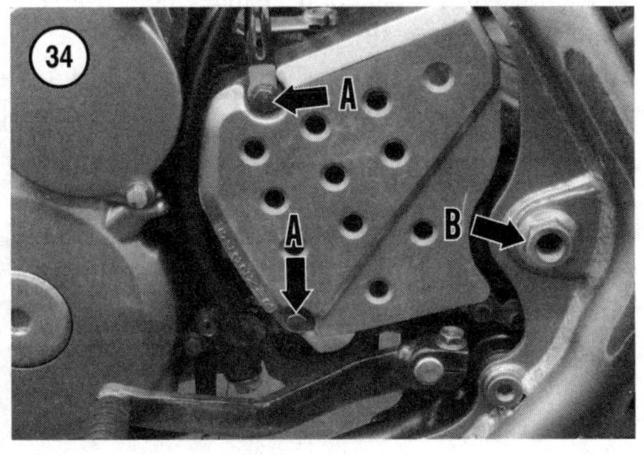

turer. Work the grease into the cavities between the balls and races.

8. Place a bearing squarely over the bearing bore.
9. Place a driver or socket over the bearing that seats against the outside diameter.
10. Press the bearing into place, seating it in the hub (**Figure 29**).
11. Turn the hub over and install the spacer.
12. Press the remaining bearing, seating it in the holder.
13. Install the seals as described in this section.

SPROCKETS

Check the condition of both sprockets and the drive chain, as described in Chapter Three. If either the chain or sprockets are worn, replace all drive components. Using new sprockets with a worn chain, or a new chain on worn sprockets shortens the life of a new part.

Front Sprocket Removal/Installation

1. Put the transmission in gear and set the parking brake.
2. Loosen the axle carrier bolts and slide the rear axle forward in the swing arm to take tension off the chain.
3. Remove the two bolts (A, **Figure 34**) securing the sprocket cover.
4. Remove the two bolts securing the front sprocket (**Figure 35**).
5. Remove the keeper by turning it slightly to align it with the shaft splines (**Figure 36**).
6. Remove the front sprocket.

7. Clean and inspect the front sprocket and chain (Chapter Three).
8. Installation is the reverse of removal. Tighten the sprocket bolts to 10 N•m (89 in.-lb.).

Rear Sprocket Removal/Installation

1. Put the transmission in gear and set the parking brake.
2. Loosen the axle carrier bolts and slide the rear axle forward in the swing arm to take tension off the chain.
3. Remove the right rear tire and hub as described in this chapter.
4. Remove the four sprocket mounting bolts (**Figure 37**).
5. Clean and inspect the rear sprocket and chain (Chapter Three).
6. Installation is the reverse of removal. Tighten the sprocket bolts as specified in **Table 3**.

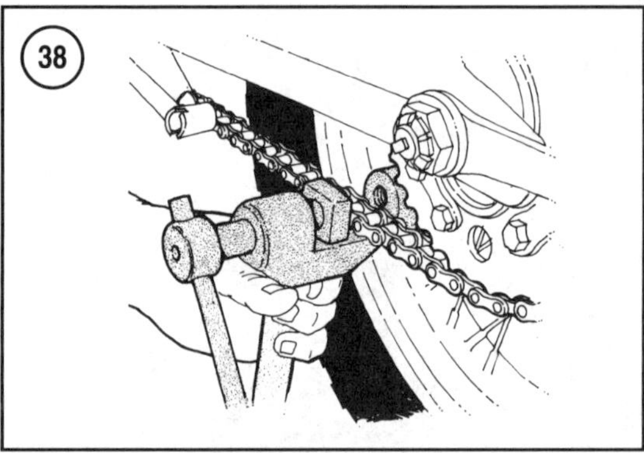

DRIVE CHAIN

Refer to Chapter Three for drive chain cleaning, lubrication, adjustment and measurement. Refer to **Table 1** in this chapter for chain specifications.

When checking the condition of the chain, also check the condition of the sprockets (Chapter Three). If either the chain or sprockets are worn, replace all drive components. Using new sprockets with a worn chain, or a new chain on worn sprockets shortens the life of the new part.

To remove the O-ring type chain, the swing arm must be partially disassembled so the chain can pass out of the swing arm pivot.

Chains that use press fit master links can be removed with a chain breaker tool (**Figure 38**) and link riveting tool (**Figure 39**).

Chain With No Master Link Removal/Installation

1. Park the ATV on level ground and block the front wheels.
2. Support the ATV with a jack until the rear wheels are off the ground.
3. Remove the rear wheels as described in this chapter.
4. Remove the parking brake cable guides from the swing arm (**Figure 40**).
5. Remove the shock absorber linkage bolt (**Figure 41**) as described in this chapter.
6. Loosen the axle housing bolts, then push the axle forward and lift the chain off the rear sprocket.
7. Remove the bolts (A, **Figure 34**) securing the front sprocket cover and lift the chain from the front sprocket.
8. Remove the swing arm pivot bolt (B, **Figure 34**) and pull the swing arm back.
9. Lower the swing arm and remove the chain.

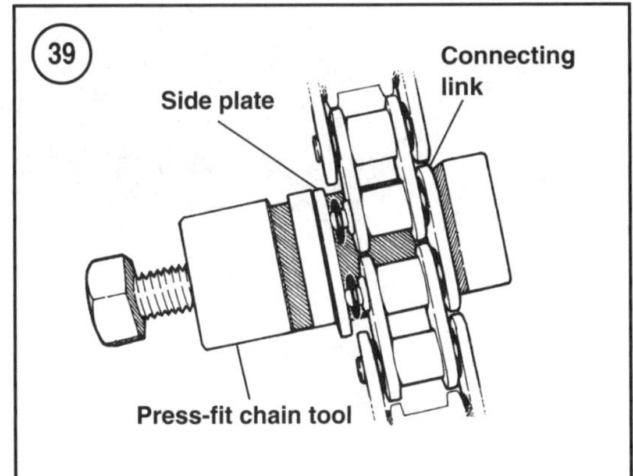

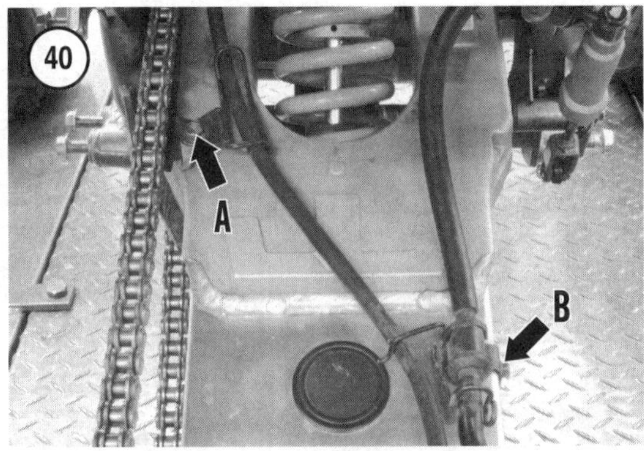

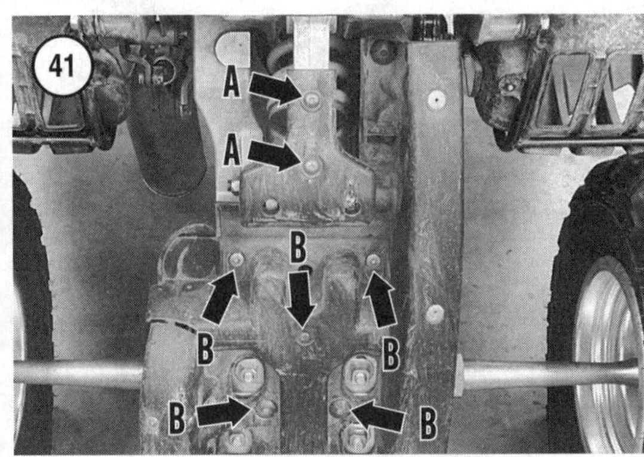

10. Reverse this procedure to install the chain. Note the following:

   a. Clean and inspect the bores in the swing arm, engine cases and frame.
   b. Apply waterproof grease to the bolts and bearings.
   c. Tighten the swing arm pivot bolt as specified in **Table 3**.
   d. Adjust the chain as described in Chapter Three.

Chain With Press-Fit Master Link Removal/Installation

1. Park the ATV on level ground and block the front wheels.
2. Loosen the axle hub nuts and chain adjusters.
3. Raise the ATV so the rear wheels are off the ground, then push the axle forward to create maximum chain free play.
4. Choose a convenient location along the drive chain for attaching a chain breaker tool **(Figure 38)**.
5. Attach the tool to the drive chain and drive a link pin from the chain. Remove the chain.
6. Install the new chain and route it over the sprockets.
   a. Put the transmission in neutral.
   b. If necessary, attach a wire to the end of the chain to route it behind the sprocket guard and over the drive sprocket.
   c. After the chain is routed over the sprockets, position the ends together. Put the transmission in gear to prevent the drive sprocket from rotating.
7. Secure the chain ends with the master link. Check that the O-rings are on the master link pins. Insert the link from the back side of the chain.
8. Place the chain link side plate on the master link. The identification marks must face out.
9. Stake the link pins using a chain riveting tool (**Figure 39**).
10. Make sure the brake hose guide (A, **Figure 40**) and the parking brake cable guide (B) are properly routed and secured.
11. Adjust the chain (Chapter Three).

SHOCK ABSORBER

The single shock absorber is a spring-loaded, hydraulically damped unit with an integrated oil/nitrogen reservoir. Refer to *Shock Absorbers* in Chapter Three if adjustment is required.

Removal/Installation

NOTE
It is not necessary to completely remove all the swing arm guards to remove the shock. They are shown removed for clarity.

12

1. Remove the rear fender as described in Chapter Fourteen.
2. Block the front wheels and support the ATV with a jackstand placed at the rear of the engine.
3. Remove the bolts (A, **Figure 41**) securing the cushion lever cover and the swing arm under cover bolts (B).
4. Support the swing arm and remove the cushion rod to cushion lever bolt (**Figure 42**).
5. Remove the bolt securing the shock to the linkage arm (**Figure 43**).
6. Remove the upper bolt securing the shock to the frame (**Figure 44**) and remove the shock from the swing arm (**Figure 45**).
7. Inspect the shock absorber as described in this section.
8. Installation is the reverse of removal, note the following:
   a. Install the mounting bolts from the left side of the frame.
   b. Tighten the upper shock absorber mounting bolts as specified in **Table 3**.
   c. Tighten the cushion rod to cushion lever bolt to 78 N•m (58 ft.-lb.).

Inspection

The shock absorber is spring-controlled and hydraulically damped. It cannot be serviced. If any part is damaged, replace the shock absorber.

1. Clean and dry the shock absorber.
2. Check the damper unit (**Figure 46**) for leaks or other damage.
3. Inspect the upper and lower shock bushings for deterioration, excessive wear or other damage.

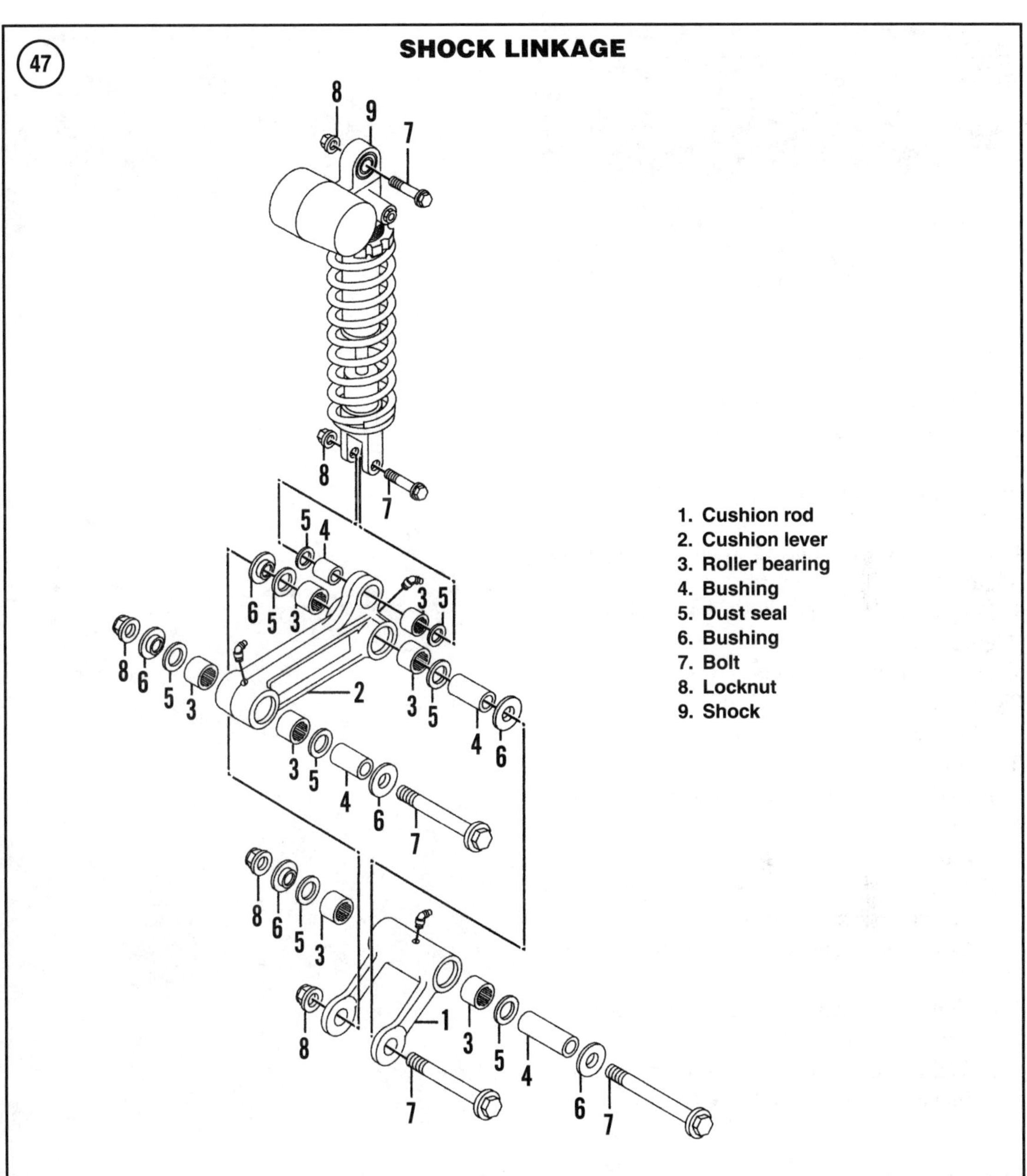

4. Inspect the shock spring for cracks or other damage.

SHOCK LINKAGE

The shock linkage (**Figure 47**) consists of the cushion rod, cushion lever, pivot bolts, dust caps, seals, pivot spacers and bushings. Since the linkage is often subjected to harsh conditions, disassemble and lubricate the linkage at the interval indicated in the maintenance and lubrication schedule (Chapter Three).

Cushion Rod and Cushion Lever Removal/Installation

1. Remove the rear fender as described in Chapter Fourteen.

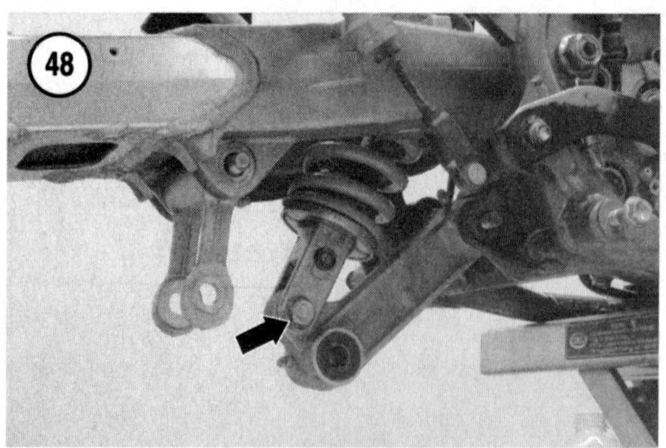

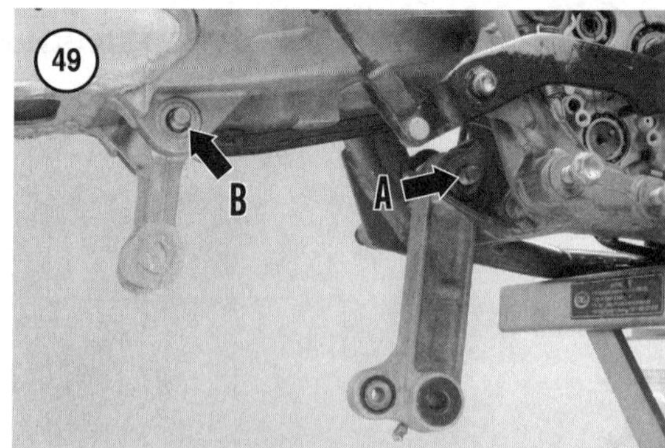

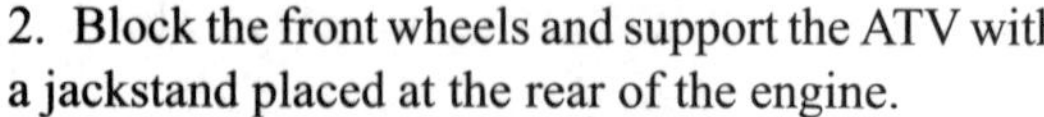

2. Block the front wheels and support the ATV with a jackstand placed at the rear of the engine.
3. Remove the bolts (A, **Figure 41**) securing the cushion lever cover and the swing arm under cover bolts.
4. Remove the cushion rod to cushion lever bolt (**Figure 42**).
5. Disconnect the shock from the cushion lever (**Figure 48**).
6. Disconnect the cushion lever from the frame (A, **Figure 49**).
7. Disconnect the cushion rod from the swing arm (B, **Figure 49**).
8. Inspect the linkage as described in this section.
9. Installation is the reverse of removal. Note the following:
   a. Lubricate all bushings, seals and pivot spacers with waterproof grease.
   b. Install the mounting bolts from the left side of the frame.
   c. Tighten the cushion rod and cushion lever bolts to 78 N•m (58 ft.-lb.).
   d. Tighten the lower shock absorber mounting bolt as specified in **Table 3**.

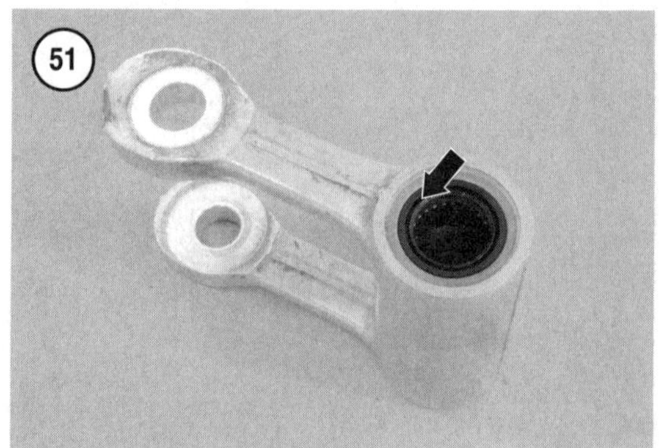

Inspection and Repair

During inspection and repair, keep all parts (**Figure 50**) identified so they may be reinstalled in their original locations.

1. Remove the dust caps and pivot spacers.
2. Pry out the seals **Figure 51**.
3. Inspect the cushion rod and the cushion lever for cracks and other damage, particularly around the bores and bosses.
4. Inspect the pivot bolts, spacers and dust caps for wear or damage.

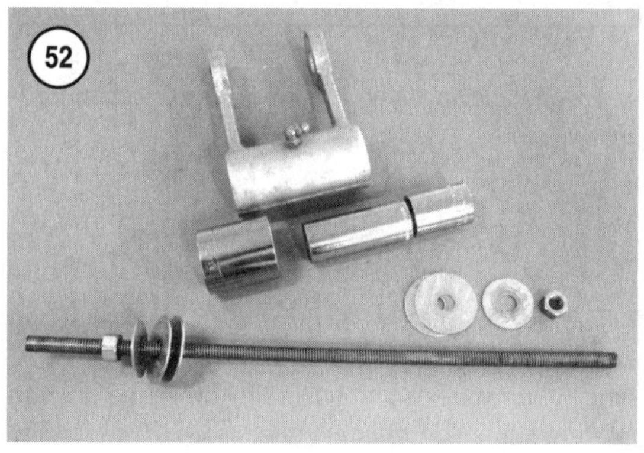

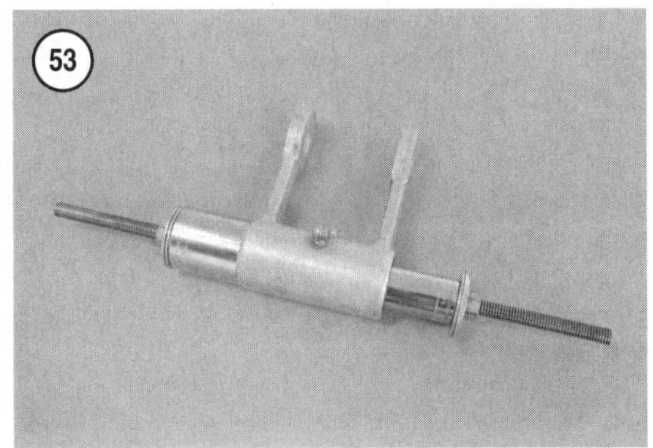

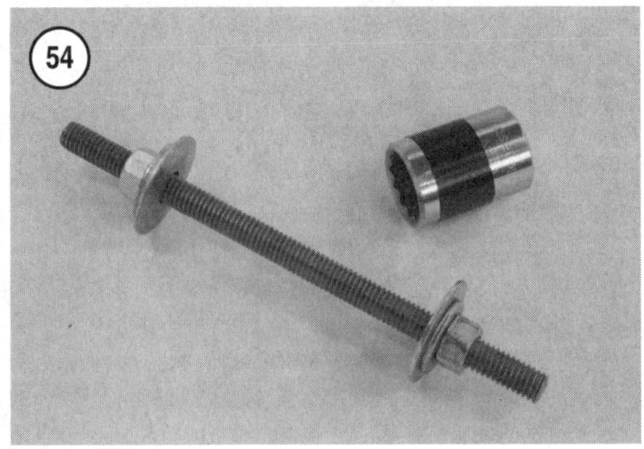

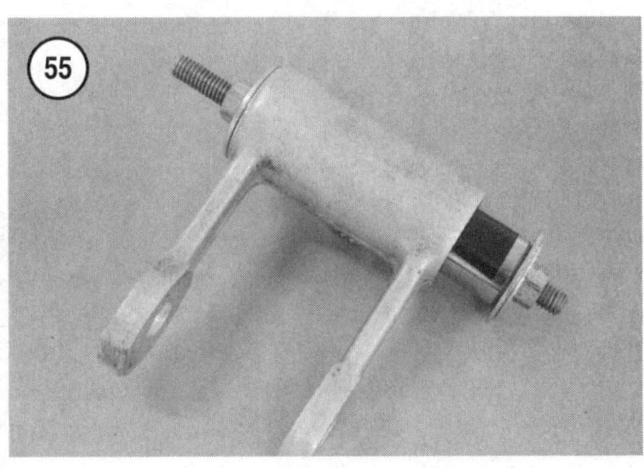

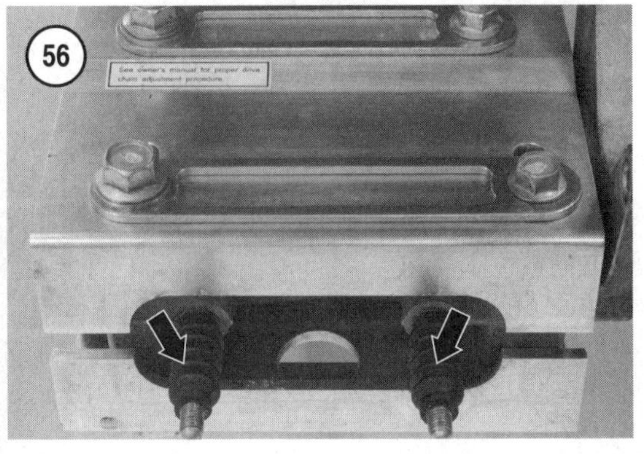

5. Check the fit of all bolts in their respective mating parts. Bolts should pass straight through the parts with no binding or difficulty.

6. Check the fit of all pivot spacers in their bearings. The spacers should turn freely and smoothly with no play. Replace if worn.

7. Inspect the bearings for wear and damage.

8. Remove the bearings using one of the following:
   a. An expanding bearing puller (Suzuki part No. 09923-73210) and slide hammer (Suzuki part No. 09923-30104).
   b. A draw bolt and a variety of sockets (**Figure 52**).
   c. A hydraulic press.

9. Install the bearings using one of the following methods:
   a. A bearing installer set (Suzuki part No. 09924-84510).
   b. A draw bolt and a variety of sockets (**Figure 52**).
   c. A hydraulic press.

10. Replace the bearings using a draw bolt as follows:
   a. To press the bearing out of the linkage, use a larger socket on one end of the draw bolt to receive the bearing (**Figure 53**).
   b. Use tape on the socket to mark the bearing depth (**Figure 54**).
   c. Turn the nuts of the draw bolt to press the bearing into the linkage to the tape mark (**Figure 55**).

11. Lubricate the bearings with waterproof grease.

12. Install new dust seals before reassembling.

SWING ARM

When servicing the swing arm it is necessary to remove the rear axle; however, the axle can remain in the rear housing. This can be done by removing the rear caliper, wheels, hubs, and rear sprocket hub from the rear axle as described in this chapter. If the axle housing is removed, remember to remove the chain adjustment plate and the rubber boots (**Figure 56**) from the chain adjustment bolts so they do not get torn when removing and reinstalling the housing.

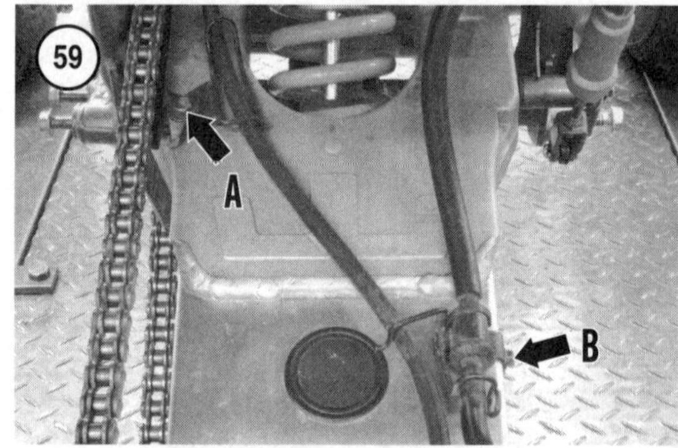

Bearing Inspection

The general condition of the swing arm bearings can be inspected with the swing arm mounted on the machine. Periodically check the bearings for play, roughness or damage. If the swing arm will be removed from the frame, make the check prior to removing the swing arm pivot bolt. If the swing arm will not be removed from the frame, perform the following steps before making the inspection.

1. Park the vehicle on level ground and block the front wheels.
2. Place a jack under the vehicle and lift the rear wheels off the ground.
3. Remove the rear wheels.
4. Disconnect the cushion lever from the cushion rod (**Figure 57**).
5. Loosen the axle hub nuts and drive chain adjusters and push the axle forward and lift the chain from the rear sprocket (Chapter Three).
6. Make sure the swing arm pivot bolt (**Figure 58**) is tightened as specified in **Table 3**.
7. Check the bearings as follows:
   a. Grasp the ends of the swing arm and leverage it from side to side. There should be no detectable play.
   b. Pivot the swing arm up and down. The bearings must pivot smoothly.
   c. If there is play or roughness in the bearings, remove the swing arm and inspect the bearing and pivot assembly for wear.
8. Install the cushion lever-to-cushion rod bolt and nut and tighten to 78 N•m (58 ft.-lb.).
9. Install the wheels as described in this chapter.
10. Adjust the chain (Chapter Three).

Removal/Installation

1. Park the vehicle on level ground and block the front wheels.
2. Place a jack under the vehicle and lift the rear wheels off the ground.
3. Remove the rear wheels as described in this chapter.
4. Remove the shock linkage as described in this chapter.
5. Remove the lower swing arm cover (B, **Figure 41**).

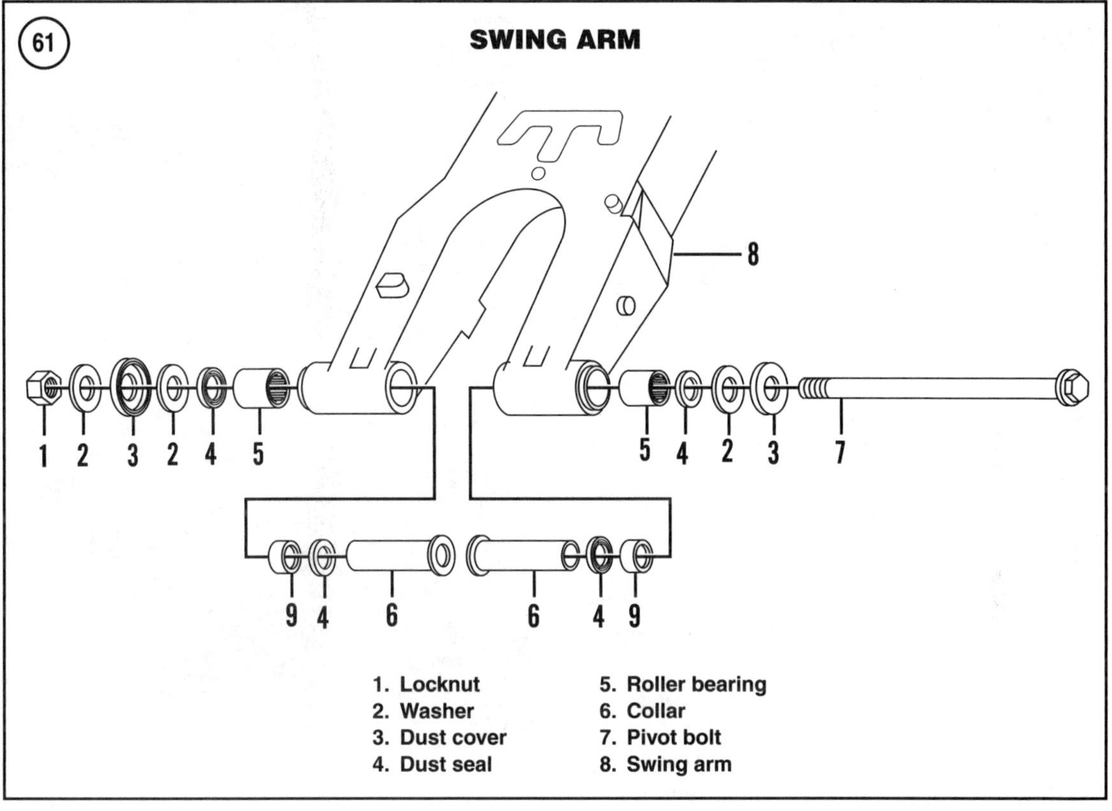

NOTE
It is not necessary to completely remove the shock, just the lower mounting bolt from the shock linkage.

6. Remove the rear brake caliper as described in Chapter Thirteen.
7. Remove the brake hose guide (A, **Figure 59**) and the parking brake cable guide (B).
8. Remove the left rear wheel hub as described in this chapter.
9. Loosen the axle housing bolts and chain adjusters, then push the axle forward and lift the chain off the sprockets (Chapter Three).
10. Remove the rear sprocket as described in this chapter.
11. Remove the rear axle housing from the *right* side of the swing arm (**Figure 60**).
12. Remove the swing arm bolt (**Figure 58**) and pull the swing arm back.
13. Inspect and service the swing arm as described in this section.
14. Installation is the reverse of removal. Note the following:
   a. Check that the chain is routed above and below the swing arm before inserting and tightening the swing arm pivot bolt.
   b. Tighten the brake hose guide bolts as noted in **Table 3**.
   c. Tighten the swing arm pivot bolt as specified in **Table 3**.
   d. Adjust the chain (Chapter Three).

Inspection and Repair

Keep all parts identified so they may be inspected and reinstalled in their original locations. Refer to **Figure 61**.

1. Remove the dust caps (A, **Figure 62**), washers (B) and collars (C).
2. Pry out the seals (D, **Figure 62**).
3. Inspect the swing arm for cracks and other damage, particularly around the bushing bores and rear axel housing.
4. Inspect the pivot bolt, collars and dust caps for wear or damage.
5. Check the fit of all pieces in their respective mating parts. The collars should fit into the bushings

12

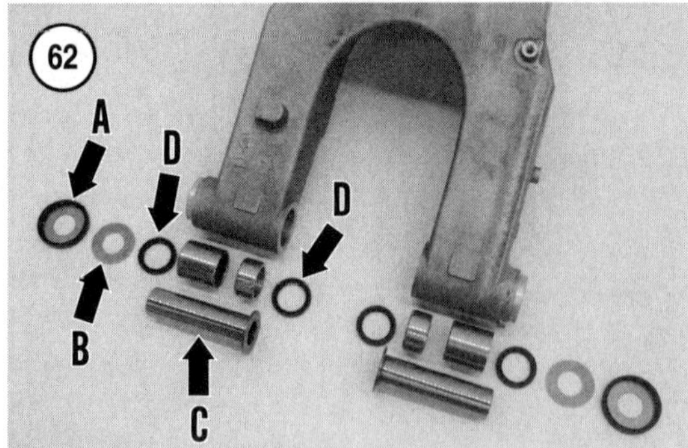

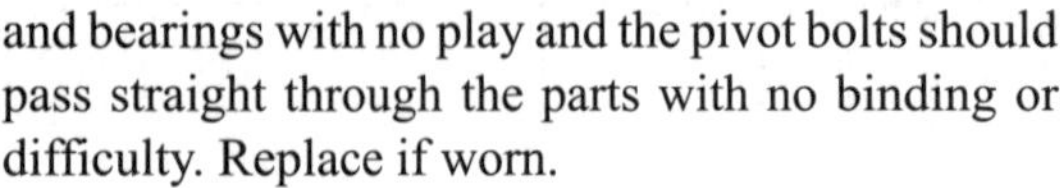

and bearings with no play and the pivot bolts should pass straight through the parts with no binding or difficulty. Replace if worn.

6. Clean and inspect the chain slider (**Figure 63**). Replace the slider if it is worn. Damage can occur to the swing arm if the chain wears through the slider.

7. Clean and inspect the chain roller attached to the frame (**Figure 64**). Replace the roller if worn or seized.

8. Inspect the bushings and bearings for wear and damage.

9. Clean and inspect the swing arm pivot at the engine (**Figure 65**). Lubricate the pivot with waterproof grease.

10. Assemble the swing arm as follows:
   a. If necessary, replace the bearings and bushings as described in this section.
   b. Apply waterproof grease to the parts as they are assembled.
   c. Install the inner and outer seals.
   d. Install the collars on the inside of the swing arm pivots.
   e. Install the dust caps and washers on the outside of the swing arm pivots.

Bushing and Bearing Replacement

Keep all parts identified so they may be inspected and reinstalled in their original locations. Refer to **Tabe 1** for the bearing and bushing installed depth.

1. Remove the dust caps (A, **Figure 62**), washers (B) and collars (C).
2. Pry out the seals (D, **Figure 62**).
3. Remove the bushings and bearings using one of the following methods:
   a. An expanding bearing puller (Suzuki part No. 09923-74511) and slide hammer (Suzuki part No. 09923-30104).
   b. A hydraulic press.
   c. A draw bolt and a variety of sockets (**Figure 52**).
4. Install the bearings and bushings using one of the following methods:
   a. A bearing installer set (Suzuki part No. 09913-70210).
   b. A hydraulic press.
   c. A draw bolt and a variety of sockets available at any hardware store (**Figure 52**).
5. Replace the bearings or bushings using a draw bolt as follows:

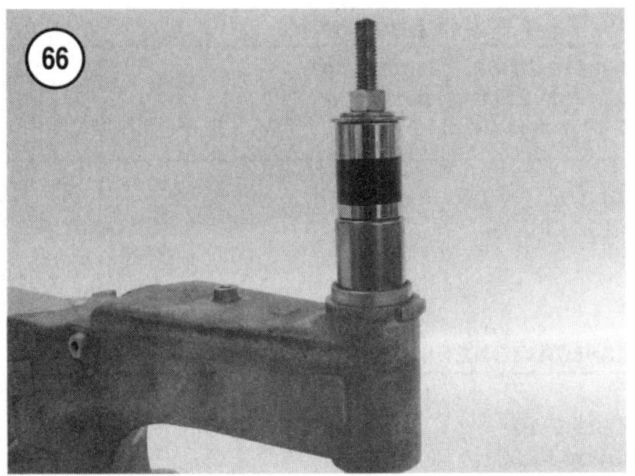

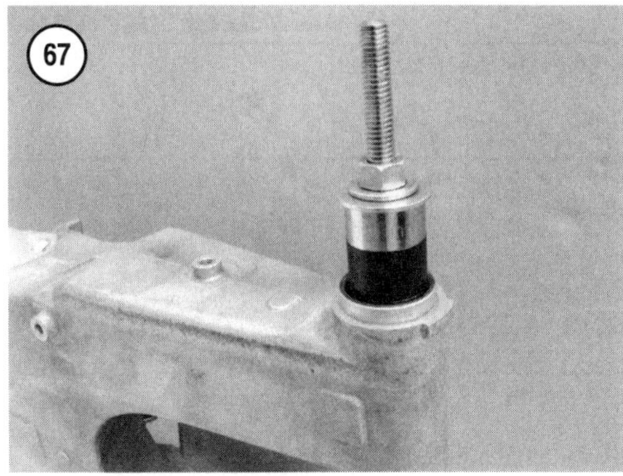

a. To press the bearing or bushing out of the linkage use a larger socket on one end of the draw bolt to receive the bearing (**Figure 53**, typical).
b. Use tape on the socket to mark the bearing depth (**Figure 66**).
c. Turn the nuts of the draw bolt and press the bearing into the linkage to the tape mark (**Figure 67**).

6. Lubricate the bearings and bushings with waterproof grease.
7. Install new dust seals before reassembling.

Table 1 REAR SUSPENSION SPECIFICATIONS

Wheel travel	230 mm (9.1 in.)
Rear axle runout service limit	6.0 mm (0.24 in.)
Cushion rod bearing depth	4.5 mm (0.18 in.)
Cushion lever bearing depth	4 mm (0.16 in.)
Shock mount	4.5 mm (0.18 in.)
Swing arm bearing depth	5 mm (0.2 in.)
Swing arm bushing depth	12 mm (0.47 in.)
Spring preload adjustment	
Standard	233 mm (9.17 in.)
Softest	238 mm (9.37 in.)
Stiffest	228.5 mm (9.00 in.)

(continued)

Table 1 REAR SUSPENSION SPECIFICATIONS (continued)

Drive chain service limit	No more than 319.4 mm (12.57 in.) between 21 chain pins
Drive chain free play	30-40 mm (1.2-1.6 in.)

Table 2 TIRE SPECIFICATIONS

Front tire	
Size	AT22 × 7-10
Original equipment	Dunlop KT331
Minimum tread depth	4 mm (0.16 in.)
Rear tire	
Size	AT20 × 10-9
Original equipment	Dunlop KT335
Minimum tread depth	4 mm (0.16 in.)
Inflation pressure (cold)*	
Standard	
Front	30 kPa (4.4 psi)
Rear	27.5 kPa (4.0 psi)

*Tire inflation pressure for original equipment tires. Aftermarket tires may require different inflation pressures.

Table 3 REAR SUSPENSION TORQUE SPECIFICATIONS

Item	N•m	in.-lb.	ft.-lb.
Brake hose guide bolts			
6 mm	12	106	–
8 mm	29	–	21
Cushion rod and cushion lever bolts/nuts	78	–	58
Front sprocket mounting bolt	10	89	–
Rear axle housing bolts			
Brake side (M10)	73	–	54
Drive chain side (M12)	100	–	74
Rear brake disc mounting bolts	23	–	17
Rear hub nut	100	–	74
Rear shock absorber locknuts			
Upper	60	–	44
Lower	55	–	41
Rear axle nuts			
2003-2004 models	180	–	133
2005-on models	240	–	177
Rear shock absorber locknuts			
2003-2004 models			
Upper	60	–	44
Lower	55	–	41
2005-on models			
Upper and lower	60	–	44

(continued)

Table 3 REAR SUSPENSION TORQUE SPECIFICATIONS (continued)

Item	N•m	in.-lb.	ft.-lb.
Rear sprocket mounting bolts			
2003 models	54	–	40
2004 models	55	–	41
2005-on models	60	–	44
Swing arm pivot bolt			
2003 models	84	–	62
2004-on models	95	–	70
Wheel lug nuts			
2003-2004 models	50	–	37
2005-on models	60	–	44

CHAPTER THIRTEEN

BRAKE SYSTEM

This chapter provides service procedures for the front and rear brake system including the brake pads, master cylinder, calipers, discs and brake pedal. Refer to Chapter Three for brake maintenance and adjustment.

The front brakes are actuated by the hand lever on the right side of the handlebar. The rear brake is actuated by the brake pedal. The clutch lever is also equipped with a lock that allows it to be used as a parking brake.

The brakes are hydraulically actuated. When pressure is applied to the brake lever, the brake fluid in the lines is compressed and pushes the brake pads against the brake disc. When pressure is relieved, the pads slightly retract from the disc, allowing the wheel to spin freely. As the pads wear, the piston in the caliper extends, automatically keeping the pads adjusted close to the disc.

When inspecting the brake system, compare any measurements to the brake specification in **Table 1**. Replace any component that is damaged or out of specification. During assembly, torque fasteners to the specification in **Table 2**. **Table 1** and **Table 2** are at the end of the chapter.

BRAKE SERVICE

Observe the following practices when working on the brake system.

1. Keep brake fluid off painted surfaces, plastic and decals. The fluid will damage these surfaces. If fluid does contact these surfaces, flush the surface thoroughly with clean water.
2. Keep the fluid reservoirs closed except when changing the fluid.
3. Replace brake fluid often. The fluid absorbs moisture from the air and causes internal corrosion of the brake system. Fresh fluid is clear to slightly yellow. If the fluid is obviously colored, it is contaminated.
4. Do not reuse brake fluid, and do not use leftover fluid that has been stored in an open container for any length of time.
5. When rebuilding brake system components, lubricate new parts with fresh fluid before assembly. Do not use petroleum based solvents. These can cause rubber components to swell and damage them.

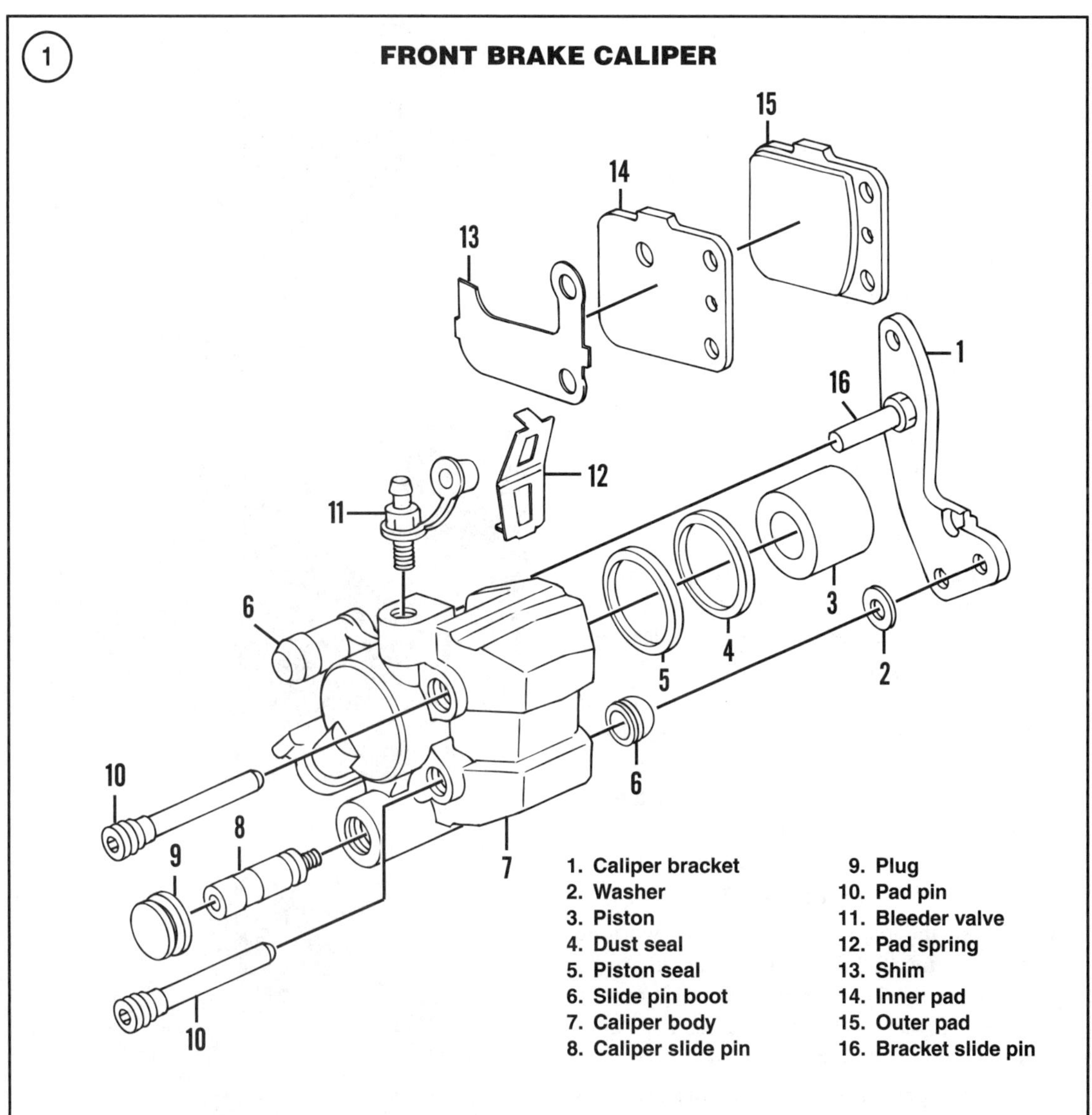

6. Bleed the brake system whenever a banjo bolt or other connector in the brake line has been loosened. Air will be in the system and brake action will be spongy.

FRONT BRAKE PADS

Removal/Installation

Refer to **Figure 1**.

1. Remove the front wheel, outer disc guard and hub hardware (Chapter Eleven).
2. Loosen the pad pins (A, **Figure 2**).
3. Remove the caliper mounting bolts (B, **Figure 2**), then slide the hub, disc and caliper out of the inner disc guard. Remove the caliper from the disc. Avoid kinking the brake hose.
4. Press down on the pads to relieve the pressure on the pad pins, then remove the pins.
5. Remove the pads.

CAUTION

In the following step, monitor the master cylinder fluid level. Brake fluid will back flow to the reservoir when the caliper piston is pressed into the bore. Do not allow brake fluid to spill from the reservoir.

NOTE
Do not operate the brake lever with the pads removed. The caliper piston can come out of the bore.

6. Grasp the caliper and press the piston (A, **Figure 3**) down into the bore, creating room for the new pads.
7. Remove the pad spring (B, **Figure 3**).
8. Clean the interior of the caliper using alcohol and inspect for the following:
   a. Leaks or damage around the piston, bleeder valve and hose connection.
   b. Damaged or missing boots.
   c. Excessive drag when the caliper is moved in and out on the slide pins. If there is corrosion or water around the rubber boots. Clean and lubricate the parts.
9. Inspect the pad pins, pad spring and mounting bolts (**Figure 4**). The pins and spring must be in good condition to allow the inner pad to slightly move when installed. Check that both small tabs on the spring are not corroded or missing.
10. Inspect the pads and shim (on back of inner pad) for wear and damage (**Figure 5**).
   a. Replace the pads when they are worn to within 1 mm (0.040 in.) of the backing plate, as shown by the wear indicator (**Figure 6**). Always replace pads that have been contaminated with oil or other chemicals.
   b. If the pads are worn unevenly, the caliper is probably not sliding correctly. The caliper must be free to float on the caliper slide pin and bracket slide pin. Buildup or corrosion on the parts can hold the caliper in one position, causing brake drag and excessive pad wear.
11. Install the pad spring with the small tabs pointing out.
12. Install the inner pad and shim, seating the pad under the caliper bracket and against the piston.
13. Install the outer pad.
14. Press down on the pads, then align and install the pad pins finger-tight. Do not fully tighten the pad pins until the caliper is installed.
15. Spread the pads so there is clearance to fit the caliper over the brake disc (**Figure 7**).

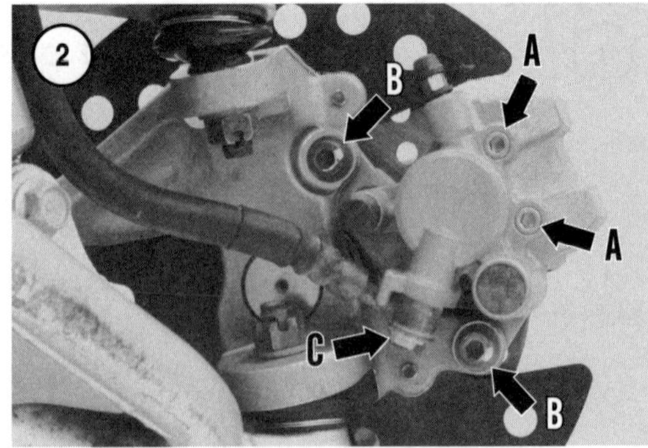

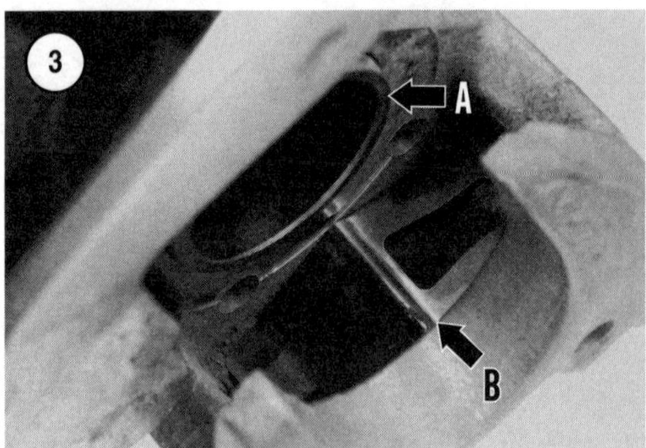

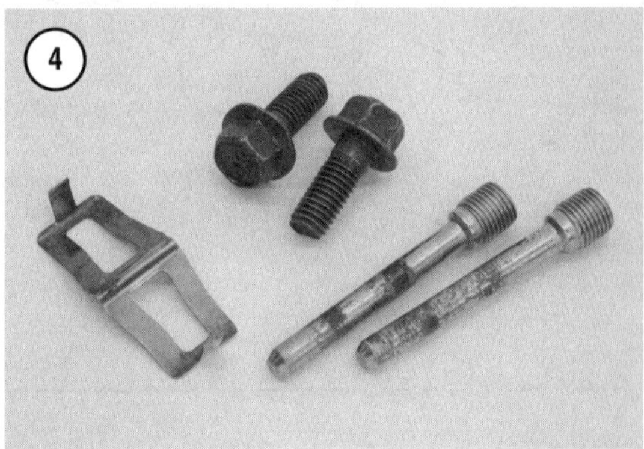

16. Position the caliper over the brake disc and hub assembly, then slide the caliper into the inner disc guard.
17. Install and tighten the caliper mounting bolts to 26 N•m (19 ft.-lb.).
18. Tighten the pad pins to 18 N•m (13 ft.-lb.).
19. Install the hub hardware (Chapter Eleven).
20. Operate the brake lever several times to seat the pads.
21. Check the brake fluid reservoir and replenish or remove fluid, as necessary.

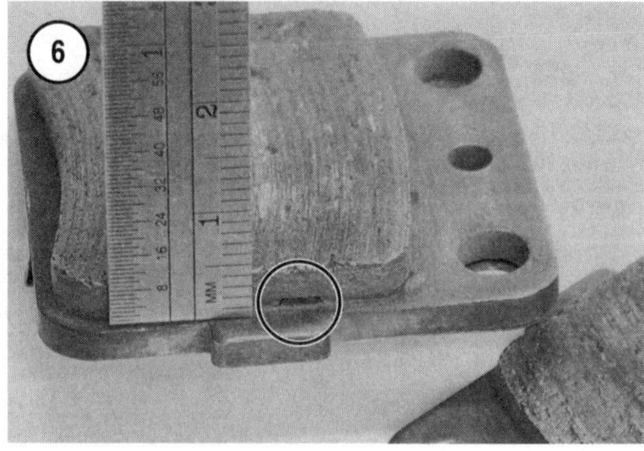

22. With the front hub raised, check that the hub spins freely and the brake operates properly.

23. Install the outer disc guard and front wheel (Chapter Eleven).

FRONT BRAKE CALIPER

Removal and Installation

1. Remove the front wheel, outer disc guard and hub hardware (Chapter Eleven).

2. If the caliper will be disassembled, drain the system as described in this chapter. After draining, loosen the brake hose banjo bolt (C, **Figure 2**) while the caliper is mounted. Leave the bolt finger-tight. It will be removed in a later step.

3. Remove the caliper mounting bolts (B, **Figure 2**), then slide the hub, disc and caliper out of the inner disc guard. Remove the caliper from the disc. Avoid kinking the brake hose.

4A. If the caliper will be left attached to the brake hose, but not disassembled and serviced:

a. Suspend the caliper with a length of wire. Do not let the caliper hang by the brake hose.

b. Put a wooden block between the brake pads. This prevents the caliper piston from extending out of the caliper if the brake lever is operated.

4B. If the caliper will be disassembled, do the following:

a. Remove the banjo bolt and seal washers from the brake hose. Have a shop cloth ready to absorb brake fluid that drips from the hose.

b. Wrap the hose end to prevent brake fluid from damaging other surfaces.

c. Drain excess brake fluid from the caliper.

d. Repair the caliper as described in this section.

5. Reverse this procedure to install the caliper. Note the following:

a. Install and tighten the caliper mounting bolts to 26 N•m (19 ft.-lb.).

b. Install new seal washers on the banjo bolt. Seat the brake hose in the guide on the caliper, then tighten the banjo bolt to 23 N•m (17 ft.-lb.).

6. Install the hub hardware (Chapter Eleven).

7. If the caliper is rebuilt, or the brake hose is disconnected from the caliper, fill and bleed the brake system as described in this chapter.

8. Operate the brake lever several times to seat the pads.

9. Check the brake fluid reservoir and replenish or remove fluid, as necessary.

10. With the front hub raised, check that the hub spins freely and the brake operates properly.

11. Install the outer disc guard, and front wheel (Chapter Eleven).

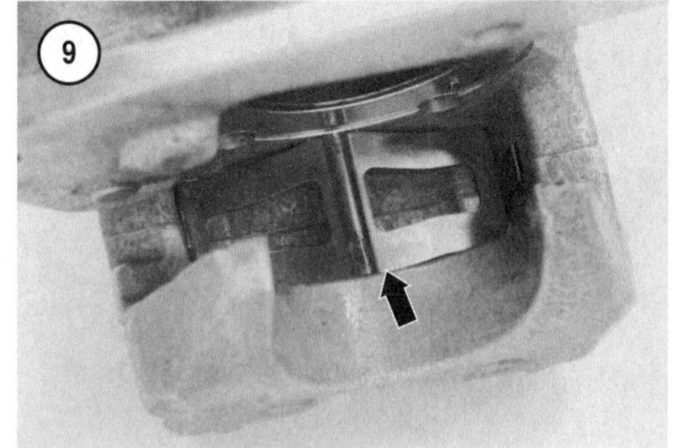

Repair

Use the following procedure to disassemble, inspect and assemble the brake caliper, using new seals. Refer to **Figure 1**.

1. Remove the caliper as described in this section.
2. Remove the pad pins (**Figure 8**). Press down on the pads to relieve the pressure on the pad pins while removing them.
3. Remove the brake pads and pad spring (**Figure 9**).

WARNING
Wear eye protection when using compressed air to remove the piston. Keep fingers away from the piston discharge area.

4. Remove the piston from the caliper bore using compressed air (**Figure 10**). To perform this technique, an air nozzle is tightly held in the brake hose fitting and air pressure ejects the piston. Do not pry the piston out of the caliper. Remove the piston from the caliper as follows:
   a. Place the caliper on a padded work surface.
   b. Close the bleed valve so air cannot escape.
   c. Place a strip of wood, or similar pad, in the caliper. The pad will cushion the piston when it comes out of the caliper.
   d. Lay the caliper so the piston will discharge downward.
   e. Insert an air nozzle into the brake hose fitting. If the nozzle does not have a rubber tip, wrap the nozzle with tape. This allows the nozzle to seal tightly and prevent thread damage.
   f. Place a shop cloth over the entire caliper to catch any spray that may discharge from the caliper.

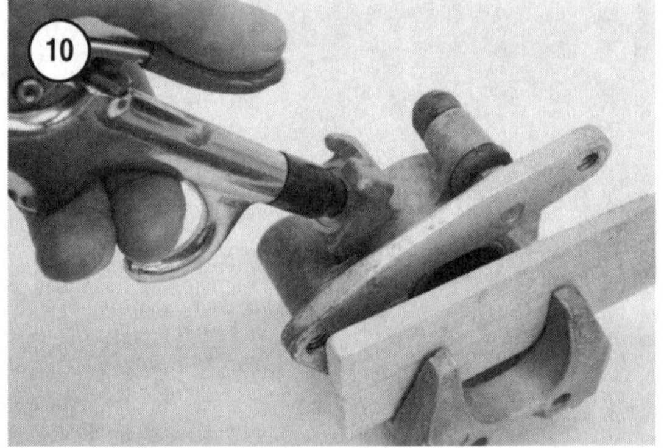

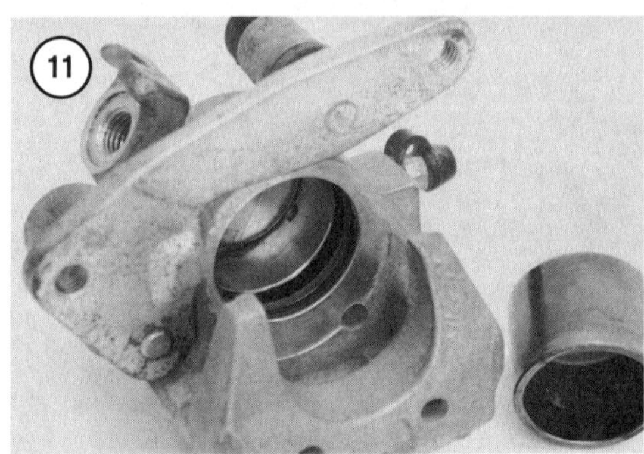

   g. Apply pressure and listen for the piston to pop from the caliper (**Figure 11**).

5. Remove the plug, caliper slide pin and boot (A, **Figure 12**). Remove the boot from the bolt before pulling it out of the caliper.
6. Remove the caliper bracket and washer (B, **Figure 12**).
7. Remove the slide pin boot (C, **Figure 12**).
8. Remove the bleeder valve and cap (D, **Figure 12**).

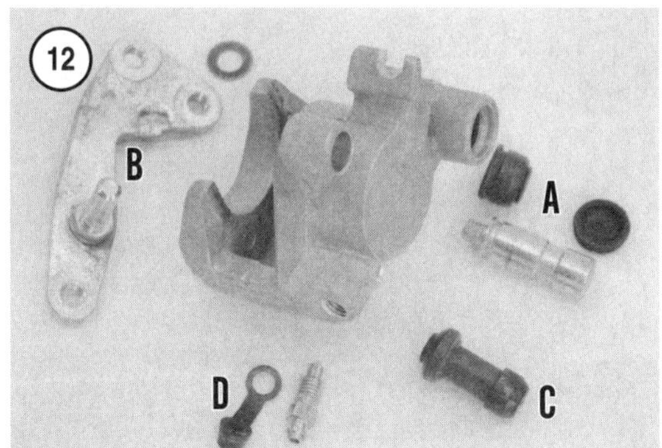

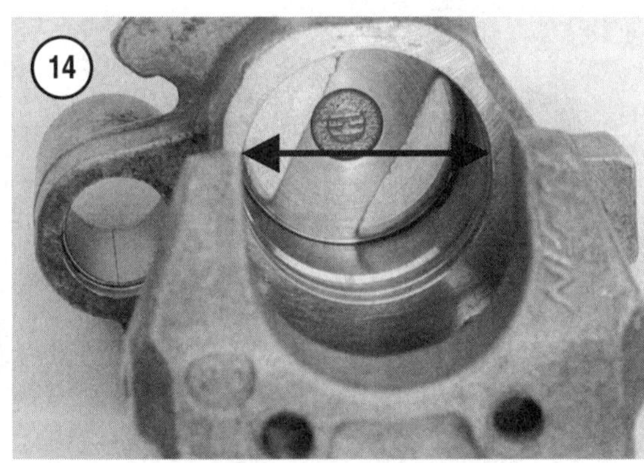

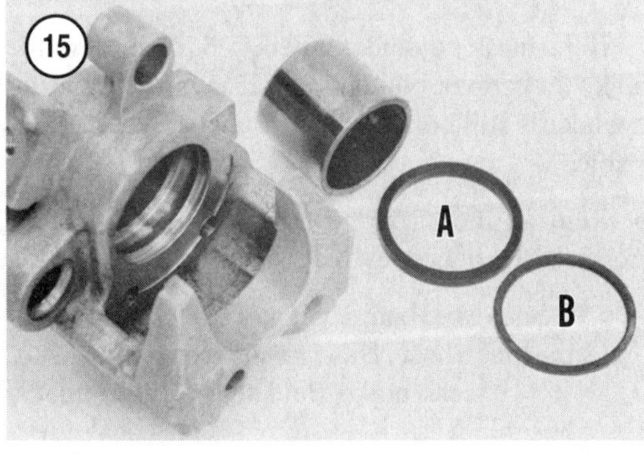

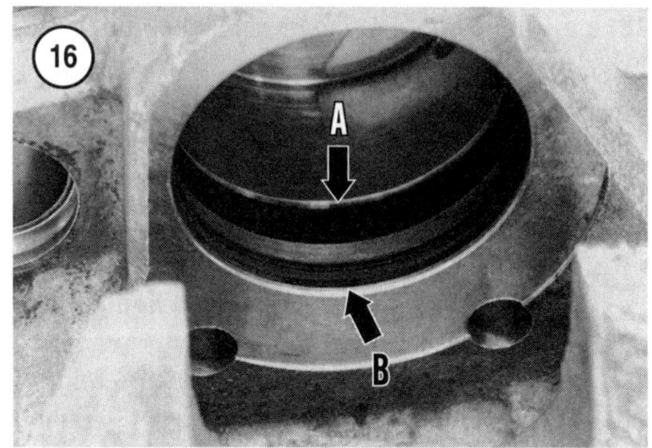

9. Remove the dust seal and piston seal (**Figure 13**).

10. Inspect the caliper assembly.

   a. Clean all parts that will be reused with fresh brake fluid or isopropyl (rubbing) alcohol. Use a wood or plastic-tipped tool to clean the seal and boot grooves.
   b. Inspect the caliper bore for wear, pitting or corrosion.
   c. Measure the inside diameter of the caliper bore (**Figure 14**). Refer to **Table 1** for specifications.
   d. Inspect the pad pins, pad spring and mounting bolts (**Figure 4**). The pins and spring must be in good condition to allow the inner pad to slightly move when installed. Check that both small tabs on the spring are not corroded or missing.
   e. Inspect the caliper slide pin and bracket slide pin for wear, pitting or corrosion.
   f. Inspect the boots for deterioration.
   g. Inspect the bleeder valve for clogging and damage.
   h. Inspect the brake pads as described in this section.

11. Install the new piston seal (A, **Figure 15**) and dust seal (B) as follows:

   a. Soak the seals in brake fluid for 15 minutes.
   b. Coat the caliper bore and piston with brake fluid.
   c. Seat the piston seal (A, **Figure 16**), then the dust seal (B) in the caliper grooves. The piston seal goes in the back groove.
   d. Install the piston, with the open side facing out (A, **Figure 17**). Twist the piston past the seals, then press the piston to the bottom of the bore.

12. Install the boots and caliper bracket pin as follows:
   a. Install the slide pin to the bracket and tighten to 18 N•m (13 ft.-lb.).
   b. Apply silicone brake grease to the interior of the boots and to the bracket slide pin.
   c. Install the slide pin boot onto the caliper (B, **Figure 17**). If necessary, apply a light coat of silicone brake grease on the exterior of the boot, to aid in passing it through the caliper.
   d. Pass the bracket pin through the caliper, then install the boot (C, **Figure 17**) over the end of the bolt.
13. Install the caliper to the bracket as follows:
   a. Lubricate the slide pin with silicone brake grease, then install it through the caliper.
   b. Apply a threadlock compound to the slide pin threads.
   c. Align the bracket with the slide pin. Place the washer over the pin, then tighten the pin (**Figure 18**).
   d. Tighten the caliper slide pin to 23 N•m (17 ft.-lb.) and install the rubber plug.
14. Install the bleeder valve and cap. Tighten to the specification in **Table 2**.
15. Install the pad spring with the small tabs pointing out (**Figure 19**).
16. Install the inner pad and shim, seating the pad under the caliper bracket and against the piston.
17. Install the outer pad.
18. Press down on the pads, then align and install the pad pins (**Figure 8**). Tighten the pins to 18 N•m (13 ft.-lb.).
19. Spread the pads so there is clearance to fit the caliper over the brake disc (**Figure 20**).
20. Install the caliper as described in this section.

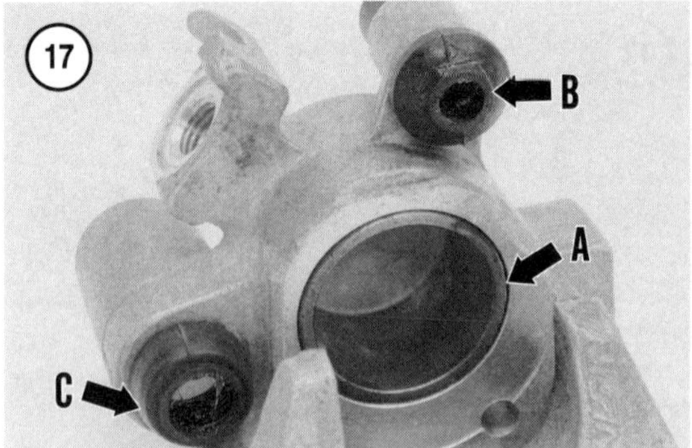

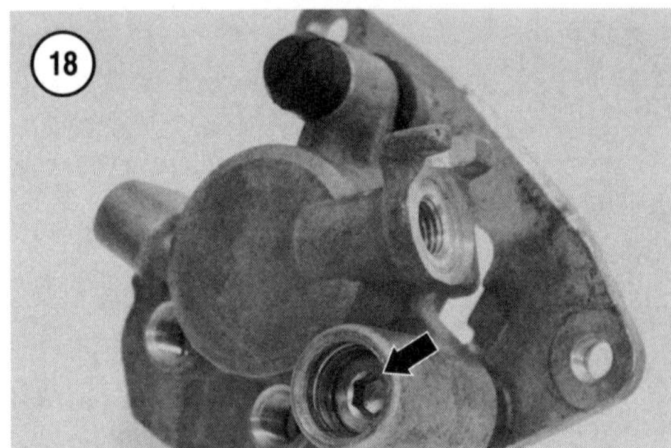

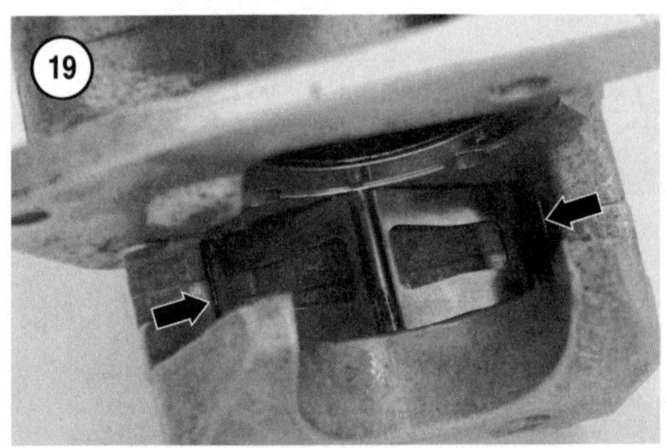

FRONT MASTER CYLINDER

Removal/Installation

1. Cover the bodywork and area surrounding the master cylinder.
2. Drain the brake system as described in this chapter.
3. Remove the cap and diaphragm and verify that the master cylinder is empty (**Figure 21**). Wipe the interior of the reservoir to absorb all remaining fluid.
4. Remove the brake light switch connector. Pull the connector (A, **Figure 22**) from the switch (B).
5. If the master cylinder will be rebuilt, remove the brake lever pivot bolt (**Figure 23**) while the master cylinder is still bolted to the handlebar and remains stable.
6. Remove the brake hose banjo bolt (C, **Figure 22**) from the master cylinder as follows:
   a. Remove the banjo bolt and seal washers from the brake hose. Have a shop cloth ready to absorb excess brake fluid that drips from the hose.

20

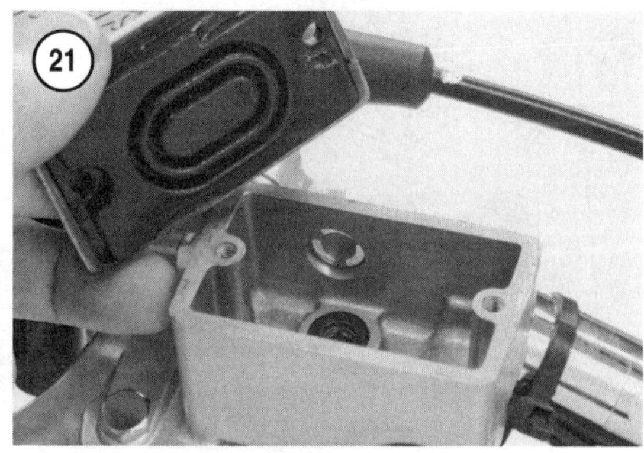
21

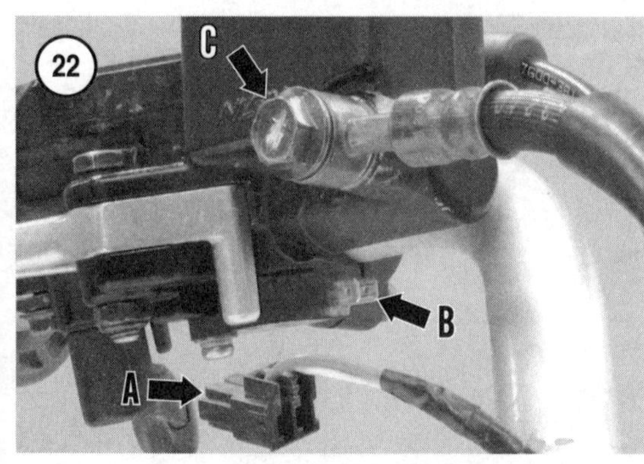

22

23

24

b. Wrap the hose end to prevent brake fluid from damaging other surfaces.

7. Remove the bolts (**Figure 24**) securing the master cylinder to the handlebar, then remove the master cylinder.

8. Repair the master cylinder as described in this section.

9. Reverse this procedure to install the master cylinder. Note the following:

a. Check that the indentations on the handlebar collar are engaged with the throttle assembly and master cylinder.

b. Install the mounting bracket so UP and the arrow are facing up. Tighten the upper bolt first, then the bottom bolt. Tighten the bolts (**Figure 24**) to 10 N•m (89 in.-lb.).

c. Position the brake hose fitting so it is slightly angled downward, keeping the hose straight.

d. Install new seal washers on the banjo bolt. Tighten the bolt to 23 N•m (17 ft.-lb.).

e. Check that the brake light operates when operating the lever.

10. Fill the brake fluid reservoir and bleed the brake system as described in this chapter.

Repair

The piston, seals and spring are only available as a complete assembly. Refer to **Figure 25**.

1. Remove the master cylinder as described in this section.

2. Remove the boot from the piston. The boot is a friction fit. To avoid damaging the boot on removal, apply penetrating lubricant around the perimeter of the boot. Carefully pull the bottom edge back so the lubricant can loosen the boot.

3. Remove the snap ring (**Figure 26**) from the master cylinder as follows:

25

FRONT MASTER CYLINDER

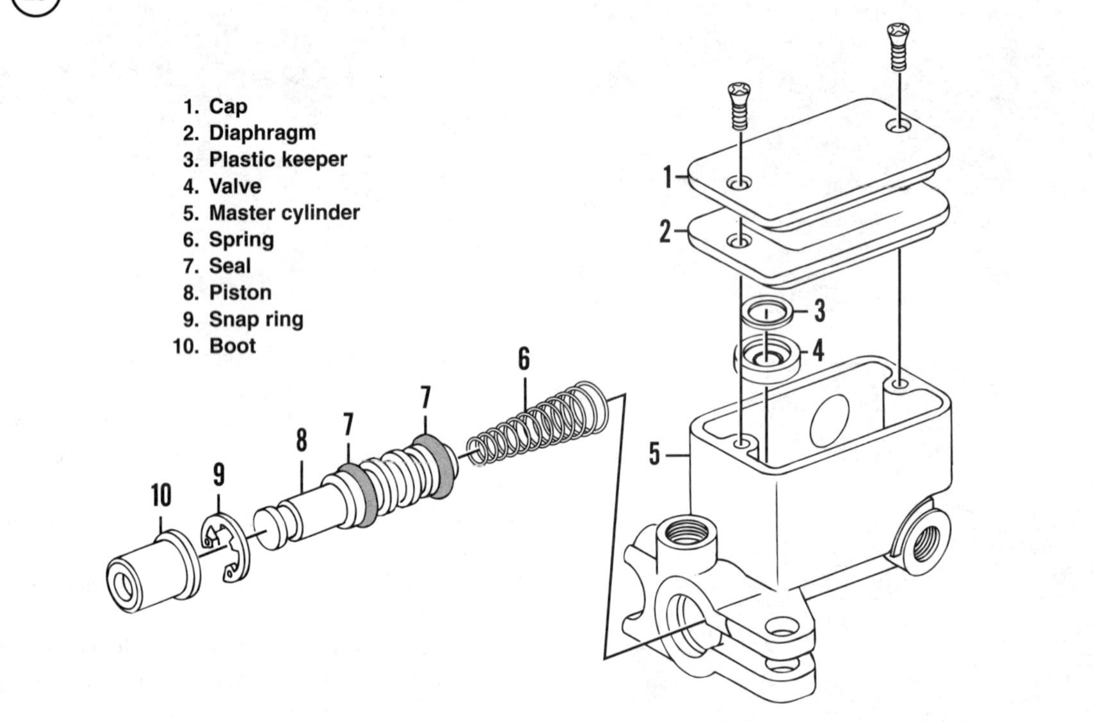

1. Cap
2. Diaphragm
3. Plastic keeper
4. Valve
5. Master cylinder
6. Spring
7. Seal
8. Piston
9. Snap ring
10. Boot

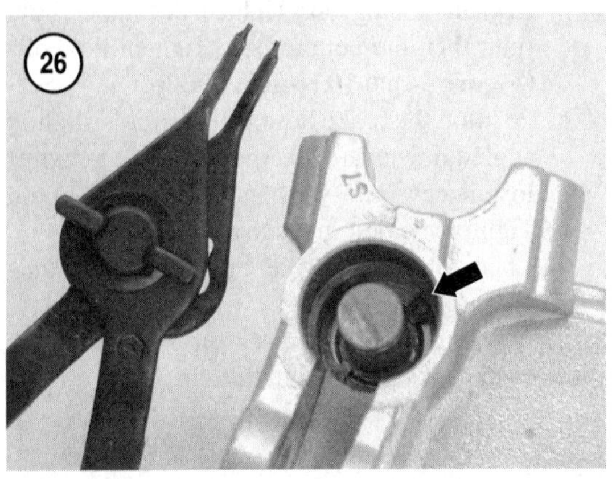

26

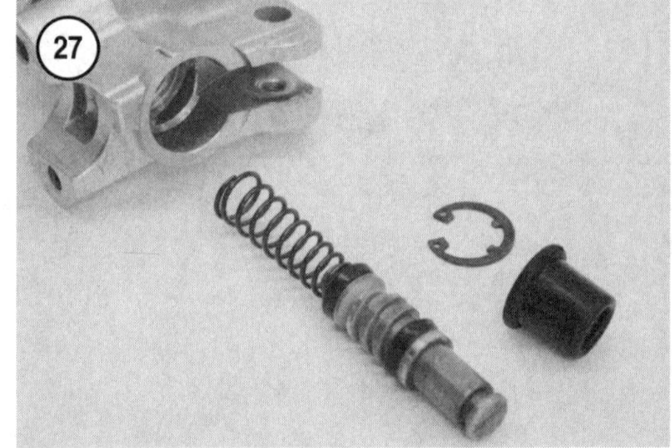

27

a. Press down on the piston to relieve pressure on the snap ring, then remove the snap ring.

b. Slowly relieve the pressure on the piston.

4. Remove the piston assembly from the bore (**Figure 27**).

5. Remove the valve from the bottom of the reservoir (**Figure 28**).

6. Inspect the master cylinder assembly.

a. Clean all parts that will be reused with fresh brake fluid or isopropyl (rubbing) alcohol.

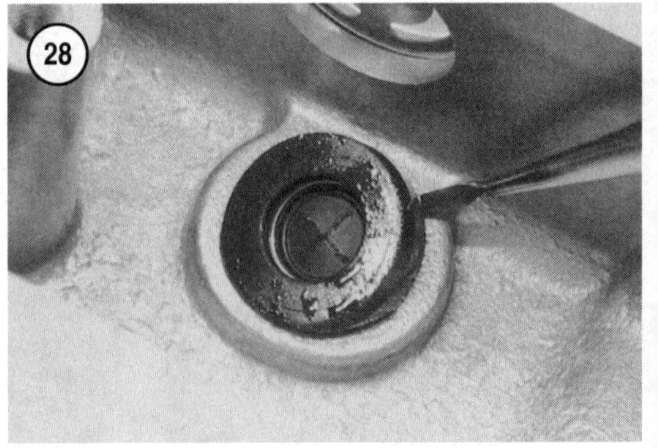

28

29

30

31

32

33

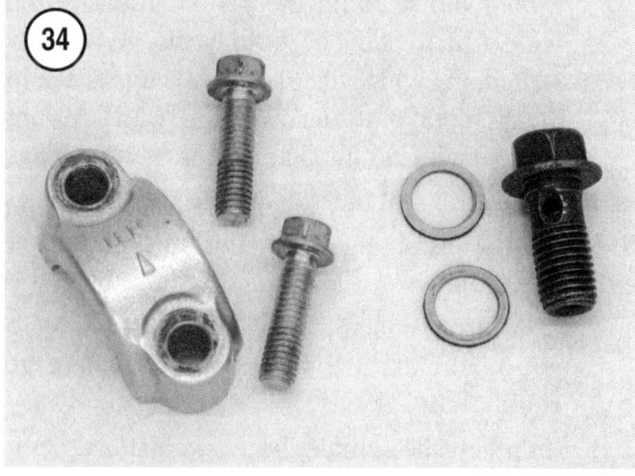
34

b. Inspect the cylinder bore for wear, pitting or corrosion.

c. Measure the inside diameter of the cylinder bore (**Figure 29**). Refer to **Table 1** for specifications.

d. Inspect and clean the threads and recessed passages in the reservoir (**Figure 30**). Clean with compressed air.

e. Inspect the brake lever bore and pivot bolt for wear (**Figure 31**).

f. Inspect the valve for cleanliness (**Figure 32**).

g. Inspect the diaphragm and reservoir cap for damage (**Figure 33**).

h. Inspect the mounting hardware and banjo bolt (**Figure 34**) for corrosion and damage. Install new seal washers on the banjo bolt.

7. Assemble the piston, seals and spring (**Figure 35**) as follows:

a. Soak the seals in fresh brake fluid for 15 minutes. This softens and lubricates the seals.

b. Apply brake fluid to the piston so the seals can slide over the ends.

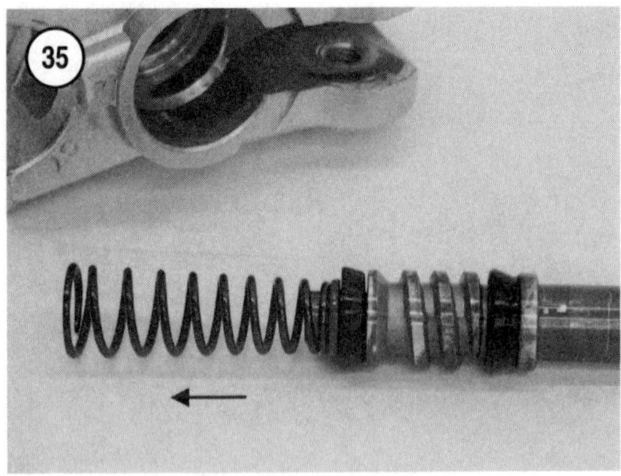

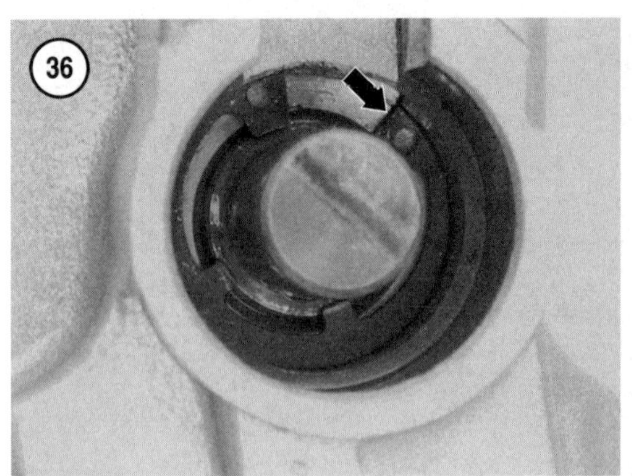

c. Mount the seals on the piston. Identify the wide (open) side of both seals. When installed, the wide side of the seals must face in the direction of the arrow (**Figure 35**). Mount the seal with the small hole nearest the spring.

d. Install and seat the spring onto the piston.

8. Install the piston and snap ring into the master cylinder as follows:

a. Lock the cylinder in a vise with soft jaws. Do not overtighten the vise or cylinder damage could occur.

b. Lubricate the cylinder bore and piston assembly with brake fluid.

c. Rest the piston assembly in the cylinder.

d. Place the snap ring over the end of the piston, resting it on the edge of the bore. The flat side of the snap ring must face out.

e. Place a screwdriver over the end of the piston and compress the snap ring with snap ring pliers.

f. Press the piston into the cylinder while guiding the snap ring into position. If the snap ring does not easily seat, release the snap ring and use the tip of the pliers to press it into the groove. Keep the screwdriver in position until the snap ring (**Figure 36**) is seated.

9. Apply silicone brake grease to the inside of the boot. Seat the boot into the cylinder.

10. Install the lever and pivot bolt. Apply waterproof grease to the pivot bolt (A, **Figure 37**) and lever contact point (B).

11. Install the valve in the bottom of the reservoir. Install the valve with the concave side down.

12. Loosely screw the diaphragm and cap onto the reservoir.

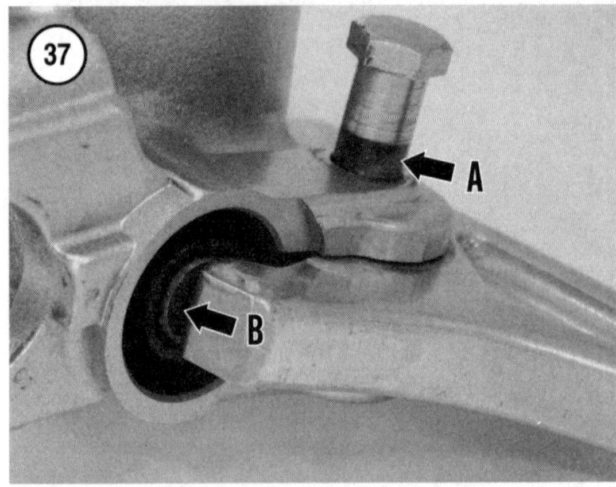

13. Install the master cylinder as described in this section.

REAR BRAKE PADS

Removal/Installation

Refer to **Figure 38**.

1. Bend the tabs (**Figure 39**) on the lockwasher away from the pad pins, then loosen the pad pins.
2. Remove the caliper mounting bolts (**Figure 40**). Avoid kinking the brake hose.
3. Press down on the pads to relieve the pressure on the pad pins, then remove the pins (**Figure 41**).
4. Remove the pads.

CAUTION

In the following step, monitor the level of fluid in the master cylinder reservoir. Brake fluid will back flow to the reservoir when the caliper piston is pressed into the bore. Do not allow brake fluid to spill from the reservoir,

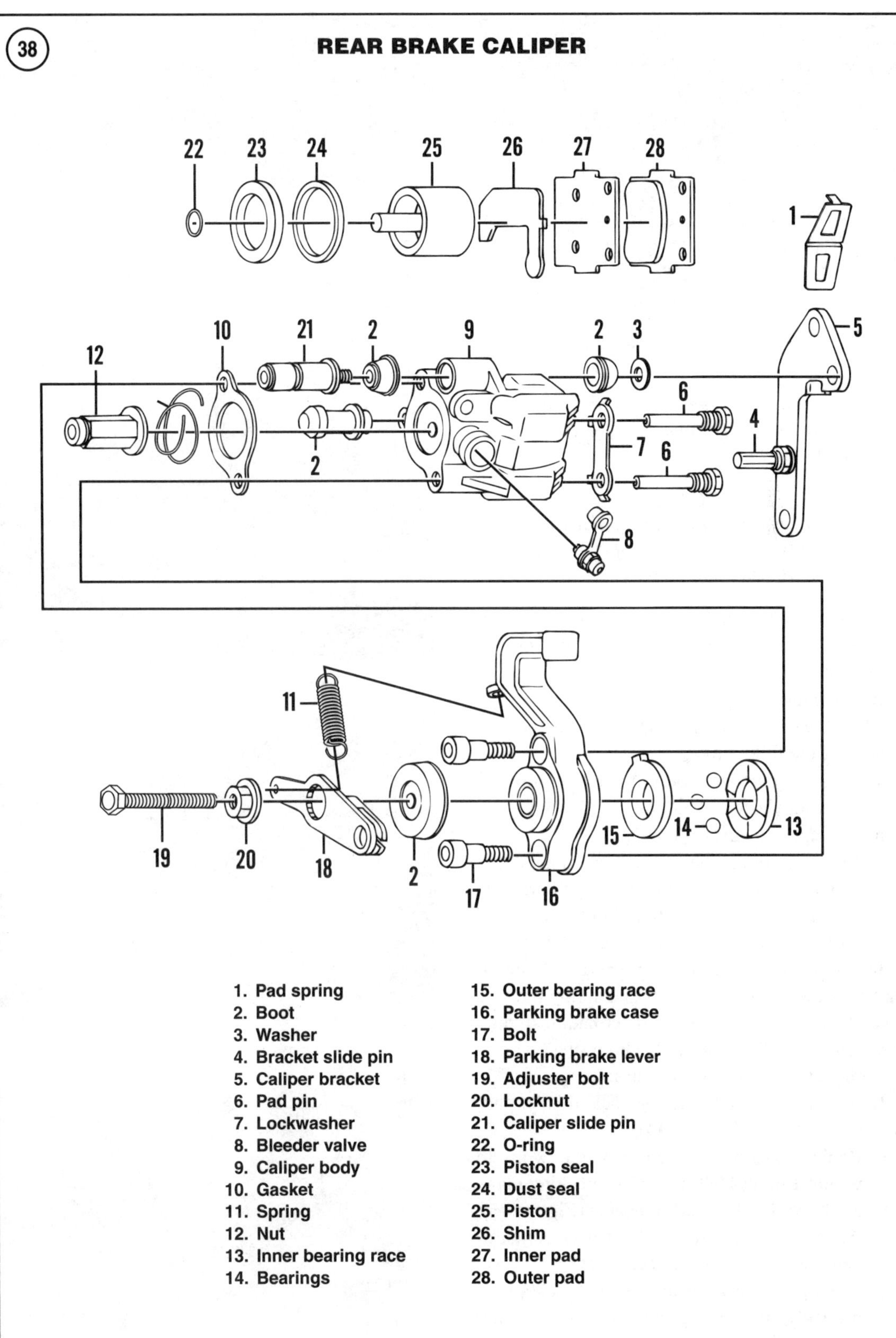

38

REAR BRAKE CALIPER

1. Pad spring
2. Boot
3. Washer
4. Bracket slide pin
5. Caliper bracket
6. Pad pin
7. Lockwasher
8. Bleeder valve
9. Caliper body
10. Gasket
11. Spring
12. Nut
13. Inner bearing race
14. Bearings
15. Outer bearing race
16. Parking brake case
17. Bolt
18. Parking brake lever
19. Adjuster bolt
20. Locknut
21. Caliper slide pin
22. O-ring
23. Piston seal
24. Dust seal
25. Piston
26. Shim
27. Inner pad
28. Outer pad

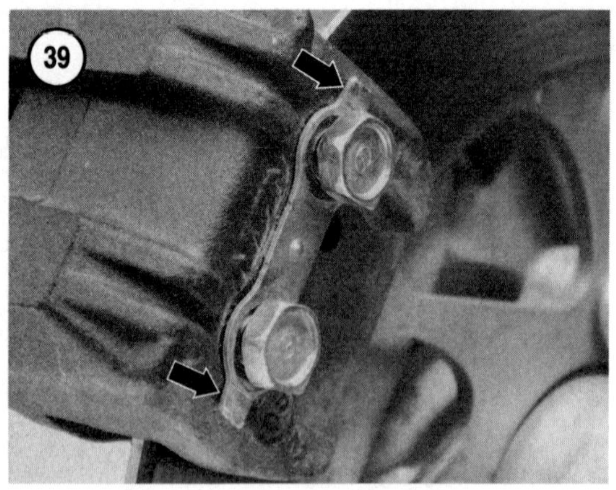

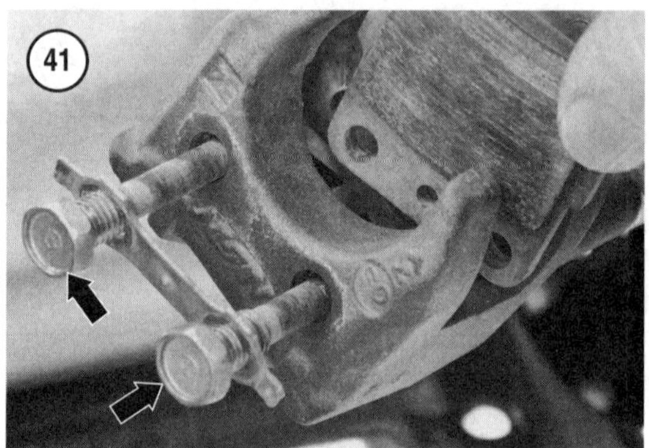

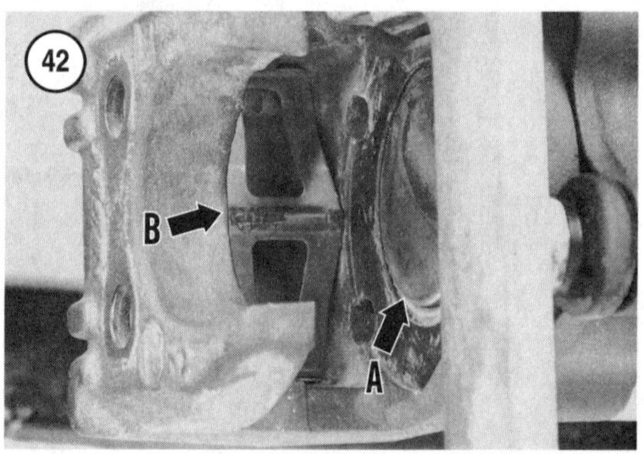

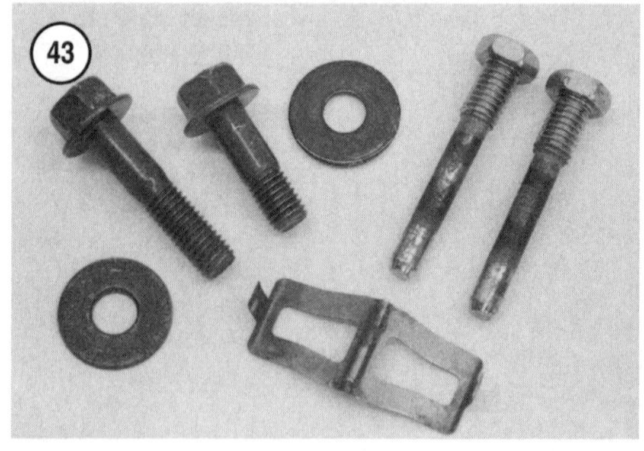

or damage can occur to painted and plastic surfaces. Immediately clean up any spills.

NOTE

Do not operate the brake pedal with the pads removed. The caliper piston can come out of the bore.

5. Grasp the caliper and press the caliper piston (A, **Figure 42**) down into the bore, creating room for the new pads.
6. Remove the pad spring (B, **Figure 42**).
7. Clean the interior of the caliper with alcohol and inspect for the following:
   a. Leaks or damage around the piston, bleeder valve and hose connection.
   b. Damaged or missing boots.
   c. Excessive drag when the caliper is moved in and out on the slide pins. If there is corrosion or water around the rubber boots, clean and lubricate the parts with silicone brake grease.
8. Inspect the pad pins, and pad spring and mounting bolts (**Figure 43**). The pins and spring must be in good condition to allow the inner pad to slightly move when installed. Check that both small tabs on the spring are not corroded or missing.
9. Inspect the pads and shim (on back of inner pad) for wear or damage (**Figure 44**).
   a. Replace the pads when they are worn to within 1 mm (0.040 in.) of the backing plate, as shown by the wear indicator (**Figure 45**). Always replace pads that have been contaminated with oil or other chemicals.
   b. If the pads are worn unevenly, the caliper is probably not sliding correctly. The caliper must be free to float on the caliper slide pin

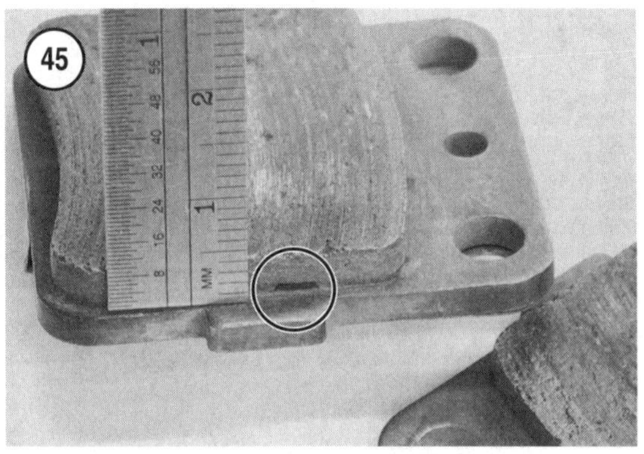

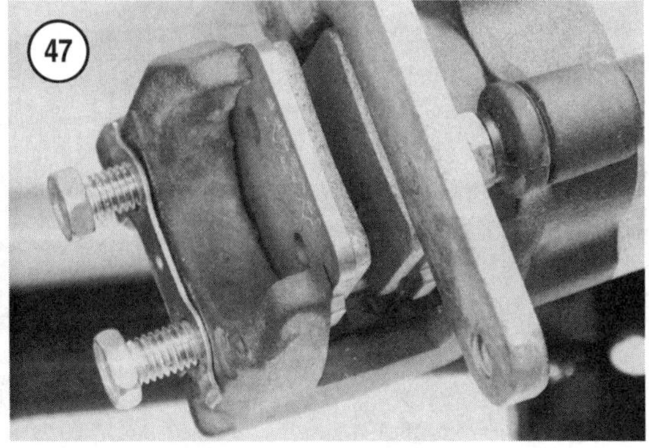

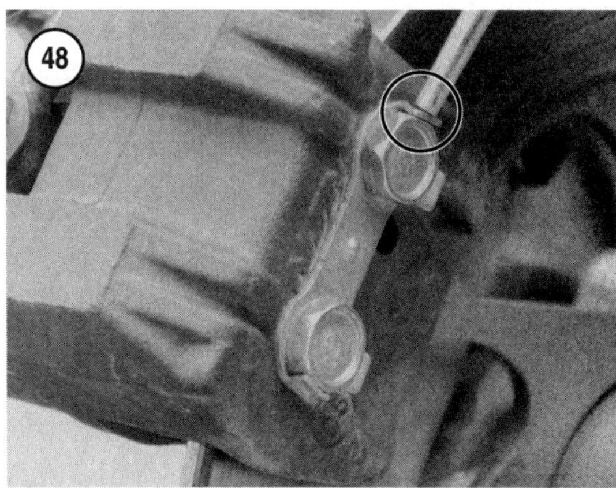

and bracket slide pin. Buildup or corrosion on the parts can hold the caliper in one position, causing brake drag and excessive pad wear.

10. Install the pad spring with the small tabs pointing out.
11. Install the inner pad and shim (**Figure 46**), seating the pad under the caliper bracket and against the piston.
12. Install the outer pad.
13. Press down on the pads, then align and install the pad pins and the *new* lockwasher. Do not fully tighten the pad pins until the caliper is installed.
14. Spread the pads so there is clearance to fit the caliper over the brake disc (**Figure 47**).
15. Position the caliper over the brake disc, then install and tighten the caliper mounting bolts to 26 N•m (19 ft.-lb.).
16. Tighten the pad pins to 18 N•m (13 ft.-lb.).
17. Bend the lockwasher tabs (**Figure 48**) against the mounting bolts.
18. Operate the brake lever several times to seat the pads.
19. Check the brake fluid reservoir and replenish or remove fluid as necessary.
20. With the rear axle raised, check that the axle spins freely and the brake operates properly.

REAR BRAKE CALIPER

Removal/Installation

1. If the caliper will be disassembled, do the following:
   a. Drain the system as described in this chapter. After draining, loosen the brake hose banjo bolt (A, **Figure 49**) while the caliper is

mounted. Leave the bolt finger-tight. It will be removed in a later step.

b. At the handlebar, loosen the locknut (A, **Figure 50**) and turn the cable adjuster (B) until there is enough slack in the cable to remove it from the parking brake lever (B, **Figure 49**).

2. Remove the caliper mounting bolts (C, **Figure 49**). Remove the caliper from the disc. Avoid kinking the brake hose.

3A. If the caliper will be left attached to the brake hose, but not disassembled and serviced, do the following:

a. Suspend the caliper with a length of wire. Do not let the caliper hang by the brake hose.

b. Insert a small wooden block between the brake pads. This prevents the caliper piston from extending out of the caliper if the brake lever is operated.

3B. If the caliper will be disassembled, do the following:

a. Remove the banjo bolt and seal washers from the brake hose. Have a shop cloth ready to absorb excess brake fluid that drips from the hose.

b. Wrap the hose end to prevent the brake fluid from damaging other surfaces.

c. Drain excess brake fluid from the caliper.

d. Repair the caliper as described in this section.

4. Reverse this procedure to install the caliper. Note the following:

a. Install and tighten the caliper mounting bolts to 26 N•m (19 ft.-lb.).

b. If removed, install the new seal washers on the banjo bolt. Seat the brake hose against the guide on the caliper (**Figure 51**), then tighten the banjo bolt to 23 N•m (17 ft.-lb.).

c. If the caliper was rebuilt, or the brake hose was disconnected from the caliper, fill and bleed the brake system as described in this chapter.

5. Operate the brake lever several times to seat the pads.

6. Check the brake fluid reservoir and replenish or remove fluid as necessary.

7. If necessary, adjust the parking brake (Chapter Three).

8. With the rear wheels raised, check that the disc spins freely and the brakes operate properly.

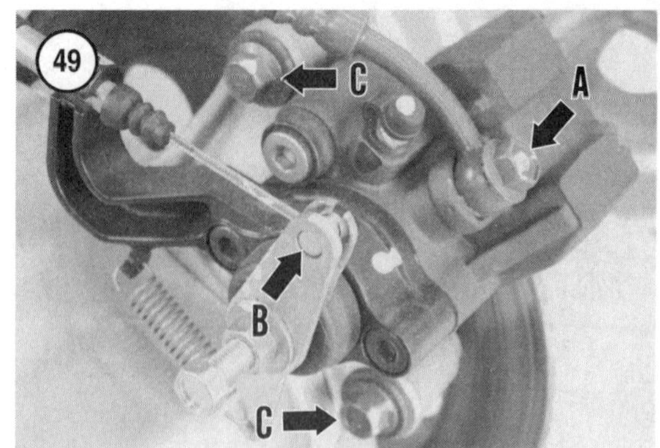

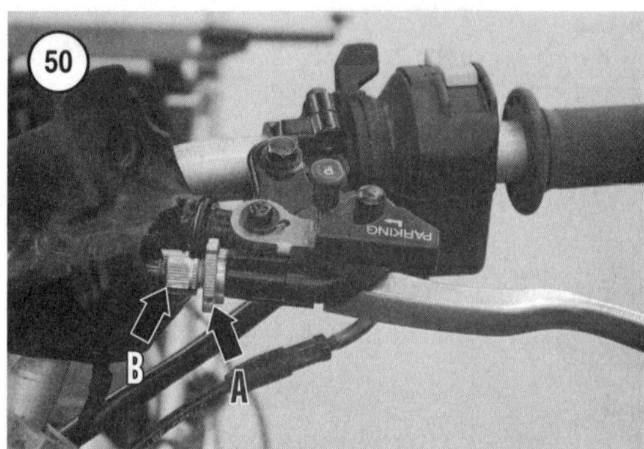

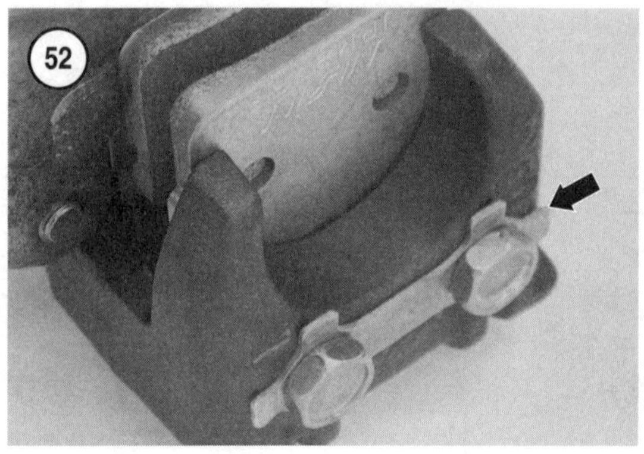

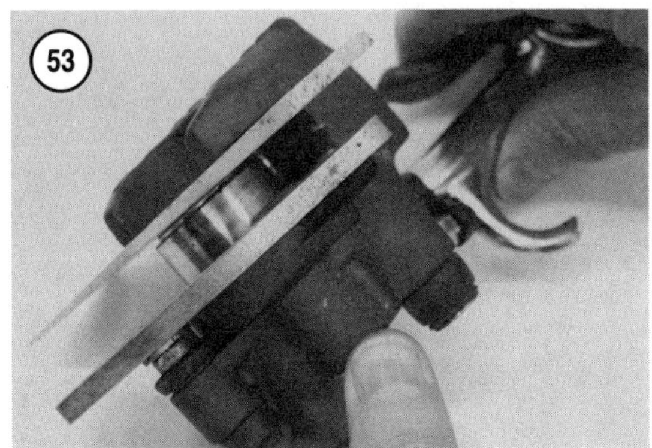

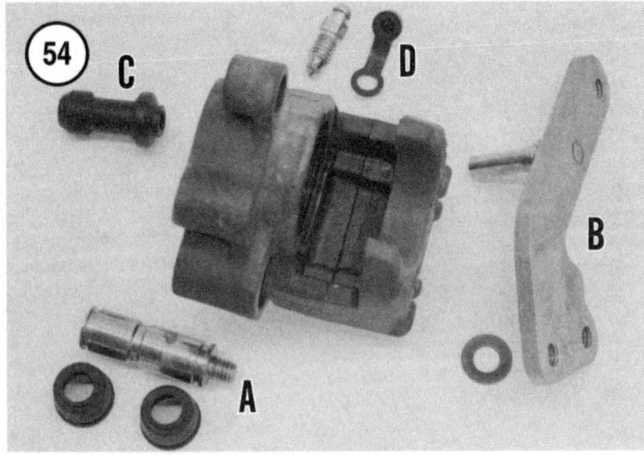

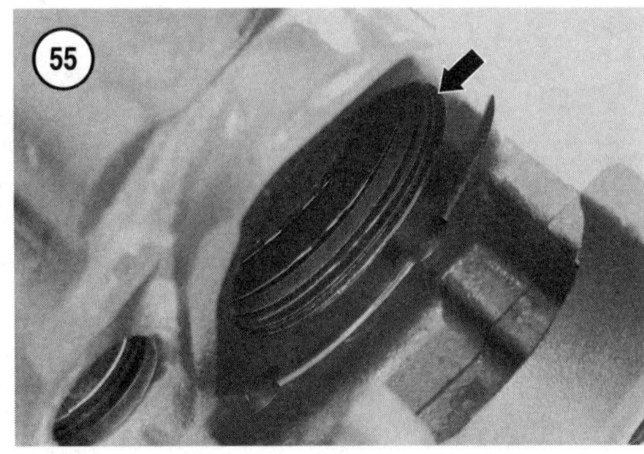

Repair

1. Remove the caliper as described in this section.

2. Remove the two bolts securing the parking brake assembly to the caliper.

3. Bend the tabs on the lockwasher (**Figure 52**) away from the pad pins, then loosen the pins.

4. Press down on the pads to relieve the pressure on the pad pins, then remove the pins.

5. Remove the pad pins and spring.

WARNING
Wear eye protection when using compressed air to remove the piston. Keep fingers away when removing the piston and keep fingers away from the piston discharge area. Injury can occur if an attempt is made to stop the piston by hand.

6. Remove the piston from the caliper bore using compressed air (**Figure 53**). To perform this technique, an air nozzle is tightly held in the brake hose fitting and air pressure ejects the piston. Do not attempt to pry the piston out of the caliper. Remove the piston from the caliper as follows:
   a. Place the caliper on a padded work surface.
   b. Close the bleeder valve on the caliper so air cannot escape.
   c. Place a strip of wood, or similar pad, in the caliper. The pad will cushion the piston when it comes out of the caliper.
   d. Lay the caliper so the pistons will discharge downward.
   e. Insert an air nozzle into the brake hose fitting. If the nozzle does not have a rubber tip, wrap the nozzle tightly with tape to seal it and prevent thread damage.
   f. Place a shop cloth over the entire caliper to catch any discharge from the caliper.
   g. Apply pressure and listen for the piston to pop from the caliper.

7. Remove the caliper slide pin and boots (A, **Figure 54**). Carefully remove the pin to prevent tearing or pinching the boots.

8. Remove the caliper bracket and washer (B, **Figure 54**).

9. Remove the slide pin boot (C, **Figure 54**).

10. Remove the bleeder valve and cap (D, **Figure 54**).

11. Remove the dust seal and the piston seal (**Figure 55**).

12. Remove the O-ring from the back side of the piston bore (**Figure 56**).

13. Inspect the caliper assembly.
   a. Clean all the parts that will be reused with fresh brake fluid or isopropyl (rubbing) alcohol. Use a wood or plastic-tipped tool to clean the seal and boot grooves.
   b. Inspect the caliper bore for wear, pitting or corrosion.

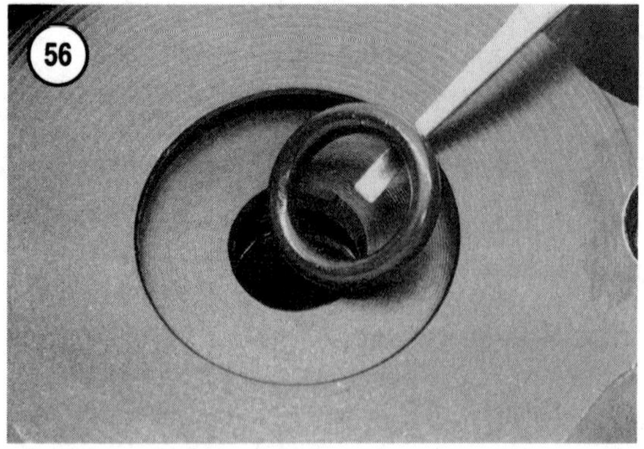

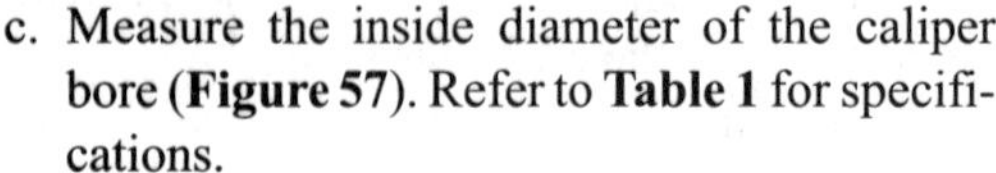

c. Measure the inside diameter of the caliper bore (**Figure 57**). Refer to **Table 1** for specifications.
d. Inspect the pad pins, pad spring and mounting bolts (**Figure 43**). The pins and spring must be in good condition to allow the inner pad to slightly move when installed. Check that both small tabs on the springs are not corroded or missing.
e. Inspect the caliper slide pin and the bracket slide pin for wear, pitting or corrosion.
f. Inspect the boots for deterioration.
g. Inspect the bleeder valve for clogging and damage.
h. Inspect the brake pads as described in this section.

14. Install a new O-ring into the back side of the piston bore (**Figure 56**).
15. Install the new piston seal (A, **Figure 58**) and dust seal (B) as follows:
    a. Soak the seals in brake fluid for 15 minutes.
    b. Coat the caliper bore and piston with brake fluid.
    c. Seat the piston seal, then the dust seal in the caliper grooves. The piston seal goes in the back groove.
    d. Install the piston with the flat side facing out. Twist the piston past the seals, then press the piston to the bottom of the bore.
16. Install the bracket slide pin and boot as follows:
    a. Install the slide pin to the bracket and tighten to 18 N•m (13 ft.-lb.).
    b. Apply silicone brake grease to the interior of the boots and to the bracket slide pin.
    c. Seat the slide pin boot in the caliper grooves and pass the slide pin through its bore. If necessary, apply a light coat of grease on the exterior of the boot, to aid in passing it through the caliper.
    d. Carefully twist the bracket pin through the caliper, then install the boot over the end of the slide pin.
17. Install the caliper slide pin as follows:
    a. Lubricate the slide pin with silicone brake grease, then install it into the caliper.
    b. Apply a threadlock compound to the threads of the slide pin.

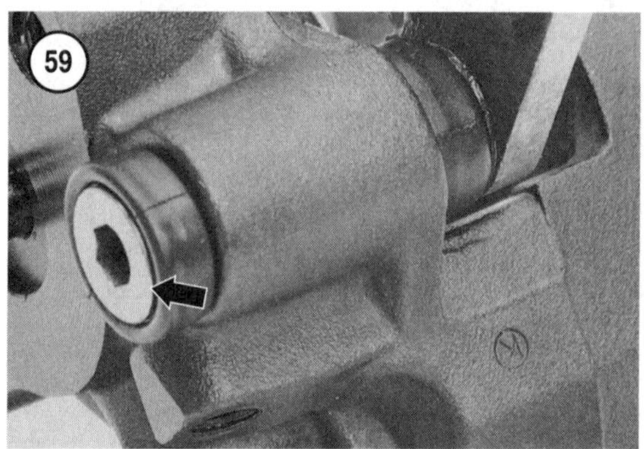

60

61

62

c. Align the bracket with the caliper slide pin. Place the washer over the pin, then tighten the pin (**Figure 59**).

d. Tighten the pin to 23 N•m (17 ft.-lb.).

18. Install the bleeder valve and cap. Tighten to the specification in **Table 2**.

19. Install the pad spring with the small tabs pointing out (**Figure 60**).

20. Install the inner pad and shim (**Figure 61**), seating the pad under the caliper bracket and against the piston.

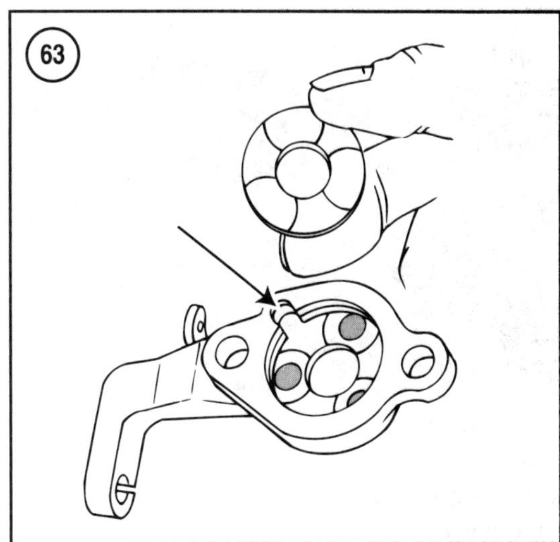
63

21. Install the outer pad.
22. Press down on the pads, then align and install the pad pins. Tighten the pins to 18 N•m (13 ft-lb.).
23. Bend the lockwasher tabs against the mounting bolts (**Figure 62**).
24. Assemble the parking brake assembly as shown in **Figure 38**.
    a. Apply waterproof grease to the balls and bearing races.
    b. Engage the tab on the outer race with the matching notch in the brake case (**Figure 63**).
    c. Apply threadlocking compound to the threads of the two mounting bolts.
    d. Tighten the parking brake bolt to 28 N•m (20.5 ft.-lb.).
25. Spread the pads so there is clearance to fit the caliper over the brake disc.
26. Install the caliper as described in this section.

13

REAR MASTER CYLINDER

Removal and Installation

1. Drain the brake system as described in this chapter.
2. Remove the right foot guard and frame as described in Chapter Fourteen.
3. Remove the cap and diaphragm and verify that the reservoir is empty. Wipe the interior of the reservoir dry, then remove the bolt (**Figure 64**) securing the reservoir to the frame.
4. Remove the banjo bolt and seal washers from the brake hose (A, **Figure 65**). Have a shop cloth ready

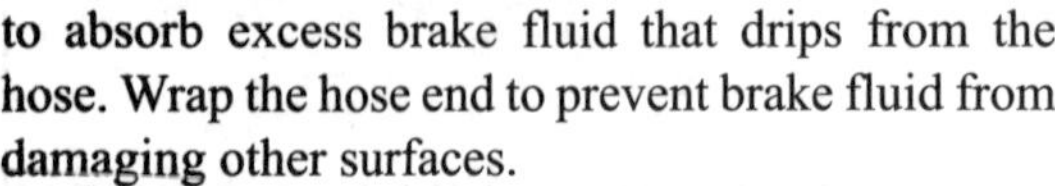

to absorb excess brake fluid that drips from the hose. Wrap the hose end to prevent brake fluid from damaging other surfaces.

5. Remove the cotter pin, washer and clevis pin (**Figure 66**) that secure the master cylinder clevis to the brake pedal.

6. Remove the master cylinder mounting bolts (B, **Figure 65**). Remove the snap ring (**Figure 67**) that retains the hose fitting against the master cylinder, then remove the fitting and internal O-ring (**Figure 68**).

7. Repair the master cylinder as described in this section.

8. Reverse this procedure to install the master cylinder and reservoir. Note the following:
   a. Tighten the master cylinder mounting bolts to 10 N•m (89 in.-lb.).
   b. Install new seal washers on the banjo bolt. Tighten the bolt to 23 N•m (17 ft.-lb.).
   c. Install a new cotter pin on the clevis pin.

9. Fill the brake fluid reservoir and bleed the brake system as described in this chapter.

Repair

Refer to **Figure 69**.

1. Remove the master cylinder and reservoir as described in this section.

2. Remove the snap ring from the master cylinder as follows:
   a. Unseat the boot from the cylinder bore and fold it toward the shaft (**Figure 70**). The boot is a friction fit. To avoid damaging the boot on removal, apply penetrating lubricant around the perimeter of the boot. Carefully pull the bottom edge back so the lubricant can loosen the boot.

69

REAR MASTER CYLINDER

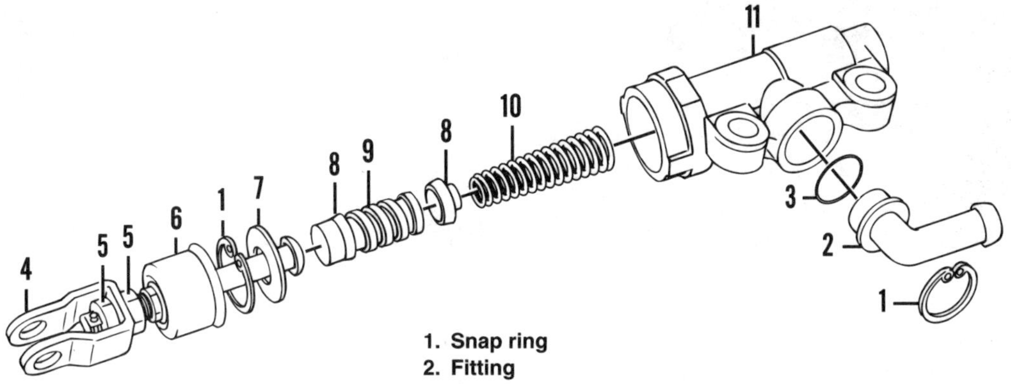

1. Snap ring
2. Fitting
3. O-ring
4. Clevis
5. Locknut
6. Boot
7. Washer
8. Seal
9. Piston
10. Spring
11. Master cylinder

b. If desired, lock the cylinder in a vise with soft jaws.

c. Press and tilt the pushrod to relieve pressure on the snap ring, then remove the snap ring (**Figure 71**) with snap ring pliers.

d. Slowly relieve the pressure on the piston.

3. Remove the piston (**Figure 72**) and pushrod assembly from the bore.

4. Inspect the master cylinder assembly.

a. Clean all parts that will be reused with fresh brake fluid or isopropyl (rubbing) alcohol.

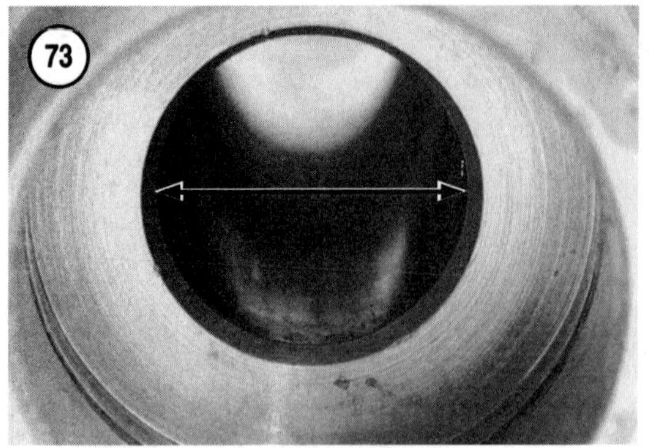

b. Inspect the cylinder bore for wear, pitting or corrosion.

c. Measure the inside diameter of the cylinder bore (**Figure 73**). Refer to **Table 1** for specifications.

d. Inspect and clean the threads and orifices in the master cylinder (**Figure 74**). Clean with compressed air.

e. Inspect the pushrod assembly (**Figure 75**). Check the parts for corrosion and wear. Install a new snap ring on the pushrod, with the sharp edge of the snap ring facing out. Remove/install the old/new snap ring by passing it around the washer as shown in **Figure 76**. Do not expand the new snap ring when installing it on the pushrod.

f. Inspect the clevis pin, banjo bolt and mounting hardware for wear or damage.

g. Inspect the reservoir, diaphragm, diaphragm holder and reservoir cap (**Figure 77**) for damage.

5. Assemble the piston, seals and spring as follows:

a. Soak the seals in fresh brake fluid for 15 minutes. This softens and lubricates the seals.

b. Apply brake fluid to the piston so the seals can slide over the ends.

c. Mount the seals on the piston. The loose seal must be installed on the top of the spring. Identify the wide (open) side of both seals. When installed, the wide side of the seals must face in the direction of the arrow (**Figure 78**).

d. Install and seat the spring onto the piston.

6. Install the piston and pushrod assembly into the master cylinder as follows:

a. Lubricate the cylinder bore and piston assembly with brake fluid.

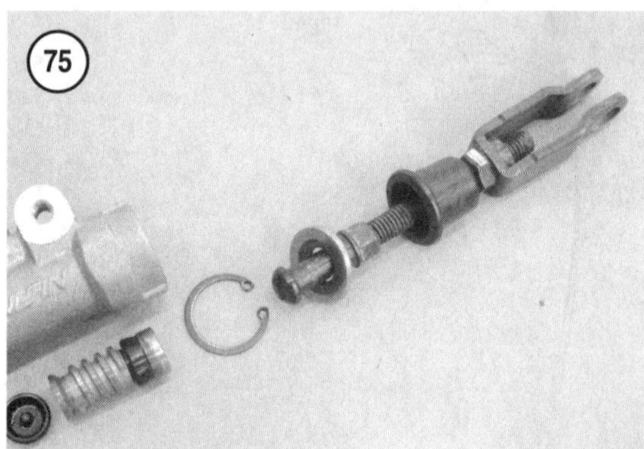

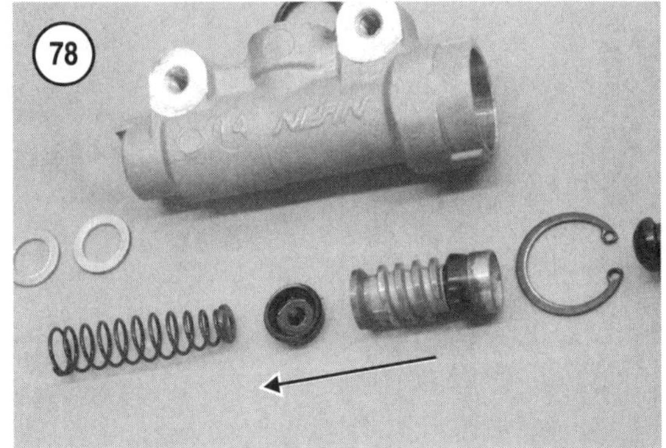

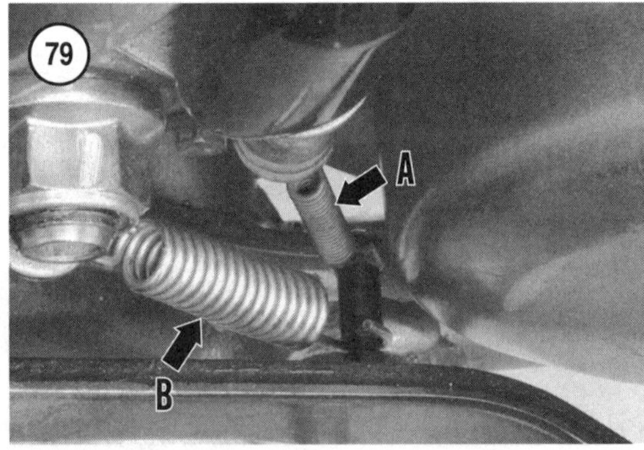

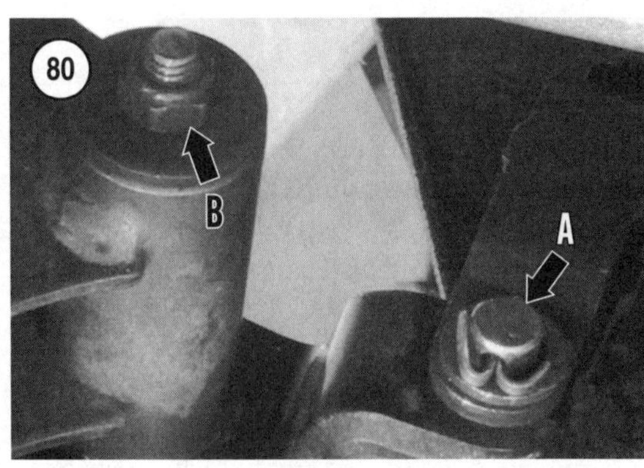

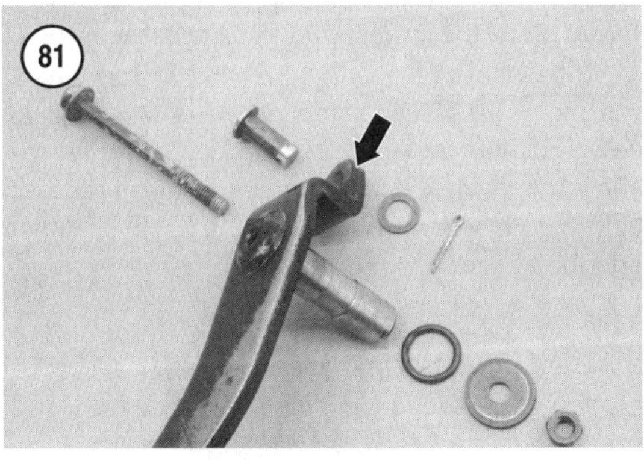

b. Apply a small amount of silicone brake grease to the contact area of the pushrod.
c. Insert the piston into the cylinder.
d. If desired, lock the cylinder in a vise with soft jaws. Do not overtighten the vise or cylinder damage could occur.
e. Compress the snap ring with snap ring pliers.
f. Press and tilt the pushrod in the cylinder while guiding the snap ring into position. If the snap ring does not easily seat, release the snap ring and use the tip of the pliers to press it into the groove. Keep the pushrod compressed until the snap ring is seated.

7. Apply silicone brake grease to the inside of the boot. Seat the boot into the cylinder (**Figure 70**).
8. Install a new, lubricated O-ring into the master cylinder (**Figure 68**), then lock the hose fitting into the O-ring. Install a new snap ring with the flat side facing out.
9. Attach the reservoir and hose to the fitting, then clamp into place.
10. Install the diaphragm, diaphragm holder and cap onto the reservoir.
11. Install the master cylinder as described in this section.

REAR BRAKE PEDAL

Removal and Installation

1. Remove the right footpeg assembly and frame (Chapter Fourteen).
2. Remove the following parts:
   a. Brake light switch spring (A, **Figure 79**).
   b. Pedal return spring (B, **Figure 79**).
   c. Master cylinder clevis pin, cotter pin and washer (A, **Figure 80**).
   d. Brake pedal pivot bolt (B, **Figure 80**).
3. Remove the pedal (**Figure 81**) from the bore.
4. Clean and inspect the parts for wear and damage.
5. Reverse this procedure to install the pedal. Note the following:
   a. Apply waterproof grease to the bore and pedal shaft.
   b. Put the O-ring (**Figure 82**) onto the base of the pivot shaft.
   c. Install a new cotter pin in the clevis pin.
   d. Check brake operation.
   e. Check pedal height. If necessary, adjust the pedal (Chapter Three).

f. Check brake light operation. If necessary, adjust the switch (Chapter Three).
g. If necessary, adjust the parking brake (Chapter Three).

BRAKE SYSTEM DRAINING

CAUTION
Brake fluid can damage painted and finished surfaces. Use water to immediately wash any surface that becomes contaminated with brake fluid.

NOTE
*Before disconnecting any brake hose(s) on the front brakes, remove the cap and diaphragm and verify that the master cylinder (**Figure 84** or **Figure 85**) is empty. Wipe the interior of the reservoir to absorb all remaining fluid.*

1. Attach one end of the tubing to the bleeder valve and place the other end into the container (**Figure 83**).
2. Open the bleeder valve so fluid can pass into the tubing.
3. Pump the brake lever/pedal to force the fluid from the system.
4. When the system no longer drips fluid, close the bleeder valve.
5. Dispose the brake fluid in an environmentally safe manner.

BRAKE SYSTEM BLEEDING

Whenever the brake fluid is replaced, or if the brake lever or pedal feels spongy, bleed the brake system. Check all brake components for leaks, and fittings and hoses for deterioration, damage or looseness. The brake system can be bled manually or by using a vacuum pump. Both methods are described in this section.

CAUTION
Brake fluid can damage painted and finished surfaces. Use water and immediately wash any surface that becomes contaminated with brake fluid.

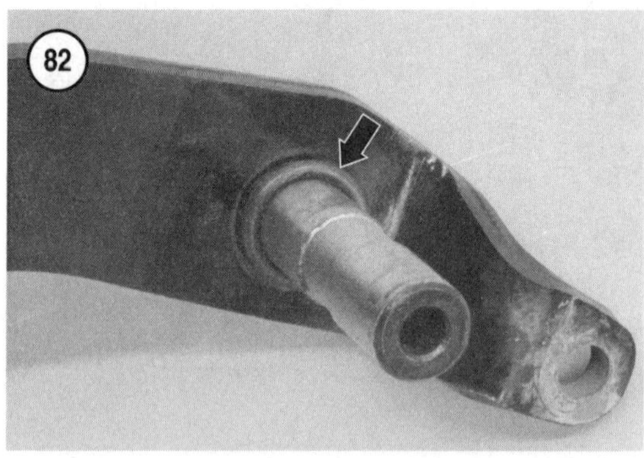

Manual Bleeding

An 8 mm wrench, tip-resistant container and a length of clear tubing that fits snugly on the brake bleeder are required to manually bleed the brake system.

1. Attach one end of the tubing to the bleeder valve and place the other end into the container (**Figure 83**).
2. Fill the reservoir to the upper level with DOT 4 brake fluid.
3. Apply pressure (do not pump) to the brake lever or pedal, then open the bleeder valve. As the fluid is forced from the system, the lever/pedal will travel its full length of operation. When the lever/pedal can move no farther, hold the lever/pedal in the down position and close the bleeder valve. Do not allow the lever or pedal to return to its up position before the bleeder valve is closed. Air will be drawn into the system.

CAUTION
In the following step, release the lever/pedal slowly. This minimizes the chance of fluid splashing out of the

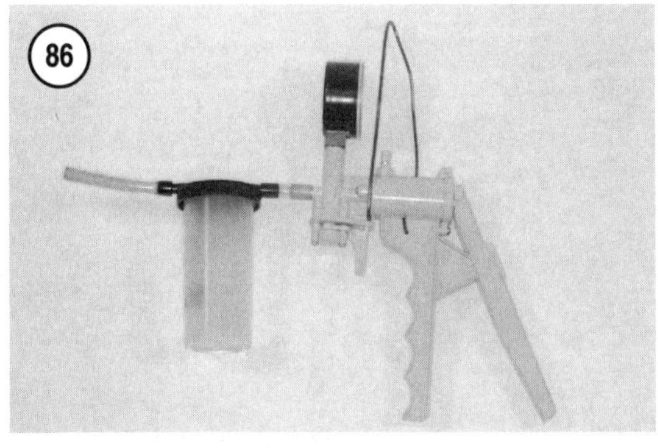

reservoir, as excess fluid in the brake line is returned to the reservoir.

4. When the bleeder valve is closed, release the lever/pedal so it returns to its up position. Check the fluid level in the reservoir and replenish, if necessary.

NOTE
The reservoir must contain fluid during the entire procedure. If the reservoir becomes empty, air will be in the system and the bleeding process will have to be repeated.

5. Repeat Step 3 and Step 4 until clear fluid (minimal air bubbles) is seen passing out of the bleeder valve. Unless the bleeder valve threads are wrapped with Teflon tape, or coated with silicone brake grease, a small amount of air will enter the system when the bleeder valve is opened.

NOTE
If small bubbles (foam) remain in the system after several bleeding attempts, close the reservoir and allow the system to stand undisturbed for a few hours. The system will stabilize and the air can be purged as large bubbles.

6. The bleeding procedure is completed when the feel of the lever/pedal is firm.
7. Check the brake fluid reservoir and fill the reservoir to the upper level, if necessary.
8. Tighten the bleeder valve to the specification in **Table 2**.
9. Dispose the waste brake fluid in an environmentally safe manner.

Vacuum Bleeding

An 8 mm wrench and a vacuum pump, such as the Mityvac pump shown in **Figure 86** are required to vacuum-bleed the brake system. Use the following procedure to bleed either the front or rear brake.

NOTE
The reservoir must contain fluid during the entire procedure. If the reservoir becomes empty, air will be in the system and the bleeding process will have to be repeated.

1. Make sure the banjo bolts are tight at the master cylinder and caliper.
2. Attach the vacuum pump to the bleeder valve. Suspend the tool with wire. This will allow the tool to be released when the fluid reservoir needs to be refilled.
3. Fill the reservoir to the upper level with DOT 4 brake fluid.
4. Pump the handle on the brake bleeder to create a vacuum.
5. Open the bleeder valve and draw the air and fluid from the system. Close the valve before the fluid stops moving. If the vacuum pump is equipped

with a gauge, close the bleeder before the gauge reads 0 in. Hg. Replenish the fluid level in the reservoir.

6. Repeat Step 4 and Step 5 until clear fluid (minimal air bubbles) is seen passing out of the bleeder. Unless the bleeder valve threads are wrapped with Teflon tape, or coated with silicone brake grease, a small amount of air will enter the system when the bleeder valve is opened. The bleeding procedure is completed when the feel of the lever/pedal is firm.

7. Check the brake fluid reservoir and fill the reservoir to the upper level, if necessary.

8. Tighten the bleeder valve to the specification in **Table 2**.

9. Dispose the waste brake fluid in an environmentally safe manner.

BRAKE DISC

The condition of the brake discs and pads are often a reflection of one another. If disc scoring is evident, inspect the pads and disc as soon as possible. If there is damage, perform the inspection described in this section.

Thickness and Runout Inspection

1. Measure the thickness of each disc at several locations around their perimeter (**Figure 87**). Refer to **Table 1** for the service limit. Replace the disc(s) if it is out of specification.

2. Measure disc runout as follows:

NOTE

If the disc runout is out of specification, check the condition of the hub bearings before replacing the disc. If the bearings are not in good condition, replace the bearings before determining disc runout.

a. Mount a dial indicator on a stable surface and in contact with the disc (**Figure 88**, typical).

b. Zero the gauge.

c. Turn the wheel and watch the amount of runout measured on the gauge.

d. Refer to **Table 1** for the service limit. Replace the disc if it is out of specification.

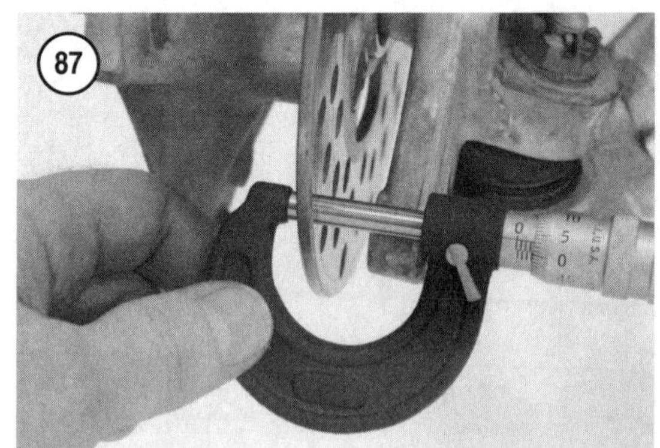

87

88

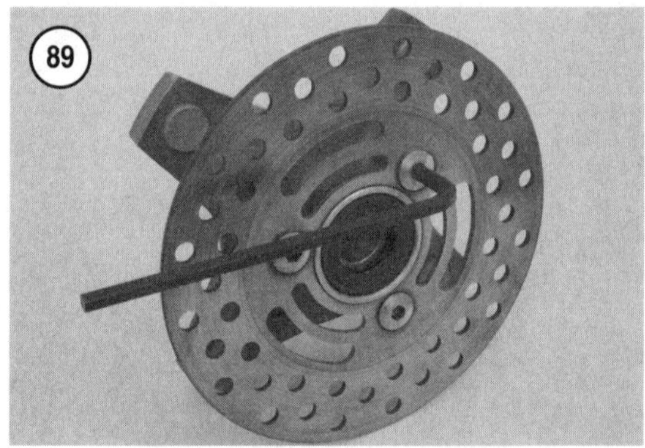

89

90

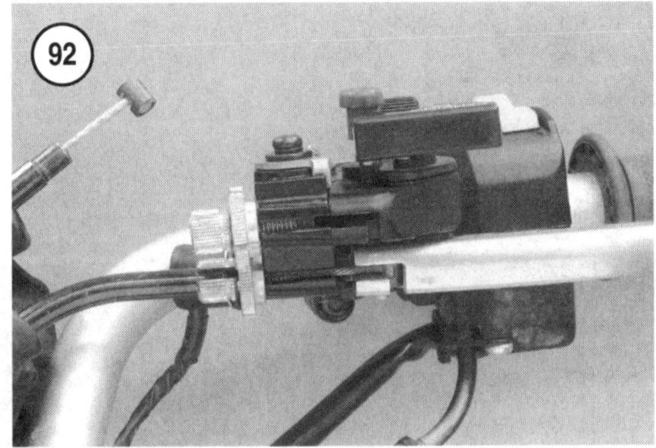

Front Brake Disc Removal and Installation

The discs are mounted to the hubs with bolts. Remove and install the discs as follows:

1. Remove the brake hub (Chapter Eleven).
2. Remove the bolts (**Figure 89**) that secure the disc to the hub.
3. Clean the bolts and mounting holes.
4. Reverse this procedure to install the discs. Note the following:
   a. Apply a threadlocking compound to the bolt threads.
   b. Tighten the bolts in several passes and in a crisscross pattern.
   c. Tighten the bolts to 23 N•m (17 ft.-lb.).

Rear Brake Disc Removal and Installation

Refer to Chapter Twelve.

PARKING BRAKE/CLUTCH LEVER

Disassembly/Assembly

1. Turn the adjusters (**Figure 90**) all the way in to provide slack in the cable and align the slots in the adjusters with the slots in the lever.
2. If the cables cannot be removed from the lever, adjust further slack by turning the barrel of the inline adjusters (**Figure 91**) for the parking brake and clutch cable.
3. Remove the cables from the lever (**Figure 92**).
4. Disconnect the clutch switch from the lever by depressing the tab in the bottom of the switch with a small screwdriver (**Figure 93**).
5. Remove the nut securing the parking brake mechanism on the bottom of the lever (**Figure 94**).
6. Remove the parking brake mechanism (**Figure 95**).
7. Remove the screw securing the plunger pin and the spring. Examine the parts for wear and apply a light lubricant before reassembly.
8. Remove the screw securing the parking brake catch lever (**Figure 96**).
9. Examine the parts for wear and apply a light lubricant before reassembly.
10. Reassemble in the reverse order.

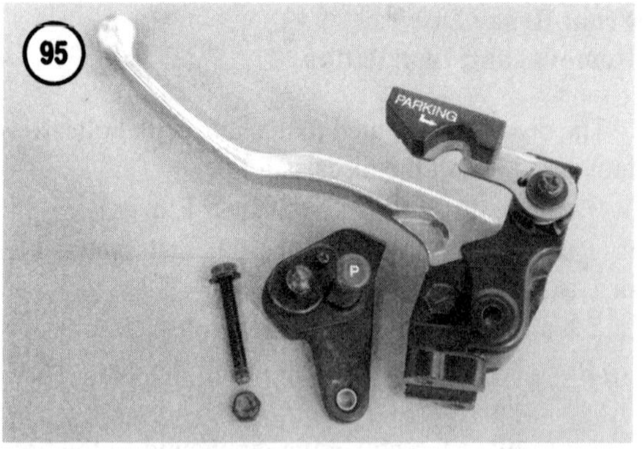

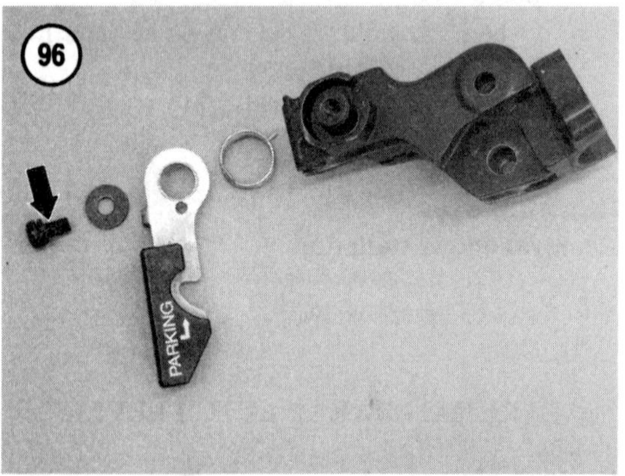

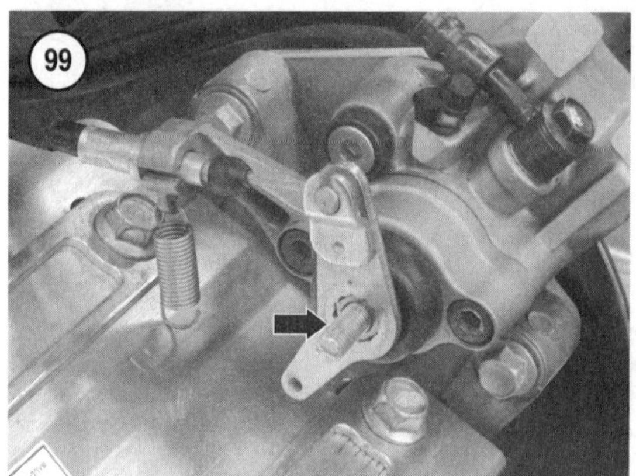

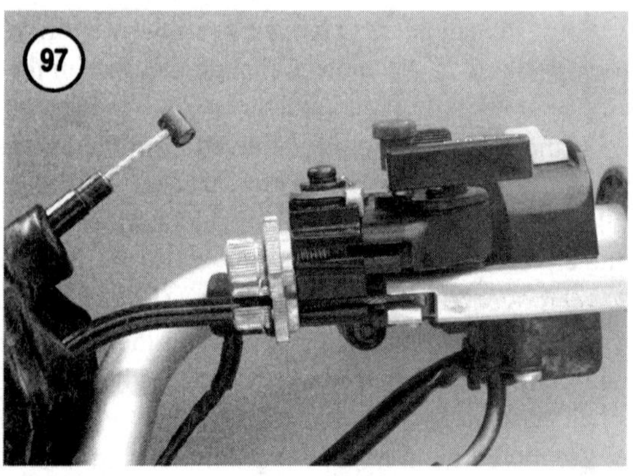

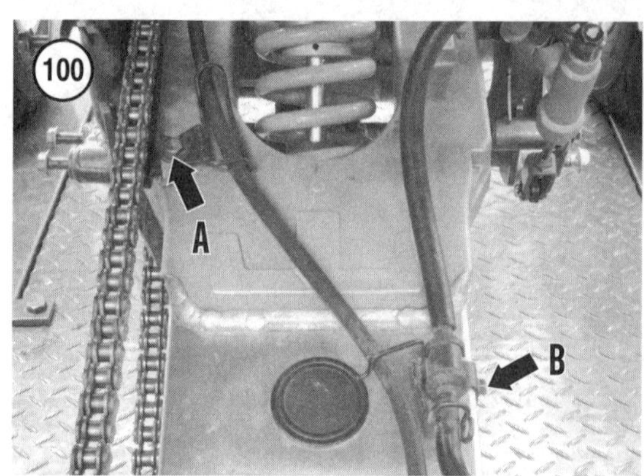

Parking Brake Cable Replacement

1. Turn the barrel adjuster for the parking brake cable all the way in and remove the parking brake cable from the parking brake/clutch lever assembly (**Figure 97**).

2. Remove the cable end from the parking brake lever on the rear brake caliper (**Figure 98**). If there is not enough slack in the cable to remove it from the bracket, remove the nut securing the lever to the caliper in order to remove the cable (**Figure 99**).

3. Remove the brake hose guide (A, **Figure 100**) and the parking brake cable guide (B).

4. Remove the cable while noting how it is routed through the frame.

5. Reassemble in the reverse order. If necessary, perform the *Parking Brake Cable Adjustment* as described in Chapter Three. Tighten the brake hose guide bolts as noted in **Table 2**.

Table 1 BRAKE SYSTEM SPECIFICATIONS

Item	New mm (in.)	Service limit mm (in.)
Rear brake pedal height	0-10 (0-0.4)	–
Brake caliper cylinder bore		
Front	32.03-32.08 (1.261-1.263)	–
Rear	33.96-34.01 (1.337-1.339)	–
Brake piston caliper diameter		
Front	31.948-31.998 (1.2578-1.2598)	–
Rear	33.878-33.928 (1.3338-1.3357)	–
Disc thickness		
Front	2.8-3.2 (0.11-0.13)	2.5 (0.10)
Rear	3.8-4.2 (0.15-0.17)	3.5 (0.138)
Disc brake runout	–	0.30 (0.012)
Master cylinder bore		
Front	12.70-12.743 (0.500-0.502)	–
Rear	14.00-14.043 (0.5512-0.5529)	–
Master cylinder piston diameter		
Front	12.657-12.684 (0.4983-0.4994)	–
Rear	13.957-13.984 (0.5495-0.5506)	–
Pad lining minimum thickness	–	1.0 (0.04)

Table 2 BRAKE SYSTEM TORQUE SPECIFICATIONS

Item	N•m	in.-lb.	ft.-lb.
Bracket slide pin	18	–	13
Brake bleed valve			
2003 models	7.5	66	–
2004-on models	6.0	53	–
Brake disc bolts*	23	–	17
Brake hose banjo bolt	23	–	17
Brake hose guide bolts			
6 mm	12	106	–
8 mm	29	–	21
Brake hose mounting bolt	23	–	17
Brake pipe	16	–	12
Caliper bleed valve	7.5	66	–
Caliper mounting bolts	26	–	19
Caliper pad pins	18	–	13
Caliper slide pin*	23	–	17
Master cylinder mounting bolts	10	89	–
Parking brake bolt	28	–	20.5

*Apply threadlocking compound.

CHAPTER FOURTEEN

BODY

RETAINING CLIPS

The body panels are held on with a system of interlocking tabs, plastic expanding clips, bolts and screws. In order to remove the plastic clips push in the center pin using a blunt punch or screwdriver, then lift the clip out around the edges. If the clip is difficult to remove, make sure the body panels are aligned and not binding on the clip.

If necessary, the clip can be loosened by inserting a thin, flat tool under the edge and carefully prying it out. The body panel plastic is soft and easily scratched. By using a plastic prying device such as a small plastic putty knife, scratching the bodywork can be minimized.

To reinsert the clips, push the center pin out so it sticks out from the surface of the clip. This allows the clip to be inserted into bodywork holes. Once in place, push the center pin in to expand the clip and hold the body panels in place.

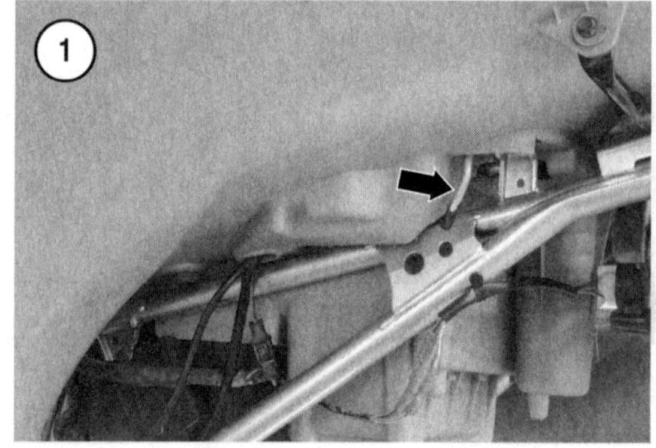

SEAT

Removal/Installation

1. Locate the seat latch under the left side of the rear fender (**Figure 1**).
2. Move the latch lever toward the rear of the vehicle to release the seat and lift on the rear of the seat at the same time.

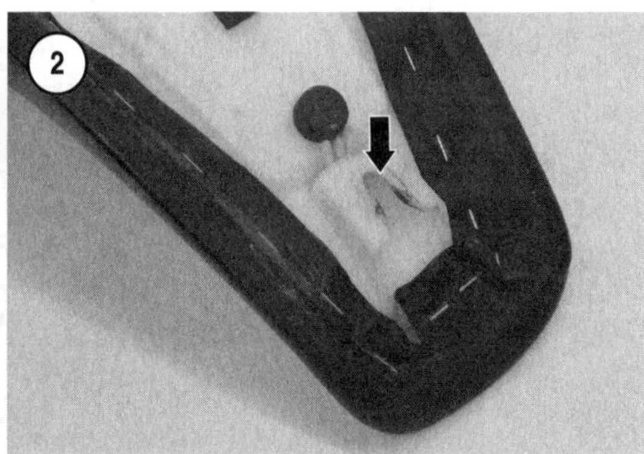

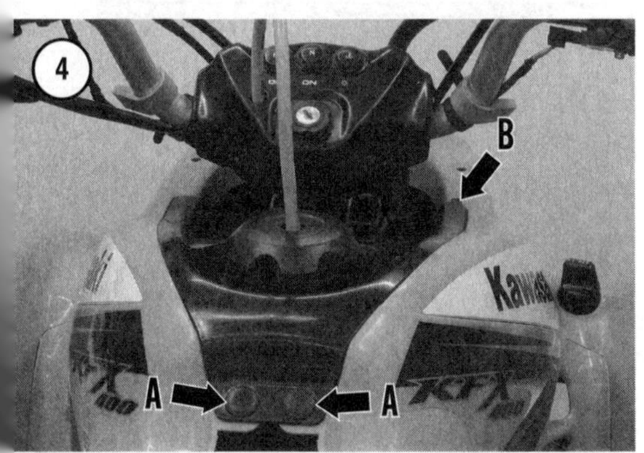

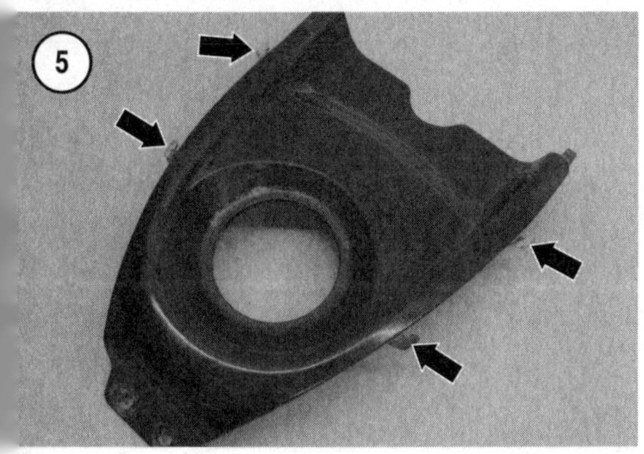

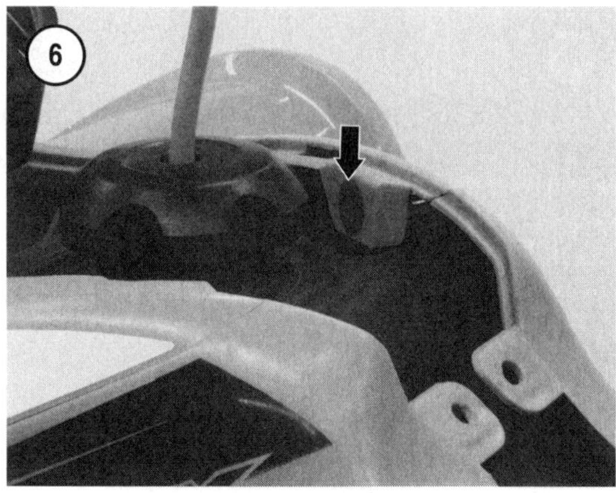

3. Lift and pull the seat to the rear of the vehicle to disengage the slotted tongue of the seat (**Figure 2**) from the plastic pin on the fuel tank (**Figure 3**).

4. Installation is the reverse of removal. Make certain the seat tongue engages with the fuel tank pin. Press on the rear of the seat until the latch clicks.

UPPER FUEL TANK COVER

Removal/Installation

1. Remove the seat as described in this chapter.
2. Remove the two plastic clips from the rear of the cover (A, **Figure 4**).
3. Remove the fuel tank cap.
4. Pull the tank cover rearward to release the tabs (**Figure 5**) from the side cover.
5. Installation is the reverse of removal. Make sure the tabs holding the front of the cover to the front fender slots (B, **Figure 4**) are properly seated.

SIDE COVERS

Removal/Installation

1. Remove the seat as described in this chapter.
2. Remove the fuel tank cover as described in this chapter.
3. Remove the upper plastic clip securing the side panel to the front fender assembly (**Figure 6**).
4. Remove the lower plastic clip securing the side panel to the rear fender assembly (**Figure 7**).
5. Pull the lower section of the side panel to the rear of the vehicle to disengage the tabs from the rear fender assembly (**Figure 8**).

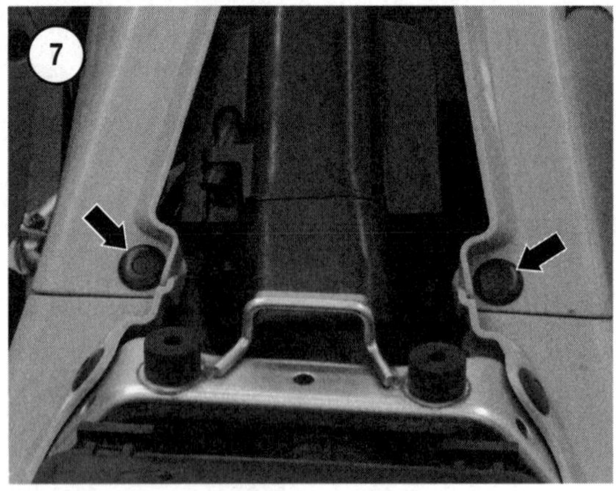

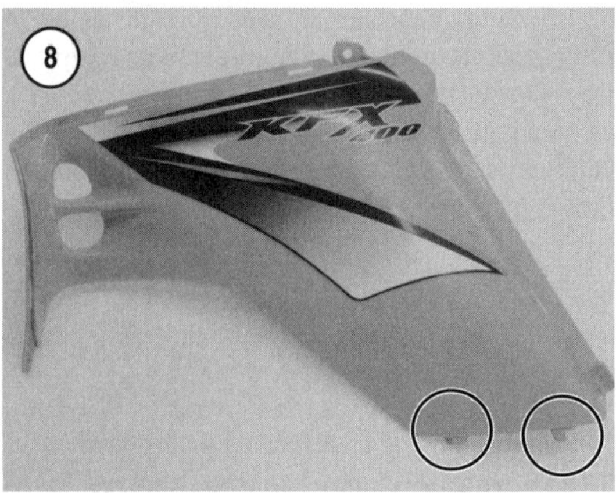

6. Push the upper part of the side panel toward the front of the bike to disengage it from the front fender tabs (**Figure 9**).

7. Installation is the reverse of removal.

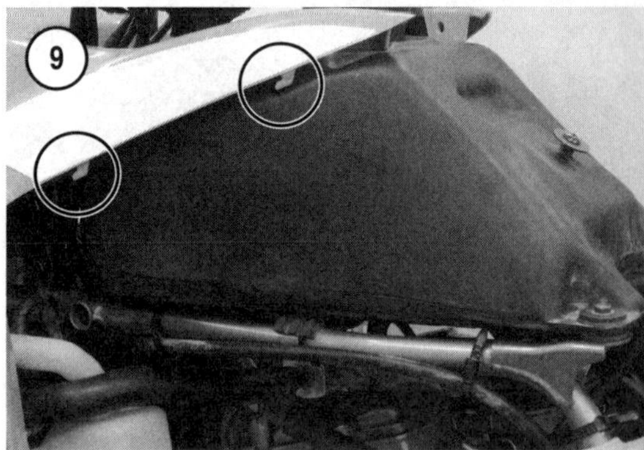

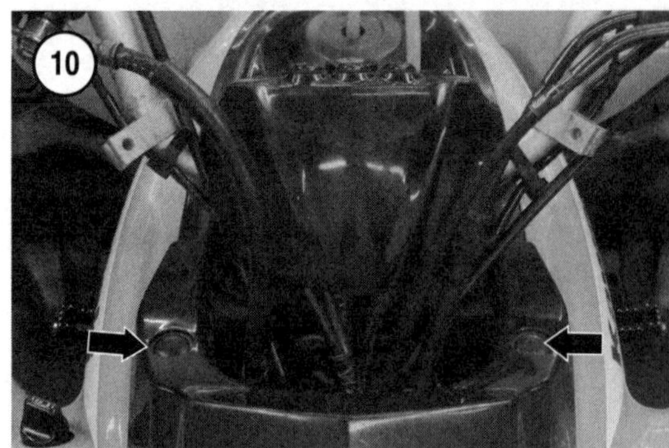

HEADLIGHT COVER

Removal/Installation

1. Remove the two plastic clips at the top of the headlight cover (**Figure 10**).

2. Remove the two screws on the inside of the front fender assembly securing the cover to the headlight assembly (**Figure 11**).

3. Lift the headlight cover off the headlight assembly.

4. Installation is the reverse of removal.

FRONT FENDER

Removal/Installation

1. Remove the seat as described in this chapter.

2. Remove the upper fuel tank cover as described in this chapter.

3. Remove the side panels as described in this chapter.

4. Remove the bolts from the fender brackets under the front fenders (A, **Figure 12**).

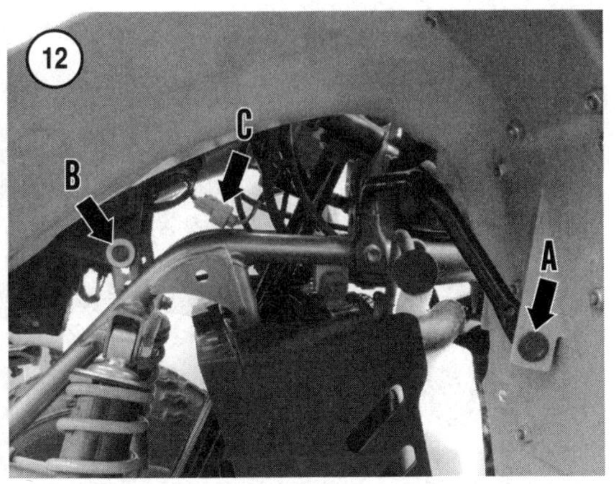

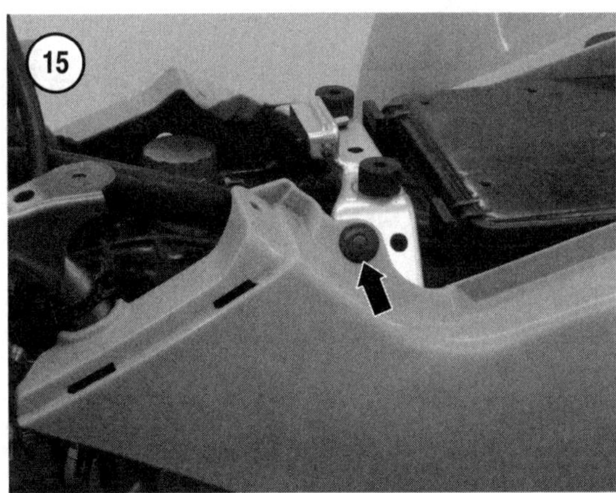

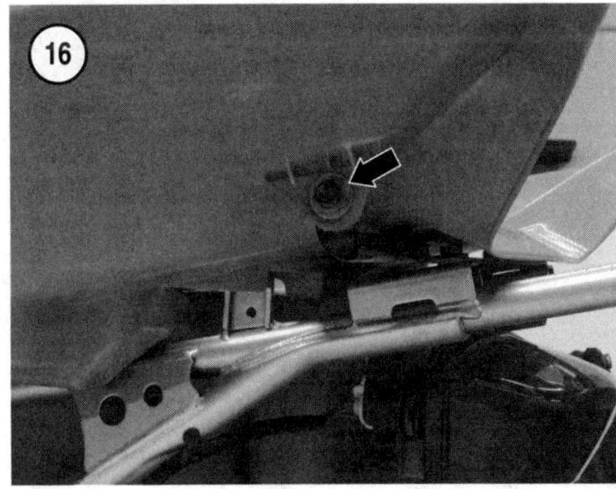

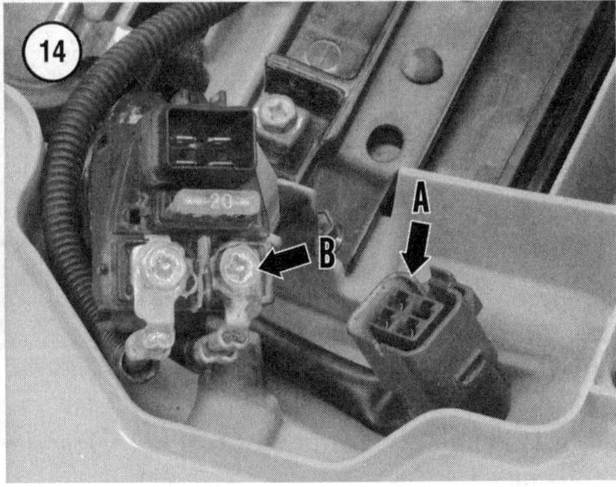

5. Remove the bolts that secure the headlight assembly to the frame (B, **Figure 12**).

6. Disconnect the headlight plug from the wiring harness (C, **Figure 12**).

7. Remove the two screws securing the reverse selection cable to the front fender (**Figure 13**).

8. Spread the sections of the front fender surrounding the tank outward and lift the fender clear, then rotate it forward and away from the machine.

9. Installation is the reverse of removal. Remember to reconnect the headlight plug.

REAR FENDER

Removal/Installation

1. Remove the seat as described in this chapter.
2. Remove the battery bracket and battery as described in Chapter Three.
3. Depress the tab on the wiring harness connector and remove it from the starter relay (A, **Figure 14**).
4. Remove the starter lead wire from the starter relay (B, **Figure 14**).
5. Remove the two plastic clips securing the rear fender to the frame near the fuel tank (**Figure 15**).
6. Remove both bolts holding the rear fender to the frame on both sides of the taillight (**Figure 16**).

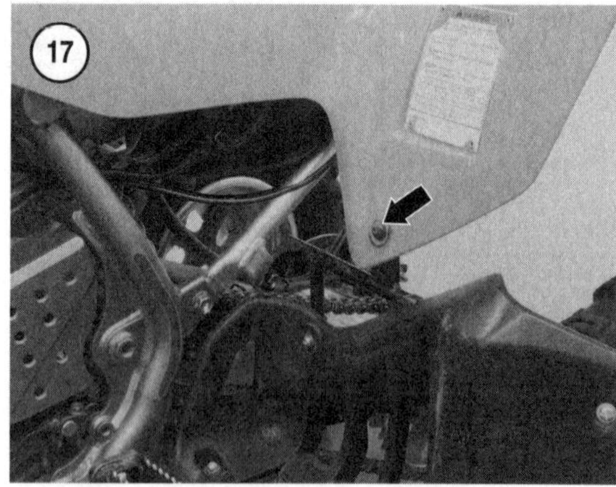

7. Remove the two bolts securing the lower part of the rear fender to the footrests (**Figure 17**).
8. Pull the wiring for the starter and wiring harness through the hole in the fender to make it easier to remove (**Figure 18**).
9. Lift the rear fender assembly straight up to remove.
10. Installation is the reverse of removal.

FOOTPEGS AND FOOTGUARD

Removal/Installation

1. Remove the four screws securing the mudguard to the footguard frame (**Figure 19**).
2. Remove the three bolts securing the footguard frame to the ATV (**Figure 20**).
3. Remove the remaining bolt securing the footpeg (**Figure 21**).

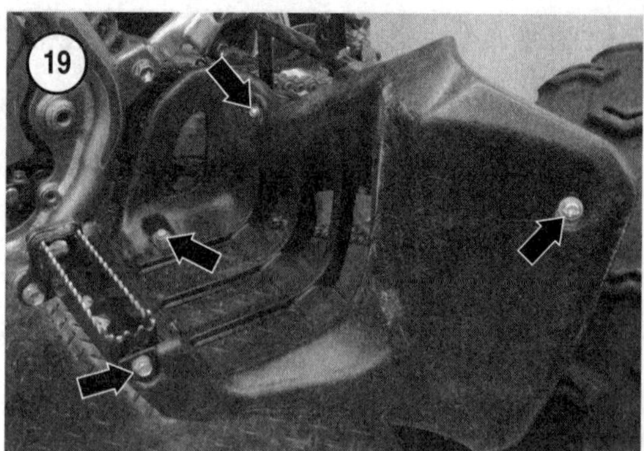

4. Installation is the reverse of removal. Note the following:
   a. Apply threadlock to the bolts securing the footgaurd to the frame. Tighten the bolts securely.
   b. Apply threadlock to the footpeg bolts. Tighten the bolts to 55 N•m (41 ft.-lb.).

TABLE 1 BODY TORQUE SPECIFICATIONS

	N•m	in.-lb.	ft.-lb.
Footrest mounting bolts*	55	–	41
*Apply threadlock.			

INDEX

T

U

V

W

LT-Z400 (2003-ON MODELS)

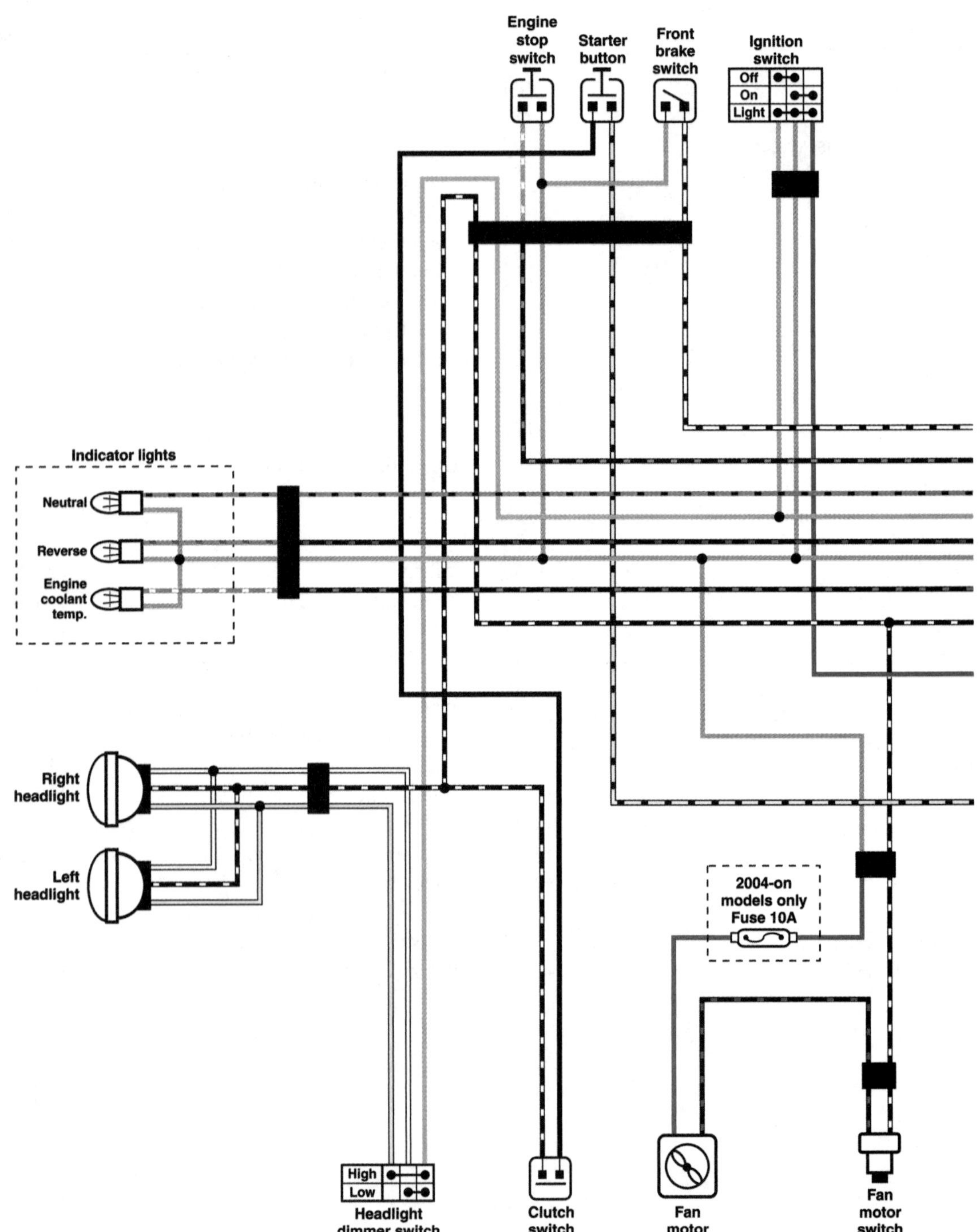

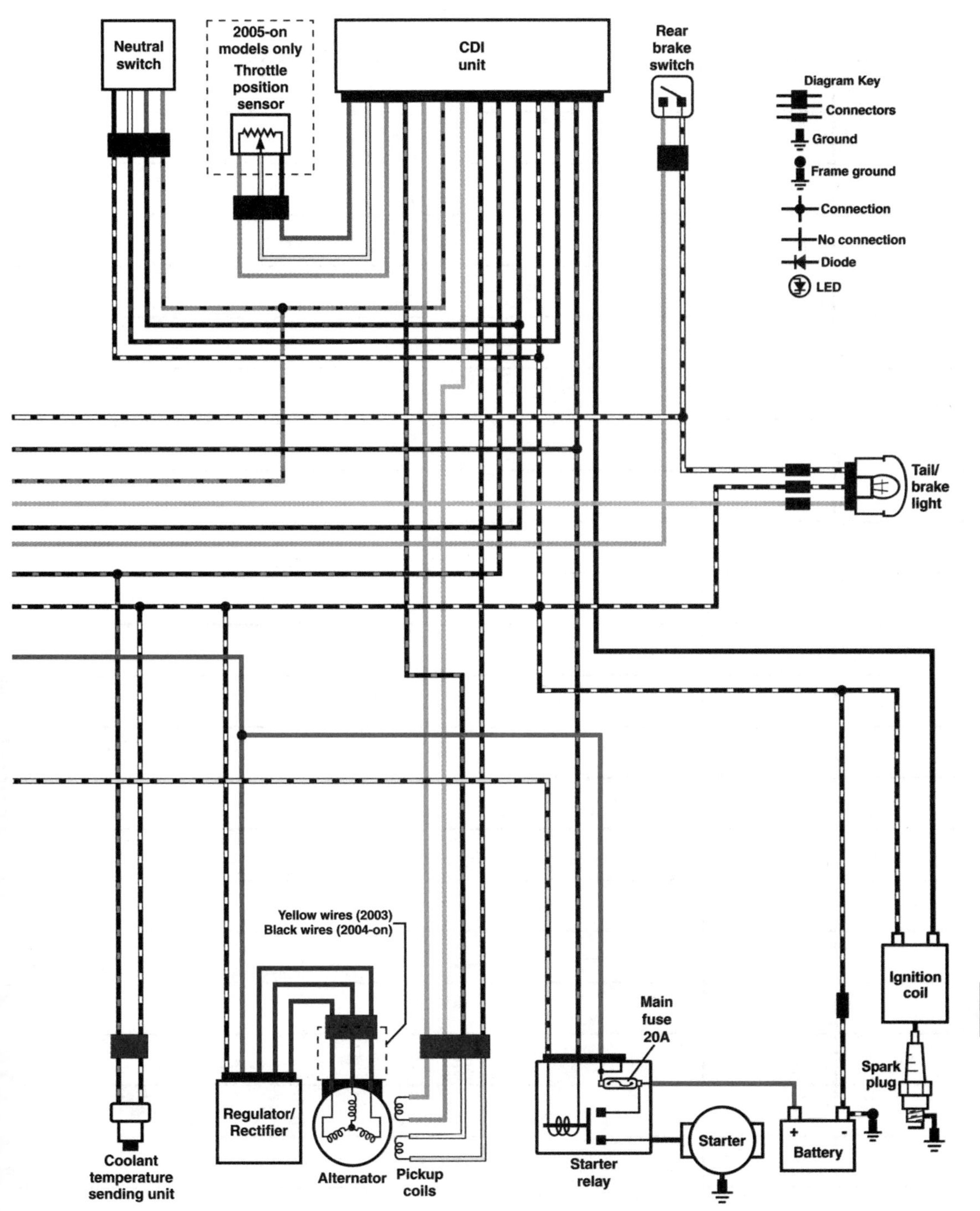

Neutral switch
2005-on models only
Throttle position sensor
CDI unit
Rear brake switch
Diagram Key
Connectors
Ground
Frame ground
Connection
No connection
Diode
LED
Tail/ brake light
Yellow wires (2003)
Black wires (2004-on)
Ignition coil
Main fuse 20A
Spark plug
Coolant temperature sending unit
Regulator/ Rectifier
Alternator
Pickup coils
Starter relay
Starter
Battery

16

MAINTENANCE LOG

Date	Hours	Type of Service